Contents

100646850

341.
242
2
STO

iv

CONTENTS

Guide to the book

In the Unlocking the Law books all the essential elements that make up the law are clearly defined to bring the law alive and make it memorable. In addition, the books are enhanced with learning features to reinforce learning and test your knowledge as you study. Follow this guide to make sure you get the most from reading this book.

AIMS AND OBJECTIVES

Defines what you will learn in each chapter.

SECTION

Highlights sections from Acts.

ARTICLE

Defines Articles of the EC Treaty, Treaty on the Functioning of the EU (TFEU) or of the European Convention on Human Rights or other Treaty.

CLAUSE

Shows a Bill going through Parliament or a draft Bill proposed by the Law Commission.

CASE EXAMPLE

 Illustrates the law in action.

JUDGMENT

 Provides extracts from judgments on cases.

QUOTATION

Encourages you to engage with primary sources.

ACTIVITY

Enables you to test yourself as you progress through the chapter.

KEY FACTS

Draws attention to essential points and information.

SAMPLE ESSAY QUESTIONS

Provide you with real-life sample essays and show you the best way to plan your answer.

SUMMARY

Concludes each chapter to reinforce learning.

LEGISLATION

Provides extracts from EU legislative provisions, such as the Treaty on European Union (TEU), the Treaty on the Functioning of the European Union (TFEU), Regulations and Directives.

SAMPLE PROBLEM QUESTION

Provides you with real-life sample problem questions and suggests the best way to plan your answer.

List of figures

Table of cases

TABLE OF CASES

Chronological Cases before the Court of Justice and the General Court

TABLE OF CASES

Table of treaty articles and legislation

Table of international legislation

TABLE OF INTERNATIONAL LEGISLATION

Table of equivalents

lxv

TABLE OF EQUIVALENTS

EC Treaty and Treaty on the Functioning of the European Union pre and post Treaty of Lisbon

EC Treaty.. TFEU

Previous numbering.................... New numbering

TABLE OF EQUIVALENTS

1

The historic origins and character of the EU legal order

AIMS AND OBJECTIVES

After reading this chapter you should be able to:

- Understand the reasons for the development of a single Europe
- Understand the background to the Treaties and the idea of the Community
- Understand the main aims and objectives of the Treaties
- Understand the concept of supranationalism
- Understand how the Treaties have developed through subsequent Treaties
- Understand the principles and consequences of enlargement of territory and scope
- Understand the significance of the EU Constitution and the Reform Treaty
- Analyse the development of the EU
- Analyse the consequences of enlargement

1.1 The origins of and background to the Treaties

1.1.1 The background to the idea of a single Europe

One problem that appears to confront students of EU law is an apparent assumption in the United Kingdom that Europe is something foreign, that it refers to a place and to people across the English Channel that have nothing to do with the United Kingdom. This is, of course, not the truth, since the United Kingdom has been a member of the European Community (now called the European Union – the use of the term Community/Community law tends to historically refer to the pre-2009 version of the Union) since signing the Treaties and ratifying membership in the European Communities Act 1972. The United Kingdom has been a member of the European Community since 1 January 1973. It has remained so after a majority vote for membership in a popular referendum in 1975 in which there was freedom for MPs of whatever party to support the campaign to deliver a 'yes' or a 'no' vote according to the way that their consciences and their commitment led them. Nevertheless, Euro-scepticism is not uncommon within the country and it would not be unreasonable to suggest that this, in part at least, follows the encouragement of certain elements of the media. This Euro-scepticism seems to be founded in two critical misconceptions about the nature and the role of the Community (now the Union since the Treaty on European Union signed at Maastricht in 1992):

▪ That the idea of European unity is a new and modern political concept – in fact it is anything but. The idea is certainly as old as Europe itself and has been put into place before but in different political form.

▪ That the Community was based mainly on co-operation between the Member States that may or may not be followed. Again, this is not the truth. The Community legal order was:

> based on the objectives of the Treaties that have been agreed by all Member States, and it works towards the achievement of the single dominant purpose of the Community: the full economic integration of the Member States towards a truly united Europe.

In fact, it is unusually appropriate that the Treaty responsible for creating and framing the concept of the Community should be referred to commonly as the Treaty of Rome (this is, of course, the second Treaty of Rome, the first being the EURATOM Treaty). It is appropriate because it is possible to see the Roman Empire as the first real attempt to unify Europe. Of course, in this case it was by a colonial power and through military dictatorship. Nevertheless, the whole purpose of the empire was economic, increasing availability of resources and markets and control of trade.

Following the Romans, it is possible to identify a number of situations demonstrating the same aspiration of a united Europe:

▪ The original view of Christendom expounded by the Roman Catholic Church, or more precisely of the Papacy that led it, was very much a European ideal, and everything outside Europe was considered to be barbarian.

▪ Charlemagne moulded and reigned over the so-called 'Holy Roman Empire' which covered much of modern Europe. This was obviously a political empire and it soon fell apart after his death as it passed to his sons, becoming the principalities that form the basis of many of the modern nation states.

▪ Henry IV of France also tried very hard to create a Christian Commonwealth of Europe.

▪ In the nineteenth century, Napoleon Bonaparte declared a stated ambition and policy for a European empire.

▪ In the twentieth century, Hitler's expansionist philosophy was also aimed at a Reich that would control most of Europe.

▪ Even besides the above, there have been numerous philosophers, including Kant, Rousseau, Marx and Neitzsche, who have all presented a united Europe as an ideal, and this despite them representing the widest spectrum of political philosophy, from Fascism to Communism.

There has always been, in the widest sense, a European identity and the desire for European unity; and historically, the so-called 'Euro-sceptics' were in a minority. However, Euro-scepticism has been on the rise across Europe, and whilst it had a particular foothold in the United Kingdom which previously was seen as marginal, the referendum on the membership of the UK in the EU on 26 June 2016 revealed a deeper rooted sense of disenfranchisement from the European project.

The 'Euro-sceptics' have always shown hostility towards the concept of a federal Europe, despite the fact that in its foundations the Community looked towards an eventual political unity as well as an economic unity. The British hostility towards federalism is even stranger since the idea of a federal Europe originated in Britain. It was suggested by Winston Churchill (who was Prime Minister during the war years) before the Second World War and supported then because of the fear of a fascist Germany. In fact, Jean Monnet, who is accepted as being the 'intellectual father' of the concept of European Union (EU), himself credited the origins of the ideal to the British. Yet today, the UK is set to exit the EU under the Article 50 TEU procedure, which was introduced by the Treaty of Lisbon and is being used for the very first time. This is a historic phenomenon which is deemed to change not only the nature of the relationship between the UK and the EU, but will also have repercussions for the development of the EU as a polity and for the UK as a non-EU country.

A further point worth making when considering the origins of the concept is that whatever philosophy has ever been put forward for EU has always included incorporation of a binding legal order as well as any economic, social or political union.

1.1.2 The origins of the Union as a Community

It must be remembered that the idea of European unity is based on a very noble and worthwhile principle: the avoidance of war in Europe. War between various nation states, most notably France and Germany, had been an almost constant feature for several centuries before the absolute devastation in the two 'World Wars' of the twentieth century.

The late nineteenth and early twentieth centuries saw various attempts at European integration of different types with this object in mind. The French 'Briand Plan' of 1929–30 is a classic example.

Nevertheless, economic and political imperatives conspired to create even more disruptive conflicts. As a result, following the Second World War there was an even stronger recognition of the need to avoid future conflicts. Certain other key points were also recognised in the immediate post-war period:

- that the Treaty of Versailles, while devised to prevent German hostility, had actually been a total failure and had led in part to the rise of Nazi Germany;
- that the only successful means of preventing war in Europe was not to repress the German state but to tie Germany into a European partnership.

Churchill (Prime Minister during the war) in fact encouraged the idea of a form of European unity. In a speech in Zurich in 1946, shortly after the close of the war, Churchill (by then Leader of the Opposition) suggested:

> We must build a kind of United States of Europe. In this way only will hundreds of millions of toilers be able to regain the simple joys and hopes which make life worth living.... The structure of the United States of Europe, if well and truly built, will be such as to make the material strength of a single state less important.
>
> I Ward, *A Critical Introduction to European Law* (Butterworths, 1996), pp. 6–7

It is worth noting that Churchill was not so much concerned with all nations losing power as he was with Germany losing power.

A European Union of Federalists was then established in 1946. Its supporters on the Continent argued that the way forward was the creation of 'supranational' bodies. In the Montreux Resolution of 1947 the group suggested:

> 'unification in Western Europe means escaping the risk of power politics. Federalists must declare without compromise that it is absolute sovereignty that must be abated ... a part of that sovereignty must be entrusted to a federal authority.'

A variety of intergovernmental conferences quickly followed at which agreements were reached to set up new organisations on either a global or merely a European scale. These organisations included:

- the **International Monetary Fund** (IMF);
- the **General Agreement on Tariffs and Trade** (GATT);
- the **Organisation for European Economic Co-operation** (OEEC) (this in effect was the creation of the United States through the 'Marshall Plan' of 1947 – the idea being to create an organisation that would administer the financial aid that was needed to repair the damage done to Europe during the Second World War);
- the **Council of Europe** (this was a most significant development for its creation of a European Convention on Human Rights and a European Court of Human Rights);
- the **BENELUX Union** (a union between the countries of Belgium, the Netherlands and Luxembourg – still among the smallest nations in the EU – significantly, though, the origins of supranationalism can be seen in this organisation for economic co-operation).

If the institutional origins of European Unity began with the 'Marshall Plan' then the next major phase was the 'Schuman Plan'. Robert Schuman was the French Foreign Minister and Jean Monnet was another French politician with responsibility for economic planning, who actually drafted the plan for Schuman. Both men were strong supporters of the idea of European co-operation.

The basis of the plan was the integration of French and German coal and steel production under the control of what was referred to as a 'higher authority'. This is the narrow agenda of the plan. The broader agenda was that it should represent the first stage towards a federal state of Europe.

The plan then led to and formed the basis of the first Treaty: the European Coal and Steel Community Treaty, formally signed as the Treaty of Paris in 1951. A significant point concerning all the various 'plans' for a united Europe is the concern to incorporate a legal order as well as economic and political union. This was demonstrated in the Treaty of Paris which created a Community with supranational institutions.

1.1.3 The creation of the Treaties

As a result of the Schuman Plan, the first of the Treaties creating the European Community, later to develop into the EU, was the European Coal and Steel Community Treaty (ECSC Treaty) – the Treaty of Paris 1951.

Focusing on the production of steel and coal was not a random choice. The Treaty had as a distinct aim the prevention of further hostilities within Europe and the establishment of stable relations between countries that had formerly been at war. That both France and Germany had regions where steel and coal were a major factor in the economy was also an actual and potential cause of conflict between the two countries. Establishing close economic co-operation in these specific fields was a logical means of preventing conflict. Not surprisingly, Monnet was made the first President of the ECSC.

The Treaty in essence devised the institutional framework of all the Communities. At first this was based on the political institutions: a 'High Authority' (later to be the Commission) to act as the executive arm, controlling production, a political assembly of representative members from the various Member States, and a Special Council of Ministers, with a partly legislative and a partly consultative role. Of course, since it was always envisaged that economic integration must be backed by a legal order, a Court of Justice was also added later.

The Treaty was in the end signed by only six European nations:

- France
- Germany
- Italy
- Belgium
- the Netherlands and
- Luxembourg.

The last three were already closely linked through the BENELUX Union. The UK significantly declined the opportunity to join the Community. Britain had suffered a lot less devastation than many of the mainland European nations and political thinking of the time leaned towards the so-called 'special relationship' with the United States of America as having more to offer than membership of an economically integrated Europe, and it saw its main market as the Commonwealth.

However, economic integration was established with the Treaty although there were still setbacks in terms of achieving unity. For instance, another initiative aimed at preventing conflict, the European Defence Community, collapsed in 1953.

Nevertheless, the move towards greater economic integration continued. The Spaak Committee Report of 1952 recommended the placing of atomic energy under a single authority and also called for the creation of a 'Common Market':

QUOTATION

'a vast area with a common political economy which will form a powerful productive unit and permit a steady expansion, an increase in stability, a more rapid rise in the standard of living, and the development of harmonious relations between member states'.

The report led directly to the creation of two more Treaties. These were the two Treaties of Rome that were signed by all six members of the ECSC on the same day in 1957, the European Atomic Energy Community Treaty (EURATOM) and the European Economic Community Treaty (later to be re-named the EC Treaty).

From the start, the three Communities shared the Common Assembly and also the European Court of Justice (ECJ). Initially the High Authority of the ECSC and the two Commissions of the other two Communities remained separate.

1.2 The basic aims and objectives of EC law and the concept of supranationalism

The major aim of the Treaties was economic integration, but the Treaties also reflect the wider purpose behind that integration. In the preamble to the EC Treaty it is clearly stated that the central objective of the signatories to the Treaties was to 'lay the foundations of an ever closer union among the peoples of Europe [by] pooling their resources to preserve and strengthen peace and liberty'.

The union was to be achieved by integration of the Member States' economic and monetary policies for the creation of a Common Market free from internal barriers to trade. The objectives of the EC in seeking to attain this Common Market were quite simply stated in the EC Treaty itself and as it has later been amended and built on by the subsequent Treaties:

- to promote throughout the Community a harmonious development of economic activities;
- a continuous, balanced expansion;
- an increase in stability;
- an accelerated raising of the standard of living and quality of life and closer relations between the states belonging to it and sustainable development of economic activities;
- a high level of employment and of social protection;
- equality between men and women;
- sustainable and non-inflationary growth;
- a high degree of competitiveness and convergence of economic performance;
- a high level of protection and of improvement of the quality of the environment;
- economic and social cohesion among the Member States.

The objectives dictated the structure of the Communities that were created in the Treaties. Key features of the structure can be identified in the EC Treaty:

- the introduction of four basic freedoms – freedom of movement of workers, the right to establish a trade or profession and to provide services freely, the free movement of goods, and the free movement of capital within the Community – all with a view to the removal of internal barriers to trade;
- the progressive approximation of economic policies of the Member States and the harmonisation of national laws in key economic areas such as agriculture, transport and trade;
- the creation of a Common Customs Tariff to regulate imports into the Community from other countries;
- the creation of a Common Commercial Policy to regulate trade between Member States and other countries.

Inevitably, different Member States had different things to gain from the Treaties and the creation of the three Communities. As a result, from the start proper integration was always hampered by national self-interest. This ensured that development could only be 'incremental' and that, often, principle would be sacrificed to what was achievable.

In fact, even before the creation of the Treaties there was a division in attitudes between those who retained a full federalist ideal and those who preferred a more co-operative progress towards integration, this latter group often being referred to as the 'functionalists':

- the **federalists** believed in the creation of a single supranational body that would in effect take over all of the functions of the individual Member States;

- the **functionalists** preferred to focus on individual areas of the economy and put these under joint management to improve efficiency and with the view that co-operation would then naturally spread from one economic area to another.

The ECSC was based on the attitudes of the functionalists. This gave way to 'neo-functionalism' which is demonstrated in the broader principles of the EC Treaty, and which reflects the need to limit the power of national governments to legislate in certain areas. This is the basis of supranationalism.

One of the major problems in achieving integration is in defining the constitution of the Community and how it becomes part of the law of the individual Member States. It is of course possible to argue that the constitution of the EC is represented by what is laid down in the Treaties and the objectives that they contain. However, the EC constitution has the added complication of being founded in Treaty relationships that are then entered into by sovereign states.

In this way another problem concerns the way that the Treaties are incorporated into Member States' law because of the different natures of the constitutions of the different Member States. These are of two distinct types:

- **Monist** constitutions: of the original six members these included both France and the Netherlands. In such constitutions the Treaty is automatically incorporated into the national legal system at the point of ratification.
- **Dualist** constitutions: of the original six these included Germany, Italy and Belgium. Significantly, of course, they also include the UK where the Treaty could only be incorporated into English law after enactment. In the case of the UK this was as the result of the passing of the European Communities Act 1972.

The result of the different methods of incorporation is that there can be a wide variance in how the Treaties are then interpreted and applied in the individual Member States. As a result, in order for the legal order of the Community to have any effect the Community institutions must be 'supranational' in character. In other words, in relation to those areas that are covered by Treaty obligations, the institutions and those Community obligations must take precedence over national law and institutions.

As a result of this the European Court of Justice (ECJ) has proved to be one of the most significant institutions both in administering and defining EC law, and also in developing the principle of 'supranationalism'. Both have been vital in ensuring the universal application of the Treaties.

Commentators have frequently accepted the importance of the Court in furthering the objectives laid down in the Treaties. 'To avoid disparities arising out of different national approaches to the incorporation of EC law and to ensure uniformity in its application, the Court of Justice has developed its own jurisprudence on the Supremacy of EC law' (P Kent, *Law of the European Union* (Longman, 2001), p. 55).

> ECJ has uniformly and consistently been the most effective integration institution in the Community. Its role was established in A220 [Article 164]: 'The Court shall ensure that in the interpretation and application of this Treaty the law is observed.' From its very inception in the Treaty, the ECJ set about establishing its hierarchical authority as the ultimate court of constitutional review. In this area two areas in particular are important. First there is the role of the ECJ in controlling member state courts, and, second, there is the role of the Court in managing the incessant inter-institutional struggles.
>
> I Ward, *A Critical Introduction to European Law* (Butterworths, 1996), p. 52

1.3 The development of the Treaties (from the European Coal and Steel Community Treaty to the Treaty of Nice)

During the early years of the Community, between 1958 and 1965, there was some successful progress towards economic integration. The period in any case was one of economic boom. The creation of a 'Customs union' was underway, with the removal of tariffs. However, there was much less progress towards the creation of an actual Common Market. Some competition policy was put in place and there was some movement made to achieve the free movement of workers. Nevertheless, there was perhaps over prominence of the Common Agricultural Policy (CAP). The ECJ did, of course, do much even in these early years to define the character of the legal order.

Nevertheless, the Common Market should have been achieved within the so-called 'transitional period' referred to throughout the EC Treaty. This comprised three four-year periods or a total of 12 years from 1957, so the Common Market should have been in place by 1969.

However, in the 1960s even the neo-functionalists faced problems with their proposed method of achieving integration. Much of this was the fault of France and in particular President De Gaulle. In 1965–66 De Gaulle created a crisis over qualified majority voting, with France withdrawing from participation in the Council. This was partly resolved by the Luxembourg Accords, which effectively created a sort of veto for the Member States on major issues. This compromise created what has been described as the **intergovernmentalist approach**. In effect, what it did was to shift more power to the council and away from the supranational bodies.

In any case the years between then and 1986 and the adoption of the Single European Act are commonly characterised as years of stagnation in terms of integration. It is possible to explain the lack of development during this time by the economic recession and also the retreat into national interest. This could particularly be said of the UK from 1979 to 1997.

There were, of course, other areas in which the Community did develop:

- by enlargement of the number of Member States;
- by a broadening of policy both inside and outside the original Treaty objectives;
- by the judicial activism of the ECJ (specifically in the development of the concept of supremacy, and by the development of the means of securing enforcement of the objectives of the Treaty through the processes of direct effect and its associated alternatives).

Another major development has been the creation of further Treaties developing and expanding the original Treaties. To start with, the Merger Treaty of 1965 established a single set of institutions to preside over all three Communities.

The Single European Act

The Single European Act (SEA) of 1986 represents the effective 're-launch' of the Community. A Commission White Paper of 1985 identified that there were a number of pressing problems facing the Community. One of the most critical of these was the fact that the Single Market had not yet been achieved even 16 years after it should have been in place. The Commission therefore proposed to set a new deadline for achieving this aim and to create the means of making it more attractive to the Member States. It was able to push forward for four main reasons:

- the dynamism of the then Commission President, Jacques Delors;
- a commitment to further integration by key political figures within the Member States themselves, the most important among these being Chancellor Kohl of Germany and President Mitterand of France;
- the relative economic prosperity at the time of many of the Member States, which meant that they also had fewer urgent national problems to deflect them from their Community objectives;
- a growing realisation in any case that survival depended on an effective EC.

The result was the Single European Act 1986. This set a new time scale for the implementation of the Single Market of 31 December 1992.

Besides refocusing on the principal aim of the original Treaty, the SEA also included constitutional and institutional reform:

- a new law-making process was devised – the co-operation procedure – that gave Parliament much greater involvement in certain measures and aimed to reduce the 'democratic deficit';
- the European Council was formally recognised and this provided for regular twice-yearly meetings of the heads of state;
- a new Court of First Instance (CFI) was created to support the ECJ through its massively increased workload;
- procedural changes also meant that there was an increase of qualified majority voting in Council to speed up the decision-making process;
- there was also a move towards the idea of European political co-operation and Community competency was extended beyond pure economic objectives to include areas such as social policy and environmental policy.

Nevertheless, the SEA still had its critics who claimed that it had done nothing more than to begin again the process of integration that should have already been achieved and that it did nothing in effect to remove the veto of individual Member States.

The Treaty on European Union

Commonly referred to as the Maastricht Treaty, the Treaty on European Union (TEU) was signed at Maastricht in 1992. The Treaty was concluded following two intergovernmental conferences in 1989, the first concerning the Commission President's three-stage plan for European Monetary Union (EMU), and the second concerning political union.

The Treaty itself took a further year to gain force because of difficulties in the ratification process in certain of the Member States and objections to the federalist character of the word 'union'.

While the Treaty fell short of what many Member States wanted, it did include some major developments:

- it did create the Union by identifying all the states comprising the Community as being part also of the Union;
- it also created the concept of European citizenship, although, unlike those rights enjoyed by workers, citizenship did not fall within the legal order;
- some constitutional and institutional changes were achieved with the creation of a new co-decision procedure for legislating and the inclusion of a Parliamentary Ombudsman and a Committee of the Regions;

- the objectives of the Community were amended to include EMU, environmental protection and social policy and the activities were to include research and technical development, trans-European networks, health, education, culture, consumer protection, energy, civil protection and tourism;

- it also created the 'three-pillar' structure of the EU (which has now disappeared since the reforms brought on by the Treaty of Lisbon): added to the central pillar of the Communities would be a second pillar to cover co-operation in foreign policy and security, and a third pillar to cover co-operation in justice and home affairs.

At Maastricht 11 of the then 12 Member States also agreed on the Social Charter but the UK opted out, thus necessitating the Protocol procedure.

The Treaty of Amsterdam 1997

The Treaty of Amsterdam 1997 (ToA) was the result of intergovernmental conferences in 1996 and 1997. It was agreed in 1997 but did not gain force for another two years. One of the principal problems facing the EU at the time of the Treaty was future enlargement, but in fact the Treaty did very little on this. It is possibly seen as not being so wide-ranging as the TEU but there were a number of key developments:

- It broadened the objectives of the EU from pure economic aims to the inclusion of some social and political objectives. For instance, where the original Treaty prohibited discrimination based on nationality and Article 141 provides for limited controls in relation to sex discrimination, the Treaty of Amsterdam gave Council the power to introduce laws to prevent discrimination based on racial or ethnic origin, religion or belief, disability, age and sexual orientation. Fundamental human rights are also given greater protection under the Treaty of Amsterdam.

- The new UK Labour government had accepted the Social Policy Agreement, so the Protocol on Social Policy from the TEU giving the UK an opt-out was repealed in the Treaty of Amsterdam.

- The Treaty repealed many of the Articles of the original Treaty that were now obsolete and it also grouped together the Articles as amended by the TEU and renumbered them.

- Institutionally, there was some reform, with the co-decision procedure extended in scope so that only EMU matters fell under the co-operation procedure.

- There were also some changes to the pillar structure created in the TEU. Under the second pillar, on common foreign policy and security, the Council was given the power to make certain international agreements on behalf of the Member States. Under the third pillar many provisions were moved under the main pillar and the name of the pillar was changed to 'Police and Judicial Co-operation in Criminal Matters'.

- A concept of close co-operation was also introduced which allows Member States to co-operate and use the institutions and procedures on areas which are not yet the subject of legislation. This is aimed at reducing some of the tension that exists in certain policy areas.

The Treaty of Nice 2000

The Treaty of Nice (ToN) was agreed in December 2000 but did not gain force until 1 February 2003 because of difficulties in ratifying the Treaty in Ireland, where a referendum initially voted against ratification.

One of the major purposes of the Nice summit was to prepare the necessary Treaty amendments and institutional changes to deal with enlargement of the Union.

- Institutional changes included changes to the composition of the institutions, with a new allocation of seats in Parliament, an extension to the number of Commissioners and judges in the ECJ.
- They also incorporated changes to the voting procedures, with the extension of qualified majority voting in Council to account for a new 25-state Union.
- There was also change to the judicial system, with the creation of a 'Chamber' attached to the CFI.
- The Treaty also approved the Charter of Fundamental Human Rights, with provision for suspension of voting rights where there are breaches.
- Besides this, measures were introduced for the provision of 'enhanced co-operation'.

This is the basic idea that some states can be at different levels of integration at the same time by agreeing on certain areas but opting out of others. An example of this would be both Greece and Denmark opting out of EMU. It is sometimes also referred to as 'variable geometry' or as 'multi-speed Europe'.

1.4 Enlargement

Enlargement of the EU has occurred and continues to occur in two ways, sometimes referred to as 'widening' and 'deepening'.

'Deepening' refers to the increasing scope of influence of the EU over its Member States. As has been seen above, the extension to the three-pillar structure of the EU has widened its influence. There has been a move gradually, through recent Treaties, to a social and political agenda well beyond the limited economic context of the original Treaties. There has been a widening and redistribution of the power of the different institutions and the creation of extra institutions. Besides this, the ECJ had steadily defined the scope and effect of EC law.

The current context of the word 'enlargement' is more towards the widening of the EU by territory. This grew significantly since the original Treaties which were entered into by only six nations: Germany, France, Italy and the three BENELUX countries:

- in 1973 the six became nine, with the addition of the UK, Ireland and Denmark;
- in 1981 Greece also joined, making for a Community of ten countries;
- in 1986 Portugal and Spain also joined, to make it 12;
- in 1995 the EU was enlarged to a group of 15 with the accession of Austria, Finland and Sweden;
- 2004 saw the biggest single expansion, with ten nations joining: the Czech Republic, Hungary, Poland, Slovakia, Slovenia, Estonia, Lithuania, Latvia, Malta and Cyprus;
- Romania and Bulgaria joined the EU in 2007, while other countries (e.g. Turkey and Macedonia) are in various stages of negotiation for entry into the EU.

Between 1957 and 2013, then, the number of Member States has risen from six to 28. The EU is already the largest trading bloc in the world and the population covered by the Union is now more than 450 million. Gaining membership is not as simple as just making an application.

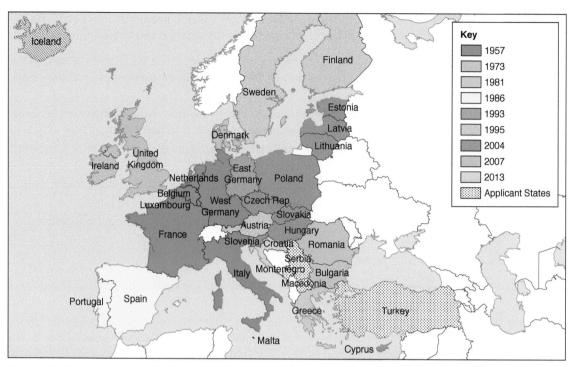

Figure 1.1 Member States of the European Union

Before a country can be considered for membership it must now meet three specific requirements:

- it must show that its institutions are democratic and guarantee the rule of law, protect human rights, and specifically is able to protect minorities;

- it must show that it operates a market economy that is capable of surviving within the Single Market;

- it must show that it is able to apply the laws of the EU and can meet the aims of economic, political and monetary union.

One significant point to make about the Union, when considering it in the context of one of the central aims of the devisers of the original Treaties, is that peace within the Member States has been maintained throughout that period.

1.5 The EU Constitution

1.5.1 The Constitutional Treaty

Later Treaties, as well as the intergovernmental conferences, focused on the difficulties of expanding the EU, and the impact that had on the institutions and the administration of the law. A year after the Nice Treaty was signed, at a meeting of the European Council in Laeken, a 'Declaration of the Future of the European Union' was adopted.

The Laeken Declaration committed the Union to becoming more democratic, more transparent and more effective, and therefore recognised the need to create a Constitution. The meeting also recognised that the traditional method for reviewing and developing the Treaties, through intergovernmental conferences of the heads of state, lacked transparency and democracy. A decision was taken to convene a Convention of representatives of governments of all the Member States and of the countries which had applied for membership as well as representatives from the institutions and the various committees: a Convention of 105 members in total.

This Convention looked into the various problems associated with taking the Union forward and eventually prepared a Draft Constitution which was presented to the inter-governmental conference at Thessaloniki in June 2003. The Draft Constitution was sub-sequently agreed by the Member State governments, identified as the EU Constitution and was referred to the Member States for ratification. A number of Member States rati-fied the EU Constitution by parliamentary vote. Certain Member States, including founder members such as France, decided to ratify by a national referendum. The rejec-tion of the EU Constitution in the French referendum in May 2005, followed by the Netherlands' rejection in June 2005, created doubts as to whether the EU could proceed with the EU Constitution at all.

One of the principal purposes of the EU Constitution was to put into a single docu-ment all of the existing Treaties so that it should be readable and clear. The Constitution itself was made up of four separate parts:

- The first part contained all of the provisions that related to the objectives, powers and decision-making processes of the Union and those relating to its institutions.
- The second part incorporated the Charter of Fundamental Rights agreed upon at Nice.
- The third part focused on the policies of the Union and incorporated many of the provisions already contained in the existing Treaties.
- The fourth part, as usual, was referred to as the Final Clauses and in this instance contained the procedures for adopting and reviewing the Constitution.

Many of the specific developments contained in the Constitution are indicated in later chapters of this book where relevant.

1.5.2 The Reform Treaty (the Lisbon Treaty)

Following the effective collapse of the Constitutional Treaty, the Brussels European Council in 2007 decided that the relative inertia resulting from this collapse, as well as the need to develop the institutional reforms begun in the Treaty of Nice 2001, meant that the position needed to be resolved and so the Treaty of Lisbon, the so-called Reform Treaty, was also drafted in 2007.

While argument has raged in UK politics on the question of whether the Lisbon Treaty is just the Constitutional Treaty in a different guise, there are significant differ-ences, although many important aspects of the Treaty remain unchanged.

One of the most important changes for students of EU Law is in the different form and structure of the two Treaties:

- The Constitutional Treaty proposed in effect to create a single written constitution, incorporating but repealing all previous Treaties. Unfortunately, to overcome the objections to the Constitutional Treaty, the Lisbon Treaty follows the format of previous amending Treaties, keeping the other Treaties in place while amending them. As a result, significant cross-referencing is still required between all the various Treaties and the Lisbon Treaty.
- The proposed change to EU laws and EU framework laws in the Constitutional Treaty is not repeated in the Lisbon Treaty and the traditional legislation, regula-tions, directives and decisions remain.
- The Charter of Fundamental Rights would have been incorporated in the Con-stitutional Treaty; instead, under the Lisbon Treaty, Article 6 TEU was amended to

provide only that the Charter of Fundamental Rights has the same legal value as the Treaties, to which it is annexed. However, Protocol 30 allows that, in the UK and Poland (and since 2009 in the Czech Republic), the Charter will create no justiciable rights beyond those already in existence within the national law of those two states.

- Institutional reforms remain mainly intact. Qualified Majority Voting is extended to other areas, as in the Constitutional Treaty. The introduction of Double Majority Voting remains, although its full introduction was delayed up to March 2017. Parliament was given increased powers, as in the Constitutional Treaty, with the extension of the co-decision procedure (now known as the ordinary legislative procedure) to a wider range of areas.
- Where the Constitutional Treaty proposed to abandon the rather complex three-pillar structure of the TEU, and place foreign affairs and justice and home affairs within the constitution, the existing structure in essence is to be retained.
- One contentious issue of the Constitutional Treaty, the creation of a flag, anthem and motto, has been abandoned in the Lisbon Treaty.

Originally the Treaty was rejected in an Irish referendum. A further successful referendum led to the Treaty being ratified by Ireland in 2009, and Poland also ratified the Treaty, so that it is now in force.

1.5.3 The Charter of Fundamental Rights of the European Union

Purpose and content

At the Cologne European Council in June 1999, the heads of states and government of the EU Member States decided that the system of fundamental rights protection, developed under the doctrine of general principles of EU law, should be consolidated in a charter of rights in order to make the latter more visible to the citizens of the EU. Despite the fact that fundamental rights were not considered or included in the original founding Treaties, the European Council nevertheless stressed that they constitute a 'founding principle of the Union'. Therefore the use of the term 'consolidate' is a key operative word which characterises the nature of the Charter of Fundamental Rights (CFR). The Convention which was charged with drafting the CFR included representatives of the Member States, the European Commission and Parliament, as well as representatives of the Member States' national parliament and civil society. The Convention did not technically create any new rights but instead catalogued in a single document all pre-existing fundamental rights which form part of the Union *acquis communautaire* (Union body of law). The European Council qualified fundamental rights protection as 'an indispensable prerequisite to the Union's legitimacy', therefore the CFR makes these existing rights accessible and visible for the citizens of the EU.

The CFR encompasses 50 rights, freedoms and principles across six chapters on Dignity, Freedoms, Equality, Solidarity, Citizens' Rights and Justice. The final Chapter VII relates to the interpretation and scope of application of the CFR.

The range of rights covered in the CFR is wider and more inclusive than those of the European Convention on Human Rights (ECHR) and other international instruments. Indeed, the CFR brings together an amalgamation of socio-economic, cultural and moral freedoms, along with civil and political rights in one document, which is a remarkably advanced consolidation of traditional, modern and aspiring rights and freedoms.

Scope of application

From its initial proclamation at the Nice Council in 2000 (which merely made the Charter 'politically binding' on the institutions and Member States of the Union), the CFR was eventually given legal force by the Treaty of Lisbon.

Article 6(1) TEU now ensures that the CFR is primary legislation. Although annexed to the Treaties in a declaration, the CFR has nevertheless the same constitutional value as the TEU and the TFEU in the EU legal order, as recognised by the CJEU in *Kücükdeveci* (Case C–555/07).

Following Article 6(1)(3) TEU, the Charter comes with a full package of mandatory interpretative assistance, including the horizontal provisions of Title VII and the Convention *Praesidium's* explanations of the Charter's rights, principles and details of their sources.

On the scope of application of the CFR, the ECJ has held that, with regards to Article 51, the application of EU law implies the application of the CFR. Therefore where national legislation falls within the scope of EU law, provisions of the CFR will be applicable (*Åkerberg Fransson* (Case C–617/10)). The ECJ adds that under Article 53 national courts may apply 'standards of protection of fundamental rights, provided that the level of protection provided for by the Charter, as interpreted by the Court, and the primacy, unity and effectiveness of EU law are not thereby compromised' (*Melloni* (Case C–399/11)). The ECJ's interpretation of the scope of application of the CFR seems closely linked to ensuring the primacy and effectiveness of EU law, as seen in *Kadi* (Joined Cases C–402/5 P and C–415/05 P) in which the ECJ held that the CFR cannot be overridden by a Member State's obligation under an international agreement where the application of the latter would contravene a provision of the CFR.

Finally, Article 1(1) of Protocol 30 states that the ECJ has no competence to scrutinise the UK and Poland (now extended to the Czech Republic), and their respective domestic courts' conformity with Charter provisions. However, the ECJ has taken a rather minimalist approach to the interpretation of this 'opt-out' Protocol by stating in *N.S.* (Joined Cases C–411/10 and C–493/10) that the protocol does not exempt the UK and Poland or their respective domestic courts from complying with the CFR provisions. In effect, the opt-out Protocol seems to be a paper tiger with little chance of effectively curtailing the application of the CFR.

In light of the above, it is apparent that the CFR is set to become a substantial instrument in the evolving politico-legal nature of the Union and the expanding reach of its legal order.

1.5.4 Post Treaty of Lisbon: from Community to Union

Prior to the ratification of the Lisbon Treaty it was important to understand the different concepts of Community and Union because the European edifice was built on a three-pillar structure. From the foundation of the original Treaties to the time of the TEU there was a Community; first the EEC and later the EC. The choice of the term 'community' by the founding fathers of the EU may have been used as an alternative to the f-word in order to assuage any concerns from the anti-federalist section. 'Community' is also a denomination that had no prior political definition and so could be distinguished from the more traditional types of international organisations. Therefore the neutral characteristic of the term 'Community' was ideal for the new European venture of peace-building and integration through co-operation and solidarity between Member States.

More concretely, the initial founding Treaties comprised not only the (economic) objectives of the Community but also the blueprint for its legal (and public) order.

Following the TEU, which also established EU citizenship, the more political incarnation of the EU was created. Between the TEU (1992) and the Lisbon Treaty (2009) there was both the EC and the EU at the same time (under the now defunct three-pillar system). In very general terms, the EC was founded by the Treaties, as amended, and was based on law; whilst the EU, stemming from the agreements made at Maastricht, was based on co-operation. This was a cumbersome and unsatisfactory structure which has been reformed by the Treaty of Lisbon. Today, the EU is one entity with legal personality and is based on law (with some exceptions, such as for the CSFP). Whilst it may be helpful, in studying the law of the EU, to understand the difference between the EC and the EU; for this textbook's purpose to introduce and simplify EU law, suffice to know that any Community and EC law related terminology refers to the EU pre-Treaty of Lisbon.

1.6 The future

1.6.1 Enlargement – nationally

Although the EU underwent its biggest expansion, in May 2004, the Union is not yet at 'capacity'. Indeed, any nation satisfying the basic admission criteria for membership is entitled to apply for membership. One country became a new Member State in 2013 and four more are at different stages in the process of application to become Member States:

- Turkey – the country which has undergone the most complicated and protracted application process ever, is still at an early negotiating stage with the European Commission. Concerns about Turkey's human rights record remain. There was a prediction that Turkey would access the Union in 2015. The implications of Turkish accession would have been enormous. Not only would Turkey's population of around 82 million make it the second most populous country in the EU, but its geographical location, on the very edge of Europe, its predominantly Muslim population and largely agricultural economy all pose significant (but not insurmountable) problems in terms of its successful integration. Nevertheless, Turkey is a member of NATO and its geopolitical significance, as the biggest predominantly Muslim state with a secular government in the world, is huge.

- The Former Yugoslav Republic of Macedonia – first applied for membership in 2004 and was given candidate country status in 2005. In 2009 the Commission recommended that accession negotiations should begin and in 2012 a High Level Accession Dialogue was opened.

- Montenegro – another part of the former Yugoslavia, declared its independence from the post Yugoslavia state of Serbia and Montenegro in 2006 and applied for membership in 2008. The Commission issued a favourable opinion on its application in 2010 subject to fulfilment of seven key priorities and it was given candidate status with accession negotiations beginning in 2012. Montenegro also enjoys visa free entry into Shengen agreement states.

- Serbia – first applied in 2009 and was granted candidate status in 2012 but is waiting for a date to be set for full negotiations towards membership to begin.

- Albania – first made a formal application in 2009 but the opinion delivered by the Commission in 2010 identified that Albania needed to deliver on 12 key priorities before accession negotiations could begin. In 2012 the Commission did recommend that Albania could be granted EU candidate status, but only subject to completion of key measures in judicial and public administration reform and reform of parliamentary rules of procedure. Albania was awarded candidate status in 2014.

There are also currently three countries which are potential applicants but which have not yet received candidate status:

- Bosnia and Herzegovina – the EU has reached a number of agreements with Bosnia and Herzegovina, for instance on the requirement of visas. However, the EU still has a significant military presence under the Common Foreign and Security Policy (CFSP) and the European Security and Defence Policy (ESDP), although with an improved security situation, forces have been reduced to 600.

- Kosovo – the EU since 1999 has played an enormous role in the reconstruction and redevelopment of Kosovo through the EULEX rule of law mission, in assisting towards independence and in helping to create a constitution.

1.6.2 Enlargement – scope of legislation

Over the last 20 years, the scope of EU legislation has expanded significantly, taking in new topics such as discrimination on grounds of sexual orientation and race (discussed in Chapter 18 of this book) and environmental protection (see Chapter 19).

1.6.3 Brexit

In 2016, the British government held a referendum on the United Kingdom's membership of the EU. After a highly politicised and controversial debate (often lacking in factual accuracy or convincing arguments) between the Leave and Remain campaigns, 52 per cent of the British people voted to withdraw from the EU. The submission of Prime Minister Theresa May's letter to the President of the European Council on 29 March 2017 under Article 50 TEU triggered the two-year process of negotiation between the institutions of the EU and the UK for its withdrawal from the European bloc, which will become effective on 29 March 2019 (European time).

The negotiations are far from straightforward and have been hampered by the British government's lack of clear withdrawal strategy as well as forward planning on future UK–EU relationship plans; and its wish to maintain as many economic and trading privileges as possible despite its apparent desire to leave the Customs Union.

On 19 June 2017, the UK government and the European Commission jointly published the terms of reference for the negotiations under Article 50 TEU, which are to focus primarily on reaching an agreement on the terms of the UK's 'orderly withdrawal' from the EU. Following the European Council's guidelines, any discussions on the future nature of the relationship between the UK and the EU can only take place once certain red lined areas have been satisfactorily agreed (e.g. the financial settlement for leaving the EU or 'divorce bill'; the protection of EU citizens' rights living in the UK; ensuring the sustainability of the Good Friday agreement; dispute and enforcement settlements mechanisms for the application and enforcement of the withdrawal agreement; etc.).

Whilst the British government insists that 'Brexit means Brexit', without a clear explanation from the British government as to what this might imply as regards its shape, form or long-term ramifications for the UK, Brexit (to paraphrase Winston Churchill) is for now a riddle wrapped in a mystery inside an enigma. However, it is worth noting that besides the impact that Brexit will have on the future of the UK, it has already started to impact on the EU as well.

1.6.4 Towards full union ...?

As discussed in Chapter 10 of this book, for many years, the EU stayed the course on its way to achieving full economic and monetary union, with the single European currency, the euro, successfully launched in 1999 (for electronic transactions) and in 2002 (for all other transactions), and the establishment of the European Central Bank. The next logical step would be for those participating states to hand over further control of their economic policies to a central European authority. This could in turn lead to the next step in integration terms – a full **political union** – which would probably involve conferring far greater powers on the Council and/or European Parliament at the expense of national Parliaments, especially in the fields of foreign policy and security. However, the 2008 economic crisis and Brexit have both altered this trajectory and forced the EU to start reflecting on its future.

Without the above mentioned events, the next step in integration terms would have been the ultimate step – full union – which would entail the complete unification of all national economies. That would mean the end of such fiercely protected national policies as the setting of rates of income tax and, with it, national identities. The EU would then become a state in its own right, albeit a federal state with a certain amount of autonomy devolved to the former Member States, which would be re-classified as 'regions' of the EU, in accordance with the principle of subsidiarity. A name-change would then be necessary, the obvious contender being 'the United States of Europe'. The EU does, after all, have its own Constitution already!

Significantly one of the events that have made closer political integration more likely has been the so-called Eurozone crisis. Economic monetary union was always a necessary step along the road to a true Single Market. However, it proved controversial and unpopular with a number of Member States including the UK.

Nineteen out of twenty-eight Member States in fact joined a single currency. Because of the problems of differences in economic stability of different Member States, convergence criteria were created and it has been argued that certain states were not really in a position to match the criteria. The problems resulting from the world banking crisis and recession also led into major problems in a number of Member States in the Eurozone. The EU has effectively had to provide financial support to a number of Member States in the Eurozone and as a result has had to intervene also to create greater fiscal discipline in those states; which has led to plans for greater fiscal integration.

In March 2017, on the eve of celebrating the 60th Anniversary of the EU, the European Commission published the *White Paper on the Future of Europe and the Way Forward*. The White Paper presents five different scenarios on the possible avenues in which the Member States might wish to take the EU in the future. The question is whether the Member States wish to further, pause or decrease the European integration process. The five scenarios are as follows:

- Scenario 1 – Carry on: the EU would pursue its current reform agenda (including on climate and sustainable development issues, financial stability policies, and defence and security strategies) as set out in the European Commission in 2014 and the European Council's Bratislava declaration of 2016.

- Scenario 2 – Nothing but the Single Market: the EU would decrease its intervention in wider policy areas beyond the Single Market (e.g. migration, security) and would essentially be an economic union with less regulatory activities.

- Scenario 3 – Those who want more do more: the EU would allow different speeds to the integration process, facilitating the means for a 'coalition of the willing' to work closer with each other in certain policy areas, whilst allowing other Member States to step back or join in as suits them.

- Scenario 4 – Doing less more efficiently: the EU would revise its key developmental priorities and ring-fence its resources to a selected few – in other words, the EU would do less but better in those chosen policy areas.
- Scenario 5 – Doing much more together: the EU would decide to deepen the integration process by 'sharing more power, resources and decision-making across the board' (a.k.a. go full union).

The aim of the White Paper is to open discussion and debate on the future direction of the EU; something that has arguably been much needed since the creation of the citizenship of the EU by the Maastricht Treaty 1992, i.e. since the EU became a more recognisable (if yet undefined) form of political community. The Nice summit and the Laeken Declaration already alluded to the need for reflecting on the nature of the European venture. The Treaty of Lisbon (as a different incarnation of the failed Constitutional Treaty) failed to answer the Union's existentialist question. It is Brexit (which was set to inspire a potential Grexit, Frexit or Nexit if national populists are to be believed) that acted as a catalyst for the White Paper's call to reflect on the EU's future. Whatever the outcome of the Brexit negotiations, the debate on the future, nature and purpose of the EU that ensues is worthwhile if the EU is to remain relevant to the future generations of European citizens.

ACTIVITY

Self-assessment questions

1. In what ways is it wrong to suggest that the idea of a united Europe is a new idea?
2. What was the main reason why the idea of an integrated Europe was so important and so desirable during the 1940s and 1950s?
3. What is the importance of the Marshall Plan?
4. What part did the Schuman Plan play in the creation of the EC?
5. What resulted from the Spaak Report?
6. What were the main objectives of the EC Treaty and how were they to be achieved?
7. What were the basic differences between the 'federalists' and the 'functionalists' and in what way were the 'neo-functionalists' a development?
8. What exactly is meant by the term 'supranationalism'?
9. In what ways did the SEA help to develop the original Treaties?
10. What institutional and constitutional reform was made in the SEA?
11. What were the main objectives of the TEU?
12. What major changes were made by the TEU?
13. What changes were made in the Treaty of Amsterdam?
14. What was the central purpose of the Treaty of Nice?
15. What further developments were made in the Treaty of Nice?
16. What precisely is the meaning of 'enlargement'?
17. To what extent has the EC been enlarged?
18. What are the problems associated with enlargement?
19. Why was it felt necessary to introduce a Draft Constitution?
20. What did the drafters wish to be the key features of the Draft Constitution?
21. What are the major differences between the Constitutional Treaty and the Reform Treaty (the Treaty of Lisbon)?
22. What is the scope of application of the Charter of Fundamental Rights?

Origins	
Background	Many examples of desire for a united Europe: • early Roman Catholic Church; • Charlemagne and the 'Holy Roman Empire'; • Henry IV of France and the Christian Commonwealth of Europe; • Napoleon Bonaparte declared ambition for a European empire; • Hitler's expansionist philosophy; • also, Kant, Rousseau, Marx and Nietzsche all advocated a united Europe.
Growth of organisations	IMF, GATT, OEC, Council of Europe, BENELUX Union.
Schuman Plan	Drafted by Jean Monnet – led to ECSC.
Spaak Report	Led to EURATOM.
Overall aim	No more wars in Europe.
Members	Six countries: France, Germany, Italy, Belgium, the Netherlands and Luxembourg.
Objectives of EC law	
Aim of EC Treaty	• To 'lay the foundations of an ever closer union among the peoples of Europe [by] pooling their resources to preserve and strengthen peace and liberty'. • To be achieved by integration of Member States' economic and monetary policies for creation of a common market free from internal barriers to trade.
Key objectives	• Introduction of 'Four Freedoms' – freedom of movement of workers, right to establish and provide services, free movement of goods, free movement of capital within the Community. • Progressive approximation of economic policies of Member States and harmonisation of national laws in e.g. agriculture, transport and trade. • Creation of Common Customs Tariff. • Creation of Common Commercial Policy.
Development of the Treaties	
ECSC	• Created the Communities and the legal order.
EURATOM, EC	• Created the institutions.
SEA	• Put in place the Common Market. • Introduced co-operation procedure for legislation. • Created European Council and Court of First Instance. • Extended qualified majority voting (QMV) in Council.
TEU	• Created the Union and the idea of citizenship. • Added two more pillars: foreign affairs and security, and justice and home affairs (based on co-operation). • Introduced co-decision procedure for legislation. • Introduced EMU. • Some institutional reform and extended QMV in Council. • Subsidiarity.

ToA	• Renumbered original EC Treaty and repealed many obsolete Articles. • Some institutional reform and extension of QMV in Council. • Broadened objectives e.g. new discrimination law. • Introduced 'closer co-operation'.
ToN	Institutional reforms for enlargement in 2004.
ToL	More institutional reform, amended provisions of the TEU; altered the EC Treaty to Treaty on the Functioning of the European Union (TFEU); elevated the CFR to primary legislation status.
CFR	Legally binding since the ToL; catalogue of rights ensuring visibility and accessibility of citizens' freedoms; binding on Member States and EU institutions.
Enlargement	
1973	UK, Ireland and Denmark.
1981	Greece.
1986	Portugal and Spain.
1995	Austria, Finland and Sweden.
2004	Czech Republic, Hungary, Poland, Slovakia, Slovenia, Estonia, Lithuania, Latvia, Malta and Cyprus.
2007	Romania and Bulgaria
2013	Croatia
Applications	Turkey, Macedonia, Montenegro, Serbia and Albania
The EU Constitution	
Purpose	Laeken Declaration committed Union to becoming more democratic, more transparent and more effective, so need to create a constitution (single document in readable form) – set up Convention for this purpose.
Form of Draft Constitution	• First part – objectives, powers and decision-making processes of the Union. • Second part incorporates the Charter of Fundamental Rights. • Third part – policies of the Union. • Fourth part – Final Clauses (includes procedures for adopting and reviewing Constitution.
The Reform Treaty (the Treaty of Lisbon)	Following failure to ratify Constitutional Treaty, Reform Treaty introduced – retains much of Constitutional Treaty but an amending Treaty not a single Constitution.

SUMMARY

- There are many examples of former attempts at a united Europe.
- The EU (formerly the EC) was created following the Second World War with its key aim being: to 'lay the foundations of an ever closer union among the peoples of Europe [by] pooling their resources to preserve and strengthen peace and liberty', and this was to be achieved by integration of Member States' economic and monetary policies for creation of a common market free from internal barriers to trade.

- The original six Member States has expanded to 27.
- A variety of Treaties has expanded the scope of the original Treaties.
- The Lisbon Treaty, while an amending treaty, introduces wide scale institutional reform and gives legal fore to the Charter of Fundamental Rights.

Further reading

Articles

Lenaerts, K, 'Exploring the Limits of the EU Charter of Fundamental Rights' (2012) 8 *EuConst* 375–403.

Meyring, B, 'Intergovernmentalism and Supranationality: Two Stereotypes for a Complex Reality' (1997) 22 *ELR* 221.

Wouters, J, 'Institutional and Constitutional Challenges for the European Union: Some Reflections in the Light of the Treaty of Nice' (2001) 26 *ELR* 342.

Books

Douglas-Scott, S, *Constitutional Law of the European Union* (Longman, 2002), Chapter 1.

Kaczarowska-Ireland, A, *European Union Law* (Routledge, 2016).

Ward, I, *A Critical Introduction to European Law* (3rd edn, Cambridge, 2011), Chapter 1.

Websites

More information on the European Union can be obtained on the website at: http://europa.eu.

2

The political and legal institutions of the European Union

AIMS AND OBJECTIVES

After reading this chapter you should be able to:

- Understand the origins and development of the different institutions
- Understand the composition and role of the Council of Ministers
- Understand the function of the European Council
- Understand the composition and role of the European Commission
- Understand the composition and role of the European Parliament
- Understand the role and composition of the Court of Justice and of the General Court
- Understand the rationale for and character of the other major institutions
- Evaluate the effectiveness of each institution
- Analyse the interrelationship between the institutions
- Evaluate the democratic nature and accountability of the institutions

2.1 The origins and development of the institutions

Both the original concept and indeed the major character of the key institutions of the EU actually came about in the ECSC Treaty. The framers of the Treaty realised that in order to have the sort of Community envisaged by the founders such as Jean Monnet, which could work effectively and prevent outbreak of another European war, it was vital to have both a legal order and a legislative system that could work independently of the Member States.

The next realisation was that this in itself would require the creation of institutions that were demonstrably supranational, bodies that could work independently of the Member States for the achievement of the aims of the Treaty.

In this way the ECSC Treaty introduced the essential concept of 'community', as we know it now. The European Coal and Steel Community was created with a number of significant features in mind:

- that the Community should have a distinct legal personality;
- that it should work through and be represented by entirely autonomous institutions;
- that Member States which became signatories to the Treaty should agree to cede (or more precisely pool) certain aspects of **their** national sovereignty in order to achieve defined objectives identified in the Treaty.

The institutions of the new 'Community' were created on this basis. The first of these institutions was originally known as the 'High Authority'. This body was to effectively control the production of coal and steel and was given power by the Treaty to make legally binding decisions as well as recommendations.

This body was supplemented by the creation of a 'Common Assembly'. This was a representative assembly to be made up of members from the various signatory states. It would have only very limited supervisory powers.

To these bodies was added a 'Special Council of Ministers' of the Member States. The Council's powers were partly legislative and partly consultative.

The final body devised in the Treaty was a 'Court of Justice'. The straightforward role of the Court was laid out in Article 31 of the Treaty, 'to ensure that in the interpretation and application of this Treaty ... the law is observed'.

When both the EEC Treaty and the EURATOM Treaty were created they followed exactly the same pattern, establishing 'Communities' with four key institutions, all autonomous, and all able to exercise powers stipulated in the Treaties creating them.

In these two Treaties, bodies called 'Commissions' in fact replaced the 'High Authority' of the ECSC. These Commissions initially had more limited powers and ranked behind both the Assembly and the Council.

At the same time that these two later Treaties were signed, a Convention created a single Assembly and a single Court of Justice that would represent all three Communities rather than having separate institutions for each.

Much later, in the Brussels Treaty 1967 (referred to as the Merger Treaty), a single Council was introduced for all three Communities. Also in the same Treaty the High Authority of the ECSC and the two Commissions of the other two Communities were merged into a single Commission. The Communities were nevertheless kept separate and the powers exercised by the individual institutions would be by reference to the specific Treaty.

The institutional structure of the EU is in fact quite unique. For instance it is not like the governing structure of any international organisation since the institutions are able to exercise sovereign powers that are in effect transferred to them by the Member States on joining.

Neither is it like any normal parliamentary democracy. There is of course no clear separation of powers between the executive and legislative functions as there would be in the constitutions of the Member States. However, there is a separation of interests.

There are complex legislative processes with both the Commission and the Council being potential sources of interpretation for legislation and the possibility of amendment or consultation by Parliament before legislation is in fact passed or created by the Council. Indeed there are even other bodies before which draft legislation might be presented before it is actually passed by the Council.

The nature of the different institutions and the various powers or responsibilities given to them means that the Commission is in fact a sort of executive but one without real executive powers. The Court of Justice is not a court of the type that we are familiar with but exercises a supervisory function and ensures that the division of power between the other institutions and between the EU and the Member States is maintained and preserved.

In keeping with the wishes of the founders of the Treaties the institutions all have broad autonomy and also their own rules of procedure. However, whatever the power of the individual bodies the overriding ruler of the EU is in fact the Treaties themselves. Everything done by the institutions must be for the furtherance of the objectives set in the Treaties.

These four basic institutions are still the main ones but they have also been added to over the years through provisions in the original Treaties or in the different subsequent Treaties:

- Article 4 of the EC Treaty allowed for the setting up of both an Economic and Social Committee and a Court of Auditors (to audit the accounts of the institutions). These two bodies have been created and the latter was made an independent body as the result of the TEU.
- Article 4 also allowed for the creation of COREPER, the Committee of Permanent Representatives. This is a vital part of the legislative process.
- The SEA 1986 then also established the Court of First Instance, a vital addition to ease the burden on the ECJ.
- A Committee of the Regions was also added by the TEU 1992.
- The TEU also provided for a European Investment Bank as well as a European Central Bank.

Besides new institutions being added to the original four, the role of the original institutions has also changed over the years. The new institutions have created extra complexity in the overall administration but have not necessarily improved it.

The balance of power between the Council and the Commission has shifted in a way that was never envisaged in the Treaties. As a result, intergovernmental decision-making took precedence over supranational authority. In fact, the power of the Council increased because of the evolution of the European Council, the importance of the presidency and the co-operation procedure (today known as the Ordinary Legislative Procedure). Besides this, the work of COREPER in many ways supports the individual states.

The role of the European Parliament (EP) has also increased. It now has a much greater and more significant role in legislation as a co-legislator with the council of the EU, which makes the European Parliament (EP) a key player in the law-making and decision-making processes in the EU public order. It also has in effect control over a significant part of the budget and in its supervisory capacity was able to react dramatically in forcing the resignation of the Commission in 1999.

2.2 The Council of Ministers and the European Council

2.2.1 The Council

The Council is governed by Articles 237–243 TFEU and Article 16 TEU. While the Treaty itself merely refers to it as 'Council' it was traditionally referred to as the 'Council of Ministers'. However, following the TEU the Council chose to change its name to the 'Council of the European Union'. The Lisbon Treaty also refers to 'Council'.

Composition

The Council in terms of its membership is in fact a fluid concept with what amounts to a floating membership. In this sense it is unlike other bodies with similar functions.

According to Article 16(6) TEU: 'The Council shall consist of an authorised representative of each Member State at ministerial level, authorised to commit the government of that State', although the original intention was that the Council should in effect be a college of delegates with each state appointing a Minister for the specific purpose.

The consequence of the definition is that the specific identity of a Minister attending a meeting of the Council depends entirely on the subject of discussion at the meeting. If the meeting concerns agriculture it will be the Agriculture Minister. If it concerns transport it will be the Transport Minister, and so on. The important point is that each Minister has the power to commit the whole government of the Member State but is then accountable to his national Parliament which is said to ensure democratic legitimacy. The composition of the Council would also have been changed significantly under the Constitutional Treaty.

The role of Council

Article 16(1) TEU identifies the role of Council in the following way: 'Council shall, jointly with the European Parliament, exercise legislative and budgetary functions. It shall carry out policy-making and co-ordinating functions as laid down in the Treaties.' In fact, Council actually has six key responsibilities:

- Legislation – it is often said that 'the Commission proposes and Council disposes'. Council, through the different legislative procedures, acts on proposals from the Commission and with the advice of Parliament passes EU law. In this respect Council is the key decision-maker within the EU.

- Co-ordinating economic policy within the Union – the EU is an economic union and the Common Market is a significant part of that.

- Forming international agreements on behalf of the Member States – possibly on trade, technology, development, etc.

- Approving the EU budget – the budget is in two parts: compulsory (for instance agricultural) and non-compulsory (which deals with the upkeep of the institutions). Both Council and Parliament must agree on the budget.

- Developing common foreign and security policies – this is only based on co-operation as Member States retain their own independent control over, e.g. defence. But there is much to be gained by working together and there is for instance an EU 'Rapid Reaction Force' of military personnel.

- Co-ordinating co-operation of justice systems of the Member States – different Member States have different legal systems but the EU can usefully work in co-operation on areas such as drug-trafficking, international fraud and terrorism.

The presidency

The Council has a rotating presidency which is for a six-month period. Each period is headed by a different Member State.

Indeed, since the Treaty of Lisbon (ToL), the Council presidency operates under the 'trio' mechanism or programme, whereby Member States are each called to preside over the Council activities in groups of three. For instance, Estonia, Bulgaria and Austria are the current presidency trio for the (respectively) following periods July–December 2017, January–June 2018, and July–December 2018. The trios work closely together to ensure the continuity of the EU's legislative agenda and key areas of policy activities. The main tasks of the Council presidency is to plan and chair Council meetings; and to represent the Council vis-à-vis other EU institutions. Because the Council meets with a different make up according to the area covered, this allows each configuration to be headed by a representative of each Member State on rotation.

As with the former system there are advantages to being President since the President sets the agenda.

Voting

Council is the major legislative organ, although there are some limited exceptions to this. It does consult both Parliament and the Economic and Social Committee but nevertheless it makes the final decision on any legislation. On this basis the voting system in Council is also very important.

Voting procedure is identified in Article 205 and it is of two main types:

- **Unanimous.** This is required for a number of areas, notably common foreign and security policy, taxation, and asylum and immigration. Since the 'Luxembourg Accords' it was always available if vital national interests were at stake. The consequence of a unanimous vote is that Member States in effect have a veto on issues. With enlargement it would seriously damage the development of the EU if too many issues required unanimous voting. As a result the Treaty of Nice reduced quite drastically the number of areas requiring unanimity. In any case the Treaties envisaged that all voting after the transitional period would be by qualified majority.

- **Qualified Majority Voting.** Since the 1960s, when numerous vetoes by France caused stagnation, this has been the most common method of voting. Under the old system of 87 votes a minimum of 62 votes was needed to carry a measure. The process was obviously also designed to prevent large states from abusing their power at the expense of the smaller ones. Since 1995, therefore, 26 votes represented a blocking minority, well within the capability of smaller states joining together.

All decisions are voted on. Because of the diversity of the countries that are members of the EU voting is inevitably weighted. Countries are given more votes according to the size of their populations and their economic influence. However, the weighting is also artificial in these terms to favour the smaller countries.

Before 1 May 2004 there were only 15 Member States and the voting system was limited to 87 votes as follows:

Germany, France, Italy, UK	10 votes each
Spain	8 votes
Belgium, Netherlands, Portugal, Greece	5 votes each
Sweden, Austria	4 votes each
Finland, Denmark, Ireland	3 votes each
Luxembourg	2 votes

Enlargement in 2004 increased membership of the EU by a further ten countries. The weighting of votes inevitably had to change to accommodate the new members. There was a new system of weighting from 1 November 2004, with the total number of votes 321, broken down as follows:

Germany, France, Italy, UK	29 votes each
Spain, Poland	27 votes each
Netherlands	13 votes
Belgium, Czech Republic, Greece, Hungary, Portugal	12 votes each
Austria, Sweden	10 votes each
Denmark, Ireland, Lithuania, Slovakia, Finland	7 votes each
Cyprus, Estonia, Latvia, Luxembourg, Slovenia	4 votes each
Malta	3 votes

From 1 November 2004 a Qualified Majority Vote occurs in the following circumstances:

- a majority of Member States (in some cases a two-thirds majority) approve the measure; and
- a minimum of 232 votes is cast in favour of the measure – this represents 72.3 per cent of the votes available (and is roughly the same as the previous 62 votes from 87).

In addition, under the new system Member States are able to ask for confirmation that the vote represents at least 62 per cent of the total population of the EU. If not, then the measure may not be adopted.

As from 1 January 2007, reflecting the membership of Romania and Bulgaria, the allocation of votes under the procedure was as follows:

Germany, France, Italy, UK	29 votes each
Spain, Poland	27 votes each
Romania	14 votes
Netherlands	13 votes
Belgium, Czech Republic, Greece, Hungary, Portugal	12 votes each
Austria, Sweden, Bulgaria	10 votes each
Denmark, Ireland, Lithuania, Slovakia, Finland,	7 votes each
Cyprus, Estonia, Latvia, Luxembourg, Slovenia	4 votes each
Malta	3 votes

Following the addition of Croatia as the newest Member State on 1 July 2013 the votes under the procedure is as follows:

Germany, France, Italy, UK	29 votes each
Spain, Poland	27 votes each
Romania	14 votes
Netherlands	13 votes
Belgium, Czech Republic, Greece, Hungary, Portugal	12 votes each
Austria, Sweden, Bulgaria	10 votes each
Denmark, Ireland, Lithuania, Slovakia, Finland, Croatia	7 votes each
Cyprus, Estonia, Latvia, Luxembourg, Slovenia	4 votes each
Malta	3 votes

This amounts to 352 votes and now a qualified majority will be reached either:

- where a majority of the 28 Member States votes in favour (sometimes even two-thirds); and
- at least 260 of the 352 votes are in favour of the measure.

From then the definition of qualified majority will be a double majority so that, to be adopted, an act must have the support of at least 55 per cent of the EU Member States and must represent at least 65 per cent of the population of the EU. A blocking minority must include at least four Member States. However, between November 2014 and March 2017, any Member State may request that the current weighted voting system be applied.

After 2014 the means of identifying the votes available to each Member State is to change. After that time a double majority system is to be introduced based on the number of states and population.

2.2.2 The European Council

The European Council is not a creation of the Treaties. It was devised and agreed on by a meeting of heads of state in 1974 and was formally put in place in the Single European Act in 1986. Following the Lisbon Treaty it is now an established institution of the EU governed by Articles 235–236 TFEU and Article 15 TEU.

Its role is to 'provide the Union with the necessary impetus for development [and to] define the general political guidelines'.

It involves twice-yearly meetings of the heads of state of the Member States together with their Foreign Ministers. These are usually referred to as 'summits'. These involve general policy-making and also the two pillars that do not have the force of Community law: common foreign and security policy, and police and judicial co-operation in criminal matters.

One other useful aspect of these meetings is that they provide the means of assuring approval of measures proposed by the Commission. If the European Council has accepted proposals then it is unlikely that they would be rejected by vote in the Council of Ministers. This helps to streamline the process of legislation.

Presidency of the European Council used to rotate with the presidency of Council between Member States. The Lisbon Treaty created a new system. The President is elected by a qualified majority of the members for a period of two-and-a-half years. This term of office can be extended once. The President represents the EU in common foreign and security policies, and also acts as chair.

2.3 The European Commission

The Commission is governed by Articles 244–250 TFEU. Of all the EU institutions it probably has the clearest claim to being a supranational body of the type envisaged by the founders of the Treaties.

The Commission actually refers to two groups of people. It refers to the Commissioners themselves, those representatives appointed from Member States who run the various departments. It also of course refers to the whole staff of the Commission, administrative officials, translators, secretaries and other staff of which there are about 38,000 with about 23,000 working in Brussels.

The Commission essentially acts as an executive arm of the EU. It is sometimes compared to a civil service but in fact it has much broader powers and roles than any civil service.

Composition and appointment

Prior to enlargement the Commission comprised 20 Commissioners. According to Article 213 there should be at least one from each Member State but not more than two. In practice, then, traditionally the larger states – France, Germany, Italy, the UK and Spain – had two Commissioners while the other states had one each.

Because of impending enlargement the Treaty of Nice provided in an amended Article 213(1) that from 1 January 2005 the Commission should include one national of each Member State. This means that the larger states will lose their extra Commissioner and this is to prevent the Commission from becoming too large and unmanageable with enlargement. The amended Article also stipulates that once there are 27 Member States there will be fewer Commissioners than Member States so that the Council will introduce a rotation system. However, the Accession Treaty for the entry of Romania and Bulgaria provided for both to gain a Commissioner, and Croatia also gained a Commissioner on entry in 2013 so the number is now 28. However, under the Reform Treaty, if ratified, from 2014 the number of Commissioners will reduce to a number equivalent to two-thirds of the number of Member States, and these will be selected on a strict rotational basis. A fixed-term presidency would also be introduced.

The Draft Constitution proposed that the composition should be modified, with a President, the Minister of Foreign Affairs (who would have the title of Vice-President) and 13 Commissioners. These would be selected on the basis of an equal rota system between the Member States. Besides these, the President would have the power to appoint additional 'Commissioners' from all other Member States, who would have no voting rights. However, because of the first Irish referendum on ratification of the Lisbon Treaty, the European Council has agreed to keep to the current system of one member for each Member State.

A new Commission is appointed every five years. Commissioners are chosen on grounds of general competence, from persons 'whose independence is beyond doubt'. In practice they are nominated by their Member States but the process of approval and appointment involves the approval of Parliament too.

Commissioners, although they are nominated by their Member States, are required by Article 213 to take an oath to be independent and neither to seek nor to take instructions from their Member State. The Member State also undertakes not to influence the

Commissioners. Each Commissioner is appointed for a five-year term and is appointed a Directorate General with specific responsibilities, for example for employment or transport or the Internal Market.

The President

The Commission is headed by a President. The President is nominated by the governments of the Member States but must be approved as part of the whole Commission by Parliament.

Post-Treaty of Lisbon, for the first time in Union history, the appointment of the Commission President became politicised and somewhat democratised as EU citizens' vote for members of the European Parliament could influence the latter's choice of Commission President. The main European Parliament political parties each put forward their designated candidate for nomination – this practice, which originates from Germany, is known as spitzenkandidaten. The European People's Party (EPP) lead candidate for the Commission 2014–2019 term won as Jean-Claude Juncker became President.

According to Article 250 TFEU, 'The Commission shall work under the political guidance of its President.' The President has the authority to decide on the internal organisation of the Commission and the President clearly has the authority within this to allocate responsibilities among the Commissioners.

The role of the Commission

The Commission is collegiate in character and it tends to act on the basis of simple majority votes.

Its key responsibilities are:

- **To initiate legislation.** The Commission proposes legislation and can draft proposals on anything covered by the Treaties which it presents to Parliament and the Council. In doing so it takes advice from the Economic and Social Committee and the Committee of the Regions. So that it does not interfere in issues that can be better dealt with by the Member States themselves, the Commission also operates according to the 'subsidiarity' principle.

- **To enforce the law.** The Commission has often been referred to as the 'watchdog' or 'guardian' of the Treaties. Article 4(3) TEU demands that all Member States are obliged to achieve the objectives of the Treaties. The Commission must then ensure that all Member States are applying EU law properly. It can then deal with breaches of EU law by Member States through Article 258 proceedings. Initially the Commission would use the 'infringement procedure' but if a Member State fails to respond then it can take the matter to the ECJ.

- **To implement policy and the EU budget.** The Commission has executive functions. As a result, it is responsible for managing policy. For instance, traditionally it had a key role in EU competition law. It is also responsible for the compulsory budget. Even though it is actually national and local authorities that usually spend the money the Commission still has supervisory responsibility. In particular, the Commission would be responsible for the European Social Fund and the Regional Development Fund.

- **To represent the EU internationally.** The Commission speaks for all the Member States in international meetings such as in the World Trade Organisation or the United Nations. It also negotiates international agreements for the EU, an example being the Cotonou Agreement which is a trade agreement between the EU and certain developing nations in Africa and the Caribbean.

Through a process known as **comity** the Council can delegate power to the Commission for it to produce detailed regulations following the passing of a framework regulation by the Council.

It must be remembered, though, that the Commission is also accountable to Parliament in certain ways. Parliament is able to pass a motion of censure on the Commission under Article 234 TFEU, causing the Commission to resign. This in fact happened in 1999 following a lengthy inquiry into fraud.

2.4 The European Parliament

In the original EC Treaty Parliament was identified as the Assembly and its role was to 'exercise the advisory and supervisory powers' conferred upon it. It was not a democratically elected body and it was made up of appointed nominees from the Member State governments. The limited powers of the Assembly were another reason for the complaint of a democratic deficit since it had no legislative power and could only act in a consultative capacity.

Since 1979, however, it has been an elected body with elections every five years using proportional representation. Parliament is governed by Articles 123–234 TFEU.

Composition

Prior to enlargement the total membership of Parliament was 626 MEPs. Membership in fact depends on the size and importance of the particular Member State. The Treaty of Amsterdam amended Article 189 to provide a maximum number of 700 MEPs. Because of impending enlargement Article 189 was subsequently amended also in the Treaty of Nice to provide for a maximum number of 732 MEPs.

The number of seats in the European Parliament for the 2009–14 term is 736. The allocation of MEPs by country from the start of the parliamentary term from 2009–14 was as follows:

Member State	Number of MEPs each
Germany	99
France, Italy, UK	72
Poland, Spain	50
Romania	33
Netherlands	25
Belgium, Greece, Portugal, Czech Republic, Hungary	22
Sweden	18
Austria, Bulgaria	17
Denmark, Finland, Slovakia	13
Ireland, Lithuania	12
Latvia	8
Slovenia	7
Cyprus, Estonia, Luxembourg	6
Malta	5

Because there were delays in ratifying the Treaty of Lisbon, elections for this Parliament took place under the cap created under the Treaty of Nice. An amendment to the Treaty in 2011 allowed for 18 further MEPs to be elected prior to 2014 and Croatia on entry was allowed 12 MEPs. As a result the membership of Parliament went up to 766. However, since the 2014 European Parliament elections, the number of MEPs is now capped at 751 (750 MEPs and 1 President). The allocation by country is now as follows:

Member State	Number of MEPs each
Germany	96
France	74
Italy, UK	73
Spain	54
Poland	51
Romania	32
Netherlands	26
Belgium, Greece, Portugal, Czech Republic, Hungary	21
Sweden	20
Austria	18
Bulgaria	17
Denmark, Finland, Slovakia	13
Ireland, Lithuania, Croatia	11
Latvia	8
Slovenia	7
Cyprus, Estonia, Luxembourg, Malta	6

MEPs are elected for a period of five years. They in fact sit in Parliament according to loose political groupings including representatives from a number of Member States rather than according to any national interest. In this respect there is no mandatory voting for Member State interests, as MEPs are representatives and not delegates.

Parliament sits for one week in each month except August, although it can also sit at other times when certain items require discussion. Voting is on a simple majority basis. There are also a number of specialist parliamentary committees. Parliament also elects its own President and various officials.

The role of Parliament

Parliament currently enjoys three main powers:

- It has a role in **legislation**. In the Ordinary Legislative Procedure (OLP and previously known as the co-decision procedure), now the most common method for introducing legislation, Parliament has an important role and can make amendments to legislative proposals, as set out in Article 294 TFEU. In some cases, the EP can exercise a veto (under the special legislative procedure as set out by the Treaties, such as the consent procedure). Under the co-operation procedure, which was introduced in the SEA and is now another special legislative procedure (SLP) known as the consent procedure, the European Parliament also has a consultative role, where the Council is required to seek the EP's opinion although it is not bound to follow it. Special legislative procedures are not specifically defined and their use is determined by certain provisions of the Treaties. Nevertheless, their legal base is found in Article 289(2) TFEU. Parliament is further able to examine the annual work programme of the Commission.

- It has a **supervisory** role over other EU institutions. This is particularly the case with the Commission. Parliament must approve each new Commission. It can also pass a motion of censure on the Commission. The effect of such a censure was seen in 1999 when it led to the resignation of the entire Commission. It is also able to send questions to the Council and also can express its views to each meeting of the European Council. The supervisory power of Parliament over the Commission has also been extended. Article 17(7) TEU requires that the commissioners, including the President and the High Representative of the Union for Foreign Affairs and Security Policy, are subject to the consent of Parliament subject to taking up office.

- It has powers over the **budget**. Parliament is required to approve each annual budget. In the case of a failure to accept the budget the effect is dramatic since this includes the day-to-day payment of all officials in the institutions. The Treaty of Lisbon extended the power of Parliament over the budget. Now under Article 314(4) TFEU it has the power to amend any part of the budget, whether the compulsory or the non-compulsory.

Despite the increasing powers afforded by the Treaty of Lisbon, criticisms of democratic deficit are still levelled against the European Parliament. There is still some discontent that the EP is unable to initiate legislation itself, despite the introduction of Article 225 in the TFEU which give the EP a right of initiative – indeed, the provision enables the EP to request a legislative proposal from the Commission, however, the latter can decline provided it can justify its refusal to oblige. Also, the censure facility only covers the whole Commission and some feel there should be the power to censure and remove individual Commissioners. It is also felt by some that the Council should be more accountable to Parliament. The main suggestion in the EU Constitution affecting Parliament is for an extension of the co-decision procedure in legislating.

2.5 Court of Justice of the European Union (and the General Court)

2.5.1 The Court of Justice
The Court of Justice is not like any court in the English legal system. In fact, it is a court with few meaningful comparisons. As can be seen in Chapters 7, 8 and 9, the Court has played an absolutely vital role in the development of EU law.

The rules governing the Court of Justice are found in Articles 251–281 TFEU and by the Statute of the Court of Justice, but also in the Protocol on the Statute of the Court of Justice of the European Community. The latter is added to the Treaty in effect as an annex and contains all the procedural rules of the Court. The procedures must be voted on by Council but since the Treaty of Nice this is done with a Qualified Majority Vote rather than requiring a unanimous vote as was the case before. The Court and the CFI (now the General Court) made representations at the Nice summit that they should be able to determine and adapt the procedure themselves but this has not been accepted.

The composition of the Court
The CJEU is composed of *juges rapporteurs* (the judges) who are assisted by *Advocates-General*. Article 253 identifies the requirements for appointment of both:

> '[they] shall be chosen from persons whose independence is beyond doubt and who possess the qualifications required for appointment to the highest judicial offices in their respective countries or who are jurisconsults of recognised competence'.

As a result of this the judges are chosen from high-level judges from the Member States or highly competent lawyers who are independent beyond doubt so that they can be relied upon to show impartiality. Indeed, they must all swear an oath of impartiality.

In terms of numbers, before enlargement Article 19 TEU provided that 'The CJEU shall consist of 15 judges'. This did in fact reflect the number of Member States and a judge for each one. The Treaty of Nice amends Article 221 to provide that the Court will consist of 'one judge per Member State'. Following the accession of Bulgaria, Romania and Croatia the number is currently 28.

Both the judges of the CJEU and the Advocates-General are appointed by joint agreement of the governments of the Member States.

Article 19 TEU, stipulates that there shall be one judge appointed from each Member State. The Treaty also provides for the appointment of eight Advocates-General to assist the Court. Both judges and Advocates-General serve for a six-year term. There is a staggered re-appointment system and it is possible to be re-appointed for a further one or two periods of three years. Removal of a judge is possible only if all colleagues agree that the judge in question is unfit to serve.

Under Article 254 TFEU, the judges appoint a President from among themselves. The President serves for a three-year period. The President generally directs the business of the Court, appoints a specific *juge rapporteur* to manage a specific case, and tends also to deal with all interlocutory matters.

The role of the Court

By Article 13(2) TEU the Court of Justice and the General Court can only act in areas where jurisdiction has been specifically given to them in the Treaties.

There are three central objectives in the work of the Court:

- to ensure that in application and interpretation the law is observed;
- to provide a forum for resolving disputes between institutions, Member States and individuals;
- to protect individual rights.

The Court hears five main types of action:

- Article 267 references from Member States for a preliminary ruling on an interpretation of EU law (known also as indirect actions) (see Chapter 6).
- Article 258 actions against Member States for failing to implement Treaty obligations (a direct action known also as infringement proceedings).
- Article 263 actions against an institution for abuse of power.
- Article 265 actions against an institution for a failure to act.
- Article 340 actions for damages against an institution that has been responsible for loss to the individual (for example where the Commission has failed to address a decision to a body engaging in anti-competitive practices and an individual suffers loss as a result).

(See Chapter 5 for the last four.)

Procedure

Traditionally, most issues involving Member States or an institution were heard by a full court. There were some straightforward issues where it was possible for a bench of three or five judges to reach a decision. This was appropriate where the Court was limited in size to 15 judges. Obviously, enlargement means that a plenary session of the Court could involve a very large number of judges. Therefore, for the sake of efficiency, the Treaty of Nice allows the Court to sit as a 'Grand Chamber' of fewer judges instead of always having to meet in plenary session. In any case, Article 17 of the Statute of the Court of Justice provides that a decision of the Court is valid only if the Court comprises an uneven number of judges.

Decisions of the Court are thus based on a majority. Procedure is essentially inquisitorial. There is no provision for individual judges to deliver dissenting judgments.

Cases are submitted through the 'registry' and the President of the Court assigns the case to a specific judge to manage. In the first stage all parties make written submissions on which the judge writes a report and then passes everything on to an Advocate-General assigned to the case. The Advocate-General then produces a reasoned opinion for the Court. This does not have to be followed by the Court but it may be. Following the introduction of the reasoned opinion the judge prepares a draft ruling which is passed to the other members of the Court.

A public hearing of the action is held before the whole court in plenary session (or post-enlargement a grand chamber of the Court) or, depending on the type and complexity of the issue, a chamber of three or five judges. All parties can put their case and the Court can ask questions.

2.5.2 The General Court

Because of the excess workload of the Court of Justice and the long delays that resulted from this, a Court of First Instance (CFI) was created in the SEA. Since the Treaty of Lisbon this is now the General Court. The Court is governed by Article 256 TFEU which also identifies the types of case that could be heard by the Court.

The jurisdiction of the General Court when it was the CFI was limited to actions including staff cases and some actions under competition law.

An amendment in the TEU added another category:

- actions by natural or legal persons under either Article 230 or Article 232 (now Articles 263 and 265 TFEU), including anti-dumping cases.

Originally the Court was specifically excluded from hearing Article 267 references. Following the Treaty of Nice, the Court can hear references for preliminary rulings on specific areas although there are as yet no specific areas identified in the Treaty.

The Treaty of Nice expanded the jurisdiction of the CFI, now the General Court, so that it can hear all actions under Articles 263, 265, 268, 270 and 272 TFEU that are not already attached to a 'judicial panel' or those that are required by the Statute of the Court of Justice to be heard in the CJEU. Judicial panels annexed to the General Court (formerly the CCFI) were another creation of the Treaty of Nice. The Council may set up such panels to hear specific types of action in specific areas to deal with issues speedily.

The regulations and requirements for the General Court are similar to those for the CJEU. Membership of the Court again is based on a representative from each Member State, with similar qualifications needed (although the General Court does not have advocates-general). While independence again is an absolute requirement, members of the Court must merely 'possess the ability required for appointment to judicial office'. From 2019, the membership of the General Court will increase from 28 to 56 judges.

In diagram form, the courts can be represented as shown in Figure 2.1.

ACTIVITY

Quick quiz

In each of the situations below, identify which institution or institutions is or are likely to be mainly involved (your answer should only refer to the main institutions).

1. Antoinette, a French national and a nurse, has complained that she is being discriminated against because her employer pays her less than is paid to a male hospital administrator, even though Antoinette argues that her work is of equal value to the employer. The French court has identified that an interpretation of EU law would be decisive.
2. Research by various bodies has indicated that a regulation should be introduced on levels of a particular chemical in certain foodstuffs because the chemical is potentially harmful to children.
3. The Commission has been exposed for financial irregularities in relation to certain aspects of the budget.
4. Various Member States wish there to be a meeting to determine a combined foreign and security policy in the light of various civil disturbances in parts of the old Soviet Union which are close to the eastern borders of the EU.

Member State governments appoint:

Juges rapporteurs (one for each Member State) together with eight Advocates-General

Both sit for a six-year (renewable) period

Judges must hold high judicial office and be independent and act impartially.

They sit in:

The European Court of Justice –

Different types of actions are heard:

Against Member States:	**Against EU institutions:**	**References from Member States:**
Enforcement proceedings for a failure to honour Treaty obligations (Art 258).	• For annulment of acts beyond the capacity of the institution (Art 263). • For failing to act (Art 265). • For a claim of damages where the institution has caused claimant loss (Art 340).	**For preliminary rulings on the meaning of EU law provisions (Art 267).**

General Court (one Judge from each Member State) hears different actions:
- direct actions by natural and legal persons (not anti-dumping);
- staff cases;
- now jurisdiction is expanded after Treaty of Nice.

Figure 2.1 The work of the CJEU and the General Court

ACTIVITY

Self-assessment questions

1. What was the significance of the 'High Authority' in the ECSC?
2. How does it compare with the modern EU institutions?
3. What are the four main institutions of the EU?
4. Which is the main legislator of the EU?
5. What powers, if any, does Parliament have over the Commission?
6. How did the TEU alter the role of Parliament?
7. How has the Council managed to extend its influence?
8. In what ways is this damaging to the original objectives of the Treaties?
9. What are the main functions of the Commission?
10. In what ways is the Court of Justice different from any English court?
11. What are the major functions of the Court?
12. What are the functions of the General Court?
13. How did the role of the General Court develop after the Treaty of Nice?
14. How important is the Commission in achieving the objectives of the Treaties?
15. Why is there a weighted voting system in the Council?
16. What are the major consequences of the Qualified Majority Voting system?
17. Why do different Member States have different numbers of MEPs?
18. To what extent is the weighting fair?
19. Can small states ever have an influence on policy-making in the EU?
20. What advantage is the use of Advocates-General to the CJEU?
21. What were the major changes to the institutions made by the Treaty of Nice in anticipation of enlargement?
22. What are the major institutional reforms made by the Lisbon Treaty?

ACTIVITY

Essay-writing skills

Read the extract below and give brief answers to the questions that follow it.

> It is suggested that Maastricht, even if it does not effect it, symbolises the respectability of supranationalism as a political idea. The enhancement of the power of the Commission, particularly in A171.2, where it is empowered to enforce ECJ decisions, is at least a gesture of significance.... However, the Commission remains a fundamentally undemocratic institution, whilst the increasingly democratic Parliament remains unacceptably ineffective. The intergovernmental Council remains, after Maastricht as before, the most powerful institution, and whilst it does so, the Community will, in the last resource, remain in the service of the nation states. In conclusion, it might be suggested that Maastricht represents a spiritual victory for supranationalism. Ultimately, however, integration still remains subject to intergovernmental control. The Community remains, after the SEA and Maastricht, a sui generis constitutional order, beyond sovereignty but not federal, characterised by a 'pooling of sovereignty'.
>
> Adapted from I Ward, *A Critical Introduction to European Law* (Butterworths, 1996), p. 44

1. In what ways is the Commission a 'fundamentally undemocratic institution'?
2. To what extent is Parliament 'increasingly democratic but unacceptably ineffective'?
3. What justifications are there for saying that Council is 'the most powerful institution'?

2.6 The other major institutions

2.6.1 The Committee of Permanent Representatives (COREPER)

COREPER is the Committee of Permanent Representatives. The name is an acronym from the French way of referring to the committee. The committee was not a product of the original Treaties but was created by Article 4 of the Merger Treaty in 1965 and now under Article 240 TFEU forms part of the decision-making procedure.

COREPER is a permanent body of representatives from all of the Member States. It was felt to be necessary because of the fluid Membership of Council as a means of informing Ministers from the Member States and streamlining the process of legislation.

In this way individual representatives prepare items of discussion at Council meetings and examine the Commission's legislative proposals for the individual Ministers. Generally, if a proposal can be agreed upon by COREPER before the Council meeting then it will be accepted without need for lengthy discussion.

2.6.2 The Court of Auditors

Again, this body is not a product of the original Treaties but was created by a Secondary Budget Treaty in 1975 and inserted into the Treaty and was eventually made a full institution in the TEU.

The basic role of the Court is to control and supervise the EU budget. It examines the accounts of all revenue and expenditure and in effect checks that the EU budget is correctly implemented by those institutions that are responsible for it. In this way it can investigate the paperwork of any body handling EU funds and can carry out spot checks if appropriate. It also prepares an annual report for Parliament and the Council. It will in any case produce an 'opinion' before any financial measure is adopted. However, it does not have any legal powers of its own but passes information on to the other bodies for them to deal with.

It has qualified members from each Member State who are independent and who are chosen for these qualities.

2.6.3 The Economic and Social Committee

The Economic and Social Committee was established in Article 257 of the EC Treaty and Article 165 of the EURATOM Treaty. It now falls under Article 300 TFEU.

Its purpose is clearly to give advice to either the Council or the Commission on social and economic matters. Advice is given in the form of an opinion. The committee is not officially recognised as one of the institutions so there is no overall obligation to consult it. These institutions do consult the committee then whenever there is a specific obligation in the Treaty. However, where the Council or the Commission fails to consult on a matter where consultation is called for it is possible for the ECJ to annul the measure in question so the committee does actually have some influence. It can in any case deliver an opinion even where it has not been called for.

Article 301 TFEU identifies that after enlargement the committee shall not exceed 350 in number. Council appoints the members of the committee for a period of five years, although this is renewable. Representation on the committee is based on the size of the Member State. After enlargement it is as follows:

Member State	Members
Germany, France, Italy, UK	24 each
Poland, Spain	21 each
Romania	15
Austria, Belgium, Bulgaria, Czech Republic, Greece, Hungary, Netherlands, Portugal, Sweden	12 each
Croatia, Denmark, Finland, Ireland, Lithuania, Slovakia	9 each
Estonia, Latvia, Slovenia	7 each
Cyprus, Luxembourg	6 each
Malta	5

Membership is based on representation of various social or economic activities so it includes various interest groups such as farmers, carriers, dealers and craftsmen of different types.

2.6.4 The Committee of the Regions

The Committee of the Regions is also not recognised as one of the institutions and was not a product of the original Treaties. The committee was created in 1994 after the Treaty of Lisbon under Articles 305–307 TFEU.

It is essentially an advisory body to represent local and regional interests. It will be consulted within the legislative process on matters of regional and local concern such as education, public health, culture and other matters of social concern.

By Article 300 its membership must come from elected members of local and regional bodies (although not national government).

It has the same ceiling on numbers as the Social and Economic Committee and allocation of representation from each Member State is on the same basis.

2.6.5 The European Central Bank

The European Central Bank (ECB) was a creation of the TEU in which provision was made in the Protocol (and now under Articles 282–284 TFEU) to have a Central Bank to act for the EU.

The purpose of setting up such a body is clear. It is an essential element of the policy of European Monetary Union (EMU) and the move to a single currency.

The bank has been in place since 1 January 1999 and has responsibility for monetary policy in the EU. Its primary aim is to maintain price stability. It is the only body allowed to issue euro banknotes.

2.6.6 The European Investment Bank

The Investment Bank was set up by Article 7 of the EC Treaty. The bank's basic mission is to invest in projects that promote the objectives of the EU. It is not financed by the EU budget but by borrowing in the financial markets and also from the Member States.

The bank only invests in projects according to strict criteria:

- the project must help achieve EU objectives, e.g. making small businesses more competitive;
- the project must help mainly disadvantaged regions;
- the project must help to attract other sources of funding.

2.6.7 The European Ombudsman

The position of Ombudsman was created in the TEU. The European Ombudsman operates in the same way as all Ombudsmen and is an intermediary between European citizens and EU institutions. The Ombudsman is elected by the European Parliament for a period of five years.

The Ombudsman acts independently and listens to complaints from EU citizens and investigates examples of maladministration. In an EU context 'maladministration' can concern:

- unfairness;
- discrimination;
- abuse of power;
- lack of information or refusal to give information;
- unnecessary delay in making decisions;
- using incorrect procedures.

The Ombudsman can refer matters to the other institutions to take appropriate action but will not investigate a complaint that has been the subject of a court case.

2.6.8 The impact of Brexit on the EU institutions

Once the UK withdraws from the EU, it can be assumed that with regards to the Council of Ministers of the EU, this would simply mean one less Member States representative in the various Council configurations.

However the issue would require a more creative response to the European Commission staffing and budgetary issues, as well as in relation to the European Parliament's vacated seats.

Although the number of British representatives working in the EU institutions has been in decline in the past decade and only represents 3.8 per cent of the Commission staff, it is still approximately 1126 British nationals who will have to cease their duties as EU civil servants come 29 March 2019.

The number of members' seats at the EP may also be revised and decreased. However, there have also been suggestions that following the departure of the 73 British MEPs, all or some of these seats should be allocated to a pan-European list of candidates. In other words, besides voting for an MEP in their respective host/home countries, EU citizens would also be able to vote for another representative of a European political party from any of the Member States. This approach would foster a more federalist sense of belonging through political participation at a transnational level.

ACTIVITY

Self-assessment questions

1. Which of the other institutions have been created after the original Treaties?
2. What is the major role of the Economic and Social Committee?
3. Why are there different weightings between the different Member States for membership of the committee?
4. Why was the creation of COREPER necessary or desirable?
5. What was the prime purpose of creating a European Central Bank?
6. What is the major function of the European Investment Bank?
7. What is the role of the Court of Auditors?
8. How does a European Ombudsman help citizens of the Union?

'The relationship between the institutions is important because it is the different powers ascribed to the institutions and the way they have to work together that provides the 'checks and balances' within the Union legal order.' [Josephine Steiner and Lorna Woods, *EU Law* (11th edn, Oxford University Press, 2012)].

Discuss the role and composition of the political institutions of the EU in the light of the above statement.

Explain that there are three main political institutions:

- Council, the Commission and Parliament

Explain the basic role of each:

- Council – main law maker; composed of ministers from each MS; fluid membership based on subject of legislation; but also co-ordinates economic policy and reaches international agreements; votes with a 'qualified majority' voting system
- Commission – main proposer and drafter of legislation; membership is one for each MS, Commissioners also have individual areas of responsibility; also acts as 'watchdog' of Treaties and has *locus standi* in court actions against institutions and against MSs; act independently of MSs
- Parliament – elected body, number of MEPs per MS based on importance of MS; originally no legislative power; but now is consulted on legislation and has power to make amendments

---

Discuss the relationship between the different institutions:

- The original undemocratic nature of the institutions and the existence of a so-called 'democratic deficit'
- Council was always subject to national self interest by Member States – hence Luxembourg Accords – now subject mostly to qualified majority voting – still the main law making body and since co-decision it must work more closely with the other bodies
- Commission oath bound to EU but drafting legislation has to work more cooperatively because of the co-decision process
- Parliament until Nice lacked power or real impact on the legislative process, but after 1979 became a democratically elected body – and since the Treaty of Nice has a much greater influence through the co-decision procedure – and has other checks on the power of the Commission, e.g. 1999

Discuss the involvement of other institutions:

- After Treaty of Lisbon, consideration also should be given to policy-making powers of the European Council
- Social and Economic Committee and the Committee of the Regions are also involved in either policy-making or legislation
- ECJ in achieving the objectives of the Treaty and ensuring that the Treaty is observed is probably the most effective check

KEY FACTS

The Council of Ministers	
Role	Main legislator of the EU. Represents Member States' interests. Co-ordinates economic policy. Concludes international agreements. Approves EU budget. Develops co-operation between Member States on justice and foreign policy.
Membership	One Minister for each Member State.
Presidency	Trio mechanism.
Voting	Changes to Treaties by unanimous vote – on most things now by 'Qualified Majority' (different votes for size and importance of state).

The European Council	
Role	In Art 4 of the TEU – impetus for development and policy-making. Deals with policy.
Meetings	Twice-yearly summits of heads of state and foreign ministers.
Presidency	Appointed by European Council to serve a two-and-a-half year term which is renewable once.

The Commission	
Role	Proposes and prepares draft legislation. Manages budget. Acts as 'watchdog' of the Treaties – enforcing EC law.
Membership	One Commissioner from each Member State for period of five years – have responsibility for heading different departments.

The Court of Justice	
Role	Ensures that law from Treaties is observed – five main actions: • Art 258 TFEU infringement proceedings against Member States; • Art 263 TFEU against institutions for exceeding powers; • Art 265 TFEU against institutions for failure to act; • Art 340 TFEU by natural/legal persons for damage caused by institution; • Art 267 TFEU references from Member State courts for interpretations of EU law.
Membership	One *juge-rapporteur* for each Member State plus eight Advocates-General. Appointed for six-year period.

The General Court	
Role	Eases workload of ECJ – hears specific types of action, e.g. staff cases, competition law, Arts 263 and 265 etc. as directed.
Membership	Similar to ECJ although the number of judges is going up to 56 from 2019, and the GC does not have advocates-general.

The other institutions	
COREPER	Permanent staff to support individual Ministers prior to meetings of Council.
The Court of Auditors	Checks that EU funds are properly used – has member from each state.
The Economic and Social Committee	Membership on basis of size of country – is consulted by Commission and Council prior to some legislation on social or economic policy – can give opinions on own initiative or where asked for.
The Committee of the Regions	Membership as for Social and Economic Committee but represents local or regional government – consulted on local or regional issues.
European Central Bank	An independent body to oversee European Monetary Union (EMU) – controls money supply and monitors pricing trends.
European Investment Bank	Invests in projects that support small businesses.
European Ombudsman	Investigates complaints of maladministration.

SUMMARY

- There are four main EU institutions.
- Council is the major legislator – using proposals from the Commission and with input from Parliament.
- The Commission prepares draft legislation, is the major administrator and is also 'the watchdog of the Treaties'.
- Parliament – is the only elected body and has powers to make amendments to legislation as well as having some control over the budget.
- The Court of Justice, which provides preliminary rulings on interpretation, hears actions against Member States for breaches of EU law, hears judicial review for abuses by the institutions and for their failure to act, and actions for damages by citizens.
- There are also other institutions including COREPER, the Economic and Social Committee, the Committee of the Regions, the Court of Auditors and the European Central Bank – and the Court of Justice is also supported by the General Court.

Further reading

Articles
Bradley, K, 'Institutional Design in the Treaty of Nice' (2001) 38 *CMLR* 1095.

Books
Douglas-Scott, S, *Constitutional Law of the European Union* (Longman, 2002), Chapters 2 and 5.

Tillotson, J and Foster, N, *Text, Cases and Materials on European Union Law* (4th edn, Cavendish Publishing, 2003), Chapters 4 and 7.

Ward, I, *A Critical Introduction to European Law* (3rd edn, Cambridge, 2011), Chapter 1.

3

The sources of EU law

AIMS AND OBJECTIVES

After reading this chapter you should be able to:

- Understand that EU law derives from a number of different sources
- Understand the binding character of the primary source, the Treaties
- Understand the binding character of the secondary sources, EU legislation in the form of regulations, directives and decisions, and the persuasive effect of recommendations, opinions and 'soft law'
- Understand the nature of the tertiary sources, case law of the Court of Justice (binding), the general principles (part of the interpretation process of CJEU) and other acts, e.g. international treaties entered into by the EU
- Analyse the interrelationship of the different sources
- Evaluate the binding or persuasive nature of each source
- Evaluate the effect of different sources on national law

Just as with English law, where the law is found in a number of different sources, so also EU law is made up of a number of different sources. The major sources of law can be very easily identified from the following table – and all of them constitute what is termed the *acquis communautaire* (i.e. the entire body of law of the EU legal order):

Primary sources	**The Treaties –** ECSC, EURATOM, EC, SEA, TEU, ToA, ToN, ToL and CFR – divide into:	
	Procedural Treaty Articles: e.g. Art 288 after Lisbon Treaty which identifies the legislation; or Art 258 an action against a Member State.	Substantive Treaty Articles: e.g. Art 157 TFEU ensuring equal pay for men and women; or Art 45 TFEU the free movement of workers.
Secondary sources	**Legislation** – identified in Art 288 TFEU and including:	
	Regulations	Automatically become law in Member States. They are generally applicable, binding in their entirety and directly applicable.

	Directives	Binding as to the effect to be achieved. Member States have an implementing period within which they must be incorporated into national law by their chosen means.
	Decisions	Addressed to a specific party, whether a company, individual or Member State. They are then binding in their entirety on the party to whom they are addressed.
	Recommendations	Have no legal force but are persuasive.
	Opinions	Have no legal force but are persuasive.
	'Soft law'	e.g. Commission guidelines or notices – no legal force but a good way of influencing policy.
Tertiary sources	**Case law of Court of Justice of the European Union** – vital because of:	
	The power to ensure observance of Treaty objectives through Art 267 TFEU references.	The judicial creativity of the CJEU in comparison with the relative inertia of the legislative bodies.
	General principles: proportionality, equality, legal certainty, natural justice, protection of fundamental human rights, subsidiarity.	
	Acts adopted by representatives of Member State governments meeting in Council. National law of Member States. International Treaties negotiated by the EU.	

3.1 Primary sources – the Treaties

3.1.1 The importance of the Treaties

The Treaties are the most significant source of EU law and primary legislation, which is the equivalent to a constitution and why they are also referred to as 'the founding Treaties'. The original founding Treaties – the ECSC, the EURATOM Treaty and the EC Treaty (now TFEU) – are all primary law which have been amended and now been consolidated by the Treaty of Lisbon in the form of the Treaty on the European Union (TEU) and the Treaty on the Functioning of the European Union (TFEU).

As the Community expanded and the Union was created, a number of related Treaties have been introduced. These all have the force of Community [now EU] law and create enforceable rights and obligations. They include:

- the various Accession Treaties expanding the original Community territorially;
- the Merger Treaties 1965;
- the Single European Act 1986 (which put in place the processes to eventually achieve the Common Market);
- the Treaty on European Union 1992 (which created the Union and its three-pillar structure);
- the Amsterdam Treaty 1997 (which rationalised the existing structure and renumbered the original TFEU);
- the Treaty of Nice 2000 (which focused on institutional reform);
- the Charter of Fundamental Rights of the European Union 2001 (which provides a codified catalogue of socio-economic, political, civil and human rights for the protection of individuals across the EU Member States);

the Treaty of Lisbon, which was introduced in place of the rejected Constitutional Treaty (has introduced further institutional reform as well as amending both the TEU and the EC Treaty and renaming the latter as the TFEU. It also gave legal binding force to the CFR).

Whilst the TEU sets out the objectives, governing principles and institutional framework of the European edifice, the TFEU, as the title suggests, provides the structural foundations for the more detailed organisation and function of the EU.

The TEU and TFEU, along with the CFR, form the constitutional basis of the EU legal order. In addition, with general principles of EU law and international agreements, the Treaties form the primary legislation block of the EU. As such, all subsequent law must fulfil the objectives of those founding Treaties, respect the provisions of the CFR and the general principles of EU law (as developed by the ECJ), as well as the terms of the international agreements that form part of the EU legal order.

The Treaties are directly applicable as they become part of the Member States domestic legal system without the need for national implementing measures.

ACTIVITY

Self-assessment questions

1. What are the key Treaties in the development of the European Community and the European Union?
2. Why are the Treaties referred to as 'primary law'?

3.2 Secondary sources – legislation under Article 288 TFEU

3.2.1 Introduction

'Secondary legislation' is a collective term that is used to describe all of the various types of law that the institutions can make and the legal instruments which they can use to regulate the policy areas within the competence of the EU. Secondary legislation is of major importance since it is the way in which EU law is expanded and developed out of the broad principles contained in the Treaties themselves. Nevertheless, it is also important to remember that secondary legislation is still subordinate to the primary law of the Treaties and must only be used for the furtherance of the objectives of the Treaties. As a result, the legislation cannot amend, repeal or alter the scope of the Treaties.

In this way the institutions may only act in secondary legislation:

- in order to carry out the tasks assigned to them by the Treaties;
- in strict accordance with the provisions of the Treaties for the fulfilment of the objectives of the Treaties;
- and only within the strict limits of the powers that are actually conferred upon them in the Treaties, and specifically those identified in Article 288 of the TFEU.

The introduction of the ordinary legislative procedure (OLP) under Article 289 TFEU has created a distinction between a legislative act (thus adopted by OLP with the participation of the EP, Council and Commission) and a regulatory act (which usually originate from the Commission through delegated powers). However, it is Article 288 TFEU that defines the role of the institutions in producing legislation:

ARTICLE

'To exercise the Union's competences, the institutions shall adopt regulations, directives, decisions, recommendations and opinions.'

As well as defining the power of the institutions to introduce legislation, Art 288 also defines the different kinds of legal instruments or legal acts in which secondary legislation can take form. As can be seen from the wording of Art 288, it is their scope and effect which distinguish them from each other.

3.2.2 The different types of secondary legislation
Binding secondary legislation
Regulations
Regulations are defined in paragraph 2 of Article 288:

ARTICLE

'A regulation shall have general application. It shall be binding in its entirety and directly applicable in all Member States.'

The terminology used in the Article needs to be understood in order to appreciate the scope and effect of a Regulation:

- 'General application' (otherwise referred to as 'general applicability') simply means that the measure applies generally to all Member States.
- 'Binding in its entirety' means that the Member States have no choice whether to give effect to the measure. They are bound by the regulation in its entirety.
- 'Directly applicable' (again commonly referred to as 'direct applicability') means that the measure automatically becomes law in each Member State on the date specified. The consequence of this is that there is no requirement for the state to implement the measure. (See section 8.1.)

It would be easy from the description given to compare regulations with Acts of Parliament in the UK. They automatically become law on the date specified and are absolutely binding.

Obviously, they also operate in this sense slightly differently from the Treaties themselves. Having a dualist constitution, the UK only became bound by the Treaties once they had been ratified and incorporated into UK law by the European Communities Act 1972. Once the UK had signed the Treaties and incorporated them into English law there is no similar requirement for the introduction of Regulations into English law. They are binding once introduced.

Regulations are also capable of creating rights and obligations which are then directly enforceable in the national courts through the principle of direct effect (see Chapter 8): *Leonesio v Ministero dell'Agricoltora & delle Foreste* (Case 93/71) [1972] ECR 287.

Directives
Directives are defined in paragraph 3 of Article 288:

ARTICLE

'A directive shall be binding, as to the result to be achieved, upon each Member State to which it is addressed, but shall leave to the national authorities the choice of form and methods.'

Again, the wording in Article 288 indicates the scope and effect of Directives, although in this case there are more significant problems in terms of their possible effects as legislative measures.

The two key aspects to the paragraph are:

- 'binding as to the object to be achieved'; and
- 'shall leave to the national authorities the choice of form and methods'.

The wording here is significant. It indicates that Directives are quite unlike Regulations which are directly applicable and demand absolute uniformity. Instead, Directives are not directly applicable but are used to ensure that Member States adapt their own laws for the application of common standards. They are about the harmonisation of Member State law on specific issues.

As such, they leave an element of discretion to the Member States and allow the Member States to select what is for them the most appropriate method of implementation. However, they are bound to do so within a set deadline.

Because they are harmonising measures they are mainly used in those areas where the diversity of national laws could prevent the proper establishment or even the effective functioning of the Single Market. A classic example of this harmonising process can be found in the so-called 'sectoral Directives' introduced for the recognition of different professional and vocational qualifications under Article 49 for the furtherance of freedom of establishment. This also applies to the more generalised Directives 89/48 and 92/51 and the 'Slim Directive' 2001/19 (see Chapter 13).

In contrast, then, whereas a Regulation is applicable to all Member States as well as individual citizens alike, a Directive is really only intended to create legal obligations on the Member States. In this way directives were not originally seen as being intended to create rights that could be directly enforced by individuals. Nevertheless, to avoid the possibility of EU law being ignored by the Member States the ECJ has created the means to ensure that they can be enforced. This has been controversial and a more detailed explanation is given in Chapter 8, but the main ways are:

- **Vertical direct effect.** This is a process by which individuals may enforce an unimplemented Directive, provided that the date for implementation has passed (*Publico Ministero v Ratti* (Case 148/78) [1979] ECR 1629 and the claim is against either the state (*Marshall v Southampton and South West AHA (No 1)* (Case 152/84) [1986] QB 401 or an 'emanation of the state' (*Foster v British Gas plc* (Case C–188/89)) [1991] 1 QB 405.

- **Indirect effect.** This is the principle developed in *Von Colson v Land Nordhein–Westfalen* (Case 14/83) [1984] ECR 1891 and *Marleasing SA v La Commercial Internacional de Alimentacion SA* (Case C–106/89) [1990] ECR I–4135. The ECJ has held that, because Article 10 (now Article 4(3) TFEU) of the EC Treaty demands that Member States fulfil all Treaty obligations, national courts should interpret national law so as to give effect to the Directive whether it is ineffectively implemented or not implemented at all.

▨ **State liability.** This principle, stemming from the case of *Francovich v Italy* (Cases C–6 and 9/90) [1991] ECR I–5357 holds that while there can be no horizontal direct effect based on a Directive as between ordinary individuals, an individual who has suffered loss as a result of the Member State's failure to implement a Directive may claim damages from the state.

Decisions

Decisions are defined in paragraph 4 of Article 288:

ARTICLE

'A decision shall be binding in its entirety. A decision which specifies those to whom it is addressed shall be binding only on them.'

The two key elements of the definition are:

▨ 'binding in its entirety'; and

▨ 'upon those to whom it is addressed'.

In terms of scope and effect, obviously the first point about a decision is its effect. A decision is immediately and totally binding on the party to whom it is addressed. As a result of this it is equally clear that a decision is capable of creating obligations that are then enforceable by third parties. For instance, see *Grad v Finanzamt Traustein* (Case 9/70) [1970] ECR 825.

The next point to make is that a decision is clearly not generally applicable as it may be addressed to a limited range of parties and not to the EU generally.

What is also clear is that decisions are the least easy form of legislation to define. They could be legally binding measures created according to a specific legal form. However, they could also be non-binding, informal acts which lay down guidelines. A common context for the use of decisions has been in EU competition law. (See Chapter 16.)

Non-legally binding secondary legislation: recommendations and opinions

Article 288 also gives the Commission the power to 'formulate recommendations' and also to 'deliver opinions'. The Article also identifies these as having no binding force.

As law, then, such measures can be seen as ineffective. Nevertheless, they are a useful means of clarifying issues in a less formal way than by introducing binding legislation.

While the measures are not enforceable as law, it is possible for them to have a persuasive effect on the Court of Justice in its decision-making. In fact, in *Grimaldi v Fonds des Maladies Professionelles* (Case 322/88) [1989] ECR 4407 the ECJ considered that national courts were bound to take recommendations and opinions into account in deciding cases. However, it is unlikely that this would be followed in practice.

	General applicability	Direct applicability	Direct effect (see Chapter 8)
Treaty Articles	These apply generally throughout the whole EU (so are generally applicable)	Once a Treaty is incorporated there is no need for further enactment of Articles	Will have if they conform to the *Van Gend* (1963) criteria
Regulations	These apply generally throughout the whole EU (so are generally applicable)	These require no further implementation (so are directly applicable)	Will have if they conform to the *Van Gend* (1963) criteria
Directives	Usually addressed to all Member States (in which case are generally applicable)	These are an order for Member States to comply (so need implementation and are not directly applicable)	Vertical direct effect only (if unimplemented/ incorrectly implemented and past implementation date)
Decisions	Addressed to particular individuals (so are not generally applicable)	These are an order that must be complied with by the addressee	May confer rights on other individuals affected by them – so can be directly effective

ACTIVITY

Self-assessment questions

1. What are the three main secondary sources of law?
2. What is the significance of Article 288 TFEU?
3. What does the term 'direct applicability' mean?
4. In what ways does a Directive differ from a Regulation?
5. On whom would a Decision be binding? How wide could this definition be?
6. What is the legal effect of a recommendation?

3.3 Tertiary sources

3.3.1 The case law of the CJEU (formerly the ECJ)

The CJEU (formerly ECJ) has played a vital role in the development of EU law. The Article 267 procedure is the major means by which the application of EU law in the Member States is tested (see Chapter 6). References from national courts under this procedure lead to binding interpretations of Treaty provisions and legislation.

The importance of the Court in illuminating principles of EU law is obvious since the Treaties are framed in broad terms and cover broad principles. To a degree, the same point can be made of the secondary legislation. The CJEU adds detail and context to these broad principles and provides more precise principles for the national courts in the Member States to follow.

The CJEU is unlike any court that we are familiar with in the UK. In character it is based on the continental 'civil' or 'Roman' law systems. As such, there is no strict system of binding precedent as exists in English law and, in theory, the Court is not bound by its past decisions, as an English court would be.

In this way the Court could be said in the strictest sense to have moral rather than legal authority and in a technical sense the Court's decisions could be argued not to be a formal source of law. Nevertheless, a number of points could be made:

- first, it is true that the Court will not depart from its past decisions without good reason;

- second, in its reasoning and in its judgments the courts as well as the General Court have shown a remarkable consistency over the years;

- in any case the rules in *CILFIT v Ministry of Health* (Case 283/81) [1982] ECR 3415 on application of the preliminary reference procedure under Article 267 in essence prevents repetitious references by Member States trying to gain different rulings on the same principle of law;

- finally, the Court in any case has proved to be very 'legislatively active' in its eagerness to achieve the *'effet utile'* (effectiveness) in ensuring the attainment of the objectives of the Treaties.

In this sense the case law of the CJEU is in fact a major source of EU law and has been a key element in the development of EU law in two ways:

- It has defined the principles that apply in all of the main areas of substantive law, e.g. the 'Four Freedoms', discrimination law, competition law etc. (see Chapters 10–19).

- It has ensured that the objectives of the Treaties are achieved in the Member States by developing the principles of supremacy and direct effect (see Chapters 7 and 8).

3.3.2 General principles of EU law (GPEUL)

There was nothing in the original Treaties that directed the ECJ (now the CJEU) to apply general principles of law in deciding cases. Article 6(1) of the TEU, as amended by the Treaty of Amsterdam, does identify that the Union is founded on principles of liberty, democracy and the rule of law as well as respect for human rights and fundamental freedoms, and also principles that are common to the Member States.

However, the Court has developed a number of unwritten principles that it will use when it interprets the Treaties and the secondary legislation. In doing so the Court relied on the authority of Article 220 which obliges it to interpret provisions so as to ensure that the law is observed by the Member States. In this way the general principles of law have been recognised as binding on the institutions, the Member States and, indeed, on individual citizens.

Subjecting interpretation of the law to general principles is not a novel idea. In fact, the practice is a familiar one in those states that have a 'civil' or 'Roman' law tradition. The general principles of law are in essence a statement of essential values and basic standards which are broad enough to be generally acceptable as principle. The process itself is not particularly controversial. It is the application of the general principles in specific situations that has been felt to be so at times.

Because a lot of EU law is essentially administrative, certain of the principles have derived quite naturally from the administrative law of both France and Germany. Nevertheless, some of the principles have their origins in UK law.

The main ones are:

- proportionality;
- equality;
- legal certainty;
- natural justice;
- the protection of fundamental human rights;
- subsidiarity.

Proportionality

Proportionality is a concept that comes from German administrative law and is known as *'verhaltnismassigkeit'*. The basic principle is that any measure or any action taken must be proportionate to the actual end to be achieved. A simpler explanation would be to say that nothing should be done that is more than is necessary to achieve the end.

The idea of applying the principle of proportionality in EC (now EU) law first came about in the *Internationale Handelsgesselschaft* case (*Internationale Handelsgesselschaft GmbH v Einfuhr und Vorratsstelle fur Getreide und Futtermittel* (Case 11/70) [1970] ECR 1125). Here, the ECJ adopted the principle in the following terms:

JUDGMENT

'No burdens should be placed on the citizens except to the extent that it is necessary to achieve the purpose.'

The principle of proportionality is now laid down in Article 5 TEU. The Court will apply the principle in relation to legislation, for instance by determining whether the legislation goes beyond what is necessary to achieve the actual purpose in the Treaty provision behind the legislation.

CASE EXAMPLE

R v Intervention Board, ex p Man (Sugar) Ltd (Case 181/84)

Here, a sugar trader did not apply for export licences within the specified time. The bank where securities had to be lodged acted in accordance with Regulation 1880/83 and forfeited the securities, amounting to a loss of £1670 to the trader. The ECJ, in a preliminary reference, accepted that this total forfeiture provided for by the Regulation was disproportionate to the actual offence committed by the trader when the licensing requirement under the Regulation was only intended to ensure sound management of the market. The Court felt that the forfeiture procedure under the Regulation was therefore invalid.

The Court also applies the principle when reviewing acts of the institutions, again, for example, in determining whether the action imposes too great a burden for the actual breach of EU law. An obvious context for this is the fines imposed for breaches of Articles 101 and 102 (see Chapter 16).

Another way in which the Court has exercised the principle is in reviewing the actions of Member States when claiming derogations under the various freedoms, particularly those in Article 36 in relation to the free movement of goods (see Chapter 14) and under Article 45(3) and Directive 2004/38 in relation to the free movement of workers (see Chapter 12).

CASE EXAMPLE

Italy v Watson and Belmann (Case 118/75) [1976] ECR 1185

A young English woman had settled in Italy with her Italian boyfriend but without obtaining the necessary work permit. When they split and the boyfriend reported her to Italian immigration authorities the penalty under Italian law was deportation. The ECJ held that this action was disproportionate to the required objective.

Equality

The concept of equal treatment or non-discrimination is not just a general principle; it is also one of the founding principles of the EU. The TFEU includes three specific prohibitions against discrimination:

- Article 18 prohibits any discrimination based on nationality (this is a base Article that also operates behind the various Treaty Articles creating the Common Market through the 'Four Freedoms').

- Article 157 demands that men and women shall receive equal pay for equal work (and has subsequently been extended to cover all discrimination between the sexes as well as other areas such as race and religion).

- Article 40 prohibits discrimination between producers and consumers in relation to the Common Agricultural Policy (CAP).

Besides this, the principle of equality was extended in the Treaty of Amsterdam, so the Treaty now includes a general aim of 'equality between men and women'. This is a major development since it is not restricted to work as it previously was. An even more impressive development gives the Council the power to legislate on discrimination in a much more general sense. Article 19 TFEU now allows the Council the power to take action to remove discrimination based on 'sex, race or ethnic origin, religion and belief, disability, age, and sexual orientation'. In fact, even before this the Commission was active in tackling discrimination and promoting equality. While English law included no specific provisions for tackling sexual harassment (so that women claiming had to use the residual category of 'subjecting to any other detriment' under s6(2)(b) of the Sex Discrimination Act 1975) a Commission Code of Practice had defined 'sexual harassment' as any 'unwanted conduct of a sexual nature, or other conduct based on sex affecting the dignity of women and men at work'.

The ECJ has also been proactive in combating discrimination and advancing equality. In implementing the principle in Article 157 the Court has identified in *Bilka-Kaufhaus GmbH v Weber von Hartz* (Case 170/84) [1986] ECR 1607 that unequal pay can only be accepted if it is based on objective justification. In defining 'objective justification' the Court also relied on the principle of proportionality (see above). The idea of objective justification itself has subsequently been extended to apply to any inequality in *Graff v Hauptzollamt Kohn-Rheinau* (Case C–351/92) [1994] ECR I–3361.

Similarly, while English courts have accepted the legitimacy of discrimination against both transsexuals and gay people, the ECJ has been more prepared to apply the principle of equality in such cases. In *P v S and Cornwall County Council* (Case C–13/94) [1996] All ER (EC) 397 the Court applied the principle of equality to the dismissal of a transsexual. While in *Grant v South West Trains Ltd* (Case C–249/96) [1998] All ER (EC) 193 the Court did not feel bound to apply the principle to same-sex couples, who it felt were not in an 'equal situation' to heterosexual couples; this now falls under Directive 2000/78.

SOURCES OF EU LAW

The Court has in any case already taken the principle of equality to extend to discrimination on religious grounds in *Prais v The Council* (Case 130/75) [1976] ECR 1589 (see further discussions in Chapters 17 and 18).

Legal certainty

This is not a novel concept and it is one that is familiar to most legal systems. The basic principle is that the law in its application must be both certain and predictable. This was identified at a very early stage in *Da Costa en Schaake NV v Nederlandse Belastingadministratie* (Cases 28 to 30/62) [1963] ECR 61. The Court has subsequently stated in *Officier van Justitie v Kolpinghuis Nijmegen BV* (Case 80/86) [1987] ECR 3969 that it is the duty of national courts to interpret EU law in such a manner that is 'limited by the general principles of law' and also that in particular national courts should observe 'the principles of legal certainty and non-retroactivity'.

There are a number of potential consequences of applying the principle. One obvious consequence is that there should be no retroactive laws. This indeed was at least partly the case for refusing to say that Article 157 was retrospectively directly effective in *Defrenne v SABENA (No 2)* (Case 43/75) [1981] All ER 122. Of course, the judgment was affected by the objections by both the UK and Irish governments and the ECJ did accept that this principle would only apply in exceptional cases where extreme difficulties would otherwise occur.

Legal certainty is also the basis of application of measures such as the Acquired Rights Directive 77/187. This in itself is demonstration of the fact that there is respect for acquired rights that cannot later be withdrawn. This in effect feeds into another aspect of the principle, that there should be protection of legitimate expectations. In simple terms it means that 'assurances relied on in good faith should be honoured'.

CASE EXAMPLE

Mulder v Minister of Agriculture and Fisheries (Case 120/86) [1988] ECR 2321

Here, a dairy farmer entered into an agreement not to supply milk for a period of five years in return for a payment. A regulation on milk quotas was then introduced during the period while this agreement was still in force. There was no provision within the quota system for farmers who had been party to the agreement, the effect of which was that the farmer would be prevented from supplying milk once the agreement was ended. The ECJ held that, on the basis of legitimate expectation, the farmer must be entitled to resume production and supply at the end of the agreement.

However, it must also be remembered that the institutions are still bound to act in furtherance of the objectives of the Treaties and the principle cannot be employed to frustrate that end.

CASE EXAMPLE

R v Ministry of Agriculture, Fisheries and Food, ex p Hamble (Offshore) Fisheries Ltd [1995] 2 All ER 714

The Ministry introduced a more stringent system for the granting of fishing licences in order to protect overworked fish stocks in UK waters. In the event, the Court of First Instance (now the General Court) held that there was no infringement of the legitimate expectations of the holders of fishing licences since such arrangements must be allowed to cater for changes in circumstances.

JUDGMENT

'The principles of legal certainty and the protection of legitimate expectation are fundamental to European Community (now Union) law. Yet these principles are merely general maxims derived from the notion that the Community (now Union) is based on the rule of law and can be applied to individual cases only if expressed in enforceable rules ... other principles ... run counter to legal certainty and ... the right balance will need to be struck.'

Natural justice

This is another concept that will be familiar to students of English constitutional law. In fact, the ECJ has on occasions referred to it simply as 'fairness'.

Within English law there are two distinct strands to the principle:

- the right to a fair and unbiased hearing; and
- the right to be heard before the making of a potentially adverse decision is made.

A third aspect that is explicit in many areas of EU law is:

- the right to a reasoned decision.

The ECJ first addressed the right to a hearing at quite an early stage:

CASE EXAMPLE

Transocean Marine Paint Association v The Commission (Case 17/74) [1974] ECR 1063

Here, in a case involving an alleged breach of Article 81 (now Article 101), the Commission addressed a decision to the applicants but failed to make known a specific condition which was later applied against them. The ECJ accepted the applicants' argument that this aspect of the decision should be annulled. As the Court identified, the applicants would be adversely affected by the condition but had never had the opportunity of a hearing to challenge it.

EU law in any case includes many express provisions that guarantee the principle. If Member States choose to claim the derogations under Directive 64/221 (now in Directive 2004/38) as applied to Articles 45, 49 or 56 then they must provide both a proper hearing and a right to appeal. Indeed, this is also the case when Member States make decisions on recognition of qualifications for establishment under Article 43 or provision of services under Article 49: Directives 89/48, 92/51 and the overarching 'Slim Directive' 2001/19 (now incorporated in the Qualifications Directive 2005/36) (see Chapter 13). The ECJ has also enforced the principle in the case law on those areas.

Those Directives also guarantee the right to a reasoned decision. The ECJ has also upheld this right in the case law.

CASE EXAMPLE

Union Nationale des Entraineurs et Cadres Techniques Professionels du Football (UNECTEF) v Heylens (Case 222/86) [1987] ECR 4097

A Belgian football trainer with a Belgian diploma was refused the right to practise his trade in France but no hearing was held and no reason given for the decision. The ECJ held that this was a breach of process.

The Court stated:

JUDGMENT

'[in] a question of securing the effective protection of a fundamental right conferred by the Treaty on Community (now EU) workers [they] must be able to defend that right under the best possible conditions and have the possibility of deciding, with a full knowledge of the relevant facts, whether there is any point in applying to the courts'.

The protection of fundamental human rights

There was no mention of human rights in the original EC Treaty. This is actually not all that surprising since the major concern of the initial Treaties was the creation of the Common Market, so it was essentially economic in its direction.

The first statement of the ECJ on the matter came in *Stauder v City of Ulm* (Case 29/69) [1969] ECR 419. Here, the Court did little more than to confirm that there was nothing in the provision that was being challenged that was 'capable of prejudicing the fundamental human rights enshrined in the general principles of Community law and protected by the court'.

In *Internationale Handelsgesellschaft* (1970) the Court was more explicit and more expansive in its statement:

JUDGMENT

'respect for fundamental human rights forms an integral part of general principles of law protected by the Court of Justice. The protection of such rights, while inspired by the constitutional traditions common to the member states, must be ensured within the framework of the structure and objectives of the European Community (now EU)'.

It became apparent that there was a lacuna in the Union legal order in regards to the protection of human rights, as the impact of Union legislation and actions on individual lives grew in importance. If we consider the federalist ambitions of the founding fathers, and the constitutionalisation process of the Union, in order to appear more like a democratic and legitimate political entity, the need to protect human rights, i.e. the rights of both its citizens and the people residing and working across the Union became imperative. Therefore, the absence of a system of checks and balances enabling acts of the Union to be reviewed for breach of individual human rights became a real issue. Consequently, answering the need for a Union approach to human rights, since 1974, the ECJ started affirming and proclaiming in its case law that Union institutions are bound by fundamental principles of basic human rights, despite a lack of specific written provision in the founding Treaties.

The meeting of the European Council at Cologne in 1999 decided that a Charter of Fundamental Rights for the EU should be drawn up in order to provide a more visible means of protection of the citizens of the Union. A Draft Charter has subsequently been produced which was signed and solemnly declared by all of the then 15 Member States at Nice in 2000. As seen in Chapter 1 the CFR has since been given legal binding force since 2009 by Article 6 TEU as amended by the Treaty of Lisbon.

Subsidiarity

Subsidiarity is also not a new concept. In fact, there were references to the principle in the founding Treaties which identified that decisions should be taken as closely as possible to the citizens that are affected by them. In other words, subsidiarity underpins the principle of conferral which is enshrined in Article 5 TEU. This provision essentially requires that, in areas of non-exclusive EU competence, the EU should leave Member States to act in the furtherance of the EU's objectives wherever appropriate.

Article 5 provided:

ARTICLE

1. The limits of Union competences are governed by the principle of conferral. The use of Union competences is governed by the principles of subsidiarity and proportionality.

2. Under the principle of conferral, the Union shall act only within the limits of the competences conferred upon it by the Member States in the Treaties to attain the objectives set out therein. Competences not conferred upon the Union in the Treaties remain with the Member States.

3. Under the principle of subsidiarity, in areas which do not fall within its exclusive competence, the Union shall act only if and insofar as the objectives of the proposed action cannot be sufficiently achieved by the Member States, either at central level or at regional and local level, but can rather, by reason of the scale or effects of the proposed action, be better achieved at Union level ...

In simple terms, then, the principle is that the institutions of the Union should only act to introduce measures where it is more appropriate than for the Member States to act individually. The result is in effect a two-part test:

- it must be determined that the measure is one which is within the competence of EU law to deal with; and
- introduction of EU measures can only then be justified if this serves an end which:
  - cannot be achieved satisfactorily at national level; and
  - can be achieved in a more satisfactory way by the EU.

3.3.3 Other tertiary sources

There are certain other tertiary sources of less certain legality. These are of three main types:

- **Acts adopted by representatives of Member State governments meeting in Council** (The Council is part of the legislative process under Article 288. However, meetings of representatives of the Member States in the Council are also used to decide on various joint action. This is a quick and easy method of making decisions that fall outside the competence of the EU. While resolutions coming out of such meetings do not have the full force of law, the ECJ will consider them. An example is *Commission v Council (Re ERTA).* (Case 22/70) [1971] ECR 263 on the legality of an agreement to co-ordinate approaches in negotiation towards a European Road Transport Agreement.)

- **National law of Member States** (National law is not formally recognised as being part of EU law. There are, however, two instances when it will be taken into account: first, where Community law actually makes reference to national law, as, for example, in determining the legal status of individuals, i.e. capacity; second, where national law has developed EU law and the ECJ looks to that law for guidance when there is a gap in the law.)

- **International Treaties negotiated by the EU** (This refers to multinational Treaties to which the EU is a party. An example would be the General Agreement on Tariffs and Trade (GATT). In *International Fruit Co NV v Produktschap voor Groenten en Fruit* (Cases 21 and 22/72) [1972] ECR 1219 the ECJ held that GATT could be referred to when determining what practices breach Community (now EU) commercial policy.)

ACTIVITY

Self-assessment questions

1. In what ways has the case law of the ECJ (now CJEU) been an important source of law?
2. In what ways do the judges of the ECJ (now CJEU) apply the 'general principles of law'?
3. What does the term 'proportionality' mean and what is its practical effect?
4. What are the differences between 'legal certainty' and 'natural justice'?
5. In what ways is it true to say that the principle of 'human rights' has developed in significance?
6. How does the principle of 'subsidiarity' affect the supranational character of the EU?

SAMPLE ESSAY QUESTION

'Discuss the relative importance of the different sources of law of the European Union to the development of EU law.'

Explain that there are different sources:

- Primary – the Treaties (particularly TFEU)
- Secondary – the legislation – regulations, directives and decisions (and also recommendations and opinions)
- Tertiary – the CJEU case law and the general principles of law

---

Explain the character of the different legislation under Article 288:

- Regulations – generally applicable, binding in their entirety, and directly applicable
- Directives – binding as to the effect to be achieved – so subject to implementation by MSs within time limit
- Decisions – binding in their entirety on the party to whom they are addressed
- Recommendations/opinions – persuasive only

Explain the character of the tertiary sources:

- Case law of the CJEU – all MSs are bound by the rulings of the Court which then becomes binding on national law
- General principles of law underpins judgment, e.g. proportionality

Discuss the significance of the Treaties:

- These regulate the Union but also contain much substantive law
- MSs have signed Accession Treaty and so accept all of the objectives of the Treaty and all subsequent legislation which becomes part of the law of each MS
- Treaties provide only a framework and broad objectives – so the interpretation given by CJEU allows EU law to be applied harmoniously

Discuss the significance of the secondary sources:

- All other sources of law are invalid unless they achieve the objectives of the Treaty
- The binding nature and general applicability of regulations means they present no problem
- The binding nature of decisions – but also the narrow focus
- The key purpose of directives is harmonisation – but they are conditional and may be implemented in different ways – so problems of enforceability
- Other secondary legislation is non-binding

Discuss the significance of tertiary sources:

- CJEU has been proactive in the creation of supremacy, direct effect, etc. – so the development of the legal order has really depended on the judges
- Unique nature and effectiveness of the general principles of law

KEY FACTS

Primary sources	
The Treaties	• ECSC (1951), EURATOM (1957), EC Treaty (1957) – created the Community – based on legal order. • Merger Treaty (1965) – merged communities and institutions. • Single European Act (SEA) (1986) – put in place the Common Market. • Treaty on European Union (TEU) (1992) – created the Union and some new institutions. • Treaty of Amsterdam (1997) – renumbered the Articles of the EC Treaty – some institutional reform. • Treaty of Nice (2000) – institutional reform in preparation for enlargement. The Charter of Fundamental Rights (2001), legally binding since 2009 – consolidates and guarantees the visibility of individual rights and freedoms protected under EU law. • The Lisbon Treaty – introduced the TFEU. N.B. The TFEU identifies the aims, tasks and activities of the Community (and the Union).

Secondary sources	
Defined in Art 288	
Regulations	• Binding in their entirety. • Generally applicable. • Directly applicable. • Directly effective if satisfy *Van Gend en Loos* (1963) criteria (*Leonesio v Ministero dell'Agricoltora & delle Foreste* (1972)).
Directives	• Binding as to the result to be achieved. • But method of implementation left to Member State. • Cannot be 'horizontally' directly effective because dependent (*Marshall v Southampton AHA (No 1)* (1986)). • But can be 'vertically' directly effective if time for implementation passed (*Pubblico Ministero v Ratti* (1979)) and if against state or emanation of the state (*Foster v British Gas plc* (1991)).
Decisions	• Binding in their entirety on party to whom addressed. • Can be directly effective if satisfy *Van Gend en Loos* (1963) criteria (*Grad v Finanzamt Traustein* (1970)).
Recommendations and opinions	• 'Soft law' – not binding. • But can be persuasive (*Grimaldi v Fonds des Maladies Professionelles* (1989)).
Tertiary sources	
Case law of ECJ (now CJEU)	Instrumental in developing, e.g. supremacy, direct effect etc.
General principles of law:	
Proportionality	No measure should place a burden on a citizen beyond what is necessary to achieve the purpose (*Internationale Handelsgesselschaft* (1970)).
Equality	Evidence in Art 18 no discrimination on nationality, Art 157 equality between men and women.
Legal certainty	The law must be both certain and predictable (*Da Costa en Schaake v Nederlandse Belastingadministratie* (1963)).
Natural justice	The right to an unbiased hearing, the right to be heard, the right to a reasoned decision (*UNECTEF v Heylens* (1987)).
Human rights	Now in Art 6 – The Union is founded on the principles of liberty, democracy, respect for human rights and fundamental freedoms, and the rule of law.
Subsidiarity	Now in Art 5 – EU should only act if result cannot be achieved satisfactorily at national level; and can be achieved in a more satisfactory way by the Community.
Other sources	• Acts of Member States in Council. • National law. • International Treaties negotiated by EU.

SUMMARY

- The sources of EU law are of three types: primary, secondary and tertiary.
- Primary sources are the Treaties themselves and, as well as outlining the objectives and indicating the roles of the institutions and processes, these also contain much substantive law.
- Secondary sources are the legislation from Article 288 TFEU – the main three types are regulations, directives and decisions.
- The main tertiary sources are the case law of the Court of Justice and the general principles of law – many of the major principles of EU Law, e.g. supremacy – have developed from the case law.

Further reading

Articles

Meyring, B, 'Intergovernmentalism and Supranationality: Two Stereotypes for a Complex Reality' (1997) 22 *ELR* 221.

Wouters, J, 'Institutional and Constitutional Challenges for the European Union: Some Reflections in the Light of the Treaty of Nice' (2001) 26 *ELR* 342.

Books

Ward, I, *A Critical Introduction to European Law* (3rd edn, Cambridge, 2011), Chapter 1.

4

The legislative process

AIMS AND OBJECTIVES

After reading this chapter you should be able to:

- Understand the different legislative processes
- Understand the role of the institutions in the different legislative processes
- Understand the context in which the different legislative processes operate
- Analyse the reasons for the development of different processes
- Evaluate the democratic effectiveness of the processes

4.1 The role of the institutions

The process of legislating within EU law appears to be quite complex. One of the reasons for this is that all rules and procedures for legislating are laid down in the Treaties at different points. Every EU law is based on a specific Treaty Article, in this case referred to as the 'legal basis' of the legislation. The second reason is that there are different processes of legislating and the appropriate process depends on the particular area of the Treaty objectives that requires legislating.

The process of legislating has been modified very significantly since the original Treaties, as the result of the different subsequent Treaties. The introduction of new legislative procedures arose from the criticism of the early legislative process that there was a so-called 'democratic deficit', in other words that those institutions that existed on the basis of appointment rather than election controlled the processes. This democratic deficit was considered to be particularly true of the role of Parliament which originally had little effect on the legislative process other than to suggest amendments. The Lisbon Treaty has modified and simplified the legislative process and now most legislation is created under the co-decision procedure.

The three institutions mainly involved in the legislative process are:

- The **Commission** (the body mainly responsible for 'proposing' legislation and producing draft legislation; in short it is for the Commission to initiate legislation except where the Treaties provide otherwise).

- **Parliament** (is one of the two key bodies responsible for passing legislation in the EU. It can also have either a consultative role or a right of veto under SLP).
- **Council** (the second half of the legislative duo with the EP).

Other institutions also have a role in terms of receiving draft proposals for legislation and providing consultation, particularly the Economic and Social Committee and the Committee of the Regions. COREPER, of course, has a role to play in supporting Council through all legislation.

Prior to the Treaty of Lisbon there were basically four types of legislative procedure that were possible within the EU legal order. However, it is also true that there are limited circumstances where the Commission is authorised to legislate on its own and there are other instances where the Council and Commission can act without consulting Parliament, although in practice they still do.

The four main processes were:

- the proposal (or consultation) procedure;
- the co-operation procedure (this has now been discontinued);
- the co-decision procedure (this is now the main legislative process now known as the ordinary legislative procedure under Article 294 TFEU);
- the process of assent.

The proposal procedure was in fact the original legislative procedure which was used prior to the SEA.

Because of the criticism that there was insufficient accountability, the so-called 'democratic deficit', a new procedure was introduced in the SEA to give Parliament a greater and more meaningful role. This was the **'co-operation procedure'**. It was introduced to provide a relatively straightforward means of involving the European Parliament, which would have two readings of the draft proposals. It was also based entirely on Qualified Majority Voting by Council. Its main context was for Internal Market measures. Although it was introduced to reduce the democratic deficit and did indeed succeed in giving Parliament a greater level of involvement, the procedure was still criticised:

QUOTATION

'Although it increased the involvement of the Parliament, the cooperation procedure was criticised for having the following weaknesses: that the Council of Ministers could still overrule the Parliament in any case and that the Parliament had been given a dubious benefit in the power to hinder EC legislation (as the Parliament prefers to be seen as a positive force in the legislative process). In fact by 1997, only 21 per cent of Parliament's amendments had been accepted by the Council at the second reading. However [it] did instil changes in inter-institutional relationships ... greater dialogue between Council and Parliament [and] between the Parliament and the Commission, which introduced considerable internal reforms to accommodate the ... procedure.'

S Douglas-Scott, *Constitutional Law of the European Union* (Longman, 2002), p. 119

The TEU then introduced the predominant process nowadays: the 'co-decision procedure, now the **ordinary legislative procedure** under Article 294 TFEU. A complex process originally, it has subsequently been somewhat modified by the Treaty of Amsterdam for the sake of simplification. Use of the procedure was expanded by the Treaty of Nice and has now become the main legislative process for adopting EU law since the Treaty of Lisbon. The ordinary legislative procedure has put the EP on an equal footing as the Council in the adoption of EU law and has thus contributed to the democratic credential of the EU.

The European Parliament may also participate in the law-making process in special legislative procedure, such as the consent and consultation procedures.

Following the Treaty of Lisbon coming into force, the ordinary legislative procedure (formerly the co-decision procedure) is the major process for legislating. It involves an active role by all three institutions, including Parliament.

As a result of the Treaty of Lisbon, Article 5(1) TEU requires for a process of conferral to limit the competences of the EU to legislate in particular areas. Where the EU institutions are not granted competence in the Treaties then there may be shared competence with the Member States, or the EU may act to support, co-ordinate or supplement the actions of Member States.

Areas where the EU institutions have exclusive competence are: the Customs Union, competition rules, monetary policy for Member States in the euro zone, marine biology and fisheries policy, and international agreements.

4.2 The ordinary legislative procedure (formerly the co-decision procedure)

The TEU introduced the process known as the 'co-decision procedure', whereby the European Parliament and Council must both agree on a legislative proposal before it can become law – in some way, it is like a bicameral structure to the EU legislative process. The aim was to give far greater power to Parliament by allowing it not only to suggest significant amendments but also ultimately to have some right of veto on draft legislation. In this respect it can be said that Council and Parliament share legislative power. The process was amended and simplified by the Treaty of Amsterdam and to a lesser extent by the Treaty of Nice. Following the Treaty of Lisbon this is now the ordinary legislative procedure used for most legislation. The ordinary legislative procedure is enshrined in Article 289 TFEU which states it 'shall consist in the joint adoption by the European Parliament and the Council of a regulation, directive or decision on a proposal from the Commission'. The procedure for adopting legislation under the ordinary legislative procedure is laid down in Article 294 TFEU.

Parliament gains more power because after it proposes amendments Council must then consider them before it acts and if Parliament rejects the proposals then the act is not adopted. Both Council and Parliament have two readings of the proposal and if they cannot agree then the measure is put before a 'conciliation committee' which is made up of members from both institutions in equal numbers. Both bodies then hold a third reading so that they may finally adopt the proposal as law.

After the first consultation of Parliament Council may adopt the proposal by Qualified Majority Vote if either:

- it agrees with all of Parliament's amendments; or
- Parliament has not made any amendments.

If this is not the case then Council adopts a 'common position' by Qualified Majority Vote which is then communicated to Parliament. Within three months if Parliament either approves the common position or does nothing then Council can adopt the common position.

Parliament can, however, within this three-month period:

- reject the common position by absolute majority of MEPs – in which case this acts like a veto and the measure cannot be adopted; or
- propose new amendments by an absolute majority.

If new amendments are introduced these are forwarded to the Commission which itself has three choices:

- it can accept them all; or
- it can reject them all; or
- it can selectively accept some and reject others.

On receiving Parliament's amendments Council also has choices:

- it can approve them all and adopt the amended measure by Qualified Majority Vote; or
- it can fail to adopt the proposal and convene a 'Conciliation Committee'.

Within six weeks the committee then has two choices:

- it can approve a new joint proposal decided upon by the committee which can then be adopted by Parliament by absolute majority and Council by qualified majority; or
- it can fail to find any possible compromise, in which case the measure is not adopted.

The procedure can be explained in diagram form as in Figure 4.2.

The development of the procedure through both the Treaty of Amsterdam and the Treaty of Nice means that the procedure is now used for most areas of legislation. These now include:

- non-discrimination on the basis of nationality;
- the right to move and to reside;
- the free movement of workers and social security for migrant workers;
- the right of establishment;
- transport;
- employment;
- Customs co-operation;
- the fight against social exclusion;
- equal opportunities and equal treatment;
- implementing decisions involving the European Social Fund or the Regional Development Fund;
- education and vocational training;
- culture;
- health;
- consumer protection;
- trans-European networks;
- research;
- the environment;
- transparency;
- the prevention of fraud;
- statistics;
- the setting up of a data protection advisory body.

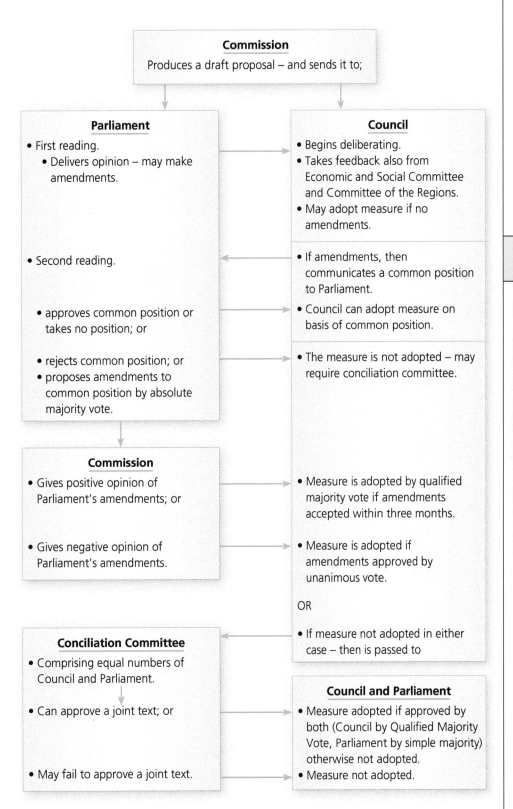

Figure 4.1 The different stages in the ordinary legislative procedure (formerly the co-decision procedure)

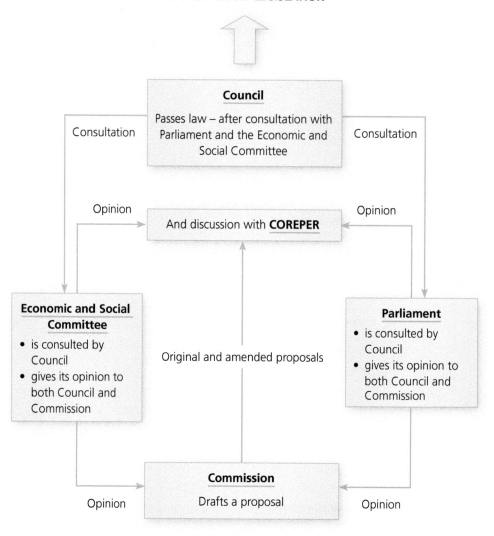

EU SECONDARY LEGISLATION

Council
Passes law – after consultation with Parliament and the Economic and Social Committee

Consultation   Consultation

Opinion   Opinion

And discussion with **COREPER**

Economic and Social Committee
- is consulted by Council
- gives its opinion to both Council and Commission

Original and amended proposals

Parliament
- is consulted by Council
- gives its opinion to both Council and Commission

Commission
Drafts a proposal

Opinion   Opinion

Figure 4.2 The different stages in the proposal (consultation) procedure

QUOTATION

'Initial reactions were ... critical. "the effective balance of power indisputably weighted toward the Council". However, following Amsterdam, the legislative balance seems to have shifted in Parliament's favour. Parliament may reject outright the Council's common position at the second reading, thus effectively having the final say in adoption of legislation. ... Parliament at last has some real power.'

S Douglas-Scott, *Constitutional Law of the European Union* (Longman, 2002), p. 120

4.3 Special legislative procedure

Article 289(2) TFEU states that 'in the specific cases provided for by the Treaties, the adoption of a regulation, directive or decision by the European Parliament with the participation of the Council, or by the latter with the participation of the European Parliament, shall constitute a special legislative procedure'. The adoption of the special legislative procedure is stipulated by specific Treaty provisions and is therefore used on an *ad hoc* basis.

One form of special legislative procedure is the **consent procedure**, formerly known as the 'assent' procedure, which gives Parliament the power to veto any legislative proposal. Under this procedure the EP can vote to either accept or reject a proposal, but cannot amend it. Failure to secure the EP's consent means that a given proposal cannot be adopted into law.

By contrast, under the other special legislative procedure known as the **consultation procedure**, the EP participates in the law-making process in a purely consultative capacity. Whilst the Council is bound to seek the opinion of the EP, it is however not bound to follow it.

This was the original process used for all legislation. Following the Treaty of Nice, it was still the basis for the adoption of certain general EC (now EU) instruments or policy areas. Examples are in Article 64(3) TFEU and Article 86(1) TFEU.

This procedure most accurately represents the notion that it is the Commission that 'proposes' and the Council that 'disposes'.

Nevertheless, the process still depends on some consultation with Parliament as well as with the Economic and Social Committee or the Committee of the Regions, and discussions in COREPER. Failure genuinely to consult may amount to a breach of an essential procedural requirement. On this basis it may result in the measure being declared void.

The importance of consultation was recognised by the ECJ in *Roquette Frères SA v Council* (Case 138/79) [1980] ECR 3333.

JUDGMENT

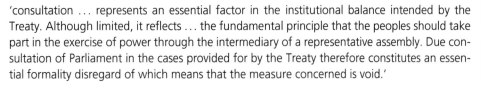

'consultation ... represents an essential factor in the institutional balance intended by the Treaty. Although limited, it reflects ... the fundamental principle that the peoples should take part in the exercise of power through the intermediary of a representative assembly. Due consultation of Parliament in the cases provided for by the Treaty therefore constitutes an essential formality disregard of which means that the measure concerned is void.'

The process involves the Commission sending its proposal to both Council and Parliament, as well as one of the committees if appropriate. The measure cannot then become law until Parliament has delivered its opinion. Even so, Council has the final say.

QUOTATION

'this ... is undermined somewhat by the fact that there is no requirement that Council actually take account of the Parliament's opinion, nor indeed, give any reason for rejecting it. Thus in the context of the Consultation procedure, the Parliament may not force its opinion on the Council as a lower house could in most ... systems.'

S Douglas-Scott, *Constitutional Law of the European Union* (Longman, 2002), p. 118

Whilst the above was one more justification that there was a democratic deficit in the administration and law-making of the EC, this assertion may lack some of its sting since the institutional reforms brought on by the Treaty of Lisbon, especially with regards to the increased role of Parliament.

The most significant difference between the various legislative procedures is the involvement and therefore democratic influence of Parliament in the law-making process. Under the consultation procedure Parliament only gives its opinion on draft legislation, so under this procedure the Council is the main law-maker. By contrast, under the consent procedure, the power of veto of the EP makes it the ultimate law-maker under this special legislative procedure. However, the balance of power is equalised under the ordinary legislative procedure where both the EP and the Council are co-legislators and share the power to make law in the EU.

ACTIVITY

Self-assessment questions

1. What institutions have a role to play in the legislative process?
2. In what way is COREPER important to the legislative process?
3. Why was the co-decision procedure introduced?
4. In what ways is Parliament's role different under the co-decision procedure?
5. How is a 'conciliation committee' comprised and what does it do?
6. What is the effect on the Commission of the changes in the legislative process?
7. What has been the effect on (i) unanimous voting and (ii) Qualified Majority Voting in Council of the changes to the legislative procedure?

KEY FACTS

The role of the institutions	Three main institutions involved: • Commission – drafts new legislation (proposes); • Parliament – has consultative role or can make amendments and sometimes veto, depending on process; • Council – votes on legislation. Three others involved in process: • COREPER – permanent body supporting Council Ministers; • Social and Economic Committee – consultative role; • Committee of the Regions – consultative role.
The co-operation	Introduced by SEA to give Parliament more involvement, but its use was limited after ToA. Now only used for EMU.
The ordinary legislative procedure (formerly the co-decision procedure)	Introduced by TEU and simplified by Treaty of Amsterdam and Treaty of Nice retained after Treaty of Lisbon and now the main legislative procedure. Involves two readings by both Parliament and Council – and possibly a 'conciliation committee': • draft legislation sent by Commission to Council and Parliament which sends an 'opinion'; • Parliament may suggest amendments; • Council can adopt proposal by qualified majority if either: • agrees with all of Parliament's amendments; or • Parliament has made no amendments. Or: • Council adopts 'common position' by qualified majority and sends to Parliament; • within three months Parliament can approve common position; or • if does nothing then Council can adopt the common position.

The ordinary legislative procedure (formerly the co-decision procedure (*continued*)	Or: • Within three-month period Parliament can: • reject common position by absolute majority of MEPs – acts like veto and measure cannot be adopted; or • propose new amendments by an absolute majority; • if amendments introduced, then are sent to Commission which can: • accept them all; or • reject them all; or • selectively accept some and reject others. • Council can then either: • approve them all and adopt by qualified majority; or • fail to adopt and convene a 'Conciliation Committee'. • Within six weeks, committee has two choices: • can approve new joint proposal decided upon by committee which can then be adopted by Parliament by absolute majority and Council by qualified majority; or • can fail to find any compromise, then measure is not adopted. Procedure is now used for most areas.

SUMMARY

- Originally most legislation was introduced through the proposal procedure which had a very limited role for Parliament.

- Complaints of a 'democratic deficit' led to the introduction of the co-operation procedure, which involved greater consultation of Parliament but still little power to influence legislation.

- Following the ToA, and with modification by ToN, the co-decision procedure was introduced – this is now known as the ordinary legislative procedure, it is used for most legislation and gives Parliament greater powers to make amendments and influence their outcome.

Further reading

Articles

Dashwood, A, 'The Constitution of the European Union after Nice: Law-making Procedures' (2001) 26 *ELR* 215.

Books

Douglas-Scott, S, *Constitutional Law of the European Union* (Longman, 2002), Chapter 3.

Fairhurst, J, *Law of the European Union* (8th edn, Pearson, 2010), Chapter 4.

Woods, L, Watson P and Costa M, *Steiner and Woods EU Law* (13th edn, Oxford University Press, 2013), Chapter 3.

5

Enforcement of EU law (through 'direct' and 'indirect' actions)

AIMS AND OBJECTIVES

After reading this chapter you should be able to:

- Understand the nature and purpose of enforcement actions
- Understand the procedure for indirect actions against Member States for breaches of EU obligations
- Understand which breaches give rise to an action and the defences that can be raised by a Member State
- Understand the processes for direct actions against EU institutions for exceeding their powers, for a failure to act and actions for damages
- Understand the significance of *locus standi*
- Understand the grounds for review of acts of EU institutions
- Understand the rules relating to claims for damages
- Evaluate the effectiveness of enforcement procedures

5.1 The nature and purpose of enforcement

'Enforcement' in simple terms refers to the actions created in the EC Treaty (now TFEU) for the purpose of ensuring that both the Member States and the institutions of the EU comply with their relative obligations within the Treaties.

The Treaties and their secondary legislation clearly create many and various substantive rights and obligations by which all parties to the Treaties are bound. These substantive rights and obligations granted under Treaties would, nevertheless, be left completely ineffective if they were left merely to the co-operation of Member States without the means of enforcing them.

Similarly, it would also be possible that the individual rights might be abused by the institutions of the EU themselves.

For these reasons the framers of the EC Treaty were wise enough to include a variety of enforcement proceedings, and the methods for reviewing the actions of both the institutions and the Member States. These were then placed under the scrutiny of the ECJ, with individuals able to gain remedies following actions in their favour.

These procedures are generally referred to as the 'direct actions'. They supplement the 'indirect actions' of the Article 267 reference procedure (considered in Chapter 6).

The measures are broadly based in that they allow a wide range of applicants to take the initiative in setting an action in motion and bringing proceedings. So this might include, for example, other institutions of the EU, as well as private citizens in certain circumstances.

There are essentially four types of action to be considered here:

- Actions under Article 258 TFEU (formerly Article 226 EC) are taken by the Commission against Member States for a failure to honour their Treaty obligations (and generally known as 'infringement proceedings').

- Actions under Article 263 TFEU (formerly Article 230 EC) can be brought against any institutions of the EU for acting in excess of their actual powers – since the powers of the various institutions are defined in the Treaties, and since, in legislating, the institutions are only capable of acting for furtherance of the actual objectives of the Treaties. This is more commonly known as the judicial review procedure.

- Actions under Article 265 TFEU (formerly Article 232 EC) are taken against the institutions of the EU where they have failed to act when they are required to act (hence it is known as an action for failure to act).

- Actions under Article 340 TFEU (formerly Article 288 EC) is an action for damages brought against the institutions to compensate a citizen for any loss caused by one of the institutions, so it is inevitably linked with grievances pursued under the previous two.

5.2 Indirect actions – Article 258 infringement proceedings against Member States

5.2.1 Actions against Member States under Articles 258 and 259

It is in the very nature of EU law that it depends on a partnership between the Member States and the institutions. This can be seen, for instance, in the implementation of Directives where the legislation is created under the various processes (see Chapter 4 and also section 3.2.2) but in the form of a written obligation containing various objectives that the Member States must incorporate into their national law but in a manner of their choosing and within an implementation period set by the Council.

While this partnership exists, it is not uncommon for Member States to show carelessness in implementing them (e.g. this was the case in the deficiencies in UK sex discrimination law in relation to the issue of different retirement ages for men and women based on state pension ages highlighted in the case of *Marshall v Southampton and South West AHA* (Case 152/84) [1986] QB 401). It is even possible that Member States may show real reluctance in fulfilling their obligations. (An obvious example of this is the arguments presented by the Tory government before 1997 in refusing to implement the Working Time Directive, despite its argument of an opt-out applying to the provision having been rejected out of hand by the ECJ.)

It is because of these possibilities that the Treaty sensibly provided the means of calling Member States to account for their failures to honour Treaty and legislative obligations. The process can be initiated in one of two ways:

- in most cases the process would normally be invoked by the Commission under Article 258;
- however, it is also possible for proceedings to be initiated by other Member States under Article 259.

5.2.2 Actions by the Commission under Article 258

The Commission has always been described as the 'watchdog of the Treaties' and so it was empowered by Article 258 to act in such manner monitoring the behaviour of Member States and, if necessary, enforcing compliance with Treaty and other obligations. It therefore has *locus standi* in Article 258 actions.

Article 258 itself provides the following:

ARTICLE

'Art 258 … if the Commission considers that a member state has failed to fulfil an obligation under the Treaty it shall deliver a reasoned opinion on the matter after giving the state concerned the opportunity to submit its observations. If the state concerned does not comply with the opinion within the period laid down by the Commission, the latter may bring the matter before the Court of Justice of the European Union.'

As a result, it is possible to identify three clear purposes of the Article 258 action:

- to ensure that Member States comply with their Treaty obligations;
- to provide a procedure for resolution of disputes between the Commission and Member States (it must be noted in this respect that four-fifths of disputes are actually settled within the preliminary stages);
- where proceedings do nevertheless end up in the CJEU, the action also provides a means of clarifying the law for all Member States to follow in the future.

There are in fact three formal stages in the procedure. However, these are usually preceded by an informal stage.

The informal stage
Mediation
Once the possibility of non-compliance has been notified, the Commission at first engages in informal discussions with the Member State. The Commission identifies the nature of the breach by the Member State and will prescribe a time limit within which it expects the Member State to comply. Usually the Member State is prepared to remedy its mistake at this point, as a result of which the action is generally then suspended.

Formal stages
Formal notice of default
It may be that the Commission is dissatisfied with the response of the Member State. If this is the case then the Commission issues a notice inviting the Member State to submit its own observations on the alleged non-compliance.

It is this stage that in effect defines exactly what the failure by the Member State is and therefore also the terms of reference of the action. These are then fixed and the Commission cannot afterwards extend the scope of the action.

CASE EXAMPLE

Commission v Italy (Re Payment of Export Rebates) (Case 31/69) [1970] ECR 25

Here, Italy was alleged to be in breach of its Community (now EU) obligations by failing to pay certain rebates to farmers, in line with Community policy. The Italian government then rectified the breach and to a certain extent paid rebates in respect of breaches falling before 1967. It did not, however, pay for certain rebates occurring after that time. Since the Commission's notice of default had not included those breaches either, the ECJ was unable to refer to them or give judgment.

Reasoned opinion

If the notice of default fails to force the Member State into remedial action and it has still not complied with its obligations then the Commission issues a reasoned opinion.

This formal document sets out all the reasons why the Commission considers that the Member State is in default. The reasoned opinion also sets a time limit within which the Commission expects the Member State to act.

Nevertheless, the reasoned opinion is not a binding act in its own right, as a result of which action in the Court of Justice may still be necessary.

CASE EXAMPLE

Alfons Lütticke GmbH v Hauptzollamt Sarrelouis (Case 57/65) [1966] ECR 205

Here, Lütticke was unable to ask the Commission to bring an action under Article 169 [now Article 258 TFEU]. His complaint concerned a tax on powdered milk by Germany. However, the German government had already withdrawn the tax to comply with the Commission and Lütticke was unable to use either Article 173 or Article 175 [now Articles 263 and 265] in respect of losses that had been suffered before the proceedings.

Court proceedings in the CJEU

Court proceedings depend on the action taken by the Member State following the earlier proceedings. If the Member State still fails to comply even after the other stages then the Commission will bring an action in the CJEU.

Nevertheless, it is still possible for the action to be settled even without a decision of the Court. Interim relief under Article 243 is an example of this. In fact, something in the region of 44 per cent of cases are settled at this point without further court action.

There are, of course, many defences that Member States have attempted to use, but most have failed:

  Member States have tried to claim that internal difficulties have genuinely prevented them from meeting their obligations:

CASE EXAMPLE

Commission v Belgium (Case 77/69) [1970] ECR 237

Here, Belgium was in breach of Article 90 [now Article 110 TFEU] for a discriminatory tax on wood. The Belgian government argued that an amendment was actually put before its Parliament but never gained force because Parliament was dissolved in the meantime. It argued that it was thus prevented from legislating and that the breach was, therefore, beyond its control. The ECJ would not accept this reasoning.

The Court identified:

JUDGMENT

'liability under [Article 258] arises whatever the agency of the State whose action or inaction is the cause of the failure to fulfil its obligations'.

- Reciprocity has also been argued – that national compliance is dependent on compliance by the other Member States:

CASE EXAMPLE

Commission v France (Re restrictions on lamb imports) (Case 232/78) [1979] ECR 2729

Here, the French government tried to argue that its ban on British lamb could be justified on the ground that it was not the only state in breach. The argument had no substance in law and failed.

- Member States have also argued the application of *force majeure* – that they are excused from acting when the circumstances are beyond the control of the national authorities:

CASE EXAMPLE

Commission v Italy (Case 101/84) [1985] ECR 2629

Here, it was held that the concept of force majeure could not be used as a defence where the Italian state had failed to provide statistical data as required, with the excuse that the database had been destroyed in a bomb attack. This was rejected because the data could easily have been replaced by the time the action took place.

- Failing to act because of internal political difficulties such as objections by trade unions has also been rejected as a defence:

CASE EXAMPLE

Commission v UK (Case 128/78) [1978] ECR 419

Here, there was much controversy surrounding the proposed introduction of tachographs to which many hauliers were objecting. This was not accepted by the ECJ as sufficient justification for avoiding obligations under EC [now EU] law.

- Member States have also tried to justify breaches of EU law on ethical grounds:

CASE EXAMPLE

Commission v Poland C–165/08 [2009] ECR I–6843

Poland tried to argue that its law prohibiting the growing of genetically modified foods was justified on ethical and religious grounds, despite the law being inconsistent with an EU directive, and that the government was bound to respect the wishes of the Catholic majority. The Court of Justice held that Poland had breached its obligation, which could not be justified on populist grounds, although it made no decision on whether ethical or religious grounds are a justification.

Enforcement

Before the signing of the Maastricht Treaty (TEU) decisions made by the CJEU lacked the possibility of actual enforcement. Because of this, repeated failure by a Member State to comply would simply lead to further Article 258 proceedings.

Following the TEU it was possible under Article 258 for a financial penalty to be imposed on the Member State. An example of this is in *Commission v Greece* (Case C–387/97) [2000] ECR I–5047 which concerned the dumping of toxic waste. The Court of Justice applied a penalty, taking into account guidelines issued by the Commission. The penalty is based on a basic sum for every day of the breach, multiplied by other significant factors such as the seriousness and length of the breach, and also takes into account the ability of the Member State to pay. The Lisbon Treaty has made procedural improvements to the enforcement procedure through Article 260 TFEU, although in merely stipulating that Member States 'are required to take the necessary measure to comply with a judgement of the Court' under Article 258, some have argued that these rulings mostly have declaratory force. Nevertheless, the imposition of pecuniary penalties for a Member State's non-compliance with obligations under EU law is still a persuasive enforcement mechanism.

Now, where a Directive has not been implemented, the CJEU can apply a penalty against a Member State at the same time that it gives its ruling. Also, in the case of other breaches, it does not have to provide a reasoned opinion.

It is possible for a Member State to present a defence against an action under Article 258 TFEU, whether on procedural grounds (i.e. for failure to comply with the procedural requirements laid down in Article 258) or on substantive grounds (e.g. unlawful obligation, force majeure, uncertain meaning of the obligation).

5.2.3 Actions by other Member States under Article 259

It was always intended in the Treaty that the Commission should be the prime body in enforcing EU law against Member States that were failing to comply with their obligations. For this reason also, while it is possible for other Member States to bring action, it was always intended to be an exceptional procedure rather than the norm. This is reflected in the wording of the Article:

ARTICLE

'Art 259 A Member State which considers that another Member State has failed to fulfil an obligation under this Treaty may bring the matter before the Court of Justice.

Before a Member State brings an action against another Member State for an alleged infringement of an obligation under this Treaty, it shall bring the matter before the Commission.'

However, the ability of other Member States to use the procedure is nevertheless a very useful safeguard against possible errors of judgement by the Commission.

It involves similar processes to those that we have looked at above. However, the Article clearly demands that the Member State must inevitably work closely with the Commission in the preliminary stages.

To date, whilst there have been four cases heard before the ECJ, only one has actually been successful:

CASE EXAMPLE

France v UK (Case 141/78) [1979] ECR 2923

Here, France, using the procedure, was able to show that the United Kingdom's rules on the mesh size of fishing nets was in fact a unilateral action, contrary to EU law and thus in breach of its obligations.

Nevertheless, the possibility of such action can be useful in focusing the attention of the Commission on the issue. This was the case when the EU lifted its ban on British beef but both the French and German governments declined to do so.

ACTIVITY

Self-assessment questions

1. Which institution would normally take action against a Member State under Article 258?
2. What are the stages in an action under Article 258? Why would the action proceed to a hearing in the Court of Justice?
3. For what reasons can Member States take a similar action under Article 259?
4. How successful have Member States been in trying to raise a defence to Article 258 proceedings?

5.3 Direct actions against EU institutions

5.3.1 Article 263 TFEU actions against EU institutions for exceeding powers

The action for annulment of an EU instrument under Article 263
Article 263 provides one of the few circumstances in which ordinary individuals are able to bring an action in the CJEU. While such an action is possible, it is nevertheless true that the ability of citizens to do so is much more restricted than it is for the institutions.
  The procedure is a very specific one and it has two major functions:

- it provides a means of questioning and indeed controlling the legality of binding acts of EU institutions;
- it offers a form of legal protection to those who are subject to the instruments of the EU and who are adversely affected by instruments that are in fact illegal.

There are three key aspects to Article 263 actions that must be considered:

- the identity of those who may bring an action, in other words the *locus standi* of individuals;
- the type of actions by the institutions that are capable of being reviewed under the procedure and the grounds on which an action may be brought;
- the actual procedure itself.

Locus standi *(the right to sue)*
Article 263 is quite explicit on those who have *locus standi*. There are three significant groups enjoying slightly different *locus standi*:

- The **Member States**, the **Commission** and the **Council** are all named as possible parties to an action. In this respect they are all classed as 'privileged claimants' and possess virtually unlimited rights of challenge against any act of any of the institutions. The exception to this is recommendations and opinions. The necessary requirement for being a privileged claimant is that the body is bound by the measure in question. This will be determined by the CJEU on studying the context and legal effect.

- **Parliament** and the **European Central Bank** are also privileged claimants. However, they have more limited powers of challenge. Traditionally, it was held that they could only use the procedure if it was 'for the purpose of protecting their prerogatives'. An example of this is *Parliament v Council (Chernobyl)* (Case 70/88) [1991] ECR I–4529. The Treaty of Nice, however, has identified Parliament as having full status as a privileged claimant.

- **Natural** and **legal persons** are also identified in Article 263 as having *locus standi*. Their rights of challenge before the Treaty of Lisbon were initially limited to 'a Decision addressed to that person, or a decision which, although in the form of a Regulation or a Decision addressed to another person, is of direct and individual concern to the individual'. Since the Treaty of Lisbon reforms, Article 263(4) TFEU extends the challenges available to individuals to include:

  - 'an act addressed to that person' (e.g. a decision)

  - 'or which is of direct and individual concern to them' (i.e. a legislative act)

  - 'and against a regulatory act which is of direct concern to them and does not entail implementing measures'

The distinction between a legislative act and a regulatory act is essential in that it will determine the judicial test which the ECJ will apply to establish whether a natural/legal person has *locus standi* under Article 263 TFEU.

Whilst the threshold for challenging a legislative act is cumbersome (the non-privilege applicant (NPA) must prove both individual and direct concern), the threshold for challenging a regulatory is less taxing as the NPA only has to fulfil the criteria for direct concern.

The distinction is made with regards to the procedure through which a legal act of the EU is adopted. If, according to Article 289(3) TFEU, a legal act is adopted by a legislative procedure, whether the ordinary legislative procedure or special legislative procedure, then the measure is a legislative act. This was confirmed in *Inuit Tapiriit Kanatami* (ITK) (Case C–583/11 P) [2014] QB 648 in which the ECJ stated that acts of the EU institutions that are legally binding and which cover 'acts of general application, legislative or otherwise, and individual acts' can only be challenged by NPA if they show individual and direct concern. It follows then that regulatory acts 'must be understood as covering all acts of general application apart from legislative acts'. In other words, acts which are not adopted through a legislative procedure, but are instead adopted by the European Commission through delegated powers (e.g. Article 290 TFEU) or for the exercise of implementing powers (Article 291(2) TFEU). This was confirmed in *Microban* (Case T–262/10) [2011] ECR II–7697.

All challenges by natural and legal persons are now brought in the General Court. There is the possibility of an appeal to the CJEU but on a point of law only.

Looking at the requirements above, it is clear that, apart from in the case of decisions addressed to an individual, three key issues need to be considered in establishing whether or not there is *locus standi*:

- what amounts to 'individual concern';

- what amounts to 'direct concern';

- the circumstances in which a Regulation may be of individual or direct concern.

Individual concern

In order for a private applicant to make a claim, 'individual concern' must mean that the Decision or Regulation must affect the applicant. How an applicant could claim to be affected by the measure was explained in *Plaumann v Commission* (Case 25/62) [1963] ECR 95.

CASE EXAMPLE

Plaumann v Commission (Case 25/62) [1963] ECR 95

Plaumann was one of 30 German importers who were all complaining about a Commission refusal to suspend certain Customs duties on mandarin oranges and tangerines. The thing that defeated their argument was that any individual in Germany might have imported the fruit, so it was impossible to show 'individual concern'.

It would be:

JUDGMENT

'by reason of certain attributes which are peculiar to them or by reason of circumstances in which they are differentiated from all other persons and by virtue of these factors distinguishes them individually just as in the case of the person addressed'.

However, this basic test has subsequently been modified so that now it must be possible to determine the number and the identity of those persons affected at the time that the measure complained about was adopted.

CASE EXAMPLE

Toëpfer v Commission (Cases 106 and 107/63) [1965] ECR 405

Here, Toëpfer challenged a protectionist German measure which had the effect of preventing Toëpfer from obtaining a licence to import maize. The Commission then accepted the legitimacy of the measure and Toëpfer challenged this decision. It was accepted that there was individual concern and that Toëpfer had *locus standi* because it was possible to identify precisely all of the people applying for a licence before the decision.

This has also been modified further by the ECJ which, in *International Fruit Co v Commission* (Cases 41 to 44/70) [1971] ECR 411, has stated that there will be individual concern and therefore *locus standi* is possible if there is a 'closed group' of people affected by the decision. In the case there was such a 'closed group' because the decision only applied to a limited number of importers who had been granted licences before a specific date.

However, the Court of Justice has not always shown consistent application of the criteria that it has set:

CASE EXAMPLE

Piraiki-Patraiki v Commission (Case 11/82) [1985] ECR 207

In this case Greek exporters challenged a decision which allowed a French quota system to be imposed on imports of Greek yarn. The ECJ acknowledged that the exporters had *locus standi* because they had been contracted during the period in which the quota was in place. This appears to fit the *Plaumann* reasoning, but not that in the International Fruit case, since the exporters could not fit into the category of a closed group.

Nevertheless, the definition of individual concern in *Plaumann* (1963) is restrictive and makes it difficult for individuals to protect themselves against breaches of their rights resulting from EU legislation. The test has been consistently criticised. The definition has recently been reviewed and a more liberal approach suggested. However, the Court of Justice has ultimately confirmed *Plaumann* as the appropriate test.

In *Union de Pequenos Agricultores (UPA) v Council* (Case C–50/00) [2003] QB 893 UPA, a trade association, had unsuccessfully challenged a Regulation in the CFI (now the General Court), being unable to show individual concern. The CFI (now the General Court) had also pointed out that UPA could instead have brought an action in the national courts and then asked for an Article 267 reference to be made. When the case came before the ECJ the Advocate-General identified that a challenge under Article 263 was a more appropriate procedure and recognised that there were inherent difficulties in trying to take the course of action suggested by the CFI (now the General Court). First, a national court would not have the power to annul the measure and so could only consider whether there was sufficient doubt as to its legality to justify a reference being made. Second, certain measures could not give rise to an action in a national court and so would be beyond any challenge by the individual. He also felt that the definition of 'individual concern' was too restrictive and that there was no reason why an individual should have to show a difference from other individuals affected by the measure. He preferred a test based on an individual having suffered a substantial adverse affect because of his particular circumstances.

Between the Advocate-General's opinion and the ruling in the ECJ the CFI in another case, *Jego-Quere et Cie v Commission* (Case T–177/01) [2003] QB 854, suggested a different test for individual concern based on the Advocate-General's opinion in *UPA*. Individual concern would be shown if the measure: 'affects his legal position in a manner which is both definite and immediate, by restricting his rights or imposing obligations on him'.

The ECJ in *UPA*, however, confirmed the *Plaumann* (1963) test on individual concern so that there is unlikely to be change without amendment to the Treaty.

Direct concern

'Direct concern' has a somewhat different meaning, and once again has been subject to some inconsistent interpretation by the Court of Justice.

It does not only refer to the causal connection between the decision and any loss suffered but has also been said to refer to the 'immediate, automatic and inevitable disadvantageous legal effects' without need for further intervention.

CASE EXAMPLE

Alcan Aluminium Raeren v Commission (Case 69/69) [1970] ECR 385

Here, several aluminium refining companies applied for annulment of a refusal by the Commission to meet a request by Belgium and Luxembourg on additional tariffs for imports of aluminium. There was no direct concern because the decision in effect conferred no rights and the Member States were in fact given discretion to act.

However, this somewhat strict approach was later relaxed in *Bock v Commission* (Case 62/70) *(The Chinese Mushrooms Case)* [1971] ECR 897 where the applicant who had applied for a licence to import Chinese mushrooms was granted *locus standi* because only he had been affected.

When a Regulation is of individual or direct concern

Because of their nature genuine Regulations can never be capable of challenge by an individual applicant. This was stated clearly in *Calpak SpA v Commission* (Case 789/79) [1980] ECR 1949.

Because of this it is vital to determine whether or not a particular Regulation conforms to the standard definition, otherwise there can be no *locus standi* in any application challenging it. In *Confederation Nationale des Producteurs de Fruits et Legumes v Council* (Cases 16 and 17/62) [1962] ECR 901 Advocate-General Lagrange identified:

JUDGMENT

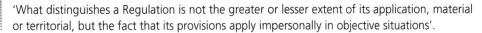

'What distinguishes a Regulation is not the greater or lesser extent of its application, material or territorial, but the fact that its provisions apply impersonally in objective situations'.

In this way a Regulation can only be challenged when it is not a provision having general application within the meaning given in Article 288 but is rather 'a bundle of individual Decisions taken by the Commission, each of which, although taken in the form of a Regulation, affected the legal position of the applicant' (*International Fruit Co v Commission* (1971)).

The substantive grounds for review

Once admissibility of an application has been established then it is for the applicant to show that the challenge to the decision concerns one of four specific grounds identified in the Article:

- lack of competence;
- infringement of an essential procedural requirement;
- infringement of the Treaties or of any rule that relates to the application of the provision of the Treaties;
- misuse of power.

Lack of competence

This ground for complaint has no real comparison in English administrative law. However, Lasok and Bridges have suggested that it is 'broadly comparable' with the *ultra vires* doctrine with which we are all familiar.

In simple terms it is possible to identify lack of competence when an EU institution appears to exercise a power that is not in fact conferred upon it by EU law; or where it appears to exercise a non-existent power; or where it in fact encroaches on the power given to another institution.

The ECJ has defined the ground in the case law but it will rarely accept a challenge by one institution against another because, first, the powers of the different institutions are clearly laid out in the Treaty and, second, because it will in any case usually interpret these powers broadly.

CASE EXAMPLE

Commission v Council (Re European Road Transport Agreement) (Case 22/70) (The ERTA case) [1971] ECR 263

Here, the ECJ rejected a claim by the Commission that the Council lacked the power to take part in the shaping of the agreement in question despite the fact that the Commission is the body that negotiates international agreements while it is the Council's role to conclude them.

In this way it is more likely for the ground to be used in respect of powers that are not possessed at all by the institution challenged in the application.

CASE EXAMPLE

Ford (Europe) v Commission (Cases 228 and 229/82) [1984] ECR 1129

Here, the Commission had delivered an interim decision on a ban by Ford on the sale of right-hand drive Ford vehicles to dealers in Germany. A challenge was possible because the Commission had no power to make interim decisions.

Most commonly, the ground will be accepted in the case of an improper delegation of power. This was the case in *Meroni v High Authority* (Case 9/56) [1956–58] ECR 133 where the Commission (High Authority) had delegated powers to make a decision to another body that did not in fact have any authority to make decisions. The action of the Commission in this instance was invalid.

Infringement of an essential procedural requirement

EU law puts in place a number of procedural mechanisms in order to act as safeguards in protection of natural justice. Such essential procedural requirements fall into distinct categories:

- First, there are procedural requirements in relation to the preparation of the measure, for instance the requirement of prior consultation. For example, in *Roquette Frères v Council* (Case 138/79) [1980] ECR 3333 the Council had failed to consult Parliament, as required, on agricultural budgeting measures and so the measure was invalid.

- Also, there are requirements in respect of the form by which the measure is created. An example of this would be the requirement to give reasons so that any party affected by the measure can understand how the institution has applied the law. Such an infringement occurred in *Germany v Commission* (Case 24/62) [1963] ECR 63 where a decision addressed to Germany concerning wine imports provided no reasons and so was invalid.

Infringement of the Treaties or of any rule relating to their application

This ground is easily explained. It clearly allows the CJEU to review how the acts of the institution in question conform with EU law. The law in this instance includes the general principles of law so that any kind of violation of EU law of whatever type may be declared invalid under this ground.

CASE EXAMPLE

Transocean Marine Paint Association v Commission (Case 17/74) [1975] 2 CMLR D75

Here, the association had been in receipt of an exemption from Article 81 (now Article 101 TFEU) for ten years. The Commission then unilaterally reviewed the exemption and imposed entirely new conditions. This was a general breach of the right to be heard, and thus a breach also of the general principle of legal certainty and was thus invalid.

Misuse of powers

This ground quite simply refers to the situation where an institution is using a power that it does in fact possess but for an objective that is contrary to those for which the power was given. It might therefore include any illegitimate use of a power.

CASE EXAMPLE

Bock v Commission (Case 62/70) [1971] ECR 897 (The Chinese Mushrooms case)

Here, although the case was actually decided on the issue of proportionality, the question of misuse of power was also considered and it was found that there was evidence of collaboration between the Commission and the German government in the issuing of a decision.

The time limit of the procedure

The most important procedural requirement in making an application is the existence of a strict time limit for bringing an action. According to Article 263(6), the time limit is within two months of the date on which the measure was published, or from the date on which the applicant was notified of the decision, or on which it came to the applicant's attention.

However, Article 50 of the Rules of Procedures of the Court of Justice (RPCJ) (L 265/1) further provides that the actual time limit for proceedings against a measure adopted by an institution will be calculated from the end of the 14th day after publication. Therefore, the countdown would technically only start 15 days after the Regulation was published in the OJ. Taking into account distances which may hinder or slow down the process of publication or notification, NPAs may also benefit from an additional 10 days (Article 51 RPCJ). Finally, the Court of Justice may also decide to extend the time limit allocated to the applicant (Article 52 RPCJ).

Nevertheless, the time limit criterion is generally strictly applied. Derogations could only apply where unforeseeable events, force majeure or excusable errors have delayed the submission of the claim for annulment (*Transportes Evaristo Molina* (Case C–36/09 P) [2010] ECR I–145); or where an EU measure is deemed defective if, for instance, its legal basis or the rights/obligation it creates are unascertainable. The ECJ held that 'such a measure produces no legal effects and may be challenged outside the limitation periods' (*BASFAG & Others v Commission of the European Communities* (Joined Cases T–79, 84–86, 89, 91, 92, 94, 96, 98, 102 and 104/89) [1992] ECR II–315).

The effects of a successful application

Article 263 is essentially an action for the annulment of an EU measure which infringes a substantive or procedural rule of law. The procedure under Article 263 is thus essentially concerned with first establishing the admissibility of a claim from the applicant (especially NPA), and second to determine whether the disputed EU measure is in fact illegal.

If the ECJ finds that the measure is indeed legally defective, the claim is successful and the outcome is stipulated by Article 264 TFEU which provides that such a measure shall be declared void. The effect of this is that the measure is treated as though it never existed in the first place.

A defunct measure becomes void, wholly or partially, upon the delivery of the ECJ ruling (*ex tunc*). The ruling declaring the annulment applies to everyone who might be concerned or affected by that measure (*erga omnes*), as confirmed in *Commission v AssiDomän* (Case C–310/97 P) [1999] ECR I–5363 and may also have retroactive effects (*Corus v Commission* (Case T–171/99) [2001] ECR II–2967).

The consequence of an application being successful is that the instrument is declared void by the CJEU. The effect of this is that the measure is treated as though it never in fact existed.

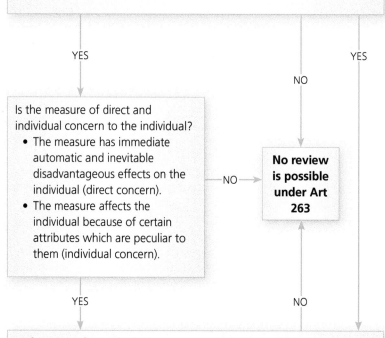

Figure 5.1 The requirements for an action for annulment under Article 263

5.3.2 Article 265 actions against institutions for a failure to act

Article 265 gives both the Member States and the EU institutions the right to call to account any of the Council, the Commission, Parliament and the European Central Bank for failing to take action when they would be required to. This is an obviously necessary addition to the annulment proceedings in Article 263. Just as there are times when the institutions go beyond the powers given to them by the Treaties, then there is also the possibility that in situations where one of the institutions would be bound to act according to the law, it fails to act. A classic example is where the Commission fails to issue a decision following a breach of competition law under Article 101 or Article 102. In such situations the Treaty has provided a form of redress to the injured party through the Article 265 action. Applicants are required to satisfy a test for admissibility and also to show that there are suitable grounds for the review.

Admissibility

There is no set time limit for a claim under Article 265 but in order for the Court to accept that there is an admissible claim it will first see whether three conditions are met:

1. First, the applicant must be able to show *locus standi*. The 'privileged claimants' in this case are described in the Article as 'the member states and other institutions'. This includes Parliament since *Parliament v Council* (Case 377/87) [1988] ECR 4051. Following the TEU it also includes the European Central Bank. 'Natural and legal persons' are also able to bring an action against a Community institution which failed to address to that person any instrument other than a recommendation or an opinion. Inevitably, this means that the instrument must be a binding act. It also obviously means that there would have been a requirement to address the instrument to the applicant had it been enacted.

2. Second, there must be what is referred to as an 'Indictable Institution'. The institutions covered by the Article are the Council, the Commission, Parliament and the Central Bank. For the claim to be admissible there must have been a failure to act by that institution in circumstances where it was in fact legally required to act.

3. Third, there must have been a prior approach to the institution. Before the CJEU will consider an application it must be satisfied that the applicant has already approached the institution seeking redress. This approach must be explicit in its terms and refer to the possibility of a challenge under Article 265 if no reply is received within two months.

Grounds for review

The grounds under which the CJEU will undertake a review are where the applicant is able to show that they were entitled to a decision and none was actually addressed to them. An alternative ground is where an action has not been taken which is of direct and individual concern to them.

In fact, few cases are found to be admissible and so there are few guidelines. Generally, if there is a result to be achieved and an obligation is sufficiently well defined then any attempt to disregard it will fall within the scope of Article 265.

CASE EXAMPLE

Parliament v Council (Case 13/83) [1987] ECR 1513

Here, there was an alleged failure by the Council to ensure freedom to provide international transport and to establish the conditions in which non-resident transporters were able to operate in another Member State. This was accepted as a ground for review.

5.3.3 Article 340 TFEU actions against institutions for damages

Article 340 in para 2 states:

> In the case of non-contractual liability the EU shall, in accordance with the general principles common to the laws of the member states, make good any damage caused by the institutions or by its servants in the performance of their duties.

It is possible, then, to see the similarity between the Article 340 action and a form of general tort action. However, it should be remembered that five of the original six members of the EC had forms of civil liability based on the French Civil Code. As a result, liability under Article 340 is more accurately seen as based on this form of liability.

The Treaty in any case provides that the CJEU should hear all actions under Article 340. There are two significant issues to consider:

- the requirements for admissibility of claims; and
- the conditions for liability.

Admissibility

Locus standi in such claims is necessarily almost unrestricted. As a result, any natural or legal person is capable of bringing an action. The key requirement for admissibility is that the individual making the claim can make out a *prima facie* case that he has personally suffered damage resulting from an act or omission of an institution or of its servant. In this way the action could not, for instance, be brought by a trade union on behalf of a member or members.

The ECJ ruled in *Werhahn Hansamuhle v Council* (Cases 63 to 69/72) [1973] ECR 1229 that the claim must be alleged specifically against an institution or its servant. Therefore a claim could not be made against the EU as a whole.

The appropriate time limit on claiming is five years from the date of the event that it is alleged caused the damage and gave rise to the action.

Conditions for liability

There are three elements that must be satisfied for a successful claim to be made: First, the occurrence of **damage** suffered by the applicant:

- This might include any physical damage as well as economic loss, including both actual damage and loss of earnings. The general qualification is that the damage is certain, provable and quantifiable.
- Future loss is also recoverable but only in limited circumstances. In *Kampffmeyer et al. v Commission* (Cases 5, 7 and 13 to 24/66) [1967] ECR 245 a claim for a future loss was accepted where the cancellation of contracts had already occurred by the time of the creation of the wrongful measure.
- Even highly speculative and non-material loss has been accepted in some circumstances:

CASE EXAMPLE

Adams v Commission (Case 145/83) [1986] QB 138

Adams worked for Hoffmann La Roche, the pharmaceutical company, and he discovered that the company was in breach of EC [now EU] competition law, as a result of which he informed the Commission, for which there was legitimate provision within the law. Nevertheless, he was then arrested for industrial espionage and his wife hanged herself. This was accepted as recoverable damage giving rise to liability.

Second, the presence of **fault** on the part of the institution complained about:

- It is sufficient in this sense to show that the applicant was owed a duty which was then breached by the institution, as was the case in *Adams v Commission* (1986).
- However, the CJEU may be less likely to conclude that there is fault where the institution was involved in making policy decisions and made errors of judgement leading on to the damage suffered.

CASE EXAMPLE

Zuckerfabrik Schoppenstedt v Council (Case 5/71) [1971] ECR 975

Here, a Regulation laid down measures to offset the differences between national sugar prices and Community [now EU] reference prices that were applicable from a particular date. The applicant complained that the criteria were in fact erroneous and had caused him loss, but failed in his complaint. The ECJ laid down some criteria for determining fault, known as the 'Schoppenstedt formula':

i. there must be a legislative measure which involves choices of economic policy; and
ii. this must involve a breach of a superior rule of law;
iii. which is sufficiently serious; and
iv. the superior rule is of a type which was for the protection of individuals.

Only if all parts are satisfied will fault be shown.

Third, it must be possible to show a **causal connection** between the measure complained of and the damage suffered:

- On this basis the mere existence of damage by itself is insufficient to give rise to an action for damages under Article 340.
- Proof of damage alone is insufficient for liability without proof also that the act of the institution challenged directly caused the damage.
- In this way remoteness of damage is clearly an important factor to be taken into account:

CASE EXAMPLE

Pool v Council (Case 49/79) [1981] ECR 569

An English cattle farmer claimed that the conversion rates for sterling (UK currency) in the agricultural sector, known as 'green rates', had caused him loss. The ECJ rejected his claim since it was too speculative.

ACTIVITY

Exercise

Identify and explain which type of enforcement action might be brought in the following situations:

a. A large French wine-producing company, Vin Francais, has been found to have infringed Article 102 by refusing discounts that it normally gives to all retailers of its wines unless these traders cease to order wine from a small English company, Anglovin. Twelve months have now passed and the Commission has not addressed a Decision to Vin Francais.

b. As a result of the Commission not issuing a Decision, many European wine retailers have ceased buying products from Anglovin in order to retain the discounts from Vin Francais. Anglovin has lost a significant amount of its trade and is now facing liquidation.

c. A Council Regulation has been issued requiring a measured reduction of the overall production of wine in the EU based on percentage reductions in all wine-producing Member States. The Commission has subsequently addressed a Decision to the UK government demanding a total halt to wine production in the UK.

ACTIVITY

Self-assessment questions

1. In an action to annul a measure under Article 263, against which institutions are actions usually brought?
2. In an Article 263 action, which bodies are privileged applicants?
3. When can a natural or legal person take action under Article 263?
4. How is the phrase 'direct concern' defined?
5. What is the meaning of the phrase 'individual concern'?
6. When can a Regulation be subject to review under Article 263?
7. What are the grounds for review under Article 263?
8. How broadly has the term 'misuse of powers' been defined?
9. What is the basic difference between an action under Article 263 and an action under Article 265?
10. What are the requirements for admissibility for an action under Article 265?
11. What is the usual context for an action under Article 265?
12. What does the case of *Werhahn Hansamuhle v Council* state about who an action can be brought against under Article 340?
13. What are the three conditions that must be proved for there to be liability under Article 340?
14. What guidelines were issued in the case of *Zuckerfabrik Schoppenstedt v Council*?

KEY FACTS

Infringement proceedings against Member States under Arts 258 and 259	
• Usually brought by the Commission as 'watchdog' of Treaties.	
• Three clear purposes:	
• ensure Member States comply with Treaties;	
• provide a procedure for dispute resolution;	
• provide means of clarifying law.	
• Starts with mediation – then three formal stages:	
• notice of default;	*Commission v Italy (Re Payment of Export Rebates)* (1970)
• reasoned opinion;	*Alfons Lütticke* (1966)
• proceedings in CJEU.	*Commission v Belgium* (1970)
• Penalties possible in Art 260.	
• An action by another state possible under Art 259.	*France v UK* (1979)

Actions against institutions for an abuse of power under Art 263	

• Two major functions:
  • provides a way of controlling legality of binding acts;
  • gives legal protection to those subject to Community
    instruments adversely affected by illegal ones.
• Commission, Council and Member States are privileged claimants.
	*Parliament v Council
	(Chernobyl)* 70/88 (1991)

• Natural and legal persons gain *locus standi* for a decision addressed to them or a Regulation or a Decision addressed to another person of direct and individual concern to them. • 'Individual concern' means decision affects them because of attributes. • 'Direct concern' means 'immediate, automatic and inevitable disadvantageous legal effects'.	*Plaumann v Commission* (1963) *Alcan Aluminium Raeren et al v Commission* (1970)
• A Regulation may be challenged if has no general application but is a 'bundle of individual Decisions'. • Grounds for review include: • lack of competence;	*International Fruit Co v Commission* (1971) *Ford (Europe) v Commission* (1984)
• infringement of an essential procedural requirement;	*Roquette Frères v Council* (1980)
• infringement of Treaties or procedural rules;	*Transocean Marine Paint Association v Commission* (1975)
• misuse of powers.	*Bock v Commission* (1971)

Actions against institutions for a failure to act under Art 265	
• Can challenge Commission, Council, Parliament and European Central Bank. • Privileged claimants are Member States and institutions. • Natural and legal persons must show institution failed to address to them any instrument other than an opinion or recommendation. • Grounds for review are where applicant can show he was entitled to a Decision and none was addressed to him, or an action has not been taken which is of direct and individual concern to him.	*Parliament v Council* (1987)

Actions for damages against institutions under Art 288	
• 'To make good any damage caused by institutions'. • Almost unrestricted *locus standi*. • Defendant must be an institution or its servant, not Community as a whole. • Conditions for liability are: • damage suffered by claimant;	*Werhahn Hansamuhle v Council* (1973) *Adams v Commission* (1986)
• fault of institution;	*Zuckerfabrik Schoppenstedt v Council* (1971)
• causal connection.	*Pool v Council* (1981)

SAMPLE ESSAY QUESTION

'Discuss the scope of the infringement procedures and judicial review of the EU.'

Explain EU infringement procedures:
- Usually brought by Commission against Member States for breaches of EU law
- Starts with mediation – then formal stages, notice of default, proceedings in CJEU
- And penalties possible under Article 260
- And action by another state possible

Discuss the purpose and scope of the procedure:
- Three main purposes – ensures Member States comply with Treaties, provides procedure for dispute resolution and means of clarifying law
- Fact of penalties and possible action by other Member States gives broad scope

Explain action for abuse of power:
- Privileged claimants are Council, Commission and Member States – but individuals also, although must generally show direct concern
- Grounds for review include: lack of competence, infringement of an essential procedural requirement, infringement of Treaties or procedural rules, misuse of powers

Discuss the purpose and scope of the procedure:
- Provides a way of controlling legality of binding acts
- Gives legal protection to those subject to EU instruments adversely affected by illegal ones

Discuss the purpose and scope of the procedure:
- Grounds for review are where applicant can show he was entitled to a decision and none was addressed to him, or an action has not been taken which is of direct and individual concern to him
- So provides protection against failures to act

Explain action for damages:
Conditions for liability are:
- damage suffered by claimant
- fault of institution
- causal connection

Discuss the purpose and scope of the procedure:
- Aimed at making good any damage caused by institutions
- Almost unrestricted *locus standi* – so wide scope
- Must involve an institution or its servant, not EU as a whole – so some restriction there

SUMMARY

- Other than references for preliminary rulings there are four types of action in the Court of Justice – infringement proceedings under Article 258, judicial review of acts by EU institutions under Article 263, and for a failure to act under Article 265, and damages claims under Article 340.

- Infringement proceedings are against Member States for breaches of EU law and penalties are possible.

- Judicial review of abuse of powers by EU institutions have two major functions: to ensure the legality of binding acts, and to give legal protection to those subject to EU instruments who are adversely affected by illegal ones.

- Actions against EU institutions for a failure to act allow privileged claimants and natural and legal persons to claim where the institution has failed to act, for instance where a decision should have been issued.

- Claims for damages against EU institutions allow for making good any damage caused by those institutions.

Further reading

Books

Douglas-Scott, S, *Constitutional Law of the European Union* (Longman, 2002), Chapters 10, 11 and 12.

Fairhurst, J, *Law of the European Union* (8th edn, Pearson, 2010), Chapter 4.

Kaczarowska-Ireland, A, *European Union Law* (Routledge, 2016), Chapter 15.

6

Article 267 TFEU and the preliminary reference procedure

AIMS AND OBJECTIVES

After reading this chapter you should be able to:

- Understand the purpose of the preliminary rulings procedure
- Understand the meaning of the phrase 'court or tribunal'
- Understand the difference between those courts and tribunals which 'may' seek a preliminary ruling and those that 'shall' do so
- Understand the circumstances in which national courts may refrain from seeking rulings, in particular the *'acte clair'* doctrine
- Understand why reform of the preliminary rulings procedure is regarded as important
- Analyse critically the various reform proposals that have been made

ARTICLE

'Art 267 The Court of Justice of the European Union shall have jurisdiction to give preliminary rulings concerning:

(a) the interpretation of the Treaties;
(b) the validity and interpretation of acts of the institutions, bodies, offices or agencies of the Union;

Where such a question is raised before any court or tribunal of a Member State, that court or tribunal may, if it considers that a decision on the question is necessary to enable it to give judgment, request the Court of Justice to give a ruling thereon.

Where any such question is raised in a case pending before a court or tribunal of a Member State against whose decisions there is no judicial remedy under national law, that court or tribunal shall bring the matter before the Court.

If such a question is raised in a case pending before a court or tribunal of a Member State with regard to a person in custody, the Court of Justice of the European Union shall act with the minimum of delay.'

6.1 The relation with Member States

The Article 267 procedure allows any national court or tribunal in any of the Member States to request that the ECJ interpret provisions of EU law. It is crucial to remember that the ECJ simply **interprets** EU law: the national court then has the task of **applying** that law, as interpreted. As Lord Denning explained in the Court of Appeal in *Bulmer v Bollinger* [1974] Ch 401:

JUDGMENT

'It is important to distinguish between the task of interpreting the Treaty – to see what it means – and the task of *applying* it – to apply its provisions to the case in hand. [First], the task of applying the Treaty. On this matter in our courts the English judges have the final word. They are the only judges who are empowered to decide the case itself. They have to find the facts, to state the issues, to give judgment for one side or the other, and to see that the judgement is enforced. Before the English judge can apply the Treaty, they have to see what it means and what is its effect. In the task of *interpreting* the Treaty, the English judges are no longer the final authority.... They are no longer in a position to give rulings which are of binding force. The supreme tribunal for *interpreting* the Treaty is the European Court of Justice.'

It is crucial to appreciate that Article 267 is **not** an appeal procedure. It is triggered by national courts or tribunals during the course of litigation itself. This is why it is known as the 'preliminary reference' procedure, and the Court's judgments are known as 'preliminary rulings'. The rulings are designed to assist the national court or tribunal to reach a final ruling.

There is, therefore, a shared jurisdiction between the national courts and the ECJ. The national courts decide questions of fact and national law; it is also the national courts who apply national and EU law. The ECJ determines abstract questions of the interpretation of EU legislation only (and deals with issues involving the validity of EU secondary legislation). In the first ever preliminary reference case, *De Geus v Robert Bosch* (Case 13/61) [1962] ECR 45, Advocate-General Lagrange said that the 'provisions of [Article 267] must lead to a real and fruitful collaboration between the municipal courts and the Court of Justice with mutual respect for their respective jurisdiction'.

Much more recently, in *Gintec* (Case C–374/05) [2007] ECR I–9517, Advocate-General Ruiz-Jarabo Colomer offered the following culinary metaphor as a means of explaining the operation of the preliminary rulings procedure:

JUDGMENT

'The various ingredients which go into the recipe for a preliminary ruling are clearly enough set out in the European Union cookbook, but theory comes up against the varying circumstances which apply each time the dish is prepared, as the chosen heat source, the pans, the condition and origin of the ingredients and even the state of mind of whoever is cooking are always different.... While the national courts take primary responsibility for the dish, the Court of Justice merely provides them with the all-important [Union] seasoning, without interfering in matters which do not concern it. Nevertheless, the European and national elements frequently become mixed up and, to allow them to perform their functions, each must absorb and refine the flavours of the other.... It falls to the Court of Justice, like a reliable kitchen hand who is unable to create a whole meal but acts as the chef's adviser, to provide the [national court] with some guidelines ... by offering it a valuable tool for resolving the dispute.'

6.2 The character of the reference procedure

6.2.1 References seeking interpretation of EU law

If a dispute as to the proper interpretation of a provision of EU legislation arises during a legal dispute before a court or tribunal in one of the Member States, a request may be made for a ruling on the interpretation of the disputed provision. The national court or tribunal suspends the case until the ECJ gives its ruling. When the ECJ has made its decision, the national court or tribunal then continues from where it left off, applying the EU law as interpreted by the ECJ.

This is supposed to achieve uniformity or consistency of interpretation of all EU law, because once the ECJ has made its preliminary ruling, this establishes a precedent for all the courts and tribunals in the Member States to follow in future cases. Having one court to interpret all EU law means that the same meaning is given throughout the Union; if it was left to national courts they might all come up with different interpretations. This would be likely given that the EU presently has 24 official languages. The Treaties are reproduced in all of them. Given that translation is not a precise science, there are bound to be differences between all the different versions; but using the ECJ helps keep the differences to a minimum. If the preliminary reference procedure did not exist, courts and tribunals in the Member States would have to make their own interpretations of EU law. This would create a very real risk of divergent meanings being given to the same provisions of EU law in different Member States and, if that happened, the whole fabric of EU law could begin to unravel.

The Court can give interpretations of provisions in both of the Treaties, and 'acts of the institutions, bodies, offices or agencies of the Union' – which basically means all secondary EU legislation (primarily Regulations and Directives). It can also rule on the interpretation of international treaties entered into by those institutions (*Hageman* (Case 181/73) [1974] ECR 449). An 'act' need not be directly effective in order to be capable of interpretation (*Mazzalai* (Case 111/75) [1976] ECR 657).

The EU's approach to interpretation

Any court in the world has a choice as to its approach to interpretation, and the ECJ is no exception. There are three main methods:

1. **Literal.** The ordinary dictionary meaning. Popular with English courts, but not with the ECJ. The multi-lingualism situation makes this method impracticable.

2. **Contextual.** Look to EU law as a whole, not just the particular piece of legislation.

3. **Purposive.** Interpret the legislation in the way which most furthers the purposes of the Union. EU legislation (whether primary or secondary) lends itself to this approach because of the presence of a 'preamble' setting out the aims and objectives of the legislation.

Generally, the ECJ takes a 'teleological' approach, which may be described as a combination of the second and third approaches. The position is summed up in the following extract from *Re Adidas AG* (Case C–223/98) [1999] ECR I–7081:

JUDGMENT

'In interpreting a provision of [EU] law it is necessary to consider not only its wording but also the context in which it occurs and the objects of the rules of which it is part ... where a provision of [EU] law is open to several interpretations, only one of which can ensure that the provision retains its effectiveness, preference must be given to that interpretation.'

Using the teleological approach allows the ECJ to update the law and meet new social and political developments.

Language differences

The Court has frequently dealt with the issue of linguistic divergences in EU legislation. For example, it held in *Stauder v Ulm* (Case 29/69) [1969] ECR 419:

JUDGMENT

'The necessity for uniform application and accordingly for uniform interpretation makes it impossible to consider one version of . . . text in isolation but requires that it be interpreted on the basis of both the real intention of its author and the aim he seeks to achieve, in the light in particular of the versions in all [the] languages.'

The role of the ECJ in the preliminary reference procedure

The ECJ is supposed to be 'reactive', that is, it responds to questions submitted to it by the national courts. Occasionally, the ECJ will take a more 'proactive' approach and reformulate a question so that the answer it gives is more useful to the national court. Even more rarely, the ECJ will answer a question that was **not actually asked**, if the Court thinks that this will assist the national court in giving judgment. A good example of this is *Marks & Spencer v Customs and Excise Commissioners* (Case C–62/00) [2003] QB 866. The Court of Appeal had asked a question of the ECJ relating to Directive 77/388. The ECJ noted that the question was based on a mistaken premise regarding direct effect and, having put the Court of Appeal straight on that point, concluded that it (the ECJ) therefore needed to rephrase the question (otherwise the answer would not make sense). The Court stated:

JUDGMENT

'In the procedure laid down by [Article 267] for co-operation between national courts and the [ECJ], it is for the latter to provide the referring court with an answer which will be of use to it and enable it to determine the case before it. To that end, the Court may have to reformulate the question referred to it.'

The ECJ is not allowed to consider the validity of national law. If it is asked to do so, it may reformulate the question and return an abstract answer on the point of (EU) law involved (*Costa v ENEL* (Case 6/64) [1964] ECR 1141) or simply refuse to answer the question asked (see *Foglia v Novello* (Case 104/79) [1981] ECR 745; *Bacardi-Martini v New-castle United* (Case C–318/00) [2003] ECR I–905). Nor is the Court supposed to consider how EU legislation should be applied by the national courts; however, it has done this in the past by giving 'practical' rulings (*Stoke-on-Trent City Council v B&Q* (Case C–169/91) [1993] 2 WLR 730). This is unsurprising, given that the line between interpretation and application is likely to be very fine.

The role of the national courts

The national courts, having requested a preliminary ruling, are then expected to apply it to the facts of the case and give judgment. However, legal history was made in 2003 in *Arsenal FC v Reed* (Case C–206/01) [2003] Ch 454, when Laddie J in the English High Court refused to apply a preliminary ruling of the ECJ that he himself had requested.

Arsenal Football Club had accused Matthew Reed of infringing its trademarks by selling unofficial merchandise such as scarves and shirts bearing Arsenal's logos (a shield and a cannon) outside the club's ground, Highbury Stadium in north London. During the course of the subsequent trademark infringement action, Laddie J had requested a preliminary ruling on the interpretation of certain provisions in Directive 89/104. However, when the ruling was delivered, Laddie J decided that the ECJ had overstepped its interpretative jurisdiction and had made certain findings of fact (with which he disagreed) regarding the question of whether or not Arsenal supporters were likely to confuse Arsenal's official merchandise with Reed's unofficial merchandise. Strictly speaking, the ECJ is only supposed to make rulings on the interpretation of points of EU legislation and, thus, if Laddie J was correct then he was perfectly entitled to reach this conclusion. Nevertheless, it was a controversial decision. However, a potential crisis in the relationship between the ECJ and the High Court was averted. Having lost the case in the High Court, Arsenal FC appealed to the Court of Appeal which found, reversing Laddie J's decision, that the ECJ had not overstepped its jurisdiction. The Court of Appeal therefore applied the preliminary ruling in full and gave judgment to Arsenal.

6.2.2 References challenging validity of EU law

Special considerations apply where the question is the **validity** of EU law rather than **interpretation**. First, the ECJ may not rule on the validity of the Treaties. It is therefore only secondary EU legislation that can be challenged on validity grounds. Second, whereas a national court may declare EU law **valid** and not refer, it may not declare EU law **invalid** (*Firma Foto-Frost v Hauptzollamt Lübeck-Ost* (Case 314/85) [1987] ECR 4199). The ECJ has exclusive authority in this situation. Where a national court suspects that a provision of EU secondary legislation may be invalid, therefore, a reference **must** be made. A good example is *R (on the application of British American Tobacco) v Secretary of State for Health* (Case C–491/01) [2002] ECR I–11453.

CASE EXAMPLE

R (on the application of British American Tobacco) v Secretary of State for Health (Case C–491/01) [2002] ECR I–11453

Directive 2001/37 had been adopted by the Council on the basis of Article 114 (measures to ensure the functioning of the Internal Market) and Article 207 (Common Commercial Policy). According to Article 1 of the Directive, its aim was to

> approximate the laws, regulations and administrative provisions of the Member States concerning the maximum tar, nicotine and carbon monoxide yields of cigarettes and the warnings regarding health and other information to appear on unit packets of tobacco products, together with certain measures concerning the ingredients and the descriptions of tobacco products, taking as a basis a high level of health protection.

In September 2001, British American Tobacco and Imperial Tobacco sought permission from the High Court in London to apply for judicial review of 'the intention and/or obligation' of the UK government to transpose the Directive into national law. The application was based on several grounds, including inappropriate legislative base. The case was referred to the ECJ for a ruling, and in due course the Court held that the Directive was valid; Article 114 was the correct legislative base. Article 207 should not have been used in addition but this was a purely formal defect and did not affect the validity of the Directive.

6.2.3 'Docket control': inadmissible references

The ECJ rarely refuses a request for a preliminary ruling. Provided that the question referred to the ECJ is one of interpretation, the ECJ is bound in principle to respond. However, there are three situations when requests for preliminary rulings have been declared inadmissible.

Contrived dispute

In *Leur-Bloem* (Case C–28/95) [1998] QB 182, the ECJ stated:

JUDGMENT

'A reference by a national court can be rejected only if it appears that the procedure laid down by [Article 267] has been misused and a ruling from the Court elicited by means of a contrived dispute, or it is obvious that [Union] law cannot apply, either directly or indirectly, to the circumstances of the case referred to the Court.'

This situation arose in *Foglia v Novello (No 2)* (Case 244/80) [1981] ECR 3045:

CASE EXAMPLE

Foglia v Novello (No 2) (Case 244/80) [1981] ECR 3045

Ms Novello, a French national, ordered a number of cases of an Italian liqueur wine from Foglia, an Italian wine merchant. The sales contract specified that Novello should not be liable for any charges imposed by either the Italian or French authorities contrary to (Union) law. The French Customs authorities imposed an allegedly unlawful tax on the wine when it entered France. Foglia paid this and then instituted proceedings against Ms Novello to recover the cost from her. In the Italian court, the judge requested a ruling regarding the interpretation of Article 110 (the prohibition of discriminatory internal taxation – see Chapter 15). However, the ECJ refused to answer the question, saying the proceedings had been created by the parties to test the validity of the French tax rules, and were 'artificial'.

This decision has been criticised, but is understandable: there was no real issue of EU law for the ECJ to determine. In *Meilicke v Meyer* (Case C–89/91) [1992] ECR I–4871, the ECJ, following *Foglia v Novello* (1981), refused to consider a series of questions referred to it from the Hanover Regional Court, as they all related to Professor Meilike's theories regarding EU company law and there was no genuine dispute between the parties. The Court announced that the purpose of Article 267 was to contribute to the administration of justice in the Member States, not to deliver advisory opinions on general or hypothetical questions.

In a number of subsequent cases the ECJ has accepted that the dispute was genuine, despite suggestions to the contrary by an interested observer. For example, in *Idéal Tourisme* (Case C–36/99) [2000] ECR I–6049 the ECJ rejected a suggestion by the Belgian government that a dispute over VAT (between a Belgian company and the Belgian tax authorities) was contrived, holding:

JUDGMENT

'The documents in the case contain nothing to show that the parties to the main proceedings manifestly colluded to obtain a ruling from the Court by means of an artificial dispute, as was the case in *Foglia v Novello*. On the contrary, it is plain that the parties disagree on a number of important points, and it is clear from the documents that Idéal Tourisme did not come to an agreement with the Belgian State to refer hypothetical questions to the Court for a preliminary ruling.'

In *Bacardi-Martini v Newcastle United FC* (2003), the ECJ refused to respond to a request from the English High Court on facts not dissimilar to those in *Foglia v Novello* (1981).

CASE EXAMPLE

Bacardi-Martini v Newcastle United FC (Case C–318/00) [2003] ECR I–905

A contract had been signed between Bacardi and NUFC to advertise the former's products on advertising hoardings at the latter's ground during a UEFA Cup match involving NUFC and a French club, Metz, in December 1996. However, NUFC pulled out of the deal when it discovered that the game was to be televised live on French television via satellite – because French law prohibits the TV advertising of alcohol. Bacardi brought an action against NUFC and the case was heard in the High Court, which requested a ruling on the interpretation of Article 56 (the free movement of services). The ECJ refused to deal with the reference, stating that it had to apply 'special vigilance' when a reference request came in from a court in one Member State seeking to question the compatibility of legislation in another Member State with EU law.

Irrelevance

Where the request relates to provisions of EU law that are incidental to the actual dispute, the request may be refused by the ECJ. According to the ECJ in *BP Supergas v Greece* (Case C–62/93) [1995] ECR I–9883, a request will be refused if it is 'quite obvious' that the question bears 'no relation' to the actual subject-matter of the litigation.

Insufficient information of factual/legal background

In *Telemasicabruzzo* (Cases C–320 to 322/90) [1993] ECR I–393, the ECJ rejected a reference that had insufficient information about the factual background or the legal dispute between the parties. This was confirmed in *La Pyramide* (Case C–378/93) [1994] ECR I–3999, the ECJ stating that this would be the case especially where the factual situation was complex.

KEY FACTS

The character of the reference procedure	
The procedure allows national courts and tribunals to seek rulings on the interpretation of EU legislation.	Art 267 TFEU
The procedure seeks to ensure that words or phrases in EU legislation are given the same, uniform interpretation throughout the EU, helping to ensure that EU law is applied consistently.	*Stauder v Ulm* (1969)
The procedure can also be used to challenge the validity of EU secondary legislation, as only the ECJ has authority to declare EU legislation invalid.	*Firma Foto-Frost* (1987)
In interpretation cases, the ECJ usually takes a 'teleological' approach, looking to interpret EU legislation in such a way as to promote the underlying purpose of the legislation, and taking into account the context.	*Re Adidas* (1999)
References will be declared inadmissible if the procedure has been abused (contrived dispute), or if the question is irrelevant, or if insufficient factual/legal background information is provided.	*Foglia v Novello* (1981); *BP Supergas v Greece* (1995); *Telemasicabruzzo* (1993)

6.3 The meaning of 'court' or 'tribunal'

There are limitations on who can request a ruling. Only a 'court or tribunal' may do so. The phrase 'court or tribunal' has been interpreted very widely. (Article 267 has itself been interpreted by the ECJ, after national courts referred questions to it, under the Article 267 procedure!) It is certainly not required that a forum have the name 'court' or 'tribunal'.

6.3.1 The *Dorsch Consult* factors

According to the ECJ in *Dorsch Consult* (Case C–54/96) [1997] ECR I–4961:

JUDGMENT

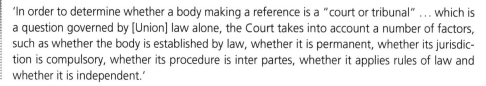

'In order to determine whether a body making a reference is a "court or tribunal" … which is a question governed by [Union] law alone, the Court takes into account a number of factors, such as whether the body is established by law, whether it is permanent, whether its jurisdiction is compulsory, whether its procedure is inter partes, whether it applies rules of law and whether it is independent.'

This is a very important case, as it establishes what might be described as a 'functional' test for establishing which bodies may invoke the Article 267 procedure. The practical result is that more bodies can seek preliminary rulings than would have been the case had the ECJ adopted a 'literal' approach, that is, only answering requests from bodies actually called 'court' or 'tribunal'. The advantages of this 'functional' approach are:

- Many bodies which do not have the name 'court' or 'tribunal' nevertheless carry out judicial functions, that is, they are deciding disputes between parties. The functional approach helps to ensure that these bodies do not have to decide on the interpretation of EU legislation themselves, which in turn means that the legislation is more likely to be applied accurately in order to resolve the disputes.

- The functional approach means more bodies can request rulings on different provisions of EU law, which allows the ECJ to give definitive rulings on ambiguous provisions of EU legislation which may not have otherwise reached the ECJ at all.

- The functional approach reduces the need for expensive and time-consuming appeals in the national legal systems. Often, appeals are available against decisions made by various bodies to 'courts'. Without a functional approach, these appeals might be triggered in order to get a case into a 'court' in order for a request for a preliminary ruling to be made. With a functional approach, any body performing a judicial function can seek a ruling itself.

A good example of the 'functional' approach is *Broekmeulen* (Case 246/80) [1981] ECR 2311. Dr Broekmeulen's registration as a GP had been refused. His appeal, to the Appeals Committee of the Royal Netherlands Society for the Protection of Medicine, was based on EU law. References were made to the ECJ, one of which asked whether or not the Appeals Committee was a 'court or tribunal'. The ECJ held:

JUDGMENT

'In the practical absence of an effective means of redress before the ordinary courts, in a matter concerning the application of [Union] law, the Appeals Committee, which performs its duties with the approval of the public authorities and operates with their assistance, and whose decisions are accepted following contentious proceedings and are in fact recognised as final, must be deemed to be a court or tribunal for the purpose of [Article 267].'

The wide scope of 'court or tribunal' can be seen in the following cases:

- *Royal Copenhagen* (Case C–400/93) [1995] ECR I–1275 – administration board in Copenhagen, Denmark;
- *O'Flynn v Adjudication Officer* (Case C–237/94) [1996] ECR I–2617 – Social Security Commissioner, UK;
- *Gebhard* (Case C–55/94) [1995] ECR I–4165 – Milan Bar Council;
- *El-Yassini* (Case C–416/96) [1999] ECR I–1209 – immigration adjudicator, UK;
- *Abrahamsson and Andersson* (Case C–407/98) [2000] ECR I–5539 – Universities Appeals Board, Sweden;
- *Cadbury Schweppes* (Case C–196/04) [2006] ECR I–7995 – Special Commissioners of Income Tax, UK;
- *Jia* (Case C–1/05) [2007] ECR I–1 – Alien Appeals Board, Sweden;
- *Torresi* (Cases C–58 and 59/13) [2015] QB 331; [2015] 2 WLR 29 – National Bar Council, Italy.

In *El-Yassini* (1999), the ECJ gave very careful consideration to the question of whether or not an immigration adjudicator in the UK qualified as a 'court or tribunal'. In the end it decided that an adjudicator did qualify. Read this quote from the judgment and note how many of the *Dorsch Consult* (1997) factors are satisfied:

JUDGMENT

'It should be first noted that the office of Immigration Adjudicator was established by the Immigration Act 1971. That statute confers on the Immigration Adjudicator jurisdiction to hear and determine disputes concerning the rights of foreigners to enter and remain on the territory of the UK. Further, Immigration Adjudicators constitute a permanent organ. Their determinations are to be made in accordance with the law, pursuant to the 1971 Act and in compliance with the rules of procedure. That procedure is inter partes in nature. Immigration Adjudicators are required to give reasons for their determinations, which are binding and may, in certain circumstances, be appealed against to the Immigration Appeal Tribunal. Lastly, Immigration Adjudicators are appointed by the Lord Chancellor for a renewable ten-year or one-year term, depending on whether they sit on a full-time or part-time basis. During their period of office, they enjoy the same guarantees of independence as judges. It follows that the Immigration Adjudicator must be regarded as a court or tribunal within the meaning of [Article 267].'

Conversely, in *Nordsee* (Case 102/81) [1982] ECR 1095, an independent arbitrator was held not to be a court. This was because the arbitrator lacked compulsory jurisdiction. A similar decision was reached in *Denuit & Cordenier* (Case C–125/04) [2005] ECR I–923, where the Court stated:

JUDGMENT

'An arbitration tribunal is not a "court or tribunal of a Member State" within the meaning of [Article 267] where the parties are under no obligation, in law or in fact, to refer their disputes to arbitration and the public authorities of the Member State concerned are not involved in the decision to opt for arbitration nor required to intervene of their own accord in the proceedings before the arbitrator.'

In *Procura Della Republica v X* (Case C–74/95) [1996] ECR I–6609, the ECJ held that questions referred to it by the Italian Public Prosecutor were inadmissible, as he did not constitute a 'court or tribunal'. And in *Victoria Film A/S* (Case C–134/97) [1998] ECR I–7023 a reference from a body within the Swedish tax administration was held inadmissible (it did not carry out a judicial function). Rather, the body carried out a purely administrative function. If anything, the body tried to prevent disputes arising in the first place, as opposed to resolving disputes which had already arisen.

Even a court may not be a 'court' if it is carrying out an administrative (as opposed to judicial) function. In *Salzmann* (Case C–78/99) [2001] ECR I–4421, the ECJ held that the District Court, Bregenz, Austria was not a 'court' when it was acting as a land registry. Similarly, in *Lutz & Others* (Case C–182/00) [2002] ECR I–547, the Regional Court, Wels, Austria was not a 'court' when acting as a company's registry. The ECJ held:

JUDGMENT

'A national court may refer a question to the [ECJ] only if there is a case pending before it and if it is called upon to give judgment in proceedings intended to lead to a decision of a judicial nature … when it makes an administrative decision without being required to resolve a legal dispute, the referring body, even if it satisfies the other conditions [identified in *Dorsch Consult* (1997)], cannot be regarded as exercising a judicial function.'

The wide scope given to the words 'court or tribunal' has allowed for a much greater number of bodies to invoke the preliminary rulings procedure. This has obvious benefits: it means that those bodies are able to apply EU legislation after it has been interpreted by the ECJ, rather than having to try to interpret the law themselves; it allows the ECJ to clarify the law on legislative provisions which may otherwise not have reached the Court; it may even reduce the number of appeals at national level. However, there has been persistent criticism of the Court's policy – from one of the Court's own advisers. In several opinions – starting with *De Coster* (Case C–17/00) [2001] ECR I–9445, repeated in *Österreichischer Rundfunk* (Case C–195/06) [2003] ECR I–4989 and most recently in *Umweltanwalt von Kärnten* (Case C–205/08) [2009] ECR I–11525 – Advocate-General Ruiz-Jarabo Colomer has complained that the ECJ's interpretation of 'court or tribunal' is 'too flexible', opening up the preliminary rulings procedure to what he calls 'quasi-judicial bodies', by which he means administrative bodies outside the 'ordinary judicial structure'. He has invited the Court to 'lay down a stricter and more consistent body of rules' on admissibility, and to redefine the concept of 'court or tribunal', to mean only 'bodies forming part of the judicial power of every State' with only occasional exceptions. However, the Court has (so far) ignored the Advocate-General's advice.

6.3.2 'Independence'

This criterion has generated some important case law. In England, a number of tribunals are closely connected with government departments whose decisions they are called upon to examine. Does this satisfy the criterion of independence? This issue arose in a case involving the Austrian legal system. In *Köllensperger & Atswanger* (Case C–103/97) [1999] ECR I–551, a reference had been made by the Procurement Office of the *Land* of Tyrol, Austria. Its members were appointed by the Tyrol government, and could be removed 'if the conditions for appointment are no longer met or if circumstances occur which prevent proper exercise of the office and are likely to do so for a long time'. According to the ECJ, this 'appears *prima facie* too vague to guarantee against undue intervention or pressure on the part of the executive'. However, the Court found that there were guarantees of independence in other provisions of Austrian law, including a provision expressly prohibiting the giving of instructions to members of the Procurement Office in the performance of their duties.

Two other cases illustrate the problem of ensuring 'independence'. In the first case, *Gabalfrisa & Others* (2000), the request was declared admissible, but in the second case, *Schmid* (2002), the Court declared that the ruling was inadmissible.

CASE EXAMPLE

Gabalfrisa & Others (Cases C–110 to 147/98) [2000] ECR I–1577

This case involved several references from the Regional Economic/Administrative Court (EAC) in Catalonia, Spain. There was a question regarding the independence of this court from the tax authorities whose decisions it reviewed. In the end, the Court stated that it was satisfied that Spanish law:

> ensures a separation of functions between, on the one hand, the departments of the tax authority responsible for management, clearance and recovery and, on the other hand, the [EAC] which rule on complaints lodged against the decisions of those departments without receiving any instruction from the tax authority.

CASE EXAMPLE

Schmid (Case C–516/99) [2002] ECR I–4573

This case involved a reference from the Appeal Chamber of the Regional Finance Authority of Vienna. The ECJ declared the reference inadmissible: the Appeal Chamber lacked independence. The problem was that the Appeal Chamber had five members, two of whom were also members of the regional tax authority whose decisions the Chamber was intended to examine. (Indeed, the President of the regional tax authority was automatically also the President of the Appeal Chamber.)

In *Schmid*, the ECJ held that a body cannot be regarded as an independent 'court or tribunal' for the purposes of Article 267 where it has 'an organisational and functional link' with a government department whose decisions it is called upon to review.

In *Wilson* (Case C–506/04) [2006] ECR I–8613, the Court offered extensive guidance on the 'concept of independence', as follows:

JUDGMENT

'The concept of independence, which is inherent in the task of adjudication, involves primarily an authority acting as a third party in relation to the authority which adopted the contested decision. The concept has two other aspects. The first aspect, which is external, presumes that the body is protected against external intervention or pressure liable to jeopardise the independent judgment of its members as regards proceedings before them. That essential freedom from such external factors requires certain guarantees sufficient to protect the person of those who have the task of adjudicating in a dispute, such as guarantees against removal from office. The second aspect, which is internal, is linked to impartiality and seeks to ensure a level playing field for the parties to the proceedings and their respective interests with regard to the subject-matter of those proceedings. That aspect requires objectivity and the absence of any interest in the outcome of the proceedings apart from the strict application of the rule of law. Those guarantees of independence and impartiality require rules, particularly as regards the composition of the body and the appointment, length of service and the grounds for abstention, rejection and dismissal of its members, in order to dismiss any reasonable doubt in the minds of individuals as to the imperviousness of that body to external factors and its neutrality with respect to the interests before it.'

KEY FACTS

The Court can only accept requests from a national 'court or tribunal'… but this means any body carrying out a judicial function.	*Broekmeulen* (1981); *Dorsch Consult* (1997); *El-Yassini* (1999)
Arbitrators, prosecutors and administrative bodies are not 'courts or tribunals'.	*Nordsee* (1982); *Procura Della Republica v X* (1996); *Victoria Film* (1998); *Salzmann* (2001)
The body requesting a ruling must be independent. It must have no 'organisational or functional link' with any government department.	*Schmid* (2002)
The body must be protected from external intervention or pressure and it must be impartial.	*Wilson* (2006)

6.4 The discretionary reference procedure

The decision on when to refer questions, and on what issues, is left entirely up to the national courts (*Pigs Marketing Board v Redmond* (Case 83/78) [1978] ECR 2347). It is normal, but not essential, that one or more of the parties will have attempted to rely upon some provision of EU legislation during the case. However, the national court may issue a reference of its own volition if it deems it necessary to reach a decision (*Verholen* (Cases C–87 to 89/90) [1991] ECR I–3757). It is essential that the request for a ruling be made while the case is still proceeding in the national court. After that point it is too late, because the ECJ decision would no longer be 'necessary' to enable the national court to give judgment (*Pardini* (Case 338/85) [1988] ECR 2041).

For those national courts or tribunals falling within the second paragraph of Article 267 (and this is the vast majority of them), there is a discretion whether or not to refer the case to the ECJ (note the word 'may'). This discretion cannot be removed by national rules as to precedent (*Rheinmuhlen-Dusseldorf* (Case 166/73) [1974] ECR 33). A lower court may refer a matter to the ECJ despite a superior court's ruling to the contrary.

The fact that the ECJ has already decided a particular matter should not of itself prevent a further reference. In *Da Costa en Schaake* (Cases 28 to 30/62) [1963] ECR 61, the ECJ declared it had the right to depart from previous decisions.

In the Court of Appeal case of *Bulmer v Bollinger* (1974), Lord Denning MR noted that national courts need only seek a ruling when it was 'necessary' to enable them to give judgment. He continued:

JUDGMENT

'It is to be noticed … that the word is "necessary". This is much stronger than "desirable" or "convenient". There are some cases where the point, if decided one way, would shorten the trial greatly. But, if decided the other way, it would mean that the trial would go to its full length. In such a case it might be "desirable" or "convenient" to take it as a preliminary point…. But it would not be "necessary" at that stage. When the facts were investigated, it might turn out to have been quite unnecessary. The case would be determined on another ground altogether. As a rule you cannot tell whether it is necessary to decide a point until all the facts are ascertained. So, in general, it is best to decide the facts first.'

He went on to list various factors that should be considered by national judges in deciding whether or not to invoke the procedure:

- time;
- cost;
- the workload of the ECJ;
- the wishes of the parties.

The words of the Master of the Rolls (as Lord Denning was at the time) are obviously important, but remember that the above guidance does not necessarily reflect the view of the ECJ. Nevertheless, time is obviously particularly relevant in criminal cases, where a defendant may have to wait on remand while the ECJ is considering its ruling. This issue has recently been addressed: the fourth paragraph of Article 267, requiring the ECJ to act 'with the minimum of delay' in cases involving 'a person in custody', was added by the Lisbon Treaty.

6.5 The mandatory reference procedure

6.5.1 Introduction

Under the second paragraph of Article 267, the court or tribunal '**may**' make a request; under the third paragraph of Article 267, courts or tribunals, against whose decisions there is no judicial remedy under national law, '**shall**' refer. So, only for certain courts or tribunals is it mandatory to refer. The question is: which courts are they? In *Costa v ENEL* (Case 6/64) [1964] ECR 1141, a request had come from an Italian magistrates' court. There was no appeal from the magistrates' decision, because of the small amount of money involved. The ECJ stated (emphasis added): 'By the terms of this Article ... national courts against whose decision, **as in the present case**, there is no judicial remedy, **must** refer the matter to the Court of Justice.'

Although slightly ambiguous, this has been taken to imply that certain courts (such as the English Court of Appeal), although generally subject to the second paragraph, could find themselves subject to the third paragraph if no appeal was available in a particular case. Initially, the view of the Court of Appeal itself was that it was never subject to the third paragraph. In *Bulmer v Bollinger* (1974), Lord Denning MR said that 'short of the House of Lords, no other English court is bound to refer a question' to the ECJ. However, in *Chiron Corporation v Murex Diagnostics (No 8)* [1995] All ER (EC) 88, Balcombe LJ pointed out:

JUDGMENT

'[Article 267] refers to "a court ... against whose decisions there is no judicial remedy under national law". For convenience, I will refer to such a court as the court of last resort. ... Where there is no right even to apply to the House of Lords for leave to appeal from a decision of the Court of Appeal – e.g. on a refusal by the Court of Appeal for leave to appeal against the decision of the court below, or a refusal by the Court of Appeal, on a renewed application, to grant leave to apply for judicial review – then the Court of Appeal will be the court of last resort. So Lord Denning MR stated the matter too widely [in *Bulmer v Bollinger*].'

Note: in 2009, the House of Lords was replaced by the Supreme Court of the United Kingdom as the UK's 'court of last resort'. This issue has been examined by the ECJ, albeit in the context of the Swedish judicial system.

CASE EXAMPLE

Lyckeskog (Case C–99/00) [2003] 1 WLR 9

The ECJ was asked whether a rule of Swedish procedural law, which required a 'declaration of admissibility' to be obtained before a case could be appealed from the Court of Appeal to the Supreme Court, meant that the former court was, in effect, a 'court of last resort' (to borrow Balcombe LJ's expression). According to its own Code of Procedure, the Supreme Court may declare an appeal admissible only if:

- it is important for guidance in the application of the law that the appeal be examined by the Supreme Court; or
- there are special grounds for examination of the appeal, such as the existence of grounds of review on a point of law, formal defect, or where the outcome of the case before the Court of Appeal is manifestly attributable to negligence or serious error.

The ECJ held that these procedural rules did not convert the Swedish Court of Appeal into a court of last resort:

JUDGMENT

'Decisions of a national appellate court which can be challenged by the parties before a supreme court are not decisions of a "court or tribunal of a Member State against whose decisions there is no judicial remedy under national law" within the meaning of [Article 267]. The fact that examination of the merits of such appeals is subject to a prior declaration of admissibility by the supreme court does not have the effect of depriving the parties of a judicial remedy.'

The decision in *Lyckeskog* was followed and applied in *Cartesio* (Case C–210/06) [2008] ECR I–9641. That case raised the question whether the Regional Court of Appeal in Hungary was subject to the third paragraph of Article 267, given that its decisions were final, subject to an 'extraordinary' appeal to the Hungarian Supreme Court. The ECJ ruled that, because appeals were available, albeit only in limited circumstances, the Regional Court of Appeal was not subject to the mandatory reference procedure.

6.5.2 Mandatory references and hypothetical questions

Although national supreme courts are obliged to make references to the ECJ when a question is raised before them, that does not mean they have to seek rulings if the question raised is actually irrelevant to the case. However interesting the question may be, if it is not essential to the outcome of the case it is hypothetical. In *CILFIT* (Case 283/81) [1982] ECR 3415, the ECJ held:

JUDGMENT

'National courts or tribunals are not obliged to refer to the Court of Justice a question concerning the interpretation of [Union] law raised before them if that question is not relevant, that is to say, if the answer to that question, regardless of what it may be, can in no way affect the outcome of the case.'

6.5.3 Mandatory references and previous rulings

Does a national court of last resort have to make a preliminary reference even if the point has already been decided? If so, that would generate a large number of 'repeat' references, which would be very inefficient. Hence, the ECJ has decided that national courts of last resort do not have to make references in such cases. In *Da Costa* (1963), the ECJ stated:

JUDGMENT

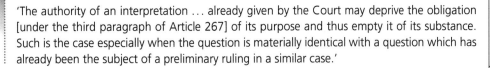

'The authority of an interpretation ... already given by the Court may deprive the obligation [under the third paragraph of Article 267] of its purpose and thus empty it of its substance. Such is the case especially when the question is materially identical with a question which has already been the subject of a preliminary ruling in a similar case.'

This was subsequently endorsed by the ECJ in *CILFIT* (1982). The ECJ referred to *Da Costa* and added that 'the same effect ... may be produced ... even though the questions at issue are not strictly identical'. And in *Bulmer v Bollinger* (1974), Lord Denning said:

JUDGMENT

'in some cases ... it may be found that the same point ... has already been decided by the [ECJ] in a previous case. In that event it is not necessary for the English court to decide it. It can follow the previous decision without troubling the [ECJ].'

A good example of this was seen recently in the UK Supreme Court case of *Mirga; Samin* [2016] UKSC 1; [2016] 1 WLR 481. Despite being the UK's 'court of last resort', the Supreme Court declined to seek a preliminary ruling because the question raised had already been decided by the ECJ in *Dano* (Case C–333/13) [2015] 1 CMLR 48; [2015] 1 WLR 2519 and *Alimanovic* (Case C–67/14) [2016] 1 CMLR 29; [2016] QB 308. All of these cases will be discussed later (see Chapter 11).

6.5.4 Mandatory references and *acte clair*

According to the ECJ in *CILFIT* (1982), 'the correct application of [Union] law may be so obvious as to leave no scope for any reasonable doubt as to the manner in which the question raised is to be resolved'. This would entitle a national 'court of last resort' to decide not to invoke the Article 267 procedure. A decision not to request a ruling because the provision is 'so obvious as to leave no scope for reasonable doubt' is an example of *acte clair* (literally, 'clear act'), a doctrine developed from French law. However, in *CILFIT* (1982), the ECJ gave very clear instructions that *acte clair* must be used with caution:

JUDGMENT

'Before it comes to the conclusion that such is the case, the national court or tribunal must be convinced that the matter is equally obvious to the courts of the other Member States and to the Court of Justice. Only if those conditions are satisfied may the national court or tribunal refrain from submitting the question to the Court of Justice and take upon itself the responsibility for resolving it.'

The Court went on to list those conditions in the next paragraph:

JUDGMENT

'To begin with, it must be borne in mind that [Union] legislation is drafted in several languages and that different language versions are equally authentic. An interpretation of a provision of [Union] law thus involves a comparison of the different language versions. It must also be borne in mind, even when the different language versions are entirely in accord with one another, that [Union] law uses terminology which is peculiar to it. Furthermore, it must be emphasised that legal concepts do not necessarily have the same meaning in [Union] law and in the law of the various Member States. Finally, every provision of [Union] law must be placed in its context and interpreted in the light of the provisions of [Union] law as a whole, regard being had to the objectives thereof and to the state of its evolution at the date on which the provision in question is to be applied.'

The instruction not to abuse *acte clair* was subsequently emphasised in *Intermodal Transports* (Case C–495/03) [2005] ECR I–8151, where the Court stated that the national court or tribunal must 'in particular' be convinced that the other Member States' national courts and the ECJ itself would find the matter 'equally obvious'.

In *X & Van Dijk* (Cases C–72, 197/14) [2016] 1 CMLR 27, the Supreme Court of the Netherlands asked the ECJ whether it was entitled to treat the interpretation of a provision of EU legislation as *acte clair* (which it was inclined to do) notwithstanding the fact that a lower court had, coincidentally, requested a preliminary ruling on the same provision (albeit in a different case) and therefore did not regard the matter as *acte clair*. The ECJ held that *CILFIT* gave the national court of last resort 'sole responsibility' for determining whether the correct application of EU law was so obvious as to leave no scope for any reasonable doubt. It therefore followed that it was for the national court of last resort 'alone' to take upon themselves 'independently' the responsibility for determining whether the provision of EU legislation in question was *acte clair*. The fact that a lower court had requested a ruling did 'not preclude the supreme court of a Member State from concluding, from its examination of the case and in keeping with the criteria laid down in the judgment in *CILFIT*, that the case before it involves an *acte clair*'.

In *Ferreira da Silva e Brito & Others v Portugal* (Case C–160/14) [2016] 1 CMLR 26, decided on the same day as *X & Van Dijk*, the ECJ reiterated that, in general, 'the fact that other national courts or tribunals have given contradictory decisions is not a conclusive factor capable of triggering the obligation' set out in Article 267/(3). The Court added that a national court of last resort 'may take the view that, although the lower courts have interpreted a provision of EU law in a particular way, the interpretation that it proposes to give of that provision, which is different from the interpretation espoused by the lower courts, is so obvious that there is no reasonable doubt'. However, in the case in hand, the ECJ held that the Portuguese Supreme Court should have referred the question, involving the interpretation of the phrase 'transfer of an undertaking' in Directive 2001/23, to the ECJ under Article 267(3). This was because of the 'conflicting lines of case law at national level' combined with 'the fact that that concept frequently gives rise to difficulties of interpretation in the various Member States'. (This aspect of the case is discussed in more detail in Chapter 9 on State Liability.)

6.5.5 *Acte clair* and the courts in the UK

In *Bulmer v Bollinger* (1974), Lord Denning MR in the Court of Appeal enthusiastically endorsed *acte clair*: 'the English court may consider the point is reasonably clear and free from doubt. In that event there is no need to interpret the Treaty but only to apply it, and that is the task of the English court.' Similarly, Lord Diplock in *Garland v BREL* [1979] 1 WLR 754 in the House of Lords said that where there was a 'considerable and consistent line of case law' such that the answer was 'obvious and inevitable' then a reference would not be required. In *Commissioners of Customs & Excise Commissioners v Samex* [1983] 1 All ER 1042, however, Lord Bingham MR in the Court of Appeal said that national courts should be mindful of the differences between national and EU legislation, of the pitfalls if they got it wrong and of the overriding need for uniform interpretation throughout the EU. Lord Bingham MR stated:

JUDGMENT

'We understand the correct approach in principle of a national court (other than a final court of appeal) to be quite clear; if the facts have been found and the [Union] law issue is critical to the court's final decision, the appropriate course is ordinarily to refer the issue to the ECJ unless the national court can with complete confidence resolve the issue itself.... In considering [this], the national court must be mindful of the difference between national and [EU] legislation, of the pitfalls which face a national court when venturing into an unfamiliar field, of the need for uniform interpretation throughout the [Union] and of the great advantages enjoyed by the ECJ in construing [EU legislation].'

The *acte clair* doctrine is extremely important in cutting out unnecessary, time-consuming requests. However, it can be abused, as happened in *R v Chief Constable of Sussex, ex parte International Trader's Ferry Ltd* [1998] 3 WLR 1260, where the House of Lords declined to seek rulings on the interpretation of the word 'measures' in Article 35 and the phrase 'public policy' in Article 36 (see Chapter 14 for discussion of these issues). Academic reaction to the ITF case was hostile:

> *ITF* is far from an exemplary illustration of the courts discharging their duty to apply [Union] law. Although it is probable that the end result is the correct one, it is impossible to be certain. At least three moot points lie buried in the case. Therefore, despite the palpable reluctance of the House of Lords to make use of the preliminary [rulings] procedure in order to seek clarification from the Court of Justice, there is a persuasive argument that a reference should have been made.
> E Baker, 'Policing, Protest and Free Trade' (2000) *Crim LR 95*

Erika Szyszczak, in 'Fundamental Values in the House of Lords' (2000) 25 *ELR* 443, made the same point, observing that it was 'surprising that the House of Lords did not make an [Article 267] reference'.

A more recent example of the UK Supreme Court displaying 'palpable reluctance' when it comes to invoking the preliminary rulings procedure – despite its obligation to do so in the third paragraph of Article 267 – is the case of *Abbey National plc v OFT* [2009] UKSC 6; [2009] 3 WLR 1215. Although all five judges decided that the case should not be referred to the ECJ, only one – Lord Mance – actually paid any attention to the *CILFIT* conditions. He decided that the possibility of the disputed provision having a different meaning in other versions of the legislation was 'very limited' and that the likelihood of the ECJ or the other Member States' courts coming up with a different interpretation to that of the Supreme Court was 'remote'. In contrast, Lord Walker simply stated that 'we should treat the matter as *acte clair*'. Meanwhile, Lord Phillips said that the matter was not *acte clair*, but should not be referred anyway because 'it would not be appropriate'. Academic reaction was again critical. Paul Davies pointed out that the High Court judge and the three judges in the Court of Appeal at earlier stages in the litigation had all reached a different conclusion to that reached by the Supreme Court. He described the Supreme Court's ruling on the *acte clair* point as 'dubious' on the basis that 'four experienced judges [in the High Court and the Court of Appeal] disagreed with the Supreme Court's interpretation' (Davies, P, 'Bank charges in the Supreme Court' (2010) 69 *CLJ* 21).

There are several other cases examined in this book in which the UK Supreme Court decided a case which involved a disputed point of EU law – but without seeking a preliminary ruling. When you read about them later you should consider whether or not the Supreme Court was acting in accordance with Article 267(3): *Russell & Others v Transocean International Resources Ltd* [2011] UKSC 57 (see Chapter 17); *Jivraj v Hashwani* [2011] UKSC 40; [2011] 1 WLR 1872, *X v Mid-Sussex Citizens Advice Bureau* [2012] UKSC 59, [2013] 1 All ER 1038 and *North & Others v Dumfries & Galloway Council* [2013] UKSC 45 (all discussed in Chapter 18). In a more recent case, *Magmatic Ltd v PMS International* [2016] UKSC 12; [2016] 4 All ER 1027, better known as the 'Trunki' case, the UK Supreme Court decided that the point of EU law involved was *acte clair*. This attracted criticism from Sara Ashby, who said that it was both 'disappointing' and 'surprising' that the Supreme Court did not seek a preliminary ruling (Ashby, S, 'The UK Supreme Court and the Trunki case: Missed Opportunities, Mysteries and Misunderstood' (2016) 38 *EIPR* 527).

6.5.6 Academic reaction to *acte clair*

Academic reaction to the doctrine of *acte clair* itself has been mixed. The consensus seems to be that the ECJ in *CILFIT* (1982) was right to endorse *acte clair*. However, opinion is divided about the criteria to be satisfied by national courts before invoking the doctrine.

> The effect of the *CILFIT* decision ... would be to enable national judges to justify any reluctance they might feel to ask for a preliminary ruling.... Of the factors to be borne in mind by national courts before they concluded that the meaning of a provision of [Union] law was clear, only the requirement that the different language versions be compared ... had any teeth.... In short, the overall effect of *CILFIT* would be to encourage national courts to decide points of [Union] law for themselves.
>
> A Arnull, 'The Use & Abuse of Article 177 EEC' (1989) 52 *MLR* 622

On the other hand, Professor Rasmussen is perhaps the most highly critical commentator of *CILFIT* (1982). While he endorses the ECJ's decision to allow national courts of last resort to decide questions of EU law for themselves, he believes that the *CILFIT* (1982) criteria are so stringent that, taken as a whole, the judgment achieves the opposite of what the Court said it intended to do. Writing in 1984, he said:

> The author believes that ... *CILFIT* means something very different from what it *prima facie* establishes.... The real strategy is different from the apparent strategy. The real strategy of *CILFIT* is not to incorporate an *acte clair* concept into [Union] law. It is to call the national judiciaries to circumspection when they are faced with problems of interpretation and application of [Union] law.
>
> H Rasmussen, 'The European Court's *Acte Clair* Strategy in *CILFIT*' (1984) 9 *ELR* 242

He repeated his criticism in 2000, calling for the ECJ to rewrite the *CILFIT* (1982) judgment to make *acte clair* more easily available:

> The Court of Justice's present predicaments are self-inflicted ... I refer to the submission straightjacket designed by the Court in *CILFIT*. This judgment has functioned as a magnet, drawing numerous, and often less-than-necessary, cases up to the Court. The ECJ ought ... to rewrite *CILFIT*'s submission criteria, thereby watering down some of the stringency of the conditions to which it subjects national courts' duty to make use of [Article 267].
>
> H Rasmussen, 'Remedying the Crumbling EC Judicial System' (2000) 37 *CMLR* 1071

KEY FACTS

Discretionary and mandatory referral	
Most national courts and tribunals have a discretion whether to invoke the procedure.	Art 267, para 2
National courts and tribunals against whose decisions there is no judicial remedy under national law 'shall' invoke the procedure. This means it is mandatory for them to refer cases to the ECJ (subject to certain exceptions).	Art 267, para 3
There is no obligation to refer hypothetical or irrelevant questions.	*CILFIT* (1982)
There is no obligation to refer questions which have already been answered by the ECJ in a previous ruling.	*Da Costa* (1963)
There is no obligation to refer questions where the answer is 'obvious'. This is 'acte clair'. However, national courts must be convinced that other Member States' courts and the ECJ would find the answer 'equally obvious'.	*CILFIT* (1982); *Intermodal Transports* (2005)

6.6 Reform of the preliminary reference procedure

The ECJ is faced with a very large backlog of cases, such that the average waiting time (from a national court or tribunal requesting a preliminary ruling until the ruling itself) is approximately 15 months. Although the average waiting time has reduced from an all-time high of 25 months in 2003 (largely thanks to the appointment of new judges following the 2004 and 2007 accessions), the fact that the typical case involves a wait of more than a year means that national judges may be inhibited from asking questions, instead attempting to answer the questions themselves, which threatens both individual rights (if the judges get the answer wrong) and the 'co-operation' between the various courts.

One thing about which there is academic agreement is that the preliminary reference procedure is in need of reform. According to Professor Rasmussen ('Remedying the Crumbling EC Judicial System' (2000) 37 *CMLR* 1071): 'It is a generally shared view today that the case for a comprehensive and profound judicial reform has become compelling.' Johnston ('Judicial Reform and the Treaty of Nice' (2001) 38 *CMLR* 499) agrees: 'Clearly, there is a serious workload problem for the Court, due to a number of factors. It is particularly serious in the context of references for a preliminary ruling.'

The delay has been caused by, among other things:

- The expansion of the EU (from six in 1958 to nine in 1973, to ten in 1981 and 12 in 1986, to 15 in 1995 and 25 in 2004, to 27 in 2007 and 28 Member States in 2013), allowing more courts and tribunals to refer questions.

- The associated growth in the number of official EU languages (from four in 1958 to six in 1973, to seven in 1981, nine in 1986, 11 in 1995 and now 24). This imposes massive burdens on the ECJ in terms of the translation of judgments.

- The width of the ECJ's own definition of 'court or tribunal' in cases such as *Dorsch Consult*.

- The ever-increasing scope and volume of EU secondary legislation. For example, during 2003 two new discrimination Directives (Directive 2000/43, the 'Race Directive', and Directive 2000/78, the 'Framework Directive') entered into force. Both Directives – especially the Framework Directive – have generated a number of preliminary rulings over the years and are likely to generate many more in the years to come. These Directives will be examined in detail in Chapter 18.

- The ECJ's development of concepts such as fundamental rights and state liability, and the reliance placed on the Charter of Fundamental Rights (2000), all of which have triggered waves of new requests for preliminary rulings.

Against this, the ECJ's own tentative steps to reduce its workload through *acte clair* in *CILFIT* in 1982 has had negligible impact. All of this has led to a net increase in the number of preliminary references which the Court has to deal with, as the table shows:

Year	Number of preliminary references
1961	1
1971	37
1981	108
1991	186
2001	237
2011	423
2016	470 (an all-time high)

6.6.1 Conferral of jurisdiction on the General Court

In the future, some preliminary rulings will be transferred to the General Court, albeit in 'specific areas' and with the possibility of reference to/review by the ECJ. The procedure is set out in Article 256(3):

ARTICLE

'Art 256(3) The General Court shall have jurisdiction to hear and determine questions referred for a preliminary ruling under Article 267, in specific areas laid down by the Statute.

Where the General Court considers that the case requires a decision of principle likely to affect the unity or consistency of Union law, it may refer the case to the Court of Justice for a ruling.

Decisions given by the General Court on questions referred for a preliminary ruling may exceptionally be subject to review by the Court of Justice, under the conditions and within the limits laid down by the Statute, where there is a serious risk of the unity or consistency of Union law being affected.'

Although the General Court has been in operation since 1989, it has never actually handled preliminary rulings. When the General Court was created, it had no jurisdiction in this area. That changed when Article 256(3) was inserted into what was then the EC Treaty in 2003. However, the procedure has not yet been brought into operation, the main stumbling block being the lack of any decision on what the 'specific areas' should be. Numerous suggestions have been made (see in particular P Dyrberg, 'What Should the Court of Justice be Doing?' (2001) 26 *EL Rev* 291) but, as yet, none of the suggestions has been adopted.

Assuming that the General Court is allowed to start hearing preliminary rulings at some point, there are likely to be teething problems until the new procedure is fully developed. For example:

- The General Court 'may' refer cases on to the ECJ when a 'decision of principle' is involved – but what does that mean?

- Although the ECJ is only to review General Court rulings 'exceptionally', this nevertheless undermines the authority of all those rulings. Can any national court apply any General Court ruling whilst a possible review is still pending? Should the ECJ be given a time limit by which it must decide whether it is to invoke its review power?

Academic reaction to the conferral of preliminary ruling jurisdiction on the General Court has been mixed, although mostly positive. Tridimas described the procedure as setting an 'acceptable balance between competing demands' – the need for consistent interpretation of EU legislation on one hand, and the need for a reduction in the waiting time on the other. He described the idea of the ECJ and General Court sharing jurisdiction over preliminary rulings as 'preferable over alternative reforms' (T Tridimas, 'Knocking on Heaven's Door: Fragmentation, Efficiency and Defiance in the Preliminary Reference Procedure' (2003) 450 *CML Rev* 9). Another commentator described the new procedure as 'very important', adding 'the sooner this possibility is exercised the better' (B Vesterdorf, 'The Community Court System Ten Years from Now and Beyond: Challenges and Possibilities' (2003) 28 *EL Rev* 303). However, Heffernan was less enthusiastic, suggesting that 'there is every reason to believe that [the General Court's] contribution will be limited' (L Heffernan, 'The Community Courts Post-Nice: A European *Certiorari* Revisited' (2003) 52 *ICLQ* 907).

6.6.2 The urgent preliminary ruling procedure

In March 2008, a new urgent preliminary rulings procedure was adopted, to be used in exceptional cases. The Court of Justice explained the thinking behind the new procedure as follows:

> This procedure is applicable as from 1st March 2008 and should enable the Court to deal far more quickly with the most sensitive issues relating to the area of freedom, security and justice, such as those which may arise, for example, in certain situations where a person is deprived of his liberty and the answer to the question raised is decisive as to the assessment of the legal situation of the person detained or deprived of his liberty; or, in proceedings concerning parental authority or custody of children, where the jurisdiction under [Union] law of the court hearing the case depends on the answer to the question referred for a preliminary ruling.

The new procedure cuts the waiting time by:

- restricting the number of parties entitled to submit written observations;
- referring all cases involving the area of freedom, security and justice to a special chamber of five judges who will decide whether to apply the new procedure and, if they decide to do so, to give their ruling shortly afterwards;
- using only electronic communication.

The new procedure was used for the first time in *Rinau* (case C–195/08 PPU) [2008] ECR I–5271; [2009] 2 WLR 972. On 30 April 2008, a preliminary ruling was requested by the Supreme Court of Lithuania in a case involving child custody. Luisa Rinau's parents were divorced and she lived with her mother in Lithuania, but her father, who lived in Germany, was seeking custody. The ECJ applied the new procedure and the ruling was delivered on 11 July, a little over ten weeks later. The Court explained that the urgency was justified by the need to protect Luisa from harm, the need to avoid damaging her relationship with her father and the need to ensure a 'fair balance' between Luisa's interests and those of her parents.

An even faster turnaround was achieved in *Santesteban Goicoechea* (case C–296/08 PPU) [2008] ECR I–6307. Here, the Court of Appeal in Montpellier, France, requested a preliminary ruling in a case involving the possible extradition of a Spanish national from France to face criminal charges in Spain. The ruling was requested on 3 July 2008 and the ECJ ruling was given on 12 August, less than six weeks later. Here, the urgency was justified because the individual concerned was being held in detention in France following the completion of a prison sentence there pending his possible extradition to Spain.

Academic reaction to the new procedure has been positive, but Koutrakos ('Speeding up the Preliminary Reference Procedure: Fast but not too Fast' (2008) 33 *EL Rev* 617) has pointed out that 'there is a balance which must be struck' between delivering judgments as quickly as possible (on the one hand) and providing sufficient time for the ECJ's judges 'to reflect on the questions put before them, assess the arguments … and consider the wider ramifications of their conclusions' (on the other). He notes that taking time to deliver a judgment is not a 'luxury' but 'an essential prerequisite for the proper administration of justice'.

6.6.3 Other reform proposals

Numerous proposals for reform of the preliminary rulings procedure have been advanced over the years. These proposals fall into two distinct groups:

1. those proposals which seek to reduce the volume of requests coming into the ECJ; and
2. those that seek to boost or streamline the European Union's judicial capacity for dealing with these cases.

(The conferral of jurisdiction on the General Court, noted above, falls into the latter group.) Group 1 proposals include:

- Restricting the range of national courts or tribunals with the discretion to seek rulings. This could entail removing the right of 'first instance' national courts and tribunals (such as magistrates' and county courts plus most tribunals in England) from seeking rulings. This would probably have little practical impact as 'first instance' courts tend not to seek many references anyway.
- Removing the right of 'first tier' appeal courts and tribunals (such as the High Court and the Employment Appeal Tribunal (EAT)) from seeking rulings. This would

probably have a significant impact in terms of cutting down requests. Statistics indicate that a large proportion of the preliminary rulings requested by British courts come from the High Court and the EAT. If these bodies lost the right to seek rulings, they would have to interpret EU legislation themselves (with the risk of divergent rulings being made).

- Tightening up the *Dorsch Consult* (1997) criteria, thereby cutting out requests from bodies such as 'appeal boards' and 'adjudicators'.

- Abolishing mandatory referral for national courts of last resort. Arguably, this has already been achieved through the doctrine of *acte clair*.

- Rewording Article 267 to require national judges to consider the importance, difficulty and/or novelty of the ruling requested.

Group 2 proposals include:

- Allowing the ECJ to filter questions. Most national courts of last resort can filter out cases deemed to be insufficiently important or novel. There are grounds for saying that the ECJ should be given the same power.

- Setting up regionalised courts with EU legal specialism, with the ECJ restyled as a 'European High Court of Justice' overseeing the new regionalised courts. This is not dissimilar to the organisation of federal courts in the United States, with the Supreme Court in Washington DC at the apex, overseeing the decisions of the various federal 'circuit' courts, which in turn oversee the federal courts in the states within each 'circuit'. The latter suggestion was first proposed by the academics Jacque and Weiler:

> At the apex of the system will remain the [ECJ], renamed perhaps as the European High Court of Justice. We propose the creation of four new Community Regional Courts which will have jurisdiction to receive preliminary references from, and issue preliminary rulings to, national courts within each region. Upon the decision or preliminary ruling of the Regional Court being issued, a party to the proceedings and the Commission, Council, Parliament or Member States as interveners, may appeal to the European High Court of Justice.
>
> J P Jacque and J Weiler, 'On the Road to European Union: A New Judicial
> Architecture' (1990) 27 *CMLR* 185

The academics Veerle Heyvaert, Justine Thornton and Richard Drabble proposed a different version of decentralisation. Extrapolating from the creation of the General Court in 1989 and the Civil Service Tribunal in 2005, they argue that:

> It would be possible to expand the range further by establishing specialised bodies for questions that are typically considered to require a high level of technical specialisation and expertise to resolve, such as trademarks and competition disputes. Environmental decision-making might qualify as a domain for which a specialised court is needed. The addition of new EU courts or tribunals could further cut down on delays or, accounting for the continuing rise in proceedings lodged over time, at least keep them on an even keel.
>
> V Heyvaert, J Thornton and R Drabble, 'With Reference to the Environment:
> The Preliminary Reference Procedure, Environmental Decisions and the
> Domestic Judiciary' (2014) 130 *LQR* 413

All of these proposals would reduce the workload of the ECJ and hence reduce the time delay, but at what cost?

- Restricting national courts' ability to seek rulings will probably lead to more appeals in the national courts as disappointed litigants try to get a case into a national court which has retained the power to request rulings.

- Filtration may undermine the 'co-operation' that exists between the ECJ and the Member States' courts and tribunals. This may deter national courts from seeking rulings in cases where, now, they would seek such a ruling, possibly leading to inconsistency of interpretation in different Member States and stifling the development of EU legal principles (key doctrines such as direct effect, indirect effect, state liability and fundamental rights were all developed during preliminary ruling cases).

- Regionalisation threatens uniformity, and setting up several new courts will incur considerable cost in terms of infrastructure, staffing, communications and IT. There may also be squabbles as to the location of any new regional courts.

KEY FACTS

Reform of the preliminary rulings procedure	
The General Court has jurisdiction to give preliminary rulings in 'specific areas', subject to referral to/review by the ECJ. But no 'specific areas' have been identified.	Art 256(3) TFEU
An urgent procedure was introduced in 2008, to deal with child custody disputes and cases where a person's liberty is at stake.	*Rinau* (2008); *Santesteban Goicoechea* (2008)
Other reform proposals have been made, including restricting the range or ability of national courts and tribunals to seek rulings, redefining the phrase 'court or tribunal', or abolishing mandatory referrals.	
Other proposals include allowing the ECJ to filter questions, or setting up specialised, regionalised courts.	

SAMPLE ESSAY QUESTION

'The biggest problem facing the Court of Justice of the European Union is the unacceptable delays resulting from its preliminary rulings caseload. This problem does not just affect the parties to the individual cases, but threatens the future development of the EU itself. There are several causes of the problem, not least of which is the Court's own "functional" test for deciding whether or not a body may request a ruling. However, there are also several possible solutions to the problem. Discuss.'

Outline the purpose and operation of the preliminary rulings procedure:

- Allows ECJ to give definitive interpretations of EU law, ensuring consistency throughout the EU (*Stauder v Ulm*)
- National courts and tribunals may, at their discretion, request rulings; national 'courts of last resort' are obliged to do so, unless the point of law has already been decided by the ECJ in a previous case (*Da Costa*), is irrelevant to the dispute or is '*acte clair*', meaning that the answer is obvious (*CILFIT*)
- Once the ECJ gives its ruling, it must then be applied in all cases
- There is an urgent procedure for cases raising sensitive issues relating to the area of freedom, security and justice, such as child custody disputes (*Inga Rinau*)

Explain the 'functional' test for deciding whether a body is a 'court or tribunal':

- The name of a body is immaterial; the key question is whether a body performs a judicial function
- Factors to determine this question include whether the body: is established by law, is independent, is permanent, has compulsory jurisdiction, has an *inter partes* procedure and applies rules of law (*Dorsch Consult*)
- Give some examples of cases where requests were denied, e.g. *Nordsee*, *Victoria Film*
- Independence is crucial (*Schmid*)

Discuss implications of the delays in the procedure:

- The dispute in the national court is prolonged
- National courts and tribunals may be discouraged from seeking rulings, and may decide to interpret EU legislation themselves. This could lead to EU law fragmenting (with different meanings in different Member States)
- The preliminary rulings procedure has allowed the ECJ to develop several key principles of EU law, such as direct effect, supremacy and state liability. The ECJ relies on new cases to continue to develop EU law

Discuss potential solutions:

- The Nice Treaty conferred jurisdiction on the General Court, but only in 'specific areas', as yet undecided, subject to referral to/review by the ECJ
- Redefine 'courts or tribunals'
- Restrict the national courts with access to the ECJ
- Abolish mandatory referral for national supreme courts
- Introduce a system of case filtering
- 'Decentralisation' – the creation of new EU courts with the ECJ restyled as a European High Court of Justice to hear appeals
- All reform options must be carefully considered. The key point is that the procedure must continue to ensure consistency of EU legislation

SUMMARY

Article 267 TFEU allows any 'court or tribunal' of a Member State to request the Court of Justice to interpret provisions of EU legislation. The national court or tribunal then has the task of applying that law, as interpreted. Having one court to interpret all EU legislation ensures uniform application (*Stauder v Ulm*).

The Court usually adopts a 'purposive' approach to interpretation, seeking to interpret ambiguous EU law in a way which most promotes the purpose behind the legislation (*Adidas*).

Only a 'court or tribunal' may request a ruling, but this means that the body must be carrying out a judicial function, taking into account various factors such as permanence, an *inter partes* procedure, compulsory jurisdiction (*Dorsch Consult*). Independence is crucial (*Schmid*).

Arbitrators, public prosecutors and administrative bodies are not a 'court or tribunal' (*Nordsee, Victoria Film*). Even a court may not be a 'court' if it is carrying out an administrative function (*Salzmann, Lutz*).

Under Article 267(2), any court or tribunal 'may' request a ruling. Under Article 267(3), 'courts of last resort' must do so where a point of EU law is involved, subject to three exceptions: previous rulings (*Da Costa*), irrelevance (*CILFIT*) and 'acte clair', i.e. the national court is convinced that the answer to the question is obvious (*CILFIT*). *Acte clair* must be used with caution. In particular, the national court must be convinced that the matter is equally obvious to the courts of the other Member States and to the Court of Justice (*Intermodal Transports*).

The ECJ is bound in principle to respond to a request for a ruling, subject to requests declared to be inadmissible: contrived disputes (*Foglia v Novello*), irrelevance, lack of background factual and/or legal information.

Under the urgent procedure, certain cases may be dealt with very quickly. Typical cases involve child custody (*Rinau*) or where a person is in custody (*Santesteban Goicoechea*).

The ECJ is faced with a very large backlog of cases; the **average** waiting time (from a national court requesting a ruling until the ruling itself) is around 16 months. If the delay is not reduced further, national judges may be inhibited from asking questions, instead attempting to answer the questions themselves, which threatens the whole point of the procedure and the 'co-operation' between the ECJ and the national courts.

- The delay has been caused by, *inter alia*, the expansion of the EU (from six to 28 Member States), allowing more courts and tribunals to refer questions; the associated growth in the number of official EU languages; the width of the ECJ's own functional definition of 'court or tribunal'; the ever-increasing scope and volume of EU secondary legislation.

- One solution is to confer jurisdiction on the General Court in 'specific areas' (Article 256(3) TFEU). As yet, no 'specific areas' have been decided. Under this procedure, there will be the possibility of cases involving 'decisions of principle' being referred on to/reviewed by the ECJ.

- Other proposals for reform include: appointing more judges; restricting the range of national courts and tribunals with the discretion to seek rulings; abolishing mandatory referral for 'courts of last resort'; filtering questions; setting up regional courts with EU legal specialism (decentralisation). All of these proposals would reduce the workload of the ECJ and hence reduce the time-delay, but there are risks, especially to consistency.

Further reading

Articles

Anagnostaras, G, 'Preliminary Problems and Jurisdiction Uncertainties: The Admissibility of Questions referred by Bodies Performing Quasi-judicial Functions' (2005) 30 *EL Rev* 878.

Arnull, A, 'Judicial Architecture or Judicial Folly? The Challenge Facing the European Union' (1999) 24 *ELR* 516.

Barnard, C, 'The PPU: Is it Worth the Candle? An Early Assessment' (2009) 34 *EL Rev* 281.

Broberg, M and Fenger, N, 'Variations in Member States' Preliminary References to the Court of Justice: Are Structural Factors (Part of) the Explanation?' (2013) 19 *ELJ* 488.

Jacque, J P and Weiler, J, 'On the Road to European Union: A New Judicial Architecture' (1990) 27 *CMLR* 185.

Johnston, A, 'Judicial Reform and the Treaty of Nice' (2001) 38 *CMLR* 499.

Komarek, J, 'In the Court(s) We Trust? On the Need for Hierarchy and Differentiation in the Preliminary Ruling Procedure' (2007) 32 *EL Rev* 467.

Lord Mance, 'The Interface between National and European Law' (2013) 38 *EL Rev* 437.

Rasmussen, H, 'Remedying the Crumbling EC Judicial System' (2000) 37 *CMLR* 1071.

Vesterdorf, B, 'The Community Court System Ten Years from Now and Beyond: Challenges and Possibilities' (2003) 28 *EL Rev* 303.

7

The relationship between EU law and national law – supremacy

AIMS AND OBJECTIVES

After reading this chapter you should be able to:

- Understand the meaning of supranationalism and the reasons for it
- Understand the meaning of supremacy and its link with supranationalism and why it was created by the ECJ
- Understand how supremacy was developed and how it is defined
- Understand the attitudes of the UK and other Member States to supremacy
- Analyse the effects and consequences of supremacy for Member States and for the EU

7.1 The origins of supremacy and the link with supranationalism

7.1.1 The basic meaning of 'supremacy'

The EU is a unique international organisation based on a co-operative partnership between its 28 Member States. The latter voluntarily pooled their resources and sovereign powers in certain areas of policy (e.g. agriculture, fisheries, competition, etc.) and have tasked the supranational institutions of the EU (e.g. the Council, the European Parliament, the Commission, the ECJ, etc.) to drive its relevant policy agendas by legislating and regulating the activities of the Union. The various fields of competence of the EU represent areas of mutual and common interests which the Member States have decided are better addressed collectively via co-operation. These fields are divided into three main categories: Article 3 TFEU exclusive competencies (e.g. customs union, monetary policy, common commercial policy); Article 4 TFEU shared competences (e.g. internal market, social policy, energy, environment); and Article 6 TFEU supporting competencies (e.g. health, culture, tourism, education). In these areas of transferred powers given to the EU institutions by the Member States, the latter have thus agreed to limit their ability to legislate unilaterally.

On that basis, 'supremacy' in simple terms means no more than that, in areas where EU law is relevant to a case before a national court (i.e. in a matter which is within the sphere of competence of the EU), EU law prevails over national law. This mirrors in some senses the way that we are told in English law that parliamentary law, in the form of Acts of Parliament, prevails over all other forms of English law. The practical consequence, then, of this supremacy is that wherever there is a conflict between the national law of a Member State and EU law itself it is EU law that must be applied.

Supremacy is one of the key doctrines, or constitutional pillars, created by the European Court of Justice that ensure the enforceability of the legal order. The other is the doctrine of direct effect, which also encompasses the principles of indirect effect and state liability. These are all discussed in Chapters 8 and 9.

It would be fair to describe all of these as fundamental principles without which EU law could not have developed. So the European Court of Justice has been active in ensuring the success of the EU and its gradual evolution.

Supremacy has probably become one of the most entrenched of all principles associated with EU law. Nevertheless, despite the inevitable political tensions between Member States and the EU institutions and some testing times between the Court of Justice and the national courts, it is possibly also fair to say that it has ultimately proved to be one of the least controversial aspects.

7.1.2 The reasons for a doctrine of supremacy

While there is no actual mention of the principle within the Treaties, it is simple to see why the European Court of Justice created and then developed the principle of supremacy (or 'primacy of EU law', as it is sometimes known):

- The fundamental objective of creating a single Internal Market demands that there should be harmonisation between Member States, which in itself then depends on a uniform application of EU law within the Member States.

- The whole structure of the Community was founded on the idea of supranationalism. Without supremacy of EU law the institutions would be deprived of supranational effect and uniformity might instead be sacrificed to national self-interest.

In this way the real justifications for the existence of a doctrine of supremacy are twofold:

- First, it prevents any possibility of a questioning of the validity of EU law within the Member States themselves to ensure the effectiveness of the European edifice.

- Second, it fulfils what is sometimes referred to as the 'doctrine of pre-emption', and it does so in two ways:

  - the fact that EU law is supreme means that the national courts in Member States are prevented from producing alternative interpretations of EU law, so that EU law is interpreted uniformly across the block;

  - the existence of such a doctrine also means that the legislative bodies of the individual Member States are prevented from enacting legislation that would conflict with EU law, so that EU law is applied in a consistent and coherent manner in the domestic systems of the Member States.

However, as has already been noted, there is nothing in the Treaties that specifically states that EU law, in whatever form, takes precedence over national law. The closest the

Treaties come is in the principle of sincere co-operation contained in Article 4(3) TEU (formerly so-called 'duty of loyalty' in Article 10 EC Treaty) which can be paraphrased in the following terms:

ARTICLE

'Art 4(3) ... Member States shall take any appropriate measure ... to ensure fulfilment of the obligations arising out of the Treaties or resulting from the acts of the institutions of the Union ... [they] shall ... refrain from any measure which could jeopardise the attainment of the Union's objectives.'

The Court of Justice, then, has been proactive and instrumental in ensuring that the objectives of the Treaties are achieved in the Member States, and in doing so supremacy has been a powerful tool in its hands.

Quite simply, the full economic integration necessary for the achievement of a Single Market would have proved unmanageable if it had been possible for Member States to ignore or even deliberately defy the supranational powers of the institutions of the EU.

Taking a long-term view, probably the most logical basis for supremacy is that without it a full integration, including the political integration required for a federalist system, would also prove impossible.

Whilst the abandoned Constitutional Treaty included an EU law primacy clause, this provision was not included in the Treaty of Lisbon as it proved too controversial for many Member States. Following the Inter-Governmental Conference 2007 on the adoption of the Lisbon Treaty, the European Council acknowledged the doctrine of primacy in Declaration 17 appended to the Treaty of Lisbon and which states that:

> in accordance with well settled case law of the Court of Justice of the European Union, the Treaties and the law adopted by the Union on the basis of the Treaties have primacy over the law of Member States, under the conditions laid down by the said case law.

Compared to protocols and annexes which have legal force, declarations attached to the Treaties are merely politically binding. Still, this political declaration validates the ECJ jurisprudence and reinforces the fundamental principle that where EU law applies, EU law will prevail over national law.

7.2 The development of a doctrine of supremacy

7.2.1 The early definitions of 'supremacy'

The earliest indication of a concept of supremacy comes from the judgment of the ECJ in the case of *Van Gend en Loos v Nederlandse Administratie der Belastingen* (Case 26/62) [1963] ECR 1; [1963] CMLR 105. (The case principally concerns the issue of direct effect and is therefore more fully discussed in Chapter 8.) The case involved an introduction of a Dutch law which was contrary to obligations imposed on Member States in an EC Treaty Article. Because the Article implicitly conferred rights on individuals and the litigant suffered financial loss as a result of the Dutch law, an Article 177 (now Article 267 TFEU) reference posed the question for the ECJ of whether or not the Treaty created rights on behalf of individuals that national courts must then protect.

In the reasoned opinion the Advocate-General declared that this was not the case and that the appropriate means of resolution in such circumstances was in an action against the Member State under Article 169 (now Article 258 TFEU). The judges in the ECJ disagreed and in their judgment identified:

'The Community constitutes a new legal order in international law for whose benefits the states have limited their sovereign rights, albeit within limited fields.'

This is not a complete definition of 'supremacy'. Nevertheless, the ECJ avoided the problems that would go with classing EU law as international law, to which different Member States, because of their different constitutions, would adopt completely different approaches. What the ECJ identified in the case was that the EU must be viewed as a different and unique legal order distinct from either national law or international law because of the transfer of powers from the Member States over to the EU institutions. Therefore the key point was the clear statement that, by accepting entry into the (then) Community, the Member States were limiting their otherwise sovereign rights to legislate contrary to the requirements of EU law in those areas affected by it.

The ECJ had to wait only two years to produce a more complete definition and more extensive explanation. This came in another reference (now under Article 267 TFEU) this time from an Italian court. Again, it involved legislation that was passed after accession to the Treaties that was inconsistent with provisions of EU law.

CASE EXAMPLE

Costa v ENEL (Case 6/64) [1964] ECR 585; [1964] CMLR 425

ENEL (more formally known as Ente Nazionale per l'Energia Elettrica) was a state electric company under which the Italian government had nationalised (put under state ownership) both the production and distribution of electricity. Costa was a lawyer who had owned shares in one of the pre-nationalised electric companies. He had argued in his local court that the law nationalising the industry was unlawful because it contravened EC monopoly laws. The Court used the Article 177 (now Article 267 TFEU) procedure to refer several questions to the ECJ. The Italian government, following a judgment of the Italian constitutional court between the parties, argued that the proceedings themselves were flawed since the Italian court should have followed the law nationalising the industry, which came later than the law ratifying the EC Treaty. The ECJ repeated the line that it had taken in *Van Gend en Loos* (1963) but expanded on it:

JUDGMENT

'By contrast with ordinary international treaties, the EC Treaty has created its own legal system which on entry into force of the Treaty became an integral part of the legal systems of the member states and which their courts are bound to apply. By creating a Community of limited duration having … powers stemming from a limitation of the sovereignty, or a transfer of powers from the states to the community, the member states have limited their sovereign rights, albeit within limited fields, and have thus created a body of law which binds both their nationals and themselves.'

EU AND NATIONAL LAW – SUPREMACY

The Court also continued by identifying the clear consequence of the transfer of powers:

JUDGMENT

'The transfer, by member states from their national orders in favour of the Community order of its rights and obligations arising from the Treaty, carries with it a clear limitation of their sovereign right upon which a subsequent unilateral law, incompatible with the aims of the community cannot prevail.'

In reaching its decision the Court identified that supremacy was confirmed by the wording of Article 288 which refers to the concept of direct applicability (see section 3.2) and also the binding nature of Community legislation. In its conclusion it explains fully its reasoning:

JUDGMENT

'It follows from all these observations that the law stemming from the Treaty, an independent source of law, could not, because of its special and original nature, be overridden by domestic legal provisions, however framed, without being deprived of its character as Community law and without the legal basis of the Community itself being called into question.'

Three clear propositions emerge from the statements in these two cases:

- the Member States, by joining the EU, had willingly transferred some of their national competence and thus given up certain of their sovereign powers to make law on certain issues;
- both the Member States themselves as well as their citizens are bound by EU law;
- the Member States, as a result, cannot unilaterally introduce new national laws that would then contradict EU law.

Supremacy or primacy?

Whilst the majority of EU law textbooks will use the term 'supremacy', it is not the one chosen by the ECJ, the drafters of the former Constitutional Treaty or the Treaty of Lisbon. It is worth noting that the EU has 24 official languages across the 28 Member States. It appears that any use of the word 'supremacy' has tended to be found in the English translation of two ECJ case laws (*Wilhelm* (Case 14/68) [1969] ECR 1 and *Fratelli Variola* (Case 34/73) [1973] ECR 981) – whereas the 'primacy' terminology seemed to be favoured in the language versions of these judgments.

The term 'supremacy' evokes a state of superiority or hierarchical relationship whereby EU law would have a 'higher' ranking or status over national law. 'Primacy', by contrast, denotes a more pragmatic and jurisdictional relationship – it is about determining which law (EU or national) shall have precedence in a given situation by establishing which jurisdiction/competence (either EU or national) governs that situation.

Avbelj (2011) suggests that the difference between supremacy and primacy matters as, more than a question of semantics, it reveals how the doctrine shapes the EU legal order. The distinction between conceptualisations is pertinent to the nature of the EU and to the relationship between EU law and its application in the domestic legal systems of the Member States.

7.2.2 The wider application of the doctrine of supremacy

The ECJ has had the opportunity to restate the principle on a number of occasions. On one occasion it was able to expand by explaining that EU law cannot be invalidated by any measure of national law, from whatever source.

CASE EXAMPLE

International Handelsgesellschaft GmbH v EVGF (Case 11/70) [1970] ECR 1125; [1972] CMLR 255

Here, an applicant in a German court was challenging the legitimacy of a Regulation. The Regulation required the introduction of export licences in respect of certain agricultural products falling under the Common Agricultural Policy (CAP). One further requirement was for payment of deposits which would be forfeited in the event that there was no export of the products during the period of the licence, as a result of which the individual in the case had lost a deposit. The German court accepted his argument that the measure was unconstitutional under the German Constitution because it infringed basic guaranteed rights to run a business freely and to be free of compulsory payment without proof of fault. Nevertheless, the German court felt that it was necessary to make an Article 177 (now Article 267 TFEU) reference asking the question of whether or not national constitutional law took precedence over EC law. The ECJ responded:

JUDGMENT

'Recourse to the legal rules or concepts of national law in order to judge the validity of measures adopted by the Institutions ... would have an adverse effect on the uniformity and efficacy of EC law. The validity of such measures can only be judged in the light of Community law.... The validity of a Community measure or its effect within a member state cannot be affected by allegations that it runs counter to either fundamental rights, as formulated by the constitution of the state or the principles of a national constitutional structure.'

The message from the ECJ was very clear: in determining any 'pecking order' of laws, EU law takes precedence over even the constitutions of the Member States.

In further restating the principle of supremacy the ECJ has subsequently made it abundantly clear that, in the event of any conflict or inconsistency between national law and EU law, the domestic court has an absolute requirement to give effect to EU law over any conflicting law, whatever the date of passing of that law.

CASE EXAMPLE

Simmenthal SpA v Amministrazione delle Finanze dello Stato (Case 70/77) [1978] ECR 1453; [1978] 3 CMLR 670

Simmenthal imported beef into Italy from France. Under an Italian law introduced in 1970, he was bound to pay for an inspection of the goods at the frontier. However, this national law was inconsistent not only with the requirements of Article 30 (now Article 34 TFEU) but also with EC Regulations introduced in 1964 and in 1968. The Italian court made a reference to the ECJ on the question of whether it must follow the EC law or should wait for the provision of Italian law to be annulled by the Italian constitutional court according to the usual state procedure.

The ECJ in its response made the following observations:

JUDGMENT

'in accordance with the principles of precedence of Community law, the relationship between the provisions of the Treaty and directly applicable measures of the institutions on the one hand and the national law of the member states on the other is such that those provisions and measures not only by their entry into force render automatically inapplicable any conflicting provision of current national law but, insofar as they are an integral part, and take precedence in, the legal order applicable in the territory of each of the member states, also preclude the valid adoption of new national legislative measures to the extent that they would be incompatible with Community provisions'.

In its conclusions the ECJ again clearly stated the consequences for Member State courts:

JUDGMENT

'it follows that every national court must, in a case within its jurisdiction, apply Community law in its entirety and protect rights which the latter confers on individuals and must accordingly set aside any provision of national law which may conflict with it, whether prior or subsequent to the Community rule'.

Over time, EU law has been held to have primacy over conflicting national law in many cases. What the cases clearly identify is that supremacy applies whatever the particular type of EU law. We have already seen the applicability of the doctrine in relation to Treaty Articles and also Regulations. EU law has also been held to be supreme in the case of:

- **Directives** – *Becker v Finanzamt Munster-Innenstadt* (Case 8/81) [1982] ECR 53, [1982] 1 CMLR 499 (where the applicant was then permitted to enforce a VAT Directive against the German tax authorities);
- **Decisions** – *Salumijico di Cornuda* (Case 130/78) [1979] ECR 867;
- **general principles of law** – *Wachauf v Germany* (Case 5/88) [1989] ECR 2609;
- **international agreements made between EU and non-EU states** – *Nederlandse Spoor-wegen* (Case 38/75) [1975] ECR 1439.

The doctrine of supremacy also will apply not merely where there is national law that directly conflicts with a provision of EU law. The doctrine will apply also in circumstances where a contradictory provision in national law, while not directly conflicting, nevertheless by its existence encroaches on the field of EU legislative powers.

CASE EXAMPLE

Commission v France (Re French Merchant Seamen) (Case 167/73) [1974] ECR 359; [1974] CMLR 216

The case here concerned a French statutory provision requiring that a certain percentage of crew on French registered merchant ships had to be French nationals. The provision had inevitably come into conflict with the rules on free movement of workers under Article 45. The Commission brought an action under Article 169 (now Article 258 TFEU), seeking to declare the French law contrary to the objectives of the Treaty and thus unlawful. The French argued in their defence that they were not acting in breach of their EC obligations since they no longer actually operated the law and that there was nothing in the Treaty requiring that Member States must specifically repeal outdated incompatible law. Nevertheless, the ECJ held that the continued existence of conflicting national law in itself created an ambiguity that was unsustainable and unacceptable in the pursuit of harmony.

7.2.3 The extreme consequences of a doctrine of supremacy

The ECJ has had many opportunities to state and restate the rule. This occurred not just in the early years of the Treaties but has surfaced in recent times too.

Possibly the most far-reaching application of the rule has come in a case involving the UK. The case is dramatic because in the most positive terms it conflicts with the notion of parliamentary supremacy within the English Constitution and directs English judges to exercise a power that would have formerly been considered to be beyond them: to suspend operation of and in effect declare invalid provisions of an Act of Parliament.

CASE EXAMPLE

R v Secretary of State for Transport, ex parte Factortame Ltd (Case C–213/89) [1990] ECR 1–2433; [1990] 3 CMLR 375

The case involved companies registered in the UK but where the majority ownership was in the hands of Spanish nationals. The companies had in fact been registered in the UK, with the specific object of purchasing trawlers registered in the UK. Provisions of the Merchant Shipping Act 1988 and the Merchant Shipping (Registration of Fishing Vessels) Regulations 1988 had inserted a nationality requirement so that for registration of the vessel more than a certain percentage of ownership had to be in the hands of UK nationals. The applicants argued before the English court that these requirements violated the 'non-discrimination on nationality' rule in Article 12 (now Article 18 TFEU) and as a result of their operation that they were denied rights to fish that would otherwise have been guaranteed by EC law (now EU). The House of Lords was confronted with the difficult question of an Act of Parliament enacted after accession to the Treaties in 1972 which specifically contradicted EC (now EU) law. As the applicants had also sought an injunction if the Court was to grant this, it would have the effect of suspending operation of an Act of Parliament until the inconsistency issue could be settled on reference to the ECJ. The Divisional Court decided that a reference should be made under Article 177 (now Article 267 TFEU) and had granted the injunction. As a result, it had ordered that the Secretary of State should be prevented from applying the parts of the Act in question until a preliminary ruling had been given under the reference. The Secretary of State appealed and the Court of Appeal granted the appeal and set aside the order of the Divisional Court. Appeal was then made to the House of Lords. Their Lordships were faced with a difficult situation. As they identified in the judgment, there was no rule in English constitutional law that would allow the type of interim relief granted by the Divisional Court; neither could it see that there existed such an overriding principle in EC (now EU) law allowing a national court to suspend operation of a national law. As a result, it made a reference to the ECJ, posing the question whether, in order to protect EC (now EU) rights, a national court must grant the interim suspension of an Act of Parliament.

The ECJ restated the relationship between national law and Community (now EU) law:

JUDGMENT

'In accordance with the case law of the court, it is for the national courts in application of the principle of co-operation laid down in Article 10 [now repealed] ... to ensure the legal protection which persons derive from the direct effect of provisions of EC law ... any provision of a national legal system and any legislative, administrative, or judicial practice which might impair the effectiveness of Community law by withholding from the national court having jurisdiction to apply such law the power to do everything necessary at the moment of its application to set aside national legislative provisions which might prevent, even temporarily, Community rules from having full force and effect are incompatible with those requirements which are the very essence of EC law.'

In its conclusions the ECJ was clear on the course of action to be taken by the national court and the effect of supremacy on the situation:

JUDGMENT

'the full effectiveness of Community law would be just as much impaired if a rule of national law could prevent a court seized of a dispute governed by Community law from granting interim relief in order to ensure the full effectiveness of the judgment to be given on the existence of the rights claimed under Community law. It therefore follows that a court which in those circumstances would grant interim relief, if it were not for a rule of national law, is obliged to set aside that law.'

Factortame (1990) then represents a major statement of supremacy by the ECJ over national courts and of EU law over national law and demonstrates the supranational power of the institutions of the EU.

ACTIVITY

Self-assessment questions

1. Why is a doctrine of supremacy of EU law necessary?
2. What precisely is the 'doctrine of pre-emption' and how does it affect the Member States?
3. What was the relationship between the former Article 10 of the EC Treaty and the concept of supremacy of EU law?
4. In *Van Gend en Loos* (1963) the ECJ identified that 'the Community constitutes a new legal order in international law'. What exactly does this mean?
5. What is the significance of the definition of supremacy given by the ECJ in *Costa v ENEL* (1964)?
6. What effect does the doctrine of supremacy of EU law have upon the sovereignty of the Member States?
7. To what extent is supremacy the sole creation of the ECJ and to what extent does it actually derive from the obligations in the Treaty?
8. How broadly have the effects of supremacy been interpreted by the ECJ?
9. Why is *Factortame* (1990) such an important case?

7.3 Supremacy and the UK

In *Factortame* (1990) the English judges recognised the supremacy of EU law and applied the clear direction given in the reference by granting the interim relief that had been applied for.

The Treaty creates 'a new legal order' under which Member States have 'limited their sovereign rights, albeit within limited fields'. *Van Gend en Loos v The Netherlands*

The Treaty carries with it a clear limitation of (Member States') sovereign right upon which a subsequent unilateral law, incompatible with the aims of the Community cannot prevail. *Costa v ENEL*

The validity of a Community measure or its effect within a Member State cannot be affected by allegations that it runs counter to either fundamental rights, as formulated by the constitution of the state or the principles of a national constitutional structure. *International Handellsgesellshaft case*

Every national court must, in a case within its jurisdiction, apply Community law in its entirety … and must accordingly set aside any provision of national law which may conflict with it, whether prior or subsequent to the Community rule. *Simmenthal*

It is for national courts … to set aside national legislative provisions which might prevent even temporarily, Community rules from having full force and effect. *Factortame*

Figure 7.1 The development of a definition of supremacy of EU law

Nevertheless, English judges have not always reacted in this manner and there has inevitably been much discussion on the key provisions of the European Communities Act 1972 and the extent to which the Treaties are entrenched in English law.

7.3.1 UK membership of the European Union

Having signed the Treaty of Accession, the UK ratified its membership of the then EC (now EU) and incorporated EC (now EU) law into English law with the passing of the European Communities Act 1972.

Initially, the key provision accomplishing this incorporation was s2(1):

SECTION

'All such rights, powers, liabilities, obligations and restrictions from time to time created or arising by or under the Treaties, as in accordance with the Treaties, are without further enactment to be given legal effect or used in the UK and shall be recognised and available in law, and be enforced, allowed and followed accordingly, and the expression "enforceable Community right" and similar expressions shall be read as referring to one to which the subsection applies.'

This would appear to be a simple enough statement of intent: all existing EC law would automatically be incorporated into English law, and all future legislative provisions of the Community would become law and be recognised as enforceable.

In any case, the section seems to have been further reinforced by s2(4), which states:

SECTION

'any enactment passed or to be passed, other than one contained in this part of the Act, shall be construed and have effect subject to the foregoing provision of this section'.

Following the enactment of the Act the existence of previous English law that might conflict with EU objectives would appear to present no real problem. On achieving membership the Act ensured that EU law would in any case prevail over any inconsistent national law. Besides this, by virtue of the doctrine of implied repeal, the very fact that the Act itself came after this law meant that, even without repealing statutes, the EU law would prevail.

The major problem, then, concerns English law made after the passing of the Act which is inconsistent with provisions of EU law. The problem seems to hinge on the extent to which the above sections are in fact entrenched or whether they are merely aids to construction.

Note that the jurisdiction of the ECJ post-Brexit is a contentious matter in the negotiations. The Prime Minister initially insisted that the UK 'would take back controls of its laws' after its withdrawal from the EU and would therefore not be subject to the ECJ judgments. However, the UK government has since conceded that the ECJ may have a degree of judicial supervision over both the withdrawal and transition agreements. Like so many elements of this 'divorce', the extent of the ECJ's future authority remains to be negotiated and agreed between the UK and the EU.

7.3.2 The attitude of English judges

Certainly, membership has meant that EU law has affected the interpretation of statutes by UK judges who are now more likely to use a purposive approach. EU law has possibly introduced another rule of statutory interpretation in its own right. Different judges at different times have in any case taken a different line.

In *Garland v British Rail Engineering Ltd (BREL)* [1982] 2 All ER 402, HL the House of Lords considered an exemption in respect of death and retirement in the Equal Pay Act 1970 and its compatibility with EC (now EU) law. The House held that the provision must be construed in order to conform with EC (now EU) law. The Law Lords took s2 of the European Communities Act 1972 as creating a rule of construction and Lord Diplock identified that the English courts were used to interpreting national law in this way.

A similar approach was taken in both *Pickstone v Freemans plc* [1988] 2 All ER 803 and *Litster v Forth Dry Dock and Engineering Co* [1989] 1 All ER 1134. In both cases the Court felt that UK law had to be construed in a manner that was consistent with EC (now EU) law. In the latter case the House of Lords observed that when applying EC (now EU) law a purposive approach to interpretation must be taken.

However, courts have not always accepted this approach. In *Duke v GEC Reliance* [1988] 2 WLR 359 the House of Lords decided that it was not bound to interpret the Sex Discrimination Act 1975 so that it gave full effect to Directive 76/207 (the Equal Treatment Directive).

Lord Templeman concluded that the effect of s2(4) of the 1972 Act is not to allow the court to 'distort a statute to enforce a directive which has no direct effect between individuals'.

The House also refused to allow a reference on the issue despite the ruling in *Marshall*.

Obviously, the doctrine of supremacy of EC (now EU) law creates fewer problems in relation to national law that pre-dates entry into the EC (now EU). Parliament in the 1972 Act accepted that all existing EC (now EU) law should be incorporated into English law. In this way it is national law and also EC (now EU) law coming after the Act that is the cause of difficulties for the judges. Judges have tried hard to ensure that EU law is observed and that national law is interpreted so that it can be seen as harmonious with EU law. Nevertheless, it is not just a question of interpretation: English judges are called on to **enforce** rights granted under EU law, but they also feel the need to reconcile this with parliamentary supremacy by which they still feel bound.

Lord Denning, at an early point in the UK's membership, identified the impact of membership on English law in quite poetic but nevertheless quite abrupt terms, in the case of *Bulmer v Bollinger* [1974] Ch 401, CA:

JUDGMENT

'The Treaty is like an incoming tide. It flows into the estuaries and up the rivers. It cannot be held back.'

The major problems will occur when Parliament appears to act inconsistently with the objectives of the Treaties or their subsidiary legislation and in the early years it was this that caused much debate among English judges. As we have seen, they would try to interpret national law, as far as possible, to be in harmony with EU law. The more dramatic problem comes if it can be seen that Parliament appears to be legislating deliberately contrary to the requirements of EU law. In *Felixstowe Dock and Railway Co v British Transport and Docks Board* [1976] 2 CMLR 655 Lord Denning again commented on the difficulties that this presented for English judges in the context of parliamentary supremacy. He concluded that all the judge could do was to follow the provision in the Act.

He later reaffirmed this in *Macarthys v Smith* [1979] WLR 1189 where he observed:

JUDGMENT

'if the time should ever come when our Parliament deliberately passes an Act with the intention of repudiating the Treaty or any provisions in it, or intentionally of acting inconsistently with it, and says so in express terms, then I should have thought that it would be the duty of our courts to follow the statute of our Parliament'.

The view was expressed at a point when membership was fairly recent and when judges had spent their careers as lawyers in a common law tradition, with parliamentary supremacy as an absolute rule. It is not surprising at this stage that judges would reject the suggestion that the provisions of the European Communities Act 1972 were entrenched against either express or implied repeal by later Acts of Parliament.

Nevertheless, a greater acceptance of the consequences of membership has developed over time. The statements of judges in more recent cases demonstrate this. In the case of *Stoke-on-Trent City Council v B&Q plc* [1990] 3 CMLR 897 the issue involved was the compatibility of the then UK Sunday trading laws and Article 34 which guarantees free movement of goods. Hoffmann J, as he then was, commented on the effects of EU law on UK legislation:

JUDGMENT

'The EC Treaty is the supreme law of the UK taking precedence over Acts of Parliament. Entry into the EC meant Parliament surrendered its sovereign right to legislate contrary to the provisions of the Treaty on matters of social and economic policy which the Treaty regulated. Entry into the EC and its attendant partial surrender of sovereignty was more than compensated for by the advantages of membership.'

The current attitude of the English courts is that demonstrated by Lord Bridge in *Factortame* (1990):

JUDGMENT

'If the supremacy within the EC of Community law over national law was not always inherent in the EC Treaty, it was certainly well established in the jurisprudence of the Court of Justice long before the United Kingdom joined the Community. Thus, whatever limitation of its sovereignty Parliament accepted when it enacted the European Communities Act 1972 was entirely voluntary. Under the terms of the Act of 1972 it has always been clear that it is the duty of a United Kingdom court, when delivering final judgment, to override any rule of national law found to be in conflict with any directly enforceable rule of Community law.'

Lord Bridge's choice of the word 'voluntary' is clearly very important. It allowed the judges to ensure observance of Treaty objectives while also maintaining the principle of parliamentary supremacy. All EU law will be followed in preference to inconsistent national law, either by harmonious interpretation or simply by declaring EU law superior, because that is what Parliament volunteered for on membership. The clear inference is that when Parliament's voluntary participation in the EU ceases then parliamentary supremacy would be observed.

7.3.3 The European Union Act 2011

While the UK judiciary has now for the most part accepted the supremacy of EU law the same cannot be said of UK politicians. There has always been a rump of Euro-scepticism in parliament from the onset of membership of the EU (at the time the EEC). This was also apparent in the referendum on membership in 1975 called by the then Labour Prime Minister Harold Wilson. At the time the Labour government was split on the issue with a number of cabinet ministers being against continued membership, although those occupying the four key posts of government were all in favour of membership. The Conservative Party in parliament at that time was mostly in favour of continued membership. This is unsurprising since it was that party which had taken the UK into the then EEC in 1973. This contrasts with the significant number of Euro-sceptic Conservative MPs in successive parliaments since 1990 particularly.

In the 2010 general election the Conservative Party, while gaining the largest number of seats, failed to gain an overall majority resulting in a coalition government with that party and the Liberal Democrats. As a result of this the Prime Minister, who supports continued membership, has been consistently under pressure from right wing anti-EU backbench MPs, and even cabinet ministers have declared their preference for an exit from membership.

Surprisingly, in the case of the Liberal Democrats since that party declares itself as the most supportive of the EU, the coalition government in 2011 passed the European Union Act which makes a number of statutory qualifications to the development of the EU and even continued membership.

Under s2 any Treaties which amend or replace the TEU and/or the TFEU will not be ratified unless this is approved by Act of Parliament or even by referendum. Under s3 the same applies in respect of amendments of the Treaties made under the simplified revision procedure under Article 48(6). Under s4 a referendum is required if an Article 48(6) decision involves:

a. the extension of the objectives of the EU as set out in Article 3 of TEU;

b. the conferring on the EU of a new exclusive competence;

c. the extension of an exclusive competence of the EU;

d. the conferring on the EU of a new competence shared with the Member States;

e. the extension of any competence of the EU that is shared with the Member States;

f. the extension of the competence of the EU in relation to

    i. the co-ordination of economic and employment policies, or

    ii. common foreign and security policy;

g. the conferring on the EU of a new competence to carry out actions to support, co-ordinate or supplement the actions of Member States;

h. the extension of a supporting, co-ordinating or supplementing competence of the EU;

i. the conferring on an EU institution or body of power to impose a requirement or obligation on the United Kingdom, or the removal of any limitation on any such power of an EU institution or body;

j. the conferring on an EU institution or body of new or extended power to impose sanctions on the United Kingdom;

k. any amendment of a provision listed in Schedule 1 that removes a requirement that anything should be done unanimously, by consensus or by common accord;

l. any amendment of Article 31(2) of TEU (decisions relating to common foreign and security policy to which qualified majority voting applies) that removes or amends the provision enabling a member of the Council to oppose the adoption of a decision to be taken by qualified majority voting;

m. any amendment of any of the provisions specified in subsection (3) that removes or amends the provision enabling a member of the Council, in relation to a draft legislative Act, to ensure the suspension of the ordinary legislative procedure.

A more important question over supremacy of EU law is to be found in s18 which in essence makes membership subject to the continuing will of Parliament. The section states:

SECTION

'18 Status of EU law dependent on continuing statutory basis

Directly applicable or directly effective EU law (that is, the rights, powers, liabilities, obligations, restrictions, remedies and procedures referred to in section 2(1) of the European Communities Act 1972) falls to be recognised and available in law in the United Kingdom only by virtue of that Act or where it is required to be recognised and available in law by virtue of any other Act.'

In other words the Act identifies that a simple Act of Parliament is all that is needed for exit from the EU. Whilst previously considered an unlikely scenario, that is exactly what is happening today with Brexit.

The European Union Withdrawal Bill

Since the UK Government initiated the withdrawal mechanism contained in Article 50 TEU ('Any member state may decide to withdraw from the Union in accordance with its own constitutional requirements'), all that is needed to complete the process is for the adoption of the **European Union Withdrawal Bill** (presented by the Government in June 2017).

The Bill will repeal the European Communities Act 1972 and, as such, will:

- entrench the UK withdrawal from the EU;

- confirm the termination of EU law primacy over British law (and arguably end the jurisdiction of the ECJ in the UK);

- transfer all EU legislation *en bloc* into UK law (to be repealed, amended and improved *ad hoc*, as required, after Brexit).

7.4 Supremacy and other Member States

The UK is not on its own in experiencing constitutional problems with the supremacy of EU law over national law. The extent of the problem depends on the character of the particular constitution in question. In the BENELUX countries, for instance, the problems are limited and those Member States are able to accept supremacy with little difficulty because of the general effect of international Treaties in their constitutions. In France, Germany and Italy, on the other hand, there are issues that have been the subject of concern for national courts.

7.4.1 Belgium and supremacy of EU law

The Belgian Constitution operates according to a 'monist' system, in contrast to the dualist constitution of the UK. In simple terms, a monist constitution operates so that international Treaties automatically become part of the national legal order on signing of the Treaty. In contrast, a dualist approach requires that, besides becoming a signatory to a Treaty, the state in question is required to ratify and incorporate the provisions into its national law by further legislation. This was the reason the UK passed the European Communities Act 1972.

In Belgium, then, the Treaties automatically became incorporated in national law once entry into the EC was achieved by signing the Treaty of Accession.

The issue of supremacy was in any case settled in subsequent case law:

CASE EXAMPLE

Ministère des Affaires Economiques v SA Fromagerie Franco–Suisse ('Le Ski')
[1972] CMLR 330, Court of Cassation, Belgium

Article 12 (now Article 18 TFEU) required the gradual removal of Customs duties during the transitional period. This was the same issue that was under discussion in the leading case of *Van Gend en Loos*, as we have already seen. The Belgian government had removed certain import duties on dairy products, but had also passed later law preventing the return of money already paid in duties. The Customs duties had been identified as unlawful in Article 169 (now Article 258 TFEU) proceedings before the ECJ. The Court identified that the normal rule, that a later legislative provision repealed an earlier one, could not apply here. The second Belgian law was unlawful in the context of Article 12 (now Article 18 TFEU), and the consequence is that the supremacy of EU law was firmly established.

7.4.2 France and supremacy of EU law

In France the judiciary has been divided in its attitude towards the supremacy of EU law over national law. This division initially manifested itself between the appeal courts, which had no problem in accepting supremacy, and the administrative court, the Conseil d'État, which originally did not.

At quite an early stage, the appeal court in *Von Kempis v Geldof (Cour de Cassation)* [1976] 2 CMLR 462 accepted both the reasoning and the case law of the ECJ in declaring that EU law takes precedence over French legislation.

However, in *Minister for the Interior v Cohn-Bendit (Conseil d'État)* [1980] 1 CMLR 543, on Directives issued under Article 39 (now Article 45 TFEU), the French constitutional court stated that a Directive could not be used as a means of challenging internal administrative law. However, the Conseil d'État has subsequently been more prepared to accept supremacy.

7.4.3 Italy and supremacy of EU law

The Italian constitutional court initially took quite a hard line, as has been seen earlier in *Costa v ENEL* (1964). At this point the view clearly expressed was that Italian legislation coming after the Treaty must be followed and this was the argument presented in the reference at that time.

However, the court then moved sharply away from that position, accepting the supremacy of EC (now EU) law:

CASE EXAMPLE

Frontini [1974] 3 CMLR 381

Here, a cheese importer was challenging the legitimacy of levies imposed as a result of EC (now EU) law in that, under the Italian Constitution, taxes could only be imposed by Italian statutory provision. The Italian constitutional court was clear that EC (now EU) law was both separate and superior and that Italian constitutional law does not apply to issues subject to EC (now EU) law. In reaching its decision the Court based its judgment almost entirely on the reasoning of the ECJ. It held that there could be no further questioning of the validity of the incorporation of Article 249 (now Article 189 TFEU) into Italian law.

Since that time Italy has been firm in its observance of the principle of supremacy. It has tended to operate towards a constructionist approach: that construction of Italian law must be consistent with the demands of EU law.

7.4.4 Germany and supremacy of EU law

Initially, Germany was unwilling to accept supremacy as an absolute principle because of the potential conflict with the protections of human rights contained in the German Constitution. This position was clearly demonstrated in the position taken by the German court in *International Handelsgesellschaft GmbH v EVGF* (1970) discussed in section 7.2.2.

It was also discussed at length in *Wunsche Handelsgesellschaft* [1987] 3 CMLR 225. Here, the German constitutional court reversed its position in the former case and accepted the principle of supremacy provided that the EU law could guarantee the protection of human rights.

In a different context, in *Kloppenberg* [1988] 3 CMLR 1, where the tax courts had originally held against the direct effect of a Directive on VAT, the constitutional court reversed this and upheld the supremacy of EU law in clear terms.

There is, then, some discrepancy between the attitude of different courts to supremacy. This debate has continued. In *Brunner v The European Treaty* [1994] 1 CMLR 57 the applicant had challenged the constitutional legitimacy of Germany signing the Treaty on European Union. The German constitutional court disagreed and upheld the validity of German membership of the new Treaty. Nevertheless, the judges passed significant comment on the relationship between the German state and the EU:

JUDGMENT

'[the TEU] can only have binding effects ... by virtue of the German instruction that its law be applied. Germany is one of the "Masters of the Treaties" which have established their adherence to the Union Treaty ... but could ultimately revoke that adherence by a contrary act. The validity and application of European law in Germany depends on the application-of-law instruction of the Accession Act. Germany thus preserves the quality of a sovereign state in its own right.'

In the same vein as the above, in the *Treaty of Lisbon judgement* [2 BvR 182/09] pronounced 30 June 2009 the German constitutional court confirmed the conditionality of the doctrine of EU law. The Court stated that it has the competence to review the compatibility of EU law, including EU Treaties amendments and transfer of powers from Germany to the EU, should that threaten the identity of the German constitution.

The ECJ's stance that EU law has primacy and the doctrine is absolute is based on the premise that the EU is *sui generis* – a unique supranational organisation with its own institutions and competences following a transfer of powers from the Member States (thus limiting their individual/unilateral action). However, it is exactly that last point which underscores the argument of the German constitutional court. The Court argues that, far from being absolute, EU law primacy is conditional *because* the powers of the EU and its institutions derive from a (partial) transfer of national sovereignty. In other words, the authority of the EU was given by the Member States, *ergo* the primacy of EU law is only valid insofar as it is permitted by their national constitutions.

This constitutional conditionality theory of EU law primacy was also confirmed in the *Danish Maastricht Treaty Ratification judgement* [1999] 3 CMLR 854.

ACTIVITY

Self-assessment questions

1. In what ways does the European Communities Act 1972 actually define the relationship between the UK and the EU?
2. What is the importance of s2(4) of the European Communities Act 1972?
3. To what extent have the English courts willingly accepted a doctrine of supremacy of EU law?
4. Is the reaction of English courts significantly different from those in other Member States?
5. How important are national constitutions to the reactions of different Member States to the issue of supremacy?
6. Why is *International Handelsgesellschaft* (1970) particularly significant to the development of a doctrine of supremacy of EU law?

KEY FACTS

The meaning of and need for supremacy	Treaty provision/case

Supremacy simply means that in any conflict between national law and EU law, EU law prevails.
Supremacy is necessary because full economic integration would be impossible if the institutions were denied supranational status.
 	
There are two main justifications:
• it prevents Member States from questioning the validity of EU law; and
• the doctrine of pre-emption,
  • prevents Member State courts from giving judgments inconsistent with EU law,
  • prevents Member State governments from legislating contrary to EU law.	

The definition and application of supremacy	Treaty provision/case
EU law first identified as creating a 'new legal order' under which Member States have partially surrendered sovereignty.	*Van Gend en Loos* (1963)
Definition and consequences expanded so that EU law 'cannot be overridden by domestic legal provisions, however framed'.	*Costa v ENEL* (1964)
EU law prevails over all inconsistent national law whether coming before or after the Treaty.	*Simmenthal* (1978)
EU law prevails even over a national constitutional provision.	*International Handelsgesellschaft* (1970)
And allows judges to suspend operation of a national legislative provision.	*Factortame* (1990)

The UK and supremacy	Treaty provision/case
UK approach originally one of construction.	*Garland v BREL* (1982)
And would not apply a Directive that would not be enforceable between individuals.	*Duke v GEC Reliance* (1988)
Judges were clear that if Parliament deliberately passed conflicting law they would have to give effect to parliamentary supremacy.	*Macarthys v Smith* (1979)
But now are prepared to accept supremacy because limiting of sovereignty was a voluntary concession in European Communities Act 1972.	*Factortame* (1990)

Other Member States and supremacy	Treaty provision/case
Belgium – accepts because it is a monist constitution.	*Le Ski* (1972)
France – appeal courts accepted but more reluctance from Conseil d'Etat.	*Von Kempis* (1976); *Cohn-Bendit* (1980); *Costa v ENEL* (1964)
Italy – originally more inclined to follow Italian Constitution but later accepted the principle.	*Frontini* (1974)
Germany – at first was prone to follow constitution because of human rights but later accepted supremacy if human rights upheld although still prone to insist that sovereignty survives.	*International Handelsgesellschaft* (1970); *Wunsche Handelsgesellschaft* (1987); *Brunner* (1994)

SAMPLE ESSAY QUESTION

'Discuss the argument that "Despite there being no mention of supremacy in the Treaty, even in the UK the doctrine of supremacy of EU Law has proved an uncontroversial creation of the European Court of Justice." '

Explain the basis of supremacy from ECJ case law:

- A new legal order ... for whose benefits the states have limited their sovereign rights, *Van Gend en Loos*
- 'The Treaty has created its own legal system which on entry into force ... became an integral part of the legal systems of the Member States and which their courts are bound to apply.... The transfer ... carries with it a clear limitation of their sovereign right upon which a subsequent unilateral law, incompatible with the aims of the Community cannot prevail', *Costa v ENEL*

Explain the basis for the doctrine:

- Under the Treaty – MSs should do everything in their power to achieve the objectives of the Treaty and refrain from doing anything that would prevent achieving those objectives
- The supranational character of the EU institutions including the ECJ

Discuss the justifications for the doctrine:

- The absence of a specific reference to supremacy in the Treaty
- The fact that the supranational character of the institutions and the law would be impaired without a doctrine of supremacy
- The objectives of the EU might be compromised

Discuss the position in the UK and whether the doctrine is 'uncontroversial':

- Supremacy of EU Law conflicts with this parliamentary supremacy
- Section 2(1) 1972 Act gives force to EU law
- Supremacy appears to be guaranteed by s2(4) 'any enactment passed or to be passed ... shall be construed and have effect subject to the foregoing provision of this section'
- The original view of judges was that ultimately the UK Parliament was supreme – Lord Denning in *Macarthys v Smith*
- But that now HL in *Factortame* has accepted: 'whatever limitations of its sovereignty Parliament accepted when it enacted the EC Act 1972 was entirely voluntary. Under the terms of the 1972 Act it has always been clear that it is the duty of a UK court ... to override any rule of national law found to be in conflict with any directly enforceable rule of Community law'

SUMMARY

- There is no mention of supremacy in the Treaties, however supranationalism would be impossible without some recognition of supremacy of EU Law and institutions.

- It is the creation of the Court of Justice that, in a very early statement, identified that states have given up certain of their sovereignty to a new legal order.

- The clearest definition is that it involves a limitation of sovereign rights upon which subsequent unilateral law, incompatible with the aims of the EU, cannot prevail – so where there is any inconsistency between national law and EU law it is the latter that takes precedence.

- Ultimately a national court can do everything necessary to set aside national legislative provisions which might prevent EU rules from having full force and effect.

Further reading

Books

Douglas-Scott, S, *Constitutional Law of the European Union* (Longman, 2002), Chapter 7.

Kaczarowska-Ireland, A, *European Union Law* (Routledge, 2016), Chapter 9.

Weatherill, S, *Cases and Materials on EU Law* (12th edn, Oxford University Press, 2016), Chapter 3.

Woods, L, Watson P and Costa M, *Steiner and Woods EU Law* (13th edn, Oxford University Press, 2017), Chapter 4.

Articles

Avbelj, M, 'Supremacy or Primacy of EU law – (Why) Does it Matter?' (2011) 17 *ELJ* 744.

8

The relationship between EU law and national law – direct effect

AIMS AND OBJECTIVES

After reading this chapter you should be able to:

- Understand the concept of direct effect and why it was developed by the ECJ
- Understand the criteria for achieving direct effect
- Differentiate between horizontal direct effect and vertical direct effect
- Understand the application of direct effect to Treaty Articles, Regulations and Decisions
- Understand the difficulty of applying direct effect to Directives
- Understand how the ECJ has got round the problem using vertical direct effect and how it has expanded the meaning of the state to include emanations of the state
- Understand the concept of indirect effect
- Evaluate the difficulties of applying indirect effect
- Understand the principle of incidental horizontal direct effect
- Analyse the effectiveness of the processes

8.1 Introduction

If supremacy defines the relationship between the Member States and the EU, then direct effect defines the relationship between the citizens of the various Member States and the EU in the form of its laws. Direct effect is therefore another major element in ensuring that EU law is applied harmoniously throughout the Member States.

Supremacy gives practical effect to the concept of supranationalism by ensuring that the Member States cannot put national self-interest before the law of the EU. Direct effect again demonstrates the supranational nature of EU law by ensuring that citizens are able to enforce it in the Member States' courts.

Direct effect was not created in the Treaties and so neither is it defined in them. It is entirely a creation of the European Court of Justice. It does in some ways relate to, and therefore must be distinguished from, other concepts that are identified in the Treaties. Article 288 TFEU, in establishing and defining the various types of legislation, for instance refers to:

General applicability

This merely refers to the fact that the measure in question applies universally throughout every Member State of the EU. In this way a Regulation is described as being generally applicable, whereas a Decision could never be generally applicable because it is addressed to a specific party.

Direct applicability

Direct applicability refers to the legal standing of the measure. A measure that is directly applicable automatically becomes law in the Member States once issued by the Council and the European Parliament through either the ordinary or special legislative procedure. Once again, a Regulation is described as directly applicable. The Regulation automatically becomes law in the Member States and there is no requirement for implementing legislation by the Member States. What may be appropriate is for them to produce law which repeals what would otherwise be inconsistent national legislation. However, even without this the EU measure has effect and, because of the doctrine of supremacy, must be applied in preference to the national law. A Directive, on the other hand, requires implementation by Member States within a set period and cannot, therefore, be directly applicable.

Direct effect, on the other hand, refers to the actual enforceability of EU law, of whatever type, in the national courts of Member States. Where the law creates actual rights and obligations then the concept can be applied to Treaty Articles, and to Regulations, and even to Decisions. However, the concept is much more problematic when it is applied to Directives.

Inevitably, this means that there are significant distinctions between direct applicability and direct effect:

- A measure may be directly applicable without necessarily creating rights that are enforceable. This would be the case with a procedural Regulation. Therefore the fact that a measure is directly applicable does not ensure that it will also have direct effect.

- It is possible that a measure can create rights and therefore be directly effective although not being directly applicable. This is the case with Directives, but only in limited circumstances.

- However, it is also of course possible that a measure could be both directly applicable and directly effective. .

Therefore whilst direct applicability relates to the automatic legal force of a given EU legislation (i.e. it is part of the domestic legal system and body of law); direct effect is concerned with the enforceability of that measure (i.e. whether individuals can invoke that legislation in domestic judicial proceedings to ensure the enjoyment of the rights it bestows upon them).

There is no doubt that direct effect is one of the most important of the creations of the ECJ. It has been instrumental in ensuring that the broad objectives of the Treaties have been observed by the Member States and incorporated into national law.

Various academics have commented on the significance of the concept: '[Direct effect is] the first step in the judicial contribution to federalism' (P Craig, 'Once Upon a Time in the West: Direct Effect and the Federalisation of EC Law' 1992 *OJLS* 453), 'a second principle of western jurisprudence to run alongside supremacy; namely the rule of law' (I Ward, *A Critical Introduction to European Law* (Butterworths, 1996), p. 57) and '[The most powerful justification for the creation of the concept is that it] enhances the effectiveness or *effet utile* of binding norms of Community law' (J Shaw, *European Community Law* (Macmillan Professional Masters, 1993), p. 151).

As with supremacy, one of the most interesting aspects of the area is that it is entirely the creation of the ECJ. It is difficult to imagine where the EU would have stood today without the ECJ taking such an uncompromising stance in creating through supremacy and direct effect the means by which the broad objectives of the Treaties can become established in national law. Inevitably, the uncompromising nature of the Court has resulted in conflict with Member States. This in turn has led to even more uncompromising behaviour by the ECJ in developing the principles of indirect effect (see section 8.4.2) and state liability (see Chapter 9).

Nevertheless, the ECJ has still been dependent on the national courts to develop the principle. F Mancini identifies the significance of this:

> The national courts … by referring to Luxembourg sensitive questions of interpretation of Community law … have been indirectly responsible for the boldest judgments the Court has made. Moreover, by adhering to these judgments in deciding the cases before them, and therefore by lending them the credibility which national judges usually enjoy in their own countries, they have rendered the case-law of the Court both effective and respected throughout the Community.
>
> F Mancini, 'The Making of a Constitution for Europe' (1989) 26 *CMLR* 595

8.2 The concept of direct effect

8.2.1 The origins of direct effect

Direct effect, as a concept, is not mentioned anywhere in the Treaties. It is entirely the creation of the ECJ. In fact, the ECJ had the opportunity to consider the enforceability of EU law first in the same case in which it also effectively developed the doctrine of supremacy.

Inevitably, the two concepts go hand in hand and are essential for the ultimate success of the Treaties and the principle of supranationalism on which the Common Market is based.

Direct effect was relevant to the case because there was a conflict between what fell within national law and how it conflicted with EU law. The citizen would have had no protection if he had been unable to rely on EU law in the case.

CASE EXAMPLE

Van Gend en Loos v Nederlandse Administratie der Belastingen (Case 26/62) [1963] ECR 1

In *Van Gend en Loos*, as we have already seen in Chapter 8, the Dutch government had reclassified certain import duties and this reclassification had meant an increase in duty on a chemical product imported from Germany, and which therefore caused increased cost to a Dutch bulb grower. Van Gend was objecting to paying the increase and argued that the reclassification in fact contravened the then Article 12 (now Article 30 TFEU) of the EC Treaty. The Dutch court made an Article 267 reference seeking a correct interpretation of the requirements of Article 12 (now Article 30 TFEU), which was then what was known as a 'standstill' Article requiring that there should be no increases on existing duties and no introduction of new duties during the transitional period. The Dutch court, since it was taking a dualist view of the Treaties and challenging the right of a citizen to invoke rights granted under the Treaties, also posed the question in the reference as to whether Article 12 (now Article 30 TFEU) was capable of creating rights in favour of individuals which a national court was then bound to protect.

The Advocate-General initially prepared a reasoned decision which took a purely literalist interpretation of the Article and suggested as a result that, since the Article contained no explicit mention of individual rights, it could not be construed as granting individual rights. He was also of the opinion that, if the reclassification of the duty was indeed contrary to EC law, then the appropriate action should be by the Commission against the Dutch state in Article 258 TFEU (then Art. 169) proceedings.

The *juges* in the ECJ, however, preferred a teleological (purposive) interpretation of the Article. It held that, since the Treaty was clearly intended to affect individuals, even though it made no specific mention of rights, it must clearly be capable of creating rights that would be enforceable by individuals in national courts.

JUDGMENT

'Independently of the legislation of the member states Community law ... not only imposes obligations on individuals but is also intended to confer upon them rights which become part of their legal heritage. These rights are granted not only where they are expressly granted by the Treaty, but also by reason of obligations which the Treaty imposes in a clearly defined way upon individuals as well as upon member states and the institutions of the Community.'

The ECJ pointed out then that, since the Treaty was clearly intended to affect individuals as well as Member States, it must also be capable of creating rights that would also be enforceable by individuals within the national courts.

In this way the Court concluded that since Article 12 (now Article 30 TFEU):

JUDGMENT

'contains a clear and unconditional prohibition ... it [is] ideally adapted to produce direct effects between member states and their subjects'.

The Court was also conscious of the limited value of the course of action that had been proposed by the Advocate-General, an action against the Dutch State under Article 258. The Court explored this possibility and gave its reasons against it.

JUDGMENT

'The implementation of Article 12 [now Article 30 TFEU] does not require any legislative intervention on the part of the states. The fact that under this Article it is the Member States who are made the subject of the negative obligation does not imply that their nationals cannot benefit from this obligation.... The argument based on Articles 169 and 170 [now Articles 258 and 259 TFEU] ... is misconceived. The fact that the Article enables the Commission and the Member States to bring before the Court a State which has not fulfilled its obligations does not mean that individuals cannot plead these obligations.... A restriction of the guarantees against infringement of Article 12 [now Article 30 TFEU] by Member States to the procedures under Articles 169 and 170 [now Articles 258 and 259 TFEU] would remove all direct legal protection of the individual rights of their nationals. There is the risk that recourse to the procedure under these Articles would be ineffective if it were to occur after the implementation of a national decision taken contrary to the provisions of the Treaty.'

The original method used to ensure that EU law was in fact enforced in Member States was by an action against the state through the enforcement proceedings in Articles 258 and 259 TFEU. As seen in the passage above, the ECJ established the concept of direct effect because it was a more effective means of ensuring that citizens of Member States could enforce the rights given to them by the Treaties than the traditional means.

8.2.2 The criteria for direct effect

Of course, the effect of *Van Gend en Loos* (1963) was initially quite limited in that direct effect only had to be applied to what are often referred to as 'standstill' Articles, or in other words prohibitive Treaty Articles. Of course, the action was in any case against the state itself.

The ECJ was able to develop the doctrine in *Van Gend* (1963) because the Article in question involved an obligation on the part of the Member States not to increase existing Customs duties or indeed create new ones. In this way the ECJ could quite easily justify enforcement of the provision because it was, as the Court described it, 'clear, precise and unconditional' and did not depend on any further action being taken for its implementation, either by the Community institutions or by the Member States themselves.

However, the original limitations in *Van Gend* (1963) soon disappeared in later judgments, with the ECJ extending the scope of direct effect. In this way not only could a wider range of EU law be enforced but also measures could be directly effective against other individuals as well as against the state.

Later judgments did confirm the criteria for establishing direct effect developed by the Court in *Van Gend* (1963), for instance that in *Reyners v Belgian State* (Case 2/74) [1974] ECR 631. The criteria for direct effect are nevertheless most commonly referred to as the '*Van Gend en Loos* criteria':

▧ The provision must be **sufficiently clear and precisely stated** – the ECJ in *Defrenne v SABENA* (Case 43/75) [1976] ECR 455 was satisfied that the principle that 'men and women shall receive equal pay for equal work' was sufficiently precise to create direct effect even though the exact meaning of 'equal pay' and 'equal work' would inevitably require further definition by the courts.

▧ The provision must be **unconditional or 'non-dependent'** – in the sense that it should not depend on the intervention of another body or require further legislative action either by the Community institutions or by Member States.

Added to this, of course, for individuals to gain enforceable rights from the provision:

▧ There must in fact be an identifiable right granted by the Treaty or legislative provision and on which the citizen can then rely (*Francovich v Italy* (Cases C–6 and 9/90) [1991] ECR I–5357).

Not all provisions do conform to the criteria, even though they may appear to be worded in unconditional terms. In *Casati* (Case 203/80) [1981] ECR 2595 the ECJ was concerned with whether the provision under the old Article 71 (now repealed) that 'member states shall endeavour to avoid introducing … new exchange restrictions' was directly effective. The Court held that the words 'shall endeavour' were in fact insufficient to create unconditional obligations and that therefore the provision could not be directly effective.

8.2.3 Vertical direct effect and horizontal direct effect

Because the action was against the state, the case of *Van Gend en Loos* (1963) did not deal with the issue of whether or not a citizen could rely on the principle of direct effect to enforce a provision against another citizen as the case had confirmed they could against the state.

This was one of the questions for the Court in *Defrenne v SABENA* (1976), which involved a claim for equal pay made against an employer under Article 157 (see Chapter 18). The ECJ rejected the argument that direct effect was a means only of enforcing substantive EU laws against the Member States. The Court identified that there were two types of direct effect: **vertical** direct effect and **horizontal** direct effect. This was necessary because otherwise citizens would be denied effective remedies where they were granted rights under EU law.

JUDGMENT

'the reference to "Member States" in [Article 141, now Article 157] cannot be interpreted as excluding the intervention of the courts in the direct application of the Treaty. . . . Since [Article 119, now Article 157] is mandatory in nature, the prohibition on discrimination between men and women applies not only to the action of public authorities, but also extends to all agreements which are intended to regulate paid labour collectively, as well as to contracts between individuals.'

The Court, in essence, then, also clarified the distinctions between the two:

Vertical direct effect in one sense concerns the relationship between EU law and national law:

- measures of EU law creates obligations on the state to ensure their observance;
- a failure on the part of Member States to honour Treaty obligations would usually give rise to an action against the state under Article 258 TFEU;
- but vertical direct effect means that the process is not necessary since an individual can rely on the measures in an action against the state (as was the case in the original *Van Gend en Loos* case and in both *Van Duyn v Home Office* (Case 41/74) [1974] ECR 1337 and *Pubblico Ministero v Ratti* (Case 148/78) [1979] ECR 1629 which were both fought against government departments);
- indeed the principle has been extended to cover other 'public bodies' other than the state itself, and these are known as 'emanations of the state'.

Horizontal direct effect, on the other hand, is concerned instead with the relationship between individuals and other individuals:

- this could include any private body including companies;
- where a measure is horizontally directly effective it creates rights between citizens and is therefore enforceable by them in national courts;
- inevitably, because of the nature of a Directive, the ECJ has stated that Directives do not have horizontal direct effect (which is why the ECJ has been so active in ensuring that citizens will not lose out merely because the provision in question is a Directive).

As a result, the distinction between the two can be critical in determining whether or not a citizen is able to enforce the law and has an action where there is a breach of EU law.

ACTIVITY

Self-assessment questions
1. What is the difference between general applicability and direct applicability?
2. What is the difference between direct applicability and direct effect?
3. What is the relationship between supremacy and direct effect?
4. What are the *Van Gend en Loos* (1963) criteria and why did the ECJ create them?
5. How did the ECJ in the case justify ignoring the normal method of dealing with the problem?
6. What is the major difference between vertical direct effect and horizontal direct effect?

The relationship between horizontal direct effect and vertical direct effect can be shown in diagram form as in Figure 8.1.

8.3 The application of direct effect

The Court of Justice has developed the principle of direct effect so that it applies generally to most types of EU law, both primary and secondary. It has generally followed its

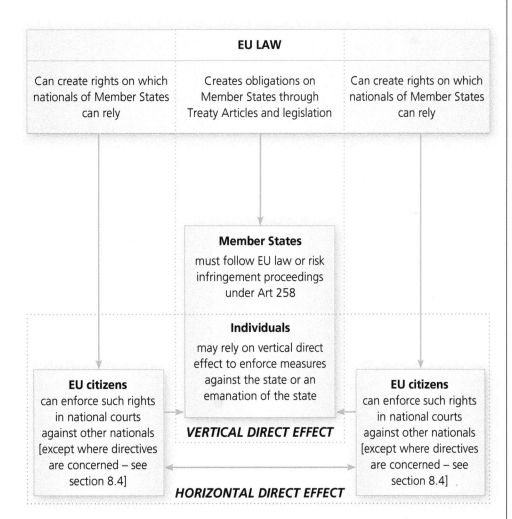

Figure 8.1 The relationship between vertical direct effect and horizontal direct effect

own criteria in *Van Gend en Loos* (1963). However, the test from the case was originally strictly applied but the ECJ has also gradually taken a more relaxed approach to ensure that citizens can take advantage of the rights given to them in the Treaties.

There are a number of consequences of this relaxation:

- the Court has in effect assumed responsibility for ensuring the effective integration of EU law;

- provided that the criteria are generally met, then direct effect of a substantive measure is almost assumed;

- the direct effect of a provision is only likely to be denied when there would be serious political or social consequences;

- as a result, direct effect has become essentially a question of policy for the ECJ.

8.3.1 Direct effect and Treaty Articles

The concept of direct effect was first accepted in *Van Gend en Loos* (1963) and this case of course involved a Treaty Article, Article 12 (now Article 30).

This was a so-called 'standstill' Article. The principle of direct effect was also applied in respect of Treaty Articles imposing a duty on Member States to act, which would have been the case with removal of features from their national laws during the transitional period that would be detrimental to the attainment of the Common Market.

The principle, however, has been extended to cover all of the main substantive Treaty Articles. So, for example, it has been applied to both Article 34 and Article 35 on the free movement of goods in *Dansk Supermarked A/S v A/S Imerco* (Case 58/80) [1981] ECR 181 (see Chapter 14).

It has also been applied to the free movement of workers under Article 45 in *Van Duyn v Home Office* (1974) (see Chapter 12) as well as to rights of establishment under Article 49 in *Reyners v Belgium* (1974) and the freedom to provide services under Article 56 in *Van Binsbergen v Bestuur van de Bedrijfsvereniging voor de Metaalnijverheid* (Case 33/74) [1974] ECR 1299 (see Chapter 13). Both Article 49 and Article 56 envisage the introduction of Directives for the harmonisation of qualifications throughout the EU. The argument that this made the Articles conditional and dependent and that they could not as a result be directly effective was expressly rejected in the *Reyners* (1974) case.

Besides this, the principle has also ensured enforceability of EU competition law under Article 101 and Article 102 in *Brasserie de Haecht SA v Wilkin-Janssen (No 2)* (Case 48/72) [1973] ECR 77 (see Chapter 16).

We have also seen already that the principle of equal pay for equal work in Article 157 was declared directly effective in *Defrenne v SABENA* (1976). The Court did, however, take the unique step of declaring the Article only prospectively directly effective.

The role of the ECJ in declaring the major EU policies directly effective has clearly been critical in defining those Treaty provisions as well as in ensuring that citizens can rely on them. One further point to add, which is of course apparent from the cases above, is that a Treaty Article will be both vertically and horizontally directly effective.

Charter of Fundamental Rights

As stated in Chapter 1, the CFR is primary legislation and has legal force and the same constitutional value as the Treaties. Therefore the applicability principles of the doctrine of direct effect for the CFR are the same as for Treaty provisions – albeit within the scope of application of Article 51 CFR. Essentially the CFR will have vertical effect as it is binding upon the Member States in the 'implementation' of EU law.

The ECJ has found that the CFR may produce horizontal effect (i.e. in proceedings between private parties) where a provision of the Charter is also found in the general principle of EU law (see *Kücükdeveci v Swedex* (Case C–555/07) [2010] ECR I–365).

8.3.2 Direct effect and Regulations

The definition of 'Regulations' under Article 288 means that they are both of 'general application' and 'directly applicable'. The consequence of this is that they may also create obligations without need for further enactment by either the institutions or the Member States.

It therefore follows that they are also capable of direct effect provided that they satisfy the *Van Gend en Loos* (1963) criteria. Because a Regulation is directly applicable it can never be construed as conditional. On this basis, provided also that it contains a recognisable right, the only real test for the ECJ is whether or not the provision is stated in sufficiently clear and precise terms. However, it naturally follows that where a Regulation is too vague in its terms then it may not be directly effective.

CASE EXAMPLE

Leonesio v Ministero dell'Agricoltora & delle Foreste (Case 93/71) [1972] ECR 287 (The widow Leonesio)

Here, the Regulation concerned the provision of subsidies for dairy farmers prepared to slaughter their dairy herds. The provision was introduced with a view to easing the 'milk lake' (overproduction of milk within the Community). The applicant here had killed her cows as directed by the Regulation but was being refused the subsidies by the Italian state. On a reference under Article 267 the ECJ held that the Regulation did indeed conform to the Van Gend en Loos (1963) criteria, was very precisely stated and in no way ambiguous, as a result of which it was also directly effective and enforceable.

Again, where the ECJ accepts the direct effect of a Regulation, then direct effect is both vertical and horizontal, as was confirmed in *Muñoz* (Case C–253/00) [2002] ECR 7289.

8.3.3 Direct effect and Decisions

As we have seen, a 'Decision' is defined in Article 288 as being 'binding in its entirety on the party to whom it is addressed'.

Since Decisions generally are addressed to parties who are in breach of EU obligations there is a clear need for the citizens who suffer as a result of those breaches to be able to rely on the decisions. The ECJ has itself accepted that.

CASE EXAMPLE

Grad v Finanzamt Traustein (Case 9/70) [1970] ECR 825

This case involved a challenge by a German company to a tax imposed upon it. The company argued that the tax was in contravention of a Directive that required amendment to national VAT laws and in effect also of a decision which gave a time limit for doing so. The question for the ECJ, therefore, was whether the company was entitled to rely on the decision.

The ECJ concluded that it could and identified that it would be:

> 'incompatible with the binding nature of decisions ... to exclude the possibility that persons affected may invoke the obligation imposed by a decision ... the effectiveness of such a measure would be weakened if ... nationals ... could not ... invoke it ... and the national courts could not take it into consideration'.

Of course, once again, all of the criteria for direct effect would need to be present. The above case law, which relates to an instance where a decision was combined with a Treaty provision and directive, was later confirmed in a case which only involved a decision (*Hansa Fleisch* (Case C–156/91) [1992] ECR I–5567).

The fact that decisions are binding only on the party to whom the decision is addressed means that there is not the same problem of lack of direct applicability that occurs with Directives. Nevertheless some of the problems that occur with Directives in relation to private parties could occur where that party is not the one to whom the decision is addressed.

8.4 The problem of enforceability of Directives

8.4.1 Direct effect and Directives

Again, the character of a Directive is defined in Article 288. Under the Article, Directives are said to be 'binding as to the result to be achieved' but 'leave to the national authorities the choice of form and method'. This means that Directives have distinct objectives but in effect create obligations on Member States to pass national laws within a set time to achieve those objectives.

In this way Directives cannot in themselves automatically create substantive rights that citizens are then able to enforce.

- First, they are not directly applicable. They do not automatically become laws in the Member States. On the contrary, the Member States are allowed to achieve the objects contained in the Directives in whatever way they choose.

- Second, because they fail one part of the test in *Van Gend en Loos* (1963). They are conditional, they are not non-dependent and they are entirely dependent on implementation by the Member States.

The problem first came to the attention of the ECJ in a situation where it was not so vital in one sense because it was in effect the Member State that was trying to plead that the Directive was enforceable. The important point for the citizen involved was whether the procedural safeguards contained in the Directive bound the Member State.

Van Duyn v Home Office (Case 41/74) [1974] ECR 1337

Here, the issue was whether the UK could make use of the derogations from free movement of workers under both Article 45 and more precisely in Directive 64/221 (now under Directive 2004/38) (see Chapter 12). The ECJ considered the problem of the direct effect of Directives and reached an important conclusion, identifying:

JUDGMENT

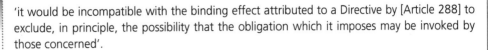

'it would be incompatible with the binding effect attributed to a Directive by [Article 288] to exclude, in principle, the possibility that the obligation which it imposes may be invoked by those concerned'.

The ECJ was thus prepared to overlook the potential limitation involved in the definition of 'Directives' given by Article 288 again to ensure the *effet utile* (usefulness) of the measure. The Court foresaw that this type of legislation could be made ineffective without allowing direct effect. Another way of looking at it is to say that there would be no purpose to this type of legislation if Member States were allowed to plead their own failure to implement as the reason for the right not being enforced.

As the Court also observed in *Van Duyn* (1974):

JUDGMENT

'where the Community authorities have, by directive, imposed on Member States the obligation to pursue a particular course of conduct, the useful effect of such an act would be weakened if individuals were prevented from relying on it before their national courts and if the latter were prevented from taking it into consideration'.

On this basis, while the Court gave little other reasoning it identified that a Directive can indeed be enforced by the means of direct effect provided that the remaining criteria from *Van Gend en Loos* (1963) are met.

Nevertheless, it must be remembered that, because Directives include objectives that are left for Member States to enact in their own chosen method, if the Member States carry out their obligations the rights identifiable in the Directives would not be enforceable through EU law but rather through the national law as enacted. For this reason, Directives are only a problem where they are unimplemented or improperly implemented.

Of course, there is nothing to stop the ECJ or the national courts from referring to the Directive after its implementation into national law in order to ensure that its objectives have indeed been achieved. This was confirmed in the case of *Verbond van Nederlands Ondernemingen v Inspecteur der Invoerrechten en Accijzen* (Case 51/76) [1977] ECR 113.

However, it is equally true that during the implementation period the rights contained in the Directive are not enforceable by any means. This would clearly be unfair since the Member States have been given a time limit within which to comply. For this reason the Court of Justice added an extra criterion to the *Van Gend en Loos* (1963) test in respect of Directives. In *Pubblico Ministero v Ratti* (1979) the ECJ stated that direct effect of a Directive is not in question until such time as the implementation period has expired.

Another significant point is that a Directive can only ever be vertically directly effective. It could never be horizontally directly effective. This means that an unimplemented or improperly implemented Directive can only be relied upon and enforced against the state which, according to the reasoning in *Van Duyn* (1974), the member state is prevented from its own failure to implement to avoid the obligation owed under the Directive.

CASE EXTRACT

In the case extract below a significant section of the judgment has been reproduced in the left hand column. Individual points arising from the judgment are briefly explained in the right hand column. Read the extract including the commentary in the right hand column and complete the exercise that follows.

Extract adapted from the judgment in *Marshall v Southampton and South West Hampshire AHA (No 1)* (Case 152/84) [1986] QB 401

Facts

The claimant was made to retire, and so was dismissed, at 62 by her employer, a health authority. A reference was made under Art 234 [now 267] on the issue of whether different retirement ages for men and women in the UK amounted to discrimination under directive 76/207, the 'equal treatment directive' (see Chapter 18). The Court of Justice confirmed that it was. It also identified that the applicant was able to use the directive against her employer but only because her employer was in fact the health service, an organ of the state.

The basic facts

The basis of the reference

Judgment of the Court of Justice

The second question

39 ... it is necessary to consider whether Article 5(1) of Directive No 76/207 may be relied upon by an individual before national courts and tribunals.

One of the questions in the referral

40 The appellant and the Commission consider that the question must be answered in the affirmative. They contend in particular, with regard to Articles 2(1) and 5(1) of Directive 76/207, that those provisions are sufficiently clear to enable national courts to apply them without legislative intervention by the Member States, at least so far as overt discrimination is concerned.

The Commission's argument that a citizen should be able to rely on the Directive

41 In support of that view, the appellant points out that Directives are capable of conferring rights on individuals which may be relied upon directly before the courts of the Member States; national courts are obliged by virtue of the binding nature of a Directive, in conjunction with Article 5 of the EEC Treaty [now Article 4(3) TFEU], to give effect to the provisions of Directives where possible, in particular when construing or applying relevant provisions of national law (judgment of ... Case 14/83 Von Colson and Kamann v Land Nordrhein-Westfalen (1984) 1891). Where there is any inconsistency between national law and Community [now EU] law which cannot be removed by means of such a construction, the appellant submits that a national court is obliged to declare that the provision of national law which is inconsistent with the Directive is inapplicable.

The reasoning that national courts should interpret national law to give effect to relevant EU law

42 The Commission is of the opinion that the provisions of Article 5(1) of Directive No 76/207 are sufficiently clear and unconditional to be relied upon before a national court. They may therefore be set up against section 6(4)

The Commission argument that national UK law on retirement ages is incompatible with EU anti-discrimination law

EU LAW AND NATIONAL LAW – DIRECT EFFECT

of the Sex Discrimination Act, which according to the decisions of the Court of Appeal, has been extended to the question of compulsory retirement and has therefore become ineffective to prevent dismissals based upon the difference in retirement ages for men and for women.

43 The respondent and the United Kingdom propose, conversely, that the second question should be answered in the negative. They admit that a Directive may, in certain specific circumstances, have direct effect as against a Member State in so far as the latter may not rely on its failure to perform its obligations under the Directive. However, they maintain that a Directive can never impose obligations directly on individuals and that it can only have direct effect against a Member State qua public authority and not against a Member State qua employer. As an employer a state is no different from a private employer. It would not therefore be proper to put persons employed by the state in a better position than those who are employed by a private employer.

The UK argument that Directives can be enforced against the state but not an individual

Qua means in the capacity of

44 With regard to the legal position of the respondent's employees the United Kingdom states that they are in the same position as the employees of a private employer. Although according to United Kingdom constitutional law the health authorities, created by the National Health Service Act 1977, as amended by the Health Services Act 1980 and other legislation, are Crown Bodies and their employees are Crown servants, nevertheless the administration of the National Health Service by the health authorities is regarded as being separate from the government's central administration and its employees are not regarded as civil servants.

The UK argument that the state as employer is the same as a private employer

45 Finally, both the respondent and the United Kingdom take the view that the provisions of Directive 76/207 are neither unconditional nor sufficiently clear and precise to give rise to direct effect. The Directive provides for a number of possible exceptions, the details of which are to be laid down by the Member States. Furthermore, the wording of Article 5 is quite imprecise and requires the adoption of measures for its implementation.

The UK argument that the provisions in the Directive fail the Van Gend en Loos criteria

46 It is necessary to recall that, according to a long line of decisions of the court (in particular its judgment ... in Case 8/81 Becker v Finanzamt Munster-Innenstadt (1982) ECR 53), wherever the provisions of a Directive appear, as far as their subject matter is concerned, to be unconditional and sufficiently precise, those provisions may be relied upon by an individual against the state where that state fails to implement the Directive in national law by the end of the period prescribed or where it fails to implement the Directive correctly.

The Court identifies that there is existing principle that the provisions of a Directive which is sufficiently precise and unconditional on its terms can be relied on against the state (vertical direct effect)

47 That view is based on the consideration that it would be incompatible with the binding nature which Article 189 [now Article 288 TFEU] confers on the Directive to hold as a matter of principle that the obligation imposed thereby cannot be relied on by those concerned. From that the court deduced that a Member State which has not adopted the implementing measures required by the Directive within the prescribed period may not plead, as against individuals, its own failure to perform the obligations which the Directive entails.

It explains that to do otherwise would be to ignore the binding nature of EU legislation as identified in the Treaty

48 With regard to the argument that a Directive may not be relied upon against an individual, it must be emphasised that according to Article 189 of the EEC Treaty [now Article 288 TFEU] the binding nature of a Directive, which constitutes the basis for the possibility of relying on the Directive before a national court, exists only in relation to 'each member state to which it is addressed'. It follows that a Directive may not of itself impose obligations on an individual and that a provision of a Directive may not be relied upon as such against such a person. It must therefore be examined whether, in this case, the respondent must be regarded as having acted as an individual.

But a Directive cannot be relied on against an individual (horizontal direct effect)

49 In that respect it must be pointed out that where a person involved in legal proceedings is able to rely on a Directive as against the state he may do so regardless of the capacity in which the latter is acting, whether employer or public authority. In either case it is necessary to prevent the state from taking advantage of its own failure to comply with Community [now EU] law.

Can rely on a Directive against the state in any capacity

50 It is for the national court to apply those considerations to the circumstances of each case; the Court of Appeal has, however, stated in the order for reference that the respondent, Southampton and South West Hampshire Area Health Authority (Teaching), is a public authority.

51 The argument submitted by the United Kingdom that the possibility of relying on provisions of the Directive against the respondent qua organ of the state would give rise to an arbitrary and unfair distinction between the rights of state employees and those of private employees does not justify any other conclusion. Such a distinction may easily have been avoided if the Member State concerned has correctly implemented the Directive in national law.

UK argues that distinction between state and private employer is arbitrary and unfair
Court responds that this could have been avoided if UK implemented the Directive properly

[...]

55 It follows that Article 5 of Directive No 76/207 does not confer on the Member States the right to limit the application of the principle of equality of treatment in its field of operation or to subject it to conditions and that that provision is sufficiently precise and unconditional to be capable of being relied upon by an individual before a national court in order to avoid the application of any national provision which does not conform to Article 5(1).

The Court identifies that UK bound by the Directive and cannot limit its application

56 Consequently, the answer to the second question must be that Article 5(1) of Council Directive No 76/207 ... which prohibits any discrimination on grounds of sex with regard to working conditions, including the conditions governing dismissal, may be relied upon as against a state authority acting in its capacity as employer, in order to avoid the application of any national provision which does not conform to Article 5(1).

The provisions of the Directive can be relied upon against the state acting in any capacity and to all aspects of employment including retirement

ACTIVITY

In the key points list that follows try to insert the two points made in the judgment that are missing from the list below using the commentary in the right hand column in the extract above to help you.

Key Points from the case of Marshall v Southampton and South West Hampshire AHA (No 1) (Case 152/84) [1986] QB 401 above:

There are ... key points that result from the judgment of the Court of Justice:

- National courts are bound to interpret national law so as to give effect to relevant EU law.
- UK law on different retirement ages for men and women at the time was incompatible with EU anti-discrimination law.
- There was existing EU law identifying that the provisions of a Directive could be enforced against the state.
-

  ....

- There can never be horizontal direct effect of a Directive.
- A Directive can be enforced against the state in whatever capacity the state acts including as employer.
- Any arbitrary distinction or unfairness that results from the claimant being able to enforce the Directive against the state as her employer when an employee of a private body could not is the fault of the UK for failing to implement the Directive properly.
-

  ....

- The Directive applies to all aspects of employment and this includes dismissal which itself includes retirement.

The ECJ subsequently identified that the national courts should decide against what bodies a Directive could be enforced using vertical direct effect. It has explained also that vertical direct effect may affect not only the state itself but also bodies that could be described as an 'emanation of the state' (or 'arm of the state'). The Court also has devised the test of which bodies can be classed as emanations of the state.

CASE EXAMPLE

Foster v British Gas plc (Case C–188/89) [1990] ECR I–3313

The applicant was making the same basic claim as that in the *Marshall* (1986) case, that British Gas was in breach of Directive 76/207 (now the Recast Directive) by compelling her to retire at 60 when male employees retired at 65 (a legitimate difference under s6(4) of the Sex

Discrimination Act 1975 – but later repealed in the Sex Discrimination Act 1986). At the time of her complaint British Gas was not a private company but was still owned by the state. The House of Lords, in a reference to the ECJ under Article 267, posed the question of whether British Gas was a body against which the Directive could be enforced. The ECJ developed a test for determining whether a body could be classed as an emanation of the state. The Court declared (in paragraph 18) that a Directive could be relied on against any organisation or body which was 'subject to the authority or control' of the state, or had 'special powers' that would not be available to a private body.

In paragraph 20, the Court then ruled on whether British Gas at the material time (before it was privatised) was such a body. The Court noted it was definitely an 'emanation of the state' because it provided a public service, was under the control of the state and was able to exercise special powers. However, when the case returned to the House of Lords, the Law Lords adopted paragraph 20 as the test for determining an 'emanation of the state', rather than paragraph 18. According to this test, a body must satisfy three criteria. It must:

- be one that provides a public service; and
- be under the control of the state; and
- be able to exercise special powers that would not be available to a private body.

It is obvious that the paragraph 20 test is much more difficult to satisfy than the paragraph 18 test. Nevertheless, a number of subsequent British cases have considered and applied the three-part paragraph 20 test. In *Doughty v Rolls Royce plc* [1992] 1 CMLR 1045 a publicly owned manufacturing company was held not to be an emanation of the state since it failed the first and third criteria. On the other hand, in *Griffin v South West Water* [1995] IRLR 15 the national court considered that a privatised water company was an emanation of the state. While the body itself was not as such under the control of the state, certain of the services it operated were.

There is inconsistent application of the principles regarding when a body can be classed as an emanation of the state. Nevertheless, there have been quite liberal interpretations by the ECJ, so that a private company has been held to be an emanation of the state where it is carrying out a public duty.

CASE EXAMPLE

Rieser Internationale Transporte GmbH v Autobahnen-und-Schnellstrasse Finanzierungs AG (Asfinag) C–157/02 [2004] ECR I-1477

An Austrian company, Asfinag, was involved in the construction of motorways in Austria. Besides this it was involved in and had certain involvement in respect of planning, maintaining and financing motorways. More importantly it was able to levy tolls on users. It was shown in the case that the Austrian state was the sole shareholder in the company, had the right to check everything done by the company, and could impose rules regarding construction, safety and the organisation of traffic. Besides this Asfinag was required to submit detailed plans to the Austrian state each year as well as having to provide details of estimated costs for the year. As a result, for the purposes of enforcing the provisions of a directive, the ECJ held that Asfinag was engaged in a public service, was under the control of the state, and also had special powers beyond those normally enjoyed by private companies and so was an emanation of the state, and therefore subject to vertical direct effect of the directive.

Where a body is deemed to be an emanation of the state according to the *Foster* criteria, that body becomes an agent of the state and must therefore take all necessary measures to fulfil the aims prescribed by the EU Directive. In other words, the state as well as its various emanations are all subject to the duty to comply with their obligations under EU law (*Portgás* (Case C-425/12) [2014] 2 CMLR 30).

The fact that Directives may generally only have vertical direct effect inevitably creates major anomalies and injustices where an applicant's case is against another individual or a private body. This can be seen in the contrasting decisions above and also in *Duke v GEC Reliance* [1988] 2 WLR 359. The case involved the identical point to that in *Marshall* (1986), but the employer was not the state but a private company. The House of Lords held that it was not bound to apply Directive 76/207 (now the Recast Directive) because the Directive could not be effective horizontally. Even though the UK was at fault for failing to implement the Directive fully, the availability of a remedy then was entirely dependent on the identity of the employer.

Clearly, the process of ensuring vertical effect of Directives in actions against the state or an emanation of the state was one way of getting round the defects in the definition of 'Directives' in Article 288. Nevertheless, the absence of horizontal effect still meant that there were problems in enforcing rights granted by Directives.

> In *Marshall* the Court held that an individual may rely upon a directive against the State, regardless of whether the State is acting as a public authority or employer. The consequence of this ruling is that, for example, a private employee may not rely on a directive but a state employee may. The ruling has been attacked as provoking unjust and anomalous situations, particularly in the field of labour law, where the scope of the Equal Treatment Directive has been reduced. The decision also led to the necessity for an impossibly rigorous definition of the state which proved very difficult to apply in case law.
>
> S Douglas-Scott, *Constitutional Law of the European Union*
> (Longman, 2002), p. 296

Nevertheless, the ECJ will pursue its function to ensure that EU law is observed, which implies protecting the doctrine of primacy from any adverse interference by domestic courts which may undermine the effectiveness of the EU legal order should a contradicting national legislation be allowed to trump EU legislation. Following *Mangold v Helm* (Case C–144/04) [2005] ECR I–9981, the ECJ suggests that it is possible for a Directive which contains a general principle of EU law (such as non-discrimination based on age) to have horizontal direct effect. Essentially, the ECJ in this case does not allow the horizontal application of the Directive *per se*, but focuses on ensuring the horizontal application of the fundamental right protected under the General Principles of EU Law (GPEUL). It is worth noting that this judgment has been highly debated and does not in fact settle the question of the horizontal application of Directives.

The means for determining the direct effect of a Directive can be represented in diagram form as shown in Figure 8.2.

Where a Directive does not fulfil the Van Gend en Loos (1963) criteria for direct effect, the ECJ will nevertheless endeavour to ensure that EU law is still applied through the principle of consistent interpretation, also known as indirect effect.

8.4.2 Indirect effect

Making use of vertical direct effect was one way in which the ECJ was able to ensure that rights gained through a Directive could be enforced but of course it had severe limitations.

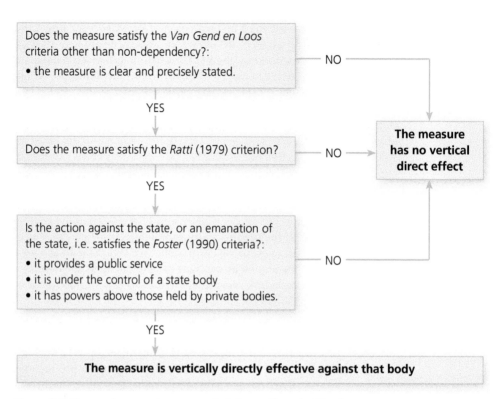

Figure 8.2 The requirements to prove vertical direct effect of a Directive

Another way round the problem was the introduction of the process of sympathetic interpretation (or indirect effect).

The ECJ identified that since Member States had an obligation at that time under Article 10 to 'take all appropriate measures … to ensure fulfilment of the obligations arising out of this Treaty' then the national courts also had a duty to interpret national law so that it would give full effect to EU law (irrespective of whether or not it is directly effective).

This is the principle of indirect effect, known also as the *Von Colson* principle, and it applies to EU law in general, not only to Directives, but it can obviously be useful in avoiding the problem of the lack of horizontal effect of Directives. The ECJ explained the principle in two cases that were referred to the Court by the German Labour Court:

CASE EXAMPLE

Von Colson and Kamann v Land Nordrhein-Westfalen (Case 14/83) [1984] ECR 1891; *Harz v Deutsche Tradax GmbH* (Case 79/83) [1984] ECR 1921

The cases both involved improper implementation of Directive 76/207 by the German government. The failure by Germany was one that was also highlighted in the second of the Marshall cases (*Marshall v Southampton and South West Hampshire AHA (No 2)* (Case C–271/91) [1993] ECR 586) on the provision of inadequate compensation in contrast with the full compensation required by the Directive.

Von Colson applied to work for a state body, the prison service, while Harz applied to work for a private company. The ECJ identified that the failure to provide compensation did amount to improper or incomplete implementation. Even so, while a remedy would have been available to Von Colson through vertical direct effect, Harz would have been denied a remedy because of the anomaly resulting from lack of horizontal effect. The ECJ took a different and at the time a very novel approach by using the obligation in Article 10 (now repealed) of the EC Treaty to introduce the principle of indirect effect. The German court was bound to give full effect to the Directive and so must order full compensation in both cases.

JUDGMENT

'Since the duty under [Article 10] to ensure fulfilment of [an] obligation was binding on all national courts ... it follows that ... courts are required to interpret their national law in the light of the wording and purpose of the Directive.'

The ECJ in *Von Colson* (1984) in this way ignored the problem of horizontal and vertical effect, and in fact ignored direct effect in general so it was a means of overcoming the problems seen above in section 8.4.1. Nevertheless, the judgment did leave ambiguous the question of to which national law the process of indirect effect could actually apply. This then allowed the House of Lords to refuse to apply the principle in *Duke* (1988) even though it would have been a means of providing a remedy for the applicant.

Another limitation in the case itself was that it also left ambiguous or unexplained just how far national courts should go in order to ensure conformity of their own national law and EU law. However, subsequent development or clarification of the principle may have overcome these problems.

CASE EXAMPLE

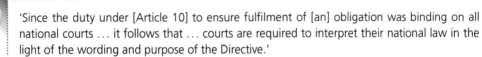

Marleasing SA v La Commercial Internacional de Alimentacion (Case C–106/89) [1990] ECR I–4135

Whereas Von Colson involved an improperly implemented Directive, this case concerned a Directive that had not been implemented at all. On a reference from the Spanish court the question for the ECJ was whether the applicant could rely on the rules on the constitution of companies in Directive 68/151, the Directive on company law harmonisation. Spain had not implemented the Directive and Spanish law conflicted with its provisions. The ECJ applied the principles of indirect effect and expanded on the definition given in Von Colson.

JUDGMENT

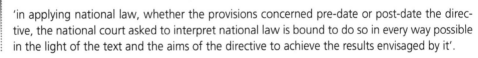

'in applying national law, whether the provisions concerned pre-date or post-date the directive, the national court asked to interpret national law is bound to do so in every way possible in the light of the text and the aims of the directive to achieve the results envisaged by it'.

The scope of indirect effect provided for by *Marleasing* (1990) is potentially very wide, then, and it has the effect of introducing horizontal direct effect but by indirect means, hence the title given to the process. However, there does seem to be a significant difference between the *Von Colson* (1984) approach, which is to do 'everything possible' to achieve conformity, and the original approach in *Simmenthal SpA v Amministrazione delle Finanze dello Stato* (Case 70/77) [1978] ECR 1453, which was to do 'everything necessary'. The ECJ has more recently held that the principle of indirect effect extends beyond directives and can apply also to a framework decision (*Pupino* C–105/03 [2005] 2 CMLR 63).

The ECJ does seem to have linked the concepts of direct effect and indirect effect as different ways of dealing with the same problem. In *Johnston v Chief Constable of the RUC* (Case 222/84) [1986] ECR 1651 the Court suggested that it was the duty of national courts to interpret national law in conformity with EU law (indirect effect) and only if this was not possible to then enforce EU law in preference to inconsistent national law (direct effect).

The ECJ also confirmed the Marshall jurisprudence in *Dominguez* (Case C–282/10) [2012] 2 CMLR 14, whereby whilst Directives do not have horizontal effect, it is for the national courts to determine whether a Directive could be used by an individual against a private body, particularly if a sympathetic interpretation of national law is not possible in the circumstance.

In *Pfeiffer & Others* (Joined Cases C–397–403/01) [2004] ECR I–8835, the ECJ further added that when interpreting national law in light of EU law, domestic courts should take the whole body of national legislation into consideration and not just the implementing measure – so that domestic courts may select the relevant national legislation to interpret in a way that is consistent with the EU Directive and facilitates the fulfilment of its objectives.

There are limitations to the process. In *Arcaro* (Case C–168/95) [1996] ECR I–4705 the ECJ held that the provisions of an unimplemented Directive cannot be imposed on an individual where to do so would lead to criminal liability. The most important limitation, of course, is that the process is entirely dependent on the willingness of the national courts to use it. As has been seen in *Duke* (1988), the national courts are not always so willing so that there is the possibility of lack of uniformity throughout the EU. Inconsistency indeed has been shown. The House of Lords in *Litster v Forth Dry Dock and Engineering Co* [1989] 1 All ER 1134 had to consider the incompatibility of the then English TUPE law and provisions of the Acquired Rights Directive 77/187. The Court, taking a different approach from that in *Duke* (1988), felt bound to interpret the English Regulations in a way that would give full effect to the Directive.

> the indirect application of EC directives by national courts cannot be guaranteed. This reluctance on the part of the national courts to comply with the *Von Colson* principle, particularly as applied in Marleasing, is hardly surprising. It may be argued that in extending the principle of indirect effect in this way the ECJ is attempting to give horizontal effect to directives by the back door, and impose obligations, addressed to Member States, on private parties, contrary to their understanding of domestic law. Where such is the case, as the House of Lords remarked in *Duke* this could be most unfair.
>
> J Steiner and L Woods, *Textbook on EC Law* (8th edn, Oxford University Press, 2003), p. 109

8.4.3 'Incidental' horizontal effect

In *Faccini Dori v Recreb Srl* (Case C–91/92) [1994] ECR I–3325 Advocate-General Lenz argued that Directives should be capable of horizontal direct effect because of changes in the TEU and also because the fact that they were not meant that individuals were being denied rights that they otherwise might claim legitimately through EU law. However, the ECJ did not follow his argument but instead applied the *Marshall* (1986) criteria in the case.

Three arguments were originally used to deny the horizontal effect of Directives:

- The **lack of legal certainty** – however, now that all Directives are published, the argument cannot apply and it is in fact the lack of horizontal effect and now the main uncertainties are what bodies will be considered public for vertical effect and the circumstances in which national courts will be prepared to impose indirect effect.

- The **estoppel argument**, that since individuals had no control over the implementation of Directives they were not at fault and should not be fixed with fault – however, the widening of the concept of the state in *Foster* in effect means that that is precisely what is happening.
- That to allow horizontal effect to Directives was to **blur the distinction** between Regulations and Directives – this again is not really an argument since, if Member States implemented Directives as national law, there would effectively be no distinction anyway.

One interesting off-shoot of the problems associated with direct effect of Directives has arisen in situations where individuals have tried to exploit the principle of direct effect to establish the illegal nature of the national law rather than to try to enforce any EU rights. The way that such situations have been dealt with has become known as 'incidental' or 'triangular' horizontal effect. Some recent cases stand out and they appear to go against the eventual stance taken in *Dori* and seem to indicate a way in which Directives can indeed be horizontally effective.

The first allowed a party to use a Directive in effect horizontally in a defence against another private party where that party was relying on national law which had not fully followed the Directive.

CASE EXAMPLE

CIA Security International SA v Signalson and Securitel (Case C–194/94) [1996] ECR I–2201

Signalson brought an action against CIA for a breach of Belgian law on unfair trading in the marketing of security products. CIA argued that the Belgian regulations could not be applied because Directive 83/189 required that Member States should obtain clearance from the Commission before introducing such measures and Belgium had not notified the Commission. The ECJ accepted the argument, as a result of which Signalson's action failed. There was no EC (now EU) right being relied on: the Directive was merely being used to disapply national law, hence 'incidental' horizontal effect.

A similar result has been achieved in a contractual dispute where the Directive was merely incidental to proving the breach of contract and had nothing to do with enforcing an EU right.

CASE EXAMPLE

Unilever Italia SpA v Central Food SpA (Case C–443/98) [2000] ECR I–7535

Here, the conflict was over the relevance of different labelling requirements and the question of which requirements should be complied with. Again, Directive 83/189 was involved since Italy had introduced labelling requirements for geographical origin on olive oil. Under the Directive Italy should have notified the Commission of its intention to regulate. The Commission intended to regulate itself Community-wide and so under the Directive Italy should not have introduced the regulation but had done so. Central Food was supplied by Unilever without the labelling required under the Italian regulation and was refusing to pay because the labelling did not conform with Italian law. Unilever argued that the Italian law could not apply since it was in effect in breach of the Directive. The ECJ held that the Italian law could not apply and that this did not conflict with the rules on horizontal direct effect of Directives since the Directive in this case did not involve rights on which individuals might rely.

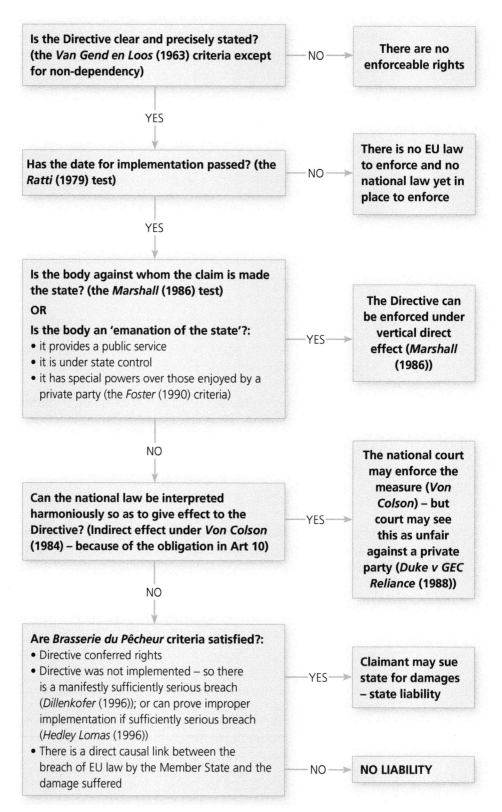

Figure 8.3 The possible means of enforcing rights contained in Directives

The above cases relate to the 'incidental' effect of Directives whereby national law is dis-applied due to a failure by the Member States to meet the measure's procedural or technical requirements – there is creation or application of individual rights through the Directive.

By contrast, the 'triangular' horizontal effect of a Directive implies that a Directive is given effect against the state which has an incidental effect on a third party. In Case C–201/02 *Wells* a company had been granted a mining permission to carry out work in a quarry near the claimant's dwelling. However, contrary to Directive 85/337, no environmental impact assessment (EIA) had been performed prior to the permit being granted. The ECJ allowed the claimant to invoke the Directive against the UK Secretary of State for Transport for its failure carry out an EIA. Whilst the obligation under the Directive was imposed on the UK, the effect of this judgment is that the mining permit could be suspended or revoked. This jurisprudence was confirmed in *Arcor* (Cases C–152 and 154/07) [2008] ECR I–5959.

ACTIVITY

Applying the law

Study the scenarios below and consider how, if at all, the principles of:

- direct effect
- indirect effect

could be applied in the light of the **fictitious** Council Directives.

The Council passed two Directives concerning air levels of two different chemicals, Directive 99/4004 [fictitious] on the chemical CCO1, and Directive 99/5200 [fictitious] on the chemical OTT66, both of which are common in the production of paint. The two Directives were passed after scientific research demonstrated that both chemicals are dangerous if certain levels of the chemicals in the air are exceeded, and also that they are likely to cause respiratory illnesses. Both Directives had an implementation date of 31 August 2004 and set maximum levels of the chemical in the air. An additional requirement of each Directive was compulsory testing for the chemical and allied industries.

1. The UK government has not yet implemented Directive 99/4004. A paint manufacturer, Coverall, uses CCO1 extensively in its paint production. Residents living near to the factory have commissioned a survey of the air around the plant which has revealed levels of CCO1 in the air that are well beyond those identified in the Directive. Several local residents have recently developed asthmatic complaints.

   Suggest whether the residents can rely on Directive 99/4004 against either Coverall or the UK government.

2. The UK did implement Directive 99/5200 within the time limit but in its legislation did not provide for compulsory testing as required in the Directive. Lawyers representing the residents above believe the lack of testing has allowed Coverall to adopt dangerous practices and that these have led to leaks of OTT66 into the atmosphere, causing higher levels of the chemical than if proper scrutiny had occurred.

   Advise the lawyers as to whether the residents are able to use Directive 99/5200 in a claim against the UK government.

ACTIVITY

Self-assessment questions

1. What were the original problems of allowing direct effect of Directives?
2. Why did the ECJ feel in *Van Duyn* (1974) that Directives should be enforceable through direct effect?
3. How did the ECJ overcome this problem?
4. What are the major effects of the decision in *Marshall (No 1)* (1986)?
5. What impact does the test in *Foster v British Gas* (1990) have on the principle of direct effect?
6. What shortcomings are there in using vertical direct effect as a means of enforcing Directives?
7. How does the principle in *Von Colson* (1984) assist individuals to enforce rights that are granted them by EU law?
8. How effective is the *Von Colson* (1984) principle?
9. In what ways does the case of *Marleasing* (1990) extend the principle in *Von Colson* (1984)?

KEY FACTS

Direct applicability
Direct applicability: • the measure becomes part of national law without need for further enactment; • it applies to Regulations but not to Directives because Directives require implementation by Member States.

Direct effect	
• Accepted that certain measures should be enforceable by citizens of Member States – if they were clear, precise and unconditional, and conferred rights on individuals. • Not all provisions do conform to the criteria. • This is straightforward in the case of substantive Treaty Articles. • And in the case of Regulations. • And even in the case of Decisions. • But not for Directives which are not a complete legal instrument. • Direct effect can be vertical (against the state) or horizontal (against another citizen).	*Van Gend en Loos v Nederlands Administratie der Belastingen* (1963) *Casati* (1981) *Reyners v Belgium* (1974) *Leonesio v Ministero dell'Agricoltora & delle Foreste* (1972) *Grad v Finanzamt Traustein* (1970) *Defrenne v SABENA* (1976)

Direct effect of Directives	
• Recognised that it would be incompatible with the binding nature of a Directive in Art 288 if they could not be enforced. • So can be directly effective if date for implementation passed. • But only 'vertically' against the state itself. • Or an 'emanation of the state' – must provide public service, be under control of state, have powers over and above those of private bodies. • Creates unfair anomalies when claim is against private party.	*Van Duyn v Home Office* (1974) *Pubblico Ministero v Ratti* (1979) *Marshall v Southampton and SW Hants AHA (No 1)* (1986) *Foster v British Gas plc* (1990) *Duke v GEC Reliance* (1988)

Indirect effect	
• Since Member States have obligation formerly under Art 10 to give full effect to EU law then national court should interpret improperly implemented Directive to give effect to its objectives. • Applies whether national law concerned pre-dates or post-dates the Directive. • But inconsistent approach taken by national courts – so unpredictable.	*Von Colson and Kamann v Land Nordrhein-Westfalen* (1984); *Harz v Deutsche Tradax* (1984) *Marleasing SA v La Commercial Internacional de Alimentacion* (1990) Compare *Litster v Forth Dock & Engineering* (1989) with *Duke* (1988)

SAMPLE ESSAY QUESTION

'Discuss the ways in which the European Court of Justice has been instrumental in ensuring that EU citizens have been able to enforce rights given to them by directives.'

Define Directives:
- binding as to the result to be achieved – so left to Member States to implement in their own way within a defined period
- so not automatically incorporated into national law or directly enforceable

Define direct effect:
- the criteria from *Van Gend en Loos*
- the measure must be clear, precise and unconditional

Discuss the problem of enforcing Directives:
- that they are not unconditional
- but ECJ in *Van Duyn* recognised that it would be incompatible with the binding nature of Article 288 if they were unenforceable

Discuss how direct effect can apply to Directives:
- date for implementation must have passed before they are enforceable
- the principle in *Marshall* that Directives can never be horizontally directly effective (against other citizens) but can be vertically directly effective (against the state)

Discuss the problems this created and how the ECJ overcame them:

- no horizontal direct effect – so not enforceable against a private body
- ECJ extended vertical effect to emanations of the state where *Foster* test applied
- indirect effect – sympathetic interpretation where there was partial implementation
- if no remedy then state liability if test in *Factortame III/Brasserie du Pêcheur* satisfied (see Chapter 9)

SUMMARY

- Direct effect and indirect effect and state liability are all devices created by the Court of Justice to ensure effective enforcement of the Treaties.

- Direct effect means the measure can be enforced and the Court of Justice has established a test of direct effect – the measure is clear, precise and unconditional.

- Direct effect can be both horizontal, the measure is enforceable against other citizens of the EU, or vertical, the measure is enforceable against the state or an emanation of the state.

- A problem arises in the case of unimplemented directives because directives are conditional on implementation by Member States – so the Court of Justice also created indirect effect, a means by which the national court can use the basic obligation of Member States to uphold EU law to sympathetically interpret the defective national law to incorporate the EU measure.

Further reading

Articles

Albors-Llorens, A, 'The Direct Effect of EU Directives: Fresh Controversy or a Storm in a Teacup? Comment on *Portgas*' (2014) 39 *EL Rev* 851.

Dougan, M, 'When Worlds Collide: Competing Visions of the Relationship Between Direct Effect and Supremacy' (2007) 44 *CML Rev* 931.

Drake, S, 'Twenty Years After *Von Colson*: The Impact of "Indirect Effect" on the Protection of the Individual's Community Rights' (2005) 30 *EL Rev* 329.

Mancini, F, 'The Making of a Constitution for Europe' (1989) 26 *CML Rev* 595.

Prechal, S, 'Does Direct Effect Matter?' (2000) 37 *CML Rev* 1047.

Books

Kaczarowska-Ireland, A, *European Union Law* (Routledge, 2016), Chapters 10 and 11.

9

State liability

AIMS AND OBJECTIVES

After reading this chapter you should be able to:

- Understand the basis of, and conditions necessary to establish, state liability
- Understand, in particular, the 'factors' used to determine whether a Member State has committed a 'sufficiently serious' breach
- Understand what is meant by the 'state' in this context
- Understand the principles which apply when determining the amount of compensation payable
- Analyse critically the law on state liability
- Apply the law on state liability to factual situations involving a Member State's failure to comply with its obligations under EU law

9.1 Introduction

As we have seen in Chapter 8, both direct effect (in particular, the lack of horizontal direct effect of Directives) and indirect effect have limitations and leave situations where a party could be without a remedy because of the failure of a Member State to implement a Directive or because of improper implementation. The ECJ devised a third way of avoiding the problems identified in Chapter 8 – this is state liability.

State liability for breaches of EU law was introduced in *Francovich & Bonifaci v Italy* (Cases C–6/90 and C–9/90) [1991] ECR I–5357, when the ECJ declared that the Member States were 'obliged' to compensate individuals for loss and damage caused to them by breaches of EU law. The Court stated:

JUDGMENT

'The Member States are obliged to make good loss and damage caused to individuals by breaches of [EU law] for which they can be held responsible.... The conditions under which that liability gives rise to a right to reparation depend on the nature of the breach of [EU law] giving rise to the loss and damage.'

CASE EXAMPLE

Francovich & Bonifaci v Italy (Cases C–6, 9/90) [1991] ECR I–5357

Andrea Francovich and Danila Bonifaci were both owed large amounts of back pay after their employers went into insolvency. The men brought an action against the Italian state for compensation. Under Directive 80/987, which aimed to protect workers' wages after their employer went into insolvency, Member States were required to ensure that payment of wages was guaranteed. However, the Italian government had not implemented the Directive before the implementation date, October 1983. The case was referred to the ECJ, which held that the complainants were entitled to compensation for losses incurred as a result of the state's failure to implement the Directive.

There is nothing *explicitly* in either of the Treaties to support the imposition of liability on Member States, but the Court justified its decision by finding that it was stated *implicitly*, in what is now Article 4(3) of the TEU, according to which Member States have an obligation to ensure the fulfilment of their obligations arising under the Treaties.

9.2 The conditions for state liability

Francovich & Bonifaci (1991) was concerned specifically with the failure of the Italian government to implement a Directive. The obligation imposed on states to implement Directives is clear (see Article 4(3) TEU and Article 288 TFEU). However, two issues remained unclear:

- what the position might be in relation to other breaches; and
- the level of fault required to establish liability.

The ECJ addressed these issues in *Brasserie du Pêcheur SA v Germany; Factortame III* (Cases C–46 and 48/93) [1996] ECR I–1029. The Court made it clear that state liability was a general principle, not restricted to a failure to implement Directives, and that three conditions had to be satisfied:

1. the rule of EU law infringed must have been intended to confer rights on individuals;
2. the breach must be sufficiently serious; and
3. there must be a direct causal link between the breach of the obligation resting on the state and the damage sustained by the injured parties.

The burden of proof is on the claimant to establish all three conditions. State liability claims are brought in the national court of the defendant state.

CASE EXAMPLE

Brasserie du Pêcheur v Germany; Factortame III (Cases C–46, C–48/93) [1996] ECR I–1029

In the first case, Brasserie, a brewery based in France, brought a test case against the German government claiming compensation for losses allegedly incurred as a result of being unable to sell beer in Germany between 1981 and 1987. The action followed the decision in *Commission v Germany (Beer Purity)* (Case 178/84) [1987] ECR 1227 that Germany's beer purity law (specifically the *Biersteuergesetz* of 1952, although the law could be traced back to the *Reinheitsgebot* of 1516) was in breach of Article 34 TFEU (see Chapter 14). The law provided, *inter alia*, that 'bottom-fermented' beers may be manufactured only from malted barley, hops, yeast and water. It was alleged that this restricted trade in beer between France (where much less stringent rules applied) and Germany.

In the second case, Factortame Ltd and several other Spanish-owned but British-registered fishing companies comprising the 'Anglo-Spanish' fishing fleet brought actions for damages against the UK government. This followed the ECJ's decision in *Factortame II* (Case C–221/89) [1991] ECR I–3905 that the UK's Merchant Shipping Act 1988 infringed the companies' directly effective rights under EU law, in particular their freedom of establishment under Article 49 TFEU (see Chapter 13). It was alleged that the Act prevented the companies from exercising fishing rights in UK territorial waters causing them financial losses.

The ECJ laid down the three conditions for establishing state liability (set out above). On condition (1), the Court held that both Articles 34 and 49 TFEU were intended to confer rights on individuals. The Court stated that condition (2) was, in principle, a matter for national courts, whilst condition (3) was exclusively a matter for the national courts. In determining the extent of the compensation payment (in the event that state liability was proven), national rules on recovery of damages (remoteness, mitigation, etc.) would apply. The two cases were returned to their respective national courts to apply conditions (2) and (3).

9.2.1 Condition (1): An intention to confer rights on individuals

There is a strong link here to direct effect. The case of *Köbler v Austria* (Case C–224/01) [2003] ECR I–10239, concerned an alleged breach of Article 45(2) TFEU (the right of migrant workers to work without discrimination on grounds of nationality – see Chapter 12). As A-G Léger noted in that case: 'The rule of law purportedly infringed ... is directly effective and its purpose is therefore *necessarily* to confer rights on individuals' (emphasis added). Condition (1) has been held to be satisfied in the case of several directly effective Treaty articles, including Articles 34 and 35 TFEU (the free movement of goods – see Chapter 14) and Articles 49 and 56 TFEU (the right of companies and self-employed people to 'establish' themselves in another Member State, or to provide services to someone from another Member State – see Chapter 13). A table at the end of this chapter summarises some of the provisions of EU law which have been held to satisfy the first condition of state liability.

If the first condition is satisfied, the focus shifts to the second condition; but if not then the claim fails. This happened in *Paul & Others v Germany* (Case C–222/02) [2004] ECR I–9425, where the ECJ decided that Article 3(1) of Directive 94/19 was not intended to confer rights on individuals. In *Berlington & Others v Hungary* (Case C–98/14) [2015] 3 CMLR 45, the ECJ held that whilst Article 56 TFEU (the freedom to provide services) was intended to confer rights on individuals, Directive 98/34 did not do so.

9.2.2 Condition (2): A sufficiently serious breach

The test for determining the second condition, a 'sufficiently serious' breach, is whether the Member State 'manifestly and gravely disregarded the limits on its discretion' (*Brasserie; Factortame III* (1996)). In two situations, a breach will be deemed automatically to have been serious. The first situation is when a Member State fails to take any measures to implement a Directive. In *Dillenkofer & Others v Germany* (Case C–178/94) [1996] ECR I–4845, the Court stated (emphasis added):

JUDGMENT

'Failure to take *any* measure to transpose a directive in order to achieve the result it prescribes within the period laid down for that purpose constitutes *per se* a serious breach of EU law.'

CASE EXAMPLE

Dillenkofer & Others v Germany (Case C–178/94) [1996] ECR I–4845

Directive 90/134 (the Package Travel Directive) was supposed to be implemented by 31 December 1992. Article 7 provides that the 'organiser and/or retailer party to the contract shall provide sufficient evidence of security for the refund of money paid over and for the repatriation of the consumer in the event of insolvency'. The German authorities did not implement the directive until July 1994.

In 1993, two German package tour operators went into insolvency. As a result, the various claimants (including Erich Dillenkofer) either lost their holidays (which they had already paid for) or were already on holiday and had to pay for flights to return to Germany. Being unable to obtain compensation from the operators, the claimants sued the German government, alleging that, had the authorities acted sooner, the tour operators would have been under an obligation to have sufficient security (e.g. through insurance) to pay for refunds and/or repatriation. The German government argued that it was late implementing the directive because it had needed more time to consult with bodies affected by the directive.

The ECJ held that Article 7 of the directive was intended to confer rights on individuals. The failure to implement the directive on time amounted to an automatically serious breach of EU law giving rise to a right in damages, subject to proof of causation.

The second situation is when the Member State defies clear ECJ case law. For example, in *Fuß v Stadt Halle* (Case C–429/09) [2010] ECR I-12167, the ECJ pointed out that employment conditions imposed on fire-fighters in the German city of Halle were not only contrary to Directive 2003/88 (the Working Time Directive – see Chapter 17) but at least three earlier ECJ decisions. Unsurprisingly, this was held to be a serious breach of EU law. The Court stated that (emphasis added):

JUDGMENT

'An infringement of EU law *will be* sufficiently serious where the decision concerned was made in manifest breach of the case law of the Court in the matter.'

CASE EXAMPLE

Fuß v Stadt Halle (Case C–429/09) [2010] ECR I–12167

Günter Fuß was a fire-engine driver in Halle, Germany. Under his contract of employment, he was rostered to work 54 hours per week on average. Much of this time was on 'stand-by', when Günter was not actually carrying out any tasks, but he was required to be present at the fire station in readiness for an emergency. He nevertheless argued that his working hours took him over the maximum stipulated in Directive 2003/88, which specifies a maximum working week of 48 hours on average. Günter claimed compensation (in the form of backdated overtime pay) for the hours he had worked in breach of the directive up to that date.

The ECJ held that the directive was intended to confer rights on individuals and that the imposition of a 54-hour working week was seriously in breach of it. In reaching that conclusion, the Court pointed out that in several earlier ECJ judgments dating back to 2000, 'stand-by' time had already been clearly established as 'working time'. The question of a direct causal link was a matter for the German courts.

In principle it is for the national courts to decide whether or not a breach of EU law was 'sufficiently serious'. However, the ECJ has identified various factors which may be used, as follows:

- the clarity and precision of the rule breached;
- the measure of discretion left by that rule;
- whether the infringement and the damage caused was intentional or involuntary;
- if there was an error of law, whether the error was excusable or not;
- whether the position taken by one of the Union's institutions may have contributed towards the adoption or retention of national measures or practices contrary to EU law.

Clarity and precision

Many state liability cases involve the failure to properly implement a Directive. Such breaches may or may not be sufficiently serious; it often depends on the clarity of the wording in the Directive. In *BT* (Case C–392/93) [1996] ECR I–1631 and *Denkavit International v Germany* (Case C–283/94) [1996] ECR I–5063, the failures by (respectively) the UK and Germany were held *not* to be serious, largely because the text of the Directives lacked clarity or precision. Moreover, both states had acted in good faith in trying to implement the Directive correctly (suggesting the breach was also excusable).

CASE EXAMPLE

BT (Case C–392/93) [1996] ECR I–1631

The UK implemented Directive 90/531 *via* the Utilities Supplies & Works Contracts Regulations 1992. BT alleged that the transposition had been made incorrectly, and brought a claim for damages for the expense incurred in complying with the Regulations and the damage it suffered as a result of being put at a commercial and competitive disadvantage. The ECJ held that the directive had not been implemented correctly by the UK government, but denied the claim for damages, because the breach was not sufficiently serious. There were various reasons:

- Article 8(1) of the Directive, on which the offending part of the 1992 Regulations was based, was imprecisely worded, and reasonably capable of bearing the meaning given to it by the UK (indeed, several other Member States had also misinterpreted the directive);
- the UK had acted in good faith;
- no guidance was available from ECJ case law as to the correct interpretation of the Article;
- the Commission had not raised any objections when the 1992 Regulations were adopted and notified to it.

Conversely, in *Rechberger & Others v Austria* (Case C–140/97) [1999] ECR I–3499 and *Stockholm Lindöpark v Sweden* (Case C–150/99) [2001] ECR I–493, incorrect implementation was deemed to be serious, because in both cases the relevant Directives were clearly worded (also suggesting that the breach was inexcusable).

Discretion

Where a Member State has broad discretion under EU law, it will be more difficult to prove that a breach has occurred at all, let alone that it was a serious breach. For example, in *Schmidberger v Austria* (Case C–112/00) [2003] ECR I–5659, it was alleged by the claimant, a German road haulage firm, that the Austrian government had seriously breached

Article 34 and/or 35 TFEU by authorising a road closure in order to allow an environmental demonstration to take place. The ECJ rejected the allegation, noting that the Austrian government had to be given a 'wide margin of discretion', given the need to balance competing (if not contradictory) interests: the need to protect the fundamental rights of the protestors to exercise their right to free speech (on one hand) and the economic rights of the claimants to import and export goods across international borders (on the other). The Court held (emphasis added):

JUDGMENT

'Having regard to the *wide margin of discretion* which must be accorded to them in the matter, the national authorities were therefore reasonably entitled to conclude that the legitimate objective pursued by that demonstration could not be achieved by measures less restrictive of trade.... Consequently, the Austrian authorities cannot be said to have committed a breach of [EU law] such as to give rise to liability.'

Conversely, a lack of discretion is much more likely to lead to a conclusion that the breach was sufficiently serious. For example, the breach of Article 35 TFEU by the UK in *Hedley Lomas* (Case C–5/94) [1996] ECR I–2553 was deemed to be serious because of the lack of discretion available. In that case, the Court stated (emphasis added):

JUDGMENT

'Where, at the time when it committed the infringement, the Member State in question was not called upon to make any legislative choices and had only *considerably reduced, or even no, discretion*, the mere infringement of [EU law] may be sufficient to establish the existence of a sufficiently serious breach.'

CASE EXAMPLE

Hedley Lomas (Case C–5/94) [1996] ECR I–2553

Between April 1990 and January 1993 the UK's Ministry of Agriculture, Fisheries and Food (MAFF) systematically refused to issue licences for the export to Spain of live animals intended for slaughter. This was because the MAFF was convinced that a number of Spanish slaughterhouses were not complying with an EU animal welfare directive on the stunning of animals prior to slaughter, either because they did not have the necessary equipment, or because the equipment was not being used correctly or at all. Although the MAFF had insufficient evidence as to the overall position in Spanish slaughterhouses, it believed the level of non-compliance with the directive justified a general ban on export licences. Hedley Lomas, a British company, were refused an export licence for live sheep in 1992, even though the firm had information that the particular slaughterhouse for which the sheep were intended was complying with all the relevant directives on animal welfare. Hedley Lomas brought an action alleging that the refusal to issue the licence was contrary to Article 35 TFEU (the right to export goods – see Chapter 14). MAFF argued that it was justified under Article 36 TFEU on grounds of protection of animal health. The ECJ held that recourse to Article 36 TFEU was not possible where harmonising directives necessary to achieve the same objective were already in place. Member States had to trust each other to carry out inspections in their respective territories. Consequently, the actions of the MAFF constituted a serious breach of Article 35 TFEU.

A similar outcome was seen in *Rechberger & Others v Austria* (1999). In this case, the Austrian government had unilaterally postponed the implementation date of Directive 90/134 (the Package Travel Directive), specifically Article 7 of it, something which is not permitted under any circumstances. This allegedly caused the claimants financial loss. The ECJ held that the breach was sufficiently serious, essentially because of the lack of discretion:

JUDGMENT

'Austria enjoyed *no margin of discretion* as to the entry into force, in its own law, of the provisions of Article 7. That being so, the limitation of the protection prescribed by Article 7 is manifestly incompatible with the obligations under the directive and thus constitutes a sufficiently serious breach of [EU law].'

There is often a correlation between the clarity of the rule breached and a (lack of) discretion. For example, in *Stockholm Lindöpark v Sweden* (2001), the rule of EU law breached – the Sixth VAT Directive – was clearly worded (suggesting a serious breach). Moreover, the clarity of the rule breached also meant that the Swedish government lacked discretion (confirming the seriousness of the breach). The Court held that 'Given the clear wording of the Sixth Directive, [Sweden] was *not in a position to make any legislative choices*' (emphasis added).

Intentional breach
The third factor involves asking whether or not the breach was intentional (which makes it more likely to be serious). For example, in *Factortame III* [1999] 3 WLR 1062, when the case was returned to the House of Lords from the ECJ, the House ultimately held that the breach of Article 49 TFEU by the UK was serious because the government had intentionally breached the provision in question. Lord Slynn stated (emphasis added):

JUDGMENT

'It seems to me clear that the *deliberate* adoption of legislation which was *clearly discriminatory* on the ground of nationality and which inevitably violated [Article 49 TFEU] … was a *manifest* breach of fundamental Treaty obligations. It was a *grave* breach of the Treaty both intrinsically and as regards the consequences it was bound, or at the least was most likely, to have on the respondents. It has not been shown to have been excusable.'

By way of contrast, in *Negassi v Home Secretary* [2013] EWCA Civ 151; [2013] 2 CMLR 45, the Court of Appeal held that the UK government's failure to properly implement Directive 2003/9 was insufficiently serious. One of the reasons for this decision by the Court was the lack of intent on the part of the government. Kay LJ said (emphasis added):

JUDGMENT

'The evaluation of the seriousness of the breach in the present case seems to me to be quite finely balanced. I have come to the conclusion that the breach was *not* of sufficient seriousness to satisfy the test. It was *not deliberate*. It was the result of a misunderstanding of new provisions in an area of recent EU concern. It was *not a cynical or egregious misunderstanding*.'

Excusable breach

The fourth factor is whether or not the breach was excusable. In several of the cases discussed above, the Member States had acted in good faith which suggested that any breach was excusable (*BT, Denkavit*). The breach of Article 34 TFEU by the German government in *Brasserie du Pêcheur* was ultimately deemed to be insufficiently serious because it was an excusable error (see the decision of the German Federal Court of Justice in *Brasserie du Pêcheur v Germany (No.2)* [1997] 1 CMLR 971).

Involvement of an EU Institution

This final factor is rarely invoked, but it can be important. In *BT* (1996), one of the reasons given for rejecting the claim was the involvement (or lack thereof) of the European Commission. The UK government had drafted its implementing legislation which was sent to the Commission, but no response was forthcoming. Had the Commission responded and pointed out the error, the implementing legislation could have been amended and the litigation avoided entirely.

9.2.3 Condition (3): Direct causal link

As to the third condition, the ECJ has held that it is, generally speaking, for the national courts to determine whether a direct causal link between breach and damage exists (*Rechberger & Others* (1999)). In *Leth & Others v Austria* (Case C–420/11) [2013] 3 CMLR 2, the Court stated:

JUDGMENT

'The existence of a direct causal link between the breach in question and the damage sustained by the individuals is, in addition to the determination that the breach of EU law is sufficiently serious, an indispensable condition governing the right to compensation. The existence of that direct causal link is a matter for the national courts to ascertain.'

9.3 What is the 'state'?

Most state liability cases involve actions against central government. In the UK, the vast majority of state liability actions have been brought against central government, including the cases (mentioned above) of *Factortame III, Hedley Lomas* and *BT*. Usually a specific government Minister is named, as in *Negassi v Home Secretary* [2013] EWCA Civ 151, [2013] 2 CMLR 45; *Delaney v Secretary of State for Transport* [2014] EWHC 1785, [2014] 3 CMLR 32 and *Recall Support Services Ltd & Others v Secretary of State for Culture, Media & Sport* [2014] EWCA Civ 1370, [2015] 1 CMLR 38. This is also the case when state liability claims are brought in the Republic of Ireland (see *Ogieriakhi v Minister for Justice & Equality & Others (No.2)* [2015] 3 CMLR 18).

However, state liability actions can be brought against other bodies. In *Berlington & Others* (2015), the ECJ held that the 'principle of Member State liability is applicable, *inter alia*, where the national legislature was responsible for the infringement'. In *Konle v Austria* (Case C–302/97) [1999] ECR I–3099 the ECJ decided that compensation need not necessarily be the responsibility of central government, and that state liability claims could instead be brought against regional government. The Court stated:

JUDGMENT

'In Member States with a federal structure, reparation for damage caused to individuals by national measures taken in breach of [EU] law need not necessarily be provided by the federal State.'

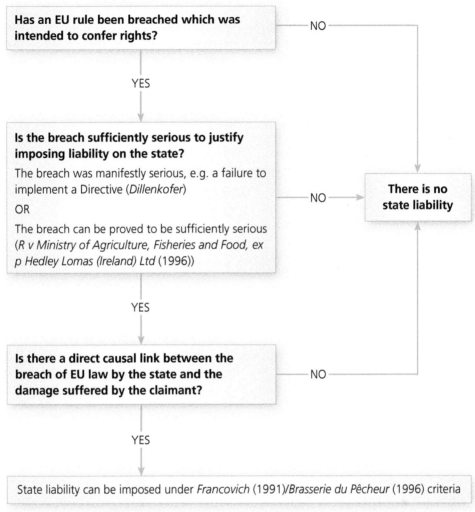

Figure 9.1 The criteria to establish state liability under *Brasserie du Pêcheur* (1996)

CASE EXAMPLE

Konle v Austria (Case C–302/97) [1999] ECR I–3099

Klaus Konle, a German national, acquired a plot of land in the mountainous Tyrol region of western Austria. Subsequently, his application to have his ownership authorised was rejected on the basis of Tyrol (i.e. regional government) legislation stipulating that land must not be used for a second residence. Although Konle claimed to have the intention of making Tyrol his primary residence, this was not accepted. Konle challenged this, alleging a breach of Article 63 TFEU (the free movement of capital – see Chapter 10), and seeking compensation. The Austrian government responded that authorisation was essential to control development in Tyrol, where only a very small amount of land could be built upon. The ECJ held that the requirement that property acquisitions had to be authorised was a breach of Article 63. Although justifiable in theory, it went beyond what was necessary. The ECJ left the question of whether this particular breach was sufficiently serious to be decided by the national courts. The Court also held that, in Member States with a federal structure, which included Austria and Germany, compensation for serious breaches of EU law did not necessarily have to be paid for by the federal government.

This is very significant as it means claimants can pursue state liability actions against regional or local governments, rather than central governments, when it is the former who are responsible for the breach in question. The proposition that regional or local authorities can be held liable extends beyond countries with a federal structure. For example, in *Combinatie & Others* (Case C568/08) [2010] ECR I–12655, a state liability case was brought against the province of Drenthe, in the north-eastern Netherlands, rather than the Dutch government. In *Barco De Vapor* [2014] EWHC 490 (the facts of which were markedly similar to those in *Hedley Lomas* (1996)), state liability was imposed on Thanet District Council in Kent. In *Haim* (Case C–424/97) [2000] ECR I-5123, the ECJ stated that state liability claims could be brought irrespective of the 'public authority ... responsible for the breach'. The Court held that (emphasis added):

JUDGMENT

'It is for each Member State to ensure that individuals obtain reparation for loss and damage caused to them by non-compliance with [EU law], *whichever public authority is responsible for the breach and whichever public authority is in principle, under the law of the Member State concerned, responsible for making reparation.* Member States cannot, therefore, escape that liability either by pleading the internal distribution of powers and responsibilities as between the bodies which exist within their national legal order or by claiming that the public authority responsible for the breach of [EU law] did not have the necessary powers, knowledge, means or resources ... there is nothing to suggest that reparation for loss and damage caused to individuals by national measures taken in breach of [EU law] must necessarily be provided by the Member State itself.'

This is intriguing but arguably begs more questions than it answers – in particular, what exactly is the meaning and scope to be given to the phrase 'pubic authority' here? In *Haim* itself, the defendant body was the Association of Dental Practitioners in the Nordrhein region of Germany. This demonstrates that professional, regulatory bodies (at least) are included in the concept of 'public authority'.

Even breaches of EU law by the judiciary may be lead to the imposition of state liability, according to the ECJ in *Köbler v Austria* (2003). Although the claim in that case (involving an alleged breach of EU law by the Austrian Supreme Administrative Court) failed, the ECJ expressly ruled that national courts 'adjudicating at last instance' could face liability albeit that such a case would have to be 'exceptional'. The Court stated (emphasis added):

JUDGMENT

'In order to determine whether the infringement is sufficiently serious when the infringement at issue stems from a decision of a national court adjudicating at last instance, the competent national court, *taking into account the specific nature of the judicial function*, must determine whether that court has manifestly infringed the applicable law. State liability can be incurred only *in the exceptional case* where the national court has manifestly infringed the applicable law and the Court's case-law in the matter.'

CASE EXAMPLE

Köbler v Austria (Case C–224/01) [2003] ECR I–10239

Gerhard Köbler, an Austrian national, had worked as a professor in various German universities but since 1986, he had been employed at Innsbruck University in Austria. In 1996, he applied for a special 15-year-service increment for professors available under Austrian law. However, this was rejected because the legislation only referred to service conducted in Austrian universities. He brought a challenge in the Austrian courts claiming a breach of Article 45(2) TFEU (see Chapter 12) on the basis that the Austrian legislation was (indirectly) discriminatory on grounds of nationality. The Austrian Supreme Administrative Court (VWG) referred the case to the ECJ. The Court responded that, as it had recently given judgment in *Schöning-Kougebetopoulou* (Case C–15/96) [1998] ECR I–47, on virtually identical facts, the VWG may want to withdraw its request. (The clear implication was that Köbler's claim would be decided successfully.) The preliminary ruling request was withdrawn but, in giving judgment, the VWG found that the increment was a 'loyalty bonus' justifying derogation from Article 45 TFEU, and rejected Köbler's claim. Subsequently, Köbler brought an action for damages against Austria, alleging that the VWG had committed a serious breach of EU law. The ECJ held that there was no reason why a state liability claim could not be brought following a breach of EU law by a national court adjudicating at last instance. The 'essential role' played by the judiciary in the protection of individuals' EU rights would be weakened if those individuals were unable, 'under certain conditions', to obtain reparation for damage caused by an infringement of EU law attributable to such a court. Ultimately, the ECJ ruled that, although the VWG's ruling was wrong and hence there was a breach of EU law, specifically Article 45(2) TFEU, it was not manifestly wrong (i.e. the breach was not 'sufficiently serious') and so Köbler was not entitled to damages.

This was confirmed in *Traghetti del Mediterraneo v Italy* (Case C–173/03) [2006] ECR I–5177, involving a claim against the Italian Supreme Court. However, the ECJ stressed that 'State liability can be incurred only in the exceptional case where the national court adjudicating at last instance has manifestly infringed the applicable law'. More recently, in *Ferreira da Silva e Brito & Others v Portugal* (Case C–160/14), [2016] 1 CMLR 26, the ECJ held that the non-referral of a question to the Court of Justice under the preliminary rulings procedure by the Portuguese Supreme Court could attract state liability. The Court of Justice pointed out that, in cases such as the present case, which was 'characterised both by conflicting lines of case-law at national level' and by the fact that the provision of EU legislation in question (Directive 2001/23) 'frequently gives rise to difficulties of interpretation in the various Member States', a national court of last resort 'must comply with its obligation to make a reference to the Court'.

This development had been predicted by Joxerramon Bengoetxea, 'Text and Telos in the European Court of Justice' (2015) 11 *ECL Rev* 184, who wrote that 'I would not exclude the possibility of the *Köbler* (or *Traghetti*) jurisprudence being applied to a stubborn national court of last instance abusively declaring *acte clair* in situations that should have been submitted for preliminary ruling'.

The decision in *Köbler* (2003) creates the possibility that a state liability claim brought against a national court could end up being decided in the same court. This actually happened in *Cooper v Attorney General* [2010] EWCA Civ 464, [2010] 3 CMLR 28, when a state liability claim brought against the Court of Appeal had to be decided by the Court of Appeal. The claimant contended that two earlier Court of Appeal decisions (in 1999 and 2000) were in serious breach of EU law. The claim was brought in the High Court, and judgment was given to the defendants, but that decision was appealed. The Court of Appeal (in 2010) decided that the earlier Courts had committed a breach of EU law, but not a *sufficiently serious* breach to justify the imposition of state liability. (NB in the 1999 and 2000 cases, the Court of Appeal had been 'adjudicating at last instance' because no appeal was available to the House of Lords.)

Finally, in *AGM v Finland* (Case C–470/03) [2007] ECR I–2749 the ECJ introduced a form of vicarious liability when it stated that EU law 'does not preclude an individual other than a Member State from being held liable, in addition to the Member State itself, for damage caused to individuals by measures which that individual has taken' in breach of EU law. Thus liability could, in principle, be imposed on a Member State for breaches of EU law made by individual government employees.

9.4 Limitations on the recovery of compensation

Member States are allowed to impose conditions on the amount of damages that the claimant can recover in state liability claims. However, any such conditions must not be less favourable than those relating to similar domestic claims (the 'principle of equivalence') or framed in such a way as to make it in practice 'impossible or excessively difficult' to obtain reparation (the 'principle of effectiveness'). These principles were held to be applicable in state liability cases by the ECJ in *Brasserie/Factortame III* (1996) in which the Court stated:

JUDGMENT

'It is for the domestic legal system of each Member State to set the criteria for determining the extent of reparation. However, those criteria must not be less favourable than those applying to similar claims based on domestic law and must not be such as in practice to make it impossible or excessively difficult to obtain reparation.'

9.4.1 The principle of equivalence

This 'principle' means that national rules on the recovery of damages via civil litigation are deemed to be also applicable in state liability actions. One question that arose in the *Factortame III* case was whether 'exemplary' (or 'punitive') damages were available in state liability. The ECJ answered yes, provided that such damages were available in the Member State in domestic civil litigation cases. The Court stated:

JUDGMENT

'[In English law] exemplary damages are based … on the finding that the public authorities concerned acted oppressively, arbitrarily or unconstitutionally. Insofar as such conduct may constitute or aggravate a breach of [EU law], an award of exemplary damages pursuant to a claim or an action founded on [EU law] cannot be ruled out.'

This was applied by the High Court in *Santos v Home Secretary* [2016] EWHC 609. Having found that the defendant, the UK Home Secretary (which at the time of the case was the UK's future Prime Minister, Theresa May), had committed a serious breach of EU law, Lang J had to decide whether to award exemplary damages. He said:

JUDGMENT

> 'Exemplary damages are, in principle, available for a breach of EU law and, in my judgment, this is a case in which the defendant has behaved in an outrageous, oppressive and unconstitutional manner.... There was a sustained and deliberate refusal to give effect to the claimant's EU rights, over several years, during which time the defendant displayed a blatant disregard for the law.... I award £25,000 by way of exemplary damages.'

Another example of the principle of equivalence is limitation periods (a period of time during which a claimant is required to bring civil litigation, after which their case becomes time-barred). National limitation periods are applied in state liability cases – subject to one proviso: they must be 'reasonable'. In *Danske Slagterier v Germany* (Case C–445/06) [2009] ECR I–2119, the ECJ stated that reasonable time limits for bringing proceedings were justifiable 'in the interests of legal certainty which protects both the taxpayer and the authorities concerned'.

9.4.2 The principle of effectiveness

This 'principle' means that any procedural rule of domestic civil litigation is deemed to be inapplicable in state liability cases where it would make the recovery of damages 'impossible or excessively difficult'. Another issue in the *Factortame III* case was whether damages for 'pure' economic loss were recoverable against the UK. In domestic English civil litigation, there is a rule that such damages are not normally available. The principle of equivalence (above) states that this rule should be applied in state liability cases against the UK. However, doing so would render it practically 'impossible' for claimants in such cases – most of whom are seeking 'pure' economic loss, typically loss of profits – to get any compensation. Therefore, the principle of effectiveness applies here to render the English rule inapplicable. In *Brasserie/Factortame III* (1996), the Court stated:

JUDGMENT

> 'Total exclusion of loss of profit as a head of damage ... cannot be accepted. Especially in the context of economic or commercial litigation, such a total exclusion ... would be such as to make reparation of damage practically impossible.'

Another potential obstacle to the recovery of damages in state liability claims is the rule of 'res judicata' (literally: let the judgment rest), which is a typical feature of domestic civil litigation. In essence, it means that once a case has been litigated, and judgment given, the issue should not be endlessly re-litigated. This is important in the interests of legal certainty, but is potentially problematic if a claimant in a state liability action has already brought an action in domestic civil litigation (and hence there is now a judgment on the matter). Is it possible to bring a state liability action despite *res judicata*? The answer is yes – because of the principle of effectiveness. In *Ferreira da Silva e Brito & Others v Portugal* (2016), the Court stated (emphasis added):

Table of EU law provisions found to satisfy the first condition of State Liability: an intention to confer rights on individuals

EU law provision	Right conferred on individuals	Case(s)
Article 34 TFEU	To import goods from other Member States	*Brasserie du Pêcheur v Germany (1996); Schmidberger v Austria (2003); Danske Slagterier v Germany (2009)*
Article 35 TFEU	To export goods to other Member States	*Hedley Lomas (1996); Barco De Vapor (2014)*
Article 45(2) TFEU	To work in another Member State without discrimination on grounds of nationality	*Köbler v Austria (2003)*
Article 49 TFEU	To establish a business in another Member State	*Factortame III (1996); Haim (2000)*
Article 56 TFEU	To provide services in another Member State	*Berlington & Others v Hungary (2015)*
Article 63 TFEU	The free movement of capital	*Konle v Austria (1999)*
Directive 85/337	To have the environmental effects of a project assessed by the competent authorities	*Leth v Austria (2013)*
Article 7 of Directive 90/314	To a refund and/or repatriation in the event of a tour operator's insolvency	*Dillenkofer & Others v Germany (1996); Rechberger & Others v Austria (1999)*
Directive 98/37	To import and export machinery	*AGM v Finland (2007)*
Article 2(1) of Directive 2000/78	To work without discrimination on grounds of age	*Specht & Others (2015)*
Directive 2001/23	The safeguarding of employees' rights in the event of a transfer of undertakings	*Ferreira da Silva e Brito & Others v Portugal (2016)*
Article 6(b) of Directive 2003/88	To work for no more than 48 hours per week on average	*Fuß v Stadt Halle (2010)*
Articles 9 and 10 of Directive 2004/38	The entitlement of migrant citizens and their family members to Residence Cards	*Santos v Home Secretary (2016)*
Article 16(2) of Directive 2004/38	To work in another EU Member State (as the family member of an EU citizen)	*Ogieriakhi v Minister for Justice & Equality & Others (No.2) (2015)*
Articles 13 and 18 of Directive 2004/83	To the grant of refugee or 'subsidiary protection' status	*D v Home Secretary (2015)*

JUDGMENT

> 'A significant obstacle, such as that [in the present case] to the effective application of EU law and, in particular, a principle as fundamental as that of state liability for infringement of EU law, **cannot** be justified either by the principle of *res judicata* or by the principle of legal certainty.'

In *Târşia v Romania* (Case C–69/14) [2016] 1 CMLR 47, the ECJ held that where it was discovered that a national supreme court had reached an incorrect decision on a point of EU law (and potentially committed a sufficiently serious breach of EU law), but where it had subsequently become impossible to re-litigate the point in the domestic courts because of *res judicata*, 'individuals cannot be deprived of the possibility of rendering the State liable in order to obtain legal protection of their rights'.

The table of EU law provisions found to satisfy the first condition of state liability an intention to confer rights on individuals.

SAMPLE PROBLEM QUESTION

La Vitesse, a French car dealership, specialises in selling sports cars imported from Germany and Italy. Six months ago, the French Minister of Trade announced a ban on the importation of sports cars on the ground that they were damaging France's domestic car manufacturing industry. The Minister explained that German and Italian sports cars in particular were so popular that France's national standing as a motorcar manufacturer was under threat, as were the jobs of thousands of employees in French car factories.

La Vitesse unsuccessfully challenged the import ban in the French courts. Yesterday, the French Constitutional Court rejected their final appeal. The Court did not seek a preliminary ruling on the basis that the import ban was 'undoubtedly' justifiable under EU law.

La Vitesse's profits for the last six months are 50 per cent lower than they were last year. La Vitesse are considering bringing a claim for damages under state liability principles but are unsure what they would need to prove and against whom they should bring their claim.

Advise La Vitesse.

Explain the scope of state liability:

A remedy which allows for individuals to recover loss caused by a Member State's breach of EU law. Explain that 'individuals' includes corporate claimants, such as La Vitesse.

Explain the three tests laid down in *Brasserie du Pêcheur v Germany/ Factortame III*:

(1) Rule of EU law breached must have been 'intended to confer rights on individuals'.

(2) Breach must be 'sufficiently serious'. This means a 'manifest and grave' disregard of the limits on the state's discretion. Explain the 'factors' used here: clarity and precision of the rule breached; amount of discretion available to the national authorities; whether breach intentional; whether breach voluntary; whether breach excusable.

(3) 'Direct causal link' between breach of EU law and individual's loss. This is a matter for the national courts (*Leth v Austria*).

Explain the meaning of the 'State':

- *Haim* recognises any 'public' body as part of the state. Therefore, the French Ministry of Trade is part of the state. Although the Minister is named personally, his Ministry would be vicariously liable (*AGM v Finland*).

- *Köbler* and *Traghetti del Mediterraneo* recognise the potential state liability of national courts adjudicating at last instance albeit only in 'exceptional' circumstances. The refusal to seek a preliminary ruling in defiance of Article 267(3) TFEU by abusing *acte clair* qualifies as such a circumstance (*Ferreira da Silva e Brito & Others*).

Discuss the extent of reparation:

This is governed by national law, subject to the overriding EU principles of equivalence and effectiveness. Compensation for 'pure' economic loss IS available in state liability cases, even if not available under national law (*Factortame III*). State liability claims have to be brought in accordance with 'reasonable' national limitation periods (*Danske Slagterier*) and claimants are expected to mitigate their losses.

Apply the law to the facts:

(1) The Minister's import ban clearly engages EU law on the free movement of goods, specifically Article 34 TFEU. Article 34 TFEU undoubtedly satisfies the first test (*Brasserie du Pêcheur, Schmidberger v Austria, Danske Slagterier v Germany*).

(2) Article 34 TFEU is directly effective and must therefore be clear and precise; Member States have no discretion to impose import bans for economic reasons (see *Commission v UK (French Turkeys)*, discussed in Chapter 14); the breach is clearly intentional and is almost certainly inexcusable. The import ban seems to be a sufficiently serious breach. The Constitutional Court's decision that the import ban is justifiable and/or the failure to seek a preliminary ruling could also be regarded as a sufficiently serious breach.

(3) There is evidence that the import ban has directly caused La Vitesse's loss – ultimately the French courts would decide this. As the Constitutional Court only gave its judgment 'yesterday' there is nothing to suggest that this can have caused any loss (yet).

'A claimant for damages has to prove not only a sufficiently serious breach but also a direct causal link between the breach and the damage alleged to have been sustained' – *Negassi v Home Secretary* [2013] EWCA Civ 151, per Kay LJ.

In the light of the above statement, critically evaluate the legal hurdles that have to be overcome in order to bring a successful state liability claim.

Explain origins/scope of state liability:
Explain that state liability was introduced by the ECJ in *Francovich v Italy* – Member States are obliged to compensate loss caused to individuals by breaches of EU law.

Explain the three conditions laid down in *Brasserie du Pêcheur/Factortame III*:

(1) Rule of EU law breached was intended to confer rights on individuals. Give examples: Article 34 TFEU (*Brasserie, Schmidberger v Austria, Danske Slagterier*); Article 45 TFEU (*Köbler v Austria*), Article 49 TFEU (*Factortame III, Haim*), Article 7 of the Package Travel Directive (*Dillenkofer, Rechberger*).

(2) Breach must be sufficiently serious. This means a 'manifest and grave' disregard of the limits on the state's discretion. Explain the 'factors' used here: clarity and precision of the rule breached; the amount of discretion available to the Member State, whether breach intentional, whether breach excusable. Elaborate with case law such as *BT, Stockholm Lindöpark, Hedley Lomas, Denkavit*.

(3) Direct causal link between breach and loss. This is a matter for the national courts (*Leth*).

Explain the case law on the 'state':

- Explain that most state liability cases have involved central government (*Francovich, Brasserie du Pêcheur, Factortame III*).

- Point out that it is also possible to bring a state liability case against regional government (*Konle, Fuß*) or any public body (*Haim*).

- Explain that the national legislature can be sued (*Berlington & Others*).

- Explain that the 'state' includes national courts adjudicating at last instance (*Köbler, Traghetti del Mediterraneo, Ferreira da Silva e Brito & Others, Târşia*) but only in 'exceptional' circumstances.

- Explain that there is a form of vicarious state liability (*AGM v Finland*).

Explain the rules on the extent of reparation:
Explain the principles of equivalence and effectiveness – national procedural rules apply except where this would make it impossible or excessively difficult to claim compensation. Explain that compensation for 'pure' economic loss is available in state liability cases, even if not available under national law (*Factortame III*). State liability claims have to be brought in accordance with 'reasonable' national limitation periods (*Danske Slagterier*) and claimants are expected to mitigate their losses.

Critically analyse the law:

- Comment that although there are many hurdles to cross, state liability claimants have been successful, for example in *Factortame III* and *Hedley Lomas* involving the inexcusable/intentional breach of directly effective Treaty provisions.

- The *Köbler/Traghetti* decisions raise certain problems of principle (e.g. does the imposition of state liability against the judiciary affect judicial independence?) and practical difficulties about how this policy is to be put into practice.

- Comment that there is as yet no definition of 'state' in this context and the ambiguity surrounding the concept of 'public body' creates uncertainty. The ECJ has clarified some of the issues on bringing actions against national courts of last resort in *Ferreira da Silva e Brito & Others* and *Târşia*.

SUMMARY

- In *Francovich*, the ECJ created the possibility of individuals seeking compensation against a state whose breach of EU law caused that individual to suffer loss. State liability is based on Article 4(3) TEU.

- State liability is not limited to the failure by the state to implement a directive, as in *Francovich*, although that still remains a good example (*Dillenkofer v Germany, BT, Rechberger & Others, Stockholm Lindöpark*). State liability extends to breaches of EU law by Member States generally.

- In *Brasserie du Pêcheur/Factortame III*, the ECJ identified three conditions for state liability (1) the rule of EU law infringed must be intended to confer rights on individuals; (2) the breach of EU law must be 'sufficiently serious'; (3) there must be a direct causal link between the state's failure to comply with EU law and the damage suffered by the individual.

- There is a strong correlation between condition (1) and direct effect. Most state liability cases (other than those involving a failure to implement a directive) involve breaches of directly effective provisions of the TFEU. Examples include *Brasserie du Pêcheur* (Article 34 TFEU), *Hedley Lomas* (Article 35 TFEU), *Köbler* (Article 45(2) TFEU), *Factortame III* (Article 49 TFEU) and *Berlington & Others* (Article 56 TFEU).

- For condition (2), a 'sufficiently serious' breach, the decisive test is whether there had been a 'manifest and grave' disregard of the limits of the state's discretion. The ECJ has identified several 'factors' in seeking to prove this:

    - the clarity and precision of the rule breached,
    - the measure of discretion left by that rule to the national authorities,
    - whether the infringement was intentional or involuntary,
    - whether any error of law was excusable or inexcusable,
    - the fact that the position taken by a Union institution may have contributed towards the adoption or maintenance of national measures or practices contrary to EU law.

- Two breaches of EU law are automatically 'sufficiently serious':

    - Failure to implement a Directive on time (*Dillenkofer & Others*).
    - Defiance of clear ECJ case law (*Fuß v City of Halle*).

- For condition (3), it is for the national courts to determine whether the causal link exists (*Brasserie du Pêcheur/Factortame III; Leth*).

- Damages for state liability are available regardless of the origin of the state responsible for the breach. Most state liability cases involve central government (*Francovich, Brasserie du Pêcheur, Factortame III*). However, it is possible to bring a state liability case against the national legislature (*Berlington & Others*); a regional government (*Konle, Fuß*); a public body, such as a professional regulatory body (*Haim*).

- National courts adjudicating at last instance may also be held liable, albeit exceptionally (*Köbler, Traghetti del Mediterraneo*). Failing to seek a preliminary ruling when the point of EU law is not *acte clair* could lead to state liability (*Ferreira da Silva e Brito & Others*).

- An individual could be held liable under state liability in addition to the state itself, a form of vicarious liability (*AGM*).

- Reparation is subject to two principles (*Brasserie du Pêcheur, Factortame III*):

  - The principle of equivalence. Reparation must be made in accordance with national rules on civil liability, including entitlement to exemplary damages and limitation periods, but under conditions that are no less favourable than for similar domestic claims.

  - The principle of effectiveness. National rules on recovery of compensation in state liability claims cannot be so framed so as to make it in practice 'impossible or excessively difficult' to obtain compensation. Thus, total exclusion of loss of profit in the context of economic and commercial litigation is not acceptable as far as state liability claims are concerned.

Further reading

Articles

Albors-Llorens, A, 'The Principle of State Liability in EC law and the Supreme Courts of the Member States' (2007) 66 *CLJ* 270.

Anagnostaras, G, 'Not as Unproblematic as you Might Think: The Establishment of Causation in Governmental Liability Actions' (2002) 27 *EL Rev* 663.

Bengoetxea, J, 'Text and Telos in the European Court of Justice' (2015) 11 *ECL Rev* 184.

Breuer, M, 'State Liability for Judicial Wrongs and Community Law: The Case of *Köbler v Austria*' (2004) 29 *EL Rev* 243.

Davis, R W, 'Liability in Damages for a Breach of Community Law: Some Reflections on the Question of who to sue and the Concept of "the State"' (2006) 31 *EL Rev* 69.

Lock, T, 'Is Private Enforcement of EU law through State Liability a Myth? An Assessment 20 years after *Francovich*' (2012) 49 *CML Rev* 1675.

Nassimpian, D, '... And we Keep on Meeting: (De)fragmenting State Liability' (2007) 32 *EL Rev* 819.

Prechal, S, 'Member State Liability and Direct Effect: What's the Difference After All?' (2006) 17 *EBL Rev* 299.

10

The Internal Market

AIMS AND OBJECTIVES

After reading this chapter you should be able to:

- Understand the aims of the Internal Market
- Understand the law relating to the free movement of capital
- Understand differences between 'capital', 'goods' and 'services'

10.1 The aims of the Internal Market

The Internal Market principle is located in Article 26(2) TFEU. It states:

ARTICLE

'Art 26(2) The internal market shall comprise an area without internal frontiers in which the free movement of goods, persons, services, and capital is ensured in accordance with the provisions of the Treaties.'

Following the EU's enlargements in 2004, 2007 and 2013, the Internal Market is now – in population terms at least – the world's largest single trading bloc (overtaking NAFTA (the North American Free Trade Association), comprising the USA, Canada and Mexico). Moreover, the Internal Market is much more than a free trade area (which characteristically only seeks to remove trade barriers between its Member States). There is also a common policy on the imposition of Customs duties both internally and externally (known as a Customs union), and a whole series of rules promoting the free movement of persons, services and capital as well as goods. NAFTA is essentially a free trade area, as is EFTA (the European Free Trade Association) which the UK helped form in the late 1950s as a 'rival' organisation to what was then the EEC. EFTA still exists, although the only surviving members are Iceland, Norway and Liechtenstein (all of whom are members of the European Economic Area (EEA)) and Switzerland. The purpose of the EEA was to allow those European states who were not committed to full EU membership to obtain some of the benefits of the Internal Market.

The Internal Market is the cornerstone of the EU. Free movement in EU law has several mechanisms and produces numerous advantages:

- Removal of trade barriers ensures that manufacturers and producers will have easier access to more consumers.
- As a corollary, those consumers will have access to more, and better, goods.
- Economies of scale and increased competition from manufacturers and producers in other countries will also drive down the prices of goods.
- The abolition of Customs charges and other tariffs will stop individual states from protecting inefficient domestic manufacturers and producers.
- Removal of obstacles to personal movement helps workers (and potential workers) to move from areas of high unemployment and/or areas of low wages to areas of high employment and/or better wages in different countries. Mutual recognition of vocational qualifications and practical experience obtained in different countries facilitates the movement of workers and self-employed people.
- The abolition of discrimination based on nationality (except where absolutely necessary) ensures employers taking on those foreign workers cannot exploit them vis-à-vis domestic workers, further encouraging free movement.

10.2 The 'Four Freedoms'

The 'Four Freedoms' are:

1. the free movement of persons;
2. the free movement of services;
3. the free movement of goods; and
4. the free movement of capital.

The first three of these will be explored in detail in Chapters 11 and 12 (persons), 13 (services), 14 and 15 (goods). This chapter will look at some of the issues that have arisen that are common to all Four Freedoms, and those issues which involve the relationship between one or more of them. The fourth freedom, capital, will also be discussed briefly.

10.2.1 Common features

The free movements of persons, services, goods and capital all involve essentially the same basic principle: the removal of all barriers to movement imposed by national legislation, regulation or administration except those which are objectively necessary in order to protect some essential national interest. In other words, there is not 'absolute' free movement. Member States of the EU are entitled to retain in force, or even introduce new, barriers to free movement. However, they must be able to justify those barriers, either by invoking specific derogations contained in the TFEU or by invoking derogations authorised by the ECJ.

The TFEU allows Member States to derogate from the free movement of persons, services, goods and capital on the grounds of public policy and public security. These are the only derogations common to all Four Freedoms. There are other derogations which are specific to one or more of the free movements. Derogations on grounds of 'public health' are available for the freedoms of persons and services, while Article 36 allows Member States to derogate from the free movement of goods on the ground of 'human health protection'. Article 36 also allows Member States to derogate from the free movement of goods on grounds of 'public morality', 'the protection of national treasures possessing artistic, historic or archaeological value' and 'the protection of industrial or commercial property'. None of these derogations applies to the other freedoms.

In addition to the specific Treaty derogations, the ECJ has introduced and developed a doctrine under which some restrictions on the freedoms imposed by national legislation, regulation or administration can be justified on any other grounds (sometimes referred to as a 'rule of reason'). However, four criteria have to be satisfied. In *Gebhard* (Case C–55/94) [1995] ECR I–4165, the ECJ stated that, in order for a national rule which restricts any of the freedoms to be justified, it must:

i. be non-discriminatory;

ii. be justified by imperative requirements in the general interest;

iii. be suitable for the attainment of the objective which it pursues;

iv. not go beyond what is necessary in order to attain its objective (the 'proportionality' doctrine).

The application of these principles to specific cases will be dealt with in the respective chapters (and later in this chapter). However, it should be noted that the ECJ's application of a uniform, four-part test to the three freedoms of movement for persons, services and goods has attracted academic criticism. Luigi Daniele has argued that there is a lack of common ground between the movement of persons and the movement of services. The former involves the physical movement of a person to another EU Member State on a more or less permanent basis; the latter requires only that a service is provided by a person established in one Member State and received by a person from another Member State. There is no requirement of physical movement at all. Daniele suggests that applying the same rules to fundamentally different situations can create more problems than it solves. He concludes by suggesting:

> The global approach to the free movement of persons risks bringing the Court unduly to put on the same footing rather different situations. More care should be taken in future when transposing the results achieved by case law in one field to another.... The Court should refrain from relying too much on the so-called 'rules of reason'. The uncertainty of the criteria on which such rules are based often forces the Court to follow a case-by-case approach. It is therefore extremely hard for the interpreter to predict how the Court will decide a given case. This might also cause an undesirable flow of mostly ill-founded cases. Before the situation gets out of hand, a re-consideration would be welcomed.
>
> L Daniele, 'Non-Discriminatory Restrictions to the Free
> Movement of Persons' (1997) 22 *EL Rev* 191

As of 2018, however, the ECJ shows no sign of abandoning its 'globalisation' policy of applying the same 'rules of reason' to the free movements of persons, services and goods. Nor has it shown any intention of tightening up the criteria on which its 'rules' are based.

10.2.2 The free movement of capital

Space precludes a detailed analysis of the free movement of capital provisions. The key provisions are found in Articles 63–66 TFEU. Article 63(1) provides that 'within the framework of the provisions set out in this chapter, all restrictions on the movement of capital between Member States and between Member States and third countries shall be prohibited'.

The original Treaty provisions on the free movement of capital were far less sweeping, however, and liberalisation of capital movements has been a slower process than that of the other freedoms. In *Casati* (Case 203/80) [1981] ECR 2595, for example, the ECJ stated that complete freedom of movement of capital could undermine the economic policy of one of the Member States or create an imbalance in its balance of payments. According to the ECJ in *Bordessa and Others* (Cases C–358 and 416/93) [1995] ECR I–361, full liberalisation of capital movements did not occur until the Council adopted Directive 88/361.

'Capital'

The TFEU does not define 'capital', although a non-exhaustive list of capital movements can be found in the Annex of Directive 88/361. The following have been held to fall within the provisions on capital movements:

- **Shares.** In *Commission v Portugal* (Case C–367/98) [2002] ECR I–4731, where Portuguese rules precluded investors from other EU Member States from acquiring more than a fixed number of shares in Portuguese companies, the ECJ held that the rules constituted a restriction on capital movements. The ECJ extended this concept in *Commission v UK* (Case C–98/01) [2003] ECR I–4641, by holding that national rules which restricted share ownership without distinction (i.e. the restriction applied to British nationals as well as foreign investors) were capable of restricting capital movements contrary to EU law.

- **Loans.** In *Sandoz* (Case C–439/97) [1999] ECR I–7041, the ECJ held that provisions of Austrian law which imposed stamp duty, a type of tax, on all loans taken out by Austrian residents, even if the lender was based in another EU Member State, breached EU law on capital movements. The Court ruled that this law would deter Austrian residents from seeking to obtain loans from lenders based in other EU Member States, some of which did not charge stamp duty. Another case in which national provisions which restricted nationals from obtaining loans from foreign providers was *Commission v Belgium* (Case C–478/98) [2000] ECR I–7587, where the Court stated that 'measures taken by a Member State which are liable to dissuade its residents from obtaining loans or making investments in other Member States constitute restrictions on the free movement of capital'.

- **Mortgages.** In *Trummer and Meyer* (Case C–222/97) [1999] ECR I–1661, the ECJ held that provisions of Austrian legislation which prohibited the registration of mortgages in the currency of another Member State breached EU law on capital movements.

- **Acquisition of real property, i.e. land.** For example, in *Konle* (Case C–302/97) [1999] ECR I–3099, where Austrian legislation forced all foreign nationals purchasing property in certain tourist-friendly regions of Austria to obtain authorisation first, the ECJ held that a breach of EU rules on capital movements had occurred. The same result was reached in *Albore* (Case C–423/98) [2000] ECR I–5965, involving Italian legislation which required foreign nationals to obtain authorisation prior to acquiring property in areas of military importance, and in *Ospelt* (Case C–452/01) [2003] ECR I–9743, involving Austrian legislation requiring prior authorisation to be obtained before purchasing agricultural land.

- **Inheritances.** An inheritance, whether of money, personal property or 'immovable property' (land and buildings), is a movement of capital – provided there is some cross-border element. Recent examples include *Eckelkamp & Others* (Case C–11/07) [2008] ECR I–6845, involving German and Dutch residents who inherited immovable property in Belgium following their mother's death; *Arens-Sikken* (Case C–43/07) [2008] ECR I–6887, involving an Italian resident who inherited a share of immovable property in the Netherlands following the death of her husband; and *Block* (Case

C–67/08) [2009] ECR I–883, involving a German resident who inherited money invested in Spain. *Jäger* (Case C–256/06) [2008] ECR I–123 was slightly different, in that it involved a French resident inheriting an estate comprising agricultural land and forest in France following the death of his mother. However, the Court found a cross-border element: the mother was living in Germany at the time of her death.

- **Gifts.** In *Persche* (Case C–318/07) [2009] ECR I–359, the ECJ held that provisions of German legislation allowing taxpayers to deduct from their income the cost of gifts to charitable, benevolent or church organisations, but only if the recipient of the gift was a body established in Germany, breached EU law on capital movements. Gifts were a form of capital whether the gift involved money or some item of property. Similarly, in *Commission v Austria (Gifts to Research and Teaching Institutions)* (Case C–10/10) [2011] ECR I–5389 the Court held that Austrian legislation which allowed tax-payers to deduct the cost of gifts to research and teaching institutions, but only where those institutions were established in Austria, was in breach of Article 63.

- **Dividends.** In *Santander Asset Management & Others* (Cases C–338/11 to C–347/11) [2012] 3 CMLR 12, the Court held that French legislation which imposed tax on dividends paid out by French companies, but only where the shareholders were based outside France (i.e. French-based shareholders did not have to pay the tax) was prohibited by Article 63.

Derogations

Article 65 specifies certain derogations from the free movement of capital provisions. It states, *inter alia*, that Member States are entitled:

> to take all requisite measures to prevent infringements of national law and regulations, in particular in the field of taxation and the prudential supervision of financial institutions, or to lay down procedures for the declaration of capital movements for purposes of administrative or statistical information, or to take measures which are justified on grounds of public policy or public security.

Considering this provision in *Association Eglise de Scientologie de Paris* (Case C–54/99) [2000] ECR I–1335, the Court stated that these derogations had to be interpreted strictly, could not be used to serve purely economic ends and were subject to the 'proportionality' doctrine. The derogation was successfully relied upon in *Sandoz* (1999) (noted above). The ECJ accepted the argument of the Austrian government that the requirement to pay stamp duty on all loans was designed to prevent 'taxable persons from evading the requirements of domestic tax legislation through the exercise of freedom of movement of capital'. However, the derogation was unsuccessfully raised in *Commission v Belgium* (2000), the Court holding that Belgian rules preventing all Belgian residents from obtaining loans abroad was an excessive and disproportionate restriction on the free movement of capital.

In addition, the four-part test set out in *Gebhard* (1995) (see Chapter 13) has been held to apply to capital movements. The Austrian legislation in *Konle* (1999) was found to be justifiable (after certain modifications to remove the discriminatory aspects) because it helped the authorities to ensure that large numbers of properties in tourist-friendly areas were not being bought as second or 'holiday' homes, whether by foreign nationals or by Austrian nationals looking to escape from the cities and suburbia. This in turn helped to ensure that those areas retained a 'permanent population and an economic activity independent of the tourist sector' (in other words, it ensured that those areas did not turn into 'ghost towns' when there were no tourists).

The Austrian rules in *Ospelt* (2003) were also held to be justifiable, on the grounds that they helped to preserve:

> agricultural communities, maintaining a distribution of land ownership which allows the development of viable farms and sympathetic management of green spaces and the countryside as well as encouraging a reasonable use of the available land by resisting pressure on land and preventing natural disasters.

However, in both cases the Court found that the requirement of authorisation went beyond what was necessary to achieve its objective. The Court thought that there were other mechanisms available to the national authorities to ensure compliance with planning legislation in tourist-friendly and/or agricultural areas, which would achieve the same objective as authorisation but impose less of an obstacle to capital movements in doing so.

In *Commission v Austria* (2011), the ECJ rejected two potential justifications for the Austrian legislation in that case. Although the Court accepted that the promotion of research and development was a potential justification, it was not available where it concerned only research and development at the national level. The promotion of national education and training was another potential justification, but the legislation was disproportionate. The onus was on the Austrian government to show that the objective could not be achieved by less restrictive measures, and it had failed to do so.

Economic and Monetary Union

Economic and Monetary Union (EMU) dates back to 1969, when the six heads of state of the EEC agreed a plan, which would have achieved such a union by 1980, although the plan did not work. Nevertheless, by the late 1980s some progress had been made with the establishment of the Exchange Rate Mechanism (ERM), which replaced the normal fixed rate of exchange between different currencies with a floating rate for those states in the ERM. The system was relatively stable and successful until 'Black Wednesday' in October 1992 when the UK (and Italy) was forced to withdraw at the cost of billions of pounds to the British Treasury. However, this disaster prompted the Member States to concentrate on taking EMU to the next level: a single currency. First, the various advantages and disadvantages had to be examined.

Advantages and disadvantages of a single (European) currency

- **Advantages:** 'transaction costs' incurred in the form of commission as one currency is exchanged for another disappear; greater transparency in terms of price comparison between the same or similar goods on sale in different countries; elimination of exchange rate fluctuations should improve confidence for producers and retailers when setting prices.

- **Disadvantages:** Member States are often at different points in the economic cycle (i.e. some have growing economies and some have shrinking economies, with differing levels of inflation) but a single currency prevents them from responding individually to these issues, e.g. by unilaterally raising or lowering interest rates.

After weighing up these advantages and disadvantages, most of the EU's Member States decided to forge ahead. Over the 1990s, these states began to co-ordinate their economic policies and forge closer co-operation between their central banks. A body called the European Monetary Institute (EMI) was established to help. The Treaty on European Union established a set of 'convergence criteria' which would be used to determine which states would be eligible to join the single currency. These included:

- a high degree of price stability, i.e. a rate of inflation close to the three best-performing Member States;
- sustainability of government deficit at not more than 3 per cent of gross domestic product (GDP) and government debt at not more than 60 per cent of GDP;
- the observance of the fluctuation margins permitted by the ERM for at least two years.

The criterion concerning government deficit and debt did not just apply at the point of Member States joining the single currency – it continues to apply afterwards. In 1997, the Member States agreed, in the Stability and Growth Pact (SGP), to maintain 'budget discipline', i.e. to respect the requirement to keep government deficit at or below 3 per cent of GDP and, if necessary, take immediate corrective action (subject to economic sanctions for failure to do so).

Eleven Member States (Austria, Belgium, Finland, France, Germany, Ireland, Italy, Luxembourg, the Netherlands, Portugal and Spain) satisfied these convergence criteria and in January 1999 the European Currency Unit (ECU, subsequently renamed the euro) came into operation in these states for electronic payments. At the same time, the EMI became the European Central Bank (ECB). The ECB, which is based in Frankfurt in Germany, has several tasks including defining and implementing monetary policy and issuing euro banknotes (individual states issue euro coins).

National currencies continued to be used for all other transactions. Greece was deemed to have satisfied the criteria in 2001, and the so-called 'euro zone' grew to 12 members. On New Year's Day 2002, however, euro notes and coins came into operation and, two months later, national currencies of the 12 participating states were finally withdrawn. Thus, the Austrian schilling, Belgian and French francs, Dutch guilder, German mark, Greek drachma, Irish punt, Italian lira, Portuguese escudo and Spanish peseta all ceased – overnight – to be legal tender. Slovenia became the thirteenth Member State to join the 'euro zone' in 2007, followed by Cyprus and Malta in 2008, Slovakia in 2009, Estonia in 2011, Latvia in 2014 and Lithuania in 2015. At the time of writing there are therefore 19 Member States in the 'euro zone', representing over 337 million people. Nine Member States – Bulgaria, Croatia, Czech Republic, Denmark, Hungary, Poland, Romania, Sweden and the UK remain outside the euro zone although they have the option of joining in the future (subject to satisfying the 'convergence criteria').

10.2.3 The relationship between 'services' and 'goods'

No definition of 'goods' is provided in the TFEU, or in any provisions of secondary legislation. The task has been left to the ECJ. In *Commission v Italy* (Case 7/68) [1968] ECR 617, the ECJ defined 'goods' very widely:

JUDGMENT

'By "goods" … there must be understood products which can be valued in money, and which are capable, as such, of forming the subject of commercial transactions.'

There is a definition of 'services' in the TFEU, although it is a far from comprehensive definition. Article 57 states that the word includes 'activities of an industrial character', 'activities of a commercial character', 'activities of craftsmen' and 'activities of the professions'.

In a number of cases the ECJ has had to decide which of the freedoms of 'services' or 'goods' applies to the facts. *Customs and Excise Commissioners v Schindler* (Case C–275/92) [1994] ECR I–1039 is illustrative of the problem facing the ECJ when it is not immediately obvious whether the free movement of goods provisions should apply or whether those on services are more appropriate.

CASE EXAMPLE

Customs and Excise Commissioners v Schindler (Case C–275/92) [1994] ECR I–1039

Gerhart and Jörg Schindler posted envelopes from the Netherlands to various addresses in the UK. Each contained invitations to participate in the German national lottery, an application form and a pre-paid envelope. Customs in Dover confiscated the envelopes on the ground that they were in breach of UK law, the Lotteries and Amusement Act 1976, which provided that anyone who, in connection with any lottery, brought into the UK for the purposes of sale or distribution any ticket to participate in, or advertisement of, a national lottery, would be guilty of an offence. The Schindlers contested the compatibility of the 1976 Act with EU law. The first question for the ECJ was whether Article 34 (free movement of goods) or Article 56 (free movement of services) applied. In the event, the ECJ decided that the case fell within the scope of Article 56, because the UK legislation primarily restricted a service (the promotion of a lottery) rather than goods (the envelopes and their contents). The restriction on the movement of goods was an indirect consequence of the restriction on the service.

CASE EXAMPLE

Commission v Italy (Case C–158/94) [1997] ECR I–5789

One question for the ECJ was whether electricity could be regarded as 'goods'. The Italian government argued that electricity bore much greater similarity to the category of 'services' than to that of 'goods'. It was argued that electricity is 'an incorporeal substance' which cannot be stored and 'has no economic existence as such', in that it is never useful in itself but only by reason of its possible applications. Moreover, imports and exports of electricity were 'merely aspects of the management of the electricity network' which, by their nature, fell within the category of 'services'. However, the ECJ rejected the argument, citing *Almelo and Others* (Case C–393/92) [1994] ECR I–1477 in which it was accepted that EU law, and indeed the national laws of the Member States, regarded electricity as constituting 'goods'.

Conversely, in *Jägerskiöld v Gustafsson* (Case C–97/98) [1999] ECR I–7319, the ECJ held that the provisions on services, and not those on goods, applied in a case concerning disputed fishing permits. Although the permits had a tangible existence, and could be regarded as a product with a monetary value, the ECJ decided that this was ancillary to the service which the permit allowed its holder to carry out.

A similar decision was reached in *FA Premier League & Others; Murphy* (Cases C–403, 429/08) [2012] 1 CMLR 29. Karen Murphy, a publican in Portsmouth, obtained and used a Greek 'decoding' card which enabled her to broadcast, in her pub, Greek satellite TV broadcasts of live English Premier League football matches. As a result she was convicted of breaching UK legislation (s297(1) of the Copyright, Designs & Patents Act 1988), but appealed to the High Court, which referred the case of the ECJ. Given that the case involved the use of an imported product (a 'decoding' card) in order to receive a service (a satellite TV broadcast) from another Member State, the first issue for the Court was whether to apply the Treaty provisions on goods or services. It decided that the provisions on services applied, holding:

> where legislation concerns an activity in respect of which the services provided by the economic operators are particularly prominent, whilst the supply of equipment is related thereto in only a purely secondary manner, it is appropriate to examine that activity in the light of the freedom to provide services alone.

(This case is examined in more detail in Chapter 13.)

10.2.4 The relationship between 'capital' and 'goods'

Current legal tender in the form of banknotes and coins is subject to the provisions on the free movement of capital rather than the provisions on the free movement of goods (*Bordessa* (1995)). By way of contrast, old coins that are no longer legal tender have been held to fall within the provisions on the free movement of goods (*R v Thompson and Others* (Case 7/78) [1979] ECR 2247, which is examined in Chapter 14).

CASE EXAMPLE

Bordessa and Others (Cases C–358 and 416/93) [1995] ECR I–361

Aldo Bordessa (an Italian living in Spain) was stopped at Gerona on the Spanish/French border, driving through the 'nothing to declare' channel with 50 million Spanish pesetas stuffed in various hiding places in his car. Meanwhile, Vicente Marí Mellado and Concepción Barbero Maestre, a Spanish couple, were arrested at the same Customs point, heading for France with 38 million pesetas in their possession. All three were prosecuted for breaching Spanish legislation which required authorisation for the export of notes in excess of five million pesetas per person per journey. The three defendants contended that the Spanish legislation was in breach of EU rules on the free movement of goods. However, the ECJ disagreed, distinguishing its earlier judgment in *R v Thompson* (1979), and held that the exportation of current bank notes was not governed by the provisions on the free movement of goods but those concerning the free movement of capital. Applying these rules, the Court found that, although Member States were entitled to monitor exports of their own currencies, the prior authorisation requirement imposed a disproportionate restriction on legitimate capital movements. The Court stated that a prior declaration requirement would achieve the same objective while imposing less of an obstacle to capital movements.

In *Persche* (2009), discussed above, a German taxpayer had donated over €18,000 worth of bed linen, towels, zimmer frames and toy cars (all 'everyday consumer goods') to a charitable organisation in Portugal. Under German legislation, he was unable to deduct this expense from his taxable income because the organisation was based in another Member State, whereas he would have been able to do so had the organisation been based in Germany. When he challenged this, the ECJ held that Article 63 applied (and had been breached). The Court rejected a suggestion that the rules on the free movement of goods should have been applied instead. The Court noted that the German legislation applied to all gifts, whether of money or consumer goods (and in the case of the latter, regardless of where the goods were purchased).

The Internal Market	
• The Internal Market is established by Art 26 TFEU. The Internal Market is 'an area without internal frontiers in which the free movement of goods, persons, services, and capital is ensured'.	Art 26 TFEU
• 'Goods' is not defined in the Treaty but has been defined by the ECJ as covering all 'products which can be valued in money'.	*Commission v Italy* (1968)
• 'Services' is not defined in the Treaty although Art 57 states that it includes 'activities of an industrial character', 'activities of a commercial character', 'activities of craftsmen' and 'activities of the professions'.	Art 57 TFEU
• In the event of a dispute as to whether the provisions on 'goods' or 'services' or 'capital' apply then a court may need to decide.	*Schindler* (1994); *Bordessa* (1995); *Persche* (2009); *Murphy* (2012)
• 'Capital' is not defined in the Treaty but has been held to include shares, loans and mortgages.	
• The Treaty does not guarantee absolute free movement of goods, persons, services and capital. The Treaty itself contains specific limitations or derogations (such as public policy and public health) which Member States may invoke to justify the imposition of barriers to free movement. However, these derogations are strictly interpreted by the ECJ.	TFEU; Directive 2004/38
• The ECJ has established a principle that national laws and policies are capable of restricting free movement even if they are non-discriminatory. Examples include packaging requirements for goods and residence requirements for persons.	
• However, these rules can be justified provided four conditions are satisfied. They must (i) be non-discriminatory; (ii) be justified by imperative requirements in the general interest; (iii) be suitable for the attainment of the objective which it pursues; (iv) not go beyond what is necessary in order to attain its objective (the proportionality doctrine).	*Gebhard* (1995)
• Economic and Monetary Union (EMU) describes the system of financial convergence between the Member States dating back to the late 1960s. It includes the Exchange Rate Mechanism (ERM) and the single European currency, the euro. The 'euro' was adopted as a single currency in 12 Member States (the euro zone) in 2002. There are presently 19 countries in the euro zone.	

SUMMARY

▨ The internal market is an area without internal frontiers in which the free movement of goods, persons, services and capital is ensured (Article 26 TFEU).

▨ There is potential difficulty in distinguishing the free movement of goods from the free movement of services, but it is important to decide which one applies in any given case because different Treaty provisions will then operate. 'Goods' are defined as 'products which can be valued in money, and which are capable, as such, of forming the subject of commercial transactions' (*Commission v Italy*) whereas 'services' are defined as simply including 'activities of an industrial character', 'activities of a commercial character', 'activities of craftsmen' and 'activities of the professions' (Article 57 TFEU).

- A similar problem arises when distinguishing the free movement of goods from the free movement of capital. In *Bordessa*, the ECJ decided that current legal tender in the form of banknotes and coins is subject to the provisions on the free movement of capital rather than the provisions on the free movement of goods. In contrast, old coins that are no longer legal tender fall within the provisions on the free movement of goods (*R v Thompson and Others*).

- The free movements are not 'absolute' freedoms. The Member States are allowed to derogate, using justifications found in the TFEU. All Four Freedoms are subject to derogations on grounds of public policy and public security. Public health can be used to derogate from the freedoms of goods, persons and services.

- In addition, the ECJ has introduced a policy, common to all of the freedoms, of allowing Member States to justify national legislation which hinders one or more of the freedoms. The legislation must pass four tests (*Gebhard*): it must (i) be non-discriminatory; (ii) be justified by imperative requirements in the general interest; (iii) be suitable for the attainment of the objective which it pursues; and (iv) not go beyond what is necessary in order to attain its objective (the 'proportionality' doctrine).

- The free movement of capital provisions are found in Articles 63–66 TFEU.

- 'Capital' includes shares, gifts, inheritances, loans, mortgages and the acquisition of real property.

- Derogations are available to the Member States (Article 65).

- The idea of Economic and Monetary Union dates back to the late 1960s and came to fruition in the early twenty-first century with the introduction of the single European currency, the euro, in January 2002. The 'euro zone' now comprises 19 Member States.

Further reading

Articles

Barnard, C, 'Fitting the Remaining Pieces into the Goods and Persons Jigsaw?' (2001) 26 *EL Rev* 35.

Daniele, L, 'Non-Discriminatory Restrictions to the Free Movement of Persons' (1997) 22 *EL Rev* 191.

Dunnett, D, 'Some Legal Principles Applicable to the Transition to the Single Currency' (1996) 33 *CML Rev* 1133.

Flynn, L, 'Coming of Age: The Free Movement of Capital Case Law 1993–2002' (2002) 39 *CMLL Rev* 773.

Greaves, R, 'Advertising Restrictions and the Free Movement of Goods and Services' (1998) 23 *EL Rev* 305.

Nic Shuibhne, N, 'Margins of Appreciation: National Values, Fundamental Rights and EC Free Movement Law' (2009) 34 *EL Rev* 230.

Oliver, P and Roth, W-H, 'The Internal Market and the Four Freedoms' (2004) 41 *CMLL Rev* 407.

Prechal, S and De Vries, S, 'Seamless Web of Judicial Protection in the Internal Market?' (2009) 34 *EL Rev* 5.

Tryfonidou, A, 'Further Steps on the Road to Convergence among the Market Freedoms' (2010) 35 *EL Rev* 36.

11

Citizenship of the Union

AIMS AND OBJECTIVES

After reading this chapter you should be able to:

- Understand the meaning and scope of the law on EU citizenship, in particular Articles 20 and 21 TFEU and Directive 2004/38
- Understand the meaning and scope of a citizen's 'family members'
- Analyse critically the law relating to EU citizenship
- Apply the law to factual situations involving EU citizenship

11.1 Introduction

The original EC Treaty signed in 1957 made no reference to any form of European 'citizenship'. At that time, people were regarded as being citizens of their own Member States, and nothing more. That was to change when the Treaty on European Union came into force in November 1993, and several new provisions were inserted into the EC Treaty. These provisions now form Part Two of the TFEU, Articles 18–25. Article 20 provides (in part) as follows:

ARTICLE

'Art 20(1) Citizenship of the Union is hereby established. Every person holding the nationality of a Member State shall be a citizen of the Union. Citizenship of the Union shall be additional to and not replace national citizenship.

(2) Citizens of the Union shall enjoy the rights and be subject to the duties provided for in the Treaties.'

11.2 Nationality requirements: Article 20 TFEU

Thus, according to Article 20, in order to be a 'Citizen of the Union', it is first necessary to hold 'the nationality of a Member State'. Nationality is conferred purely by way of the national law of the state concerned. In *Micheletti* (C–369/90) [1992] ECR I–4239, the ECJ stated that 'it is for each Member State, having due regard to [Union] law, to lay down the conditions for the acquisition and loss of nationality'. However, 'nationality' is wide enough to include dual nationals. This is most obviously the case with people holding the nationality of two Member States (for example, *Garcia Avello v Belgium* (Case C–148/02) [2003] ECR I–11613, involving dual Belgian–Spanish nationality, and *McCarthy* (case C–434/09) [2011] ECR I–3375, involving dual British–Irish nationality). However, it is enough if a person holds the nationality of one of the Member States and that of a non-Member State, as *Micheletti* (1992) illustrates:

CASE EXAMPLE

Micheletti (Case C–369/90) [1992] ECR I–4239

Mario Micheletti, born in Argentina to Italian parents, had dual Italian–Argentinean nationality. He wished to set up as a dentist in Spain, but was rejected by the Spanish authorities, as Spanish law deemed him to have the nationality of his country of birth, Argentina. He challenged this, claiming to be entitled to invoke EU law (specifically Article 49, the freedom of establishment) because, under Italian law, the fact that he was born of Italian parents conferred on him Italian nationality – regardless of where in the world he was born. The ECJ held that he was both Italian and Argentinean, and that was enough for the purposes of Article 49.

Although *Micheletti* pre-dates the introduction of the citizenship provisions, the case is still good authority for the proposition that holders of dual nationality (only one of the nationalities being in the EU) is sufficient for Article 20 to apply, and hence Article 21 also. This was confirmed in *Collins* (Case C–138/02) [2004] 3 WLR 1236, where the ECJ held that a dual Irish-American national could rely upon EU law (specifically Article 45 TFEU, the free movement of workers). Other cases to note are Z.Z. (Case C–300/11) [2013] 3 CMLR 46; [2013] QB 1136 (involving a dual French-Algerian national) and *Iida* (Case C–40/11) [2013] 1 CMLR 47, [2013] 2 WLR 788 (involving a girl with German, Japanese and US nationality). All of these cases will be examined in detail later in this chapter.

Loss of nationality

All of the above cases involved the **acquisition** of EU citizenship. Only one case has so far addressed the **loss** of EU citizenship. *Rottmann* (Case C–135/08) [2010] ECR I–1449 involved a German national who was threatened with having his (acquired) nationality revoked. (He had been born an Austrian national but had later acquired German nationality, giving up his Austrian nationality as he did so. It subsequently emerged that he had not been entirely honest with the German authorities at the time he acquired his new nationality.) As this would also entail him losing his EU citizenship status, the ECJ was asked to provide guidance. The Court held that, in general, Member States were free to decide on matters of nationality, including loss of nationality – a point confirmed in several international conventions. The Court stated that it was 'legitimate for a Member State to wish to protect the special relationship of solidarity and good faith between it and its nationals and also the reciprocity of rights and duties, which form the bedrock of the bond of nationality'. However, the Court also held that it was incumbent on the national court to assess whether the decision to revoke nationality in any particular case was 'proportionate'. In deciding this, it would be necessary 'to take into account the consequences that the decision entails for the person concerned and, if relevant, for the members of his family with regard to the loss of the rights enjoyed by every citizen of the Union'.

11.3 Citizens' rights of free movement and residence: Article 21(1) TFEU

ARTICLE

'Art 21(1) Every citizen of the Union shall have the right to move and reside freely within the territory of the Member States, subject to the limitations and conditions laid down in the Treaties and by the measures adopted to give them effect.'

In *Kaur* (Case C–192/99) [2001] ECR I–1237 the ECJ confirmed that it was for each state to determine which persons are entitled to nationality of that state and, in turn, whether such nationality actually entitled the holder of it to entry into and residence within the state in question.

CASE EXAMPLE

Kaur (Case C–192/99) [2001] ECR I–1237

Manjit Kaur was born in Kenya in 1949 to a family of Asian origin, but became a citizen of the UK under the terms of the British Nationality Act 1948. However, she did not come within any of the categories of citizens of the UK recognised under the Immigration Act 1971 as having a right of residence in the UK. Subsequently, the British Nationality Act 1981 conferred on her the status of a 'British Overseas Citizen'. As such, she had, in the absence of special authorisation, no right under UK law to enter or remain in the UK. In 1996 she was in the UK (not for the first time) and applied for leave to remain and obtain gainful employment. However, the Home Secretary refused. She sought judicial review of this refusal, relying in part on the provisions in Articles 20 and 21. The High Court referred the case to the ECJ, which rejected her argument.

This decision must be correct. If Ms Kaur was regarded as a 'Citizen of the Union' purely because of her status as a 'British Overseas Citizen' then she would have rights to move around the EU and reside in any state of her choosing – except the UK, where British law did not confer on her a right of residence. Such an outcome would be deeply illogical. It must be the case that, before Article 21 can be invoked, the claimant must first have a right of residence in one of the Member States under its national law.

The 'direct effect' question: can Article 21(1) be relied upon in national courts?

In *Baumbast* (Case C–413/99) [2002] ECR I–7091, the ECJ held that Article 21(1) could be relied upon by EU citizens, to claim a right of residence in other EU Member States. Although Article 21(1) was subject to certain limitations and conditions, this did not deprive it of direct effect. The ECJ held that the competent authorities of the Member State and, where necessary, national courts, must ensure that those limitations and conditions were applied in compliance with the general principles of EU law and, in particular, the principle of proportionality.

CASE EXAMPLE

Baumbast (Case C–413/99) [2002] ECR I–7091

In 1990, the Baumbast family arrived in the UK. The father, a German national, was employed in the UK. He resided with his wife (who was Colombian) and their two school-age daughters, the younger one of whom, Idanella, had dual German–Colombian nationality. The elder daughter, being Mrs Baumbast's daughter from a previous relationship, held only Colombian nationality. Over the next three years, Mr Baumbast was economically active either as a worker or in a self-employed capacity in the UK. In 1993, however, economic circumstances forced him to take work outside the EU (first in China and then in Lesotho in southern Africa). In 1995, Mrs Baumbast applied for indefinite leave to remain in the UK for herself and her daughters. This was refused and she appealed. The ECJ held that Article 21(1) was directly effective and Mrs Baumbast therefore had the right to residence in the UK despite the fact that her husband was no longer working or self-employed in the UK. (Strictly speaking, Idanella would be classed as the 'Citizen of the Union', being the only member of the family other than Mr Baumbast holding the nationality of a Member State, with her mother claiming a right of residence as her primary carer. This aspect of the case is examined below (see section 11.5.3)).

Who is entitled to rely upon Article 21(1)?

The case of *Baumbast* (2002) therefore establishes that Article 21(1) is directly effective, and confers on anyone holding the nationality of a Member State a legally enforceable right of movement to, and residence in, any other EU Member State. That on its own is an important decision, as it apparently obviates the need for persons to establish some form of economic activity (whether as worker, work-seeker, self-employed person, service-provider or service-recipient) in order to claim residence rights under EU law. Over the years, the ECJ has allowed Article 21(1) to be relied upon by a variety of people who, prior to the introduction of citizenship rights, may have struggled to build a case using the more traditional free movement provisions (Articles 45, 49 and 56 – workers, the self-employed and service-providers). The cases to date can be grouped into the following categories:

- the unemployed – *Martínez Sala* (Case C–85/96) [1998] ECR I–2691; *Collins* (2004); *De Cuyper* (Case C–406/04) [2006] ECR I–6947;

- students – *Grzelczyk* (Case C–184/99) [2001] ECR I–6193; *D'Hoop* (Case C–224/98) [2002] ECR I–6191; *Bidar* (Case C–209/03) [2005] ECR I–2119; *Morgan and Bucher* (Cases C–11 & 12/06) [2007] ECR I–9161; Case C–158/07 *Förster* [2008] ECR I–8507;

- children – *Zhu and Chen* (Case C–200/02) [2004] ECR I–9925; *Schwarz* (Case C–76/05) [2007] ECR I–6849; *Ruiz Zambrano* (Case C–34/09) [2011] ECR I–1177; *Alokpa & Moudoulou* (Case C–86/12) [2017] 1 CMLR 40; *Rendón Marín* (Case C–165/14) [2017] 1 CMLR 29; [2017] 2 WLR 117;

- the retired – *Pusa* (Case C–224/02) [2004] ECR I–5763; *Turpeinen* (Case C–520/04) [2006] ECR I–10685; *Zablocka-Weyhermüller* (Case C–221/07) [2008] ECR I–9029; *Rüffler* (Case C–544/07) [2009] ECR I–3389; *Brey* (Case C–140/12) [2014] 1 CMLR 37; [2014] 1 WLR 1080;

- those incapable of working for health reasons – *Tas-Hagen* (Case C–192/05) [2006] ECR I–10451; *Nerkowska* (Case C–499/06) [2008] ECR I–3993.

The crucial threshold that has to be crossed in all citizenship cases is that 'beneficiaries of the right of residence must not become an unreasonable burden on the public finances of the host Member State' (*Grzelczyk* (2001)). That criterion itself begs the (as yet unanswered) question – what exactly is an 'unreasonable burden'? In several of the

Article 21 cases, EU citizens have been held to be entitled to claim social security or other financial benefits such as:

- a child-raising allowance – *Martínez Sala* (1998);
- a 'minimum subsistence allowance' – *Grzelczyk* (2001);
- a 'tideover allowance' – *D'Hoop* (2002);
- a student loan – *Bidar* (2005);
- a student grant – *Förster* (2008);
- a 'compensatory supplement' – *Brey* (2014).

So, it is clear that, just because the EU citizen is in need of financial help from the state, this does not make him or her an 'unreasonable burden'.

The right of citizens to invoke Article 18 TFEU to challenge discrimination based on nationality

A right of residence alone is potentially of little assistance unless it is accompanied by a right not to be discriminated against. Article 21(1) itself says nothing about such a right, but the ECJ has allowed citizens to invoke Article 18 TFEU in order to challenge discrimination based on nationality. Article 18 states:

ARTICLE

'Art 18 Within the scope of application of the Treaties, and without prejudice to any special provisions contained therein, any discrimination on grounds of nationality shall be prohibited.'

The earliest case was *Martínez Sala* (1998).

CASE EXAMPLE

Martínez Sala (Case C–85/96) [1998] ECR I–2691

María Martínez Sala, a Spanish national, had lived in Germany since 1968 and had worked there intermittently from 1976 until 1986 and again for a short time in 1989. Since then she had not worked and was in receipt of social security. When, after her daughter was born in 1993, she applied for a child-rearing benefit, this was refused, essentially on grounds of nationality. She contested this refusal. The ECJ ruled that, as a Spanish national, and therefore EU citizen, lawfully resident in Germany, María could invoke Article 18 in conjunction with Article 21(1) in order to challenge discrimination on grounds of nationality.

The Court stated:

JUDGMENT

'[Article 21(1)] attaches to the status of Citizen of the Union the rights and duties laid down by the Treaty, including the right, laid down in [Article 18], not to suffer discrimination on grounds of nationality within the scope of application *ratione materiae* of the Treaty. A citizen of the European Union ... lawfully resident in the territory of the host Member State, can rely on [Article 18] in all situations which fall within the scope *ratione materiae* of [Union] law.'

Martínez Sala was applied in *Grzelczyk* (2001), a case involving a French national in his final year as a student at a university in Belgium. He submitted a claim for financial assistance from the Belgian social service, known as the *minimex*, to allow him to concentrate on his dissertation rather than having to take part-time jobs. However, this was turned down, on the basis that he was neither a Belgian national nor a migrant worker, as required by Belgian legislation. The ECJ, however, held that, as a French national lawfully resident in Belgium, he was protected by Article 21(1) and allowed to invoke Article 18 to claim the *minimex*. The Court stated:

JUDGMENT

'Union citizenship is destined to be the fundamental status of nationals of the Member States, enabling those who find themselves in the same situation to enjoy the same treatment in law irrespective of their nationality, subject to such exceptions as are expressly provided for.'

Other cases involving students invoking the combined effect of Article 21(1) (residence) and Article 18 (non-discrimination) include *D'Hoop* (2002), considered below, and *Bidar* (2005).

CASE EXAMPLE

Bidar (Case C–209/03) [2005] ECR I–2119

Dany Bidar, a French national, had enrolled to study economics at University College London (UCL). He submitted an application for a student loan, but this was turned down on the ground that, under UK legislation, applicants had to have been 'ordinarily resident' in the UK for at least three years prior to submitting the application. Although Bidar had been resident in the UK for three years he had spent this time in full-time education and the UK legislation excluded time spent 'wholly or mainly for the purpose of receiving full-time education'. Bidar challenged this, alleging that it was (indirectly) discriminatory against someone like him, who had come to live in the UK for the purposes of full-time education. The ECJ held that (1) the British rules were indirectly discriminatory, and (2) Bidar, as a French national lawfully resident in the UK, had the right to challenge these rules using a combination of Articles 18 and 21(1). The Court stated emphatically that Article 18 'must be read in conjunction with the provisions of the Treaty on citizenship of the Union'.

The right of citizens to invoke Article 21(1) to challenge national legislation which places them 'at a disadvantage'

In a number of cases the ECJ has upheld claims brought by EU citizens challenging their home state's legislation based purely on Article 21(1), on the basis that the legislation had placed them 'at a disadvantage' because they had 'exercised their freedom to move and to reside in another Member State'. Examples include *Pusa* (2004), *Turpeinen* (2006), *De Cuyper* (2006), *Tas-Hagen* (2006) and *Morgan and Bucher* (2007). There is no requirement in such cases to establish that the legislation in question was either directly or even indirectly discriminatory (although if it was, then Article 18 could be invoked as well).

One of the cases on students, *Morgan and Bucher* (2007), illustrates this point. The case involved two German students at educational establishments in other Member States. Rhiannon Morgan was studying at the University of the West of England in

Bristol, while Iris Bucher was a student at the Hogeschool Zuyd in Heerlen, in the Netherlands. Both women applied for a training grant from the authorities in Germany, but in each case it was turned down on the basis that, although funding was available for study abroad, this was only the case where students were continuing studies that had been commenced in Germany. Both women appealed, and the ECJ agreed that in each case the women, being German nationals lawfully resident in the UK and the Netherlands, respectively, could invoke Article 21(1). The Court ruled that the restriction of funding for overseas students was simply a breach of Article 21(1) itself. The Court stated:

JUDGMENT

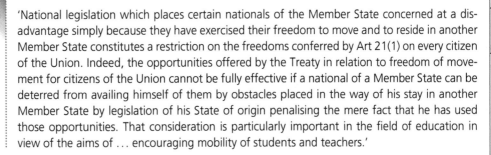

'National legislation which places certain nationals of the Member State concerned at a disadvantage simply because they have exercised their freedom to move and to reside in another Member State constitutes a restriction on the freedoms conferred by Art 21(1) on every citizen of the Union. Indeed, the opportunities offered by the Treaty in relation to freedom of movement for citizens of the Union cannot be fully effective if a national of a Member State can be deterred from availing himself of them by obstacles placed in the way of his stay in another Member State by legislation of his State of origin penalising the mere fact that he has used those opportunities. That consideration is particularly important in the field of education in view of the aims of ... encouraging mobility of students and teachers.'

This development can also be seen in *Pusa* (2004) and *Turpeinen* (2006), both involving retired Finnish nationals who went to live in Spain (presumably to take advantage of the more clement weather in Iberia compared to Scandinavia). The situation where retired persons seek to invoke citizenship rights can only increase in significance in the future, given improving health and living conditions, so these cases are clearly very significant. Both Heikki Pusa and Pirkko Turpeinen had encountered problems after having moved to Spain. Essentially the disputes involved their Finnish retirement pensions being subjected to greater tax liability, as a result of their move to Spain, than would have been the case had they remained in Finland. In each case the ECJ held that Article 21(1) was available, in principle at least, to challenge any disadvantage incurred as a result of exercising their freedom of movement rights. In *Pusa*, the Court stated:

JUDGMENT

'National legislation which places at a disadvantage certain of its nationals simply because they have exercised their freedom to move and to reside in another Member State would give rise to inequality of treatment, contrary to the principles which underpin the status of citizen of the Union, that is, the guarantee of the same treatment in law in the exercise of the citizen's freedom to move.'

The judgment in *Turpeinen* was worded almost identically. Another, similar, category of person seeking to invoke citizenship rights under Article 21(1) is those who have been forced to give up working because of health reasons. The leading case to date is *Tas-Hagen* (2006).

CASE EXAMPLE

Tas-Hagen (Case C–192/05) [2006] ECR I–10451

The case involved two Dutch nationals who had submitted claims for civilian war benefit, which was payable to any Dutch national who had suffered physical and/or mental injury during the Netherlands' involvement in the Second World War. The problem for the two claimants was that, although they had suffered such injuries, the Dutch benefit eligibility rules required claimants to be resident in the Netherlands at the date the claim was submitted. However, by the time both Mr Tas and Mrs Tas-Hagen submitted their claims, in 1999, they were both living in Spain, having moved there after being forced to give up work for health reasons in 1983 and 1987, respectively. Their claims were, therefore, rejected. When the two claimants challenged the rejections, the ECJ held that Article 21(1) had been, in principle at least, infringed. The Dutch benefit eligibility rules made it more difficult for claimants who had exercised free movement rights to claim benefits than those who had stayed in the Netherlands.

Therefore, *Tas-Hagen* decides that a restriction on the availability of civilian war benefit can be challenged using Article 21(1). Now, civilian war benefit is not something that falls within the scope of EU law generally (compare the case of *Baldinger* (Case C–386/02) [2004] ECR I–8411, discussed in Chapter 12, where war compensation was held not to fall within the scope of Regulation 1612/68). However, that appears to have no importance where an Article 21(1) claim is involved. Yuri Borgmann-Prebil ('The Rule of Reason in European Citizenship' (2008) 14 *ELJ* 328) argues this point as follows (emphasis added):

QUOTATION

'The question is whether a citizen of the EU can invoke and rely on [Article 21(1)] in all situations in which he exercises his free movement right, or whether it is a pre-requisite that, in addition to the mere exercise of the free movement right, the situation must concern a substantive area of law that is covered by [Union] law. If the latter were true, the material scope of the [Article] would be delimited by other provisions of [EU] law. If the former were correct, [Article 21(1)] itself would expand the material scope of the Treaty. . . . According to one view . . . reliance on [Article 21(1)] requires that the factual situation falls within the ambit of *other* provisions of [EU] law. The opposite view is epitomised by the Court's jurisprudence ever since Grzelczyk, where the Court held that a situation falls within the material scope *whenever a citizen exercises his free movement rights*. . . . It is submitted that, while the fact that a situation is covered by other provisions of [Union] law may help to clarify that the activity falls within the scope of [Union] law, this does not constitute a necessary pre-condition . . . citizens of the EU can even rely on the fundamental freedom enshrined in [Article 21(1)] in situations that are not specifically covered by [EU] law.'

Citizenship rights can be invoked in the citizen's 'home' state
In *D'Hoop* (Case C–224/98) [2002] ECR I–6191 the ECJ decided that Article 21(1) could be relied upon **in the citizen's home state**, provided that she had gone to another EU Member State in order to exercise her free movement rights before returning.

CASE EXAMPLE

D'Hoop (Case C–224/98) [2002] ECR I–6191

Marie-Nathalie D'Hoop, a Belgian national, had undertaken her secondary school education in France (1985–91) before studying for a degree in Belgium (1991–95). On graduating, she applied for a 'tideover allowance', a social security benefit paid to recent graduates who had undertaken their schooling in Belgium. As Ms D'Hoop had spent some years as a student in France, this was refused. She challenged this, alleging discrimination contrary to Article 18 and relying on her status as a 'Citizen of the Union' under Article 21(1). The ECJ, following *Grzelczyk*, held that she was entitled to the allowance.

Children's rights to invoke Article 21(1)

In *Zhu and Chen* (Case C–200/02) [2004] 3 WLR 1453, the question arose as to (1) whether an infant child could rely upon her status as a 'Citizen of the Union' in order to claim a right of residence in another EU Member State and, if so, (2) whether her mother, as 'primary carer', was entitled to residence with her. The ECJ answered both questions in the affirmative.

CASE EXAMPLE

Zhu and Chen (Case C–200/02) [2004] 3 WLR 1453

Man Lavette Chen and her husband, both Chinese nationals, already had one child, a son, born in 1998. The couple wished to have another child but, because of strict Chinese laws on the number of children allowed per couple, desired that it should be born outside China. When she was six months pregnant, Chen travelled to the UK and, three months later, gave birth to a daughter, named Catherine Zhu, in Belfast in Northern Ireland. Under Irish law, any child born on the island of 'Ireland' (whether the Republic or Northern Ireland) acquired Irish nationality and, thus, Catherine became an Irish citizen. Chen took her daughter to live in Cardiff in Wales. Subsequently, a question arose as to their entitlement to residence in the UK. The ECJ held that, as an Irish national and therefore 'Citizen of the Union', Catherine was entitled to reside in the UK. As her mother and 'primary carer', Chen was allowed to live in the UK with her. No time limit was placed on the right of residence of either Catherine or her mother. (The meaning and scope of the 'primary carer' doctrine is examined below – see section 11.5.3.)

The Court stated:

JUDGMENT

'A young child can take advantage of the rights of free movement and residence guaranteed by [EU] law. The capacity of a national of a Member State to be the holder of rights guaranteed by the Treaty ... cannot be made conditional upon the attainment by the person concerned of the age prescribed for the acquisition of legal capacity to exercise those rights personally.... A refusal to allow the parent, whether a national of a Member State or a national of a non-member country, who is the carer of a child ... to reside with that child in the host Member State would deprive the child's right of residence of any useful effect. It is clear that enjoyment by a young child of a right of residence necessarily implies that the child is entitled to be accompanied by ... his or her primary carer and accordingly that the carer must be in a position to reside with the child in the host Member State for the duration of such residence.'

Another case in which children were held to be entitled to invoke Article 21(1) is *Schwarz* (Case C–76/05) [2007] ECR I–6849. The Schwarz family lived in Germany. In 1998, Herbert Schwarz and his wife Marga decided to send two of their three teenage children to the Cademuir International School in Scotland which specialised in exceptionally gifted children. Under German law, however, this meant that they could not claim tax relief on school fees (around 10,000 DM per year) which would have been available had the children been schooled privately in Germany. They challenged this decision, invoking Article 56 (the freedom to receive services) or, alternatively, Article 21(1). The ECJ decided that the case would fall within Article 56 if the Cademuir School was 'essentially financed by private funds', this being a question of fact for the national court. If not, then Article 21(1) would apply. The Schwarz children had exercised their free movement rights, notwithstanding their youth (following *Zhu and Chen*). In either case, there was a breach, because there was no justification for the discrimination between schooling in Germany and schooling abroad for the purposes of conferring tax relief on school fees. On the ability of children to invoke Article 21(1), the Court stated:

JUDGMENT

'The Schwarz children, by attending an educational establishment situated in another Member State, used their right of free movement. As is shown by the judgment in Zhu and Chen, even a young child may make use of the rights of free movement and residence guaranteed by [Union] law.'

N.B. The German deutschmark ceased to be legal tender when the single European currency was introduced in 2002. The latest ECJ case involving the exercise by children of their citizenship rights under EU law is *Rendón Marín* (Case C–165/14) [2017] 1 CMLR 29; [2017] 2 WLR 117, which will be discussed later in this chapter (see section 11.6.8).

Justification for restrictions on citizens' rights
In many of the cases discussed above, the ECJ ruled that EU citizens could invoke Article 21(1) (either on its own or in conjunction with Article 18) in order to challenge national legislation which was either discriminatory or places the citizen 'at a disadvantage' as a result of he or she exercising their free movement rights. However, in most of those cases, that was not the end of the story. The Court is prepared to listen to arguments that national legislation imposing restrictions on a citizen's free movement rights constituting a *prima facie* breach of Article 21(1) can be justified by referring to 'objective considerations of public interest'. For example, in *Tas-Hagen* (2006), discussed above, the Court stated:

JUDGMENT

'Such a restriction can be justified [but] only if it is based on objective considerations of public interest independent of the nationality of the persons concerned and is proportionate to the legitimate objective of the national provisions ... a measure is proportionate when, while appropriate for securing the attainment of the objective pursued, it does not go beyond what is necessary in order to attain it.'

It is essential to note the four elements of this extract from the Tas-Hagen *judgment. In order for a restriction on a citizen's rights to be justified it must be:*

  'Based on objective considerations of public interest' – the cases of *D'Hoop* (2002), *Bidar* (2005) and *Tas-Hagen* itself, discussed below, provide examples of such 'objective considerations'.

- 'Independent of the nationality of the persons concerned' – the national legislation must either be non-discriminatory or, at the most, 'indirectly' discriminatory. This typically means legislation that, at first sight, appears not to discriminate but in practice has that effect. The most common example is a residency requirement. The cases of *Bidar* and *Tas-Hagen* both illustrate this situation. See also section 12.4.2 for more examples of 'indirect' discrimination.
- 'Appropriate' – the restriction must be capable of achieving the desired objective.
- 'Proportionate' – the restriction must be absolutely necessary. In other words, it should impose the minimum restriction needed in order to achieve the desired objective, and not go any further than that.

D'Hoop (2002), discussed above, illustrates these points. First, the Court accepted that it was 'legitimate for the national legislature to wish to ensure that there is a real link between the applicant for that allowance and the geographic employment market concerned'. In other words, the requirement that claimants had undertaken their schooling in Belgium was potentially justifiable in order to establish a 'real link'. Second, the legislation did not expressly refer to nationality. However, the Belgian legislation failed the appropriateness test. The schooling requirement was not capable of establishing the 'real link', being 'too general and exclusive in nature'.

Bidar (2005) further illustrates this point. In that case the ECJ accepted, in principle, that the UK legislation imposing a residency requirement on applicants for a student loan was *prima facie* justifiable. The Court held that it was 'legitimate' for the UK to seek to ensure

> that an applicant for assistance has demonstrated a certain degree of integration into the society of that State [which] may be regarded as established by a finding that the student in question had resided in the host Member State for a certain length of time.

However, the UK legislation also failed the appropriateness test. The Court stated:

JUDGMENT

'It is common ground that the rules at issue in the main proceedings preclude any possibility of a national of another Member State obtaining settled status as a student. They thus make it impossible for such a national, whatever his actual degree of integration into the society of the host Member State, to satisfy that condition. . . . Such treatment cannot be regarded as justified by the legitimate objective which those rules seek to secure.'

Tas-Hagen (2006) provides another example. The Dutch government argued that the requirement in Dutch law that claimants for civilian war benefit had to be resident in the Netherlands when the claim was made reflected the 'legislature's wish to limit the obligation of solidarity with civilian war victims to those who had links with the population of the Netherlands during and after the war'. Although the ECJ was prepared to accept 'the obligation of solidarity' as an 'objective consideration of public interest', the ECJ held that the residency criterion was not an appropriate means of establishing 'solidarity'. The Court stated:

> a residence criterion ... based solely on the date on which the application for the benefit is submitted, is not a satisfactory indicator of the degree of attachment of the applicant to the society which is thereby demonstrating its solidarity with him.

One case where all four elements were satisfied, including both the appropriateness and proportionality tests, is *Förster* (2008).

CASE EXAMPLE

Förster (Case C–158/07) [2008] ECR I–8507

Jacqueline Förster, a German national, enrolled on a course in educational theory at the College of Amsterdam in the Netherlands. She was initially awarded a student grant, but was subsequently ordered to repay some of the money because, under Dutch law, maintenance grants were only available to students who had been continuously resident in the Netherlands for five years. She challenged the lawfulness of this. The ECJ held that the residency period constituted indirect discrimination but also held that not only was it legitimate in principle (on exactly the same grounds as those identified in *Bidar*, i.e. the need to demonstrate a 'certain degree of integration' into the society of the host state), but that it also satisfied the appropriateness and proportionality tests. The Court stated:

JUDGMENT

'A condition of five years' uninterrupted residence is appropriate for the purpose of guaranteeing that the applicant for the maintenance grant at issue is integrated into the society of the host Member State.... A condition of five years' continuous residence cannot be held to be excessive.'

In *Patmalniece* [2011] UKSC 11, [2011] 1 WLR 783, the UK Supreme Court ruled that a provision in the State Pension Credit Act 2002 which required claimants to be 'habitually resident' in Great Britain constituted indirect discrimination. However, the Court accepted the government's argument that it was justifiable, because of the need 'to prevent exploitation of welfare benefits by people who come to this country simply to live off benefits without working here' (according to Lord Hope). More recently, in *Commission v UK (Social Security Benefits)* (Case C–308/14) [2016] 3 CMLR 41; [2016] 1 WLR 5049, the ECJ held that UK legislation (the Social Security Contributions and Benefits Act 1992 and the Tax Credits Act 2002), which required that people claiming child benefit or child tax credit, respectively, had to be 'ordinarily resident' in the UK was indirect discrimination against EU citizens. However, such discrimination was justifiable based on 'the need to protect the finances of the host Member State'.

There has been criticism of the justifications in some of the cases involving Article 21(1). Samantha Besson and André Utzinger ('Future Challenges of European Citizenship: Facing a Wide-Open Pandora's Box' (2007) 13 *ELJ* 573) criticise 'the elaboration of overbroad justifications' in some of the Article 21(1) cases, which they argue are 'quite vague and leave it to national authorities and courts to determine where to draw the line; this is quite paradoxical given the traditionally strict limitations placed by [EU] law on national restrictions to [EU] rights and principles'. *D'Hoop* and *Bidar* illustrate their point – the justifications accepted by the ECJ were a 'real link' and 'a certain degree of integration', respectively, both of which do appear to be 'quite vague'. However, the Court has offered some guidance on the factors which could be used to establish a 'real link' in *Prete* (Case C–367/11) [2013] 1 CMLR 40, which helps to clarify this area of law. In addition to 'residence in the host State for a period of time', it was possible for a citizen to establish a link 'in other ways such as registration with an employment agency, taking active steps to find work, and marrying a national of the host State'.

Citizenship of the Union	
'Citizenship of the Union' was introduced in November 1993 when the Treaty on European Union came into force.	
Anyone holding the nationality of one of the EU's Member States is a citizen of the Union.	Art 20 TFEU
This includes dual nationals.	*Micheletti* (1992); *Garcia-Avello* (2003)
Citizens of the Union have the right 'to move and reside freely within the territory of the Member States'. This is not just a political statement but is a legally enforceable right.	Art 21(1) TFEU *Baumbast & R* (2002)
Citizenship rights can be invoked by people who are not economically active. Thus the unemployed, students, children and retired people have all been held to have enforceable rights using Art 21(1) TFEU.	*Martínez Sala* (1998); *Grzelczyk* (2001); *Zhu and Chen* (2004); *Pusa* (2004); *Rendón Marín* (2017)
Art 21(1) TFEU, when combined with Art 18 TFEU, can be used to challenge discrimination based on nationality.	*Martínez Sala* (1998); *Bidar* (2005)
Art 21(1) TFEU can also be used to challenge any national legislation which places a citizen 'at a disadvantage' because they invoked their free movement rights.	*Pusa* (2004); *Tas-Hagen* (2006); *Morgan and Bucher* (2007)
Restrictions on citizens' free movement rights are justifiable, if based on objective considerations of public interest, are independent of the nationality of the persons concerned, and capable of achieving the desired objective and which are proportionate (i.e. they go no further than necessary).	*D'Hoop* (2002); *Bidar* (2005); *Tas-Hagen* (2006); *Förster* (2008)

11.4 Citizens' rights of exit, entry and residence: Directive 2004/38

The rights of a citizen to leave the territory of his or her 'home' state, to enter the territory of the 'host' state, to bring their family with them and to set up home there, and even to retire there after their working life is over, are all covered by Directive 2004/38. This repealed pre-existing legislation, Directive 68/360, although some of the case law on that directive is still of relevance today. Indeed, some of that case law has been incorporated into the new directive. This section will provide an overview of the main provisions of the new directive.

11.4.1 Rights of exit: Article 4

Article 4 deals with the right of a citizen to leave their 'home' state in order to work in another state (the 'host' state). Article 4(1)–(3) provides as follows:

ARTICLE

'Art 4(1) ...all Union citizens with a valid identity card or passport and their family members who are not nationals of a Member State and who hold a valid passport shall have the right to leave the territory of a Member State to travel to another Member State.

(2) No exit visa or equivalent formality may be imposed on the persons to whom paragraph 1 applies.

(3) Member States shall, acting in accordance with their laws, issue to their own nationals, and renew, an identity card or passport stating their nationality.'

Note: the meaning and scope of a citizen's 'family members' will be discussed in the next section of this chapter (section 11.5, below).

11.4.2 Rights of entry: Article 5

Article 5(1) provides that Member States must grant to all Union citizens the right to enter their territory with a valid ID card or passport, and must also grant family members who are non-EU nationals the right to enter their territory with a valid passport. Host Member States cannot require an entry visa from Union citizens (Article 5(1)). Member States may require a visa for non-EU national family members, in certain circumstances, but 'possession of the valid residence card referred to in Article 10 shall exempt such family members from the visa requirement' (Article 5(2)). Article 5(2) was considered in *McCarthy & Others* (Case C–202/13) [2015] 2 CMLR 13; [2015] QB 651.

CASE EXAMPLE

McCarthy & Others (Case C–202/13) [2015] 2 CMLR 13; [2015] QB 651

Sean McCarthy, a UK national, lived in Spain with his Colombian wife, Helena. She was in possession of an EU family member's residence card issued by the Spanish authorities under Article 10 of Directive 2004/38 (see below). The family also owned property in the UK, to which they travelled frequently. However, the British government refused to recognise Helena's residence card as exempting her from the visa requirement, because of a government policy which asserted that there was a 'systemic problem' of abuse of rights and fraud by third-country (i.e. non-EU) nationals involving residence cards. The British government alleged that the vast majority of residence cards issued by other EU Member States were susceptible to forgery. This meant that, whenever Helena wished to travel to the UK, she had to travel from the family home in Marbella to Madrid to apply, in person, for an entry permit which would be valid for only 6 months. The permit was not issued automatically and Helena had to provide details of her finances and employment. Eventually, the McCarthy family challenged the British government, alleging a breach of Article 5(2). The ECJ held that Article 5(2) exempted a third-country family member (such as Helena) from the requirement to possess a visa when entering a Member State. Moreover, Article 5(2) was not limited in its scope to states other than the citizen's home state. Therefore, Helena could rely on Article 5(2) in order to enter Sean's home state, the UK, using her Spanish residence card.

Article 5(4) provides:

ARTICLE

'Art 5(4) Where a Union citizen, or a family member who is not a national of a Member State, does not have the necessary travel documents or, if required, the necessary visas, the Member State concerned shall, before turning them back, give such persons every reasonable opportunity to obtain the necessary documents or have them brought to them within a reasonable period of time or to corroborate or prove by other means that they are covered by the right of free movement and residence.'

Finally, Article 5(5) provides that the host Member State may require the person concerned to report his or her presence within its territory within a 'reasonable and non-discriminatory period of time'. Failure to comply with this requirement may make the person concerned 'liable to proportionate and non-discriminatory sanctions'.

11.4.3 Rights of residence for up to three months: Article 6

Article 6(1) provides that Union citizens shall have the right of residence in the 'host' state for a period of up to three months without any 'conditions' or 'formalities' other than the requirement to hold a valid ID card or passport. Article 6(2) applies the provisions of Article 6(1) to non-EU family members who are 'accompanying or joining' the Union citizen, provided that they are in possession of a valid passport.

11.4.4 Rights of residence for more than three months: Article 7

Article 7(1) provides that Union citizens have a right of residence for more than three months in the 'host' state if they:

(a) are workers or self-employed;

(b) have 'sufficient resources' for themselves and their family members not to become a 'burden' on the social assistance system of the 'host' state during their period of residence and have 'comprehensive sickness insurance cover';

(c) are students, have 'comprehensive sickness insurance cover' and 'assure the relevant national authority' that they have 'sufficient resources'.

Article 7(1)(d) adds that the right of residence is also conferred on 'family members accompanying or joining a Union citizen who satisfies the conditions referred to in points (a), (b) or (c)'. Article 7(2) confirms that this right extends to non-EU family members.

Workers or the self-employed: Article 7(1)(a)

The meaning of the word 'worker' and the additional rights enjoyed by workers and their family members will be examined in more detail in Chapter 12; the rights enjoyed by those in self-employment will be examined in more detail in Chapter 13.

Those with 'sufficient resources' not to become a 'burden': Article 7(1)(b)

The directive does not define the phrase 'have sufficient resources' or the word 'burden'. Inevitably, this has generated case law, which has established a number of points. First, there is no requirement that the 'resources' actually belong to the citizen: the question is whether they are 'available' to him. In *Alokpa & Moudoulou* (Case C–86/12) [2017] 1 CMLR 40, the ECJ stated that 'the expression "have" sufficient resources in Article 7(1)(b) must be interpreted as meaning that it suffices that such resources are available to the Union citizens.... That provision lays down *no requirement whatsoever as to their origin'* (emphasis added). This meant that two French children, who had moved to Luxembourg with their mother (a non-EU national) could claim a right of residence in that Member State provided that funds were 'available' to them, either personally or via their mother. Similarly, in *Singh & Others* (Case C–218/14) [2016] 1 CMLR 12; [2016] QB 208, the ECJ held that the 'fact that some part of the resources available to the Union citizen derives from resources *obtained by the spouse* from his activity in the host Member State does not preclude the condition concerning the "sufficiency" of resources in Article 7(1)(b) from being regarded as satisfied'. That case involved three couples living in Ireland: a Latvian woman and her Indian husband; a German woman and her husband, a national of Cameroon; and a Lithuanian woman and her Egyptian husband. It was held to be irrelevant whether or not the three women, all EU citizens, had resources personally. Provided that their respective husbands (all non-EU nationals) had resources which were 'available' to their wives, then the women could invoke Article 7(1)(b).

A second principle which has emerged from the case law is that there is no fixed sum of money which has to be available to the citizen in order to qualify as 'sufficient' resources. In *Brey* (Case C–140/12) [2014] 1 CMLR 37; [2014] 1 WLR 1080, the ECJ held that, 'although Member States may indicate a certain sum as a reference amount, they may not impose a minimum income level below which it will be presumed that the person concerned does not have sufficient resources, irrespective of a specific examination of the situation of each person concerned'. Third, the reference to a 'burden' on the social assistance system meant an 'unreasonable burden'. It followed that the 'mere fact' that a citizen had applied for benefits in the host state was 'not sufficient to show that he constitutes an unreasonable burden on the social assistance system of the host Member State' (*Brey*). This meant that Peter Brey, a retired German national who had moved to Austria, was not necessarily a 'burden' on the Austrian social assistance system merely because he had applied for a 'compensatory supplement' – a form of social security benefit in Austria – in order to top up his income (which comprised his pension and a care allowance for his wife, amounting to just over €1100 per month). However, the fact that a non-economically active citizen, such as Peter Brey, may be eligible to receive a state benefit could be 'an indication' that he did not have 'sufficient resources' to avoid becoming an 'unreasonable' burden. The competent national authorities could not, however, draw such a conclusion without first carrying out an overall assessment of the 'specific burden' which granting that benefit would place on the national social assistance system as a whole, by reference to the 'personal circumstances' of the citizen concerned.

Finally, the reference to 'comprehensive sickness insurance cover' has been held by the Court of Appeal to mean **private** health insurance, and that access to the National Health Service does **not** satisfy this criterion (*Ahmad* [2014] EWCA Civ 988; [2015] 1 WLR 593 and *Pelltari v Southwark* LBC [2015] EWCA Civ 300).

Retention of residence rights: Article 7(3)
Article 7(3) provides that the right of residence conferred by Article 7(1)(a) is not lost by a worker if he or she:

- is temporarily unable to work as the result of an 'illness or accident';
- is in 'duly recorded involuntary unemployment' – if the period of work prior to that point was less than a year, then the 'worker' status is only retained for six months;

embarks on 'vocational training' – unless he or she is involuntarily unemployed, the retention of the status of worker shall require the training to be related to the previous employment.

Some of the provisions of Article 7(3) are ambiguous, but case law is helping to clarify its scope. Most notably, in *St Prix* (Case C–507/12) [2015] 1 CMLR 5, the ECJ held that pregnancy did **not** fall within the scope of the phrase 'illness or accident' and thus a woman who was forced to temporarily leave her job in the late stages of pregnancy was **not** protected by Article 7(3)(a). The Court stated that 'pregnancy must be clearly distinguished from illness, in that pregnancy is not in any way comparable with a pathological condition'. (However, the Court went on to hold that a pregnant woman could retain 'worker' status under Article 45 TFEU instead, subject to certain conditions being met – see Chapter 12.)

In *Samin* [2016] UKSC 1, [2016] 1 WLR 481, the Supreme Court of the UK held that Wadi Samin, an Austrian national living in the UK, could not invoke Article 7(3) because he had been declared *permanently* incapacitated from working on health grounds whereas the Directive only protected those who were 'temporarily' unable to work. Finally, in *Gusa* (Case C–442/16), (not yet reported), the ECJ held that the phrase 'involuntary unemployment' covered both employed and self-employed people whose work had ceased 'for reasons beyond their control'.

11.4.5 Registration: Articles 8–11

Article 8(1) provides that, for periods of residence longer than three months, the 'host' state may require citizens to register with the relevant authorities. Failure to do so 'may render the person concerned liable to proportionate and non-discriminatory sanctions' (Article 8(2)). This point was originally established by the ECJ in a case on Directive 68/360, *Royer* (Case 48/75) [1976] ECR 497, in which the Court ruled that it would be disproportionate to expel or imprison a migrant worker for failing to register.

Once registered, the host state must then immediately issue to the citizen a '**registration certificate**'. In order to register, Article 8(3) provides that the citizen needs to produce certain documents, depending on the capacity in which he or she is seeking to register. In all cases, a valid ID card or passport is required, plus:

- confirmation of engagement from the employer or a certificate of employment, or proof that they are self-employed persons (for those under Article 7(1)(a)); or
- proof that they satisfy the relevant conditions laid down in Article 7(1)(b); or
- proof of enrolment at an accredited establishment, proof of comprehensive sickness insurance cover and the declaration about 'sufficient resources' (for those under Article 7(1)(c)).

Article 8(5) deals with the right of family members (who are also EU nationals) to claim registration certificates. As with the citizen, a valid ID card or passport is required, plus certain additional documents proving the family member's relationship with the citizen (e.g. as spouse, partner, dependant). Non-EU nationals cannot claim such certificates. Instead, Article 9(1) states that non-EU family members are to be issued with a '**registration card**'. As above, failure to comply with the requirement to apply for a registration card may make the person concerned liable to 'proportionate and non-discriminatory sanctions' (Article 9(3)). Article 10 sets out the documents to be provided by the non-EU family member (these are essentially the same as those set out in Article 8(5)). Registration cards 'shall be valid for five years from the date of issue or for the envisaged period of residence of the Union citizen, if this period is less than five years' (Article 11(1)).

11.4.6 Effect of death or departure of the citizen: Article 12

If the citizen dies, or departs the 'host' state, then his or her family members (who are also EU nationals) do not lose their right of residence in that state (Article 12(1)). The situation for non-EU family members is slightly more complicated. Article 12(2) provides that the death of the citizen shall not entail loss of the right of residence of his or her non-EU family members, provided that they have been residing in the host Member State as family members for at least one year before the citizen's death. Article 12(3) adds that neither the death of the citizen, nor their departure from the host Member State, shall entail loss of the right of residence of either his or her children, or of the parent who has actual custody of the children, irrespective of nationality, if the children reside in the host Member State and are enrolled at an educational establishment, for the purpose of studying there, until the completion of their studies. Article 12(3) gives effect to the ECJ's decision in *Baumbast* (2002) which was discussed above.

11.4.7 Effect of divorce, annulment of marriage or termination of registered partnership: Article 13

Article 13 deals with the entitlement of former husbands, wives and partners to remain in the host state after divorce, marriage annulment or the termination of a registered partnership. Article 13 is discussed below (see section 11.5).

11.4.8 Retention of residence rights: Article 14

Article 14 deals with retention of residence rights. It states:

ARTICLE

'Art 14(1) Union citizens and their family members shall have the right of residence provided for in Article 6, as long as they do not become an unreasonable burden on the social assistance system of the host Member State.

(2) Union citizens and their family members shall have the right of residence provided for in Articles 7, 12 and 13 as long as they meet the conditions set out therein . . .

(3) An expulsion measure shall not be the automatic consequence of a Union citizen's or his or her family member's recourse to the social assistance system of the host Member State.

(4) By way of derogation from paragraphs 1 and 2 . . . an expulsion measure may in no case be adopted against Union citizens or their family members if:

(a) the Union citizens are workers or self-employed persons, or

(b) the Union citizens entered the territory of the host Member State in order to seek employment. In this case, the Union citizens and their family members may not be expelled for as long as the Union citizens can provide evidence that they are continuing to seek employment and that they have a genuine chance of being engaged.'

Article 14(4)(b) is designed to implement the ECJ decisions in *Antonissen* (Case C–292/89) [1991] ECR I–745 and *Collins* (2004), which are discussed in more detail in Chapter 12.

11.4.9 Right of permanent residence: Articles 16–21

Articles 16–18 of Directive 2004/38 deal with the acquisition of a permanent right of residence. In *Lassal* (Case C–162/09) [2010] ECR I–9217, the Court emphasised the importance of this right, describing it as 'a key element in promoting social cohesion' which was provided 'in order to strengthen the feeling of Union citizenship'. Article 16 sets out the conditions under which citizens and their family members can acquire a right of permanent residence in the 'host' state. According to Article 16(1), this right is conferred on all citizens who 'have resided legally for a continuous period of five years' in the host state. In *Ziolkowski & Szeja* (Cases C–424, 425/10) [2011] ECR I–14035, the Court held that 'resided legally' meant in accordance with the provisions of Article 7(1); in other words, it was not permissible simply to reside in a Member State for five years and then claim a right of permanent residence.

It logically followed that time spent in prison does **not** count as 'legal' residence for the purposes of Article 16(1). This was confirmed by the ECJ in *Onuekwere* (Case C–378/12) [2014] 2 CMLR 46; [2014] 1 WLR 2420. The Court also held that time spent in prison interrupted the 'continuity' of legal residence and prevented the aggregation of periods before and after imprisonment from counting towards a right of permanent residence. The Court stated:

JUDGMENT

'The EU legislature made the acquisition of the right of permanent residence pursuant to Article 16(1) subject to the integration of the Citizen in the host Member State.... The imposition of a prison sentence by the national court is such as to show the non-compliance by the person concerned with the values expressed by the society of the host Member State in its criminal law.... The taking into consideration of periods of imprisonment for the purposes of the acquisition of the right of permanent residence would clearly be contrary to the aim pursued by that directive.'

In *Lassal*, the ECJ also held that Article 16(1) may be used to claim a right of permanent residence, even though the five years in question was completed prior to the Directive's implementation date (30 April 2006). This ruling was followed in *Dias* (Case C–325/09) [2011] 3 CMLR 40 and *Ziolkowski & Szeja* (2011), in which the Court also held that time spent in a Member State by persons from a non-EU country which *subsequently* became a Member State counted as residency for the purposes of Article 16(1) – provided, of course, that the Article 7(1) criteria were met. This meant that Tomasz Ziolkowski and Barbara Szeja, both Polish nationals, who had been living in Germany since the late 1980s could invoke Article 16(1) to claim a right of permanent residence in Germany even though Poland did not accede to the EU until May 2004.

Article 16(2) provides for non-EU family members. They may also acquire a right of permanent residence provided they have 'legally resided with the Citizen in the host Member State for a continuous period of five years'. The requirement proved problematic for the family member in *Ojo* [2015] EWCA Civ 1301. Miss Ojo, a Nigerian national, entered the UK with her mother (who had acquired Austrian nationality) in July 2007. The two women lived together in the south of England until January 2009 when Miss Ojo moved to Manchester to work. Sixteen months later, Miss Ojo moved back south and returned to live with her mother. However, when Miss Ojo later claimed a right of permanent residence under Article 16(2), the Court of Appeal rejected her claim – she had not resided with her mother 'for a continuous period of five years'.

Thus both Article 16(1) and (2) require 'continuous' residence. This point is amplified in Article 16(3):

'Art 16(3) Continuity of residence shall not be affected by temporary absences not exceeding a total of six months a year, or by absences of a longer duration for compulsory military service, or by one absence of a maximum of 12 consecutive months for important reasons such as pregnancy and childbirth, serious illness, study or vocational training, or a posting in another Member State or a third country.'

Article 16(4) states that, once acquired, the right of permanent residence is lost only through absence from the 'host' state for a period exceeding two consecutive years. In *Dias* (2011), the ECJ noted that a right of permanent residence (once acquired) could be lost, according to Article 16(4), 'only' by spending at least two consecutive years out of the country. However, the Court then stated that the 'integration link' implied by Article 16(1) could also be broken by someone who had legally resided in the host state for at least five years if that was followed by a period of non-legal residence (such as time spent in voluntary unemployment) of at least two years.

Article 17 deals with certain exemptions from the normal five-year qualification period. Article 17(1) states that the right of permanent residence in the 'host' state may be acquired before completion of the continuous five-year residence period laid down in Article 16 by workers or self-employed persons who:

a. At the time they stop working, have reached the age laid down by the law of that Member State for entitlement to an old age pension or workers who cease paid employment to take early retirement, provided that they have been working in that Member State for at least the preceding 12 months and have resided there continuously for more than three years.

b. Have resided continuously in the host Member State for more than two years and stop working there as a result of permanent incapacity to work. If such incapacity is the result of an accident at work or an occupational disease entitling the person concerned to a benefit payable in full or in part by an institution in the host Member State, no condition shall be imposed as to length of residence.

c. After three years of continuous employment and residence in the host Member State, work in an employed or self-employed capacity in another Member State, while retaining their place of residence in the host Member State, to which they return, as a rule, each day or at least once a week.

The remainder of Article 17 deals with family members. Article 17(2) states that the conditions as to length of residence and employment laid down in Article 17(1)(a), and the condition as to length of residence laid down in Article 17(1)(b), shall not apply if the worker's or the self-employed person's spouse or partner is a national of the 'host' state or lost such nationality on marriage to that worker or self-employed person. Otherwise, Article 17(3) or (4) apply. These provisions are as follows:

ARTICLE

'Art 17(3) Irrespective of nationality, the family members of a worker or a self-employed person who are residing with him in the territory of the host Member State shall have the right of permanent residence in that Member State, if the worker or self-employed person has acquired himself the right of permanent residence in that Member State on the basis of paragraph 1.

(4) If, however, the worker or self-employed person dies while still working but before acquiring permanent residence status in the host Member State on the basis of paragraph 1, his family members who are residing with him in the host Member State shall acquire the right of permanent residence there, on condition that:

(a) the worker or self-employed person had, at the time of death, resided continuously on the territory of that Member State for two years; or

(b) the death resulted from an accident at work or an occupational disease; or

(c) the surviving spouse lost the nationality of that Member State following marriage to the worker or self-employed person.'

Article 17(4)(a) is slightly ambiguous – does the two-year residency have to have occurred at any time in the citizen's past, or does it have to immediately precede their death? The ECJ considered the meaning of the phrase 'resided continuously' in *Givane* (Case C–257/00) [2003] ECR I–345. The Court stated that the provision was 'intended to establish a significant connection between, on the one hand, [a] Member State and, on the other hand, [a citizen] and his family, and to ensure a certain level of their integration in the society of that State'. It therefore ruled that the residence period had to occur immediately prior to the citizen's death.

CASE EXAMPLE

Givane (Case C–257/00) [2003] ECR I–345

Rama Givane, a Portuguese national, had lived and worked in the UK for three years (between 1992 and 1995) before leaving for India for ten months. He returned to the UK in February 1996, this time accompanied by his wife Nani and their three children, all of whom were Indian nationals. Rama died in November 1997, some 21 months after his returning to the UK. His relatives argued that he had 'resided continuously' in the UK for at least two years (between 1992 and 1995); the UK Home Office argued that the residence had to be immediately preceding the death. The ECJ agreed with the Home Office.

Article 18 states that the non-EU family members of a citizen may acquire a right of permanent residence in the 'host' state after residing there legally for five consecutive years. Article 19 provides that Member States are to issue to citizens who comply with the above provisions a 'document certifying permanent residence'. Similarly, non-EU family members who comply with the above provisions are to be issued with 'a permanent residence card' (Article 20(1)). Article 21 states: 'Continuity of residence is broken by any expulsion decision duly enforced against the person concerned' (see section 11.6 for discussion of the situations in which Member States can expel other states' nationals).

11.4.10 Territorial restrictions: Article 22
Article 22 states:

ARTICLE

'Art 22 The right of residence and the right of permanent residence shall cover the whole territory of the host Member State. Member States may impose territorial restrictions on the right of residence and the right of permanent residence only where the same restrictions apply to their own nationals.'

11.4.11 Equal treatment: Article 24

Article 24(1) provides for a general principle of 'equal treatment' for all citizens (plus their family members) with the nationals of the 'host' state 'within the scope of the Treaty'. This provision has generated some important case law, primarily dealing with the question whether economically inactive EU citizens can invoke Article 24(1) in order to claim social security benefits. In the first case, *Dano* (Case C–333/13) [2015] 1 CMLR 48; [2015] 1 WLR 2519, the ECJ held that the answer was 'no': only citizens with a right of residence under Article 7(1) – discussed above – could invoke Article 24(1). That meant that the citizen had to be working, self-employed, studying, or have 'sufficient resources' not to become a 'burden' on the host state. The Court stated:

JUDGMENT

'In order to determine whether economically inactive Union citizens can claim equal treatment with nationals of that Member State so far as concerns entitlement to social benefits, it must be examined whether the residence of those citizens complies with the conditions in Article 7(1)(b) of Directive 2004/38.... Those conditions include the requirement that the economically inactive Union citizen must have "sufficient resources". To accept that persons who do not have a right of residence under Directive 2004/38 may claim entitlement to social benefits ... would run counter to an objective of the directive, namely preventing Union citizens from becoming an unreasonable burden on the social assistance system of the host Member State.'

CASE EXAMPLE

Dano (Case C–333/13) [2015] 1 CMLR 48; [2015] 1 WLR 2519

Elisabeta Dano and her son Florin, both Romanian nationals, lived in Leipzig, Germany. Elisabeta applied to the authorities for 'basic provision', a German social security benefit available to German nationals, designed to help them to meet their basic subsistence needs, accommodation and heating costs. However, this was refused, on the basis that Elisabeta had been living in Leipzig for several years (staying with her sister, who provided food and lodging) but had not entered the job market – or even attempted to do so – at any point. She challenged that refusal, but the ECJ held that as she was economically inactive, she was not legally resident in Germany, and therefore had no right to claim equal treatment with German nationals.

Dano was followed in *Alimanovic* (Case C–67/14) [2016] 1 CMLR 29; [2016] QB 308 (economically inactive Swedish nationals not entitled to social security benefits in Germany) and by the UK Supreme Court in *Mirga; Samin* [2016] UKSC 1, [2016] 1 WLR 481 (economically inactive Polish and Austrian nationals not entitled to social security benefits (income support and housing benefit, respectively) in the UK).

Article 24(2) goes on to state that 'the host Member State shall not be obliged to confer entitlement to social assistance during the first three months of residence'. This provision has been interpreted literally. Thus, in *Garcia-Nieto & Others* (Case C–299/14) [2016] 3 CMLR 5; [2016] 1 WLR 3089, the Court held that a provision of German legislation denying social security benefits during a citizen's first three months of residence in Germany was perfectly lawful. This meant that the Garcia-Nieto family who left Spain and went to live in Germany in June 2012 would have to wait until September 2012 at the earliest until becoming eligible to even apply for German social security benefits.

KEY FACTS

Citizens' rights under Directive 2004/38	
Citizens have a right to exit a Member State with an ID card or passport.	Art 4
Citizens have a right to enter a Member State with an ID card or passport.	Art 5
Citizens have an unconditional right of residence in a Member State for 3 months.	Art 6
Citizens have a right of residence in a Member State for more than 3 months if working, self-employed, studying or if they are financially self-sufficient.	Art 7
Citizens may acquire a right of permanent residence in a Member State after 5 years' continuous residency, or earlier than that in certain circumstances.	Arts 16 and 17
Citizens have a right to equal treatment with the nationals of the 'host' state.	Art 24

11.5 The rights of a citizen's family members and Directive 2004/38

11.5.1 The scope of the citizen's family: Article 2

Directive 2004/38 extends the scope of the free movement provisions to a citizen's 'family members'. This is designed to further promote the free movement of citizens: there would clearly be a massive disincentive – financial as well as emotional – if citizens were not permitted by EU law to be accompanied by their families when working or studying abroad. Article 2(2) of the directive defines the citizen's 'family members' as follows:

ARTICLE

'Art 2(2) "Family member" means:

(a) the spouse;
(b) the partner with whom the Union citizen has contracted a registered partnership, on the basis of the legislation of a Member State, if the legislation of the host Member State treats registered partnerships as equivalent to marriage and in accordance with the conditions laid down in the relevant legislation of the host Member State;
(c) the direct descendants who are under the age of 21 or are dependants and those of the spouse or partner as defined in point (b);
(d) the dependent direct relatives in the ascending line and those of the spouse or partner as defined in point (b).'

The Directive was adopted by the Council in April 2004 and its implementation date was 30 April 2006. However, it is very important to appreciate that this was not the first legislative definition of 'family members'. Article 10 of Regulation 1612/68 contained the original definition and, although Article 10 has now been repealed, case law on the earlier Regulation continues to be relevant today.

'Spouse'

The ECJ has held that 'spouse' means only marital relationships. In *Netherlands v Reed* (Case 59/85) [1986] ECR 1283 the ECJ stated:

JUDGMENT

'In the absence of any indication of a general social development which would justify a broad construction, and in the absence of any indication to the contrary in the Legislation, it must be held that the term "spouse" refers to a marital relationship only.'

This decision has attracted criticism (Clare McGlynn, 'Families and the European Union Charter of Fundamental Rights' (2001) 26 *ELR* 582) on the basis that it reinforces stereotypical assumptions about marriage. Notwithstanding this criticism, *Reed* was confirmed in *Hadj Ahmed* (Case C–45/12) (unreported), with the Court stating emphatically that 'a mere cohabiting partner cannot be considered to be a "spouse"'.

Separated, but not yet divorced, couples are still treated as spouses. In *Diatta v Land Berlin* (Case 267/83) [1985] ECR 567 the ECJ stated:

> the marital relationship cannot be regarded as dissolved so long as it has not been terminated by the competent authority. It is not dissolved merely because the spouses live separately, even where they intend to divorce at a later date.

This is so even if they live apart. The ECJ has held that it is not necessary for spouses to cohabit (*Diatta* (1985)):

> It is not for the immigration authorities to decide whether a reconciliation is possible. Moreover, if co-habitation of the spouses were a mandatory condition, the [citizen] could at any time cause the expulsion of his spouse by depriving her of a roof.

CASE EXAMPLE

Diatta v Land Berlin (Case 267/83) [1985] ECR 567

Aissatou Diatta, a Senegalese woman, married a Frenchman in 1977 and in 1978 they set up home together in Germany where he had been working for several years. From August 1978, however, they began living apart. Now separated from her husband and living in rented accommodation in Germany, Mrs Diatta intended to get a divorce as soon as possible. However, she was working in her own right and intended to stay in Germany. When her residence permit expired, in 1980, she applied for a renewal but this was refused on the ground that she was no longer a member of her husband's family. She challenged this and the ECJ held that, while separated but not yet divorced, she had not yet lost her right of residence.

Diatta was followed in *Iida* (Case C–40/11) [2013] 1 CMLR 47, [2013] 2 WLR 788, involving a German woman and her Japanese husband. Although the couple were separated, they were not divorced and therefore Mr Iida was still classed as the 'spouse' of an EU citizen. *Diatta* was followed again in *Ogieriakhi* (Case C–244/13) [2015] 1 CMLR 14; [2014] 1 WLR 3823, involving a French woman (G) and her Nigerian husband (O) living in Ireland. The couple married in 1999 but separated in 2002 and O subsequently spent several years living with another woman. The couple eventually divorced in 2009. The ECJ held that O had retained his spousal status throughout this ten-year period of marriage, even though G and O had been living separately for seven years.

Location and timing of the marriage

The ECJ has held that it is immaterial where the marriage between citizen and spouse took place. In *Metock & Others* (Case C–127/08) [2008] ECR I–6241, the ECJ pointed out that there were no provisions in Directive 2004/38 stipulating 'any requirements as to the place where the marriage of the Union citizen and the national of a non-member country is solemnised'. Moreover, it followed from that conclusion that there were no requirements that the marriage had to have taken place prior to the spouse entering the host Member State. This was despite the fact that Directive 2004/38, Article 3(1) states (emphasis added):

> This Directive shall apply to all Union citizens who move to or reside in a Member State other than that of which they are a national, and to their family members as defined in Article 2(2) who *accompany* or *join* them.

In the *Metock* case itself, a number of non-EU nationals had entered Ireland, the host state (as asylum seekers) and each had subsequently met and then married a citizen of the Union who had arrived in that state after the asylum seeker. When the Irish government decided to commence deportation proceedings against the asylum seekers (who by this stage had had their asylum applications rejected), the ECJ ruled that the order in which the citizen and his or her spouse arrived in the host state was immaterial; what mattered was that the marriage was recognised as genuine.

The Court stated (emphasis added):

JUDGMENT

'It must be determined whether, where the national of a non-member country has entered a Member State before becoming a family member of a Union citizen who resides in that Member State, he accompanies or joins that Union citizen within the meaning of Article 3(1). It makes *no difference* whether nationals of non-member countries who are family members of a Union citizen have entered the host Member State *before* or *after* becoming family members of that Union citizen, since the refusal of the host Member State to grant them a right of residence is equally liable to discourage that Union citizen from continuing to reside in that Member State.'

Although Article 3(1) proved to be no obstacle for the various spouses in *Metock & Others*, it was more problematic for the spouse in *Iida* (2013). The Court decided that Directive 2004/38 could not be invoked when the 'spouse' (and, by extension, all other family members) of the EU citizen was living in a state other than that in which the citizen was resident. This may at first appear harsh, but it is justifiable on the basis that EU law is designed to facilitate the free movement of persons from one Member State to another, which necessarily entails the right of EU citizens to take their family members with them when they move. There would be a serious obstacle to free movement otherwise.

CASE EXAMPLE

Iida (Case C–40/11) [2013] 1 CMLR 47, [2013] 2 WLR 788

Yoshikazu Iida, a Japanese national, married a German national in 1998. In 2004, when they were living in the USA, their daughter was born. In 2005, the family moved to Germany. In 2008, the wife accepted a job offer and moved to Austria, taking their daughter with her, while Mr Iida remained in Germany. Mr Iida sought a declaration that he was entitled to continue to reside in Germany under EU law. However, the ECJ held that although he was still the 'spouse' of an EU citizen under Article 2(2)(a), this did not qualify him as a family member for the purposes of Directive 2004/38, because he was still in Germany and had not moved to Austria to 'accompany or join' his wife, as required by Article 3(1).

The rule that 'spouse' means only marital relationships does not, however, mean that partners in other relationships do not have any rights (*Reed* (1986) – see below). The question whether a **divorced** spouse remained entitled to residence in another EU Member State under EU law was left undecided in *Diatta* (1985), but in *Baumbast* (Case C–413/99) [2002] ECR I–7091 the ECJ made it clear that a divorcee cannot be regarded as a 'spouse'.

Implications of divorce/marriage annulment/termination of registered partnership

Although a divorce terminates the ex-wife or ex-husband's entitlement to residence as a 'spouse', that does not mean that they are no longer protected by EU law. Likewise with the situation of a former registered partner. Article 13 of Directive 2004/38 deals with these situations. Article 13(1) states that if an ex-wife, ex-husband or ex-partner are themselves an EU citizen then they can remain in the 'host' state, based on their own personal free movement entitlements. Article 13(2) deals with the more problematical situation where the ex-wife, ex-husband or ex-partner is a non-EU citizen (as would have been the case if the Senegalese wife in *Diatta* had actually divorced her husband).

ARTICLE

'Art 13(2) ... divorce, annulment of marriage or termination of the "registered partnership" ... shall not entail loss of the right of residence of a Union citizen's family members who are not nationals of a Member State where:

(a) prior to initiation of the divorce or annulment proceedings or termination of the registered partnership ... the marriage or registered partnership has lasted at least three years, including one year in the host Member State; or

(b) by agreement between the spouses or the partners ... or by court order, the spouse or partner who is not a national of a Member State has custody of the Union citizen's children; or

(c) this is warranted by particularly difficult circumstances, such as having been a victim of domestic violence while the marriage or registered partnership was subsisting; or

(d) by agreement between the spouses or partners ... or by court order, the spouse or partner who is not a national of a Member State has the right of access to a minor child, provided that the court has ruled that such access must be in the host Member State, and for as long as is required.'

Two cases have reached the ECJ on Article 13(2): *Singh & Others* (Case C–218/14) [2016] 1 CMLR 12; [2016] QB 208 and *Ahmed* (Case C–115/15) [2017] 1 CMLR 12; [2017] QB 109. In *Singh & Others* (2016) the Court decided that Article 13(2)(a) did not apply to cases in which the citizen had already left the host state before the initiation of divorce or annulment proceedings. The Court held that Article 13(2)(a) only allowed spouses or partners to retain a right of residence (under Article 7(2)) in the event of divorce of annulment, so that if that right had already been lost, prior to the commencement of those proceedings, then Article 13(2)(a) could not 'revive' it. In *Singh & Others*, this meant that the three former spouses (ex-husbands from Cameroon, Egypt and India) were not entitled to remain in the host state (Ireland) on the basis of Article 13(2)(a) because their EU citizen wives (from Germany, Latvia and Lithuania) had already left Ireland *before* the commencement of divorce proceedings. The wives' departure from Ireland (whilst the couples were all still married) extinguished the (then) husbands' residence rights under Article 7(2), which the subsequent divorce proceedings could not revive.

Ahmed (2017) involved a different provision, Article 13(2)(c), but a similar outcome. The Court held that it was too late for a former spouse of an EU citizen to seek to invoke Article 13(2)(c) if divorce proceedings were commenced after the citizen had already left the host state. In this case, an ex-wife (from Pakistan) was not entitled to remain in the host state (the UK) on the basis of Article 13(2)(c) – notwithstanding evidence of domestic violence during the marriage – because her EU citizen ex-husband (a German national) had already left the UK (in December 2006) *before* the commencement of divorce proceedings (in September 2008). His departure from the UK extinguished her right of residence under Article 7(2) and that right could not be revived by Article 13(2)(c).

'Marriages of convenience'

Although the ECJ has held that 'spouse' means 'part of a married couple' only, it subsequently had to qualify that statement by pointing out that 'marriages of convenience' will be regarded as an abuse of this situation. This point was made in *Akrich* (Case C–109/01) [2003] ECR I–9607, the facts of which will be examined in Chapter 12. The Court held that there would be an abuse of EU law if spousal rights to residence had been invoked in the context of 'marriages of convenience', entered into in order to 'circumvent the national immigration provisions'.

In *Rosa* [2016] EWCA Civ 14, involving an alleged marriage of convenience between a Portuguese man and a Brazilian woman with the latter seeking a right of residence in the UK as a 'spouse', the Court of Appeal said that the 'legal burden of proof on the issue of marriage of convenience lies throughout on the Secretary of State', i.e. the Member State.

'Registered partners'

Some care is required here. Directive 2004/38 does not confer 'family member' status on 'partners' in the loose sense of a boyfriend or girlfriend (irrespective of the gender of the citizen). Article 2(2)(b) of the directive only confers 'family member' status on 'partners':

- who have 'contracted a registered partnership, on the basis of the legislation of a Member State'; and
- where 'the legislation of the host Member State treats registered partnerships as equivalent to marriage'.

The reference to 'the legislation of a Member State' means that a partnership registered in, say, New Zealand would not count. For UK nationals seeking to invoke Article 2(2)(b) to confer 'family member' status on a partner, the only relevant legislation is the Civil Partnership Act 2004. Section 1 of the Act defines a 'civil partnership' as 'a relationship between two people of the same sex ("civil partners") … which is formed when they register as civil partners of each other'. In other words, heterosexual couples cannot enter into registered partnerships under UK law. Even for registered partners, the host Member State must have legislation which 'treats registered partnerships as equivalent to marriage'. Not all Member States have such legislation.

However, unregistered partners – whatever their sexual orientation – may invoke Article 3(2)(b) instead. This refers to a 'partner with whom the Union citizen has a durable relationship' – clearly, a much wider concept. This will be examined in more detail below.

'Descendants'

Article 2(2)(c) confers 'family member' status on any 'direct descendants' of the citizen, or of the citizen's spouse or partner, provided that they are under 21 years of age or 'dependent'. This most obviously applies to children (e.g. the daughter in *Iida* (2013)) and grandchildren (see for example *Bigia & Others* [2009] EWCA Civ 79, [2009] 2 CMLR 42, in which the Court of Appeal had no hesitation in holding that the Indian grandchildren of two Portuguese nationals living in the UK were entitled to the protection of Article 2(2)(c)).

As well as blood-relative children, this provision is designed to ensure that the citizen's step-children are included in the family. The previous legislation, Article 10 of Regulation 1612/68, defined the 'family' in terms of a worker, his spouse and "their descendants". This was more ambiguous about the position of step-children, and the ECJ was called upon to decide the point in *Baumbast* (2002), the facts of which were given above. The question was whether a citizen's step-daughter (specifically, his wife's daughter from a previous relationship) could be classed as one of 'their descendants'. The Court – adopting a purposive rather than a literal interpretation of the legislation – held that she could.

Although the position of a citizen's step-children is now clear, the position regarding adopted children has never been raised through litigation in the ECJ and the Directive does not refer to them specifically. However, in *M* [2015] EWCA Civ 1109, [2016] 1 CMLR 45, the Court of Appeal in England had no doubt that an adopted child could be categorised as a 'descendant'. The Court stated that the 'ordinary meaning of "direct descendant" is a *natural* descendant in the direct line: child, grandchild, etc. But it is accepted on all hands that the phrase extends to a person who is a descendant by *adoption*'.

'Dependants'

The test of dependency is a question of fact, that is: does the citizen provide financial support? In *Lebon* (1987), a case on Article 10 of Regulation 1612/68 involving a worker's adult daughter, the ECJ held:

JUDGMENT

'The status of dependent member of a worker's family is the result of a factual situation. The person having that status is a member of the family who is supported by the worker and there is no need to determine the reasons for recourse to the worker's support or to raise the question whether the person concerned is able to support himself by taking up paid employment.'

There is therefore no requirement that the citizen be under a legal obligation to provide support to his or her descendants. In *Lebon* (1987), the ECJ also ruled that a member of the citizen's family does not cease to be dependent simply because they make a claim for a social welfare benefit. If it were otherwise, no member of a citizen's family (apart from the spouse or registered partner and any children under 21) could ever make such a claim without taking themselves outside the scope of the family.

CASE EXAMPLE

Lebon (Case 316/85) [1987] ECR 2811

Marie-Christine Lebon had been born to French parents working in Belgium. She had lived there ever since, apart from two years when she returned to France. On her return to Belgium she was initially granted income support but shortly afterwards this was withdrawn on the basis that she was not seeking work. By this time she was 24 years old. She claimed to be a 'dependant' and thus entitled to the benefit. The ECJ held that the test for dependency was purely a question of fact.

The ECJ looked again at the meaning of dependency in the context of a descendant in *Reyes* (Case C–423/12) [2014] 2 CMLR 39; [2014] 3 WLR 1101. Coincidentally, this case also involved a 24-year-old daughter. The Court held that in order to qualify as a dependent descendant the 'existence of a situation of real dependence' must be established. That status must be the 'result of a factual situation characterised by the fact that material support for that family member is provided', either by an EU citizen or by his/her spouse or partner. In order to determine the existence of such dependence, the host Member State must assess whether, 'having regard to [their] financial and social conditions', the descendant was 'not in a position to support' themselves.

The Court added that the 'need for material support must exist', either in the descendant's home country or in the country from which they came when they applied to join the citizen in the host state. However, there was no need to determine the reasons for that dependence. The fact that an EU citizen 'regularly' and 'for a significant period', paid a sum of money to the descendant in order for them to support themselves was evidence 'to show that the descendant is in a real situation of dependence vis-à-vis that citizen'. The descendant could **not** be required to establish that they had tried to find work or obtain subsistence support or otherwise tried to support themselves. The descendant's job prospects in the host state were irrelevant. The fact that a descendant was 'deemed to be well placed to obtain employment' because of their 'personal circumstances' such as youth, health and qualifications, and intended to start work in the host state, did **not** undermine their status as a dependant. Otherwise, a paradox would be created whereby any descendants aged 21 or over would lose the right to employment or self-employment (guaranteed by Article 23 of Directive 2004/38) on the basis that he or she was no longer a 'family member' precisely because they had good job prospects.

CASE EXAMPLE

Reyes (Case C–423/12) [2014] 2 CMLR 39; [2014] 3 WLR 1101

Flora Reyes, a Filipino national, was born in 1987. When she was three, her mother travelled to Germany in order to work. Flora remained in the Philippines with her grandmother. In due course, Flora's mother obtained German nationality, moved to Sweden and got married. In 2011 Flora, now aged 24, travelled to Sweden to join her mother and stepfather. Flora claimed residence in Sweden as a dependent descendant. The Swedish authorities disagreed and a court in Sweden rejected her appeal, pointing out that Flora was young, with qualifications and relatives in the Philippines, whilst acknowledging that Flora's mother and stepfather had been supporting her financially. On further appeal the case was referred to the ECJ which held that dependency was a question of fact and did not depend on the person's job prospects in the host state or 'personal circumstances' such as age and qualifications.

'Ascendants'

Article 2(2)(d) confers 'family member' status on 'dependent direct relatives in the ascending line', whether that be the 'line' of the citizen or their spouse or partner (as the case may be). This provision is designed to allow citizen's parents and grandparents, and in-laws, to claim 'family member' status. However, in a similar way to the situation of descendants who are aged 21 or over, 'family member' status is not automatic – the ascendant relative must be 'dependent'. The situation is demonstrated by the case of *Jia* (Case C–1/05) [2007] ECR I–1.

CASE EXAMPLE

Jia (Case C–1/05) [2007] ECR I–1

Svanja Schallehn, a German national, had been living and working in Sweden since 1995. Her husband, Shenzhi Li, a Chinese national, was living with her. In May 2003, Li's mother, Yunying Jia, was granted a 90-day single entry visitors visa by the Swedish Embassy in Beijing to visit her son and daughter-in-law in Sweden, and she duly arrived ten days later. Two months after that, she made an application for residence in Sweden as the ascendant relative of an EU citizen's spouse. In order to establish dependency she produced a certificate from her former employer, China Forestry Publishing House, stating that she was financially dependent on her son and daughter-in-law. The Swedish authorities refused and she appealed to the Aliens Appeal Board, which requested a preliminary ruling seeking clarification of Jia's rights of residence. The ECJ decided that she was entitled to reside in Sweden.

One issue in particular was the appropriate test to be used to establish 'dependency'. On this point, the ECJ stated:

JUDGMENT

'In order to determine whether the relatives in the ascending line of the spouse of a [Union] national are dependent on the latter, the host Member State must assess whether, having regard to their financial and social conditions, they are not in a position to support themselves. The need for material support must exist in the State of origin of those relatives or the State whence they came at the time when they apply to join the [Union] national.'

Jia was applied by the Court of Appeal in *Lim* [2015] EWCA Civ 1383. The case involved a Malaysian national, Mrs Lim. She was both divorced and retired; owned a property in Malaysia worth £80,000; and had sufficient savings to meet her own needs. She also had two adult daughters, one of whom lived in the UK with her Finnish husband. Mrs Lim applied to join them in the UK as a dependent relative in the ascending line, but this was rejected. Although Mrs Lim's daughter and son-in-law had regularly been sending her money, the evidence showed that she was in fact financially independent.

In *Iida* (2013), discussed above, the Court considered the possibility that Mr Iida, a Japanese national, might have a right of residence in Germany under Article 2(2)(d), on the basis that he was 'dependent' on his daughter. This was decisively rejected: it was, in fact, the 'converse situation', whereby *she* was still dependent on *him*, on the basis that he paid €300 per month towards her school fees, and not the other way around. The same decision was reached in *Alokpa & Moudoulou* (2017) and *Rendón Marín* (2017). In the former case, the Court held that Ms Alokpa, a Togolese national who lived in Luxembourg with her two young sons (both of whom were French nationals exercising their rights of residence) could not claim to be dependent on them. And in the latter case, the Court held that Mr Rendón Marín, a Colombian national who lived in Spain with his two young children (a boy with Spanish nationality and a girl with Polish nationality) could not claim to be dependent on either of them. In both cases, it was the same type of 'converse situation' as in *Iida*.

'Irrespective of their nationality'
Under Directive 2004/38, the family members may be of any nationality. Among many cases demonstrating this point are *Diatta* (1985), where the spouse was from Senegal;

Baumbast (2002), where the spouse and one child were Colombian nationals; *Givane* (2003), where the spouse and children were from India; *Akrich* (2003), where the spouse was from Morocco; *Jia* (2007), where the spouse and ascendant relatives were from China; *Iida* (2013), where the spouse was Japanese. In *Baumbast* the ECJ confirmed:

JUDGMENT

'As to the fact that the children are not themselves citizens of the Union ... suffice it to state that the descendants of a [Union citizen] who are under the age of 21 or are dependants, *irrespective of their nationality*, are to be regarded as members of his family and have the right to install themselves with that [citizen].'

No requirement that family members have lived in the citizen's home state

In *Akrich* (2003), the ECJ had appeared to suggest that, in order to qualify for residence rights as a 'family member' – in that case, as a spouse – it was necessary that the person had been lawfully resident in the citizen's home state. However, in *Jia* (2007), the ECJ stated that there was no such general requirement:

JUDGMENT

'[EU] law does not require Member States to make the grant of a residence permit to nationals of a non-Member State, who are members of the family of a [Union citizen] who has exercised his or her right of free movement, subject to the condition that those family members have previously been residing lawfully in another Member State.'

Hence, there was no legal obstacle to Mrs Jia, a Chinese national, taking up residence in Sweden as an ascendant relative of her son and daughter-in-law, despite the fact that she (Mrs Jia) had never set foot in Germany, her daughter-in-law's home state.

Situation when the citizen returns 'home'

Consider this question: what would happen if, in the *Jia* case, the German daughter-in-law were to return to Germany, her 'home' state? Would her Chinese husband and mother-in-law be entitled to come to live in Germany with her? This question was raised in *Eind* (Case C–291/05) [2007] ECR I-10719, the Court answering 'yes'.

CASE EXAMPLE

Eind (Case C–291/05) (2007)

Runaldo Eind, a Dutch national, came to the UK to work. Shortly afterwards, he was joined by his 11-year-old daughter Rachel. Prior to that point she had been living in Surinam and held Surinamese nationality. Subsequently, Runaldo returned to the Netherlands, accompanied by Rachel, but the Dutch authorities refused to recognise her claim for residency. The ECJ, however, held that Runaldo, as a Dutch national who had exercised his free movement rights by living and working in the UK before returning to the Netherlands, was entitled on his return to be accompanied by any relatives, irrespective of their nationality, falling within the definition of 'family'. Neither the fact that Mr Eind was now economically inactive (he was not working in the Netherlands because of ill health) nor the fact that Rachel had no pre-existing entitlement to residency in the Netherlands, had any relevance.

Eind was decided under Regulation 1612/68 (subsequently repealed). The question whether the same entitlement arose under Directive 2004/38 arose in *O & B* (Case C–456/12) [2014] 3 CMLR 17; [2014] QB 1163. The Court held not. Article 3(1) of Directive 2004/38 defined the 'beneficiaries' of the rights conferred by it as 'all Union citizens who move to or reside *in a Member State other than that of which they are a national*, and … their family members as defined in [Article 2(2)] who accompany or join them' (emphasis added). It followed from a 'literal, systematic and teleological' interpretation of Directive 2004/38 that it did **not** establish a derived right of residence for non-EU family members in the Member State of which the citizen was a national. However, the Court went on to hold that, in principle, Article 21 TFEU instead conferred such a right, because otherwise, an obstacle to the citizen's free movement rights would be created.

However, this was subject to the condition that 'the residence of the Union citizen in the host Member State has been sufficiently genuine so as to enable that citizen to create or strengthen family life in that Member State'. Hence, Article 21 did not require that 'every' residence in the host state by a citizen accompanied by a non-EU family member necessarily conferred a derived right of residence on that family member in the citizen's home state upon the citizen's return to it. More specifically, residence by the citizen in the host state in accordance with Article 6 of Directive 2004/38 (i.e. for up to three months) was **not** evidence of an intention 'to settle in the host Member State in a way which would be such as to create or strengthen family life in that Member State'. Short periods of residence such as weekends or holidays spent in the host state, even when considered cumulatively, remained within the scope of Article 6 and did not satisfy the condition of 'genuine residence'. Conversely, residence in the host Member State pursuant to and in conformity with the conditions set out in Article 7(1) of the directive (i.e. for more than three months) was, in principle, evidence of 'settling' there and therefore of the citizen's 'genuine residence' in the host state and went 'hand in hand with creating and strengthening family life in that Member State'. This principle applied with particular strength where the citizen had acquired the right of permanent residence in the host state (i.e. after five years' continuous legal residence) in accordance with Article 16(1) of the directive.

11.5.2 Other family members and partners in a durable relationship: Article 3(2)

Article 3(2) of Directive 2004/38 refers to some more categories of family members. It states that Member States are to 'facilitate entry and residence for the following persons':

(a) other family members, irrespective of their nationality, not falling under the definition in Article 2(2) who, in the country from which they have come, are dependants or members of the household of the Union citizen having the primary right of residence, or where serious health grounds strictly require the personal care of the family member by the Union citizen;

(b) the partner with whom the Union citizen has a durable relationship, duly attested.

'Other family members': Article 3(2)(a)

People such as a citizen's siblings, uncles, aunts, cousins, nieces and nephews, who do **not** fall within the four categories of 'family member' above, are classed as 'other family members' (OFMs). However, it is not enough for, say, a citizen's brother or nephew to claim OFM status based purely on their relationship. Article 3(2)(a) states that OFMs must, 'in the country from which they have come', be dependants **or** 'members of the household of the Union Citizen' **or** have 'serious health grounds' which 'strictly require the personal care' of the Union citizen. These concepts are all quite ambiguous, but some clarity has now been provided by the ECJ in *Rahman* (Case C–83/11) [2012] 3 CMLR 55, [2013] QB 249.

'The country from which they have come'

According to *Rahman*, this phrase is to be taken at face value, i.e. it simply refers to the country where the OFMs were living prior to joining the citizen in the host state. 'The country' does not have to be another EU Member State, and there is no requirement that the citizen had to have ever lived there. Hence, in *Rahman*, the two brothers-in-law of Roisin Rahman (an Irish national) were able to travel directly from their home country, Bangladesh, to join her and her husband (their brother) in the host state (the UK).

'Dependants'

According to *Rahman*, the objective of Article 3(2) is to 'maintain the unity of the family in a broader sense' by facilitating entry and residence for persons who are not included in the Article 2(2) definition of 'family member' but 'who nevertheless maintain close and stable family ties with a Union citizen on account of specific factual circumstances, such as economic dependence'. In terms of timing, the Court stated that, whilst it was **not** essential that this relationship of dependency had to exist at the time when the Union citizen settled in the host state, it did have to do so at the time when the OFM applied to join him or her in that state. Whether or not it did so was a question of fact for the national court to decide.

'Members of the household'

The ECJ has not provided any guidance on the meaning of this phrase, although in *Bigia & Others* (2009), Kay LJ in the Court of Appeal said that OFMs 'who seek to travel from a different country to that from which the Union citizen is moving or has recently moved cannot without more be said to be "members of his household"'. The implication here is that whilst OFMs claiming to be dependent on a citizen might live anywhere in the world, even a country where the citizen has never lived (such as the Bangladesh-based brothers-in-law in *Rahman*), OFMs claiming to be members of a citizen's 'household' must have actually lived with the citizen. This is illustrated by the Court of Appeal case of *A* [2014] EWCA Civ 1741; [2015] 2 CMLR 14. In this case, 'A' had lived with his brother 'F' in Algeria before F married an Italian national 'K' and went to live in the UK. A's claim to be an OFM of K, his sister-in-law, was rejected. There was no evidence that A was either dependent on K or that he had never been a member of K's household.

Not only that, but it is probably not enough that the citizen and OFMs had lived together at some point in the distant past. In *Bigia & Others*, Kay LJ said that 'historic but lapsed dependency or membership is irrelevant to the Directive policy of removing obstacles to the Union citizen's freedom of movement and residence rights'. The same judge reiterated this point in *Onaghise* [2014] EWCA Civ 1418, when he said that there had to be a 'nexus of recency' between the arrival of the citizen and of the OFM in the host state. This was because the purpose of Article 3(2) was 'to ensure that the EU citizen is not deterred from exercising Treaty rights by being unable to move with members of his or her household'.

Partners in a durable relationship (Article 3(2)(b))

Someone in this category is in the same position as an OFM. The concept of a 'durable relationship' is very ambiguous. For example, is 'durability' purely a question of longevity, in which case, how long? If there is more to durability than longevity, what else should be required – that the couple had moved in together? That they had children? What other criteria could be used to establish such a relationship? There is no ECJ case law to help answer these questions, but in *B & C v Home Secretary* [2012] EWHC 226 (QB), [2012] 4 All ER 276, the High Court accepted that a Swedish man and his Bolivian girlfriend were in a 'durable' relationship – the couple had been together in London for over six years, they had lived together for most of that time, and they had a five-year-old daughter together.

Rights of OFMs and partners in a durable relationship

Neither OFMs nor partners in a durable relationship have a guaranteed right of entry and residence, and nor do they have any rights to employment. Article 3(2) simply states that 'the host Member State shall … facilitate entry and residence', although it adds that the state concerned must 'undertake an extensive examination of the personal circumstances and shall justify any denial of entry or residence to these people'. In *Rahman*, the ECJ explained that Article 3(2) did not 'oblige' the Member States to accord a right of entry and residence to OFMs. However, because of the words 'shall … facilitate', it was clear that OFMs had 'a certain advantage' compared to people who had no connection to an EU citizen at all, because they were at least entitled to have their application for entry and residence carefully considered by the host state.

11.5.3 The concept of 'primary carer'

In addition to the above legislative definitions, the ECJ has added a further category of family member: the 'primary carer'. In *Baumbast and R v Home Secretary* (2002) the ECJ invented this concept as a means of conferring a continued right of residence on two mothers who would otherwise have faced deportation from the UK (and possible separation from their children):

- *Baumbast v Home Secretary*. Mrs Baumbast, a Colombian national, faced being deported because her German husband had left the UK to work, initially in China and subsequently in Lesotho in southern Africa. She was therefore no longer the spouse of an EU citizen in the UK.

- *R v Home Secretary*. Mrs R, an American national, faced deportation following her divorce from her French husband because she was no longer the **spouse** of an EU citizen.

However, the ECJ held that both women retained rights of residence as 'primary carer' of their children, who were still being educated in British schools. The 'primary carer' doctrine is technically based on Article 10 of Regulation 492/2011, which confers on all children of Union citizens who have worked in another Member State the right to be educated in that state. (Article 10 is examined in more detail in Chapter 12.) In *Baumbast and R*, the Court stated:

JUDGMENT

'The right conferred by [Article 10] necessarily implies that that child has the right to be accompanied by the person who is his primary carer and, accordingly, that that person is able to reside with him in that Member State during his studies.'

The judgment in *Baumbast and R* did leave some questions unanswered. In particular, for how long does 'primary carer' status continue? That question has now been answered by the ECJ in *Teixeira* (Case C–480/08) [2010] ECR I–1107. The ECJ held that 'in principle' children who have reached adulthood are assumed not to require parental care, but that it was possible for the 'primary carer' to be needed beyond that age to help their son or daughter complete their education.

CASE EXAMPLE

Teixeira (Case C–480/08) [2010] ECR I–1107

Maria Teixeira, a Portuguese national, had come to live in London with her husband in 1989, and their daughter Patricia had been born in 1991. Subsequently, the couple divorced and, although Patricia initially lived with her father, she subsequently went to live with her mother. However, Maria did not satisfy any of the conditions for residence in the UK under Article 7 of Directive 2004/38, so the question arose whether she was entitled to exercise a continued residence in the UK based on her being a 'primary carer'. The answer to that question was complicated by the fact that, by this time, Patricia had celebrated her 18th birthday. The Court ruled that it was possible for someone in Patricia's situation to need continued parental care in order to complete their education.

The Court stated:

JUDGMENT

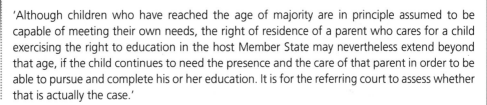

'Although children who have reached the age of majority are in principle assumed to be capable of meeting their own needs, the right of residence of a parent who cares for a child exercising the right to education in the host Member State may nevertheless extend beyond that age, if the child continues to need the presence and the care of that parent in order to be able to pursue and complete his or her education. It is for the referring court to assess whether that is actually the case.'

The 'primary carer' therefore enjoys a right of residence as long as they have a child in education who needs parental support. In *Alarape & Tijani* (Case C–529/11) [2013] 3 CMLR 38; [2013] 1 WLR 2883, the ECJ followed *Teixeira* and confirmed that a primary carer's derived right of residence potentially lasted until the 'child' completed his or her education, even if by that point the 'child' had reached adulthood. The Court added that the determination of whether an adult 'child' continued to need the presence and care of his or her parent in order to pursue and complete their education was a question of fact to be resolved by the national court. This meant that Olaitan Alarape, a Nigerian national, was **potentially** entitled to remain in the UK in order to care for her son, Olukayode Tijani, even though he was by this point in time a 24-year-old PhD student at Edinburgh University. (Olukayode qualified as the 'child' of a 'worker' because Olaitan had been married to a French national whilst the latter was working in the UK.) The ECJ did state that the circumstances and features which the national court may take into account included, *inter alia*, the age of the child, whether the child resided in the family home and whether the child needed financial and/or emotional support from the parent in order to be able to continue and to complete his or her education.

There are no other conditions or restrictions on the primary carer's rights of residence, a point that was made very clearly in *Ibrahim* (Case C–310/08) [2010] ECR I–1065, decided on the same day as *Teixeria*.

CASE EXAMPLE

Ibrahim (Case C–310/08) [2010] ECR I–1065

Nimco Ibrahim, a Somali national, had come to live in the UK with her husband Yusuf, a Danish national, and their children, all of whom were Danish nationals. Yusuf worked for around eight months. Subsequently, he left the UK but Nimco remained in London. According to the ECJ, 'she was never self-sufficient. She does not work and depends entirely on social assistance to cover her living expenses and housing costs. She does not have comprehensive sickness insurance cover and relies on the National Health Service'. In other words, she did not satisfy any of the conditions for residence in Article 7 of Directive 2004/38. Nimco's right to continued residence in the UK therefore depended entirely on her being the primary carer of her children. The Court nevertheless held that primary carer status on its own was sufficient as the basis for residency.

The Court stated:

JUDGMENT

'The children of a national of a Member State who works or has worked in the host Member State and the parent who is their primary carer can claim a right of residence in the latter State on the sole basis of [Article 10 of Regulation 492/2011], without being required to satisfy the conditions laid down in Directive 2004/38 [and] without such a right being conditional on their having sufficient resources and comprehensive sickness insurance cover in that State.'

In *Czop & Punakova* (Cases C–147, 148/11) [2013] Imm AR 104, the ECJ refused to expand the scope of the 'primary carer' concept to include the children of the self-employed. This meant that two otherwise essentially identical cases were decided differently:

- Lucja Czop, a Polish national, had come to live in the UK in 2002, initially as a student, and subsequently in self-employment. Her eldest child was born in Poland, and she had three other children, who were all born in the UK to the same father, a self-employed Polish national called Krzyzowski. The Court held that Lucja did **not** qualify as a primary carer because, despite the fact that her children were studying in the UK, none of them were the children of a 'worker'.

- Margita Punakova, a Czech national, came to live in the UK in 2001. She subsequently gave birth to three children; their father was a Lithuanian national called Buklierius, who was intermittently employed in the UK. The Court held that Margita's children were the children of a (former) worker, and therefore Margita was entitled to remain in the UK as their primary carer.

The Court explained:

JUDGMENT

'It is apparent from the clear and precise wording of [Article 10], which refers to "the children of a national of a Member State who is or has been employed", that that provision applies only to the children of employed persons ... [Article 10], which concerns only employed persons, cannot be interpreted as applying also to the self-employed.'

In *Hadj Ahmed* (Case C–45/12) (2013) (unreported) the Court refused to extend the primary carer concept to a case in which the putative primary carer (an Algerian national) had never been married to the citizen (a French national working in Belgium) and the child in question (also Algerian) was the former's daughter from a previous relationship. As the daughter was not the 'child of a national of a Member State', Article 10 did not apply to her, and hence the primary carer concept did not apply to her mother either.

In the most recent case, *Ahmed* (2017), the facts of which were given above, the ECJ held that although Nazia Ahmed was not entitled to remain in the UK under Article 13(2)(c), she would be entitled to remain under the primary carer doctrine. Her two daughters were in education in the UK and Nazia's ex-husband, the children's father, was a German national who had worked in the UK prior to his departure and so Article 10 applied to them.

11.5.4 Rights to employment: Article 23

Article 23 of Directive 2004/38 confers the right to work on the citizen's family members. It states:

ARTICLE

'Art 23 Irrespective of nationality, the family members of a Union citizen who have the right of residence or the right of permanent residence in a Member State shall be entitled to take up employment or self-employment there.'

It is particularly important to bear in mind that this right is conferred on all family members, 'irrespective of nationality', so that even non-EU nationals can work legally in the EU. Article 23 replaced Article 11 of Regulation 1612/68, which has now been repealed. However, the two leading cases on Article 11 remain relevant as a guide to the interpretation of Article 23. Both of the cases involve family members – spouses – who were non-EU nationals.

Article 11 was applied in *Gül* (Case 131/85) [1986] ECR 1573, involving a Cypriot national, a doctor, who had been refused the right to work in Germany, despite being the spouse of a UK national who was employed there. The ECJ held that such a refusal was in breach of Regulation 1612/68, and emphasised that the authorities of the host state were obliged to 'treat the spouse in a non-discriminatory fashion' in so far as access to employment was concerned.

CASE EXAMPLE

Gül (Case 131/85) [1986] ECR 1573

Dr Emir Gül, a Cypriot national, was married to an English woman working as a hairdresser in Germany. He had qualifications in medicine from Istanbul University in Turkey. He had worked as an anaesthetist in Germany on a temporary basis for some time, where he gained specialist qualifications. When he applied for permission to practise in Germany permanently, however, this was refused on the ground of his nationality. The ECJ held that Dr Gül was entitled to practise in Germany, provided only that his qualifications were recognised in German law.

It should be noted that Cyprus became a Member State of the EU in May 2004, which would have entitled Dr Gül to rely upon EU law in his own right. Nevertheless, the principle of law established remains applicable to other non-EU family members.

In *Mattern & Cikotic* (Case C–10/05) [2006] ECR I–3145, the ECJ was again asked to rule on Article 11 of Regulation 1612/68. The case involved a Luxembourg national, Cynthia Mattern, who was married to a 'Yugoslav' national, Hajrudin Cikotic. Ms Mattern had obtained work in Belgium, so clearly Mr Cikotic would have been entitled to work there, applying the precedent from *Gül*. However, the issue was whether he was entitled to work in a different state – specifically, Ms Mattern's home state of Luxembourg (the couple lived near the border between those two countries). The ECJ refused, stating:

JUDGMENT

'[EU law] does not confer on a national of a third country the right to take up an activity as an employed person in a Member State other than the one in which his spouse, a [Union] national, pursues or has pursued an activity as an employed person in exercise of her right to free movement.'

KEY FACTS

Citizens' family members and their rights under Directive 2004/38	
Citizens are entitled to be accompanied by their family members, irrespective of their nationality.	Art 3(1)
Family members include the spouse, registered partner, direct descendants (who are under 21 or dependent) and dependent relatives in the ascending line.	Art 2(2)
'Spouse' means a marital relationship. Separation does not terminate the spousal status.	*Diatta* (1985); *Reed* (1986); *Iida* (2013); *Ogieriakhi* (2014)
There are no requirements as to when or where the marriage took place.	*Metock and others* (2008)
But the marriage must be genuine. 'Marriages of convenience' do not count.	*Akrich* (2003); *Rosa* (2016)
Descendants includes step-children and adopted children. Where dependency has to be established, this is a question of fact.	*Lebon* (1987); *Baumbast and R* (2002); *Reyes* (2014); *M* (2015)
Relatives in the ascending line includes parents and grandparents. Dependency has to be shown.	*Jia* (2007); *Lim* (2015)
Family members may acquire the right of permanent residence in the Member State.	Art 17
Family members have the right to work, or self-employment, without discrimination, in the same state as the citizen.	Art 23; *Gül* (1986); *Mattern & Cikotic* (2006)
Family members have the right to equal treatment with nationals of the host state.	Art 24
Other family members have a right of entry and residence. This includes partners in a 'durable relationship'.	Art 3(2); *Rahman* (2012)
The ECJ has invented a further category: the primary carer.	*Baumbast and R* (2002)
This is based on Art 10 of Regulation 492/2011 (worker's children's rights to education) and, in principle, ends when the child reaches the age of majority – although it may be extended.	*Teixeira* (2010); *Alarape & Tijani* (2013)
The primary carer enjoys a right of residence based purely on Art 10. None of the conditions in Directive 2004/38 apply.	*Ibrahim* (2010)

11.6 Limitations on free movement – the derogations in Directive 2004/38

The right of free movement for citizens and their family members is not an 'absolute' right. Specifically, the right is subject to 'limitations justified on grounds of public policy, public security or public health'. Further guidance is given in Article 27 of Directive 2004/38:

ARTICLE

'Art 27(1) ... Member States may restrict the freedom of movement and residence of Union citizens and their family members, irrespective of nationality, on grounds of public policy, public security or public health. These grounds shall not be invoked to serve economic ends.

(2) Measures taken on grounds of public policy or public security shall comply with the principle of proportionality and shall be based exclusively on the personal conduct of the individual concerned. Previous criminal convictions shall not in themselves constitute grounds for taking such measures. The personal conduct of the individual concerned must represent a genuine, present and sufficiently serious threat affecting one of the fundamental interests of society. Justifications that are isolated from the particulars of the case or that rely on considerations of general prevention shall not be accepted.'

This provision largely replaces Articles 1–3 of Directive 64/221, which only dealt with workers and their family members, and which has now been repealed. However, many of the cases decided by the ECJ under the old Directive have continuing relevance today, given that both Directives use very similar – in some cases, identical – terms. Indeed, some of the jurisprudence of the ECJ has been adopted into the new Directive. Compare, for example, Article 27(2), above, with the quote from the case of *R v Bouchereau* (1978), below.

11.6.1 Scope of the derogations

The ECJ had handed down a number of important judgments on the scope of Directive 64/221. Although that legislation has now been repealed, many of those judgments are still relevant as a guide to the scope of the derogations under Directive 2004/38.

Directive 2004/38 only applies to restrictions placed on the movement of 'Union citizens and their family members'

This point is made explicitly in Article 27(1), but had already been stated by the ECJ in *Commission v Spain* (Case C–503/03) [2006] ECR I–1097, a case involving Directive 64/221. The ECJ stated that EU law:

enables Member States to prohibit nationals of other Member States or their spouses who are nationals of third countries from entering their territory on grounds of 'public policy' or 'public security'. The [Union's] legislature has nevertheless made reliance by the Member States on such grounds subject to strict limits.

Implicit in this judgment is a principle that Directive 2004/38 does not apply to any case only involving a non-EU national (or, as the Court describes them, 'nationals of third countries'). This can be seen in the decision in *Dem'Yanenko* (Case C–45/03) (2005), unreported, where the ECJ declined jurisdiction in a case involving the deportation of a Ukrainian national from Italy. Two cases in which a citizen's non-EU spouse claimed protection under Article 27 are *Rendón Marín* (2017) and *C.S.* (2017), which will be discussed below (section 11.6.8).

EU nationals do not need to have been lawfully resident in another Member State in order to be protected

This point was made in another case involving Directive 64/221, *Commission v Netherlands* (Case C–50/06) [2006] ECR I–1097, where the ECJ stated:

JUDGMENT

'The safeguards provided by Directive 64/221 call for a broad interpretation as regards the persons to whom they apply. Member States must take all steps to ensure that the safeguard of the provisions of the directive is available to any national of another Member State who is subject to a decision ordering expulsion. To exclude from the benefit of those substantive and procedural safeguards citizens of the Union who are not lawfully resident on the territory of the host Member State would deprive those safeguards of their essential effectiveness.'

The fact that Member States cannot deport their own nationals does not prevent them from deporting other states' nationals

This point was emphasised in *Pereira Roque* (Case C–171/96) [1998] ECR I–4607, where the ECJ stated (emphasis added):

JUDGMENT

'[EU law] permits Member States to adopt, with respect to the nationals of other Member States and on the grounds specified in that provision … measures which they **cannot** apply to their own nationals, inasmuch as they have no authority to expel the latter from the national territory or deny them access thereto. That difference of treatment between a State's own nationals and those of other States derives from a principle of international law which precludes a State from denying its own nationals the right to enter its territory and reside there, and which the [TFEU] cannot be assumed to disregard in the context of relations between Member States.'

11.6.2 'Public policy'

The situations when 'public policy' measures may be invoked are not necessarily concerned with criminal activities (see *Van Duyn v Home Offlce* (Case 41/74) [1974] ECR 1337 – permission to enter the UK refused to a member of the Church of Scientology). The ECJ has given guidance on what sort of behaviour will justify public policy measures. In *R v Bouchereau* (Case 30/77) [1978] ECR 1999, the ECJ held:

JUDGMENT

'Recourse by a national authority to the concept of public policy presupposes, in any event, the existence, in addition to the perturbation of the social order which any infringement of the law involves, of a genuine and sufficiently serious threat to the requirements of public policy affecting one of the fundamental interests of society.'

In *Adoui and Cornuaille* (1982) the ECJ noted that prostitution could amount to a threat to public policy. In *Calfa* (Case C–348/96) [1999] ECR I–11, confirmed in *Orfanopoulos and Oliveri* (Case C–482/01) [2004] ECR I–5257, the ECJ stated that 'the use of drugs constitutes a danger for society such as to justify special measures against foreign nationals who contravene its laws on drugs, in order to maintain public order'. There is no requirement that the activity be criminal according to the law of the Member State (*Van Duyn* (1974)). However, it is important that the Member State concerned is regulating the conduct of which the citizen is accused among its own nationals. This point was made in *Adoui and Cornuaille* (1982).

CASE EXAMPLE

Adoui and Cornuaille v Belgium (Case 115/81) [1982] ECR 1665

Rezguia Adoui and Dominique Cornuaille, both young French women, were employed as waitresses in a bar in Liège in Belgium, which was considered 'suspect from the point of view of morals'. They were prostitutes. The Belgian authorities refused to grant them residence permits. The particular conduct that the authorities were complaining about was that the two women were sitting semi-naked in windows. Such behaviour was subject to, at most, minor penalties in some, but not all, Belgian municipalities. In Liège minor penalties were imposed. The women challenged the refusal of the permits. The ECJ held that public policy measures could only be invoked in situations when the Member State concerned took 'repressive measures' or other 'genuine and effective measures' against its own nationals. The Court left it to the Belgian court to decide whether the test had been satisfied.

The Court stated:

JUDGMENT

'Conduct may not be considered as being of a sufficiently serious nature to justify restrictions on the admission to or residence within the territory of a Member State of a national of another Member State in a case where the former Member State does not adopt, with respect to the same conduct on the part of its own nationals repressive measures or other genuine and effective measures intended to combat such conduct.'

This point was reiterated in *Jany and Others* (Case C–268/99) [2001] ECR I–8615, involving six women who were refused residence permits despite working as self-employed prostitutes in Amsterdam. The ECJ stated that EU law did not 'impose on Member States a uniform scale of values as regards the assessment of conduct which may be considered to be contrary to public policy', before repeating its judgment in *Adoui* (1982).

In *Oteiza Olazabal* (Case C–100/01) [2002] ECR I–10981, the ECJ authorised the imposition of 'public policy' measures involving an EU citizen's residence rights in specific areas of another Member State. The ECJ stated:

JUDGMENT

'In situations where nationals of other Member States are liable to banishment or prohibition of residence, they are also capable of being subject to less severe measures consisting of partial restrictions on their right of residence, justified on grounds of public policy, without it being necessary that identical measures be capable of being applied by the Member State in question to its own nationals.'

It seems that the ECJ reached its decision because otherwise the complainant (a Spanish national convicted of terrorism offences in France) would have to be deported from France. This would not be in keeping with the fundamental requirement of proportionality.

In *Rutili* (Case 36/75) [1975] ECR 1219, the ECJ explained that the 'genuine and serious threat' test was designed to ensure compliance with Articles 8–11 of the European Convention on Human Rights (ECHR), that restrictions were available in the interests of national security or public safety only when **necessary** for the protection of those interests in a democratic society.

11.6.3 'Public security'

This is reserved for serious crimes and subversive, anti-state activities, e.g. terrorism and espionage. Public security was specifically referred to in *Oteiza Olazabal* (2002), involving a member of ETA (*Euskadi Ta Askatasuna* (Basque Homeland and Freedom)). Formed in 1959, the organisation seeks autonomy for the Basque area of northern Spain. The ECJ stated:

JUDGMENT

'The defendant in the main proceedings ... has been sentenced in France to 18 months' imprisonment and a four-year ban on residence for conspiracy to disturb public order by intimidation or terror ... he formed part of an armed and organised group whose activity constitutes a threat to public order in French territory. Prevention of such activity may, moreover, be regarded as falling within the maintenance of public security.'

An important case on the scope of the 'public security' derogation is *Tsakouridis* (Case C–145/09) [2010] ECR I–11979. The Court was asked whether involvement in criminal activity (in this case, drug trafficking) could be classified as a public security (rather than public policy) matter. It answered in the affirmative:

JUDGMENT

'A threat to the functioning of the institutions and essential public services and the survival of the population, as well as the risk of a serious disturbance to foreign relations or to peaceful coexistence of nations, or a risk to military interests, may affect public security. It does not follow that objectives such as the fight against crime in connection with dealing in narcotics as part of an organised group are necessarily excluded from that concept. Dealing in narcotics as part of an organised group is a diffuse form of crime with impressive economic and operational resources and frequently with transnational connections. . . . Illicit drug trafficking poses a threat to health, safety and the quality of life of Citizens of the Union, and to the legal economy, stability and security of the Member States. Since drug addiction represents a serious evil for the individual and is fraught with social and economic danger to mankind, trafficking in narcotics as part of an organised group could reach a level of intensity that might directly threaten the calm and physical security of the population as a whole or a large part of it.'

In *P.I.* (Case C–348/09) [2012] 3 CMLR 13, [2012] QB 799, the ECJ was asked whether the public security derogation could be applied to someone convicted of child sex offences. Again, the Court responded in the affirmative, holding that it was open to the Member

States to regard certain criminal offences, such as the sexual exploitation of children, as constituting a particularly serious threat to one of the fundamental interests of society, which might pose a direct threat to the calm and physical security of the population and thus be covered by the concept of public security 'as long as the manner in which such offences were committed discloses particularly serious characteristics'. Whether or not that was the case was for the national courts to decide.

11.6.4 'Public health'

Article 29 of Directive 2004/38 provides as follows:

ARTICLE

'Art 29(1) The only diseases justifying measures restricting freedom of movement shall be the diseases with epidemic potential as defined by the relevant instruments of the World Health Organisation and other infectious diseases or contagious parasitic diseases if they are the subject of protection provisions applying to nationals of the host Member State.

(2) Diseases occurring after a three-month period from the date of arrival shall not constitute grounds for expulsion from the territory.

(3) Where there are serious indications that it is necessary, Member States may, within three months of the date of arrival, require persons entitled to the right of residence to undergo, free of charge, a medical examination to certify that they are not suffering from any of the conditions referred to in paragraph 1. Such medical examinations may not be required as a matter of routine.'

There is no ECJ case law (yet) to provide any guidance on phrases such as 'diseases with epidemic potential', or 'other infectious diseases or contagious parasitic diseases'.

11.6.5 'Proportionality'

Article 27(2) states that 'Measures taken on grounds of public policy or public security shall comply with the principle of proportionality.' An example of this can be seen in the case of *Oulane* (Case C–215/03) [2005] ECR I–1215, where a French national had been arrested behaving suspiciously at Rotterdam railway station in the Netherlands, in an area closed off to the public. He was unable to produce any ID, nor could he give a residence address and had no luggage. He was detained and, a week later, he was deported. Subsequently he brought a legal challenge to the deportation. The ECJ decided that deportation in such circumstances would be disproportionate. The Court stated:

JUDGMENT

'Detention and deportation based solely on the failure of the person concerned to comply with legal formalities concerning the monitoring of aliens impair the very substance of the right of residence directly conferred by [Union] law and are manifestly disproportionate to the seriousness of the infringement.'

In *Tsakouridis* (2010), the Court provided further guidance on the meaning of the 'proportionality' requirement. The Court stated:

'To assess whether the interference contemplated is proportionate to the legitimate aim pursued ... account must be taken in particular of the nature and seriousness of the offence committed, the duration of residence of the person concerned in the host Member State, the period which has passed since the offence was committed and the conduct of the person concerned during that period, and the solidity of the social, cultural and family ties with the host Member State. In the case of a Union citizen who has lawfully spent most or even all of his childhood and youth in the host Member State, very good reasons would have to be put forward to justify the expulsion measure.'

The case of *Byankov* (Case C–249/11) [2013] 1 CMLR 15, [2013] 2 WLR 293, further illustrates the 'proportionality' test. The case involved Bulgarian legislation which prevented those who owed a 'considerable' debt to another person from leaving the country. This was held to be disproportionate (and therefore contrary to Article 27(1)) because the prohibition was 'absolute', that is, it was 'not coupled with any exceptions, temporal limitation' – i.e. it could last indefinitely – 'or possibility of regular review of the factual and legal circumstances underpinning it'.

Two recent decisions of the Court of Appeal further illustrate the application of the proportionality test. In *Vassallo* [2016] EWCA Civ 13, [2016] 2 CMLR 12, the Court quashed a deportation order against an Italian national who had been convicted by British courts on 31 separate occasions of a grand total of 68 offences (mainly of dishonesty offences, including numerous offences of burglary). The fact that he had lived in the UK since 1952 (i.e. for *over 60 years*), was married to a British national and had two children who were also British citizens, meant that it would be disproportionate to deport him. By way of contrast, in *X.H.* [2017] EWCA Civ 41, [2017] 2 WLR 1437, the Court of Appeal held that the Home Secretary's decision to cancel the passport of a British national was proportionate, based on the evidence that he was an 'Islamic terrorist' who was 'likely to travel overseas in the future in order to engage in further terrorism-related activity ... these activities overseas would present a risk to the national security of the United Kingdom'.

11.6.6 'Personal conduct'

Article 27(2) of the Directive states: 'measures taken on grounds of public policy or public security shall be based exclusively on the personal conduct of the individual concerned'. Applying this, the ECJ has held that Member States may not justify deportation of an individual on the ground that it will serve as an example to others. In *Bonsignore* (Case 67/74) [1975] ECR 297, the ECJ emphasised how public policy and/or public security measures 'cannot be justified on grounds extraneous to the individual'. In the same case the ECJ held that 'The concept of "personal conduct" expresses the requirement that a deportation order may only be made for breaches of the peace and public security which might be committed by the individual affected'. In *Calfa* (1999), the complainant faced automatic deportation from Greece, having committed a relatively minor drugs offence. The ECJ held that deportation was not permissible without taking account of the individual's personal conduct.

CASE EXAMPLE

Calfa (Case C–348/96) [1999] ECR I–11

Donatella Calfa, an Italian national, was convicted of the possession and use of prohibited drugs while on holiday in Greece. The Greek court sentenced her to three months' imprisonment and expelled her for life from Greece, as required by Greek law. The law in question provided for automatic expulsion for life unless there were compelling reasons, in particular family reasons, that would justify the person's continued residence in Greece. The expulsion could be revoked only by and at the discretion of the Minister for Justice. Miss Calfa appealed against the expulsion, arguing that Greece was not empowered to expel a national of another Member State for life if a comparable measure could not be taken against a Greek citizen. The ECJ held that automatic expulsion was contrary to the 'personal conduct' requirement. The Court noted that expulsion for life 'automatically' followed a criminal conviction, without any account being taken of the 'personal conduct' of the offender or of the danger that that person represented.

The Court stated:

JUDGMENT

'The existence of a previous criminal conviction can ... only be taken into account in so far as the circumstances which gave rise to that conviction are evidence of personal conduct constituting a present threat to the requirements of public policy ... an expulsion order could be made against [an EU citizen] only if, besides her having committed an offence under [national] laws, her personal conduct created a genuine and sufficiently serious threat affecting one of the fundamental interests of society.'

This seems correct. After all, there is a huge difference between, on one hand, someone who is caught with a substantial amount of a highly dangerous drug such as heroin which they clearly intend to sell and, on the other hand, someone who has only a small amount of a recreational drug for her own personal use. Yet, under Greek law, all drug offenders were subject to the same blanket rule: automatic life-time expulsion.

A similar provision of national legislation was examined by the ECJ in *Oliveri* (2004). The case concerned the *Ausländergesetz* (German law on aliens), which provided for mandatory deportation for foreign nationals in certain circumstances, one being where a foreign national committed a drugs offence or a public order offence and was sentenced to a term of imprisonment (para 47). The ECJ stated that such mandatory deportation would be incompatible with the Directive.

The Court also held that a practice adopted in Germany, whereby courts were prohibited, when reviewing the legality of national authorities' deportation orders, from taking into account any subsequent factual developments, constituted a breach of the personal conduct criterion.

CASE EXAMPLE

Oliveri (Case C–493/01) [2004] ECR I–5257

Raffaele Oliveri, an Italian national, was born in Germany in 1977 and had lived there ever since. He became a drug addict and committed several offences of theft and one offence of dealing illegally in drugs, for which he received a prison sentence. As a result of his drug-taking, he developed HIV in 1998 which subsequently became full-blown AIDS in 2001. He had been sentenced to prison in April 2000 and, in August 2000, the German authorities issued a deportation order against him. The decision was based on his lengthy criminal record for drugs offences, but his deportation order was mandatory under para 47 of the *Ausländergesetz*. In September 2000, Oliveri challenged this, claiming that he had 'gained maturity' while in prison, such that there was no risk of reoffending following his eventual release. In addition, the prison hospital service indicated that Oliveri was seriously ill and 'likely soon to die of his illness'. The ECJ upheld his challenge.

The Court stated:

JUDGMENT

'In practice, circumstances may arise between the date of the expulsion order and that of its review by the competent court which point to the cessation or the substantial diminution of the threat which the conduct of the person ordered to be expelled constitutes.... That is especially so if a lengthy period has elapsed between the date of the decision to expel the person concerned and that of the review of that decision by the competent court.'

The Court dealt with a similar issue in *Orfanopoulos* (2004). This case involved another provision of the *Ausländergesetz*, under which certain foreign nationals have 'special protection', including those living in a family relationship with a German national (para 48). This protection means that deportation is only available on 'serious' grounds of public security and policy. When a foreign national entitled to special protection commits an offence that would normally lead to mandatory deportation, such as those in para 47, he can still be deported – not automatically, but 'as a general rule'. In effect, there is a presumption in favour of deportation. The Court held that the presumption in para 48 also breached the personal conduct requirement of the directive. The Court held that it was essential in **every** case to take into account a number of factors:

- the nature and seriousness of the offences committed;
- the length of residence in the host Member State;
- the period which has elapsed since the commission of the offence;
- the family circumstances of the person concerned;
- the seriousness of the difficulties which the spouse and any of their children risk facing in the country of origin of the person concerned.

CASE EXAMPLE

Orfanopoulos (Case C–482/01) [2004] ECR I–5257

Georgios Orfanopoulos, a Greek national, had gone to live in Germany in 1972, when aged 13. In 1981, he married a German national, and they went on to have three daughters. Georgios was occasionally in employment but these jobs were interrupted by long periods of unemployment. He became a drug addict, and was convicted nine times for drug-related offences and crimes of violence. He was sentenced to six months' imprisonment in 1999 and in January 2000 he was hospitalised for detoxification. By September 2000 he was back in prison. Eventually, in February 2001, the German authorities ordered his expulsion, to take effect on his release from prison. The decision was based in part on the length and seriousness of his criminal record and partly on the risk of reoffending (because of his drug dependency). As he was married to a German national, his deportation order was based on para 48 of the *Ausländergesetz*, in that he posed a serious threat to German public policy. He challenged this outcome, and the ECJ held that para 48 breached both Article 8 of the ECHR (protection of family life) and the Directive (personal conduct requirement).

The Court stated:

JUDGMENT

'The importance of ensuring the protection of the family life of [Union citizens] in order to eliminate obstacles to the exercise of the fundamental freedoms guaranteed by the Treaty has been recognised under [EU] law. It is clear that the removal of a person from the country where close members of his family are living may amount to an infringement of the right to respect for family life as guaranteed by Article 8 of the ECHR, which is among the fundamental rights which are protected in [EU] law.'

Bonsignore (1975) was applied by the Court of Appeal in *Straszewski & Kersys* [2015] EWCA Civ 1245, [2016] 1 WLR 1173. The court dismissed the Home Secretary's appeal against decisions of the Immigration Tribunal to quash deportation orders against Jacek Straszewski (a Polish national who had been convicted of robbery and inflicting GBH), and Darius Kersys (a Lithuanian national who had been convicted of fraud). The Home Secretary argued that the decisions to quash the deportation orders failed to recognise the importance of deterring other foreign nationals from committing similar offences and the need to reflect 'public revulsion' in the offenders' conduct. Moore-Bick LJ rejected these arguments. He said that 'deterrence, in the sense of measures designed to deter others from committing similar offences, has of itself no part to play in a decision to remove the individual offender. Similarly, it is difficult to see how a desire to reflect public revulsion at the particular offence can properly have any part to play, save, perhaps, in exceptionally serious cases'.

Membership of organisations and the 'personal conduct' rule

According to *Van Duyn* (1974), membership of an organisation may constitute 'personal conduct'. Thus, members of organisations known to pose a threat to public policy or security (most obviously terrorist groups) can be made subject to deportation orders or refusals of entry purely on the basis of their membership. However, the ECJ distinguished between past and present membership.

CASE EXAMPLE

Van Duyn v Home Office (Case 41/74) [1974] ECR 1337

Yvonne Van Duyn, a Dutch national and member of the Church of Scientology, was offered a position as secretary in the UK's branch of the church, the Hubbard College of Scientology in East Grinstead. On arriving at Gatwick Airport she presented her offer of employment to immigration officials, but was refused entry, on the ground that the Home Office had declared undesirable any person entering the country to work for the Church. However, the Church itself was not banned under UK law, and no restrictions were placed on UK nationals becoming employees of the Church. Miss Van Duyn therefore sought a declaration from the High Court that this refusal infringed her right to free movement, in particular the 'personal conduct' criterion. The ECJ held that it was possible for an individual, by reason of their present membership of an organisation to be engaging in 'personal conduct'.

The Court stated (emphasis added):

JUDGMENT

'Although a person's *past* association cannot, in general, justify a decision refusing him the right to move freely within the [EU] ... *present* association, *which reflects participation in the activities of the body or the organisation as well as identification with its aims or designs*, may be considered a voluntary act of the person concerned and, consequently, as part of his personal conduct.'

This decision is highly significant, as it allows Member States to expel EU nationals who are known to be a present member of a terrorist organisation, without having to prove that the individual has committed any specific offence. For example, in *Gallagher* (Case C–175/94) [1995] ECR I–4253, the UK authorities expelled a known IRA member. Although there was evidence that he had committed a firearms offence, under the *Van Duyn* (1974) ruling this would not have been necessary. Establishing his membership of the IRA alone would have sufficed. Another case example is *Oteiza Olazabal* (2002), discussed above. Again, he had been convicted by a French court of a terrorist offence but, under *Van Duyn* (1974), restrictions could have been placed on his free movement simply by establishing his membership of the terrorist group ETA.

Van Duyn has application beyond terrorist organisations. In *R v Kraus* [1982] Crim LR 468, the Court of Appeal authorised the removal of a German national from the UK, partly on the basis of criminal activity, and partly on the basis of his membership of the Nazi party. Watkins LJ said that 'We are entitled to take notice ... that members of parties such as the Nazi party are notorious for their unswerving allegiance to the objectionable cause they seek to serve and for the ruthlessness with which they seek to achieve their aims'. More recently, in *Wahl v Iceland* (Case E–15/12) [2014] 1 CMLR 29, the EFTA Court (which has jurisdiction over the three Member States of the European Free Trade Association that are also members of the European Economic Area, i.e. Iceland, Norway and Liechtenstein) applied *Van Duyn*. The EFTA Court held that the Icelandic authorities were entitled to refuse entry on public policy grounds to a Norwegian national who was known to be a member of the Hells Angels motorcycle gang, described in the judgment as an 'international motorcycle club associated with organised crime'.

11.6.7 Excluded situations

Directive 2004/38 provides that measures taken on the grounds of public policy, security or health will **not** be justified in two situations.

'Economic ends': Article 27(1)

This would mean, for example, that a Member State could not deny entry to an EU citizen from another state on the ground that there was high unemployment in the state. The meaning of 'economic ends' was considered in *Aladzhov* (Case C–434/10) [2011] ECR I–11659. A Bulgarian businessman had been prevented from leaving Bulgaria until he paid around €22,000 in back taxes. He challenged this, arguing that it would severely impact on his business interests which required a lot of foreign travel. The ECJ held that non-payment of tax may fall within the scope of 'public policy'. Moreover, since the purpose of taxes was to ensure the 'funding of actions of the Member State on the basis of the choices which are the expression of, *inter alia*, its general policy in economic and social matters', measures adopted by a Member State in order to ensure that they were paid could not be said to have been adopted exclusively to serve 'economic ends'.

'Previous criminal convictions': Article 27(2)

Previous criminal convictions shall not 'in themselves' constitute grounds for the taking of such measures. So what significance do they have? In *R v Bouchereau* (1978) the ECJ emphasised that the individual had to represent a 'present' threat.

CASE EXAMPLE

R v Bouchereau (Case 30/77) [1978] ECR 1999

Pierre Bouchereau, a French national working in the UK, was convicted of possession of a small quantity of cannabis and amphetamine in January 1976. He was given a 12-month suspended sentence. In June 1976, Pierre was back before the courts, this time pleading guilty to a charge of possession of a small amount of LSD and amphetamine. The stipendiary magistrate contemplated a recommendation for deportation. However, he sought guidance from the ECJ, which held that deportation was permissible only when the individual posed a 'genuine and serious threat' to society. Having received this guidance, the magistrate decided that Pierre did not constitute such a threat and fined him £35 instead.

The Court offered the following guidance:

JUDGMENT

'The existence of a *previous* criminal conviction can ... only be taken into account in so far as the circumstances which gave rise to that conviction are evidence of personal conduct constituting a *present* threat to the requirements of public policy. Although, in general, a finding that such a threat exists implies the existence in the individual concerned of a propensity to act in the same way in the future, it is possible that past conduct alone may constitute such a threat to the requirements of public policy.'

This distinction between a 'previous conviction' and a 'present threat' was utilised by the English Immigration Appeal Tribunal in the following cases:

- *Monteil v Secretary of State for the Home Dept* [1984] 1 CMLR 264 – a deportation order issued against M, a French national working in the UK, was quashed, despite a string of criminal convictions. The tribunal found that there was evidence that M was a reformed character, having undertaken treatment for alcoholism while in prison.

- *Proll v Secretary of State for the Home Dept* [1985] Imm AR 118 – an immigration officer's decision to deny entry into the UK to P, a German national, was quashed, despite the fact that she was a former member of the Baader–Meinhof terrorist organisation and had served a year in prison for armed robbery. The tribunal found that there was evidence that she had reformed after her time in prison; she had also matured over the years since her time in the terrorist organisation.

The decision in *R v Bouchereau* (1978) suggested that a single conviction of a serious offence could be enough to justify deportation. This was confirmed by the English High Court in *R v Secretary of State for the Home Dept, ex p Marchon* [1993] 2 CMLR 132, involving the smuggling of a large quantity of illegal drugs.

11.6.8 Procedural safeguards

The need to examine the individual's circumstances: Article 28(1)

Article 28(1) of Directive 2004/38 provides as follows:

ARTICLE

'Art 28(1) Before taking an expulsion decision … the host Member State shall take account of considerations such as how long the individual concerned has resided on its territory, his/her age, state of health, family and economic situation, social and cultural integration into the host Member State and the extent of his/her links with the country of origin.'

This list of 'considerations' in Article 28(1) echoes the list provided by the ECJ in *Orfanopoulos* (2004). More recently, in both *Rendón Marín* (2017) and *C.S.* (2017), the ECJ (without referring to Article 28(1)), emphasised the importance of taking into account the effect of deportation of any children who might be affected. The Court stated that an expulsion decision involving a person who is the sole carer of a child (or children) can result 'only from a specific assessment by the national court of all the current and relevant circumstances of the case [including] the child's best interests…. That assessment must therefore take account [of] the age of the child at issue and his state of health, as well as his economic and family situation'.

CASE EXAMPLE

Rendón Marín (Case C–165/14) [2017] 1 CMLR 29; [2017] 2 WLR 117

Alfredo Rendón Marín, a Colombian national, lived in Spain. He was the father and sole carer of two minor children: a boy of Spanish nationality (X) and a girl of Polish nationality (Y). (The whereabouts of the children's mother, a Polish national, are unknown.) Both children were EU citizens and the Polish daughter, being resident in Spain, was exercising her free movement rights. In 2010, Alfredo applied for a Spanish residence permit but this was refused because he had a criminal record. (Spanish legislation precluded – absolutely – the granting of a residence permit to foreign nationals with a criminal record.) He challenged that refusal, arguing that to deny him a residence permit would be tantamount to ordering his expulsion from Spain; this in turn would mean his two children having to leave Spain as well in breach of EU law. The ECJ held that the automatic refusal of a residence permit, based only on Alfredo's criminal conviction and without any consideration given to his personal conduct and with no assessment of the currency or gravity of the threat (if any) which he posed to Spanish society, was contrary to Article 27.

CASE EXAMPLE

C.S. (Case C–304/14) [2017] 1 CMLR 31; [2017] QB 558

CS, a Moroccan national, married a British citizen and came to live in the UK in 2003. In 2011, their son was born and acquired British nationality. CS had sole care and custody of the child. In 2012, CS was convicted of a criminal offence and was sentenced to twelve months' imprisonment. Five months' later, CS was notified that, by reason of her criminal conviction, she was liable to be deported. (Section 32(5) of the Borders Act 2007 provides that, where a person who is not a British citizen is convicted in the UK of an offence and is sentenced to a period of imprisonment of at least 12 months, the Home Secretary must make a deportation order.) On release from prison, CS challenged the deportation order. The ECJ held that 'in exceptional circumstances', a Member State could adopt an expulsion measure provided that it was founded upon the individual's personal conduct constituting a genuine, present and sufficiently serious threat adversely affecting the society of that state, and was based on 'consideration of the various interests involved'. Ultimately, that was a matter for the national court to determine.

In *Dumliauskas & Others* [2015] EWCA Civ 145, the Court of Appeal identified another potentially relevant 'consideration': the (relative) prospects of rehabilitation in the individual's home state and the host state. Sir Stanley Burnton said that:

JUDGMENT

'Rehabilitation is not infrequently linked to the health of the offender. In Article 28(1), 'health' is expressly referred to as a factor to be taken into account in the determination of proportionality.... It is notorious that a great deal of offending is linked to illicit drugs and/or to alcohol. Addiction to drugs leads to crimes of acquisition, including theft, burglary and robbery, aimed at financing the purchase of drugs to feed the addiction. Alcohol affects self-restraint and is particularly associated with crimes of violence.... The Secretary of State must consider the relative prospects of rehabilitation, in the sense of ceasing to commit crime, when considering whether an offender should be deported.'

Special protection for those with a right of permanent residence: Article 28(2)

Article 28(2) applies to anyone with a right of permanent residence, meaning those who have been resident for at least five years in the host state. It states:

ARTICLE

'Art 28(2) The host Member State may not take an expulsion decision against Union citizens or their family members, irrespective of nationality, who have the right of permanent residence on its territory, except on serious grounds of public policy or public security.'

The ECJ has yet to consider what is meant by 'serious' policy or security grounds, but the Court of Appeal has done so. In *Bulale* [2008] EWCA Civ 806, [2009] QB 536, the Court held that there was a distinction to be drawn between crimes of dishonesty (such as theft) and crimes of violence (including robbery). Only the latter category of criminal offending would cross the 'serious' threshold, opening up the possibility of the authorities taking an expulsion decision against those with permanent residency. The case itself involved a Dutch national (B) who had resided in the UK for over five years, thereby acquiring a right of permanent residence. However, he had also committed a number of criminal offences, including robbery. The Court of Appeal held that this entitled the Home Secretary to deport B, on the basis that his involvement in violent crime constituted 'serious' public policy grounds.

Extra protection for those with ten years' residence and minors: Article 28(3)

Article 28(3) applies to those with at least ten years' residence in the host state, and to minors.

ARTICLE

'Art 28(3) An expulsion decision may not be taken against Union citizens, except if the decision is based on imperative grounds of public security, as defined by Member States, if they:

(a) have resided in the host Member State for the previous 10 years; or
(b) are a minor, except if the expulsion is necessary for the best interests of the child.'

The leading case on Article 28(3) is *Tsakouridis* (2010).

'Imperative grounds'

In both *Tsakouridis* and *P.I.* (2012), the Court was asked whether public security (rather than public policy) applied. The reason was that both cases involved EU citizens (from Greece and Italy, respectively) who had lived in the host Member State (Germany in both cases, coincidentally) for over ten years and hence could only be deported on 'imperative grounds of public security'. As well as explaining the scope of 'public security' and the 'proportionality' requirement, in *Tsakouridis* the Court offered some guidance on the meaning of the phrase 'imperative grounds', when it said (emphasis added):

JUDGMENT

'By subjecting all expulsion measures in the cases referred to in Article 28(3) to the existence of "imperative grounds" of public security, a concept which is considerably stricter than that of "serious grounds" within the meaning of Article 28(2), the EU legislature clearly intended to limit measures based on Article 28(3) to "exceptional circumstances". The concept of "imperative grounds of public security" presupposes not only the existence of a threat to public security, but also that such a threat is of a *particularly high degree of seriousness*, as is reflected by the use of the words "imperative reasons".'

'Resided ... for the previous ten years': Article 28(3)(a)

The Court in *Tsakouridis* also addressed this phrase. The question arose because the Greek national in that case had travelled extensively between Greece and Germany during the ten years preceding his conviction for drug trafficking, which called into question his entitlement to rely upon Article 28(3)(a). The Court stated:

JUDGMENT

'The decisive criterion is whether the Union citizen has lived in that Member State for the ten years preceding the expulsion decision. The national authorities ... are required to take all the relevant factors into consideration in each individual case, in particular the duration of each period of absence from the host Member State, the cumulative duration and the frequency of those absences, and the reasons why the person concerned left the host Member State. It must be ascertained whether those absences involve the transfer to another State of the centre of the personal, family or occupational interests of the person concerned. The fact that the person in question has been the subject of a forced return to the host Member State in order to serve a term of imprisonment there and the time spent in prison may, together with the factors listed in the preceding paragraph, be taken into account as part of the overall assessment required for determining whether the integrating links previously forged with the host Member State have been broken.'

CASE EXAMPLE

Tsakouridis (Case C–145/09) [2010] ECR I–11979

Panagiotis Tsakouridis, a Greek national, was born in Germany in 1978, and had lived in Germany virtually ever since. However, for eight months in 2004, he lived in Rhodes, Greece, where he ran a crêpe stall, before returning to Germany. In October 2005, he returned to Rhodes and continued running his crêpe stall. A few weeks later, a German court issued an international arrest warrant for him. He was arrested in Greece a year later and extradited to Germany in March 2007. In August 2007, he was sentenced to six years' imprisonment for drug dealing. In August 2008, the authorities in Germany decided to expel him from Germany, taking the view that such a step was justified on public security grounds. The ECJ held that it was a matter for the national authorities to decide whether his absences from Germany for several months in 2004 and again in 2005 affected his entitlement to rely upon Article 28(3), but that in any event drug trafficking was serious enough to engage the public security derogation.

In *Onuekwere* (2014), discussed above (see section 11.4.9), the Court held that time spent in prison did **not** count as 'residence' for the purpose of acquiring a right of permanent residence under Article 16. In *M.G.* (Case C–400/12) [2014] 2 CMLR 40; [2014] 1 WLR 2441, the ECJ reached exactly the same conclusion with respect to Article 28(3)(a). Moreover, the Court held that the ten-year period of residence necessary for the grant of the enhanced protection provided for in Article 28(3)(a) must be calculated by counting **backwards** from the date of the deportation order, **not** by counting forwards from the date of the individual's arrival in the host state. The Court also ruled that, in principle, 'such periods interrupt the continuity of the period of residence for the purposes of that provision'.

The effect of this is that if a deportation order is issued against an individual who is in, or has only recently been released from, prison, it will be very difficult, if not impossible, for them to invoke Article 28(3)(a). For example, in *Warsame* [2016] EWCA Civ 16, [2016] 4 WLR 77, the Court of Appeal held that Article 28(3)(a) did **not** apply to a Dutch national (W) who had arrived in the UK in April 1998 and who was issued with a deportation order in January 2012, some 13 years and 9 months' later. This was because in the interim, W had been sentenced to terms of imprisonment twice – in March 2007 and October 2009. Therefore, by starting in January 2012 and counting backwards from there but not counting time in prison, it could **not** be said that W had 10 years' continuous residence in the UK.

Children: Article 28(3)(b)

Article 28(3)(b) applies to cases involving children, ruling out deportation except where it would be in their 'best interests'. This is an intriguing concept and it will be interesting to see what guidance the ECJ offers as to when it will be in a child's 'best interests' to be deported.

Giving reasons: Article 30

Article 30(1) states: 'the persons concerned shall be notified in writing of any decision taken under Article 27(1), in such a way that they are able to comprehend its content and the implications for them'. This does not mean that the notification has to be in the individual's own language; they just have to be able to 'comprehend' it. In *Petrea* (Case C–184/16) (not yet reported), the Court held that Article 30(1) does not require 'that the removal order is to be translated into the language of the person concerned, but requires by contrast that the Member States take the necessary measures to ensure that the latter understands the content and implications of that decision'.

CASE EXAMPLE

Petrea (Case C–184/16) (not yet reported)

In 2011, Mr Petrea, a Romanian national, had been convicted of robbery by a Greek court and given a suspended prison sentence. He was also issued with a deportation order and notified (albeit not in Romanian) about his rights in an 'information bulletin'. Shortly afterwards, he declared in writing that he had waived his legal remedies and wished to return to his home country. He then returned to Romania, but subsequently (in 2014) alleged that the Greek authorities had breached Article 30(1) by ordering his removal from Greece but not providing him with a notice in Romanian. This complaint was rejected. The evidence showed that he had understood the contents of the information bulletin and had not requested a translation.

Article 30(2) adds that the person concerned should be informed of the grounds of public policy, public security or public health upon which the decision taken in his case is based, unless this is contrary to the interests of the security of the state involved. The authorities must give the person a precise and comprehensive statement of the reasons for its decision (*Rutili* (1975)). Without adequate reasons, the person cannot prepare a full defence.

There is an apparent contradiction inherent in Article 30(2) in public security cases, requiring as it does Member States' obligation to inform the person concerned of the public security grounds on which any restriction on free movement is based – unless the interests of state security take precedence. The ECJ was asked to clarify Article 30(2) in Z.Z. (Case C–300/11) [2013] 3 CMLR 46; [2013] QB 1136. The Court ruled that Article 30(2) 'must be interpreted strictly, but without depriving it of its effectiveness'. This meant that Member States were permitted not to disclose 'certain information' to the person concerned in the light of 'overriding considerations connected with State security'. More specifically, the Court acknowledged that full disclosure of evidence in public security cases may 'endanger the life, health or freedom of persons or reveal the methods of investigation specifically used by the national security authorities and thus seriously impede, or even prevent, future performance of the tasks of those authorities'.

However, the Court also held that the Member States had the task of proving that state security would in fact be 'compromised' by precise and full disclosure. It followed that there was 'no presumption that the reasons invoked by a national authority exist and are valid'. At the very least, the person concerned must be informed of 'the essence' of the grounds on which a decision refusing entry taken under Article 27(1) was based. The Court stressed that 'the necessary protection of State security cannot have the effect of denying the person concerned his right to be heard'.

CASE EXAMPLE

Z.Z. (Case C–300/11) [2013] 3 CMLR 46; [2013] QB 1136

Z.Z., a dual French–Algerian national, was refused entry to the UK on grounds of public security. He appealed, unsuccessfully, to the Special Immigration Appeals Commission. The SIAC issued two judgments: an 'open' judgment and a 'closed' judgment; the latter was provided only to the Secretary of State and to Z.Z.'s two 'special advocates'. (The 'special advocates' represented Z.Z. before the SIAC but were precluded from seeking further instructions from, or providing information to, Z.Z. or his lawyers without the permission of the SIAC.) In the 'open' judgment, the SIAC acknowledged *inter alia* that 'little of the case' against Z.Z. had been disclosed to him, that those elements 'did not really engage with the critical issues' but that for reasons explained only in the 'closed' judgment, it was satisfied that Z.Z. represented a genuine, present and sufficiently serious threat to British public security. Z.Z. appealed, contending that Article 30(2) required disclosure of the reasons for his exclusion from the UK. The ECJ explained that full disclosure could compromise state security operations and even endanger lives, but that at the very least a person whose free movement had been restricted was entitled to be informed of 'the essence' of the grounds against him.

Appeals and reviews: Article 31

Article 31 provides for appeals against, and reviews of, measures taken by Member States to restrict the free movement of other states' nationals. Article 31(1) provides:

ARTICLE

'Art 31(1) The persons concerned shall have access to judicial and, where appropriate, administrative redress procedures in the host Member State to appeal against or seek review of any decision taken against them on the grounds of public policy, public security or public health.'

This replaces Article 8 of Directive 64/221, which has been repealed, although some of the case law on that provision is of continuing relevance, for example *Royer* (1976) and *Pecastaing* (1981).

In *Royer*, the ECJ was asked whether a deportation order could be executed immediately, or whether such an order became effective only after all national judicial remedies had been exhausted. The ECJ stated:

JUDGMENT

'All steps must be taken by the Member States to ensure that the safeguard of the right of appeal is *in fact* available to anyone against whom a restrictive measure of this kind has been adopted. However, this guarantee would become illusory if the Member States could, by the immediate execution of a decision ordering expulsion, deprive the person concerned of the opportunity of *effectively* making use of the remedies which he is guaranteed by legislation.'

In *Pecastaing* (Case 98/79) [1981] ECR 691, the ECJ stated:

A Member State cannot ... render the right of appeal for persons covered by the directive conditional on *particular requirements as to form or procedure* which are less favourable than those pertaining to remedies available to nationals in respect of acts of the administration.

Duration of exclusion orders: Article 32

Article 32 deals with the duration of any exclusion order made by a Member State. Article 32(1) provides:

ARTICLE

'Art 32(1) Persons excluded on grounds of public policy or public security may submit an application for lifting of the exclusion order after a reasonable period, depending on the circumstances, and in any event after three years from enforcement of the final exclusion order which has been validly adopted in accordance with [Union] law, by putting forward arguments to establish that there has been a material change in the circumstances which justified the decision ordering their exclusion.'

Expulsion as a penalty or legal consequence: Article 33

Article 33(1) provides that Member States may not make expulsion an automatic consequence of a person from another Member State committing a criminal offence in their territory. This is consistent with pre-existing ECJ case law on the 'personal conduct' criterion, examined above, in particular *Calfa* (1999) and *Orfanopoulos & Oliveri* (2004). In that sense Article 33(1) simply confirms existing law and practice. Article 33(2) provides:

ARTICLE

'Art 33(2) If an expulsion order, as provided for in paragraph 1, is enforced more than two years after it was issued, the Member State shall check that the individual concerned is currently and genuinely a threat to public policy or public security and shall assess whether there has been any material change in the circumstances since the expulsion order was issued.'

The separation in time between a deportation order being made and its enforcement, as contemplated by Article 33(2), is likely to occur if an order is made when a convicted criminal is serving a prison sentence, with the order to take effect on release. This situation can be illustrated using the facts of *Santillo* (Case 131/79) [1980] ECR 1585. This case actually involved a different issue – the question for the ECJ was whether a trial judge's recommendation to deport could be regarded as valid some four-and-a-half years later (the ECJ ruled that this was a matter for national courts to decide). Were the facts of this case to recur now, then there would be no need to have recourse to Article 33(2) as the date when the Home Secretary's deportation order was made (September 1978) was only seven months before the date when the order was enforced (April 1979).

CASE EXAMPLE

Santillo (Case 131/79) [1980] ECR 1585

Mario Santillo, an Italian, was living in the UK. In December 1973, after a Crown Court trial, he was convicted of the rape and indecent assault of two prostitutes. In January 1974 he was sentenced to eight years' imprisonment, with a recommendation from the trial judge that it be followed by deportation. Four-and-a-half years later, in September 1978, the Home Secretary made an order for his deportation as soon as his sentence was completed. Santillo completed his sentence in April 1979 after remission for good behaviour. He was due to be released but was retained in detention pending deportation. He sought judicial review to quash the deportation order, on the basis that four-and-a-half years had passed between the 'recommendation' and the deportation order. The High Court referred the case to the ECJ, which held that a lapse in time between the judicial recommendation of deportation, and the deportation order itself, was 'liable to deprive the recommendation of its function'. Whether or not it did so was a question of fact for the national court to decide. Applying this to the facts, the High Court decided that the trial judge's recommendation was still valid, there being no evidence that the position had changed in the intervening four-and-a-half years.

11.6.9 Application to Member States' own nationals

The vast majority of the above cases in this section involve restrictions imposed by Member States on other states' nationals. However a Member State can also impose restrictions on its own nationals. An example is *Jipa* (Case C–33/07) [2008] ECR I–5157.

CASE EXAMPLE

Jipa (Case C–33/07) [2008] ECR I–5157

In September 2006, Gheorghe Jipa, a Romanian national, left Romania to go to Belgium. However, he was repatriated to Romania on account of 'illegal residence' by the Belgian authorities two months later, pursuant to a 'Re-admission Agreement' concluded between Romania and the Benelux countries. This triggered a provision of Romanian law, which provides that restrictions may be imposed on the free movement rights of Romanian citizens, for up to three years, under certain conditions. One such condition involved the citizen being repatriated by a state under a readmission agreement concluded between Romania and that state. Subsequently, in January 2007, the Romanian government sought to impose a restriction on Jipa's movement. He challenged this, and the case was referred to the ECJ. There, it was held that Directive 2004/38 applied to such a situation (especially given the 'right of exit' in Article 4) and would have to be justified using the criteria in Article 27, as described above.

The Court stated:

JUDGMENT

'The fact that a citizen of the Union has been subject to a measure repatriating him from the territory of another Member State, where he was residing illegally, may be taken into account by his Member State of origin for the purpose of restricting that citizen's right of free movement only to the extent that his personal conduct constitutes a genuine, present and sufficiently serious threat to one of the fundamental interests of society.'

There have since been other cases before the ECJ involving restrictions on Member States' own nationals, including *Aladzhov* (2012) and *Byankov* (2013), discussed earlier, both of which involved Bulgarian nationals who were prevented from leaving Bulgaria on public policy grounds linked to unpaid taxes and an unpaid debt, respectively.

Even before *Jipa*, the Court of Appeal had already addressed this point, in the context of football banning orders, in *Gough and Others* [2001] 4 All ER 289. These are orders which may be imposed under the UK's Football Spectators Act 1989 (as amended) on English football hooligans in order to prevent them travelling to watch matches in Europe involving the England national side or English clubs. When banning orders were imposed on four individuals, they challenged the legality of the orders under EU law (and the European Convention on Human Rights). Laws LJ dismissed the challenges, holding that: 'in a proper case a Member State may be justified on public policy grounds in preventing a citizen of the Union from leaving its shores'. A more recent example of a restriction being imposed by the UK on a British national is *X.H.* (2017), who had his passport cancelled because the government suspected that he intended to travel to Syria to participate in terrorist activities. *X.H.* was discussed above (in section 11.6.5).

11.7 Citizens' political rights: Articles 22–25 TFEU

Article 22(1) TFEU states that every citizen of the Union, if residing in an EU Member State of which he or she is not a national, has the right to both vote in, and even to stand as a candidate at, 'municipal elections' of the host state 'under the same conditions as nationals of that State'. This would mean, for example, that any French or German national living in the UK would be entitled to vote in any UK municipal elections provided that they were at least 18 years of age (the minimum British voting age). They could also stand for election if they were at least 18 years of age (the minimum age for British candidates) and, if elected, could then serve provided they were not disqualified (UK law disqualifies certain people from holding political office, such as some convicted criminals, undischarged bankrupts and the mentally disordered).

Article 22(2) adds:

every citizen of the Union residing in a Member State of which he is not a national shall have the right to vote and to stand as a candidate in elections to the European Parliament in the Member State in which he resides, under the same conditions as nationals of that State.

Limitations on citizens' rights of free movement and residence under Directive 2004/38	
Member States may limit the free movement and residence of EU citizens and their family members on grounds of public policy, security or health.	Art 27(1)
Any 'measures' must be based exclusively on the personal conduct of the individual. Present membership of an organisation amounts to 'personal conduct'.	Art 27(2); *Bonsignore* (1975); *Calfa* (1999); *Van Duyn* (1974)
Any 'measures' must comply with the principle of proportionality.	Art 27(2); *Oulane* (2005)
Previous criminal convictions do not, in themselves, constitute grounds for taking measures. But they may be relevant if they provide evidence of a present threat.	Art 27(2); *R v Bouchereau* (1977)
Member States may take measures (such as deportation) against citizens from other states which they cannot take against their own nationals.	*Pereira Roque* (1998)
Measures will only be permitted if the Member State imposes genuine and effective measures against its own nationals for the same conduct.	*Adoui and Cornuaille* (1982); *Jany and others* (2001)
The person must pose a genuine, present and sufficiently serious threat to society.	Art 27(3); *R v Bouchereau* (1977)
Measures must not be 'based on considerations of general prevention'.	Art 27(3); *Orfanopoulos and Oliveri* (2004)
Before taking an expulsion decision, Member States must take into consideration factors such as the citizen's age, health, family and economic situation, etc.	Art 28(1)
This is to ensure compliance with the right of all citizens to respect for their private and family life.	Art 8 ECHR; *Rutili* (1975); *Orfanopoulos and Oliveri* (2004)
An expulsion decision may only be taken against citizens with the right of permanent residence on 'serious' grounds of policy or security	Art 28(2)
An expulsion decision may only be taken against citizens with 10 years' residency, or minors, on 'imperative' grounds of public security.	Art 28(3)
Public health refers only to diseases with epidemic potential, infectious diseases and contagious parasitic diseases.	Art 29
Persons must be notified in writing of any decisions taken under the Directive.	Art 30
Persons have the right to appeal against and/or seek judicial review of any decision taken under the Directive. These remedies must be made available in fact.	Art 31; *Royer* (1976); *Pecastaing* (1981)
Expulsion from a Member State may not follow automatically from a criminal conviction.	Art 33(1); *Calfa* (1999); *Orfanopoulos and Oliveri* (2004)
Expulsion orders enforced more than 2 years after issue must be checked to ensure the person is still a present threat.	Art 33(2)
Member States may impose restrictions on the free movement of their own nationals, subject to the provisions of the Directive.	*Jipa* (2008)

Article 22(2) was examined by the ECJ in *Eman & Sevinger* (Case C–300/04) [2006] ECR I–8055. The case involved two Dutch nationals who were resident in Aruba, a Caribbean island some 15 miles off the coast of Venezuela. Aruba is classed as an overseas territory of the Netherlands. However, the Dutch authorities had refused to register them for the European Parliament elections in 2004 because of provisions in Dutch law which conferred the voting franchise on all Dutch nationals resident in the Netherlands (but excluding the Dutch Antilles and Aruba), plus other Member States' nationals resident in the Netherlands. The complainants contested that this was a breach of their rights under Article 22(2).

However, the ECJ rejected their claim on this basis. Although the Court accepted that EU citizens resident in one of the 'overseas countries and territories' (OCTs) could rely on EU law, it held that Article 22(2) did not apply to 'a citizen of the Union residing in an OCT who wishes to exercise his right to vote in the Member State of which he is a national'. The Court stated that, as a general principle, there was nothing in the present state of EU law which prevented Member States from insisting on residency as a criterion in conferring the franchise on voters and also for establishing the right to stand for election. Here the Court noted that the European Court of Human Rights had earlier held, in *Melnychenkov v Ukraine* (2004), that the obligation to be resident within national territory in order to be able to vote is a requirement which is not, in itself, unreasonable or arbitrary and which can be justified on several grounds. The ECJ concluded: 'the criterion linked to residence does not appear, in principle, to be inappropriate to determine who has the right to vote and to stand as a candidate in elections to the European Parliament'.

Article 23 TFEU confers certain diplomatic rights on citizens of the Union. Specifically, citizens have the right to protection by the diplomatic or consular authorities of other Member States if they are in a non-EU country and there is no diplomatic or consular office from that person's own state. For example, a Latvian national – and hence also a citizen of the Union – would be able to rely upon protection from a British embassy in any country in the world if there happened to be no Latvian diplomatic presence in that country.

Finally, Article 24 TFEU allows citizens of the Union to:

- petition the European Parliament;
- apply to the Ombudsman established under Article 228 TFEU; and
- write to 'any of the institutions' (namely the European Parliament, the European Commission, the Council, the European Council, the ECJ, the European Central Bank and the Court of Auditors) in any of the 'authentic' languages mentioned in Article 55(1) TEU and to receive a reply in the same language.

KEY FACTS

Citizens' political rights	
Citizens of the Union have the right to vote and stand for election in EU Member States other than their home state.	Art 22(1) TFEU
Citizens of the Union have diplomatic protection.	Art 23 TFEU
Citizens of the Union have the right to write to any of the EU's institutions (in particular the European Parliament) in any of the EU's authentic languages and to receive a reply in the same language.	Art 24 TFEU

Essay 1: 'The rights enjoyed by citizens of the Union and their family members under Articles 18 and 21(1) TFEU, and Directive 2004/38, are extensive – but not unconditional. Critically consider the extent to which Member States can legitimately restrict those rights (other than on grounds of public policy, security or health).'

Explain the concept of citizenship:
- All nationals of the EU's Member States are automatically EU citizens (Article 20 TFEU)
- This includes dual nationals (*Micheletti*)
- EU citizenship complements but does not replace nationality
- There is no minimum age limit, i.e. children can invoke citizenship rights (*Zhu & Chen*)
- There is no requirement of economic activity (*Martínez Sala*)

Explain the scope of the citizen's 'family members':
- Identify family members as defined in Directive 2004/38, Article 2(2):
  - Spouse – discuss the case law, e.g. *Reed, Diatta, Akrich, Metock, Iida*
  - Registered partners
  - Descendants under 21 or dependent
  - Dependent relatives in the ascending line
- Consider meaning of 'dependency' – *Lebon, Jia*
- Note that the nationality of each family member is irrelevant
- Note that other relatives, and partners in a durable relationship, may be entitled to join the citizen, but are not classed as 'family members' (Article 3(2))

Explain the rights enjoyed by citizens and their family members:
- The right not to be discriminated against on grounds of nationality (Article 18 TFEU; Directive 2004/38, Article 24)
- The right to free movement and residence in any Member State (Article 21(1) TFEU). Elaborate on the free movement rights by reference to Directive 2004/38, Articles 4, 5, 6 and 7
- A right of permanent residence after five years' continuous residence (Directive 2004/38, Articles 16 and 17)
- Family members – regardless of nationality – have the right to accompany or join the citizen in the host state, to take up employment or self-employment (Directive 2004/38, Article 23) and to equal treatment vis-à-vis host state nationals (Directive 2004/38, Article 24)

Discuss limitations on citizens' rights

- Citizens seeking residence rights for longer than three months need to be in work, self-employment, in education or have independent financial resources (Directive 2004/38, Article 7)
- Consider why this is
- Member States are entitled to restrict citizens' access to social benefits, typically by imposing a minimum residence period
- This is justifiable if it aims to ensure that benefit claimants have established a sufficient 'link' with the society of the host state (*Bidar, Förster*), subject to proportionality
- Again consider why this is, perhaps to discourage benefit 'tourism'?

SUMMARY

- Article 20 TFEU establishes 'Citizenship of the Union' for every person holding the nationality of a Member State, including dual nationals (*Micheletti, Collins*). The acquisition of nationality is a matter of national law (*Micheletti, Zhu & Chen*).

- The citizen need not be economically active. Citizenship rights may be invoked by: the unemployed (*Martínez Sala*); students (*Grzelczyk, D'Hoop, Bidar, Förster*); the retired (*Pusa*); those incapable of working for health reasons (*Tas-Hagen*).

- The age of the citizen is immaterial. Children can invoke citizenship status (*Zhu & Chen*).

- Citizens have 'the right to move and reside freely within the territory of the Member States' (Article 21 TFEU), which is directly effective (*Baumbast & R*). Citizens may invoke Article 21 TFEU, in combination with Article 18 TFEU, in order to challenge national legislation which discriminates (directly or indirectly) against nationals of other Member States.

- Citizens may also invoke Article 21 TFEU in order to challenge national legislation which places them at a 'disadvantage' following the exercise of free movement rights (*Pusa, Tas-Hagen*).

- Citizens must not become 'an unreasonable burden' on the host state (*Grzelczyk*). But this does not mean that citizens cannot claim financial benefits (*Martínez Sala, D'Hoop, Grzelczyk, Collins, Bidar*). The key word is 'unreasonable'.

- Certain restrictions on citizens' rights are justifiable if based on 'objective considerations of public interest', do not directly discriminate on grounds of nationality, are suitable and proportionate. One 'objective consideration' is the need to ensure that there is a 'real link' between the claimant and the State (*D'Hoop*).

- Citizens have a range of political rights, e.g. to participate in elections (Article 22 TFEU).

- Under Directive 2004/38, citizens have a right of 'exit' from their home state (Article 4); a right of 'entry' into the host state (Article 5); a right of residence in the host state for up to three months without any conditions or formalities (Article 6). For longer residence periods, the citizen should either be working, self-employed, financially independent or a student (Article 7).

- Citizens may acquire a right to remain permanently in the host state after five years' continuous residence (Article 16). Time spent in prison does not count as 'residence' (*Onuekwere*). A right of permanent residence may also be acquired on reaching retirement age (after three years' residence), or if forced to retire from work as a result of permanent incapacity (Article 17).

- Citizens are entitled to equal treatment with the nationals of that Member State 'within the scope of the Treaty' (Article 24).

- Directive 2004/38 confers rights on a citizen's 'family members', 'irrespective of their nationality':

  - 'Spouse' refers to genuine marital relationships only (*Reed*, *Akrich*). It is immaterial where or when the marriage was solemnised (*Metock & Others*). Marital status continues after separation (*Diatta*, *Iida*, *Ogieriakhi*). The spouse is not obliged to remain in the same accommodation as the citizen (*Diatta*). Divorce terminates the spouse's status (*Baumbast & R*) but under Directive 2004/38, Article 13, ex-spouses retain residence rights in some situations.

  - 'Registered partners', but only if the legislation of the host Member State treats registered partnerships as equivalent to marriage.

  - 'Descendants' of the citizen/spouse/partner, if under 21 or 'dependent'. 'Dependence' is a factual issue (*Lebon, Reyes*).

  - 'Dependent relatives in the ascending line' of the citizen/spouse/partner. The 'need for material support must exist in the State of origin' (*Jia*).

- Directive 2004/38, Article 3, confers rights of entry and residence on 'other family members', irrespective of their nationality, if 'dependants' or 'members of the household' of the citizen, or where 'serious health grounds strictly require … personal care', and on 'the partner with whom the Union citizen has a durable relationship, duly attested'.

- Family members have rights to take up 'employment or self-employment' (Directive 2004/38, Article 23), but only in the same Member State as the citizen (*Gül, Mattern & Cikotic*), and to 'enjoy equal treatment' with nationals of the host state (Directive 2004/38, Article 24).

- Under Directive 2004/38, Member States may impose 'measures' which restrict free movement on grounds of public policy, public security or public health, such as refusal of entry (*Van Duyn*), refusal of exit (*Jipa*), expulsion (*R v Bouchereau*), territorial restrictions (*Rutili*).

- Although Member States cannot refuse entry to/expel from national territory their own nationals, they are not prevented from refusing entry to/expelling other states' nationals (*Pereira Roque*).

- The concept of 'public policy' must 'be interpreted strictly, so that its scope cannot be determined unilaterally by each Member State' (*Rutili*). 'Public policy' measures require a 'genuine, present and sufficiently serious threat affecting one of the fundamental interests of society' (Directive 2004/38, Article 27(2)). States must be prepared to impose 'repressive' measures on their own nationals before invoking 'public policy' measures (*Adoui & Cornuaille, Jany*).

- Public security has been invoked in cases involving terrorism (*Oteiza Olazabal*), organised crime (*Tsakouridis*) and child sex offences (*P.I.*).

- Public policy or security measures must be based 'exclusively' on the individual's 'personal conduct', and not on considerations of general prevention (Directive 2004/38, Article 27(2); *Bonsignore, Calfa, Orfanopoulos & Oliveri*). But present membership of an organisation may constitute 'personal conduct' (*Van Duyn*).

- Previous criminal convictions must not 'in themselves' constitute grounds for the taking of measures (Article 27(2)), but may do so if they provide evidence of a 'present threat' (*R v Bouchereau*).

- Measures taken on grounds of public policy or security must comply with the principle of 'proportionality' (Article 27(2); *Oulane, Tsakouridis*).

- Before seeking expulsion, Member States must take into account how long the individual concerned has resided on its territory, his/her age, state of health, family and economic situation, social and cultural integration into the host Member State, the extent of his/her links with the country of origin (Directive 2004/38, Article 28(1)). The impact of deportation on any children is particularly important (*Rendón Marín, C.S.*).

- For individuals with a permanent right of residence, expulsion is only possible on 'serious' grounds of public policy or security (Article 28(2)). Minors, or someone with ten years' residence, may only be expelled 'on imperative grounds of public security' (Article 28(3), *Tsakouridis, P.I.*). Time spent in prison does not count as 'residence' (*M.G.*).

- States may take public health measures against those suffering from 'diseases with epidemic potential' as well as 'infectious diseases or contagious parasitic diseases' (Directive 2004/38, Article 29).

- All decisions require notification 'in writing' (Directive 2004/38, Article 30; *Z.Z.*). The individual must be able to appeal and/or seek judicial review of any decision taken against them (Article 31(1)). Persons excluded on public policy or security grounds may apply to have it lifted after three years (Article 32).

Further reading

Articles

Azoulai, L and Coutts, S, 'Restricting Union Citizens' Residence Rights on Grounds of Public Security' (2013) 50 *CML Rev* 553.

Bell, C and Bačić Selanec, N, 'Who is a "Spouse" under the Citizens' Rights Directive? The Prospect of Mutual Recognition of Same-Sex Marriages in the EU' (2016) 41 *EL Rev* 655.

Currie, S, 'Accelerated Justice or a Step too Far? Residence Rights of non-EU Family Members and the Court's Ruling in *Metock*' (2009) 34 *EL Rev* 310.

Dautricourt, C and Thomas, S, 'Reverse Discrimination and Free Movement of Persons Under Community Law: All for Ulysses, Nothing for Penelope' (2009) 34 *EL Rev* 433.

Kochenov, D, 'The Right to Have What Rights? EU Citizenship in Need of Clarification' (2013) 19 *ELJ* 502.

Łazowski, A, 'Darling You Are Not Going Anywhere: The Right to Exit and Restrictions in EU Law' (2015) 40 *EL Rev* 877.

O'Brien, C, 'Real Links, Abstract Rights and False Alarms: The Relationship between the ECJ's "Real Link" Case Law and National Solidarity' (2008) 33 *EL Rev* 643.

Reynolds, S, 'Exploring the "Intrinsic Connection" between Free Movement and the Genuine Enjoyment Test: Reflections on EU Citizenship after *Iida*' (2013) 38 *EL Rev* 376.

Solanke, I, 'Another Type of "Other" in EU law?' (2013) 76 *MLR* 383.

Wollenschlager, F, 'A New Fundamental Freedom Beyond Market Integration: Union Citizenship and its Dynamics for Shifting the Economic Paradigm of European Integration' (2011) 17 *ELJ* 1.

12

The free movement of workers

AIMS AND OBJECTIVES

After reading this chapter you should be able to:

- Understand the law relating to the free movement of workers, in particular Article 45 TFEU and Regulation 492/2011

- Understand the meaning and scope of the concept of 'worker'

- Understand the circumstances in which the free movement of workers may be restricted

- Analyse critically the law relating to the free movement of workers

- Apply the law to factual situations involving the free movement of workers in the EU

ARTICLE

'Art 45(1) Freedom of movement for workers shall be secured within the Union.

(2) Such freedom of movement shall entail the abolition of any discrimination based on nationality between workers of the Member States as regards employment, remuneration and other conditions of work and employment.

(3) It shall entail the right, subject to limitations justified on grounds of public policy, public security or public health:

   (a) to accept offers of employment actually made;
   (b) to move freely within the territory of Member States for this purpose;
   (c) to stay in a Member State for the purpose of employment in accordance with the provisions governing the employment of nationals of that State laid down by law, regulation or administrative action;
   (d) to remain in the territory of a Member State after having been employed in that State, subject to [Directive 2004/38].

(4) The provisions of this Article shall not apply to employment in the public service.'

12.1 The objectives of Article 45 TFEU

The objectives of Article 45 are, broadly speaking, twofold:

To allow for workers to move from one EU Member State to another for the purposes of employment

This benefits both individual workers and their employers. Individual workers benefit because they can move from areas of high unemployment and/or low wages to areas of low unemployment and/or higher wages. This is true whether the workers are skilled or not, and whether they possess professional qualifications or not. Readers of this book who are familiar with the TV programme *Auf Wiedersehen, Pet* will recall how the plot of the original series involved British manual workers (bricklayers, plasterers etc.) moving from the UK (where their skills were not in high demand) to Germany, where their skills were put to good use working on building sites.

A real-life example of people exploiting EU rules on the free movement of workers is provided by the huge numbers of professional footballers from across the EU who have come to play in the English Premiership and Championship, particularly since the *Bosman* ruling of December 1995, which applied Article 45 to professional sport. The wages on offer at Premiership clubs – generated by large attendances at bigger capacity grounds, by TV and satellite broadcasting revenue and by highly lucrative sponsorship deals – dwarf those on offer in most other European leagues (the obvious exception being Spain). This explains why so many top French players, in particular, have come to England in recent years; it also explains who so few British players have moved in the opposite direction. Again, the exception is Spain, specifically Real Madrid, who signed David Beckham from Manchester United in 2003, Michael Owen from Liverpool and Jonathan Woodgate from Newcastle United in 2004 and then broke the world record for football transfers in signing Gareth Bale for €100 million (£85.3 million) from Tottenham Hotspur in September 2013. All of these players were 'workers' who invoked rights under Article 45 to go from the UK to play – or, rather, work – in Spain.

Employers also benefit because they have a greater choice of potential workers to choose from. This may mean they can employ workers with better qualifications or greater experience than they otherwise would be able to if restricted to workers from the same Member State. Workers from states where there are relatively low average wages may be prepared to move to other states to take on unskilled work, or work anti-social hours (which national workers may be unwilling to do) and still receive better salaries than they would had they stayed at home. An influx of foreign workers can also help resolve 'skills shortages'. At the time of the EU's expansion in May 2004 it was widely reported in the British media that highly skilled engineers and scientists from central and eastern Europe (Poland in particular) were planning on coming to the UK to work. This benefits the individual workers (average wages in the UK being much higher than those in Poland), and their employers, who were struggling to find suitably qualified British engineers and scientists.

To prohibit discrimination on grounds of nationality against workers who have moved

Article 45(2) prohibits Member States, through legislation, and employers, through their terms and conditions of employment, from discriminating against workers who have moved under Article 45(1). After all, there would be a massive disincentive to move if employers were free openly to discriminate against migrant workers. The dual objectives of Article 45 were neatly summarised by the ECJ in the case of *Lyyski* (Case C–40/05) [2007] ECR I–99, when the ECJ stated:

JUDGMENT

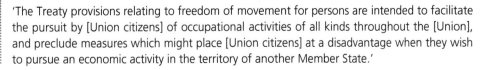

'The Treaty provisions relating to freedom of movement for persons are intended to facilitate the pursuit by [Union citizens] of occupational activities of all kinds throughout the [Union], and preclude measures which might place [Union citizens] at a disadvantage when they wish to pursue an economic activity in the territory of another Member State.'

12.2 The scope of Article 45

Article 45(1) provides that 'Freedom of movement for workers shall be secured within the Union'. This means that workers are (subject to very narrowly defined derogations) free to move from one Member State to another without restriction. The ECJ offered some guidance on this in *Graf* (Case C–190/98) [2000] ECR I–493:

CASE EXAMPLE

Graf (Case C–190/98) [2000] ECR I–493

Under Austrian law, workers who had worked a minimum three years with the same employer were entitled to a termination payment. However, that payment was forfeited if the employee resigned, left prematurely for no important reason or bore responsibility for his premature dismissal. Volker Graf had worked for the same Austrian company for three-and-a-half years when he resigned in order to go to work for a German company. His employers refused to pay up. When he challenged this, arguing Article 45, they responded that the refusal to pay him did not constitute a restriction on his mobility. The ECJ agreed: the Austrian legislation imposed no obstacle to the free movement of workers.

The Court stated:

JUDGMENT

'Provisions which, even if they are applicable without distinction, preclude or deter a national of a Member State from leaving his country of origin in order to exercise his right to freedom of movement therefore constitute an obstacle to that freedom. However, in order to be capable of constituting such an obstacle, *they must affect access of workers to the labour market*.'

The principle established in *Graf* was recently illustrated in *Casteels v British Airways* (Case C–379/09) [2011] ECR I–1379. Here, a Collective Agreement between British Airways (BA) and the relevant trade union in Germany stated, *inter alia*, that employees who transferred from a division of BA in Germany to a division of BA in another Member State (but not those who transferred within Germany) were deemed to have left the company 'voluntarily', which had adverse consequences when it came to calculating their length of service with the company, and ultimately their pension entitlement. The Court held that this provision placed workers

> who exercise their right to free movement at a disadvantage [which was] liable to dissuade workers from leaving their employer's establishment in one Member State in order to take up a position with an establishment of that same employer in another Member State.

This dissuasive effect was enough to bring the provision within the scope of Article 45.

Article 45(2) states that, having moved, workers are entitled not to be discriminated against in terms of nationality. This provision is directly effective and can be enforced in national courts in order to challenge discriminatory national legislation, or to challenge discriminatory employment practices. Article 45(2) even applies to private employers, as *Angonese* (Case C–281/98) [2000] ECR I–4139 demonstrates:

CASE EXAMPLE

Angonese (Case C–281/98) [2000] ECR I–4139

Roman Angonese, an Italian national, spoke fluent German as well as Italian. He also spoke English, Polish and Slovene. In July 1997 he applied for a job with a bank in the northern Italian city of Bolzano. One of the conditions of entry was possession of a special certificate issued in Bolzano which confirmed bilingualism in German and Italian. Angonese, who had studied languages and translation for a number of years at the University of Vienna, asked for his degree certificate to be accepted instead of the Bolzano bilingualism certificate. The bank refused. Angonese challenged this, relying upon Article 45(2). The ECJ agreed that the bank's insistence on accepting only the certificate issued in Bolzano constituted a form of discrimination based on nationality and was therefore prohibited by Article 45(2).

The ECJ has held that Article 45(2) can also be invoked by employers. In *Innovative Technology Center* (Case C–208/05) [2007] ECR I–181, the Court decided that the right of workers to be engaged and employed without discrimination necessarily entailed, as a corollary, an employer's entitlement to engage them without discrimination. That right also entailed, as a further corollary, the right of intermediaries, such as recruitment agencies, to assist work-seekers in finding employment. Hence, provisions of German law, under which the Federal Employment Agency was obliged to pay recruitment agencies for finding work for unemployed people – but only if the employment was based in Germany – constituted a *prima facie* infringement of Article 45(2).

The principle that employers can invoke Article 45 as well as employees was seen in the recent case of *Caves Krier Frères* (Case C–379/11) [2013] 2 CMLR 14. A wine producer/merchant in Luxembourg invoked Article 45 to challenge a rule of national law that offered a financial incentive to Luxembourg-based companies to recruit older workers, but only if they were resident in Luxembourg. This was held to restrict the free movement of workers based in other Member States (who would be less likely to be offered employment by companies in Luxembourg), and by corollary it restricted the freedom of Luxembourg companies to employ migrant workers.

Article 45(2) applies throughout the territories of the Member States and even extends beyond the EU itself, to workers who, although situated outside the geographical scope of the EU, have an employment relationship with their employer which is founded within one of the Member States or where the relationship retained a 'sufficiently close link' with the EU. In *SARL Prodest* (Case 237/83) [1984] ECR 3153 the ECJ ruled:

JUDGMENT

'The principle of non-discrimination applies to the case of a national of a Member State who is employed by an undertaking of another Member State even during a period in which the employee temporarily works outside the territory of the [EU].'

The scope of Art 45	
Workers are entitled to 'free movement' in the EU.	Art 45(1) TFEU
Any provisions of national legislation which 'preclude or deter' a worker from exercising their free movement rights are prohibited.	*Graf* (2000)
Workers are entitled not to be discriminated against on grounds of nationality.	Art 45(2) TFEU
The entitlement to non-discrimination can be enforced against employers in order to challenge discriminatory provisions in employment contracts.	*Angonese* (2000)
The non-discrimination provision can also be invoked by employers.	*Innovative Technology Center* (2007)

12.3 The definition of 'worker'

The definition of 'worker' has the same meaning in all EU Member States because, otherwise, Member States could define 'worker' in such a way as to prevent the access of migrant workers (*Levin* (Case 53/81) [1982] ECR 1035). However, the word is not defined in any EU legislation. The ECJ has therefore been called upon in several cases to explain the meaning and scope of the 'worker' concept. In *Lawrie-Blum* (Case 66/85) [1986] ECR 2121, the ECJ noted that the free movement of workers was a fundamental principle, and it therefore had to be defined widely. It then stated:

JUDGMENT

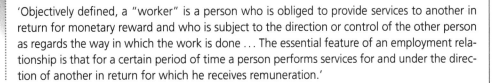

'Objectively defined, a "worker" is a person who is obliged to provide services to another in return for monetary reward and who is subject to the direction or control of the other person as regards the way in which the work is done … The essential feature of an employment relationship is that for a certain period of time a person performs services for and under the direction of another in return for which he receives remuneration.'

The employer need not necessarily be a company of any particular nationality. EU nationals employed by international organisations based in another EU Member State are entitled to the protection afforded by Article 45:

- *Echternach* (Case 389/87) [1989] ECR 723 – German national employed by the European Space Agency in Belgium;
- *Schmid* (Case C–310/91) [1993] ECR I–3011 – German national employed by Eurocontrol (the European Organisation for the Safety of Air Navigation) in Belgium;
- *Ferlini* (Case C–411/98) [2000] ECR I–8081 – Italian national employed at the European Commission in Luxembourg;
- *My* (Case C–293/03) [2004] ECR I–12013 – Italian national employed at the Council of the European Union in Brussels, Belgium;

- *Öberg* (Case C–185/04) [2006] ECR I–1453 – Swedish national employed at the European Court of Justice in Luxembourg;

- *Rockler* (Case C–137/04) [2006] ECR I–1441 – Swedish national employed at the European Commission in Brussels, Belgium;

- *Alevizos* (Case C–392/05) [2007] ECR I–3505 – Greek national and member of the Greek Air Force, seconded to the North Atlantic Treaty Organisation (NATO) in Italy;

- *Gardella* (Case C–233/12) [2013] ICR D34 – Italian national employed by the European Patent Office (EPO) in Germany;

- *Adrien & Others* (Case C–466/15) (unreported) – French nationals employed at the Court of Justice in Luxembourg.

12.3.1 Part-time and low-paid employees

The ECJ has been very flexible here. Some activity of an economic nature, even if it is poorly paid, qualifies an individual as a 'worker'. On the question of whether part-time workers are covered, the ECJ has stated (*Levin* 1982):

JUDGMENT

'Whilst part-time employment is not excluded from the field of application of the rules on freedom of movement for workers, those rules cover only the pursuit of effective and genuine activities, to the exclusion of activities on such a small scale as to be regarded as marginal and ancillary.'

The ECJ had consistently refused to lay down a rule setting any sort of **quantitative threshold** of work, either in terms of the number of hours per week or in terms of a minimum salary. Rather, what matters to the ECJ is that a basic **qualitative threshold** of work has been met.

CASE EXAMPLE

Levin (Case 53/81) [1982] ECR 1035

Mrs Levin, a British national, had gone to the Netherlands with her South African husband. It seems that the couple were financially independent and simply wanted to live there. The authorities were reluctant to allow this, so Mrs Levin took work as a chambermaid in a Dutch hotel, working 20 hours a week for which she was paid the equivalent of £25. However, this meant that her wages were below the Dutch minimum wage and so the authorities refused to regard her as a 'worker' for the purposes of EU law. When Mrs Levin challenged this, the ECJ held that whether or not a person was a 'worker' was not a question of how much money they earned but whether or not it was 'genuine'. The ECJ also rejected the argument that Mrs Levin was not a 'worker' because she had taken the chambermaid job simply to qualify for 'worker' status. The Court held that motivation was immaterial: the fact of employment is what mattered.

The fact that a worker has to supplement his income in order to subsist is also irrelevant – thereby narrowing what the ECJ suggested in *Levin* (1982): that employment must be 'effective'. This principle is clearly illustrated in *Kempf* (Case 139/85) [1986] ECR 1741.

CASE EXAMPLE

Kempf (Case 139/85) [1986] ECR 1741

Kempf, a German national, was working as a music teacher in the Netherlands. However, he was only working for 12 hours a week. His income was not enough to live on, so he claimed Dutch supplementary benefit (sickness benefit as well as more general income support). In 1981 he applied for a Dutch residence permit. This was refused on the ground that his income was insufficient to support himself. Kempf challenged this. The ECJ held that the fact that Kempf claimed financial assistance in order to supplement the income he received from teaching activities did not exclude him from the provisions of Article 45.

The Court stated:

JUDGMENT

'A person in effective and genuine part-time employment cannot be excluded from [Article 45] merely because the remuneration he derives from it is below the level of the minimum means of subsistence and he seeks to supplement it by other lawful means of subsistence. In that regard it is irrelevant whether those supplementary means of subsistence are derived from property or from the employment of a member of his family … or whether, as in this instance, they are obtained from financial assistance drawn from the public funds of the member state in which he resides, provided that the effective and genuine nature of his work is established.'

Although the ECJ has been generous with its definition of 'worker', the principle will not be taken to extremes. Where a person's activities can be described as 'marginal and ancillary', they will not be classed as a 'worker'. The ECJ has subsequently stated that the duration of the activity performed is relevant in determining whether activities amount to genuine employment or are simply marginal and ancillary (*Raulin* (Case C–357/89) [1992] ECR I–1027).

In *Ninni-Orasche* (Case C–413/01) [2003] ECR I–13187, the ECJ explicitly refused to hold that the fact that an Italian national had been employed for two-and-a-half months over a period of three years in Austria automatically excluded her from the scope of Article 45. Ultimately, whether or not she was a 'worker' was a question of fact for the national court, applying the 'effective and genuine activities' test. The ECJ stated:

JUDGMENT

'The fact that a national of a Member State has worked for a temporary period of 2½ months in the territory of another Member State, of which he is not a national, can confer on him the status of a worker within the meaning of [Article 45] provided that the activity performed as an employed person is not purely marginal and ancillary.'

Two cases have raised questions regarding whether or not work was 'genuine'. In *Bettray* (Case 344/87) [1989] ECR 1621, involving a German national who was living in the Netherlands, the ECJ held that activities described as 'social employment' which were carried out as part of a state-sponsored drug rehabilitation programme, did not constitute genuine employment. However, in *Trojani* (Case C–456/02) [2004] ECR I–7573, the ECJ took a more generous view with what was described as 'a personal socio-occupational reintegration programme'. Although the ECJ distinguished *Bettray* (1989), it conceded that the ultimate decision whether or not a person qualified as a worker was a question for the national court.

CASE EXAMPLE

Trojani (Case C–456/02) [2004] ECR I–7573

Michel Trojani, a French national, had gone to live in Belgium in 2000. He lived for a time on a campsite and later stayed in a youth hostel. By early 2002 he was living in a Salvation Army hostel, and in return for board and lodging and 'some pocket money' he did 'various jobs for about 30 hours per week as part of a personal socio-occupational reintegration programme'. The ECJ held that this was, in principle, capable of being regarded as falling within the scope of Article 45, although ultimately it was a question for the national court.

The Court stated:

JUDGMENT

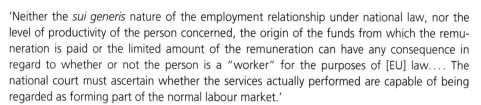

'Neither the *sui generis* nature of the employment relationship under national law, nor the level of productivity of the person concerned, the origin of the funds from which the remuneration is paid or the limited amount of the remuneration can have any consequence in regard to whether or not the person is a "worker" for the purposes of [EU] law.... The national court must ascertain whether the services actually performed are capable of being regarded as forming part of the normal labour market.'

It should be remembered that the ultimate decision as to whether or not a person qualifies as a 'worker' is a matter for the national court, applying the principles in cases such as *Lawrie-Blum* and *Levin*. For example, in *Barry v Southwark LBC* [2008] EWCA Civ 1440, [2009] 2 CMLR 11, the Court of Appeal held that a Dutch national who had worked in the UK as a security guard for about nine months followed by two weeks as a steward during the Wimbledon tennis championship qualified as a 'worker', on the basis that his employment was 'effective and genuine'. Conversely, in *B & Others v Home Secretary* [2012] EWCA Civ 1015, [2012] 3 CMLR 43, the same court held that an Italian national who had lived in the UK for over ten years but had only worked (as a cleaner) for a total of 80 hours (and had been motivated to take this employment purely in order to maintain his benefits) was not a 'worker'.

12.3.2 Trainees

Students undertaking vocational training are 'workers'. In *Lawrie-Blum* (1986), involving a British woman who had applied to become a trainee teacher in Germany, the ECJ held:

JUDGMENT

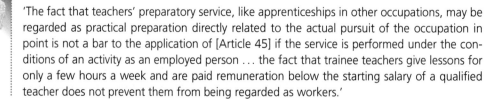

'The fact that teachers' preparatory service, like apprenticeships in other occupations, may be regarded as practical preparation directly related to the actual pursuit of the occupation in point is not a bar to the application of [Article 45] if the service is performed under the conditions of an activity as an employed person ... the fact that trainee teachers give lessons for only a few hours a week and are paid remuneration below the starting salary of a qualified teacher does not prevent them from being regarded as workers.'

Lawrie-Blum (1986) was followed in *Bernini* (Case C–3/90) [1992] ECR I–1071, involving an Italian woman working as a trainee in a furniture factory in the Netherlands. In

Kranemann (Case C–109/04) [2005] ECR I–2421, the ECJ was asked whether a trainee lawyer qualified as a 'worker'. The case involved a German national who had completed his legal education in Germany and was spending part of his legal training with a law firm in London. The ECJ had no doubt that the trainee was a 'worker':

JUDGMENT

'As regards the activities carried out by trainee lawyers … such trainees are required to apply in practice the legal knowledge acquired during their course of study and thus make a contribution, under the guidance of the employer providing them with training, to that employer's activities and trainees receive payment in the form of a maintenance allowance for the duration of their training … Such an employment relationship cannot fall outside the scope of [Article 45] merely because the allowance paid to trainees constitutes only assistance allowing them to meet their minimum needs … Given that trainee lawyers carry out genuine and effective activity as an employed person they must be considered to be workers within the meaning of [Article 45].'

12.3.3 Work-seekers

Could Article 45 be interpreted so as to give work-seekers protection? A literal reading of Article 45(3) would seem to indicate not, as it states that the freedom of movement for workers includes the right 'to accept offers of employment actually made'. However, the ECJ very rarely adopts a literal reading of EU legislation, preferring to take a purposive approach (favouring any interpretation which promotes free movement over one which inhibits it). Hence, in *Antonissen* (Case C–292/89) [1991] ECR I–745, the ECJ held that work-seekers did have certain rights:

JUDGMENT

'[Article 45(3)] must be interpreted as enumerating, in a non-exhaustive way, certain rights benefiting nationals of Member States in the context of the free movement of workers … that freedom also entails the right for nationals of Member States to move freely within the territory of the other Member States and to stay there for the purposes of seeking employment.'

The ECJ added that migrant nationals seeking employment in other EU Member States had to be able to 'appraise themselves … of offers of employment' and to take the 'necessary steps in order to be engaged'. Work-seekers could not, therefore, be deported as long as they could provide evidence that they were (a) continuing to seek employment and (b) had genuine chances of becoming employed.

CASE EXAMPLE

Antonissen (Case C–292/89) [1991] ECR I–745

Gustaff Antonissen, a Belgian national, challenged a deportation order that had been made against him following his conviction at Liverpool Crown Court for possession of cocaine. He had been looking for work in the UK for over two years, without success. Under UK law, deportation of unemployed people was permitted after six months. The Immigration Appeal Tribunal referred to the ECJ the question of the compatibility of this rule with EU law on the free movement of workers. The Court held that work-seekers were protected by EU law, but not indefinitely. The ECJ added that the six-month limit was not insufficient to enable work-seekers to appraise themselves of the work situation and, therefore, did 'not jeopardise the effectiveness of the principles of free movement'. However, that time limit could be extended if the person concerned was still actively work-seeking.

Work-seekers and social benefits

In *Collins* (Case C–138/02) [2004] ECR I–2703, the ECJ held that a work-seeker could also claim entitlement to certain social benefits, such as job-seeker's allowance. That does not guarantee they will receive those benefits, however. In *Collins*, the issue was whether a particular benefit for unemployed people in the UK could be made subject to a require-ment of 'habitual residence'. The ECJ held that this requirement was potentially indi-rectly discriminatory against foreign nationals, on the basis that UK nationals would be more likely to satisfy it, but it was nevertheless justifiable. The Court stated that it 'may be regarded as legitimate for a Member State to grant such an allowance only after it has been possible to establish that a genuine link exists between the person seeking work and the employment market of that State'.

However, the 'habitual residence' test was subject to the 'proportionality' principle. The ECJ held that its application by the national authorities 'must rest on clear criteria known in advance and provision must be made for the possibility of a means of redress of a judicial nature'. Finally, any period of residence laid down in the national rules 'must not exceed what is necessary in order for the national authorities to be able to satisfy themselves that the person concerned is genuinely seeking work in the employ-ment market of the host Member State'.

CASE EXAMPLE

Collins (Case C–138/02) [2004] ECR I–2703

Brian Collins, of dual US–Irish nationality, arrived in the UK in May 1998 to look for work. In June, he applied for job-seeker's allowance, a benefit under the Jobseekers Act 1995. In July, his application was refused on the ground that he was not 'habitually resident' in the UK as required by the Jobseekers' Allowance Regulations 1996. Although EU nationals who were 'workers' or who had a right of residence under Directive 68/360 (see below) were exempted from that requirement, neither exemption applied to Collins. He challenged this. The ECJ held that, although Collins was a work-seeker, following *Antonissen* (1991), he was protected from all discrimination based on nationality within the scope of EU law by Article 18 TFEU. The requirement of 'habitual residence' constituted 'indirect' discrimination, although it was objectively justifiable.

Collins was followed in *Vatsouras & Koupatantze* (Cases C–22, 23/08) [2009] ECR I–4585, involving two Greek nationals who had briefly worked in Germany before being made unemployed. They both applied for, but were denied, social benefits. They challenged the refusals. The Court held that, in general, work-seekers fell within the scope of Article 45 and therefore enjoyed the right to equal treatment laid down in Article 45(2). In particular, this included the right to claim financial benefits – but only if those benefits were 'intended to facilitate access to the labour market'. In *Alhashem* [2016] EWCA Civ 395, the Court of Appeal held that the claimant (a Dutch national looking for work in the UK) was *not* entitled to Employment and Support Allowance. This was 'primarily provided for those who cannot work or who are on the borderlines due to some disability or past episode in their lives'; it was therefore not a benefit which was 'intended to facilitate access to the labour market'.

Moreover, the ECJ confirmed in *Vatsouras & Koupatantze* that it was legitimate for a Member State to grant such benefits only after the work-seeker had established a 'real link' with the labour market of that state (which was for the competent national authorities and, where appropriate, the national courts to establish).

12.3.4 The previously employed

The ECJ has held that persons who have lost their job but are capable of taking another are still within the definition of 'worker'. In *Leclere and Deaconescu* (Case C–43/99) [2001] ECR I–4265 the ECJ stated:

JUDGMENT

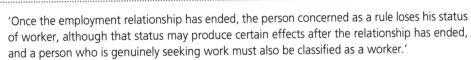

'Once the employment relationship has ended, the person concerned as a rule loses his status of worker, although that status may produce certain effects after the relationship has ended, and a person who is genuinely seeking work must also be classified as a worker.'

This is a remarkable statement – a person who is seeking work is, clearly, not actually working. However, the Court says that such a person is nevertheless to be 'classified' as a worker. It appears that this statement only applies to those persons who have at one time been workers for the purposes of Article 45. Those people who have never worked – such as the claimants in *Antonissen* (1991) and *Collins* (2004) – remain in the pure 'work-seekers' category.

12.3.5 Pregnant workers

In *St Prix* (Case C–507/12) [2015] 1 CMLR 5, the ECJ held that a woman who was obliged to (temporarily) leave employment in order to take maternity leave was entitled to retain her 'worker' status, and correspondingly her right of residence. The Court held that, where 'the physical constraints of the late stages of pregnancy and the immediate aftermath of childbirth' meant that a woman had to give up work during that period, this did not 'deprive her of the status of "worker" within the meaning Article 45'. The Court added:

JUDGMENT

'The fact that she was not actually available on the employment market of the host Member State for a few months does not mean that she has ceased to belong to that market during that period, provided she returns to work or finds another job within a reasonable period after confinement.'

In determining what is 'reasonable', the national court should take account of all the 'specific circumstances' of the case and the 'applicable national rules on the duration of maternity leave'. To date, two cases before the Upper Tribunal have examined the limit of a 'reasonable period' in the UK. In *F & Others* [2015] UKUT 502 and *Weldemichael & Obulor* [2015] UKUT 540, [2016] 1 CMLR 30, involving Dutch, Lithuanian and Portuguese women working in the UK, it was held that the 'reasonable period' will 'usually' be 52 weeks and that it starts 11 weeks before the pregnant woman's 'due date'.

12.3.6 Frontier workers

It is obvious from an examination of all of the cases above that Article 45 applies when a person moves from his or her 'home' state to work (or at least look for work) in another Member State. However, Article 45 also applies to the situation where a person lives in their 'home' state but works in a neighbouring state, effectively commuting to work across a national border. Such a person is known as a 'frontier worker'. Examples include:

- *Geven* (Case C–213/05) [2007] ECR I–6347 – Dutch national living in the Netherlands, commuted to work in Germany;

- *Erny* (Case C–172/11) [2012] 3 CMLR 31 – French national living in France, commuted to work for the Daimler car company in Germany;

- *Giersch & Others* (Case C–20/12) [2014] 1 CMLR 2 – Belgian nationals living in Belgium, and a German national resident in Germany, commuted to work in Luxembourg;

- *S & G* (Case C–457/12) [2014] 3 CMLR 18; [2014] QB 1207 – Dutch nationals living in the Netherlands, commuted to work in Belgium;

- *Depesme & Others* (Cases C–401–403/15) (unreported) – French nationals living in France, and a Belgian national living in Belgium, commuted to work in Luxembourg;

- *Eschenbrenner* (Case C–496/15) [2017] 3 CMLR 12 – French national living in France, commuted to work in Germany.

The ECJ has also been asked whether Article 45 applies in a less obvious 'frontier' situation, namely when a person has found employment in his or her 'home' state, but then moves their residence to another state, and commutes from there to their 'home' state to work. The answer is 'yes'. The cases are:

- *Hartmann* (Case C–212/05) [2007] ECR I–6303 – a German national, employed by the Post Office in Germany, moved to Austria to live but continued working in Germany;

- *Hendrix* (Case C–287/05) [2007] ECR I–6909 – a Dutch national, employed at a DIY store in the Netherlands, moved to Belgium to live but continued working in the Netherlands.

In both cases, the ECJ confirmed that Article 45 applied on these facts. In *Hartmann*, confirmed in *Hendrix*, the Court stated:

JUDGMENT

'A national of a Member State who, while maintaining his employment in that State, has transferred his residence to another Member State and has since then carried on his occupation as a frontier worker can claim the status of migrant worker.'

The case of *Hartmann* will be examined in more detail below, in the section dealing with 'social and tax advantages'.

KEY FACTS

The definition of 'worker'	
The word 'worker' has an EU-wide definition. It requires the provision of services, under the direction or control of another person, in return for remuneration.	*Lawrie-Blum* (1986)
Part-time and low-paid employees are 'workers' provided they pursue 'effective and genuine activities'.	*Levin* (1982); *Kempf* (1986); *Ninni-Orasche* (2003); *Trojani* (2004)
Trainees are 'workers'.	*Lawrie-Blum, Bernini* (1992); *Kranemann* (2005)
Work-seekers are also entitled to protection under Art 45, provided they are actively seeking work and have genuine chances of finding work.	*Antonissen* (1991); *Collins* (2004); *Vatsouras & Koupatantze* (2009)
Former workers who are seeking re-employment must be 'classified' as a worker.	*Leclere & Deaconescu* (2001)
Pregnant women retain their 'worker' status whilst on maternity leave provided they return to work, or seek alternative employment, after a 'reasonable period'	*St Prix* (2014)
Frontier workers who live in one state and commute to work in another are also regarded as 'workers' under Art 45.	*Geven* (2007); *Hartmann* (2007); *Hendrix* (2007)); *Erny* (2012); *Giersch & Others* (2014); *Eschenbrenner* (2017)

12.4 Equality in social and welfare provisions and Regulation 492/2011

An important piece of secondary legislation, Regulation 1612/68, was passed in order to elaborate the meaning and scope of Article 45(2) and (3). In 2011, the Regulation was repealed and replaced by Regulation 492/2011, although the key provisions in both pieces of legislation are identical. (In most cases, even the article numbers are unchanged, although Article 12 of Regulation 1612/68 is now Article 10 of Regulation 492/2011.) This means that any ECJ case law under the 1968 Regulation remains applicable under the 2011 Regulation.

12.4.1 Eligibility for employment: Articles 3 and 4

ARTICLE

'Art 3(1) Under this Regulation, provisions laid down by law, regulation or administrative action or administrative practices of a Member State shall not apply:

- where they limit application for and offers of employment, or the right of foreign nationals to take up and pursue employment or subject these to conditions not applicable in respect of their own nationals; or
- where, though applicable irrespective of nationality, their exclusive or principal aim or effect is to keep nationals of other Member States away from the employment offered.

This provision shall not apply to conditions relating to linguistic knowledge required by reason of the nature of the post to be filled.'

Linguistic knowledge

The proviso to Article 3(1) was invoked in the context of school teachers in *Groener v Minister for Education* (Case 379/87) [1989] ECR 3967:

CASE EXAMPLE

Groener v Minister for Education (Case 379/87) [1989] ECR 3967

Anita Groener, a Dutch national, applied for a job teaching art at the College of Marketing and Design in Dublin. Even though the classes were to be taught in English, Irish law requires all teachers to have a certificate of proficiency in Irish which, under the Irish Constitution, is the national and first official language of Ireland. Miss Groener failed a proficiency test in Irish and was thus denied the job. She appealed and the case was referred to the ECJ. The Court held that the Irish law was justified under Article 3(1). Language was an important aspect of any country's culture and identity, although this was only the case provided that it was not being used as a means of discriminating against non-Irish nationals.

The Court stated:

JUDGMENT

'Teachers have an essential role to play, not only through the teaching which they provide but also by their participation in the daily life of the school and the privileged relationship which they have with their pupils. In those circumstances, it is not unreasonable to require them to have some knowledge of the first national language.'

ARTICLE

'Art 4(1) Provisions laid down by law, regulation or administrative action of the Member States which restrict by number or percentage the employment of foreign nationals in any under-taking, branch of activity or region, or at a national level, shall not apply to nationals of the other Member States.'

Article 4(1) was infringed in *Commission v France* (Case 167/73) [1974] ECR 359, where French legislation, the *Code du Travail Maritime 1926,* imposed a ratio of three:one in favour of Frenchmen for the crew of French merchant ships. It was also used in *Bosman* (Case C–415/93) [1995] ECR I–4921, to challenge what was known as the '3+2' rule. This case is examined in the section on sport, below.

12.4.2 Article 7(1) – prohibition of discrimination in employment

ARTICLE

'Art 7(1) A worker who is a national of a Member State may not, in the territory of another Member State, be treated differently from national workers by reason of his nationality in respect of any conditions of employment and work, in particular as regards remuneration, dismissal, and should he become unemployed, reinstatement or re-employment.'

Discrimination comes in two forms: direct and indirect. Both are prohibited, although either form of discrimination could be exempted in two circumstances:

- by Article 45(3), which deals with derogations justified on grounds of 'public policy, public security or public health' (discussed in the previous chapter);
- by Article 45(4), which deals with employment in the 'public service' (discussed below).

Apart from that, however, direct discrimination cannot be justified. Indirect discrimination could be justified on the basis that it was necessary to satisfy some overriding national interest (this is discussed below – see section 12.7).

Direct discrimination
National legislation which, on its face, discriminates against workers because of their nationality, is clearly contrary to Article 45(2). For example, in order to join the British Army, applicants will be eligible only if they are a British citizen or a citizen of an independent Commonwealth country (who has lived in the UK for at least five years). Irish nationals living in the UK are eligible to join the Army Reserve. These nationality criteria clearly directly discriminate against nationals of the other 26 EU Member States and hence are a *prima facie* breach of Article 45(2). However, they would be exempted under Article 45(4).

Indirect discrimination
National rules which are not directly discriminatory (in that they appear on their face to apply regardless of nationality) may nevertheless be in breach of Article 45(2), if the effect of those rules is to discriminate either in favour of that state's nationals or against nationals of other states. *O'Flynn* (Case C–237/94) [1996] ECR I–2617 provides an example.

CASE EXAMPLE

O'Flynn (Case C–237/94) [1996] ECR I–2617

UK social security legislation provided for a benefit to cover the cost of burial or cremation of deceased persons incurred by the person taking responsibility for the arrangements – but only if the burial had taken place in the UK. O'Flynn, an Irish national working in the UK, was denied this benefit which he claimed for the cost of his father's burial because that was to take place in Ireland. The ECJ found that a greater proportion of UK nationals than nationals of other EU Member States would satisfy the burial requirement and thus it was indirectly discriminatory.

In *O'Flynn*, the ECJ explained the sort of national rules which may be found to be indirectly discriminatory:

JUDGMENT

'Conditions imposed by national law must be regarded as indirectly discriminatory where, although applicable irrespective of nationality, they affect essentially migrant workers or the great majority of those affected are migrant workers, where they are indistinctly applicable but can more easily be satisfied by national workers than by migrant workers, or where there is a risk that they may operate to the particular detriment of migrant workers ... It is not necessary in this respect to find that the provision in question does in practice affect a substantially higher proportion of migrant workers. It is sufficient that it is liable to have such an effect.'

Indirect discrimination was found in the following cases:

- *Sotgiu v Deutsche Bundespost* (Case 152/73) [1974] ECR 153 – the German Post Office paid a separation allowance to all employees forced by work to live away from their families: 10 DM per day was paid to workers whose family home was in Germany; 7.5 DM per day was paid to all other employees. The ECJ found that German nationals were far more likely to qualify for the higher allowance than migrant workers.

- *Alluè & Coonan* (Case 33/88) [1989] ECR 1591 – Italian legislation provided that foreign-language assistants could only be employed on year-long contracts. No such limits were imposed on other university workers. Evidence showed that 75 per cent of foreign-language assistants in Italian universities were from outside Italy.

- *Scholz* (Case C–419/92) [1994] ECR I–505 – the recruitment procedure adopted by the University of Cagliari in Italy took account of each candidate's previous public–sector employment, but only if it had been in Italy. The ECJ found that most Italians would satisfy this criterion but only a minority of migrant workers.

- *Schöning-Kougebetopoulou* (Case C–15/96) [1998] ECR I–47 – German legislation conferred automatic promotion on public–sector workers (such as health care workers) after eight years' employment – but only if that employment had been in Germany. The ECJ found that most Germans would satisfy this criterion but only a minority of migrant workers.

- *Köbler v Austria* (Case C–224/01) [2003] ECR I–10239 – Austrian legislation conferred a special length-of-service increment on professors who had completed 15 years' service in Austrian universities. The ECJ found that most Austrian professors would satisfy this criterion but only a minority of professors from other Member States.

Note: the German deutschmark (DM) ceased to be legal tender when the single European currency was introduced in 2002.

12.4.3 Article 7(2) – 'social and tax advantages'

Article 7(2) provides that the worker 'shall enjoy the same social and tax advantages as national workers'. Article 7(2) has been defined very widely, as the case of *Fiorini v SNCF* (Case 32/75) [1975] ECR 1085 demonstrates.

CASE EXAMPLE

Fiorini v SNCF (Case 32/75) [1975] ECR 1085

Anita Fiorini was the widow of an Italian national, Euginio Fiorini, who had worked in France since 1962 but had been killed in an industrial accident in 1968. Anita, who decided to stay in France with her four children, had never been employed. She claimed entitlement to reduced rail travel, which was granted to large families in France. Initially, her claim was refused by the French authorities, who restricted Article 7(2) to advantages granted to citizens within the ambit of work as employed persons. Mrs Fiorini appealed and the case was referred to the ECJ, which held that Article 7(2) covered all social and tax advantages, whether or not attached to contracts of employment. These rights continued even after the worker's death and so Mrs Fiorini was entitled to the rail travel reduction.

The Court stated:

JUDGMENT

'The reference to "social advantages" in Article 7(2) cannot be interpreted restrictively. It therefore follows that, in view of the equality of treatment which the provision seeks to achieve, the substantive area of application must be delineated so as to include *all* social and tax advantages, whether or not attached to the contract of employment.'

In *Even* (Case 207/78) [1979] ECR 2019 the ECJ defined 'social advantages' as follows:

JUDGMENT

'Those which, whether or not linked to a contract of employment, are generally granted to national workers primarily because of their objective status as workers, or by virtue of the mere fact of their residence on national territory and the extension of which to workers who are nationals of other member countries therefore seems suitable to facilitate their mobility within the [Union].'

This definition has been employed in many subsequent cases, mostly involving entitlement to state benefits. However, such is the width of the interpretation given to Article 7(2) that it has extended into a number of unexpected areas:

- the right to have a trial conducted in a particular language (*Mutsch* (Case 137/84) [1985] ECR 2681);
- the right to reside with an unmarried companion (*Reed* (Case 59/85) [1986] ECR 1283);
- the right to funding and maintenance to pursue full-time education (*Lair* (Case 39/86) [1988] ECR 3161).

Funding and maintenance for education

Lair established the proposition that Article 7(2) could be relied upon by a migrant worker to claim funding and maintenance to pursue full-time education. The rule established in *Lair* is controversial, as it generally entails the worker giving up their status as worker in order to pursue the course of full-time education. Hence, the ECJ has imposed limitations.

CASE EXAMPLE

Lair (Case 39/86) [1988] ECR 3161

Sylvie Lair, a French national, had spent over five years in Germany, working intermittently, with spells of involuntary unemployment, before securing a place at Hanover University to study languages and literature. She claimed a maintenance grant. This was rejected on the basis that she had not been employed in Germany for at least five years prior to enrolment, a condition applicable only to foreigners. Sylvie challenged this refusal. The ECJ held that, provided she was a 'worker', she was entitled to a grant by virtue of Article 7(2). Germany's five-year employment requirement for foreigners was clearly discriminatory and contrary to Article 7(2). Applying this, Sylvie was therefore entitled to a grant provided that she could show that her course was connected in some way to her previous employment.

The Court stated:

JUDGMENT

'Migrant workers are guaranteed certain rights linked to the status of "worker" even when they are no longer in an employment relationship. In the field of grants for university education, such a link between the status of "worker" and a grant awarded for maintenance and training with a view to the pursuit of university studies does, however, presuppose some continuity between the previous occupational activity and the course of study; there must be a relationship between the purpose of the studies and the previous occupational activity. Such continuity may not, however, be required where a migrant has involuntarily become unemployed and is obliged by conditions on the job market to undertake occupational retraining in another field of activity.'

Thus, in order for a migrant worker to be entitled for funding and/or maintenance grants to pursue education, there must be 'some continuity' unless the worker became 'involuntarily' unemployed.

Continuity

In the following cases the element of continuity was satisfied:

- *Matteucci* (Case 235/87) [1988] ECR 5589 – period of employment as a teacher of eurythmics; followed by a singing and voice-training course;
- *Bernini* (1992) – period of employment in design and planning department of a furniture factory; followed by architectural studies degree.

In *Lair*, the ECJ referred to 'the previous occupational activity', i.e. the singular, suggesting that the migrant worker's most recent employment had to be connected to the course of study. However, the ECJ has relaxed this requirement. In *Raulin* (Case C–357/89) [1992] ECR I–1027, the ECJ stated that it was:

> for the national court to assess whether *all the occupational activities* previously exercised in the host Member State, regardless of whether or not they were interrupted by periods of training or retraining, bear a relationship to the studies in question.

Involuntary unemployment

This point was addressed by the ECJ in *Ninni-Orasche* (2004), where an Italian worker had applied for a maintenance grant for a higher education course in languages at an Austrian university after losing her job as a waitress. There was clearly no 'continuity', so her claim depended entirely on her being 'involuntarily' unemployed. Her waitressing job had been on a fixed-term basis, and she had known this from the outset. It was argued that, because she knew before she took the job that she would subsequently lose it, her unemployment was in a sense chosen and thus 'voluntary'. The ECJ rejected this:

JUDGMENT

'While a contract of employment is generally the result of negotiations, it is nonetheless true that cases in which the worker has no influence over the term and type of contract of employment which he may conclude with an employer are not unusual ... in some occupations it is common practice to conclude fixed-term contracts of employment and there are various reasons for this such as the seasonal nature of the work, the fact that the relevant market is sensitive to economic fluctuations or the possible inflexibility of national employment law.'

Studying abroad

Assuming that the above conditions are satisfied, however, there are no other restrictions. Article 7(2) may even be relied upon to claim funding for migrant workers to study abroad. This point was made in *Matteucci* (1988), where the ECJ stated:

JUDGMENT

'Article 7(2) lays down a general rule which imposes responsibility in the social sphere on each Member State with regard to every worker who is a national of another Member State and established in its territory as far as equality of treatment with national workers is concerned. Consequently, where a Member State gives its national workers the opportunity of pursuing training provided in another Member State, that opportunity must be extended to [Union] workers established in its territory.'

This principle applies even if it means the migrant worker returning to their home state! This point was established in *Di Leo* (1990), involving (what is now) Article 10 of Regulation 492/2011. The daughter of an Italian national working in Germany wanted to study medicine at the University of Sienna in Italy. German legislation made provision for grants for Germans who wished to study abroad. This was extended to the children of non-Germans working in Germany, provided that the child did not return to their home state. The ECJ held that this proviso was contrary to Article 10. *Di Leo* (1990) was then applied to Article 7(2) in *Bernini* (1992):

CASE EXAMPLE

Bernini (Case C–3/90) [1992] ECR I–1071

Mrs Bernini, an Italian national who had lived in the Netherlands since she was aged two, spent ten weeks as a salaried trainee in the design and planning department of a furniture factory in Haarlem, in the Netherlands. She then began a course of architectural studies at the University of Naples in Italy. She applied to the Dutch Education Ministry for funding but this was rejected on various grounds. She claimed to be a 'worker' and therefore entitled to the funding under (what is now) Article 7(2) of Regulation 492/2011. The ECJ held that, if she was a worker (that being a question for the national court), then the question of whether she was entitled to funding required proof that a link existed between her work and her proposed course, following *Lair* (1988). However, the fact that the course was to be studied abroad was irrelevant, following *Matteucci* (1988), as was the fact that she was to be studying in her home state, following *Di Leo* (1990). It all depended simply on whether Dutch nationals would be entitled to funding from the Dutch authorities to study in Italy.

The Court stated:

JUDGMENT

'Once a Member State offers to its national workers grants to pursue studies in another Member State, that opportunity must be extended to [Union] workers established within its territory ... the fact that the studies are pursued in the State of which the person concerned is a national is without significance in this connection.'

The continuing relevance of the *Lair/Bernini* case law was demonstrated recently in two cases.

- *Commission v Netherlands* (Case C–542/09) [2012] 3 CMLR 27 – a rule of Dutch law provided for funding for higher education pursued outside the Netherlands, but only for those people who had resided lawfully in the Netherlands during at least three out of the last six years. The ECJ confirmed that 'assistance granted for maintenance and education in order to pursue university studies ... constitutes a social advantage', following *Lair* and *Bernini*. The rule was ultimately held to be contrary to Article 7(2) – it indirectly discriminated against foreign nationals working in the Netherlands compared to Dutch nationals.

- *L.N.* (Case C–46/12) [2013] 2 CMLR 37 – an EU citizen (nationality unknown), entered Denmark in June 2009 and started full-time work within a week. In August, he applied for funding in order to attend Copenhagen Business School, starting in September. However, the Danish authorities refused on the basis that, back in March, he had already applied for a place at the School and therefore his principal objective in coming to Denmark was to pursue a course of study. He challenged that refusal. The ECJ held that it was for the national court to determine whether or not he had worker status, but that if he had, he would be entitled to the funding under Article 7(2), again following *Lair* and *Bernini*.

Summary of the 'funding and maintenance' cases

Case	Home state	Host state	Course
Lair (1988)	France	Germany	Languages and literature; University of Hanover, Germany
Matteucci (1988)	Italy	Belgium	Singing and voice-training course in Germany
Raulin (1992)	France	Netherlands	Visual arts course at the Gerrit Rietveld Academy, Amsterdam
Bernini (1992)	Italy	Netherlands	Architectural studies at the University of Naples, Italy
Ninni-Orasche (2004)	Italy	Austria	Languages and literature, specialising in Italian and French; University of Klagenfurt, Austria
L.N. (2013)	Unknown	Denmark	Copenhagen Business School

All of this case law is still relevant today, despite the rapidly expanding jurisprudence on students' rights as citizens to claim funding for education (discussed in Chapter 11). This is because of Article 24(2) of Directive 2004/38, which provides as follows:

ARTICLE

'[The] host Member State shall not be obliged … prior to acquisition of the right of permanent residence, to grant maintenance aid for studies, including vocational training, consisting in student grants or student loans to persons other than workers, self-employed persons, persons who retain such status and members of their families.'

You may also recall from reading Chapter 11 that 'the right of permanent residence' is only conferred on those who have resided continuously in the host state for five years (Article 16, Directive 2004/38). In *Förster* (Case C–158/07) [2008] ECR I–8507 (discussed in Chapter 11), Article 24(2) was explicitly referred to by the ECJ to support its conclusion that the five-year continuous residency period imposed under Dutch law for students to become eligible for a maintenance grant was legitimate and proportionate.

The decision of the ECJ in *Förster* is criticised here for failing to acknowledge that the principles in *Lair*, *Matteucci* and *Bernini* applied to Ms Förster. She had actually worked in the Netherlands as a primary school teacher (and later in a 'special school providing secondary education to pupils with behavioural and/or psychiatric problems') before embarking on her degree course in educational theory. It is fairly clear that there was a very close connection between her work and her course of study, bringing her situation into line with cases such as *Lair*. Ms Förster should therefore have been able to rely upon Article 7(2) of Regulation 492/2011 in order to claim her full grant. This argument was actually put to the Court by the European Commission and A-G Mazák, but the Court completely ignored it.

Unsuccessful claims

Unsuccessful claims based on Article 7(2) are rare. In *Leclere and Deaconescu* (2001), the ECJ held that Article 7(2) could not be invoked to challenge the refusal of a benefit where the claimant was no longer working or even resident in the country in which they had been employed. More recently, in *Baldinger* (Case C–386/02) [2004] ECR I–8411, the ECJ dismissed a claim based on Article 7(2) for entitlement to war compensation. This was a benefit introduced in 2000 and payable to Austrian nationals who had been taken as prisoners of war during or immediately after the Second World War. The ECJ held that this benefit could not be classed as a 'social and tax advantage':

JUDGMENT

'An allowance such as [war compensation], apart from not being linked to the status of worker, is provided … in testimony of national gratitude. It is thus paid as a *quid pro quo* for the service they rendered to their country.'

Family members' entitlement to Article 7(2) protection

This entitlement to 'social and tax advantages' is afforded to workers' families too. The ECJ has pointed out that to allow Member States to discriminate against migrant workers' families in this respect could inhibit the free movement of those workers. In the earliest case on this point, *Fiorini v SNCF* (1975), the ECJ allowed the Italian widow of an Italian worker in France to claim reduced rail travel, but on the basis that he would have been entitled to it had he been alive. Subsequently, in *Inzirillo* (Case 63/76) [1976] ECR 2057 and *Castelli* (Case 261/83) [1984] ECR 3199 the ECJ held that migrant workers could make claims for benefits on behalf of their families. Finally, in *Bernini* (1992), the ECJ went further and held that the family members themselves could make a claim under Article 7(2). The ECJ held:

JUDGMENT

'The dependent members of the family are the indirect beneficiaries of the equal treatment accorded to the migrant worker. Consequently, where the grant of financing to a child of a migrant worker constitutes a social advantage for the migrant worker, the child may itself rely on Article 7(2) in order to obtain that financing if under national law it is granted directly to the student.'

The *Bernini* principle, that a worker's family members can invoke Article 7(2) to claim social advantages, specifically funding for education, has been confirmed in several cases subsequently. It applies to cases in which the worker's child claims funding from their working parent's 'host' state in order to study in the child's 'home' state and, in the most recent case, it has been extended to cover cases in which the worker's *step-child* claims funding.

- *Meeusen* (Case C–337/97) [1999] ECR I–3289 – the daughter of a Belgian national working in the Netherlands was able to claim funding under Article 7(2) from the Dutch authorities to study chemistry at a college in Belgium;
- *Giersch & Others* (2014) – the sons and daughters of various Belgian and German nationals working in Luxembourg were able to claim funding under Article 7(2) from the Luxembourg authorities to study in Belgium and the UK;

- *Depesme & Others* (Cases C–401–403/15) (unreported) – the stepchildren of two French nationals (who lived in France), and one Belgian national (who lived in Belgium) but who worked in Luxembourg, were able to claim funding from the Luxembourg authorities to study at universities in France or Belgium, respectively.

In *Giersch & Others*, the ECJ explained the situation as follows:

JUDGMENT

'The members of a migrant worker's family are the indirect recipients of the equal treatment granted to the worker under Article 7(2). Since the grant of funding for studies to a child of a migrant worker constitutes a "social advantage" for the migrant worker, the child may himself rely on that provision in order to obtain that funding if, under national law, such funding is granted directly to the student.'

Finally, the nationality of the worker's family member is irrelevant in this context (*Deak* (Case 94/84) [1985] ECR 1873).

Summary of cases involving Article 7(2) and family members

Case	Home state(s)	Host state(s)	Family member(s)
Fiorini (1975)	Italy	France	Wife and children
Inzirillo (1976)	Italy	Belgium	Son
Castelli (1984)	Italy	Belgium	Mother
Deak (1985)	Italy	Belgium	Son
Bernini (1992)	Italy	Netherlands	Daughter
Schmid (1993)	Germany	Belgium	Daughter
Meeusen (1999)	Belgium	Netherlands	Daughter
Giersch & Others (2014)	Belgium and Germany	Luxembourg	Sons and daughters
Depesme & Others (Cases C–401–403/15)	Belgium and France	Luxembourg	Step-children

The ECJ's flexible approach as to whether it is the worker or a family member who claims the 'social advantage' can be seen in *Hartmann* (Case C–212/05) [2007] ECR I–6303, a case involving a claim for child-raising allowance, a benefit payable under German social security legislation. The Court confirmed that this constituted a 'social advantage' and, moreover, that it was immaterial which parent claimed the allowance. The Court stated (emphasis added):

JUDGMENT

'A benefit such as child-raising allowance, which enables one of the parents to devote himself or herself to the raising of a young child, by meeting family expenses, benefits the family as a whole, *whichever parent it is who claims the allowance*. The grant of such an allowance to a worker's spouse is capable of reducing that worker's obligation to contribute to family expenses.'

12.4.4 Article 10 – access for worker's children to education

ARTICLE

'Art 10 The children of a national of a Member State who is or has been employed in the territory of another Member State shall be admitted to that State's general educational, apprenticeship and vocational training courses under the same conditions as the nationals of that State, if such children are residing in its territory.

Member States shall encourage all efforts to enable such children to attend these courses under the best possible conditions.'

Article 10 has been extended beyond conditions of entry to 'general measures to facilitate attendance', including funding in the shape of grants and loans to undertake such courses. In *Casagrande* (Case 9/74) [1974] ECR 773, the ECJ stated:

JUDGMENT

'It follows from the provision in the second paragraph of [Article 10] ... that the article is intended to encourage special efforts, to ensure that the children may take advantage on an equal footing of the education and training facilities available. It must be concluded that in providing that the children in question shall be admitted to educational courses "under the same conditions as the nationals" of the host State, Article 10 refers not only to rules relating to admission, but also to general measures intended to facilitate educational attendance.'

Age limits

For the purposes of Article 10, there is no age restriction as far as the child is concerned. This point was made in *Gaal* (Case C–7/94) [1995] ECR I–1031, where the 'child' in question was a 22-year-old biology student.

CASE EXAMPLE

Gaal (Case C–7/94) [1995] ECR I–1031

Lubor Gaal was born in Belgium in 1967 but from the age of two was brought up in Germany. He subsequently began a biology degree at a German university. In 1989, when aged 22, he applied for funds to study biology for a year at a British university. His father had died in 1987 and he was not financially dependent on his mother. The authorities in Germany refused his application, as he was over 21 and was not financially dependent on either parent. The ECJ held that the definition of 'child' for the purposes of Article 10 was not subject to any conditions (in terms of age). Gaal could therefore rely upon Article 10 to challenge the refusal to award funding.

The Court stated:

JUDGMENT

'[Article 10] encompasses financial assistance for those students who are already at an advanced stage in their education, even if they are already 21 years of age or older and are no longer dependants of their parents. Accordingly, to make the application of [Article 10] subject to an age-limit or to the status of dependent child would conflict not only with the letter of that provision, but also with its spirit.'

In Case C–529/11 *Alarape & Tijani* (Case C–529/11) [2013] 3 CMLR 38; [2013] 1 WLR 2883, the facts of which were discussed in Chapter 11, a 24-year-old PhD student at Edinburgh University was nevertheless held to be the 'child' of a worker. Article 10 may, therefore, encompass 'children' aged over 21 and no longer dependent. Otherwise, students would be rendered ineligible for state financial assistance as soon as they reached 21 and were financially independent of their parents.

Step-children

Article 10 refers to the 'children *of* a national of a Member State'. However, the Court has held that a worker's step-children are included, and that these children can be of any nationality. This has been seen in two cases:

- *Baumbast* (Case C–413/99) [2002] ECR I–7091 – German worker with Colombian step-daughter living in the UK: Article 10 applied.
- *Alarape & Tijani* (2013) – French worker with Nigerian step-son living in the UK: Article 10 applied.

Death, retirement, etc. of the 'worker'

In order for Article 10 to apply, it is essential that one of the child's parents is, **or has been**, working in the state providing the education (*Brown v Secretary of State for Scotland* (Case 197/86) [1988] ECR 3205; *Humbel* (Case 263/86) [1988] ECR 5365). However, because Article 10 refers to the children of a worker who is 'or has been' employed, provided that the working parent did work in the state at some point, it is immaterial that he has since retired, died or moved on to work in another country, as these cases illustrate:

- *Michel S* (Case 76/72) [1973] ECR 457 – Italian national worked in Belgium until his death. Son entitled to continue to rely on Article 10.
- *Casagrande* (1974) – Italian national worked in Germany until his death. Son entitled to continue to rely on Article 10.
- *Gaal* (1995) – Belgian national worked in Germany until his death. Son entitled to continue to rely on Article 10.
- *Baumbast* (2002) – German national worked in the UK until economic circumstances forced him to leave the UK and work in China and Lesotho in southern Africa. Daughter and step-daughter entitled to continue to rely on Article 10.
- *Ibrahim* (Case C–310/08) [2010] ECR I–1065 – Danish national worked in the UK, followed by a period of unemployment, and then left the country. Children entitled to continue to rely on Article 10.
- *Ahmed* (Case C–115/15) [2017] 1 CMLR 12; [2017] QB 109 – German national worked in the UK, and then left the country. Daughters entitled to continue to rely on Article 10.

A similar situation exists if the child's parents divorce and the child lives with the non-working parent (*R v Home Secretary* (Case C–413/99) [2002] ECR I–7091); *Teixeira* (Case

C–480/08) [2010] ECR I–1107). What happens if the worker leaves the host state and the child accompanies him but **then** decides to return in order to complete their education? The ECJ has held that in such circumstances the child may be covered by Article 10, in the interests of education continuity. This occurred in *Moritz* (Case 389/87) [1989] ECR 723, where M, a German national, had gone to live with his father in the Netherlands when the latter worked there. Subsequently the father returned to Germany and the son again accompanied him. However, the son later applied to return to the Netherlands to complete his education. The ECJ held that M had not forfeited his rights to complete his education in the Netherlands.

Right to education abroad
Article 10 is available to secure funding even if the course is abroad, **provided** that such right is available to nationals of the host state. In *Di Leo v Land Berlin* (Case C–308/89) [1990] ECR I–4185, the ECJ stated:

JUDGMENT

'[Article 10] lays down . . . a general rule which, in matters of education, requires every Member State to ensure equal treatment between its own nationals and the children of workers who are nationals of another Member State established within its territory. Accordingly, where a Member State gives its nationals the opportunity to obtain a grant in respect of education or training provided abroad, the child of a [Union] worker must enjoy the same advantage if he decides to pursue his studies outside the host State. That interpretation cannot be invalidated by the fact that a person seeking education or training decides to follow a course in the Member State of which he is a national.'

'Vocational training'
In *Gravier v Liège* (Case 293/83) [1985] ECR 593, the ECJ was asked to define 'vocational training' and duly provided a very generous interpretation of the phrase.

CASE EXAMPLE

Gravier v Liège (Case 293/83) [1985] ECR 593

Françoise Gravier, a French national, was studying a four-year course in strip-cartoon art at the Académie Royale des Beaux-Arts in Liège in Belgium. She refused to pay the *minerval* (supplementary fees imposed on foreign students in Belgian universities). Her enrolment was cancelled. She brought an action against the city authorities, claiming discrimination on grounds of nationality, contrary to (what is now) Article 18 TFEU. The question was whether her programme of study fell within the scope of EU law, which it would if it could be described as 'vocational training'. The ECJ defined 'vocational training' in such a way as to include most university courses, bringing them within the scope of Article 18.

The Court stated:

JUDGMENT

'Any form of education which prepares for a qualification for a particular profession, trade or employment or which provides the necessary skills for such profession, trade or employment is vocational training, whatever the age and the level of training of the pupils or students, and even if the training programme includes an element of general education.'

In *Blaizot v University of Liège* (Case 24/86) [1988] ECR 379, the ECJ went further and held that university education could constitute 'vocational training' 'where the student needs the knowledge so acquired for the pursuit of a profession, trade or employment, even if no legislative or administrative provisions make the acquisition of such knowledge a prerequisite for that purpose'.

CASE EXAMPLE

Blaizot v University of Liège (Case 24/86) [1988] ECR 379

Vincent Blaizot, a French national, was studying veterinary medicine at the University of Liège in Belgium. He wished to recover the *minerval* he had been required to pay prior to the *Gravier* decision. The question for the ECJ was whether university courses constituted 'vocational training' so as to be subject to (what is now) Article 18 TFEU. The university, supported by the Belgian government, argued that as university courses were essentially academic they were not vocational. Blaizot, supported by the Commission, argued the opposite. The ECJ agreed with Blaizot.

KEY FACTS

Workers' rights Under regulation 492/2011	
Member States must not limit employment opportunities for 'foreign nationals'.	Art 3
Member States may demand 'linguistic knowledge' where the 'nature of the post' requires it.	Art 3; *Groener* (1989)
Member States must not restrict the employment of 'foreign nationals' by reference to a number or percentage.	Art 4; *Commission v France* (1974); *Bosman* (1995)
Discrimination on grounds of nationality in the context of employment is prohibited. Both direct and indirect discrimination is prohibited.	Art 7(1)
Workers are entitled to the same 'social and tax advantages' as national workers. This provision has been defined very widely. In particular, no link is required with the worker's actual employment.	Art 7(2); *Fiorini v SNCF* (1975); *Even* (1979)
Article 7(2) includes the right to claim funding and grants for full-time education, provided there is 'some continuity' between the work and education, or the worker became involuntarily unemployed.	*Lair* (1988); *Matteucci* (1988); *Bernini* (1992); *Ninni-Orasche* (2004)
Worker's family members can rely on Art 7(2) to claim 'social and tax advantages'.	*Fiorini v SNCF, Bernini, Hartmann* (2007)
Worker's children are entitled to be educated under the same conditions as nationals.	Art 10
Art 10 extends to funding for education.	*Casagrande* (1974); *Gaal* (1995)
Art 10 is not subject to a maximum age limit. It therefore applies to university education.	*Di Leo* (1990); *Gaal* (1995); *Alarape & Tijani* (2013)
Art 10 can be used to pursue education in another Member State.	*Di Leo* (1990); *Gaal* (1995)

The child's right to education continues even if the worker is no longer working (because of death or retirement) or no longer resident in the state.	*Michel S* (1973); *Casagrande, Gaal, Baumbast and R* (2002); *Ibrahim* (2010); *Teixeira* (2010); *Ahmed* (2017)
The 'primary carer' doctrine, which is based on Art 10, allows the 'primary carer' of a child to residence rights until the child reaches the age of majority or even beyond that if continued support is needed to complete education.	*Baumbast and R* (2002); *Ibrahim* (2010); *Teixeira* (2010); *Alarape & Tijani* (2013)

12.5 Purely internal situations

If all the facts of a particular case occur within the territory of a single EU Member State, then EU law has no role to play. This point was first made in the context of Article 45, although it has since been confirmed and applied to Article 49 (freedom of establishment) and Article 56 (freedom to provide services) as well (these freedoms are discussed in the next chapter).

12.5.1 Workers and the 'purely internal' rule

CASE EXAMPLE

R v Saunders (Case 175/78) [1979] ECR 1129

Vera Saunders, from Northern Ireland, pleaded guilty to theft at Bristol Crown Court and was bound over on condition that she returned to Northern Ireland and did not return to England or Wales for three years. However, within six months she was arrested in Wales. When charged with breaching the terms of her binding over, she alleged a breach of Article 45. However, the ECJ pointed out that there was no cross-border movement and hence Article 45 did not apply.

This principle was applied in the following cases:

- *Iorio* (Case 298/84) [1986] ECR 247 – Paolo Iorio, an Italian national, was fined for not having the proper ticket on the Rome–Palermo train. He appealed, claiming that the Italian legislation imposing the fine infringed Article 45 on the basis that it inhibited free movement, but he was unsuccessful. There was no cross-border element to the case.

- *Steen* (Case C–332/90) [1992] ECR I–341 – Volker Steen, a German national, had worked for the German Post Office for 12 years. In 1985, he applied for a promotion, but withdrew from it when he discovered that this would mean classifying him as a 'civil servant'. He complained that this classification constituted a breach of Article 45, because under German law only German nationals could be appointed as civil servants. The ECJ again held that Article 45 did not apply.

12.5.2 Workers' family and the 'purely internal' rule

As with the worker, if the family member has not sought to exercise their free movement rights, EU law has no role to play. This principle has been seen in several cases:

- *Morson and Jhanhan* (Case 35/82) [1982] ECR 3723 – Surinamese nationals and parents of Dutch nationals in the Netherlands could not rely upon EU law because there was only one Member State involved;

- *Dzodzi v Belgium* (Case 297/88) [1990] ECR I–3763 – Togolese national married to Belgian national working in Belgium could not enforce EU law (only one Member State involved);

- *Uecker and Jacquet* (Cases C–64 and 65/96) [1997] ECR I–3171 – Norwegian and Russian nationals married to German nationals working in Germany could not enforce EU law (only one Member State involved);

- *Mayeur* (Case C–229/07) [2008] ECR I–8 – Peruvian national married to French national working in France could not enforce EU law (only one Member State involved).

In *Carpenter* (Case C–60/00) [2002] ECR I–6279, however, the ECJ ruled that EU law applied to the case of a Filipino woman married to a UK national and living and working in the UK. Although this case looks superficially identical to the cases of *Dzodzi*, *Uecker* and *Jacquet* above, the ECJ distinguished them. The reason was that, although the UK national lived and worked in the UK, his business involved providing services to customers in other EU Member States. The ECJ therefore held that a cross-border element had been satisfied and hence his wife could invoke EU law.

CASE EXAMPLE

Carpenter (Case C–60/00) [2002] ECR I–6279

Peter Carpenter was a self-employed UK national who provided services to customers based in other EU Member States. Specifically, he sold advertising space in various British medical and scientific journals. In 1996 he married Mary, a Philippines national. Shortly afterwards, she applied for leave to remain in the UK, but this was refused and a deportation order was made against her. (She had entered the UK in 1994 and stayed on in breach of her visitor status.) Mary sought to rely upon Article 56 (the freedom to provide and receive services – see Chapter 13), on the basis that if she were to be deported it would detrimentally affect Peter's ability to run his business and thus his freedom to provide services. In particular, she helped to look after his children from his first marriage. The question was whether the case raised any cross-border element sufficient to bring EU law into play. The ECJ held that there was, and went on to hold that Mary was entitled to rely upon EU law to remain in the UK.

Carpenter was followed in the context of Article 45 in *S & G* (Case C–457/12) [2014] 3 CMLR 18; [2014] QB 1207. The case involved two Dutch nationals (D1 and D2) who lived in the Netherlands but who worked in Belgium (i.e. they were frontier workers). Whilst working in Belgium, their children were looked after by D1's Ukrainian mother-in-law (S), and D2's Peruvian wife (G), respectively. S and G claimed rights of residence in the Netherlands, under Directive 2004/38, as D1's dependent relative in the ascending line and D2's spouse, respectively, but these claims were rejected by the Dutch authorities. When S and G challenged this, the ECJ held that Directive 2004/38 was inapplicable (that legislation only conferred rights on family members of EU citizens who had taken up residence in a Member State other than their home state) but Article 45 TFEU was applicable, by analogy with *Carpenter*, on the basis that the denial of residence status to S and G could – potentially – interfere with D1 and D2's rights to work in Belgium. Ultimately, it was a question for the national court to determine whether the grant of residence status to S and G was necessary in order to 'guarantee the effective exercise' of D1 and D2's Article 45 rights.

12.5.3 Exceptions to the 'purely internal' rule

There are two significant exceptions to the 'purely internal' rule.

First exception: returnees

First, it does not apply to 'returnees', that is, persons who have left their home state to exercise free movement rights (whether under Article 45, Article 49 or Article 56, or some other provision) and have then returned to their home state. Such persons may invoke EU law (*Singh* (Case C–370/90) [1992] ECR I–4265). Perhaps the most frequently occurring situation where EU law may be brought into play, despite a *prima facie* 'purely internal' situation, is if the person involved had exercised freedom of movement rights previously in order to obtain a qualification abroad before returning to work in their home state. In *Kraus* (Case C–19/92) [1993] ECR I–1663 the Court stated:

JUDGMENT

'If a national of a Member State, owing to the fact that he has lawfully resided on the territory of another Member State and has acquired a professional qualification there, finds himself with regard to his state of origin in a situation which may be assimilated to that of a migrant worker, he must also be entitled to enjoy the rights and freedoms guaranteed by the Treaty.'

This exception to the 'purely internal' rule can be seen in the following cases:

- *Knoors* (Case 115/78) [1979] ECR 399 – Dutch national permitted to rely on qualification obtained in Belgium while employed in the Netherlands;

- *Bouchoucha* (Case C–61/89) [1990] ECR I–3551 – French national permitted to rely on qualification obtained in the UK while employed in France;

- *Kraus* (1993) – German national permitted to rely on qualification obtained in the UK while employed in Germany;

- *Fernández de Bobadilla* (Case C–234/97) [1999] ECR I–4773 – Spanish national permitted to rely on qualification obtained in the UK while employed in Spain;

- *Dreessen* (Case C–31/00) [2002] ECR I–663 – Belgian national studied civil engineering in Germany (at Aachen State Civil Engineering College) before returning to Belgium;

- *Brouillard* (Case C–298/14) [2016] 2 CMLR 7 – Belgian national permitted to rely on his master's degree in Law, Economics & Management, awarded by the University of Poitiers in France, in order to apply for work in Belgium.

Second exception: the Ruiz Zambrano *principle*

In *Ruiz Zambrano* (Case C–34/09) [2011] ECR I–1177, [2012] QB 265, the ECJ created a second exception to the 'purely internal' rule when it decided that EU law did apply, even though there was only one Member State (Belgium) involved. The case involved two Colombian nationals who came to live in Belgium as asylum seekers. Subsequently, the couple had two children who acquired Belgian nationality – and therefore EU citizenship – by virtue of being born in Belgium. Eventually, the Belgian authorities rejected the parents' asylum application and ordered that the family be deported. However, the ECJ ruled that deportation of the parents would infringe the rights of the children 'of the *genuine enjoyment of the substance of the rights* conferred by virtue of their status as Citizens of the Union' (emphasis added). Not only that, but the Colombian parents (or at least one of them) was entitled to a work permit in order to be able to support their Belgian children.

This is an interesting development but its practical implications are quite modest. Subsequent case law has demonstrated that the 'purely internal' rule has not been abandoned. Indeed, *Ruiz Zambrano* was distinguished within a matter of weeks in *McCarthy* (Case C–434/09) [2011] ECR I–3375. This case involved Shirley McCarthy, a British national, who had resided in the UK all of her life. However, she also had Irish nationality because her mother was Irish. Shirley's husband, George, a Jamaican national, wished to be issued with a residence permit as the spouse of an EU citizen. Shirley therefore applied for a residence permit on the basis that she was an EU citizen resident in a state other than that of her nationality (Irish). The Home Office refused. She challenged that refusal, but the ECJ confirmed the continuing application of the 'purely internal' rule. The Court held that neither Article 21 TFEU, nor Directive 2004/38, applied to the situation of an EU citizen who had never exercised his or her free movement right and who had always resided in the Member State of which he or she was a national, even if the citizen was also a national of another Member State. It followed that the family members of such a citizen could not invoke any rights under that legislation either. Finally, the situation in *Ruiz Zambrano* was distinguishable, because the national measures in that case had the effect of depriving an EU citizen of 'the genuine enjoyment of the substance of the rights conferred by virtue of that status', which was not the situation in the present case.

McCarthy was then followed and applied in *Dereci & Others* (Case C–256/11) [2011] ECR I–11315, where the ECJ explained that *Ruiz Zambrano* dealt with the very specific situation where the denial of residence to a citizen's family member(s) would entail the citizen having to leave the territory of the EU entirely (and not just the host Member State). As a result, the Court held that various Nigerian, Serbian, Sri Lankan, Turkish and Yugoslavian nationals were **not** entitled to join their Austrian relatives in Austria unless a refusal of residence would entail the Austrian relatives being forced to leave the EU entirely. The Court added that the 'mere fact that it might appear desirable ... for economic reasons or in order to keep his family together in the territory of the Union' was insufficient to establish that a citizen would be forced to leave the Union if his/her non-EU family members were denied a right of residence. It was for the national court to decide whether or not the *Ruiz Zambrano* test was met. *Dereci & Others* has itself been followed in several ECJ cases, as follows:

- *O, S & L* (Cases C–356, 357/11) [2013] 2 WLR 1093 – two men of Algerian and Ivorian nationality were **not** entitled to join their Finnish relatives in Finland **unless** a refusal of residence would entail the Finnish relatives being forced to leave the EU entirely.

- *Ymeraga & Others* (Case C–87/12) [2013] 3 CMLR 33 – four Kosovan nationals were **not** entitled to join their Luxembourg relative in Luxembourg **unless** a refusal of residence would entail the Luxembourg relative being forced to leave the EU entirely.

- *C.S.* (Case C–304/14) [2017] 1 CMLR 31; [2017] QB 558 – a Moroccan national (who had been convicted of a criminal offence and was subject to a deportation order) was **not** entitled to remain in the UK **unless** her expulsion would entail her son (a British national of whom she was the primary carer) being forced to leave the EU entirely.

- *Chavez-Vilchez & Others* (Case C–133/15) [2017] 3 CMLR 35 – eight women (two from Venezuela, two from Surinam and one from Cameroon, Nicaragua, Rwanda and the former Yugoslavia) would **not** be entitled to remain in the Netherlands (and claim benefits) **unless** their removal would entail their children (all of whom were Dutch nationals and of whom the women claimed to be the primary carer) being forced to leave the EU entirely.

In *Chavez-Vilchez*, the Dutch authorities disputed the various mothers' claims to be the 'primary carer' of their children, given that, although the children all lived with their mothers, the fathers (all Dutch nationals) had apparently 'acknowledged' the children's existence. The Court held that, in such cases:

JUDGMENT

'It is important to determine which parent is the "primary carer" of the child and whether there is in fact a relationship of dependency between the child and the third-country national parent.... The fact that the other parent, a Union citizen, is actually able and willing to assume sole responsibility for the primary day-to-day care of the child is a relevant factor, but it is not in itself a sufficient ground for a conclusion that there is not, between the third-country national parent and the child, such a relationship of dependency that the child would be compelled to leave the territory of the EU if a right of residence were refused to that third-country national. In reaching such a conclusion, account must be taken, in the best interests of the child concerned, of all the specific circumstances, including the age of the child, the child's physical and emotional development, the extent of his emotional ties both to the Union citizen parent and to the third-country national parent, and the risks which separation from the latter might entail for that child's equilibrium.'

12.5.4 Circumventing the 'purely internal' rule

Given that some cross-border element is essential, is there anything to stop a UK national from going to work in Ireland for six months and then returning to the UK in order to then make a claim based on EU law? This was the situation in *Akrich* (2003). The Court held that the motives of any EU citizen intending to work in another EU Member State were irrelevant in assessing the legal situation of the couple at the time of their return to the 'home' Member State. Such conduct cannot constitute an abuse even if the spouse did not have a right to remain in the 'home' Member State at the time when the couple installed themselves in the other Member State. There would be an abuse of EU law only if the couple's marriage had been one of 'convenience', that is, if it had been entered into for cynical reasons of acquiring marital status only, as opposed to genuine feelings of love.

CASE EXAMPLE

Akrich (Case C–109/01) [2003] ECR I–9607

Hacene Akrich, a Moroccan national, married Halina Jazdzewska, a British national, in June 1996. In June 1997, Halina moved to Ireland, where she found work in a bank, before returning to the UK approximately six months afterwards. In February 1998, Hacene applied for leave to enter the UK as the spouse of a migrant worker. In September 1998 the Home Secretary refused him clearance to enter the UK. The Home Secretary took the view that Halina's move to Ireland was a temporary move designed to circumvent UK immigration law by artificially bringing EU law into play. Hacene appealed and, in October 2000, the case was referred to the ECJ, which held that Article 45 could be applied to these facts.

Directive 2004/38 now provides explicitly for situations in which free movement rights are 'abused', such as the alleged marriage of convenience in *Akrich*. Article 35 provides:

ARTICLE

'Art 35 Member States may adopt the necessary measures to refuse, terminate or withdraw any right conferred by this Directive in the case of abuse of rights or fraud, such as marriages of convenience. Any such measure shall be proportionate and subject to the procedural safeguards provided for in Articles 30 and 31.'

ACTIVITY

Applying the law

If there was no abuse of Article 45 in *Akrich* (2003), would there have been an abuse if Halina had moved to Ireland for three months, or three weeks? *Carpenter* (2002) establishes that any cross-border economic activity suffices to bring EU law into play (albeit not necessarily Article 45). If a British national goes on holiday to Spain for a fortnight before returning to the UK, has he established a cross-border economic activity sufficient to allow *Carpenter* or *Akrich* to be relied upon? Would a long weekend in Rome be enough? What about a day trip to Calais?

KEY FACTS

The 'purely internal' rule	
As a general rule, EU law does not apply if the worker is employed in their home state.	*Saunders* (1978); *Iorio* (1986); *Steen* (1992)
Worker's family members are not protected by EU law if the worker has never exercised free movement rights.	*Morson & Jhanjan* (1982); *Dzodzi* (1990); *Uecker & Jacquet* (1997)
The 'purely internal' rule does not apply in cases where there is some cross-border element.	*Carpenter* (2002); *S & G* (2014)
The 'purely internal' rule does not apply where a person has exercised free movement rights, typically by working or studying abroad and then returning 'home'.	*Knoors* (1979); *Singh* (1992); *Kraus* (1993); *D'Hoop* (2002); *Brouillard* (2016)
The 'purely internal' rule does not apply where the denial of residence to a citizen's family member(s) would entail the citizen having to leave the territory of the EU entirely (and not just the host Member State).	*Ruiz Zambrano* (2011); *Dereci* (2012); *O, S & L* (2013); *Ymeraga & Others* (2013); *C.S.* (2017); *Chavez-Vilchez & Others* (2017)
Working abroad for a few months before returning 'home' does not constitute an abuse of the 'purely internal' rule.	*Akrich* (2003)

12.6 The public service exemption and Article 45(4) TFEU

Member States are permitted to exclude foreign nationals from working in the 'public service' by virtue of Article 45(4). Member States could potentially exploit this derogation in order to limit the freedom of migrant workers to take up work in that state. It has therefore been restrictively interpreted by the ECJ. First, it only applies to **access to** employment, not **conditions of** employment after access has been granted (*Sotgiu v Deutsche Bundespost* (Case 152/73) [1974] ECR 153). In *Brouillard* (2016), the Court stressed that Article 45(4) does not allow Member States to restrict access to 'public service' employment in a case where one of its *own* nationals is the job applicant.

More significantly, the ECJ has held that Article 45(4) does not apply to **all** employment in the public service, only 'certain activities' involving the exercise of official authority (*Sotgiu*). In *Commission v Belgium* (Case 149/79) [1980] ECR 3881, the ECJ laid down the following test in determining whether a worker is employed in the 'public service':

JUDGMENT

'Classification depends on whether or not the posts in question are typical of the specific activities of the public service in so far as the exercise of powers conferred by public law and responsibility for safeguarding the general interests of the State are vested in it.'

Further guidance was given in *Lawrie-Blum* (1986), where the ECJ held that the derogation only applied to those posts which required 'a special relationship of allegiance to the State on the part of persons occupying them and reciprocity of rights and duties which form the foundation of the bond of nationality'.

CASE EXAMPLE

Lawrie-Blum (Case 66/85) [1986] ECR 2121

Deborah Lawrie-Blum, a British national, was refused entry to a teacher training course in Germany, purely on national grounds. There were two questions for the ECJ:

1. Was she a worker, given her trainee status?
2. Did the 'public service' derogation apply to teaching?

   The ECJ held:

   1. that she was a worker, because trainee teachers received a salary and would be required to teach up to 11 hours of classes per week; and
   2. that teaching was not a 'public service' occupation, because teachers did not owe 'a special relationship of allegiance to the State'.

These principles can be seen in the following cases, where the jobs in question were all held **not** to be in the 'public service':

- *Commission v France* (Case 307/84) [1986] ECR 1725 – nurses;
- *Lawrie-Blum* (1986) – school teachers;
- *Alluè & Coonan* (Case 33/88) [1989] ECR 1591 – university teachers;
- *Schöning-Kougebetopoulou* (Case C–15/96) [1998] ECR I–47 – doctors.

Colegio de Oficiales de la Marina Mercante Española (Case C–405/01) [2003] ECR I–10391 introduced further limitations on the scope of the Article 45(4) derogation.

CASE EXAMPLE

Colegio de Oficiales de la Marina Mercante Española (Case C–405/01) [2003] ECR I–10391

The case involved the post of ship's master. Under Spanish law, such posts were reserved to Spanish nationals. It was argued that the Article 45(4) derogation applied, because ship's masters had a range of public order powers while on board, which they could exercise in emergencies. The ECJ held that Article 45(4) potentially applied because ship's masters' powers to enforce public safety did 'constitute participation in the exercise of rights under powers conferred by public law for the purposes of safeguarding the general interests of the flag State'. The fact that, at any given time, masters may be employed by private individuals or companies did not affect this conclusion because they continued to act as representatives of public authority. However, it was 'necessary that such rights are in fact exercised on a regular basis by those holders and do not represent a very minor part of their activities'.

The ECJ stated:

JUDGMENT

'The scope of [Article 45(4)] must be limited to what is strictly necessary for safeguarding the general interests of the Member State concerned, which cannot be imperilled if rights under powers conferred by public law are exercised only sporadically, even exceptionally, by nationals of other Member States.'

In *Alevizos* (Case C–392/05) [2007] ECR I–3505, the ECJ considered that a Greek national and member of the Greek Air Force might be classed as working in the public service:

JUDGMENT

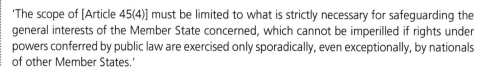

'The position occupied by Mr Alevizos in the Greek Air Force ... might fall within the concept of "employment in the public service" within the meaning of Article 45(4) in so far as it involves direct or indirect participation in the exercise of powers conferred by public law and duties designed to safeguard the general interests of the State or of other public authorities.'

KEY FACTS

The public service derogation	
Member States are permitted to exclude foreign nationals from their 'public service'.	Art 45(4) TFEU
Art 45(4) applies only to access to employment, not conditions of employment (e.g. salary, promotion).	*Sotgiu* (1974)
Art 45(4) only applies to migrant workers, not to a state's own nationals.	*Brouillard* (2016)
'Public service' is narrowly defined, requiring the 'exercise of powers conferred by public law and responsibility for safeguarding the general interests of the State'; a 'special relationship of allegiance' to the state.	*Commission v Belgium* (1980); *Lawrie-Blum* (1986)

It does not apply if public law powers are exercised only 'sporadically' or 'exceptionally'.	*Colegio de Oficiales de la Marina Mercante Española* (2003)
It does not apply to civil servants, teachers, doctors, nurses, etc.	*Lawrie-Blum, Commission v France* (1986); *Schöning-Kougebetopoulou* (1998)

12.7 Justification for non-discriminatory rules

In addition to the specific Article 45 derogations, the ECJ has created a parallel set of derogations which may be pleaded by Member States to justify restrictions on the free movement of workers. The ECJ has authorised Member States to impose restrictions on the free movement of workers, provided that the national rule in question satisfies four criteria:

i. it is non-discriminatory;

ii. it is justified by imperative requirements in the general interest;

iii. it is suitable for the attainment of the objective it pursues;

iv. it does not go beyond what is necessary in order to attain its objective (the 'proportionality' doctrine).

Two of the leading cases in this area are dealt with in the next section as they involve national rules curtailing free movement in the interests of sport (see *Bosman* (1995) and *Lehtonen* (2000)). Other cases where the ECJ has considered the application of the four-part test include *Alluè and Coonan* (1989) and *Clean Car Autoservice* (Case C–350/96) [1998] ECR I–2521. The former case involved a challenge to a provision of Italian legislation, which provided that foreign-language teaching assistants in Italian universities could only be employed on year-long contracts, and for a maximum of six years. It was argued by Ms Alluè (who was Spanish) and Ms Coonan (a British national), both of whom worked as foreign-language teaching assistants at the University of Venice, that this breached Article 45 as it restricted their freedom to work in Italy for as long as they wished. The Italian government sought to justify the restriction, and the ECJ applied the four-part test:

i. Was the rule non-discriminatory? The rule applied to all foreign-language teaching assistants, including those of Italian nationality.

ii. Was it justified by imperative requirements in the general interest? The Italian government suggested that the rule was necessary in order to ensure that foreign-language teaching assistants retained sufficient familiarity with the language that they taught.

iii. Was it suitable for the attainment of the objective which it pursues? The ECJ thought not. The Court said that the danger of foreign-language teaching assistants losing contact with their mother tongue was 'slight, in the light of the increase in cultural exchanges and improved communications'.

iv. Did it not go beyond what is necessary in order to attain its objective (the 'proportionality' doctrine)? Again, the Court thought not. It was 'open to the universities in any event to check the level of assistants' knowledge'.

In *Clean Car Autoservice* (1998), a challenge was brought to a provision of Austrian legislation which required companies to appoint a manager who was resident in Austria. CCA, an Austrian company, appointed a manager, a German national, who was resident in Berlin. Vienna City Council refused to register the company until he acquired a residence in Austria. CCA challenged this and the ECJ applied the four-part test:

i. Was the rule non-discriminatory? The rule applied to all companies operating in Austria, regardless of the nationality of their managers.

ii. Was it justified by imperative requirements in the general interest? The Austrian government argued that it could be justified on two grounds. First, to ensure that the person appointed would be in a position to act effectively as manager. Second, to ensure that he could be served with notice of any fines which may be imposed upon him, and also to ensure that any fines imposed could be enforced.

iii. Was it suitable for the attainment of the objective it pursued? The ECJ decided that the residence requirement did not serve its objective. As far as the effective management point was concerned, a person could reside in the same state but be further from the place of business than someone living just over the border in a different state.

iv. Did it not go beyond what is necessary in order to attain its objective (the 'proportionality' doctrine)? The ECJ held that the rule was disproportionate as other means, less restrictive of the freedom of movement of workers, were available. Regarding the argument about the imposition of fines, the Court held that fines could be served at the company's registered office instead.

12.8 Free movement of workers and professional sport

12.8.1 Introduction

EU law does apply to sport, but it is important to bear in mind the following basic propositions:

- Article 45, on the free movement of workers, applies to team sports such as football, rugby, basketball and hockey. Individual sportsmen and women, such as golfers and tennis players, are not protected by Article 45 because they are not employed by anyone. However, they are entitled to invoke Article 56, on the freedom to provide services. For an example, see *Deliège* (Cases C–51/96 and C–191/97) [2000] ECR I–2549, discussed in the next chapter, at section 13.3.3).

- EU law only applies to any type of sport if there is some economic activity. In other words, it applies to professional or semi-professional sport, but not to purely amateur sporting activities.

- EU law does not apply to 'questions of purely sporting interest', such as the number of players on a team or the actual rules of the sport itself, whether in a professional, semi-professional or amateur contest.

The first ECJ case to examine the compatibility of national laws regulating sporting activity with EU law, specifically the free movement provisions, occurred in *Walrave and Koch* (Case 36/74) [1974] ECR 1405. The ECJ ruled that the rule of non-discrimination on grounds of nationality found in Articles 18, 45 and 56 TFEU did **not** affect the composition of sports teams, in particular national teams, the formation of which was 'a question of purely sporting interest and as such has nothing to do with economic activity'. However, this clearly left open the possibility of invoking EU law to challenge other sporting rules which did have something 'to do with economic activity'.

CASE EXAMPLE

Walrave and Koch (Case 36/74) [1974] ECR 1405

Bruno Walrave and Longinus Koch, Dutch nationals, were motorcycle pacemakers. This entailed them riding ahead of cyclists in medium-distance cycle races, for which they received payment. In 1973, the Association Union Cycliste International (AUCI) issued a rule that pacemakers in the World Championships, which the AUCI organised, had to be of the same nationality as the cyclist. W and K challenged this rule on the basis that it interfered with their freedom to provide services under Article 56. The ECJ decided that both Articles 18 and 56 were directly effective and could, in principle, be used to challenge discriminatory treatment in the sporting context, provided that there was some economic activity involved. On the facts, however, this case involved 'a question of purely sporting interest' and EU law did not apply.

The next development was *Donà v Mantero* (Case 13/76) [1976] ECR 1333, which involved a challenge to rules of the Italian football federation, under which only Italian nationals could play in federation games. Here the ECJ ruled that Articles 18, 45 and 56 TFEU (as the case may be) could be invoked to challenge national sporting rules in the context of professional or semi-professional sport.

12.8.2 Using EU law to challenge transfer restrictions

The leading case here is the famous 'Bosman ruling', *Bosman v Royal Belgian Football Association and Union des Associations Européennes de Football (UEFA)* (1995). In this case the ECJ held that the 'transfer fee' system used in professional football whenever one player (if he was out of contract) moved to another club imposed an obstacle to the free movement of workers and was prohibited by Article 45(1). The expression 'Bosman free' to describe the free transfer of an out-of-contract football player from one club to another has now entered the vocabulary of professional football. The ECJ rejected a number of arguments advanced by the defendants to justify retention of the transfer fee system.

CASE EXAMPLE

Bosman v Royal Belgian Football Association and UEFA (Case C–415/93 [1995] ECR I–4921

Jean-Marc Bosman was a midfield football player with Liège FC in Belgium whose employment contract had expired in June 1990. He found a new football club willing to give him a new contract, Dunkerque FC in France. However, under rules adopted by all of the national football associations operating under the umbrella of the UEFA organisation, Liège retained Bosman's playing registration and would only release it to Dunkerque (or indeed anyone else) if the latter paid a 'transfer fee', set by Liège at 11.7 million Belgian francs. The transfer collapsed as a result, prompting Bosman to launch a challenge to the 'transfer fee' system which culminated, in December 1995, in a historic victory for Bosman.

Note: the Belgian franc ceased to be legal tender when the single European currency was introduced in 2002.

It is also important to note that the *Bosman* ruling meant the abolition of transfer fees for **out-of-contract** football players only. One of the first players to benefit from this ruling was Steve McManaman, who transferred from Liverpool FC to Real Madrid in the summer of 1999 on a 'Bosman free' transfer. Players who are transferred while **still under contract** are potentially subject to a transfer fee – the fee operates as compensation to the 'selling' club for the loss of the player. In some cases these transfer fees can be very large indeed. Recent examples include the transfers of German midfielder Mesut Özil from Real Madrid to Arsenal for £42.5 million, Belgian midfielder Kevin de Bruyne from Wolfsburg to Manchester City for £55 million, Spanish striker Álvaro Morata from Real Madrid to Chelsea for £60 million and French midfielder Paul Pogba from Juventus to Manchester United for £89 million. All four players were under contract to the 'selling' club at the dates of their moves to the UK and hence a transfer fee was payable.

Bosman was followed, but distinguished, in an ECJ case involving the compatibility of 'transfer deadlines' with EU law. While in *Bosman* the ECJ had held that transfer fees for out-of-contract players imposed an unjustifiable restriction on the free movement of workers, in *Lehtonen* (2000), the ECJ held that 'transfer deadlines' imposed a justifiable restriction.

CASE EXAMPLE

Lehtonen (Case C–176/96) [2000] ECR I–2681

In March 1996, towards the end of the 1995–96 basketball season, Jyri Lehtonen, a Finnish national, transferred from a team in Finland to Castors, in Belgium, who intended to play him during the final stages of the Belgian championships. However, rule 3(c) of the International Basketball Federation (FIBA) provided that European clubs were not allowed, after a deadline of 28 February, to include in their teams players who had already played in another European country during that season. Consequently, FIBA refused to issue a licence for Lehtonen to play in Belgium that season and warned Castors that the club might be penalised if it played him. However, Castors did play him in a match the next day, which they won, only to have the game awarded to their opponents by a score of 20–0. As the club ran the risk of being penalised again or even relegated if he played, Lehtonen was dropped for the remainder of the 1995–96 season. A few days later, Castors and Lehtonen brought proceedings challenging the FIBA rules. The case was referred to the ECJ, which held, first, that rule 3(c) did restrict the free movement of basketball players but, second, that it was justified. In particular, it prevented bigger clubs from 'distorting' the run-in to the league championship by trying to buy the best players from rival clubs.

Following *Bosman* and the abolition of transfer fees for out-of-contract players, UEFA introduced a new system of 'transfer windows' to try to regulate the movement of professional footballers. Under this system, players are only free to move from one club to another during the 'close season', which in Europe is June to August, and for one month mid-season (January). Although transfer windows clearly do restrict 'free' movement, they are probably justifiable by applying the precedent in *Lehtonen* (2000).

The ECJ has since given judgment in another case involving football which raised similar issues to those in *Bosman*. In *Olympique Lyonnais* (Case C–325/08) [2010] ECR I–2177, the issue was whether provisions of French law, requiring young footballers to pay damages to the club which had trained them in the event that the player did not subsequently sign professionally for that club, were compatible with Article 45. The ECJ held not.

CASE EXAMPLE

Olympique Lyonnais (Case C–325/08) [2010] ECR I–2177

Olivier Bernard spent his early playing career at Olympique Lyonnais, a football club in central France. However, he rejected the opportunity to sign a professional contract with Lyon, although one was offered, preferring to join Newcastle United in the English Premiership instead. This triggered a provision of French law, according to which he was liable to pay damages to Lyon. He refused, contending that the French rules infringed his rights as a worker under Article 45. The case reached the ECJ which held that the French rules were potentially justifiable. The Court accepted that the objective of 'encouraging the recruitment and training of young players' must be accepted as legitimate. Moreover, 'the prospect of receiving training fees is likely to encourage football clubs to seek new talent and train young players'. However, in this case, the French rules provided for the payment of damages, not compensation for training. This went beyond what was permitted, and therefore constituted an unjustified breach of Article 45.

12.8.3 Using EU law to challenge other sporting rules

Bosman also involved a challenge to a rule devised by UEFA, known as the '3+2' rule. The rule, which was enforced by all national football associations in Europe, applied to football clubs competing in certain competitions (national championships or UEFA-organised competitions – the UEFA Cup (now the Europa League), the Champions' Cup (now the Champions' League) and the European Cup Winners' Cup (now defunct)). It meant that they could only field three non-nationals plus two 'affiliated' players (meaning those players who had played in the country for an uninterrupted period of five years). The ECJ held that the rule constituted a breach of (what is now) Article 4 of Regulation 492/2011, which prohibits the imposition of 'quotas' on the employment of foreign nationals. The net result is that the '3+2' rule was disapplied as far as it concerned EU nationals, although it could still be applied to non-EU nationals. UEFA suggested several justifications for the rule, all of which were rejected. One such argument was that the rule helped to maintain a connection between clubs and local players. This was rejected, the ECJ pointing out that there was no requirement that clubs had to employ local players. Even before *Bosman* (1995), many clubs fielded players born hundreds of miles away.

The implications of this aspect of the *Bosman* ruling have been enormous, especially in the English Premiership. The amount of extra revenue that has been generated in this country through the upsurge in the game's popularity since the Premiership's introduction, higher ticket prices linked to better facilities and all-seater stadia, bigger ground capacities and Sky sponsorship, has allowed English clubs to attract large numbers of foreign nationals. Chelsea made football history in 1999 when it fielded a team containing no English players. It is quite common now for some Premiership games, say Arsenal v Liverpool, to involve mostly players from EU Member States (particularly France, Germany and Spain) and perhaps only two or three British players. This would have been unthinkable before *Bosman*.

This aspect of *Bosman* was followed in the context of another sport, handball, which is very popular in Germany, in *Kolpak* (2003). This case involved a Slovakian national playing in Germany who found his opportunities limited by a rule allowing clubs to field only two foreigners. It was argued that the rule was justified on the ground that it was intended 'to safeguard training organised for the benefit of young players of German nationality and to promote the German national team'. This was rejected. The rule did not benefit young German players because, following *Bosman*, it had already been repealed in the context of the other EU Member States and the signatories of the European Economic Area Treaty

(Iceland, Liechtenstein and Norway). The ECJ held that it could not be applied to those states with which the EU had signed Association Agreements, including Slovakia, either.

CASE EXAMPLE

Kolpak (Case C–438/00) [2003] ECR I–4135

In March 1997, Maros Kolpak, a Slovakian handball player, signed for the German club TSV Östringen. The German Handball Association (DHB) issued him with a player's permit marked 'A' for '*Auslander*' (foreigner). Under DHB rules only two squad places were available to foreigners. Kolpak challenged this, claiming that it limited his playing opportunities and was contrary to the prohibition of discrimination against foreign nationals. The ECJ held that the rules were discriminatory and could not be justified on 'purely sporting grounds'. In future, clubs were free to field an unlimited number of nationals of other EU Member States, nationals of EEA states and nationals of EU Association states.

A similar outcome to *Kolpak* was seen in *Simutenkov* (Case C–265/03) [2005] ECR I–2579, a case involving the EU/Russia Partnership Agreement. Igor Simutenkov, a Russian national, was playing in the Spanish football league with Tenerife. He was issued with a player's licence identifying him simply as a non-EU player. This meant that he could be excluded from certain games where only a limited number of non-EU players could be fielded. He contested this and the ECJ held that discrimination against Russian nationals was prohibited by the partnership agreement between the EU and Russia. The same result occurred in *Kahveci* (Case C–152/08) [2008] ECR I–6291, involving a Turkish national playing in the Spanish football league. He successfully invoked the Association Agreement between the EU and Turkey to challenge playing restrictions imposed on him.

ACTIVITY

Applying the law

1. Franco, an experienced heart surgeon, from Italy, was recently offered a professorial position at a teaching hospital in Nice, France, regarded as one of the best in Europe. He immediately accepted the offer and handed in his notice to his previous employer, a health authority in Rome in Italy. He also sold his house in Rome and most of his furniture, intending to make a fresh start in the south of France.

   Last month Franco flew to Nice, accompanied by his wife, Gisele, who is from Albania, their nine-year-old daughter Heidi, and Julio, Franco's son from a previous relationship. Julio is 23 years old but has a mental age of ten, the result of a brain tumour when he was a child. Soon afterwards, Franco started work and Heidi was enrolled at school. However, a few days after starting work, Franco arrived at his office to be told that his post was being re-advertised. He was told that new French legislation had just come into force, stating that all senior teaching posts in France had to be held by French nationals. Franco has decided to stay in Nice to fight this decision, which he regards as blatantly wrong.

   Julio loves gardens and would like to be a gardener. Franco, therefore, had arranged for Julio to be enrolled on a training course for adults with educational difficulties, run by Nice University. The course offers tuition in a variety of skills including cooking and gardening. However, when Franco applied (on Julio's behalf) for a special grant from the French government, available for victims of brain injuries to commence education, he was told that the grants are only available to French nationals.

   The strain of the move to Nice, followed by the sudden withdrawal of Franco's job, proved too much for Gisele, who has decided to seek a divorce. She has already moved out of the apartment and is renting a flat. Ideally, she would like to stay in France and get a job and a place for herself and Heidi to live, rather than return to Albania or Italy.

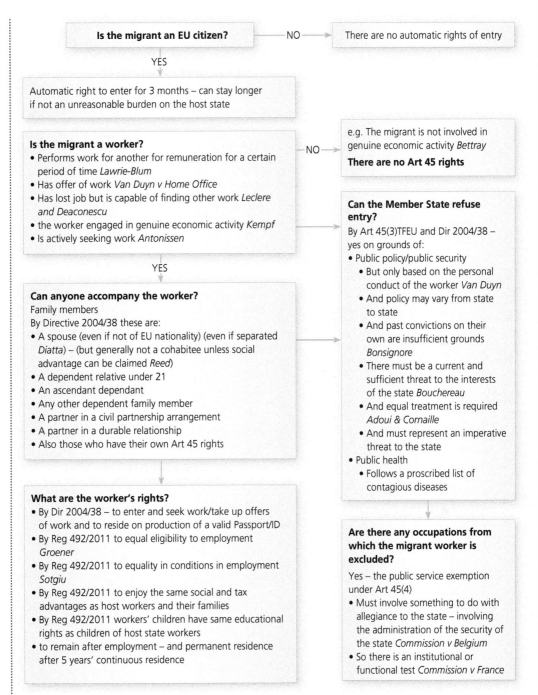

Figure 12.1 The free movement of workers under Article 45 and associated secondary legislation

Advise:

a. Franco as to his rights under EU law to challenge the Mayor's decision regarding the professorial position.

b. Gisele as to her rights to stay in France, to get accommodation there and to get a job, both in the immediate future and in the event of a divorce.

c. Julio as to his rights to the government grant.

Note: to answer this question you will also need to refer back to Chapter 11.

The application of Art 45 to sport	
Sport is subject to EU law only when there is some 'economic activity'. That means professional or semi-professional sports only.	*Walrave & Koch* (1974); *Donà v Mantero* (1976)
Sportsmen and women who play team sports such as football, basketball and handball are 'workers' and are protected by Art 45.	*Donà v Mantero*, *Bosman* (1995); *Lehtonen* (2000); *Kolpak* (2003)
Sportsmen and women who play individual sports are protected by Art 56 (the freedom to provide services).	*Deliège* (2000)
Transfer fees for out-of-contract sportsmen and women are in breach of Art 45(1) TFEU. Transfer fees for players under contract are permitted.	*Bosman* (1995)
Transfer deadlines are a justifiable restriction on the free movement of workers.	*Lehtonen* (2000)
Payments in the form of compensation for the training of young players are a justifiable restriction on the free movement of workers.	*Olympique Lyonnais* (2010)
'Quotas' restricting the number of foreign players who can be employed by a club or fielded in a game are prohibited.	Art 45(2) TFEU; Art 4, Regulation 1612/68; *Bosman* (1995)
This prohibition extends to players from EU Association countries such as Russia and Turkey.	*Kolpak*, *Simutenkov* (2005); *Kahveci* (2008)

SAMPLE ESSAY QUESTION

'Cases involving Article 45 TFEU and/or Regulation 1612/68 (now 492/2011) reveal that the ECJ is prepared to adopt a very wide interpretation of most concepts, such as the words "worker", but also a very narrow interpretation of certain concepts, such as the phrase "public service". However, this apparent contradiction is actually perfectly coherent – the ECJ is seeking to promote as much freedom for workers as possible. Discuss.'

Examine case law on meaning of 'worker':

- Cases such as *Lawrie-Blum* and *Trojani* show that the ECJ is very generous with its definition
- There is no minimum wage or minimum hourly rate threshold
- Case law has focused on the quality of the work – 'effective and genuine' activities – rather than the quantity of work
- Part-time and/or low-paid workers are covered (*Levin*, *Kempf*, *Ninni-Orasche*)
- Frontier workers are also covered (*Geven*, *Hartmann*, *Hendrix*)
- Trainees are workers (*Lawrie-Blum*, *Bernini*)
- The previously employed are also classed as workers (*Leclere and Deaconescu*)
- Even the unemployed have rights – despite not being in 'work' (*Antonissen*)
- But note that there are some limits (*Bettray*)

Examine case law on meaning 'social and tax advantages':

- In *Even* the ECJ refused to limit Regulation 1612/68, Article 7(2), to employment-related benefits and expanded the provision to include all benefits available to nationals
- Give examples from the case law, e.g. *Fiorini v SNCF, Mutsch, Reed, Lair, O'Flynn*
- Discuss how worker's family members may invoke Article 7(2) – *Fiorini v SNCF, Bernini, Meeusen,* even if they are not themselves EU citizens (*Deak*)
- Note that there are some limits (*Leclere and Deaconescu, Baldinger*)

Examine case law on meaning and scope of children's education:

- Despite referring only to 'access' to education, Regulation 492/2011, Article 10, has been defined very widely, to include funding for education up to and including University education (*Casagrande, Di Leo, Gaal*)
- The 'child' of a worker can be an adult (*Di Leo, Gaal*)
- Article 10 can even be used to claim funding for education in another Member State (*Echternach & Moritz, Di Leo, Gaal*)
- Article 10 continues to apply even after the death/retirement/departure of the worker (*Michel S, Casagrande, Gaal, Baumbast, Ibrahim*)
- Article 10 has also inspired the 'primary carer' doctrine (*Baumbast, Ibrahim, Teixeira*)

Examine case law on meaning and scope of the 'public service' derogation:

- Article 45(4) TFEU only applies to access, not conditions in, employment (*Sotgiu*)
- Explain characteristics of 'public service' employment – 'exercise of powers conferred by public law', 'responsibility for safeguarding the general interests of the state', 'a special relationship of allegiance to the state' (*Commission v Belgium, Lawrie-Blum*)
- Article 45(4) does not apply to posts where public law powers are 'exercised only sporadically, even exceptionally' (*Colegio de Oficiales*)
- Give examples of when Article 45(4) does apply, e.g. *Alevizos*

SUMMARY

- The free movement of workers is provided for by Article 45(1) TFEU. National rules which 'preclude', 'deter' or 'dissuade' nationals of one state going to work in another are prohibited (*Graf, Casteels v British Airways*).

- Article 45(2) TFEU prohibits discrimination in employment based on nationality. It can be invoked by workers to challenge discrimination in national legislation or in the policies of individual employers (*Angonese*). Article 45(2) can also be invoked by employers (*Innovative Technology Center, Caves Krier Frères*). The prohibition of discrimination is emphasised by Regulation 492/2011, Article 7(1).

- Discrimination can be direct or indirect. Direct discrimination occurs when a rule of national legislation or practice clearly applies different rules depending on nationality (*Wood*). Indirect discrimination occurs when a national rule is superficially neutral, but in practice is easier for nationals to satisfy and/or harder for non-nationals to satisfy (*Sotgiu, Allué & Coonan, Scholz, Schöning-Kougebetopoulou, Köbler v Austria*).

- Direct discrimination can only be justified using the TFEU (i.e. on grounds of public policy, security and health, under Article 45(3) (see Chapter 11), or using the public service derogation in Article 45(4) (see below)). Indirect discrimination is justifiable if it pursues a legitimate objective, is capable of achieving that objective and satisfies proportionality, i.e. it does not go beyond what is necessary to achieve that objective (*Allué & Coonan, Clean Car Autoservice, Lehtonen*).

- The word 'worker' is not defined in any EU legislation. In *Lawrie-Blum*, the ECJ established the conditions for a 'worker': provision of services, for another person, in return for monetary reward. Subsequent cases have emphasised the need for 'remuneration' (*Trojani*).

- Part-time and/or low-paid workers qualify for Article 45 protection regardless of the level of remuneration. The minimum threshold is the provision of 'effective and genuine' activities (*Levin, Kempf, Kranemann*).

- The following are also classed as workers: trainees (*Lawrie-Blum, Bernini*); frontier workers (*Hartmann, Geven, Hendrix, Giersch & Others, Eschenbrenner*); the previously employed (*Leclere and Deaconescu*); women on maternity leave, provided that they return to work within a 'reasonable' time period (*St Prix*).

- People genuinely seeking work who can provide evidence to that effect are entitled to remain in the 'host' Member State indefinitely (*Antonissen, Collins*).

- Workers and their family members (see Chapter 11) are provided with further rights under Regulation 492/2011. Under Article 3, Member States may not make eligibility for employment more difficult for foreign nationals. However, it is permissible, if the 'nature of the post' requires it, that workers have certain linguistic knowledge. This applies to teaching (*Groener*) and banking (*Angonese*).

- Under Article 4, Member States may not discriminate against other EU nationals by imposing 'quotas' on the number of foreign workers (*Commission v France (Merchant Seamen), Bosman*).

- Article 7(2) extends the anti-discrimination principle to 'social and tax advantages'. 'Social advantages' is not restricted to work-related benefits. It covers benefits which are 'generally granted to national workers primarily because of their objective status as workers or by virtue of the mere fact of their residence on the national territory' (*Even*). Examples include rail travel packages (*Fiorini v SNCF*), the right to have a partner (*Reed*), the right to funding for full-time education (*Lair, Bernini, Ninni-Orasche*).

- Workers' family members can invoke Article 7(2), regardless of their nationality (*Fiorini v SNCF, Deak, Bernini, Giersch & Others*).

- However, Article 7(2) is not without some limits (*Leclere and Deaconescu, Baldinger*).

- Under Article 10, workers' children have the 'right of access to general educational, apprenticeship and vocational training courses under the same conditions as the nationals of that State'. This extends to funding for education (*Casagrande, Di Leo, Gaal*).

- There is no age restriction; a 'child' can be an adult (*Di Leo, Gaal, Alarape & Tijani*).

- Article 10 extends to 'all forms of education, whether vocational or general, including University courses' (*Echternach & Moritz, Di Leo, Gaal*).

- Article 10 includes a right for a child's 'primary carer' to reside in the Member State with the child, irrespective of the carer's nationality (*Baumbast & R*). The primary carer acquires a right of residence 'on the sole basis' of Article 10; the residency conditions in Directive 2004/38 do not apply (*Ibrahim*). In principle, the primary carer's right of residence ends when the child reaches the age of majority, but it may continue if necessary to enable the child to complete their education (*Teixeira*).

- Purely internal situations are not covered by Article 45 (*R v Saunders*).

- Even where family members are involved, if the worker has not exercised free movement rights, Article 45 does not apply (*Morson & Jhanhan*).

- The purely internal rule does not apply to 'returnees' – workers who have exercised their right to move to another state, before returning home (*Kraus*). Nor does it apply where the denial of residence to a citizen's family member(s) would entail the citizen having to leave the territory of the EU entirely (and not just the host Member State) (*Ruiz Sambrano, Dereci, Chavez-Vilchez*). Working abroad for a few months before returning home is enough to bring Article 45 into operation (*Akrich*).

- Employment in the 'public service' is exempted from the freedom to work provisions by Article 45(4). This allows Member States to restrict access to public service employment; it does not justify discrimination against non-nationals in conditions of employment (*Sotgiu*).

- 'Public service' employment involves 'the exercise of powers conferred by public law and responsibility for safeguarding the general interests of the state' (*Commission v Belgium*) and 'a special relationship of allegiance to the state' (*Lawrie-Blum*). It does not apply if public law powers are 'exercised only sporadically, even exceptionally' (*Colegio de Oficiales de la Marina Mercante Española*).

- The following are not employed in the 'public service': doctors (*Schöning-Kougebetopoulou*); nurses (*Commission v France (Nurses)*); teachers (*Lawrie-Blum, Bleis*); university lecturers (*Alluè & Coonan*).

- Article 45(4) has been held to be applicable to the captains of merchant ships (*Colegio*) and to air force pilots (*Alevizos*). Other occupations where Article 45(4) may apply include national security services, the higher levels of the civil service and the police force.

- Article 45 applies to sport to the extent that sport is an economic activity (*Walrave and Koch, Donà v Mantero*). Article 45 applies to professional and semi-professional team sports.

- Article 45 was successfully used to challenge transfer restrictions for out-of-contract footballers and for nationality quotas in football (*Bosman*) and the requirement that young players pay damages to their first club if they chose not to sign professionally for them (*Olympique Lyonnais*). But transfer deadlines used in basketball were held to be justifiable (*Lehtonen*).

- Sportsmen and women who play individual sports are not 'workers' but are protected by Article 56, the freedom to provide services (*Deliège*).

Further reading

Articles

Busby, N, 'Crumbs of Comfort: Pregnancy and the Status of "Worker" under EU Law's Free Movement of Persons' (2015) 44 *ILJ* 134.

Currie, S, 'Pregnancy-related Employment Breaks, the Gender Dynamics of Free Movement Law and Curtailed Citizenship' (2016) 53 *CML Rev* 543.

Gardiner, S and Welch, R, 'Bosman – There and Back Again: The Legitimacy of Playing Quotas under European Union Sports Policy' (2011) 17 *ELJ* 828.

Golynker, O, 'Jobseekers' Rights in the European Union' (2005) 30 *EL Rev* 111.

O'Leary, S, 'The Curious Case of Frontier Workers and Study Finance' (2014) 51 *CML Rev* 601.

Pennings, F, 'Case Note on *Casteels*' (2012) 49 *CML Rev* 1787.

Van den Bogaert, S, 'Sport and the EC Treaty: A Tale of Uneasy Bedfellows' (2006) 31 *EL Rev* 821.

Van Elsuwege, P, 'European Union Citizenship and the Purely Internal Rule Revisited' (2011) 7 *ECL Review* 308.

13

Freedom of establishment and the freedom to provide and receive services under Articles 49 and 56 TFEU

AIMS AND OBJECTIVES

After reading this chapter you should be able to:

- Understand the law relating to the freedom of establishment, in particular Article 49

- Understand law relating to the provision of services, in particular Article 56

- Understand the law relating to the mutual recognition of qualifications, in particular Directive 2005/36

- Understand the circumstances in which the freedom of establishment and the provision of services may be restricted

- Analyse critically the law relating to the freedom of establishment and the provision of services

- Apply the law to factual situations involving the freedom of establishment and the provision of services in the EU

Article 49 provides for the freedom of establishment; Article 56 provides the freedom to provide (or receive) services. Both provisions are directly effective – *Reyners v Belgium* (Case 2/74) [1974] ECR 631 (Article 49) and *Van Binsbergen* (Case 33/74) [1974] ECR 1299 (Article 56).

- A right of **establishment** is the right to install one's self in another Member State, permanently or semi-permanently, on a self-employed basis, for the purpose of performing a particular activity there. It also gives companies the right to set up a branch or a subsidiary in another Member State.

- The right to provide **services** allows an individual, established in one Member State, to provide their services in another Member State, on a temporary or spasmodic basis. It also allows a company, established in one Member State, to provide their services to anyone in another Member State. If necessary, it allows them to visit the other Member State, on a temporary or spasmodic basis, in order to do so.

13.1 Freedom of establishment and Article 49 TFEU

ARTICLE

'Art 49 Within the framework of the provisions set out below, restrictions on the freedom of establishment of nationals of a Member State in the territory of another Member State shall be prohibited. Such prohibition shall also apply to restrictions of the setting up of agencies, branches or subsidiaries by nationals of any Member State established in the territory of any Member State.

Freedom of establishment shall include the right to take up and pursue activities as self-employed persons and to set up and manage undertakings, in particular companies or firms ... under the conditions laid down for its own nationals by the laws of the country where such establishment is effected.'

Article 49 refers to the taking up as well as the pursuit of professional activities for individual, self-employed persons. For companies, the freedom of establishment **includes** the right to set up and manage 'undertakings', in particular companies and firms; and the setting up of agencies, branches or subsidiaries; under the same conditions laid down for nationals of the state where establishment is effected. This list is non-exhaustive, and has been expanded on. In *Commission v Germany (Insurance Services)* (Case 205/84) [1986] ECR 3755, the ECJ suggested that 'establishment' could also include the presence in a state of an office managed by a company's own staff, or a person who is independent but authorised to act on a permanent basis for the company.

It is possible to be established in two Member States at the same time. *Paris Bar Council v Klopp* (Case 107/83) [1984] ECR 2971 and *Gebhard v Milan Bar Council* (Case C–55/94) [1995] ECR I–4165 are two similar cases in which qualified German lawyers (already established in Germany) wished to set up second sets in France and Italy, respectively. They were challenged by the Paris and Milan Bar Councils but successfully invoked Article 49 to overcome any objections that they could not operate from more than one set simultaneously. These cases will be discussed in more detail in section 13.9.

13.1.1 The scope of Article 49 TFEU

Article 49 abolishes restrictions on the freedom of nationals (whether individuals or companies) to establish themselves in another Member State. The ECJ has stated that, for persons, Article 49 relates not only to the taking up of an activity as a self-employed person, but also to the pursuit of that activity, in the widest sense. The most obvious situation where Article 49 will apply is to prohibit national laws which clearly discriminate against nationals from other Member States seeking to establish themselves, perhaps by imposing extra conditions on them or by denying them rights available to nationals. This discrimination could be:

- **Direct.** For example *Steinhauser v City of Biarritz* (Case 197/84) [1985] ECR 1819 – French law gave specific advantages to French nationals working as self-employed artists. This was successfully challenged by a German national who had travelled to Biarritz in south-west France to ply his trade as a landscape artist. See also *Thijssen* (Case C–42/92) [1993] ECR I–4047 – Belgian rules restricted the post of Insurance Commissioner to Belgian nationals.

- **Indirect.** For example *Stöber and Pereira* (Cases C–4 and 5/95) [1997] ECR I–511 – German law provided child benefits to self-employed nationals only if their children were habitually resident in Germany. This was held to discriminate indirectly against foreign nationals who had come to Germany to set up a business but whose family had decided to remain at 'home'.

However, Article 49 is not limited to prohibiting cases of nationality discrimination. Article 49 states that 'restrictions on the freedom of establishment of nationals of a Member State in the territory of another Member State shall be prohibited'. Thus, **any** restriction imposed by one Member State on the freedom of establishment – even if it applies equally to that state's own nationals – is potentially prohibited by Article 49. This point was first made by the ECJ in *Klopp* (1984). It has been confirmed in several cases since, including *Gebhard* (1995). However, the ECJ has also acknowledged in such cases that **non-discriminatory** national rules may be justified (see below).

In *International Transport Workers' Federation & Finnish Seamen's Union v Viking Line* (Case C–438/05) [2007] ECR I–10779, the *Viking Line* case, the ECJ was asked whether Article 49 could be invoked to challenge threatened strike action by a trade union (in other words, whether Article 49 had 'horizontal' direct effect). The Court held that it did:

JUDGMENT

'In principle, collective action initiated by a trade union or a group of trade unions against an undertaking in order to induce that undertaking to enter into a collective agreement, the terms of which are liable to deter it from exercising freedom of establishment, is not excluded from the scope of [Article 49].'

13.1.2 Rights of entry and residence and Directive 2004/38

Self-employed persons have the same rights as all citizens to enter another Member State and to live there, to be accompanied by their family members, and even to retire in that state after their working life is over. The detailed rules are set out in Directive 2004/38, which was discussed in Chapter 11.

KEY FACTS

Freedom of establishment	
Freedom of establishment allows self-employed persons to go to another EU Member State and set up in business there. Also allows companies based in one EU Member State to establish a subsidiary or branch in another state.	Art 49 TFEU
It is possible to be established in more than one state simultaneously.	*Klopp* (1984); *Gebhard* (1995)
Art 49 prohibits discrimination (whether direct or indirect) based on nationality and any other 'restrictions' on the freedom of establishment.	*Steinhauser* (1985); *Stöber and Pereira* (1997)
Art 49 is directly effective, vertically and horizontally.	*Reyners* (1974); *Viking Line* (2007)

13.2 The problem of qualifications

13.2.1 The law prior to 2007

Although Article 49 removes restrictions on the freedom of EU nationals to establish themselves in another EU Member State, it says nothing about the various conditions which may be laid down in other states by legislation or by rules of trade or professional bodies relating to the education and/or training required to practise. These may vary widely from state to state and, left to their own devices, Member States may have been slow to recognise other states' qualifications. There was thus a major barrier to the free movement of the self-employed, as well as employees whose trade is subject to national regulation.

To tackle this, the EU's legislative bodies were empowered to 'issue directives for the mutual recognition of diplomas, certificates and other evidence of formal qualifications' (Article 53). During the 1970s and early 1980s many Directives were passed, largely in the health services field. But progress was slow, especially in heavily regulated areas like architecture (Directive 85/433 was **17 years** in the making). Because harmonising by profession was proving slow, it was decided in 1984 to abandon the 'sectoral' approach, and instead adopt a general approach. This was not based on harmonisation of individual professions, but the mutual recognition of qualifications in all areas where a higher education diploma was required. The underlying rationale was that a professional person, fully qualified in one Member State, was likely to have much the same skill, knowledge and competence as that required of a counterpart in another Member State.

The result was Directive 89/48, often referred to as the Mutual Recognition Directive. Directive 89/48 essentially created a presumption that those in possession of higher-education qualifications (referred to in the directive as 'diplomas') which entitled them to practise a 'regulated profession' in one Member State were entitled to practise that profession in any other Member State, subject to certain limited derogations. Directive 89/48 was subsequently complemented by a second Mutual Recognition Directive, Directive 92/51, which applied the same principles to all post-secondary qualifications. Neither of these directives applied to professions where specific harmonising directives applied. Finally, Directive 99/42 covered the recognition of qualifications in various commercial and industrial sectors such as agriculture, carpentry, the hotel and restaurant sector, and textiles. Until 2007, therefore, there were three separate regimes:

- Professions where specific harmonising directives existed. This covered the professions of general practitioner (GP), dentist, nurse, veterinary surgeon, midwife, pharmacist and architect.

- All other professions, such as accountants, lawyers and bankers, where one of the Mutual Recognition Directives applied.

- Those commercial and industrial sectors where Directive 99/42 applied.

13.2.2 The Qualifications Directive 2005/36

Those three separate regimes have now been consolidated by Directive 2005/36 (the Qualifications Directive). All the pre-existing legislation on qualifications, including the two Mutual Recognition Directives and Directive 99/42, was repealed, although some of the case law decided under these directives may still be of relevance today. The Qualifications Directive was later amended by Directive 2013/55. All references to Directive 2005/36 in the rest of this chapter are to the amended version of it. The general purpose of Directive 2005/36 is set out in Article 1, which states:

ARTICLE

'Art 1 This Directive establishes rules according to which a Member State which makes access to or pursuit of a regulated profession in its territory contingent upon possession of specific professional qualifications (referred to hereinafter as the host Member State) shall recognise professional qualifications obtained in one or more other Member States (referred to hereinafter as the home Member State) and which allow the holder of the said qualifications to pursue the same profession there, for access to and pursuit of that profession. This Directive also establishes rules concerning partial access to a regulated profession and recognition of professional traineeships pursued in another Member State.'

Article 2 sets out the scope of the Directive as follows:

ARTICLE

'Art 2(1) This Directive shall apply to all nationals of a Member State wishing to pursue a regulated profession in a Member State, including those belonging to the liberal professions, other than that in which they obtained their professional qualifications, on either a self-employed or employed basis. This Directive shall also apply to all nationals of a Member State who have pursued a professional traineeship outside the home Member State.

(2) Each Member State may permit Member State nationals in possession of evidence of professional qualifications not obtained in a Member State to pursue a regulated profession … on its territory in accordance with its rules.'

A 'regulated profession'

A 'regulated profession' is defined in Article 3(1)(a) as a

professional activity or group of professional activities, access to which, the pursuit of which, or one of the modes of pursuit of which is subject, directly or indirectly, by virtue of legislative, regulatory or administrative provisions to the possession of specific professional qualifications; in particular, the use of a professional title limited by legislative, regulatory or administrative provisions to holders of a given professional qualification shall constitute a mode of pursuit.

It follows, therefore, that it is possible that a 'profession' may be regulated in some Member States but not necessarily all of them. It depends on whether access to the 'profession' is subject in any given state to the possession of qualifications. In *Aranitis* (Case C–164/94) [1996] ECR I–135, a case on Directive 89/48, for example, the applicant had higher-education qualifications in geology awarded in Greece. However, when he purported to rely upon these in Germany he was told that the 'profession' of geology was unregulated in Germany and hence the Directive did not apply. This was confirmed in the following cases:

- *Fernández de Bobadilla* (Case C–234/97) [1999] ECR I–4773, another case on Directive 89/48, involving the question whether the 'profession' of art restorer was regulated in Spain (the ECJ held that this was a matter for the national court to decide).

- *Gräbner* (Case C–294/00) [2002] ECR I–6515, a case on Directive 92/51, involving the question whether the 'profession' of 'health practitioner' was regulated in Austria (the ECJ answered this question in the negative).

Nasiopoulos (Case C–575/11) [2014] 1 CMLR 7, a case on Directive 2005/36, where the Court accepted that the 'profession' of 'medical masseur-hydrotherapist' was not regulated in Greece.

In *Burbaud* (Case C–285/01) [2003] ECR I–8219, another case on Directive 89/48, the ECJ held that, just because an activity was carried out in the public sector, it could still be regarded as a 'regulated profession'. The case involved a Portuguese national who wished to rely upon her hospital administrator's qualification awarded by the University of Lisbon in order to secure a managerial position within the French national health service. The French authorities refused, insisting upon possession of specific French qualifications. The Court, however, rejected the French government's arguments and held that the definition of 'regulated profession' was a matter of EU law – indeed, it had to be, otherwise national legislatures could arbitrarily and unilaterally determine what was within the scope of the EU legislation on qualifications.

Article 3(2) of the Qualifications Directive adds that a profession practised by the members of an association or organisation listed in Annex I shall be treated as a 'regulated profession'. This includes, in the UK, bodies as diverse as the British Computer Society, the Institute of Chartered Accountants, the Royal Institution of Chartered Surveyors, the Royal Aeronautical Society and the Engineering Council.

Article 4 elaborates on the 'effect' of the Qualifications Directive:

ARTICLE

'Art 4(1) The recognition of professional qualifications by the host Member State shall allow beneficiaries to gain access in that Member State to the same profession as that for which they are qualified in the home Member State and to pursue it in the host Member State under the same conditions as its nationals.

(2) For the purposes of this Directive, the profession which the applicant wishes to pursue in the host Member State is the same as that for which he is qualified in his home Member State if the activities covered are comparable.

(3) By way of derogation from paragraph 1, partial access to a profession in the host Member State shall be granted under the conditions laid down in Article 4f.'

'Partial access' is defined, in paragraph 4f, as follows:

ARTICLE

'Art 4f(1) The competent authority of the host Member State shall grant partial access, on a case-by-case basis, to a professional activity in its territory only when all the following conditions are fulfilled:

(a) the professional is fully qualified to exercise in the home Member State the professional activity for which partial access is sought in the host Member State;

(b) differences between the professional activity legally exercised in the home Member State and the regulated profession in the host Member State as such are so large that the application of compensation measures would amount to requiring the applicant to complete the full programme of education and training required in the host Member State to have access to the full regulated profession in the host Member State;

(c) the professional activity can objectively be separated from other activities falling under the regulated profession in the host Member State.'

Directive 2005/36 then divides into two broad areas:

- the free provision of services (Title II; Articles 5–9);
- freedom of establishment (Title III; Articles 10–52).

The Qualifications Directive is a lengthy, detailed and technical piece of legislation and the following is necessarily only an overview of the main provisions.

The free provision of services

The main substantive provision here is Article 5, which states:

ARTICLE

'Art 5(1) ... Member States shall not restrict, for any reason relating to professional qualifications, the free provision of services in another Member State:

(a) if the service provider is legally established in a Member State for the purpose of pursuing the same profession there (hereinafter referred to as the Member State of establishment), and

(b) where the service provider moves, if he has pursued that profession in one or several Member States for at least one year during the last 10 years preceding the provision of services when the profession is not regulated in the Member State of establishment. The condition of one year's pursuit shall not apply if the profession or the education and training leading to the profession is regulated.

(2) The provisions of this title shall only apply where the service provider moves to the territory of the host Member State to pursue, on a temporary and occasional basis, the profession referred to in paragraph 1. The temporary and occasional nature of the provision of services shall be assessed case by case, in particular in relation to its duration, its frequency, its regularity and its continuity.

(3) Where a service provider moves, he shall be subject to professional rules of a professional, statutory or administrative nature which are directly linked to professional qualifications, such as the definition of the profession, the use of titles and serious professional malpractice which is directly and specifically linked to consumer protection and safety, as well as disciplinary provisions which are applicable in the host Member State to professionals who pursue the same profession in that Member State.'

Article 6 adds that Member States may exempt service providers from the requirements which it places on professionals established in its territory relating to authorisation by, registration with or membership of a professional organisation or body. Article 7 allows Member States to require that, where a service provider first moves from one state to another in order to provide services, he or she informs the competent authority of the host state, in writing, in advance of doing so. Article 8 provides that the competent authorities of the host state may ask the competent authorities of the service provider's state of establishment 'in the event of justified doubts' to provide any information relevant to:

- the legality of that establishment;
- the service provider's 'good conduct'; and
- the absence of any disciplinary or criminal sanctions of a professional nature.

Under Article 9, the competent authorities of the host state may also require the service provider to provide the service recipient with various information, such as:

- the name and address of the competent supervisory authority (if any) in the state of establishment;
- the service provider's professional title or formal qualification and the state in which it was awarded;
- details of any insurance cover or other means of professional liability protection.

Freedom of establishment

The Title on establishment further subdivides into three chapters:

- general system for the recognition of evidence of training (Chapter 1; Articles 10–15);
- recognition of professional experience (Chapter 2; Articles 16–20);
- recognition on the basis of co-ordination of minimum training conditions (Chapter 3; Articles 21–52).

General system for the recognition of evidence of training (Chapter 1)

This Chapter applies to all 'regulated professions' not covered by Chapters 2 and 3 (Article 10). It is this Chapter which replaces the Mutual Recognition Directives. It divides professional competence into five levels:

- Level 1 – an **'attestation of competence'** issued by a competent authority in the home state on the basis of a training course not forming part of a certificate or diploma, or three years' full-time professional experience, or general primary or secondary education, attesting that the holder has acquired 'general knowledge' (Article 11(a)).
- Level 2 – a **'certificate'** attesting to successful completion of a secondary course which is either 'general' or 'technical or professional' in character, and which in either case is supplemented by a course of study or professional training (Article 11(b)).
- Level 3 – a **'diploma'** certifying either (i) successful completion of training at post-secondary level of at least one year's duration (full-time) or the equivalent part-time duration, or (ii) regulated education and training or, in the case of regulated professions, vocational training with a 'special structure', if such training provides a comparable professional standard and which prepares the trainee for a 'comparable level of responsibilities and functions' (Article 11(c)).
- Level 4 – a **'diploma'** certifying successful completion of training at post-secondary level of at least three and not more than four years' duration (full-time), or the equivalent part-time duration, at a university or equivalent establishment, plus any additional professional training which may be required (Article 11(d)).
- Level 5 – a **'diploma'** certifying successful completion of a post-secondary course of at least four years' duration (full-time), or the equivalent part-time duration, at a university or equivalent establishment, plus successful completion of any additional professional training required (Article 11(e)).

Conditions for recognition: Article 13

Article 13 is the main substantive provision of Chapter 2. It provides:

'Art 13(1) If access to or pursuit of a regulated profession in a host Member State is contingent upon possession of specific professional qualifications, the competent authority of that Member State shall permit applicants to access and pursue that profession, under the same conditions as apply to its nationals, if they possess an attestation of competence or evidence of formal qualifications referred to in Article 11, required by another Member State in order to gain access to and pursue that profession on its territory.

Attestations of competence or evidence of formal qualifications shall be issued by a competent authority in a Member State, designated in accordance with the laws, regulations or administrative provisions of that Member State.

(2) Access to, and pursuit of, a profession as described in paragraph 1 shall also be granted to applicants who have pursued the profession in question on a full-time basis for one year or for an equivalent overall duration on a part-time basis during the previous ten years in another Member State which does not regulate that profession, and who possess one or more attestations of competence or evidence of formal qualifications issued by another Member State which does not regulate the profession.

Attestations of competence and evidence of formal qualifications shall satisfy the following conditions:

(a) they are issued by a competent authority in a Member State, designated in accordance with the laws, regulations or administrative provisions of that Member State;

(b) they shall attest that the holder has been prepared for the pursuit of the profession in question.'

Trevor Tayleur ('Qualified Approval' (2007) *NLJ* 1494) provides some useful examples of how the new provisions in the Qualification Directive might operate in practice. He writes:

Under the new system the first step is to find out how the professional qualification is obtained in the Member States concerned. For example, imagine that Germany requires five years' study at university for a given profession, while the UK merely requires three years. The German qualification will be at level 5, and the British at level 4. Germany cannot reject the British qualification, as the Qualifications Directive requires Member States to accept qualifications obtained in other Member States at least equivalent to the level immediately below that which is required in the host State. Thus, Germany must accept a level 4 qualification, though may impose compensation measures. Imagine that in Hungary, members of that same profession only had to go to university for two years; that would be a level 3 qualification. The UK must accept it, subject to compensation measures, as the UK qualification is at level 4. However, Germany would not have to, as its qualification is at level 5 and level 3 is too far below that level.

In *Toki* (Case C–424/09) [2011] ECR I–2587, a case on Directive 89/48, the ECJ was asked what was meant by the reference to applicants who have 'pursued the profession' in (what is now) Article 13(2) of Directive 2005/36. (This is crucial in cases where the applicant has moved from a state where the profession is not 'regulated'.) The Court held that it required 'the continuous and regular pursuit of a range of professional activities which characterise the profession concerned'. On the other hand, time spent conducting research and teaching did **not** count as pursuit of the profession in question.

'Compensation measures': Article 14

Article 14 provides for 'compensation measures'. It states:

ARTICLE

'Art 14(1) Article 13 shall not preclude the host Member State from requiring the applicant to complete an adaptation period of up to three years or to take an aptitude test if:

(a) the training the applicant has received covers substantially different matters than those covered by the evidence of formal qualifications required in the host Member State;

(b) the regulated profession in the host Member State comprises one or more regulated professional activities which do not exist in the corresponding profession in the applicant's home Member State, and the training required in the host Member State covers substantially different matters from those covered by the applicant's attestation of competence or evidence of formal qualifications.

(2) If the host Member State makes use of the option provided for in paragraph 1, it must offer the applicant the choice between an adaptation period and an aptitude test...

(3) By way of derogation from the principle of the right of the applicant to choose, as laid down in paragraph 2, for professions whose pursuit requires precise knowledge of national law and in respect of which the provision of advice and/or assistance concerning national law is an essential and constant aspect of the professional activity, the host Member State may stipulate either an adaptation period or an aptitude test.

(4) ... "substantially different matters" means matters in respect of which knowledge, skills and competences acquired are essential for pursuing the profession and with regard to which the training received by the migrant shows significant differences in terms of content from the training required by the host Member State.

(5) Paragraph 1 shall be applied with due regard to the principle of proportionality. In particular, if the host Member State intends to require the applicant to complete an adaptation period or take an aptitude test, it must first ascertain whether the knowledge, skills and competences acquired by the applicant in the course of his professional experience or through lifelong learning, and formally validated to that end by a relevant body, in any Member State or in a third country, is of such nature as to cover, in full or in part, the substantially different matters referred to in paragraph 4.

(6) The decision imposing an adaptation period or an aptitude test shall be duly justified...

(7) Member States shall ensure that an applicant has the possibility of taking the aptitude test referred to in paragraph 1 not later than six months after the initial decision imposing an aptitude test on the applicant.'

In *Beuttenmüller* (Case C–102/02) [2004] ECR I–5405, a case under Directive 89/48, the ECJ discussed the role of the 'compensation measures' under that Directive (which are essentially the same as those set out above). The Court stated:

JUDGMENT

'The system of mutual recognition of diplomas ... does not imply that diplomas awarded by the other Member States certify that the education and training are similar or comparable to that required in the host Member State.... A diploma is not recognised on the basis of the intrinsic value of the education and training to which it attests, but because it gives the right to take up a regulated profession in the Member State where it was awarded or recognised.... Differences in the organisation or content of education and training acquired in the Member State of origin by comparison with that provided in the host Member State are not sufficient to justify a refusal to recognise the professional qualification concerned. At most, where those differences are "substantial", they may justify the host Member State's requiring that the applicant satisfy one or other of the "compensatory measures".'

In *Colegio de Ingenieros de Caminos, Canales y Puertos* (Case C–330/03) [2006] ECR I–801, another case under Directive 89/48, the ECJ again examined the role of the 'compensation measures'. The Court concluded that, just because a host Member State was *entitled* to require an applicant from another state to satisfy one of the measures before being allowed to practise a profession in the host state, it did not follow that it was *obliged* to do so. Instead, the Court created the possibility of 'partial recognition' of an applicant's qualifications, allowing him or her to practise in the areas in which they were actually qualified.

CASE EXAMPLE

Colegio de Ingenieros de Caminos, Canales y Puertos (Case C–330/03) [2006] ECR I–801

In June 1996, Mr Imo, an Italian national with an Italian civil engineering diploma (specialising in hydraulics) applied for permission to practise as a civil engineer in Spain. His application was approved by the Spanish Ministry of Development, but the Institution of Civil Engineers in Spain (the Colegio) challenged this, on the basis that the Italian diploma was very different from the Spanish diploma. Under Spanish legislation, the profession of civil engineer covers a very broad range of activities, including the design and construction of hydraulic installations; land, sea and inland waterway transport infrastructures; conservation of beaches; and town and country planning. The Spanish diploma is awarded after six years of specific post-secondary education and training. Mr Imo's Italian diploma, on the other hand, only covered certain aspects of the Spanish diploma (namely, hydraulics). The ECJ decided that Mr Imo should be allowed 'the possibility of partial taking-up' of the profession in Spain.

The Court stated:

JUDGMENT

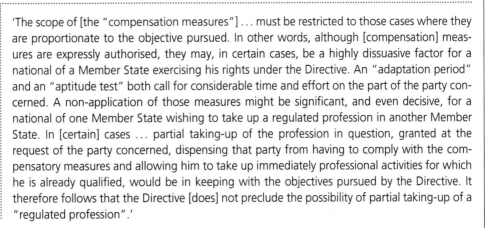

'The scope of [the "compensation measures"] ... must be restricted to those cases where they are proportionate to the objective pursued. In other words, although [compensation] measures are expressly authorised, they may, in certain cases, be a highly dissuasive factor for a national of a Member State exercising his rights under the Directive. An "adaptation period" and an "aptitude test" both call for considerable time and effort on the part of the party concerned. A non-application of those measures might be significant, and even decisive, for a national of one Member State wishing to take up a regulated profession in another Member State. In [certain] cases ... partial taking-up of the profession in question, granted at the request of the party concerned, dispensing that party from having to comply with the compensatory measures and allowing him to take up immediately professional activities for which he is already qualified, would be in keeping with the objectives pursued by the Directive. It therefore follows that the Directive [does] not preclude the possibility of partial taking-up of a "regulated profession".'

However, the Court added that the possibility of 'partial taking-up' would only be available in cases where there were such significant differences between the home and host

Member States that compensation measures would be tantamount to 'the full programme of education and training' in the latter state. Mr Imo's case was a perfect example: the Spanish Supreme Court had already found that there were significant differences between the profession of hydraulic engineer in Italy and that of civil engineer in Spain, such that requiring Mr Imo to undergo compensation measures in Spain would, in effect, force him to 'complete a fresh, complete programme of education and training'. That would be disproportionate, and hence partial taking-up was a more appropriate solution. By way of contrast, where a profession in two Member States was sufficiently similar (albeit not identical), then compensation measures would be more appropriate and 'partial taking-up' would **not** be available.

In *Colegio*, the ECJ also acknowledged that 'partial taking-up' of a profession created a risk of 'fragmenting the professions regulated in a Member State into various activities [leading] to a risk of confusion in the minds of the recipients of services, who might well be misled as to the scope of those qualifications'. However, the Court held that a blanket ban on 'partial taking-up' would be disproportionate. There were other, less-restrictive methods of protecting consumers from the 'risk of confusion'.

Colegio was followed and applied in *Nasiopoulos* (2014), involving a Greek national who qualified as a 'medical masseur-hydrotherapist' in Germany and who wished to practise as a physiotherapist in Greece. The ECJ held that it was for the Greek courts to examine the differences between the two professions (i.e. physiotherapy in Greece and medical masseur-hydrotherapy in Germany). If they were 'so great' that requiring Mr Nasiopoulos to undergo compensation measures would effectively require him to 'follow a full programme of education and training' in order to pursue the profession of physiotherapist in Greece, then 'partial taking-up' should be made available to him; otherwise, he would have to accept the compensation measures.

Generally speaking, where one of the 'compensation measures' is required, then the individual applicant can choose either to undergo an 'adaptation period' or take an 'aptitude test' (full definitions of these expressions are given below). By way of derogation from this, Article 14(3) provides that host states can specify one or the other for those professions requiring 'precise knowledge of national law'. This most obviously includes judges and lawyers – but does it extend to other professions as well? In *Price* (Case C–149/05) [2006] ECR I–7691, a case under Directive 89/48 involving an auctioneer, the ECJ considered what was meant by the phrase 'precise knowledge of national law'. The Court stated:

JUDGMENT

'The application of that requirement cannot lead to the result that only "traditional" legal professions, such as that of judge, notary or lawyer, fall within the scope of [what is now Article 14(3)].... It is not necessary for the advice and/or assistance provided to clients to concern all national law. It is sufficient that it concerns a specialised area. In order to determine the extent to which the provision of advice and/or assistance on national law is an "essential and constant" element of the activity concerned, it is necessary to refer in particular to normal practice of the relevant profession. It is for the national court to decide that issue.'

In *Van Leuken* (Case C–197/06) [2008] ECR I–2627, another case under Directive 89/48, the ECJ held that the 'profession' of estate agent in Belgium was not one 'whose practice requires precise knowledge of national law'. The Court pointed out:

it is sufficient to be the holder of a Belgian diploma in civil, agricultural, technical or industrial engineering in order to become a member of the profession of estate agent in Belgium and the education and training leading to those diplomas does not include significant legal training.

This meant that the Belgian authorities could not demand that Willem Van Leuken – a Dutch estate agent based in the Netherlands whose activities included selling property in Belgium to Dutch clients – undertake an aptitude test in Belgian property law. More recently, in *Vandorou & Others* (Cases C–422, 425 and 426/09) [2010] ECR I–12411, the Court accepted that accountancy was another profession requiring 'precise knowledge of national law'. This meant that, although Vassiliki Vandorou had qualified as a chartered accountant in the UK, she would have to pass an aptitude test (in Greek company, commercial, employment and tax law) before being allowed to practise as an accountant in Greece.

'Adaptation period': Article 3(1)(g)

An 'adaptation period' is defined in Article 3(1)(g) of the Qualifications Directive as:

> the pursuit of a regulated profession in the host Member State under the responsibility of a qualified member of that profession, such period of supervised practice possibly being accompanied by further training. This period of supervised practice shall be the subject of an assessment. The detailed rules governing the adaptation period and its assessment as well as the status of a migrant under supervision shall be laid down by the competent authority in the host Member State.

'Aptitude test': Article 3(1)(h)

An 'aptitude test' is defined in Article 3(1)(h) of the Qualifications Directive as a

> test of the professional knowledge, skills and competences of the applicant, carried out or recognised by the competent authorities of the host Member State with the aim of assessing the ability of the applicant to pursue a regulated profession in that Member State. In order to permit this test to be carried out, the competent authorities shall draw up a list of subjects which, on the basis of a comparison of the education and training required in the Member State and that received by the applicant, are not covered by the diploma or other evidence of formal qualifications possessed by the applicant.

Article 3(1)(h) goes on to provide that the test must

> take account of the fact that the applicant is a qualified professional in the home Member State or the Member State from which the applicant comes. It shall cover subjects to be selected from those on the list, knowledge of which is essential in order to be able to pursue the profession in question in the host Member State. The test may also cover knowledge of the professional rules applicable to the activities in question in the host Member State.

Recognition of professional experience (Chapter 2)

This Chapter deals with those commercial and industrial sectors where previously Directive 99/42 applied. Article 16 now provides that if, in a Member State, access to or pursuit of one of the activities listed in Annex IV of the Qualifications Directive is contingent upon possession of 'general, commercial or professional knowledge and aptitudes', that state must recognise previous pursuit of the activity in another state as sufficient proof of such knowledge and aptitudes. The list of 'activities' in Annex IV is very lengthy but, by way of example, it includes agriculture, carpentry, construction, footwear and clothing manufacturers, and the beverage, chemicals and petroleum industries. Articles 17–19 stipulate various minimum time periods over which the activities must have been pursued in the home state.

Recognition on the basis of co-ordination of minimum training conditions (Chapter 3)

This Chapter deals with those professions which previously had their own Directive. They now have their own provisions in the Qualifications Directive (GPs are covered by Articles 24–30; nurses by Articles 31–33a; dentists by Articles 34–37; vets by Articles 38 and 39; midwives by Articles 40–43b; pharmacists by Articles 44 and 45; architects by Articles 46–49), but the essential principles are the same for each of these areas. The Qualifications Directive:

- co-ordinates across all states the training required in order for qualification (as a nurse, dentist, architect, etc.); and

- provides that, once a professional in one of these areas is qualified to practise in one Member State then they are automatically entitled to practise in any other state.

13.2.3 Obligation to assess equivalence

Prior to Directive 89/48, many cases arose involving professions where no separate harmonising Directive existed. The ECJ has developed a line of case law according to which it is unlawful discrimination, and a breach of Articles 49 or 56 TFEU, to refuse permission to practise to a person whose qualifications in one state have been recognised, by the competent authorities, as equivalent to those awarded in the state in which he seeks to practise. Examples of this approach are *Thieffry* (Case 71/76) [1977] ECR 765 and *Patrick v Minister of Cultural Affairs* (Case 11/77) [1977] ECR 1199.

CASE EXAMPLE

Thieffry (Case 71/76) [1977] ECR 765

Jean Thieffry was a Belgian national with a doctorate in law from Louvain University, in Belgium, which had been recognised by the University of Paris as equivalent to a French law degree. He then undertook professional examinations and was awarded the *certificat d'aptitude a la profession d'avocat*. However, the Paris Bar Council refused to recognise his doctorate when he applied to undertake admission to the French bar. The ECJ held that this was a breach of Article 49.

CASE EXAMPLE

Patrick v Minister of Cultural Affairs (Case 11/77) [1977] ECR 1199

Richard Patrick was a qualified English architect who wished to practise in France. At the time (1973) there was no harmonising Directive on architectural qualifications. His qualifications had, however, been recognised as equivalent to the corresponding French qualifications under a Ministerial Decree of 1964. However, the French Minister of Cultural Affairs refused him permission – purely on nationality grounds. The ECJ held that this refusal was a breach of Article 49.

The ECJ then developed this rule to impose an obligation on the authorities of the host state to compare the candidate's qualifications with those awarded in the host state in order to establish whether or not they were equivalent (*UNECTEF v Heylens* (Case 222/86) [1987] ECR 4097). The person concerned must be given reasons why their qualifications are not deemed to be equivalent, and the decision must be subject to judicial review. The leading case in this area is *Vlassopoulou* (Case C–340/89) [1991] ECR I–2357.

CASE EXAMPLE

Vlassopoulou (Case C–340/89) [1991] ECR I–2357

Irène Vlassopoulou, a Greek national, was qualified as a lawyer in Greece. In 1983 she began work in a law office in Germany. In 1984 she was authorised by the German authorities to advise on Greek and EU law. In 1988 she applied to join the German Bar, but this time the German authorities refused her permission on the basis of a lack of qualifications. Conditions for entry to the German Bar included studying at a German university. The ECJ held that the German authorities were obliged to assess the level of equivalence between her Greek qualifications and those available under German study.

The ECJ held that the competent authorities are obliged to make:

JUDGMENT

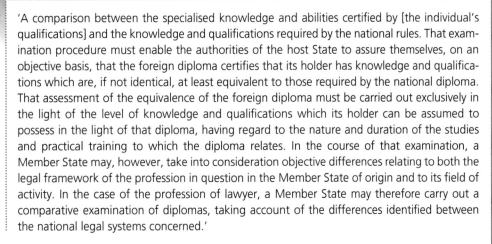

'A comparison between the specialised knowledge and abilities certified by [the individual's qualifications] and the knowledge and qualifications required by the national rules. That examination procedure must enable the authorities of the host State to assure themselves, on an objective basis, that the foreign diploma certifies that its holder has knowledge and qualifications which are, if not identical, at least equivalent to those required by the national diploma. That assessment of the equivalence of the foreign diploma must be carried out exclusively in the light of the level of knowledge and qualifications which its holder can be assumed to possess in the light of that diploma, having regard to the nature and duration of the studies and practical training to which the diploma relates. In the course of that examination, a Member State may, however, take into consideration objective differences relating to both the legal framework of the profession in question in the Member State of origin and to its field of activity. In the case of the profession of lawyer, a Member State may therefore carry out a comparative examination of diplomas, taking account of the differences identified between the national legal systems concerned.'

The ECJ laid down some guidelines as to what Member States' authorities should do after the assessment was completed. It distinguished between three situations: full, partial and no equivalence:

- **Full equivalence:** the Member State had to accept the candidate's qualification.

- **Partial equivalence:** the candidate might be required to show that he had acquired the knowledge and qualifications lacking. Any examination of documents made in order to discover which was the case had to be done in such a way as to ensure that the person's EU legal rights were protected. Any decision taken after the examination had to be capable of judicial review. The candidate had to be able to ascertain the reasons for any adverse decision, and also told of the remedies available against such a decision.

- **No equivalence:** the Member State was under no obligation to allow the candidate to practise.

These tests have since been applied in several cases (*Aguirre Borrell and Others* (Case C–104/91) [1992] ECR I–3003; *Fernández De Bobadilla* (1999); *Dreessen* (Case C–31/00) [2002] ECR I–663); *Morgenbesser* (Case C–313/01) [2003] ECR I–13467; *Peśla* (Case C–345/08) [2009] ECR I–11677. In *Dreessen* (2002), the ECJ summarised the position as follows:

JUDGMENT

'The authorities of a Member State to which an application has been made by [an EU citizen] for authorisation to practise a profession, access to which depends, under national legislation, on the possession of a diploma or professional qualification or on periods of practical experience, are required to take into consideration all of the diplomas, certificates and other evidence of formal qualifications of the person concerned and his relevant experience, by comparing the specialised knowledge and abilities so certified and that experience with the knowledge and qualifications required by the national legislation.'

The cases can be summarised as follows:

Case	Year	Candidate's nationality	Candidate's qualifications	Awarding state	Host state
Heylens	1987	Belgium	Coaching	Belgium	France
Vlassopoulou	1991	Greece	Law	Greece	Germany
Aguirre Borrell and Others	1992	UK	Estate management	UK	Spain
Fernández De Bobadilla	1999	Spain	Art restoration	UK	Spain
Dreessen	2002	Belgium	Civil engineering	Germany	Belgium
Morgenbesser	2004	France	Law	France	Italy
Peśla	2009	Poland	Law	Poland	Germany

In *Morgenbesser* (2003), Christine Morgenbesser, a French national, had studied law in France and obtained her diploma of *maîtrise en droit* in 1996, signifying completion of the academic stage of legal education. She did not, however, go on to study for her *certificate d'aptitude à la profession d'avocat* which would have allowed her to practise as a lawyer in France. Instead, she spent several months working in a law firm in Paris. Then, in 1998, she joined a firm of lawyers (*avvocati*) in Genoa, Italy. In 1999, she applied for enrolment in the register of '*praticanti*' – lawyers who have the academic qualifications but not the practical training. However, her application was refused by both the Genoa Bar Council and the National Bar Council on the basis that Italian legislation required that *praticanti* held a diploma awarded or confirmed by an Italian university. She challenged this.

The ECJ rejected her claim to rely upon Directive 89/48, on the basis that she did not have a 'diploma' as defined in that legislation. However, the Court went on to hold that, under Article 49, the Italian authorities were nevertheless obliged to undertake an examination of her French qualifications (namely, her *maîtrise en droit*) plus whatever practical experience she had acquired, and to assess that for equivalence to the Italian qualifications. She would then be in a position, if she wished, to undertake whatever additional education and/or practical training was required in order to become fully qualified as an *avvocato* in Italy. The Court relied on several of the cases described above, including *Thieffry, Heylens, Vlassopoulou* and *Fernández de Bobadilla*.

Obviously, *Morgenbesser* and all of the cases relied upon in that case pre-date the new Qualifications Directive but the principles established in those cases continue to be relevant today. If, for whatever reason, the Qualifications Directive does not apply, then the above principles will need to be invoked. There are at least two situations where this is possible:

- where an individual does not have a 'diploma';
- where a profession is unregulated in the 'host' state.

The principles established in *Vlassopoulou* were applied in a slightly different context in *Vandorou & Others* (Cases C–422, 425 and 426/09) [2010] ECR I–12411. Three Greek nationals, who had obtained qualifications (in accountancy and engineering) in other Member States (the UK and Germany), sought to rely on them in order to practise professionally back 'home' in Greece. However, because of substantial differences between the education and training undertaken abroad and that required in Greece, the Greek authorities insisted on compensation measures being undertaken. The applicants asked for practical experience which they had acquired whilst studying for their diplomas to be taken into account when determining what form the compensation measures should take. The Greek authorities refused, but the ECJ held that such experience had to be recognised, stating:

> insofar as all practical experience in the pursuit of related activities can increase an applicant's knowledge, it is incumbent on the competent national authorities to take into consideration all practical experience of use in the pursuit of the profession to which access is sought.

13.2.4 Qualifications obtained outside the EU

In *Tawil-Albertini* (Case C–154/93) [1994] ECR I–451, where the candidate, a French national, had a qualification in dentistry awarded in Lebanon and wanted to practise in France, the ECJ held that the Member States were **not** obliged to recognise qualifications obtained in a country outside the EU. This was the case even if one Member State recognises the non-EU qualification as equivalent to its own: this does not bind the other Member States. Thus, the fact that the Belgian authorities were prepared to recognise the candidate's Lebanese qualification did not oblige the authorities in France to recognise it. However, if one Member State does recognise non-EU qualifications, and allows the person to practise there, then the other Member States are required to recognise **that practical experience**. This was decided in *Haim* (Case C–319/92) [1994] ECR I–425, where an Italian national acquired a Turkish diploma in dentistry before practising in Belgium, where his diploma was recognised, and then sought to rely upon his diploma in Germany, where it was not recognised. The ECJ held that the German authorities had to take into account Haim's professional experience acquired in Belgium. This point was confirmed in *Hocsman* (Case C–238/98) [2000] ECR I–6623. Moreover, in *Hocsman* the ECJ seemed to say that the authorities would be obliged to recognise all qualifications awarded 'abroad'. This would amount to an overruling of *Tawil-Albertini* (1994), although the ECJ did not make this explicit.

CASE EXAMPLE

Hocsman (Case C–238/98) [2000] ECR I–6623

Hugo Fernando Hocsman, a Spanish national, obtained qualifications in medicine in 1976 from the University of Buenos Aires in Argentina. He was then authorised to practise in Spain, which recognised his Argentinean qualifications as equivalent to the Spanish. He went on to obtain a diploma in urology in 1982 from the University of Barcelona. However, when he attempted to obtain authorisation to practise in France in 1997, the French authorities refused to recognise his qualifications. The French authorities argued that Hocsman could not rely upon Article 49 but the ECJ disagreed, and held that Hocsman could rely on Article 49 and oblige the French authorities to examine both his Argentinean qualifications and his experience in Spain for equivalence with the French qualification requirements.

The ECJ held:

JUDGMENT

'The authorities of a Member State to whom an application has been made by [an EU] national for authorisation to practise a profession access to which depends, under national law, on the possession of a diploma or professional qualification, or on periods of practical experience, must take into consideration *all the diplomas, certificates and other evidence of formal qualifications* of the person concerned and his relevant experience, by comparing the specialised knowledge and abilities so certified and that experience with the knowledge and qualifications required by the national rules. If that comparative examination of diplomas and professional experience results in the finding that the *knowledge and qualifications certified by the diploma awarded abroad* correspond to those required by the national provisions, the competent authorities of the host Member State must recognise that diploma.'

Summary of cases involving the recognition of non-EU qualifications:

Case	Year	Nationality of complainant	Non-EU state and qualification obtained	Member State where qualification recognised	Member State refusing to recognise qualification
Tawil-Albertini	1994	French	Lebanon – dentistry	Belgium	France
Haim	1994	Italian	Turkey – dentistry	Belgium	Germany
Hocsman	2000	Spanish	Argentina – medicine	Spain	France

These case law developments have now been recognised in legislation. Article 3(3) of the Qualifications Directive provides:

ARTICLE

'Art 3(3) Evidence of formal qualifications issued by a third country shall be regarded as evidence of formal qualifications if the holder has three years' professional experience in the profession concerned on the territory of the Member State which recognised that evidence of formal qualifications in accordance with Article 2(2), certified by that Member State.'

The problem of qualification	
Persons in possession of professional qualifications obtained in one Member State may, subject to certain conditions, practise that profession in other Member States.	Directive 2005/36
Compensation measures in the form of adaptation periods of aptitude tests may apply if there are differences in the duration of training or the matters covered during training.	Directive 2005/36
If for any reason Directive 2005/36 does not apply, professionals can fall back on Art 49 TFEU, which requires the host state's authorities to undertake a comparison of qualifications and/or professional experience and recognise that if fully or even partially equivalent.	*Thieffry* (1977); *Patrick* (1977); *Vlassopoulou* (1991); *Morgenbesser* (2003)
Qualifications obtained outside the EU must be recognised by all Member States, at least where one state has recognised them and allowed the holder to practise for three years.	*Directive* 2005/36; *Haim* (1994); *Hocsman* (2000)

13.3 The freedom to provide services under Article 56 TFEU

Article 56 provides that 'restrictions on freedom to provide services ... shall be prohibited in respect of nationals of Member States who are established in a [Member State] other than that of the person for whom the services are provided'.

13.3.1 'Services'
This is defined in Article 57:

ARTICLE

'Art 57 Services shall be considered to be "services" within the meaning of the Treaties where they are normally provided for remuneration, insofar as they are not governed by the provisions relating to freedom of movement for goods, capital and persons.
   "Services" shall in particular include:

(a) activities of an industrial character;
(b) activities of a commercial character;
(c) activities of craftsmen;
(d) activities of the professions.

Without prejudice to the provisions ... relating to the right of establishment, the person providing a service may, in order to do so, temporarily pursue his activity in the State where the service is provided, under the same conditions as are imposed by that State on its own nationals.'

Article 56 therefore has a very wide scope. It covers all commercial activities, financial and legal advice, medical treatment, even holidays. *SPUC v Grogan* (Case C–159/90)

[1991] ECR I–4685 established that abortions provided by private clinics amounted to 'services' for the purpose of Article 56. In *Jany and Others* (Case C–268/99) [2001] ECR I–8615 the ECJ held that Article 56 could apply to prostitution!

13.3.2 'Freedom to provide services'

Article 56 prohibits national laws which discriminate against service providers from other Member States. This discrimination may be direct or indirect. In fact, most of the cases involve indirect discrimination. For example, in *Van Binsbergen* (Case 33/74) [1974] ECR 1299, Dutch rules required lawyers to be habitually resident in the Netherlands. This was held to discriminate indirectly against foreign nationals who were less likely to be living in the Netherlands. The ECJ stated:

JUDGMENT

'A requirement that the person providing the service must be habitually resident within the territory of the State where the service is to be provided may, according to the circumstances, have the result of depriving [Article 56] of all useful effect.'

A similar case of indirect discrimination is *Coenen* (Case 39/75) [1976] ECR 1547 – Dutch rules required insurance brokers to be habitually resident in the Netherlands. A more recent example is *Bickel and Franz* (Case C–274/96) [1998] ECR I–7637.

CASE EXAMPLE

Bickel and Franz (Case C–274/96) [1998] ECR I–7637

Italian law giving people resident in the northern Italian region of Bolzano the right to choose whether to have criminal proceedings against them conducted in either Italian or German was held to discriminate indirectly against foreign nationals. Bickel was an Austrian national visiting Bolzano on business; Franz was a German national who had gone there on holiday. Both were prosecuted for relatively minor offences (drink-driving; possession of an unlawful weapon) and asked to have the trial conducted in German; this was refused. They successfully argued that this refusal infringed Article 56.

Article 56 may even be invoked to challenge all national legislation which is not discriminatory at all (directly or indirectly), provided that it has the potential to inhibit the freedom to provide services. This was clearly acknowledged in *Säger v Dennemeyer & Co.* (Case C–76/90) [1991] ECR I–4221, where the ECJ stated:

JUDGMENT

'[Article 56] requires not only the elimination of all discrimination against a person providing services on the ground of his nationality but also the abolition of any restriction, *even if applied without distinction to national providers of services and to those of other Member States*, when it is liable to prohibit or otherwise impede the activities of a provider of services established in another Member State where he lawfully provides similar services.'

In *Scorpio Konzertproduktionen* (Case C–290/04) [2006] ECR I–9461, the ECJ offered the following guidance on when Article 56 applies:

'The provisions governing the freedom to provide services apply if the following conditions are satisfied:

– the service must be provided within the [Union];
– the provider of services must be a national of a Member State and established in a State of the [Union].

It follows that the [TFEU] does not extend the benefit of those provisions to providers of services who are nationals of non-member countries, even if they are established within the [Union] and an [intra-Union] provision of services is concerned.'

The Services Directive 2006/123

In 2006, the Council adopted the Services Directive (Directive 2006/123). Although popularly known as the Services Directive it actually applies to Establishment as well. The purpose behind the Directive is to force Member States to become more proactive in identifying and removing barriers to service providers seeking either to establish themselves in another Member State or to provide services in another state. The preamble to the Directive explains this:

LEGISLATION

'It is necessary to remove barriers to the freedom of establishment ... and barriers to the free movement of services ... and to guarantee recipients and providers the legal certainty necessary for the exercise in practice of those two fundamental freedoms of the Treaty. ... Providers should be able to choose between those two freedoms, depending on their strategy for growth in each Member State. Those barriers cannot be removed solely by relying on direct application of Articles [49 TFEU and 56 TFEU]. ... This Directive establishes a general legal framework which benefits a wide variety of services. ... That framework is based on a dynamic and selective approach consisting in the removal, as a matter of priority, of barriers which may be dismantled quickly and, for the others, the launching of a process of evaluation, consultation and complementary harmonisation of specific issues.'

The key points are:

- The Directive apples to services supplied by providers established in a Member State (Article 2(1)).
- A number of services are excluded, including 'non-economic services of general interest', financial services, electronic communications services, transport, temporary work agencies, healthcare, gambling, audiovisual, private security and social services (Article 2(2)).
- Otherwise, the Directive applies to 'any self-employed economic activity, normally provided for remuneration' (Article 4(1)).
- The Directive provides that cross-border service providers must be free to do so, except where it is justifiable to restrict that freedom 'for reasons of public policy, public security, public health or the protection of the environment' (Article 16). These derogations must 'respect the principles' of 'non-discrimination: the requirement may be neither directly nor indirectly discriminatory with regard to nationality or, in the case of legal persons, with regard to the Member State in which they are established' and 'proportionality: the requirement must be suitable for attaining the objective pursued, and must not go beyond what is necessary to attain that objective' (Article 16).

13.3.3 'Remuneration'

Article 56 applies whenever a cross-border service is provided in return for remuneration. In the vast majority of cases this proposition will be straightforward, but in certain circumstances it has prompted questions that needed to be resolved by the ECJ. For example, in *Bond van Adverteerders* (Case 352/85) [1988] ECR 2085, subsequently confirmed in *Deliège* (Cases C–51/96 and C–191/97) [2000] ECR I–2549, the ECJ held that it is not essential that the person who receives the services be the person who provides the remuneration.

CASE EXAMPLE

Deliège (Cases C–51/96 and C–191/97) [2000] ECR I–2549

Christelle Deliège, a Belgian national, had been competing in national and international judo tournaments since 1987. She complained that the Belgian judo federation was unlawfully frustrating her career by not selecting her for a number of important international competitions. Matters came to a head when she was not picked for a tournament in Paris in February 1996. She brought a claim alleging breach of Article 56. The question was: as an amateur *judoka*, could she rely upon Article 56? The ECJ held that sporting activities did fall within the scope of EU law, but only to the extent that they constituted an economic activity. However, a high-ranking athlete capable of participating in international tournaments was capable of attracting sponsorship; the presence of international standard athletes would attract the paying public, TV companies and advertisers. Thus, an athlete's participation in a tournament could be regarded as the provision of services for 'remuneration', as required by Article 57, even if the services were provided for someone other than the person(s) providing the remuneration.

Two areas of cross-border provision of services have generated controversy, because of the question of remuneration.

Educational services

In *Humbel* (Case 263/86) [1988] ECR 5365 the ECJ made it very clear that while privately funded education is covered by Article 56, state-funded education is not. *Humbel* (1988) has been followed ever since. In *Wirth* (Case C–109/92) [1993] ECR I–6447, the ECJ held that courses 'given in an establishment of higher education which is financed essentially out of public funds' do not constitute 'services', while in *Schwarz* (Case C–76/05) [2007] ECR I–6849, the Court stated:

> Article 56 is applicable where taxpayers of a given Member State send their children to a private school established in another Member State which may be regarded as providing services for remuneration, that is to say which is essentially financed by private funds.

Medical treatment

Luisi and Carbone (Cases 286/82 and 26/83) [1984] ECR 377 established that privately funded medical treatment is covered by Article 56. The principle that private medical treatment is a 'service' and therefore subject to Article 56 has been confirmed in several cases since, for example *Watts v Bedford Primary Care Trust* (Case C–372/04) [2006] ECR I–4325. The case involved Yvonne Watts, a British woman who underwent a hip replacement operation at a private hospital in France, because she would have had to wait for a year to have the operation in the UK. Regarding the question whether Article 56 applied on these facts, the ECJ stated:

JUDGMENT

'Article 56 applies where a patient such as Mrs Watts receives medical services in a hospital environment for consideration in a Member State other than her State of residence ... It must therefore be found that a situation such as that which gave rise to the dispute in the main proceedings, in which a person whose state of health necessitates hospital treatment goes to another Member State and there receives the treatment in question for consideration, falls within the scope of the Treaty provisions on the freedom to provide services.'

13.3.4 What if the 'service' is illegal?

This issue arises because a service may be permitted in one Member State but prohibited (or at least restricted) in another. Article 56 applies provided that the service is lawful in **some**, but not necessarily **all**, Member States. The best example is perhaps an English case that did not even reach the ECJ. *R v Human Fertilisation and Embryology Authority, ex p Blood* [1997] 2 CMLR 591 involved the famous case of Diane Blood. Her husband, Stephen, suddenly contracted meningitis and lapsed into a coma (from which he never recovered). The couple were childless but they had both wanted children. Mrs Blood therefore applied to the High Court for permission to use Stephen's sperm for artificial insemination. However, the Court refused because UK legislation, the Human Fertilisation and Embryology Act 1990, requires the written consent of the man concerned, and Stephen had not given this consent. Mrs Blood appealed and the Court of Appeal held that she had a right under Article 56 to take Stephen's sperm for insemination treatment in Belgium, where written consent was not required. Treatment was duly carried out, successfully, in 1998 and Mrs Blood had her first child in 1999.

Society for the Protection of Unborn Children (SPUC) v Grogan (1991) raised the question of whether Article 56 could be relied upon by students in one Member State (Ireland) to disseminate information about abortion clinics in another Member State (the UK), given that, at the time, abortion was absolutely prohibited in Ireland.

CASE EXAMPLE

SPUC v Grogan (Case C–159/90) [1991] ECR I–4685

Article 40 of the Irish Constitution contained the following provision:

> The State acknowledges the right to life of the unborn and, with due regard to the equal right to life of the mother, guarantees in its laws to respect, and, as far as practicable, by its laws to defend and vindicate that right.

Abortion was specifically prohibited by the Health (Family Planning) Act 1979. This meant that Irish women wanting an abortion were forced to travel to the UK, where abortions are lawful (subject to the conditions in the Abortion Act 1967 being satisfied). Stephen Grogan, a university student in Dublin, published information on how and where female students could get abortions in London and other British cities. The SPUC went to the Irish High Court to secure an injunction to prevent further publication, successfully arguing that abortion was unlawful in Ireland. Grogan challenged the injunction on the basis that Article 40 of the Irish Constitution was a breach of Article 56, in that it imposed a limitation on his freedom to provide information about the services of abortion clinics in the UK. The SPUC argued Article 52 (the public policy derogation) but, in the end, the ECJ avoided the issue by holding that there was too tenuous a connection between the providers of the service (the abortion clinics in the UK), and the students distributing information about it, for an injunction to be regarded as a restriction on the freedom to provide services. There was therefore no breach of Article 56, so it was unnecessary to consider whether Article 52 would apply.

13.3.5 The scope of 'cross-border' services

Although the provider of services will typically travel to another state to do so, it is not necessary. Article 56 also applies where the service **recipient** travels to a state other than their own in order to receive a service – most obviously, tourists and those seeking specialist medical treatment (see section 13.5, below). Indeed, it is not actually necessary for **either** the service provider **or** the recipient to leave their own state. Provided that they are established in different states, and the service is provided by one and received by the other, then Article 56 will apply. This allows service providers to challenge measures adopted by their own state where those measures prohibit or restrict their freedom to provide services to nationals established in other Member States. This is increasingly likely to become the case where instantaneous telecommunication systems – most obviously the Internet – are relied upon. In *Alpine Investments* (Case C–384/93) [1995] ECR I–1141, the ECJ stated that Article 56 'covers services which the provider offers by telephone to potential recipients established in other Member States and provides without moving from the Member State in which he is established'. In *Carpenter* (Case C–60/00) [2002] ECR I–6279, the facts of which were given in the previous chapter (see section 12.5.2), the ECJ confirmed *Alpine Investments* (1995) and stated:

> Services come within the meaning of 'services' in [Article 56] both in so far as the provider travels for that purpose to the Member State of the recipient and in so far as he provides cross-border services without leaving the Member State in which he is established.

KEY FACTS

The freedom to provide services	
The freedom to provide services allows a service provider, based in one Member State, to provide a service to any person based in another state.	Art 56 TFEU
The service provider must be a national of a Member State and the service must be provided within the EU.	*Scorpio Konzertproduktionen* (2006)
Art 56 prohibits discrimination (whether direct or indirect) based on nationality and any other 'restrictions' on the freedom to provide services.	*Van Binsbergen* (1974); *Säger v Dennemeyer & Co.* (1991)
Art 56 applies when there is a cross-border service, even if neither service provider nor recipient moves. This is increasingly noticeable in cases involving services provided electronically, such as financial services and gambling services.	*Alpine Investments* (1995); *Carpenter* (2002)
Art 56 is directly effective.	*Van Binsbergen* (1974)
'Services' are defined very widely, including commercial and professional activities.	Art 57 TFEU
Services must be 'normally' provided for 'remuneration', i.e. paid for, although there is no requirement that the service recipient provides it.	Art 57; *Deliège* (2000)

Education and medical treatment are 'services', but only if provided for 'remuneration'.	*Humbel* (1988); *Wirth* (1993); *Kohll* (1998); *Watts* (2006)
Art 56 applies even though a service may be prohibited in some Member States – such as abortions or gambling.	*SPUC v Grogan* (1991); *Schindler* (1994)

13.4 Distinguishing establishment and services

The difference between the two is a matter of degree – whether someone is simply providing services, or is actually established, in a Member State other than their own may simply depend on how lengthy is their stay in that other state. It is sometimes difficult to differentiate between established persons and service providers. Occasionally, the ECJ may need to decide. The leading case is *Gebhard* (1995), where the ECJ stated:

JUDGMENT

'The chapter on the right of establishment [and] the chapter on services [are] mutually exclusive.... The provisions of the chapter on services are subordinate to those of the chapter on the right of establishment.... The concept of establishment is a very broad one, allowing [an EU] national to participate, on a stable and continuous basis, in the economic life of a Member State other than his State of origin and to profit therefrom, so contributing to economic and social interpenetration within the [Union] in the sphere of activities as self-employed persons. In contrast, where the provider of services moves to another Member State, the provisions of the chapter on services envisage that he is to pursue his activity there on a temporary basis ... The temporary nature of the activities in question has to be determined in the light, not only of the duration of the provision of the service, but also of its regularity, periodicity or continuity.'

In *Schnitzer* (Case C–215/01) [2003] ECR I–14847, the ECJ offered further guidance on the difference between establishment and the provision of services. The Court stated that Article 56 may cover services 'varying widely in nature', including services which are provided 'over an extended period, even over several years, where, for example, the services in question are supplied in connection with the construction of a large building'. The Court then stated:

JUDGMENT

'No provision of the Treaty affords a means of determining, in an abstract manner, the duration or frequency beyond which the supply of a service or of a certain type of service in another Member State can no longer be regarded as the provision of "services". It follows that the mere fact that a business established in one Member State supplies identical or similar services with a greater or lesser degree of frequency or regularity in a second Member State, without having an infrastructure there enabling it to pursue a professional activity there on a stable and continuous basis and, from the infrastructure, to hold itself out to, amongst others, nationals of the second Member State, is not sufficient for it to be regarded as established in the second Member State.'

The ECJ has held that, where an enterprise is situated in one Member State, but its activities are directed **entirely** or **mainly** towards another Member State (often in order to avoid more stringent rules and regulations applying in the latter state), then the enterprise will be deemed to be established in the latter state and not simply providing services there (*TV 10* (Case C–23/93) ECR I–4795).

More recently, in *Garkalns* (Case C–470/11) [2012] 3 CMLR 52, the Court held that Article 49 (establishment) applies when an 'operator offers its services on a stable and continuous basis from an establishment in the Member State of destination'; otherwise Article 56 (services) applies. Here, Article 49 applied to the proposed development of an amusement arcade in a shopping centre in Riga, the capital of Latvia, as the gambling services in question would eventually be offered 'on a stable and continuous basis'.

13.5 The freedom to receive services

Although Article 56 refers to the right to provide services, it has been extended to the right to receive them too. The first case was *Luisi and Carbone* (1984).

CASE EXAMPLE

Luisi and Carbone (Cases 286/82 and 26/83) [1984] ECR 377

Two Italian nationals, Graziani Luisi and Giuseppe Carbone, were prosecuted under Italian law for taking excess foreign currency out of the country. Luisi had withdrawn a considerable sum in US dollars, French and Swiss francs and Deutschmarks from various Italian banks and taken this to Germany and France for a combination of tourism and medical purposes. Carbone had taken a sizeable amount of US dollars, Swiss francs and Deutschmarks to Germany on a three-month holiday. Each was convicted and fined the difference between the amount they had taken and the amount they were permitted to take. They appealed against their fines. The Italian court referred the matter to the ECJ, which held that the Italian rules constituted a breach of Article 56.

The Court stated:

JUDGMENT

'The freedom to provide services includes the freedom, for the recipient of services, to go to another Member State in order to receive a service there, without being obstructed by restriction ... and that tourists, persons receiving medical treatment and persons travelling for the purposes of education or business are to be regarded as recipients of services.'

Note: the French franc and the German Deutschmark ceased to be legal tender when the single European currency was introduced in 2002.

This ruling has since been followed in several cases:

- **tourists** – *Cowan* (Case 186/87) [1989] ECR 195; *Bickel and Franz* (1998); *Calfa* (Case C–348/96) [1999] ECR I–11;

- **persons receiving private education** (see above);

- **persons receiving medical treatment** (see above).

CASE EXAMPLE

Cowan v Trésor Public (Case 186/87) [1989] ECR 195

Ian Cowan, an Englishman on holiday in France, was violently assaulted outside a Métro station in Paris. He applied for compensation to the *Commission d'Indemnisation des Victims d'Infraction*. Under French law, compensation was payable from public funds only to French nationals and holders of French residence permits. Cowan argued that this discrimination was contrary to Article 56 in that it obstructed his freedom to move to France for the purpose of receiving services (i.e. tourism). The ECJ upheld Cowan's claim.

A variation on this theme occurred in *De Coster* (Case C–17/00) [2001] ECR I–9445, which involved the imposition of a satellite dish tax by a local authority in Belgium. One of the residents challenged this, alleging that it restricted his freedom to receive services (in the form of satellite television broadcasts) from other Member States. The ECJ agreed (although it found the tax was at least potentially justifiable because it helped to control the proliferation of satellite dishes, which was beneficial to the environment).

13.6 The 'official authority' derogation in Article 51 TFEU

Article 51 provides that 'activities … that are connected, even occasionally, with the exercise of official authority' are **not** covered by the Treaty rules on establishment and services. The derogation has, however, been given a very narrow scope. The ECJ has pointed out that Article 51 applies only to **activities** connected with the exercise of official authority; not professions or occupations **as a whole**. In *Reyners v Belgium* (Case 2/74) [1974] ECR 631, involving Belgian law restricting the profession of *avocat* (similar to barrister) to Belgian nationals, the ECJ stated:

JUDGMENT

'Professional activities involving contacts, even regular and organic, with the courts, including even compulsory co-operation in their functioning, do not constitute, as such, connection with the exercise of official authority. The most typical activities of the profession of *avocat*, in particular, such as consultation and legal assistance and also representation and the defence of parties in court, even where the intervention or assistance of the *avocat* is compulsory or is a legal monopoly, cannot be considered as connected with the exercise of official authority.'

A similar outcome was seen in *Peñarroja* (Cases C–372 and 373/09) [2011] ECR I–1785, where the Court held that Article 51 did not apply to the activities of court translators. However, in both cases, the Court implied that, although the activities of lawyers and court translators did not involve the 'exercise of official authority', the activities of judges do. In *Reyners*, for example, the Court stated that 'the exercise of these activities leaves the discretion of judicial authority and the free exercise of judicial power intact'.

The ECJ continues to insist that only activities involving a 'direct and specific' connection with official authority are covered by Article 51. In six cases decided on the same day in May 2011 the ECJ agreed with the European Commission that six Member

States – Austria, Belgium, France, Germany, Greece and Luxembourg – had breached Article 49 by requiring that notaries hold the nationality of the state concerned. Notaries in civil law countries (as opposed to common law jurisdictions) may be defined as legally qualified, public officials appointed by private parties to authenticate legal documents such as contracts, conveyances, deeds, gifts, powers of attorney and so on. In all six cases, the defendant state argued that the profession was exempted by Article 51, but the Court pointed out that the typical activity of a notary (authenticating documents), could not be said to involve a 'direct and specific' connection with the 'exercise of official authority' (see, for example *Commission v Germany* (Case C–54/08) [2011] ECR I–4355).

In *Thijssen* (Case C–42/92) [1993] ECR I–4047, the ECJ imposed another limitation on the scope of Article 51. The Court had been asked whether the post of Insurance Commissioner in Belgium was one which involved the 'exercise of official authority'. The Court answered 'no', on the basis that the post involved only 'auxiliary and preparatory functions'. It was the Belgian Insurance Inspectorate itself which had decision-making powers and therefore exercised official authority, rather than its individual employees. This limitation has been applied in other cases involving inspectors supervised by public authorities. In *Commission v Austria* (Case C–393/05) [2007] ECR I–10195 and *Commission v Portugal* (Case C–438/08) [2009] ECR I–10219, involving organic farm inspectors and motor vehicle inspectors, respectively, the Court held that Article 51 did not apply because the inspectors were supervised by the relevant public authority.

13.7 Derogation on grounds of public policy, public security or public health in Article 52 TFEU

The 'public policy' derogation is rarely invoked, although *Calfa* (1999), discussed in Chapter 11, involved the application of the public policy derogation to an Italian national convicted of possessing drugs while on holiday in Greece, that is, she was exercising her rights to receive services under Article 56. *Omega* (Case C–36/02) [2004] ECR I–9609 involved the question of whether or not the protection of human dignity, as provided for in the German Constitution, could be invoked to derogate from the freedom to provide services. The ECJ held that it could.

CASE EXAMPLE

Omega (Case C–36/02) [2004] ECR I–9609

Omega, a German company, operated a 'laserdrome' centre in the German city of Bonn. This allowed paying customers to play 'laser quest' games whereby they would attempt to shoot each other using sub-machine gun-type laser guns aimed at sensor tags attached to the jackets of the players. Omega used equipment supplied by a British company, Pulsar Advanced Games Systems Ltd. However, the local police objected and issued an order forbidding Omega from operating 'laser quest' games. According to the order, the 'acts of simulated homicide and the trivialization of violence thereby engendered were contrary to fundamental values prevailing in public opinion'. This contravened the provision in German constitutional law of respect for human dignity. Omega challenged this, alleging a breach of Article 56, in that the order would prevent Pulsar in the UK from supplying their services to Omega in Germany. The case was referred to the ECJ, which held that the order *prima facie* infringed Article 56. However, it was justifiable under Article 52.

The Court stated:

JUDGMENT

....

'The [Union] legal order undeniably strives to ensure respect for human dignity as a general principle of law. There can therefore be no doubt that the objective of protecting human dignity is compatible with [Union] law ... Since both the [Union] and its Member States are required to respect fundamental rights, the protection of those rights is a legitimate interest which, in principle, justifies a restriction of the obligations imposed by [Union] law, even under a fundamental freedom guaranteed by the Treaty such as the freedom to provide services.'

An Article 52 derogation was rejected in *Navileme & Nautizende* (Case C–509/12), unreported. People wishing to sail a boat in Portugal had to have a boating licence, issued following an examination. However, only people resident in Portugal were eligible to sit the exam. Two Portuguese nautical training schools challenged the residency requirement. The Portuguese government claimed that the requirement was necessary on grounds of public policy, in order to ensure a high level of safety at sea. The ECJ held that the requirement infringed the freedom of nautical colleges in Portugal to provide services (in the sense of nautical training services), and the freedom of EU citizens to receive those services, and was *prima facie* prohibited by Article 56 TFEU. Moreover, the requirement was **not** justifiable on public policy grounds. First, Article 52 TFEU presupposed the existence of a genuine, sufficiently serious threat affecting one of the fundamental interests of society, which was not the case here. Second, the residence requirement bore 'no relation' to the training followed or the ability to sail and hence was 'not in itself appropriate for attaining the objective in question, that is, to ensure safety of navigation at sea'. Third, the residence condition failed the proportionality test. The objective of ensuring a better level of maritime safety may be satisfied by less restrictive means such as setting the requirements of the examination for the award of a boating licence at a 'high level'.

The public health derogation is more frequently invoked. For example, in *MacQuen & Others* (Case C–108/96) [2001] ECR I–837, the ECJ held that a rule of Belgian law which meant that only those holding specific medical qualifications, such as ophthalmologists, had the right to carry out eyesight examinations, was capable of restricting the freedom to provide services. However, the Court went on to hold that the Belgian law was justified on the ground of health protection. Another example is *Corporación Dermoestética* (Case C–500/06) [2008] ECR I–5785, involving Italian legislation prohibiting the advertising of medical and/or surgical treatments at private health care clinics on national TV. The Court accepted, at least in principle, that such rules 'can be justified in the light of the objective of protection of public health'.

However, by far the most common situation in which the human health derogation has been invoked is in cases involving individuals receiving private medical treatment in a Member State other than their home state, paying for it themselves, but then seeking to recover the cost of the treatment from their social security provider or, in the case of the UK, NHS trust. Often, the authorities in the home state are very reluctant to meet these costs and seek to justify their refusal on public health grounds. Essentially, the argument is that for one state to have to use public funds to pay for private medical treatment provided in another state would potentially be such an enormous drain on the resources of the former state that it could undermine the ability of that state to provide effective health care treatment itself.

For example, in *Kohll* (Case C–158/96) [1998] ECR I–1931, the Court stated:

> the objective of maintaining a balanced medical and hospital service open to all, although intrinsically linked to the method of financing the social security system, may fall within the derogations on grounds of public health, insofar as it contributes to the attainment of a high level of health protection.

The Court added:

JUDGMENT

'Article 52 permits Member States to restrict the freedom to provide medical and hospital services in so far as the maintenance of a treatment facility or medical service on national territory is essential for the public health and even the survival of the population.'

The Court is also very conscious of the enormous amount of centralised planning that has to go into the organisation of hospitals and associated facilities in each Member State. This could be severely disrupted if large numbers of people decided to go abroad to receive private medical treatment instead. Thus, in *Watts v Bedford Primary Care Trust* (2006), discussed above, involving a British woman who received a hip replacement in a French private hospital, the Court ruled:

JUDGMENT

'It is well known that the number of hospitals, their geographical distribution, the way in which they are organised and the facilities with which they are provided, and even the nature of the medical services which they are able to offer, are all matters for which planning, generally designed to satisfy various needs, must be possible. For one thing, such planning seeks to ensure that there is sufficient and permanent access to a balanced range of high-quality hospital treatment in the State concerned. For another thing, it assists in meeting a desire to control costs and to prevent, as far as possible, any wastage of financial, technical and human resources. Such wastage would be all the more damaging because it is generally recognised that the hospital care sector generates considerable costs and must satisfy increasing needs, while the financial resources which may be made available for healthcare are not unlimited, whatever the mode of funding applied.'

There is now secondary legislation in this area. Directive 2011/24 (the Cross-border Healthcare Directive) was adopted by the Council in March 2011. Article 1(1) provides: 'This Directive provides rules for facilitating the access to safe and high-quality cross-border healthcare and promotes cooperation on healthcare between Member States, in full respect of national competencies in organising and delivering healthcare.' In the context of this chapter, the key provision is Article 7(7), which states that the home Member State may impose on an individual seeking to recover the cost of cross-border healthcare 'the same conditions, criteria of eligibility and regulatory and administrative formalities … as it would impose if this healthcare were provided in its territory'. However, no such conditions, criteria or formalities:

> may be discriminatory or constitute an obstacle to the free movement of patients … unless it is objectively justified by planning requirements relating to the object of ensuring sufficient and permanent access to a balanced range of high-quality treatment in the Member State concerned or to the wish to control costs and avoid, as far as possible, any waste of financial, technical and human resources.

The Directive's implementation deadline was 25 October 2013.

KEY FACTS

Derogations under Arts 51 and 52	
Member States may exclude non-nationals from practising activities connected with the 'exercise of official authority'.	Art 51 TFEU
This is interpreted very narrowly. It only applies to specific activities, not whole professions.	*Reyners* (1974)
Member States may restrict the freedoms of establishment and services on grounds of public policy, security and health.	Art 52 TFEU
The public health derogation allows Member States to impose restrictions on people seeking private medical treatment in order to maintain both 'a balanced medical and hospital service' and 'treatment capacity or medical competence'.	*Kohll* (1998); *Watts* (2006)

13.8 Justification for non-discriminatory rules

In addition to the specific Treaty derogations, the ECJ has created a parallel set of derogations which may be pleaded by Member States to justify restrictions on establishment or the provision of services.

In *Van Binsbergen* (1974), the ECJ was asked whether a Dutch rule requiring lawyers to be habitually resident in the Netherlands before they could exercise rights of audience before Dutch courts and tribunals was compatible with Article 56. The ECJ stated:

JUDGMENT

'A requirement that the person providing the service must be habitually resident within the territory of the State where the service is to be provided may, according to the circumstances, have the result of depriving [Article 56] of all useful effect. However, taking into account the particular nature of the services to be provided, specific requirements imposed on the person providing the service cannot be considered incompatible with the Treaty where they have as their purpose the application of professional rules justified by the general good – in particular rules relating to organisation, qualification, professional ethics, supervision and liability.'

In *Säger v Dennemeyer & Co* (1991), the ECJ stated:

JUDGMENT

'The freedom to provide services may be limited only by rules which are justified by imperative reasons relating to the public interest and which apply to all persons and undertakings pursuing an activity in the State of destination in so far as that interest is not protected by rules to which the person providing the service is subject in the State in which he is established. In particular, these requirements must be objectively necessary in order to ensure compliance with professional rules and must not exceed what is necessary to attain those objectives.'

The ECJ confirmed the applicability of these criteria in *Gebhard* (1995) (an Article 49 case). Thus, for a national rule which restricts either the freedom of establishment or the freedom to provide services to be compatible with Article 49 or Article 56, a four-part test has to be satisfied:

i. the rule must be non-discriminatory;

ii. it must be justified by imperative requirements in the general interest;

iii. it must be suitable for the attainment of the objective it pursues;

iv. it must not go beyond what is necessary in order to attain its objective (the 'proportionality' doctrine).

Commission v France (Tourist Guides) (Case C–154/89) [1999] ECR I–659 provides a good example of these conditions being applied. French legislation required all tourist guides accompanying groups of tourists to take an exam in order to become licensed. The Commission alleged that this was in breach of Article 56. France argued that it was necessary to ensure that guides gave tourists correct artistic and cultural information. The ECJ held that the French legislation was a *prima facie* infringement of Article 56, because it prevented self-employed tour guides from offering their services to tourists; it also prevented tourists from taking part in such organised tours from availing themselves at will of the services in question. However, the Court held that the licence requirement was justifiable, in principle.

i. It was non-discriminatory, as it applied to French nationals hoping to work as tourist guides as well as to other nationals.

ii. It was at least justifiable, as it sought to 'ensure the protection of general interests relating to the proper appreciation of places and things of interest and the widest possible dissemination of knowledge of the artistic and cultural heritage of the country'.

iii. It was capable of achieving this objective.

iv. The final question was whether the licence requirement was actually necessary. Here, the Court held that it went too far, at least as far as general tourist information was concerned. Forcing tourist companies to employ only licensed guides would inevitably lead some tour operators to have recourse to local guides instead of their own staff. That, in turn, could leave tourists with a guide unfamiliar with their language, their interests and their specific expectations. Moreover, the fierce competition under which tour companies operated meant that they were obliged voluntarily to exercise control over the tour guides they employed.

In *Alpine Investments* (1995), the ECJ held that the restriction under Dutch law of 'cold-calling' practices in the financial services sector was a *prima facie* infringement of Article 56. However, it was justifiable in the interests of consumer protection and the protection of the reputation of that service industry. The ECJ concluded with the wry observation that since 'the commodities futures market is highly speculative and barely comprehensible for non-expert investors, it was necessary to protect them from the most aggressive selling techniques'. The ECJ was also prepared to hold that the Dutch rules were not disproportionate:

- the legislation prohibited cold-calling **only**, i.e. it did not prohibit other forms of approaching potential clients;

- there was no prohibition on contacting existing clients by telephone;

- the legislation only prohibited cold-calling **in the commodities futures market**; i.e. brokering in other markets was not subject to the same rules.

Alpine had argued that simply requiring unsolicited telephone calls to be tape-recorded would suffice to protect customers as effectively. Moreover, in the UK, the Securities and Futures Authority had adopted similar rules. However, the ECJ was not persuaded, commenting that the fact that one Member State imposes less strict rules than another does not mean that the latter state's rules are disproportionate and hence incompatible with EU law.

In *Viking Line* (Case C–438/05) [2007] ECR I–10779, the ECJ recognised that the protection of workers was a legitimate interest capable of overriding the freedom of establishment.

CASE EXAMPLE

International Transport Workers' Federation & Finnish Seamen's Union v Viking Line (Case C–438/05) [2007] ECR I–10779

Viking Line, a Finnish ferry company, owned seven vessels which it used to sail the Baltic Sea route between Helsinki in Finland and Tallinn in Estonia. These ships were registered in Finland, which meant that the crew were protected by Finnish law and entitled to wages comparable to those payable in Finland generally. Viking Line was, however, operating at a loss as it was competing with Estonian ferry companies whose crew wages and hence operating costs were much lower. Consequently, Viking Line gave notice that it intended to re-flag one its ships, the *Rosella*, under the Estonian flag. The crew were all members of the Finnish Seamen's Union (the FSU) (which was affiliated to the International Transport Workers' Federation (the ITF)). The ITF had a 'flag of convenience' policy, which meant that it opposed ship-owners flagging their ships under the flag of a country with which it had no connection, in order to exploit lower wages and/or weaker worker protection in that country. Consequently, the FSU and ITF threatened strike action against Viking Line. Eventually, Viking Line brought an action, alleging that the threatened strike was contrary to Article 49. The ECJ ruled that (1) the threatened strike was a *prima facie* breach of Article 49 but (2) the breach was – in principle, at least – justified on the basis of worker protection.

More recently, the Court acknowledged that environmental protection (long recognised as capable of justifying restrictions on the free movement of goods – see Chapter 14) was also capable of justifying restrictions on the freedom to provide services.

CASE EXAMPLE

Regione Sardegna (Case C–169/08) [2009] ECR I–10821

Legislation in the Mediterranean island of Sardinia (which is an autonomous region of Italy) imposed a 'stopover tax' on recreational boats and tourist aircraft stopping at the island. The tax was designed to achieve two objectives: (1) 'discourage squandering of the environmental and coastal land scape heritage' and (2) finance measures to restore coastal areas. The ECJ held that the legislation was capable of restricting the freedom to provide and receive services (tourism firms being less likely to call at Sardinian ports or land at Sardinian airports because of the tax) and so amounted to a *prima facie* breach of Article 56. The restriction was potentially justifiable on environmental protection grounds by leading to a reduction in pollution. However, it was not justified, because the tax exempted tourism firms domiciled in Sardinia itself. The Court ruled that 'national legislation is appropriate to ensuring attainment of the objective pursued only if it genuinely reflects a concern to attain it in a consistent and systematic manner'.

Environmental protection was one of three justifications invoked in *Yellow Cab* (Case C–338/09) [2010] ECR I–13927. The Court held that Austrian legislation designed to encourage the operation of public transport services was capable of achieving a number of overriding reasons in the public interest: promotion of tourism, road safety (by channelling tourist traffic) and environmental protection (by offering a viable alternative to individual transportation).

In *Josemans* (Case C–137/09) [2010] ECR I–13019, the Court accepted that a policy introduced in the Dutch city of Maastricht under which non-residents of the Netherlands were barred from entering 'coffee-shops' (where cannabis can be bought and consumed alongside food and non-alcoholic drinks in strictly limited quantities and in controlled conditions) in the city was a restriction on the freedom to provide and receive services but was justified on the basis of the need to tackle 'drug-tourism' and the accompanying public nuisance. According to the local authorities, before the ban was introduced, the 14 coffee-shops in Maastricht attracted around 10,000 visitors per day (i.e. nearly four million visitors per year), 70 per cent of which were not resident in the Netherlands. These large numbers of people generated nuisance and crime, in particular dealing in hard drugs.

In *FA Premier League & Others; Murphy* (Cases C–403, 429/08) [2012] 1 CMLR 29, the Court held that the protection of intellectual property rights, and the protection of sporting events, were overriding reasons in the public interest capable of justifying restrictions on the freedom to provide and receive services (in this case, satellite TV broadcasts of live football matches).

CASE EXAMPLE

FA Premier League & Others; Murphy (Cases C–403, 429/08) [2012] 1 CMLR 29

Karen Murphy, a publican in Portsmouth, had been convicted of breaching s297(1) of the Copyright, Designs & Patents Act 1988, which prohibits the use for commercial purposes of any apparatus 'designed or adapted to enable or assist persons to access the programmes or other transmissions or circumvent conditional access technology related to the programmes or other transmissions when they are not entitled to do so'. Murphy had obtained and used a Greek 'decoding' card which enabled her to broadcast, in her pub, Greek satellite TV broadcasts of live English Premier League football matches. This was challenged by the Premier League, who had granted to Sky an exclusive licence to broadcast live Premiership football matches in the UK. (Murphy, along with many other British publicans, had obtained a foreign 'decoding' card because the subscription fee for foreign satellite channels was significantly less expensive than Sky's subscription fee.) The ECJ held that s297(1) was, *prima facie*, in breach of Article 56. It prevented satellite TV services from being received by UK residents. Such restriction could, in principle, be justified because of the need to protect intellectual property (IP) rights such as copyright. The Court held that sporting events as such did not attract copyright status, because that was reserved for the results of 'intellectual creation', whereas sporting events such as football were subject to rules of the game, 'leaving no room for creative freedom for the purposes of copyright'. However, sporting events did have a status *comparable* to IP. The Court held that sporting events have a 'unique' and, to that extent, 'original' character comparable to copyright-able works. Hence, it was permissible for a Member State to protect sporting events by putting in place specific national legislation. This justification was subject to the usual proportionality test. Here, the Court focused on the premium paid by broadcasters to secure their exclusive territorial licences (the cost of which was then passed on to the consumers, the eventual service recipients). The Court held that holders of IP (and equivalent) rights were entitled only to 'appropriate remuneration', which meant 'reasonable in relation to the economic value of the service provided'. The Court concluded that the Premier League's premiums went beyond what was necessary to ensure territorial exclusivity and so failed the proportionality test.

'Overriding reasons relating to the public interest': summary

The case law reveals that a number of different 'overriding interests' have been accepted by the ECJ. They include (bear in mind that this is not a comprehensive list – indeed, new interests may be added to the list at any time):

- consumer protection – *Alpine Investments* (1995);
- the 'sound administration of justice' – *Wouters and Others* (Case C–309/99) [2002] ECR I–1577;
- the need to 'ensure high standards of university education' – *Neri v European School of Economics* (Case C–153/02) [2003] ECR I–13555;
- the 'protection of workers' – *Viking Line* (2007);
- the 'promotion of research and development' – *Jundt* (Case C–281/06) [2007] ECR I–12231;
- environmental protection – *Regione Sardegna* (2009), *Yellow Cab* (2010);
- the need to tackle 'drug tourism' – *Josemans* (2010);
- the protection of intellectual property (such as copyright) – *Murphy* (2012);
- the protection of sporting events – *Murphy* (2012).

A non-exhaustive list of 'overriding reasons relating to the public interest' is also provided in Article 4(8) of the Services Directive 2006/123, all of which are based on cases decided by the ECJ. In that sense the Directive does not add anything new to this area of law.

Regulation of gambling

Several cases have addressed the question of whether Member States can regulate gambling services. In *Customs and Excise Commissioners v Schindler* (Case C–275/92) [1994] ECR I–1039, the facts of which were given in Chapter 10, the ECJ observed that UK anti-lottery legislation (prior to its abolition by the National Lotteries Act 1993), was capable of infringing Article 56. However, it was justifiable because it pursued the following objectives:

- to prevent crime and to ensure that gamblers would be treated honestly;
- to avoid stimulating demand in the gambling sector which has damaging social consequences when taken to excess; and
- to ensure that lotteries could not be operated for personal or commercial profit but solely for charitable, sporting or cultural purposes.

The ECJ concluded that the UK legislation was more concerned with 'the protection of the recipients of services and, more generally, of consumers' and was, therefore, justified. The ECJ was also prepared to accept the 'maintenance of order in society' as an alternative public interest reason. The ECJ observed that it was 'not possible to disregard the moral, religious or cultural aspects of lotteries, like other types of gambling'. After observing that 'lotteries involve a high risk of crime or fraud … particularly when they are operated on a large scale' it then declared, slightly pompously, that 'they are an incitement to spend which may have damaging individual and social consequences'. Consequently, the legislation did not infringe Article 56 'in view of the concerns of social policy and of the prevention of fraud which justify it'. Somewhat paradoxically, the ECJ concluded by extolling the virtues of national lotteries, pointing out how they 'may make a significant contribution to the financing of benevolent or public interest activities such as social works, charitable works, sport or culture'.

Similar outcomes were reached in *Läärä* (Case C–124/97) [1999] ECR I–6067, concerning Finnish legislation restricting the availability of gaming licences, and in *Zenatti* (Case

C–67/98) [1999] ECR I–7289, concerning Italian law regulating gambling. In the latter case, the ECJ held that the Italian law (*prima facie* contrary to Article 56 but justifiable) sought to:

- prevent gambling from being a source of private profit;
- avoid risks of crime and fraud and the damaging individual and social consequences of the incitement to spend which it represents; and
- allow gambling only to the extent to which it may be socially useful as being conducive to the proper conduct of competitive sports.

In *ANOMAR and Others* (Case C–6/01) [2003] ECR I–8621, Portuguese legislation restricted the running of games of chance to casinos within gaming zones created by decree. The *Associação National de Operadores de Máquinas Recreativas* (ANOMAR), an association of gaming machine operators in Portugal, challenged this as restricting the freedom to provide services (i.e. gambling services to foreign tourists and business people). The ECJ held that the Portuguese legislation was capable of restricting the freedom to provide services, as it prevented operators from providing gambling opportunities outside the gaming zones. However, it was justified. The ECJ referred to the familiar objectives of consumer protection and maintaining order in society.

However, the ECJ refused to apply the usual justifications in *Gambelli and Others* (Case C–243/01) [2003] ECR I–13031, which involved Italian rules restricting the provision of Internet gambling services to state-run or state-licensed organisations. The Court stated that restrictions on gambling services had to be deployed in 'a consistent and systematic manner'. This might not be the case where a Member State was providing its own gambling services, either directly or indirectly via a system of exclusive licences, whilst prohibiting private operators from doing likewise. The ECJ stated:

JUDGMENT

'In so far as the authorities of a Member State incite and encourage consumers to participate in lotteries, games of chance and betting to the financial benefit of the public purse, the authorities of that State cannot invoke public order concerns relating to the need to reduce opportunities for betting in order to justify measures such as those at issue in the main proceedings.'

The ECJ did not maintain this strict position for long. A partial retreat from *Gambelli* was announced in *Placanica* (Cases C–338, 359 and 360/04) [2007] ECR I–1891, when the Court stated that a distinction had to be drawn between the objectives of reducing gambling opportunities on one hand, and crime prevention on the other. By focusing on the latter objective, the Court held that a 'policy of controlled expansion in the betting and gaming sector' carried out under state control or licence may be 'entirely consistent with the objective of drawing players away from clandestine betting and gaming … to activities which are authorised and regulated'. The Court declared that a licensing system may 'constitute an efficient mechanism enabling operators active in the betting and gaming sector to be controlled with a view to preventing the exploitation of those activities for criminal or fraudulent purposes'.

The *Placanica* principle has been applied in numerous cases subsequently to uphold the situation in several Member States whereby certain forms of gambling are allowed but only under state control (whether the gambling services were provided by the state itself or by private operators under state licence). Although this restricts the freedom of gambling providers based in other states to provide their services, it is justifiable on the basis that state-controlled gambling services are safer for the consumer than equivalent services provided on the open market (see e.g. *Betfair* (Case C–203/08) [2010] ECR I–4695 (the Netherlands); *Sjöberg & Gerdin* (Cases C–447 and 448/08) [2010] ECR I–6921 (Sweden) and *Zeturf* (Case C–212/08) [2011] ECR I–5633 (France)).

A similar outcome to that in *ANOMAR* occurred in *Liga Portuguese de Futebol Profissional* (Case C–42/07) [2009] ECR I–7633, also known as the Santa Casa case. Portuguese legislation conferred an exclusive right on an organisation called Santa Casa to operate lotteries and all forms of sports betting (including online gambling) throughout Portugal. The Court held that, although clearly capable of restricting both the freedom of rival companies based in other Member States to provide gambling services, and the freedom of Portuguese consumers to receive those services, the Portuguese legislation was justified. In giving judgment, the ECJ focused on crime prevention, stating:

JUDGMENT

'The fight against crime may constitute an overriding reason in the public interest that is capable of justifying restrictions in respect of operators authorised to offer services in the games-of-chance sector. Games of chance involve a high risk of crime or fraud, given the scale of the earnings and the potential winnings on offer to gamblers.... Limited authorisation of games on an exclusive basis has the advantage of confining the operation of gambling within controlled channels and of preventing the risk of fraud or crime in the context of such operation.'

Berlington & Others v Hungary (Case C–98/14) [2015] 3 CMLR 45 involved Hungarian legislation banning the operation of slot machines except in casinos. The claimants operated slot machines in amusement arcades in Hungary. They challenged this legislation, alleging a breach of Article 56, on the basis that most of the people who used arcade machines were tourists from other Member States. The ECJ agreed that the legislation was a restriction on the freedom to provide services but was potentially justifiable on the basis that 'the protection of consumers against gambling addiction and the prevention of crime and fraud linked to gambling, constitute overriding reasons in the public interest capable of justifying restrictions on gambling', subject to the proportionality test. The Hungarian legislation would be appropriate for ensuring attainment of the objective relied on only if it reflected a concern to attain it in a 'consistent and systematic' manner, a matter for the national court to determine.

Internet gambling

In *Santa Casa*, the ECJ also held that, because of the particular dangers associated with internet gambling, Member States were **not** obliged to take into account the fact that the provider of a gambling service might be regulated by the national authorities in another Member State. The justification proferred for this was 'the lack of direct contact between consumer and operator', which meant that 'games of chance accessible via the internet involve different and more substantial risks of fraud by operators against consumers compared with the traditional markets for such games'. In other words, Internet gambling was singled out for special treatment because of the greater threat of criminal activity.

In subsequent cases, the Court has confirmed that Internet gambling is special, but for other reasons than the risk of crime and fraud. In *Carmen Media* (Case C–46/08) [2010] ECR I–8149, the Court focused on the need to protect against gambling addiction. The

Court held that the specific 'characteristics' of Internet gambling may prove to be a 'source of risks of a different kind and a greater order' compared with traditional forms of gambling, particularly in relation to 'young persons' and those with 'a propensity for gambling or likely to develop such a propensity'. Apart from the lack of direct contact, the Court identified a number of other specific risks, namely the 'particular ease and the permanence of access to games offered over the internet' and the 'potentially high volume and frequency' of international offers (a point A-G Mengozzi had made in his Opinion, i.e. the supply of games available online is virtually unlimited – a number of gambling windows can be opened at the same time – and it is available 24 hours a day, 365 days a year). These risks, moreover, were exacerbated by the fact that Internet gambling took place 'in an environment ... characterised by isolation of the player, anonymity and an absence of social control'.

In *Zeturf* (2011), the Court confirmed both *Santa Casa* and *Carmen Media*, namely that Internet gambling posed 'different and more substantial risks of fraud' and 'may prove to be a source of risks of a different kind and a greater order in the area of consumer protection'.

Soon afterwards, in *Dickinger & Ömer* (Case C–347/09) [2011] ECR I–8185, the ECJ again confirmed its policy of applying special rules to Internet gambling. The result was that the authorities in Austria did not have to recognise the controls imposed on the activities of Internet gambling providers established in Malta. The Maltese government, intervening in the case, had sought to distinguish *Santa Casa* (2009) on the basis that 'Malta was the first State to develop a regulatory system specifically aimed at controlling and monitoring online games of chance [and] which was designed with the objective of addressing the risks inherent in those modern modes of operation'. Specifically, Internet gambling providers based in Malta were subject 'to continued checks and monitoring' by the Lotteries and Gaming Authority, which had 'implemented advanced and robust systems of regulation'. It was further argued that, if anything, Internet gambling services can be controlled 'more effectively' than traditional gambling services 'because all operations performed on electronic media can be tracked, which makes it easy to detect problematic or suspicious operations'. However, none of these arguments persuaded the Court to change its policy. The Court explained that in the absence of EU-level harmonisation and in view of the 'substantial differences between the objectives pursued and the levels of protection sought by the legislation of the various Member States', it was not possible to compel the Member States to recognise each other's regulatory systems.

KEY FACTS

Justification for non-discriminatory rules	
Non-discriminatory restrictions on the freedoms of establishment or services may be justified by reference to 'imperative reasons relating to the public interest'.	*Säger v Dennemeyer & Co.* (1991); *Gebhard* (1995)
The restrictions must be both suitable for attaining the desired objective and proportionate.	
Examples of imperative reasons include consumer protection, the sound administration of justice, the protection of workers.	*Van Binsbergen* (1974); *Wouters and Others* (2002); *Viking Line* (2007)
Member States may restrict gambling services in order to protect consumers from the dangers of addiction, and to prevent crime and fraud.	*Schindler* (1994); *Läärä* (1999); *Zenatti* (1999); *ANOMAR and Others* (2003); *Santa Casa* (2009); *Zeturf* (2011)

13.9 The free movement of lawyers

Lawyers are called a variety of names in the EU, as the following list illustrates:

- *abogado* (used in Spain);
- *advocaat* (used in the Netherlands and parts of Belgium);
- *advocat* or *Advokat* (used in Denmark, Finland, Slovakia and Sweden);
- *advogado* (used in Portugal);
- *advokáat* (used in the Czech Republic);
- *advokāts* (used in Lithuania);
- *adwocat* (used in Poland);
- *avocat* (used in France, Luxembourg and parts of Belgium);
- *avukat* (used in Malta);
- *avvocato* (used in Italy);
- *barrister/solicitor* (used in Ireland and the UK);
- *dikigoros* (used in Cyprus and Greece);
- *odvetnik/odvetnica* (used in Slovenia);
- *rechtsanwalt* (used in Austria, Germany and parts of Belgium);
- *ügyvéd* (used in Hungary);
- *vandeadvokaat* (used in Estonia);
- *zvērināts* (used in Latvia).

13.9.1 Freedom of establishment under Article 49 TFEU

Many lawyers, particularly barristers, are self-employed. This means that there have been several cases involving the free movement of lawyers under Article 49. In *Paris Bar Council v Klopp* (1984), the ECJ was asked to rule on the compatibility of a rule of French law that said that lawyers could have only one place of establishment at a time. This was allegedly designed to ensure that lawyers 'should practise in such a way as to maintain sufficient contact with their clients and the judicial authorities and abide by the rules of the profession'. The ECJ held that this rule imposed an unjustifiable restriction on the freedom of lawyers to establish themselves in other EU Member States.

CASE EXAMPLE

Paris Bar Council v Klopp (Case 107/83) [1984] ECR 2971

Onno Klopp was a German national, a qualified *rechtsanwalt* and a member of the Düsseldorf Bar. In 1981 he applied to be registered as an *avocat* at the Paris Bar. He planned to set up chambers there, as well as retaining his chambers in Germany. However, he was refused permission by the Paris Bar Council, whose rules required *avocats* to establish chambers in one place only. The ECJ held that this rule breached Article 49. The Court stated that although Article 49 allowed Member States some flexibility to organise rules on professionals, that did not allow them to force lawyers to have only one place of establishment at a time.

The Court stated:

JUDGMENT

'In the absence of specific [EU] rules in the matter each Member State is free to regulate the exercise of the legal profession in its territory. Nevertheless that rule does not mean that the legislation of a Member State may require a lawyer to have only one establishment throughout the [Union]. Such a restrictive interpretation would mean that a lawyer once established in a particular Member State would be able to enjoy the freedom of the Treaty to establish himself in another Member State only at the price of abandoning the establishment he already had.'

However, national legal authorities may be able to justify other restrictions, such as supervision and compliance with professional rules. *Gullung v Colmar and Saverne Bar Council* (Case 292/86) [1988] ECR 111, involved a German lawyer who had been refused permission to practise in France after contravening French regulations relating to the professional ethics of those in the legal professions. The Court stated:

JUDGMENT

'Members of the legal profession, when providing services, are required to comply with the rules relating to professional ethics in force in the host Member State ... the requirement that lawyers be registered at a Bar laid down by certain Member States must be regarded as lawful in relation to [EU law] provided, however, that such registration is open to nationals of all Member States without discrimination. The requirement seeks to ensure the observance of moral and ethical principles and the disciplinary control of the activity of lawyers and thus pursues an objective worthy of protection.'

In what is now the leading case, *Gebhard v Milan Bar Council* (1995), the ECJ confirmed *Gullung*. The ECJ acknowledged that national professional regulatory bodies (such as the Solicitors Regulation Authority and the Bar Standards Board in England and Wales) have rules governing issues such as client care, confidentiality and professional ethics which are capable of imposing restrictions on the free movement of lawyers. Nevertheless, these rules are designed to protect clients and the reputation of the profession as a whole and, therefore, are justifiable.

CASE EXAMPLE

Gebhard v Milan Bar Council (Case C–55/94) [1995] ECR I–4165

Reinhard Gebhard was a German national, a qualified *rechtsanwalt* and a member of the Stuttgart Bar. Since 1978 he had resided in Milan. Initially he operated as an associate with a set of chambers in Milan, advising clients on aspects of German law. However, in 1989, he opened his own chambers there and began to use the title '*avvocato*' on the letterhead of his notepaper. Several Italian practitioners complained about this as the title is reserved for lawyers possessing Italian legal and professional qualifications. The Milan Bar Council banned him from using the title. In subsequent disciplinary proceedings, the Council held that he had also infringed Italian law which allowed professional activities to be carried out on a temporary basis by lawyers qualified in other Member States, but prohibited 'the establishment [in Italy] either of chambers or of a principal or branch office'. Gebhard was suspended for six months. On appeal, before the National Council of the Bar, Gebhard argued that Directive 77/249 (see below) entitled him to pursue his professional activities from his own chambers in Milan. The ECJ decided that, because of the amount of time he spent in Milan, he had gone beyond merely providing services and had become established there. This meant that Directive 77/249 did not apply. Nevertheless, he was entitled to rely on Article 49. However, although the Italian rules did, *prima facie*, infringe his freedom of establishment, they were justifiable in that they sought to protect clients from unscrupulous people adopting professional titles and passing themselves off as qualified lawyers.

The Court stated:

JUDGMENT

'The taking-up and pursuit of certain self-employed activities may be conditional on complying with certain provisions laid down by law, regulation or administrative action justified by the general good, such as rules relating to organization, qualifications, professional ethics, supervision and liability. Such provisions may stipulate in particular that pursuit of a particular activity is restricted to holders of a diploma, certificate or other evidence of formal qualifications, to persons belonging to a professional body or to persons subject to particular rules or supervision, as the case may be. They may also lay down the conditions for the use of professional titles.'

13.9.2 The Lawyers' Establishment Directive 98/5

Directive 98/5 confers rights on lawyers qualified in one Member State (the home state) to practise in another Member State (the host state), although they must be clearly 'badged' as a sign to potential clients that the migrant lawyer is qualified in another state's law.

Practice under the 'home country professional title'

According to Article 2, migrant lawyers are entitled to practise various activities which are listed in Article 5, but only using their original title, in the host state's language. According to Article 4, this title 'must be expressed in the official language ... of his home Member State, in an intelligible manner and in such a way as to avoid confusion with the professional title of the host Member State'. Under Article 3, migrant lawyers are required to 'register with the competent authority' in the host Member State. The areas of activity in Article 5(1) include advice on:

- the law of the home Member State;
- EU law;
- international law; and
- the law of the host Member State.

In *Torresi* (Cases C–58 and 59/13) [2015] QB 331; [2015] 2 WLR 29, the Court was asked whether Directive 98/5, in particular Article 3, applied in the case where a national of one Member State (Italy) left that state in order to acquire the qualifications necessary to practise as a lawyer in another Member State (Spain) before returning to the home state in order to practise there. The Court answered 'yes'. The Court held that the right of EU citizens to choose, on the one hand, the Member State in which they wished to acquire their professional qualifications and, on the other, the Member State in which they intended to practise their profession was 'inherent in the exercise, in a single market, of the fundamental freedoms guaranteed by the Treaties'. Moreover, the fact that a lawyer had chosen to acquire a professional qualification in a Member State other than their home state in order to benefit from 'more favourable' legislation in that other state was not, in itself, sufficient ground to conclude that there is an abuse of EU rights (which could have precluded the application of Directive 98/5).

Rules of professional conduct

When practising in the host state, even under his home state's professional title, the migrant lawyer will be expected to abide by 'the local codes of conduct in respect of all activities he pursues in its territory' (Article 6). This will extend to, for example, rules on advertising.

Disciplinary proceedings

The migrant lawyer will be subject to all the local disciplinary rules (Article 7(1)). Provision is made for his home state's professional body to be fully informed of any disciplinary action, including 'all the relevant details', i.e. the evidence on which it is based, before any action is taken (Article 7(2)). A duty of co-operation is imposed on the host state's disciplinary body, while the home state's body has a right to 'make submissions to the bodies responsible for hearing any appeal' (Article 7(3)).

The registration requirement in Article 3, as well as the professional conduct and disciplinary proceedings requirements in Articles 6 and 7, of Directive 98/5 were all examined in *Wilson* (Case C–506/04) [2006] ECR I–8613, involving a British barrister, Graham Wilson, who wished to register in Luxembourg. The Court held that Article 3 did not allow the registration of a lawyer in a Member State to be made conditional on them being proficient in the language(s) of that state. The Court stated: 'presentation … of a certificate attesting to registration with the competent authority of the home State is the only condition to which registration of the person concerned in the host Member State may be subject'. However, the Court noted that, under Article 6, a lawyer must comply with the rules of professional conduct applicable in the host state. One of those rules is an obligation not to handle matters which a lawyer knows, or ought to know, they are not competent to handle, for example, because they lack linguistic knowledge. The Court held that communication with clients, with the national authorities and/or with the professional bodies of the host state may all require a lawyer to have sufficient linguistic knowledge, or at least recourse to assistance where that knowledge is insufficient. Acting without such knowledge may amount to a breach of Article 6 of the Directive leading to possible disciplinary action under Article 7. Nevertheless, the Court concluded, the linguistic knowledge requirement did not justify the national authorities demanding an examination of the lawyer's proficiency in the language(s) of the host Member State *prior to* registration.

Admission to the legal profession in the host state

Article 10(1) provides that a lawyer practising under his home country professional title who has 'effectively and regularly' pursued an activity in the host Member State in the law of that state (including EU law) for at least three years shall, with a view to gaining admission to the profession of lawyer in the host Member State, be exempted from the conditions set out in (what is now) Article 14(1) of Directive 2005/36 (the Qualifications Directive).

Article 10 was invoked in *Ebert* (Case C–359/09) [2011] ECR I–269. Donat Ebert, a German lawyer, had practised law in Hungary under his home country title, *'rechtsanwalt'*, for several years. He applied to the Hungarian authorities for permission to use the Hungarian title, '*ügyvéd*'. This was rejected because Ebert had not become a member of the Hungarian Bar Association. He challenged this refusal. However, the Court held that Article 10 exempted certain lawyers from the need to comply with Directive 2005/36; it did **not** preclude national rules laying down a requirement to be a member of a body such as a national Bar Association in order to practise law under the title of the host Member State.

13.9.3 The Lawyers' Services Directive 77/249

Directive 77/249 harmonises the rules under which lawyers established in one Member State may provide their services in the territory of another state. Article 2 provides: 'Each Member State shall recognise as a lawyer for the purpose of pursuing the activities specified in Article 1(1) any person listed in Article 1(2)'. This is the same list as found in Directive 98/5. Article 1(1) simply states that 'This directive shall apply, within the limits and under the conditions laid down herein, to the activities of lawyers pursued by way of provisions of services.'

In *Piringer* (Case C–342/15) [2017] 3 CMLR 19, the ECJ held that Directive 77/249 covers the situation where the lawyer travels to another Member State to meet with their client and *provide* legal services there and to the corollary situation where the client travels to another Member State to meet with their lawyer and *receive* legal services there. Ms Leopoldine Piringer, an Austrian national, had travelled to the Czech Republic to meet with her lawyer in order to have her signature on a document in which she had declared her intention to sell property that she owned in Austria authenticated. The Court held that Directive 77/249 was 'capable of applying' on these facts. (Ultimately, Ms Piringer was barred from using her Czech lawyer's services in this particular case but only because of a specific derogation in the directive which provides that Member States have the option of reserving to 'prescribed categories of lawyers' the preparation of formal documents for, *inter alia*, creating or transferring rights to property.)

KEY FACTS

The free movement of lawyers	
Self-employed lawyers are entitled to establish themselves in another Member State.	Art 49 TFEU; Directive 98/5
Lawyers can establish themselves in more than one state simultaneously.	*Klopp* (1984); *Gebhard* (1995)
Member States may restrict lawyers' freedom of establishment where necessary in order to ensure compliance with professional rules on conduct, ethics, liability and consumer protection.	Directive 98/5; *Gullung* (1988); *Gebhard* (1995); *Wilson* (2006)
Self-employed lawyers are also entitled to provide legal services in another Member State.	Art 56 TFEU; Directive 77/249

ACTIVITY

Applying the law

a. Connie has been running a successful nursery and nanny agency in London for over ten years. In the past year Connie has identified a niche in the market for high-quality, stimulating pre-school education and care, particularly in demand from professional parents. Her business has gone from strength to strength and she is now ready to expand it. Following extensive market research, Connie has decided to establish a new nanny agency in Bonn. Initially, she intends to set up an office in Bonn, recruit suitably qualified nannies and place them with families.

Advise Connie whether she has any rights under EU law to carry out her plans.

b. The German Small Business Association provides free advice and consultancy to new small businesses. Connie has approached the Association for advice but has been told that she is not eligible to receive this service because she is not a German national.

Advise Connie.

SAMPLE ESSAY QUESTION

'Article 56 TFEU provides for the freedom to provide services, while Article 57 TFEU defines "services". These Articles give this freedom a very wide scope, and the case law of the European Court of Justice has expanded it even further. As a result, there are virtually no limits on this freedom. Discuss.'

Explain the meaning and scope of the 'free movement' of services:

- Article 56 TFEU applies to any cross-border service provision (*Scorpio Konzertproduktionen*)
- Article 56 applies to any national legislation which hinders the movement of services, whether or not discriminatory (*Säger v Dennemeyer*)
- Article 56 may be invoked by the service provider to challenge legislation in their 'home' state (*Alpine Investments*, *Carpenter*)
- Services must 'normally' be provided for 'remuneration', which is interpreted widely (*Bond van Adverteerders*, *Deliège*)
- Rights have been conferred on service recipients through case law. Give examples from the case law, e.g. *Luisi & Carbone*, *Kohll*, *Watts*, *Schwarz*. This case law has significantly expanded the scope of Article 56

Explain the meaning and scope of 'services':

- Article 57 TFEU defines services provided by, *inter alia*, craftsmen and professionals, including legal services (*Reyners*, *Van Binsbergen*, *Säger v Dennemeyer*)
- Case law has expanded the scope of Article 57 by including less obvious 'services' such as prostitution (*Jany & Others*), abortion (*SPUC v Grogan*) and sport (*Deliège*)
- Discuss the fact that just because a service is restricted or even prohibited in some Member States does not prevent Article 56 from applying, e.g. abortion, online gambling, artificial insemination (*Blood*)

Explain that there are limits on the scope of the freedom:

- There must be a cross-border element (*Scorpio Konzertproduktionen*)
- There must be 'remuneration' – so publicly funded services are not covered (*Humbel*)
- Article 51 TFEU exempts 'official authority' activities – although this has been interpreted narrowly (*Reyners*)
- Article 52 TFEU allows for derogations on policy, security and health grounds. 'Public policy' has also been interpreted narrowly (*Calfa*, but compare with *Omega*). Discuss the case law on 'public health' (*MacQuen*, *Kohll*, *Watts*, etc.)
- Examine the case law on 'imperative requirements' which may justify restrictions (*Van Binsbergern*, *Säger v Dennemeyer*, *Schindler*). Give example, e.g. the protection of consumers, workers, cultural heritage, the environment, human dignity; the fight against crime and prevention of fraud
- Conclude that, although Article 56 is defined widely, there are some limitations

SUMMARY

- Article 49 TFEU covers the freedom of establishment; Article 56 TFEU covers the freedom to provide services. Both are directly effective: *Reyners* (Article 49) and *Van Binsbergen* (Article 56).

- **Establishment** is the right to install oneself in another Member State, permanently or semi-permanently, on a self-employed basis, for the purpose of performing a particular activity there. It also gives companies the right to set up a branch or a subsidiary, in another Member State.

- **Provision of services** allows an individual, established in one Member State, to provide their services in another Member State, on a temporary or intermittent basis. It also allows a company, established in one Member State, to provide their services to anyone in another Member State. If necessary, it allows them to visit the other Member State, on a temporary or intermittent basis, in order to do so.

- Article 49 refers to the taking-up as well as the pursuit of professional activities for individual, self-employed persons. For companies, the freedom of establishment includes the right to set up and manage 'undertakings'. In both cases, establishment is under the same conditions laid down for nationals of the state where establishment is effected (*Steinhauser*).

- It is possible to be established in two Member States at the same time (*Klopp, Gebhard*).

- Article 49 can be invoked vertically (*Reyners*) and horizontally (*Viking Line*).

- Directive 2005/36 (as amended) consolidates the rules for the mutual recognition of qualifications required in order to pursue a 'regulated profession' in another Member State.

- A profession is 'regulated' if access to it depends on the possession of qualifications (*Aranitis*).

- Once qualifications have been recognised, the holder of them can pursue a profession in the host Member State under the same conditions as its nationals.

- Member States are allowed to impose 'compensation measures' on holders of qualifications obtained in other states in certain situations, e.g. if the duration of training is at least one year shorter than in the host state, or if training covers 'substantially different matters'.

- Where that happens, states may require the completion of an 'adaptation period' or the passing of an 'aptitude test'. Usually, the candidate can choose which, except for professions 'whose pursuit requires precise knowledge of national law', in which case the state can specify. This exception does not just apply to 'traditional' legal professions (*Price, Vandorou & Others*). Alternatively, states can offer 'partial recognition' of a candidate's qualifications (*Colegio de Ingenieros, Nasiopoulos*).

- Where Directive 2005/36 does not apply, states are obliged to undertake an assessment of a candidate's qualifications to establish the extent of equivalence, which may be full, partial or not equivalent (*Thieffry, Patrick, Vlassopoulou, Morgenbesser*).

- Where qualifications obtained outside the EU have been accepted by one Member State as equivalent to their qualifications and the candidate has practised there, other states must recognise that practical experience (*Haim, Hocsmann*).

- Article 56 TFEU provides that 'restrictions on freedom to provide services … shall be prohibited'. It is crucial that there is a cross-border element. Article 56 EC applies if two conditions are satisfied: (1) the service must be provided within the EU; (2) the provider of services must be a national of a Member State and established in a state of the EU other than that of the service recipient (*Scorpio Konzertproduktionen*).

- Article 56 may be invoked by service providers to challenge all national legislation, whether discriminatory or not, if it inhibits the freedom to provide services (*Säger v Dennemeyer & Co*).

- Article 56 may be used by service providers to challenge legislation in their state of establishment (*Alpine Investments, Carpenter*).

- Article 56 may be invoked by the recipients of services, e.g. tourists (*Luisi & Carbone, Calfa*), persons receiving private education (*Humbel, Schwarz*), persons receiving medical treatment (*Kohll, Watts*).

- 'Services' has a very wide scope, including TV broadcasting (*Bond van Adverteerders*), gambling (*Schindler*), abortions (*SPUC v Grogan*), prostitution (*Jany and Others*), sporting activities (*Deliège*).

- The service must normally be provided for 'remuneration' (Article 57 TFEU). Thus, while private education is included, public education is not (*Humbel, Schwarz*). It is not essential that the service recipient be the person who provides the remuneration (*Bond van Adverteerders, Deliège*).

- Establishment and services are mutually exclusive; the freedom to provide services is subordinate to the freedom of establishment; the concept of establishment assumes the person/company in question is in another Member State 'on a stable and continuous basis', whereas the provisions on services 'envisage that he is to pursue his activity there on a temporary basis' (*Gebhard*).

- Ultimately, whether Article 49 or 56 applies is 'determined in the light, not only of the duration of the provision of the service, but also of its regularity, periodicity or continuity' (*Gebhard*).

- 'Activities … that are connected, even occasionally, with the exercise of official authority' are *not* covered by the Treaty (Article 51 TFEU). This applies only to official authority *activities*; not professions or occupations *as a whole* (*Reyners*).

- Member States may derogate from the freedoms on grounds of public policy, security or health (Article 52 TFEU). For further explanation, see Chapter 11.

- Article 52 allows Member States, in principle, to restrict access to medical services on public health grounds. This is justifiable because it 'seeks to ensure that there is sufficient and permanent access to a balanced range of high-quality hospital treatment in the State concerned' (*Kohll, Watts*).

- National legislation restricting either of the freedoms is justifiable if it is non-discriminatory, pursues a legitimate objective, is capable of achieving that objective and satisfies proportionality, i.e. it does not go beyond what is necessary to achieve that objective (*Van Binsbergern, Gebhard*).

- Examples of legitimate objectives include 'the proper appreciation of places and things of historical interest; dissemination of knowledge of national artistic and cultural heritage' (*Commission v France (Tourist Guides)*), consumer protection (*Alpine Investments, Schindler*), the protection of workers (*Viking Line*), protection of the environment (*Regione Sardegna, Yellow Cab*), the prevention of crime (*Zenatti, Santa Casa*).

- In addition, Article 16 of Directive 2006/123 (the Services Directive), states that Member States must not make access to or exercise of a service activity in their territory subject to compliance with any requirements which do not respect the principles of non-discrimination, necessity and proportionality.

- Lawyers seeking establishment in another Member State may rely on Directive 98/5, while lawyers providing services may rely on Directive 77/249, in addition to the rights provided by Articles 49 and 56.

Further reading

Articles

Anagnostaras, G, 'Les Jeux Sont Faits? Mutual Recognition and the Specificities of Online Gambling' (2012) 37 *EL Rev* 191.

Barnard, C, 'Unravelling the Services Directive' (2008) 45 *CML Rev* 323.

Bulterman, M and Kranenborg, H, 'What if Rules on Free Movement and Human Rights Collide? About Laser Games and Human Dignity: The *Omega* Case' (2006) 31 *EL Rev* 93.

Davies, G, 'The Services Directive: Extending the Country of Origin Principle, and Reforming Public Administration' (2007) 32 *EL Rev* 232.

De La Rosa, S, 'The Directive on Cross-Border Healthcare or the Art of Codifying Complex Case Law' (2012) 49 *CML Rev* 15.

Hatzopoulos, V, 'The Court's Approach to Services (2006–2012): From Case Law to Case Load?' (2013) 50 *CML Rev* 459.

Littler, A, 'Regulatory Perspectives on the Future of Interactive Gambling in the Internal Market' (2008) 33 *EL Rev* 211.

Van den Bogaert, S and Cuyvers, A, ' "Money for Nothing": The Case Law of the EU Court of Justice on the Regulation of Gambling' (2011) 48 *CML Rev* 1175.

14

The free movement of goods and Articles 34 and 35 TFEU

AIMS AND OBJECTIVES

After reading this chapter you should be able to:

- Understand the law relating to the prohibition of 'quantitative restrictions' and measures of 'equivalent effect' on imports and exports in Articles 34 and 35 TFEU

- Understand the meaning and scope of the *Dassonville* judgment

- Understand the meaning and scope of the *Keck & Mithouard* judgment

- Understand the derogations available to Member States under Article 36

- Understand the principles established in *Cassis de Dijon*, and their application

- Analyse critically the law relating to the free movement of goods

- Apply the law to factual situations involving the free movement of goods in the EU

14.1 The removal of non-fiscal barriers to trade

In Chapter 15 we will examine how EU law has sought to prevent Member States from imposing fiscal barriers (in the forms of Customs charges and discriminatory taxation) to the free movement of goods. In this chapter, we will examine how EU law prevents Member States from imposing non-fiscal barriers. There is a potentially infinite variety of such barriers, from measures such as hygiene inspections at border crossing points to technical legislation prescribing the permitted amount of salt in bakery products or the shape of margarine tubs. National legislation making it a criminal offence to import pornographic videos or banning the advertising of junk food could all have the effect of imposing trade barriers.

14.2 Prohibition of quantitative restrictions on imports – Article 34 and exports – Article 35 and all measures having equivalent effect

14.2.1 Introduction

ARTICLE

'Art 34 Quantitative restrictions on imports and all measures having equivalent effect shall be prohibited between Member States.'

ARTICLE

'Art 35 Quantitative restrictions on exports, and all measures having equivalent effect, shall be prohibited between Member States.'

Article 34 prohibits quantitative restrictions, and all measures having equivalent effect, on imports; Article 35 does the same for exports. A measure which infringes Articles 34 or 35 is *prima facie* contrary to EU law; however, Article 36 provides that Articles 34 or 35 will not apply to certain restrictions, justifiable on various grounds, which are not disproportionate (Article 36 is discussed in section 14.5; proportionality is discussed in section 14.7). In addition to this, the ECJ has developed its own line of case law, allowing justifications on other grounds, again provided that they are not disproportionate (see *Cassis de Dijon* (Case 120/78) [1979] ECR 649, discussed in section 14.6).

14.2.2 Direct effect of Articles 34 and 35

In *Ianelli & Volpi SpA v Meroni* (Case 74/76) [1977] ECR 595, the ECJ announced:

JUDGMENT

'The prohibition of quantitative restrictions and measures having equivalent effect laid down in [Article 34] is mandatory and explicit and its implementation does not require any subsequent intervention of the Member States or [Union] institutions. The prohibition therefore has direct effect and creates individual rights which national courts must protect.'

14.2.3 Scope of Articles 34 and 35

Articles 34 and 35 are addressed to the Member States and therefore apply only to acts or omissions on behalf of the Member States. This essentially means the legislative and executive arms of each state's government although it extends beyond that. In *Aragonesa and Publivia* (Cases C–1 and 176/90) [1991] ECR I–4151, which concerned provisions of Catalan law, the ECJ stated that Article 34 'may apply to measures adopted by all the authorities of the Member States, be they the central authorities, the authorities of a federal State, or other territorial authorities'. Apart from central and local government, the actions of the following have been held capable of infringing Articles 34 and 35:

- semi-public bodies such as quangos (e.g. *Apple and Pear Development Council v K J Lewis Ltd*) (Case 222/82) [1983] ECR 4083;

- nationalised industries such as the Post Office (*Commission v France* (Case 21/84) [1985] ECR 1355);

- regulatory agencies and professional bodies established under statutory authority (*R v Pharmaceutical Society of GB, ex parte Association of Pharmaceutical Importers* (Cases 266 and 267/87) [1989] ECR 1295);
- the police force (*R v Chief Constable of Sussex, ex parte ITF Ltd* [1998] 3 WLR 1260, HL);
- even the EU's own institutions are bound to comply with the provisions of Articles 34 and 35 (*Denkavit* (Case 15/83) [1984] ECR 2171).

The word 'goods' does not appear in either Article 34 or Article 35. The word does appear in Article 36, however, which refers to 'prohibitions or restrictions on imports, exports or goods in transit'. It also appears in Article 26(2) and Article 28(1) TFEU, and it has been defined – very widely – by the ECJ (refer to Chapter 10, section 10.2.3). In practice, all products (whether manufactured or not) taken across an internal border of the EU for the purpose of commercial transactions are subject to the free movement of goods provisions – even waste (*Commission v Belgium* (Case C–2/90) [1992] ECR I–4431; *Dusseldorp* (Case C–203/96) [1998] ECR I–4075). The provisions apply equally to goods manufactured or produced in the EU and to those in 'free circulation' in the EU, regardless of their country of origin. Thus, in *Donckerwolcke and Schou* (Case 41/76) [1976] ECR 1921, where cloth originating from Syria and the Lebanon had been imported into Belgium before being re-imported into France, the ECJ held that Article 34 applied.

14.3 The definition of 'quantitative restrictions'

A 'quantitative restriction' was defined in *Geddo v Ente Nazionale Risi* (Case 2/73) [1973] ECR 865 as 'measures which amount to a total or partial restraint of, according to the circumstances, imports, exports or goods in transit'. This most obviously includes a **quota system** (*Salgoil* (Case 13/68) [1968] ECR 453), but also includes an **outright ban** on imports (*Commission v Italy* (Case 7/61) [1961] ECR 635; *Commission v UK* (Case 40/82) (the French Turkeys case) [1982] ECR 2793). In *R v Henn and Darby* (Case 34/79) [1979] ECR 3795, the ECJ held that s42 of the UK's Customs Consolidation Act 1876, which made it a criminal offence to be 'knowingly concerned in the fraudulent evasion of the prohibition of the importation of obscene articles', was a quantitative restriction. The ECJ stated:

JUDGMENT

'It is clear that [Article 34] includes a prohibition on imports inasmuch as this is the most extreme form of restriction. The expression used in [Article 34] must therefore be understood as being the equivalent of the expression "prohibitions or restrictions on imports" occurring in [Article 36].'

This was contrary to what had been earlier suggested in the Court of Appeal in the same case, by Lord Widgery CJ, that a total prohibition was not a 'quantitative' restriction because the 1876 Act made no reference to quantities of obscene articles ([1978] 3 All ER 1190).

Rosengren & Others (Case C–170/04) [2007] ECR I–4071 concerned Swedish legislation which prohibited individuals from importing spirits, wine or strong beer into Sweden, unless personally transporting it. A number of Swedish nationals had ordered cases of Spanish wine to be imported into Sweden. However, the wine was confiscated by Swedish customs. A legal challenge was brought to recover the wine, which raised a question regarding the legality of the Swedish legislation under EU law. The ECJ held that the Swedish legislation constituted a quantitative restriction on imports.

Generally speaking, it will be positive actions that infringe Articles 34 and 35. However, it will be possible for Member States to infringe Article 34, at least, by omission. This has occurred in two cases:

- *Commission v France (French Farmers)* (Case C–265/95) [1997] ECR I–6959, where the French authorities failed to take action to prevent striking French farmers from blockading ports.

- *Schmidberger v Austria* (Case C–112/00) [2003] ECR I–5659, where the Austrian authorities decided to allow a demonstration by an environmental group to go ahead. The effect was to block a major motorway to heavy goods vehicles.

In both cases the French and Austrian authorities, respectively, were held to have infringed Article 34 – although in *Schmidberger* (2003) the ECJ went on to decide that the authorities' omission was justified (this case is considered below – see section 14.6).

14.4 Defining 'measures equivalent to quantitative restrictions' (MEQRs) in Article 34: the *Dassonville* formula

Nowhere in the TFEU is the phrase 'measures equivalent to quantitative restrictions' (known as MEQRs) defined. The classic formulation was given in *Dassonville* (Case 8/74) [1974] ECR 837, a case involving a provision of Belgian law found to amount to an MEQR.

CASE EXAMPLE

Dassonville (Case 8/74) [1974] ECR 837

Under Belgian legislation, a certificate of origin was required for all imports of a range of goods, including Scotch whisky. Benoît Dassonville, a trader in Belgium, imported a consignment of 'Johnnie Walker' and 'VAT 69' Scotch whisky from France. The French distributor was unable to provide a certificate of origin, which could be issued only by the UK Customs authorities. Despite this, Dassonville went ahead with the transaction, using forged documents. The Belgian authorities discovered the forgery and he was prosecuted. He pleaded Article 34 in his defence, arguing that the certification rule constituted a potential hindrance to trade. The case was referred to the ECJ, which held that the Belgian legislation did infringe Article 34, because it was capable of hindering trade.

The Court stated:

JUDGMENT

'All trading rules enacted by Member States which are capable of hindering, directly or indirectly, actually or potentially, [intra-Union] trade are to be considered as measures having an effect equivalent to quantitative restrictions.'

This definition of an MEQR has been cited in practically every case involving Article 34 ever since. However, in some of the more recent cases, the ECJ has modified the 'formula' slightly, substituting the word 'commercial' for 'trading'.

Note that the 'formula' extends Article 34 to any measure that **might** affect trade (as well as measures that definitely or probably **would** affect trade, or have actually done so). *Dassonville* (1974) therefore gives Article 34 a very wide scope indeed, as the cases examined below illustrate. But there are some limitations. A 'charge having equivalent effect to a Customs duty' cannot also be a measure equivalent to a quantitative restriction – that is, a measure cannot be in breach of both Article 30 **and** Article 34 (*Ianelli & Volpi v Meroni* (1977)). (Article 30 is examined in Chapter 15.)

14.4.1 Distinctly applicable MEQRs

In *Dassonville* (1974), the ECJ did not distinguish between those national rules which only apply to imports (known as 'distinctly applicable' MEQRs), and those national rules which apply both to imports and domestically produced goods (known as 'indistinctly applicable' MEQRs). However, the distinction between the two types of national rules is very important, as it determines whether or not the *Cassis de Dijon* principle (discussed below) applies.

The following are some examples of 'distinctly applicable' MEQRs:

'Buy national' campaigns

Government-sponsored campaigns to encourage consumers to buy domestic products on the basis of their nationality clearly infringe Article 34. See *Commission v Ireland ('Buy Irish' Campaign)* (Case 249/81) [1982] ECR 4005:

CASE EXAMPLE

Buy Irish Campaign (Case 249/81) [1982] ECR 4005

The Irish Goods Council was a semi-public body given the task by the Irish government of promoting Irish goods on the basis of their Irish origin. The Council was given financial support to launch a major advertising campaign by the Irish Ministry of Industry. The European Commission alleged that the activities of the Goods Council infringed Article 34. It was alleged that, although incapable of passing binding measures, the Council's activities could nevertheless influence Irish traders and shoppers into discriminating against imports and thus frustrating free movement. The ECJ agreed.

However, it is **not** contrary to EU law to promote a domestic product by pointing out that it has certain qualities not found in goods from other Member States (*Apple and Pear Development Council v K J Lewis Ltd* (1983)):

CASE EXAMPLE

Apple and Pear Development Council (Case 222/82) [1983] ECR 4083

The Apple and Pear Development Council was set up to promote the consumption of apples and pears grown in England and Wales via television advertising campaigns (using the slogan 'Polish up your English'), research projects and general public relations. This was to be financed by a statutory levy. Several growers, including K J Lewis Ltd, refused to pay the levy and were sued by the Council. In defence they argued Article 34. The case was referred to the ECJ which held that no breach of Article 34 had occurred. The Council was 'under a duty not to engage in any advertising intended to discourage the purchase of products of other Member States or to disparage those products in the eyes of consumers'. Nor was it allowed to 'advise consumers to purchase domestic products solely by reason of their national origin'. The Court concluded that it was permissible to promote a national product by reference to its particular qualities. Hence it was legitimate to point out to consumers that English apples were particularly crisp.

Import licence requirements

Where national legislation insists on importers being licensed, the ECJ has held that such requirements are in breach of Article 34. *Evans Medical & Macfarlan Smith* (Case C–324/93) [1995] ECR I–563 concerned licences to import poppy seeds into the UK. The British government insisted that importers be licensed, because although poppy seeds can be converted legally into diamorphine, a powerful pain-killing drug widely used in British hospitals, if it falls into the 'wrong hands' it can end up on 'on the street' as a heroin substitute. Article 34 applies even if the granting of the licence would be a mere formality (*Commission v UK (UHT Milk)* (Case 124/81) [1983] ECR 203). This is because the cost and time taken up in having to apply for a licence could act as a barrier to trade (*Franzén* (Case C–189/95) [1997] ECR I–5909).

Similarly, national legislation requiring retailers to be licensed in order to sell a product has also been held to breach Article 34 (*Sandoz* (Case 174/82) [1983] ECR 2445; *Visnapuu* (Case C–198/14) [2016] 2 CMLR 32). However, this particular type of licensing system **may** now be regarded, after the decision in *Keck and Mithouard* (Case C–267/91) [1993] ECR I–6097, as a selling arrangement, which is exempt from Article 34.

Hygiene inspections

Hygiene inspections carried out on imported goods (typically food and drugs) may still infringe Article 34 because they involve delay, expense, etc. This was seen in the following cases:

- *Rewe-Zentralfinanz* (Case 4/75) [1975] ECR 843 (German legislation required that imported apples be subject to phytosanitary inspection (to detect the presence of San José Scale));

- *Commission v France (Italian Wines)* (Case 42/82) [1983] ECR 1013 (French legislation required imported wine from Italy to be subjected to rigorous inspections).

14.4.2 Indistinctly applicable MEQRs

The majority of the cases have involved indistinctly applicable MEQRs, that is, national rules which apply without distinction to imports and to domestically produced goods but which, nevertheless, have the potential to hinder trade.

Origin marking requirements

National laws imposing a requirement that goods be marked with their country of origin could infringe Article 34 for two reasons:

- They impose extra burdens on importers, many of whom will also not even be aware of the national law and so face difficulties in complying with it.

- They may encourage 'latent' nationalistic prejudice in shoppers, who may consciously or subconsciously select domestically produced goods in preference to imports, purely on the basis of their nationality.

In *Commission v UK (Origin Marking)* (Case 207/83) [1985] ECR 1201, the ECJ acknowledges both of these arguments:

CASE EXAMPLE

Commission v UK (Origin Marking) (Case 207/83) [1985] ECR 1201

UK law, the Trade Descriptions (Origin Marking) (Miscellaneous Goods) Order 1981, prohibited the supply or offer of supply of clothing and textiles, domestic electrical appliances, footwear and cutlery in the UK unless marked with, or accompanied by, an indication of origin. Furthermore, the indication had to be clear and legible, and 'not in any way hidden or obscured or reduced in conspicuousness by any other matter, whether pictorial or not'. The Order applied to all goods, UK included. The Commission alleged that this was capable of inhibiting the free movement of goods. The ECJ agreed that a breach of Article 34 had been committed. There were two principal reasons for this decision: (1) the ECJ accepted the argument that origin-marking of goods allowed consumers to assert latent prejudice against foreign goods and (2) the ECJ accepted an argument (put forward by the French Domestic Appliance Manufacturers' Association) that manufacturers of domestic appliances based in other EU Member States who wished to sell their products in the UK would have to mark such products systematically. This was not something they already did and so doing so in order to comply with UK law would increase the cost of the manufacturing process and could disinhibit manufacturers from so doing.

JUDGMENT

'The purpose of origin-marking is to enable customers to distinguish between domestic and imported products and this enables them to assert any prejudices which they may have against foreign products ... the Treaty, by establishing a Common Market ... seeks to unite national markets in a single market having the characteristics of a domestic market. Within such a market, the origin-marking requirement not only makes the marketing in a Member State of goods produced in other Member States ... more difficult, it also has the effect of slowing down economic interpenetration in the [Union].'

Other examples include *Dassonville* (1974) itself and *Commission v Ireland* (*Souvenir Jewellery*) (Case 113/80) [1981] ECR 1625. The *Souvenir Jewellery* case will be discussed below.

Packaging requirements
National laws which relate to how products are packaged may well infringe Article 34, because they increase the costs of manufacturers in other Member States, who will have to develop special packaging processes purely for the importing state. It will also inhibit retailers in the state in question from importing goods that do not comply with the national law. Conversely, it will be much easier for domestic manufacturers to comply with their own national requirements as to packaging. Examples include:

- *Walter Rau v De Smedt* (Case 261/81) [1982] ECR 3961 (Belgian legislation required margarine to be packaged in a cube);
- *Mars* (Case C–470/93) [1995] ECR I–1923 and *Estée Lauder Cosmetics v Lancaster* (Case C–220/98) [2000] ECR I–117 (German legislation prohibited the use of misleading packaging).

Contents and ingredients restrictions
In the following cases, national legislation prescribing or restricting the contents and/or ingredients of various products was held to breach Article 34:

- *Cassis de Dijon* (Case 120/78) [1979] ECR 649: German legislation laid down a minimum alcohol level of 25 per cent per litre for certain spirits.
- *Gilli and Andres* (Case 788/79) [1981] ECR 2071: Italian legislation required all vinegar to be made from wine.
- *Commission v Germany (Beer Purity)* (Case 178/84) [1987] ECR 1227: German legislation prohibited the use of additives in beer.
- *Muller* (Case 304/84) [1986] ECR 1511: French legislation prohibited the use of emulsifying agents in bakery products.

- *Greenham and Abel* (Case C–95/01) [2004] ECR I–1333: French legislation prohibited the sale of any food or drink containing a chemical substance called coenzyme Q10.
- *Commission v Italy (Red Bull)* (Case C–420/01) [2003] ECR I–6445: Italian legislation banned drinks with more than 125 mg per litre of caffeine (such as 'Red Bull', which has a caffeine level double that).

Many of these cases reached the ECJ via requests for preliminary rulings from criminal courts because traders had been prosecuted for selling imported goods that did not comply with the national legislation. Thus:

- Herbert Gilli and Paul Andres were prosecuted in Italy for selling apple vinegar made in Germany.
- Claude Muller was prosecuted in France for selling a cake and pastry mix called 'Phénix', imported from Germany, which contained an emulsifying agent.
- John Greenham and Léonard Abel were prosecuted in France for selling a food supplement, 'Juice Plus', to which had been added Q10. 'Juice Plus' is sold without restriction in the UK, Germany, Italy and Spain.

In all of these cases the ECJ decided that the national rules in question amounted to an indistinctly applicable MEQR, and were thus prohibited by Article 34, unless one of the Article 36 or *Cassis de Dijon* (1979) derogations applied (typically, protection of public health).

Name restrictions

National legislation that reserves particular names to products bearing very specific characteristics is capable of breaching Article 34. For example, in *Smanor* (Case 298/87) [1988] ECR 4489 (French legislation reserved the name 'yoghurt' to fresh produce only, with the result that frozen yoghurt had to be re-named as 'deep-frozen fermented milk') the ECJ decided that Article 34 had been infringed because 'it may none the less make the marketing [of imported frozen yoghurt] more difficult and thus impede, at least indirectly, trade between Member States'.

The same result occurred in the following cases:

- *Fietje* (Case 27/80) [1980] ECR 3839: Dutch legislation made the name 'likeur' compulsory for most alcoholic products of at least 22 per cent proof.
- *Miro* (Case 182/84) [1985] ECR 3731: Dutch legislation prescribed that the word 'Jenever' could only be applied to describe gin that was at least 35 per cent proof.
- *Deserbais* (Case 286/86) [1988] ECR 4907: French legislation restricted the use of the word 'Edam' to describe cheese with a minimum fat content.
- *Guimont* (Case 448/98) [2000] ECR I–10663: French legislation prescribed the contents of 'Emmenthal' cheese very rigidly, in that it had to be

    a firm cheese produced by curing, pressing and salting on the surface or in brine, of a colour between ivory and pale yellow, with holes of a size between a cherry and a walnut [and with a] hard, dry rind, of a colour between golden yellow and light brown.

- *Commission v Spain* (Case C–12/00) [2003] ECR I–459: Spanish and Italian legislation restricted the use of the name 'chocolate' to products containing only chocolate and no vegetable fats. This affected chocolate products made in the UK, Denmark, Finland, Ireland, Portugal and Sweden, which traditionally contain vegetable fats. These could be sold in Italy and Spain but only under the label 'chocolate substitute'.

Conversely, where national authorities in one Member State ban or restrict the use of a name which is used elsewhere, this could also constitute a breach of Article 34. Thus, in *Clinique Laboratories and Estée Lauder Cosmetics* (Case C–315/92) [1994] ECR I–317, where the German authorities refused to allow the name 'Clinique' to be used for cosmetics, the ECJ held that Article 34 had been infringed.

Authorisation/certification requirements

National legislation requiring all goods of a certain type to be inspected in order to ensure that they satisfy national standards, and authorised or certified as such prior to them being made available for sale to the consumer, are capable of hindering trade and are therefore in breach of Article 34. Examples include:

- *Dynamic Medien v Avides Media* (Case C–244/06) [2008] ECR I–505 – German legislation required DVDs to be inspected and classified.

- *Commission v Spain (Herbal Products)* (Case C–88/07) [2009] ECR I–1353 – under Spanish legislation, all medical products could only be placed on the market with official authorisation.

- *ASCAFOR & ASIDAC* (Case C–484/10) [2012] 2 CMLR 22 – under Spanish legislation, a number of technical requirements had to be met before reinforced steel could be used in construction projects.

- *Fra.bo* (case C–171/11) [2012] 3 CMLR 38; [2013] QB 187 – under German legislation, only products (the case itself involved copper fittings for use in the water industry) which met certain technical standards could be used in Germany.

In such cases, although a *prima facie* breach of Article 34 was identified (on the basis that the national requirements posed a potential barrier to trade), the legislation was justifiable (in principle), typically on health and/or consumer protection grounds.

Prohibitions on use

A complete ban under national legislation on the use of a product is an MEQR. In *Toolex Alpha* (Case C–473/98) [2000] ECR I–5681, Swedish legislation prohibiting the sale, transfer or use, for industrial purposes, of chemical products composed wholly or partially of trichloroethylene was held to breach Article 34 (but was justifiable under Article 36). This case is discussed in detail in the next section.

Three recent cases further illustrate this type of MEQR. In each case the Court held that a complete ban on the use of a product in a Member State breaches Article 34 (even if the product could be lawfully imported and sold) because customers in that state would have little or no interest in buying such a product, if they knew that they could not lawfully use it. Hence the ban creates a potential barrier to trade in that product. Note: in all three cases the legislation, being indistinctly applicable, was at least potentially justifiable using *Cassis de Dijon* principles.

- *Commission v Portugal (Tinted Film for Car Windows)* (Case C–265/06) [2008] ECR I–2245: Portuguese legislation prohibited (with limited exceptions) the 'affixing of tinted film to the windows of passenger or goods vehicles'.

- *Commission v Italy (Motorcycle Trailers)* (Case C–110/05) [2009] ECR I–519: Italian legislation prohibited mopeds and motorcycles from towing trailers.

- *Mickelsson & Roos* (Case C–142/05) [2009] ECR I–4273: Swedish legislation prohibited the use of 'personal watercraft' – jet-skis – except on water designated as a 'general navigable waterway'.

MEQRs and the *Dassonville* formula	
Art 34 TFEU prohibits 'measures having an equivalent effect' to quantitative restrictions (MEQRs). This phrase is defined very widely. Any national measure capable of hindering trade – whether directly or indirectly, and whether actually or even potentially – is an MEQR.	*Dassonville* (1974)
MEQRs may be distinctly applicable. These are measures which only affect domestic goods **or** imports (but not both), such as buy national campaigns, or import inspections.	*Commission v Ireland* ('Buy Irish') (1982); *Commission v France* (Italian Wine) (1983)
MEQRs may also be indistinctly applicable. These are measures which affect domestic goods **and** imports. Examples include: 　i. origin-marking rules 　ii. packaging requirements 　iii. contents and ingredients restrictions 　iv. name restrictions 　v. prohibitions on use	*Dassonville; Commission v UK Walter Rau v De Smedt* (1982); *Mars* (1995) *Cassis de Dijon* (1979); *Gilli & Andres* (1981) *Fietje* (1980); *Miro* (1985) *Toolex Alpha* (2000); *Commission v Italy* (Motorcycle Trailers) (2009)

14.5 Article 36 and the derogations from Articles 34 and 35

ARTICLE

'Art 36 The provisions of Articles 34 and 35 shall not preclude prohibitions or restrictions on imports, exports or goods in transit justified on grounds of public morality, public policy or public security; the protection of health and life of humans, animals or plants; the protection of national treasures possessing artistic, historic or archaeological value; or the protection of industrial or commercial property. Such prohibitions or restrictions shall not, however, constitute a means of arbitrary discrimination or a disguised restriction on trade between Member States.'

14.5.1 The grounds under Article 36

The grounds listed are exhaustive and may not be added to. In *Commission v Ireland* (*Souvenir Jewellery*) (1981), the ECJ stated:

JUDGMENT

'The exceptions listed [in Article 36] cannot be extended to cases other than those specifically laid down. In view of the fact that neither the protection of consumers nor the fairness of commercial transactions is included amongst the exceptions set out in [Article 36], those grounds cannot be relied upon as such in connexion with that Article.'

In particular, arguments based on economics have consistently been rejected (*Campus Oil Ltd* (Case 72/83) [1984] ECR 2727; *Evans Medical and Macfarlan Smith* (1995)). Other examples of rejected arguments include:

- consumer protection and/or the fairness of commercial transactions (*Souvenir Jewellery* (1981));
- protection of cultural diversity (*Leclerc* (Case 229/83) [1985] ECR 1).

In that case the ECJ stated:

JUDGMENT

'Since it derogates from a fundamental rule of the Treaty, [Article 36] must be interpreted strictly and cannot be extended to cover objectives not expressly enumerated therein. Neither the safeguarding of consumers' interests nor the protection of creativity and cultural diversity in the realm of publishing is mentioned in [Article 36].'

However, these two grounds have now been recognised as 'mandatory' or 'overriding' requirements under *Cassis de Dijon* (1979) principles instead (see section 14.6). The grounds under Article 36 have also been restrictively interpreted because they operate as exceptions from the fundamental freedom of movement. The burden of proving that an Article 36 derogation has been made out rests with the party seeking to rely upon it, usually the national authorities (*Denkavit Futtermittel* (Case 251/78) [1979] ECR 3369).

In *ATRAL* (Case C–14/02) [2003] ECR I–4431, the ECJ was asked whether a Member State which claims justification under Article 36 and/or *Cassis de Dijon* (1979) principles may merely rely on it in the abstract or must specifically demonstrate its genuineness. The ECJ replied (emphasis added):

JUDGMENT

'An exception to the principle of the free movement of goods may be justified under [Article 36] only if the national authorities show that it is necessary in order to attain one or more objectives mentioned in that article and that it is in conformity with the principle of proportionality. *Such justification can only be specifically demonstrated by reference to the circumstances of the case.* The same considerations necessarily apply to exceptions to the free movement of goods based on the overriding requirements recognised by [Union] case-law. The Court adopts an equally specific approach when assessing that category of derogations (see *Cassis de Dijon*).'

Public morality

The protection of public morality was successfully invoked in *R v Henn and Darby* (1979):

CASE EXAMPLE

R v Henn and Darby (Case 34/79) [1979] ECR 3795

UK law, s42 of the Customs Consolidation Act 1876, provides that it is a criminal offence to be 'knowingly concerned in the fraudulent evasion of the prohibition of the importation of obscene articles'. Maurice Henn and John Darby had imported a consignment of pornographic films and magazines into the UK from Denmark via Rotterdam. The consignment was detected by British Customs. Although the majority of the films and magazines were lawfully produced and marketed in Denmark, the two men were convicted. On appeal they relied on Article 34, while the prosecution invoked public morality under Article 36. The House of Lords referred the case to the ECJ, which held: (1) the 1876 Act imposed a quantitative restriction on imports and was *prima facie* prohibited by Article 34 and (2) the restriction was justifiable under Article 36.

The ECJ stated:

JUDGMENT

'In principle, it is for each Member State to determine in accordance with its own scale of values and in the form selected by it the requirements of public morality in its territory. In any event, it cannot be disputed that the statutory provisions applied by the UK in regard to the importation of articles having an indecent or obscene character come within the powers reserved to the Member States by the first sentence of Article 36.'

The case was distinguished by the ECJ in *Conegate* (Case 121/85) [1986] ECR 1007 (below). It has since been followed by the UK's Divisional Court, in *R v Wright* [1999] 1 Cr App R 69, a case involving the importation of pornography supposedly to be added to a private collection. The argument advanced was that this was not a fitting subject for the application of the public morality defence. The Divisional Court disagreed (*per* Kennedy LJ):

JUDGMENT

'There is a public morality purpose to be served not only in protecting the innocent but also in protecting the less innocent from further corruption, and the addict from feeding or increasing his own addiction. Furthermore ... if a substantial quantity of material is imported for private use there is an obvious risk that it will not be seen only by the importer. There is a potential for distribution which raises the question of public morality.'

The public morality ground was also invoked by the Court of Appeal in *R v Dryzner* [2014] EWCA Crim 2438. The Court held that s9 of the UK's Video Recordings Act 1984, which made it a criminal offence to supply or offer to supply a video recording in respect of which no classification certificate has been issued, was an MEQR in that it potentially hindered trade in videos, but one which was justifiable under Article 36. The Court held that the purpose of the UK legislation was to provide information to the public, in the form of the age-banded classifications determined by the British Board of Film Classification (U, PG, 12A, 15 and 18), in order to protect children and young persons from viewing unsuitable material such as extreme violence or pornography.

Public policy

Despite great **potential** width, this ground has rarely been successfully invoked. It does not provide some general fallback provision for states (*Commission v Italy* (1961)); nor can it be used for purely economic reasons (*Commission v Italy* (Securities for Imports) (Case 95/81) [1982] ECR 2187). It cannot be used to justify measures that really fall within consumer protection (*Kohl v Ringelhan* (Case 177/83) [1984] ECR 3651). It is also no justification that the activities with which the law deals are subject to criminal penalties (*Prantl* (Case 16/83) [1984] ECR 1299). However, the defence was successfully invoked in *R v Thompson* (Case 7/78) [1979] ECR 2247 (involving UK legislation that imposed an export ban on old coins).

CASE EXAMPLE

R v Thompson (Case 7/78) [1979] ECR 2247

UK legislation prohibited the export from the UK of certain goods, including silver alloy coins minted in the UK before 1947, namely sixpences, shillings, florins and half-crowns. In 1975, Ernest Thompson and two other men exported to Germany some 40 tonnes of silver alloy coins. The men were convicted of breaching the UK law. They appealed and the case was referred to the ECJ, which held that (1) the coins were no longer legal tender and could therefore be regarded as 'goods' and (2) the restrictions on exportation were *prima facie* prohibited by Article 35, however, (3) they were justified on public policy grounds, under Article 36, since the state had an interest in protecting its mint coinage. The ban was designed to ensure that there was no shortage of current coins for use by the public.

More controversially, the House of Lords used the public policy derogation in *R v Chief Constable of Sussex, ex p ITF Ltd* [1998] 3 WLR 1260, to justify the Chief Constable's decision to withdraw police officers from the port of Shoreham in Sussex. This had the effect of allowing animal-rights protestors to blockade the port and prevent companies such as ITF Ltd from exporting live animals to other EU Member States. The Lords decided that this decision was justifiable because the Chief Constable had limited police manpower resources and had to deploy his officers throughout the county, not just in one town.

The public policy derogation was successfully invoked by the Finnish government in *Ahokainen & Leppik* (Case C–434/04) [2006] ECR I–9171. The case involved a provision of Finnish law, under which a licence was required in order to import drinks containing ethyl alcohol over 80 per cent proof, breach of which was a criminal offence. Two Finnish nationals, Jan-Erik Ahokainen and Mati Leppik, were convicted of 'smuggling' – importing without a licence – nearly 10,000 litres of spirits into Finland from Germany and sentenced to prison. On appeal, they argued that the Finnish law amounted to a breach of Article 34. In response, the Finnish government invoked Article 36 – relying on both public health and public policy. The ECJ agreed, stating:

JUDGMENT

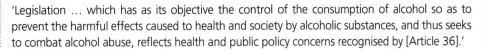

'Legislation ... which has as its objective the control of the consumption of alcohol so as to prevent the harmful effects caused to health and society by alcoholic substances, and thus seeks to combat alcohol abuse, reflects health and public policy concerns recognised by [Article 36].'

Public security

Again, purely economic reasons will not suffice. However, the presence of an economic justification for national legislation will not be fatal provided that the legislation is also justifiable on public security grounds. The defence was successfully invoked in *Campus Oil* (1984). Irish legislation restricted the importation of petroleum products, ostensibly to reduce the danger of Ireland becoming over-reliant on imports. The effect of the legislation was that petrol companies operating in Ireland were forced to obtain about 30 per cent of their supplies from Ireland's only oil refinery, in Cork. The ECJ stated:

JUDGMENT

'Petroleum products, because of their exceptional importance as an energy source in the modern economy, are of fundamental importance for a country's existence since not only its economy but above all its institutions, its essential public services and even the survival of its inhabitants depend upon them. An interruption of supplies of petroleum products ... could therefore seriously affect the public security that [Article 36] allows States to protect ... the aim of ensuring a minimum supply of petroleum products at all times is to be regarded as transcending purely economic considerations and thus as capable of constituting an objective covered by the concept of public security.'

Campus Oil (1984) was confirmed in *Commission v Greece (Petroleum Stocks)* (Case C–398/98) [2001] ECR I–7915. The ECJ acknowledged that 'the maintenance on national territory of a stock of petroleum products allowing continuity of supplies to be guaranteed constitutes a public security objective'. However, the Court went on to reject the defence on the facts, finding that the Greek legislation was primarily concerned about protecting the economic freedom of oil refineries rather than Greek public security.

Public security was also raised in *Richardt and Les Accessoires Scientifiques* (Case C–367/89) [1991] ECR I–4621, although this did not involve imports or exports. Instead, it concerned the transit of a machine used in the production of bubble memory circuits from the USA to Russia via Luxembourg. The transit company was prosecuted under Luxembourg law for failing to have acquired the requisite clearance in advance. It challenged the law, and the Luxembourg authorities relied on public security. Bubble memory circuits were a type of computer memory storage that used a thin film of a magnetic material to hold small magnetised areas, known as 'bubbles'. They were widely used in the 1970s and 1980s but eventually fell into disuse with the advent of hard discs. However, bubble memory circuits found uses through the 1980s in computer systems operating in high vibration or harsh environments. It appears that the Luxembourg authorities were concerned that the machine might have been put to military use, and hence invoked the public security derogation. The ECJ stated:

JUDGMENT

'The concept of public security within the meaning of [Article 36] covers both a Member State's internal security and its external security. It is common ground that the importation, exportation and transit of goods capable of being used for strategic purposes may affect the public security of a Member State, which it is therefore entitled to protect pursuant to [Article 36].'

Protection of the health and life of humans, animals and plants

In *Toolex Alpha* (2000), where Swedish legislation prohibited the sale, transfer or use, for industrial purposes, of chemical products composed wholly or partially of trichloroethylene, because of a perceived risk of causing cancer, the ECJ stated that 'the health and life of humans rank foremost among the property or interests protected' by Article 36. Article 36 has been used to justify many measures, typically prohibitions (or at least restrictions) on the import or sale of various foodstuffs, additives, drugs and chemicals; tests and inspections as to quality, etc.

CASE EXAMPLE

Toolex Alpha (Case C–473/98) [2000] ECR I–5681

Swedish law prohibited the sale, transfer or use, for industrial purposes, of chemical products composed wholly or partially of trichloroethylene (TE). Toolex Alpha, a manufacturer of machine parts used in the production of CDs, used TE to remove residues of grease produced during the manufacturing process. Toolex challenged the ban, alleging a breach of Article 34. The Swedish government relied upon Article 36. It was not contested that TE was a known carcinogenic substance, carrying a risk of cancer in humans and posing a threat to the environment. The Swedish authorities further submitted that TE affects the central nervous system, the liver and the kidneys. The fact that it is highly volatile increases the chances of exposure. Inhaling the substance can cause fatigue, headaches and difficulties with memory and concentration. The case was referred to the ECJ, which held: (1) the Swedish legislation, being an outright ban, was *prima facie* prohibited by Article 34; (2) the Swedish rules were justified under Article 36. The Court noted that concern regarding TE had been mounting in recent years. In particular, the International Cancer Research Agency had produced evidence that TE is a carcinogen. A German case study produced statistics indicating a link between the incidence of renal cancer and exposure to TE. Furthermore, an American epidemiological study indicated that there is an aggravated risk of renal cancer, in particular following exposure to TE at the workplace.

Sometimes the defence is successful. The Dutch restrictions on the sale of vitamin-enhanced muesli bars in *Sandoz* (1983), the Swedish ban on trichloroethylene in case *Toolex Alpha* (2000) and the French ban on 'Red Bull' in *Commission v France* (Case C–24/00) [2004] ECR I–1277 were all upheld. In *Scotch Whisky Association* (Case C–333/14) [2016] 2 CMLR 27; [2016] 1 WLR 2283, the ECJ held that Scottish legislation, the Alcohol (Minimum Pricing) (Scotland) Act 2012, which permitted the Scottish government to impose a minimum retail price for alcohol, was an MEQR (it 'significantly restricts the freedom of economic operators to determine their retail selling prices and, consequently, constitutes a serious obstacle to access to the UK market of alcoholic drinks lawfully marketed in [other] Member States') but one which was justifiable on health grounds. The Court held that the specific aim of the legislation was to raise the price of 'cheap' alcoholic drinks. A minimum price for such drinks was 'capable of reducing the consumption of alcohol, in general, and the hazardous or harmful consumption of alcohol, in particular, given that drinkers whose consumption can be so described purchase, to a great extent, cheap alcoholic drinks'. The Court then left it to the Scottish Courts to determine whether the 2012 Act was necessary, given alternative measures such as higher excise duties. Subsequently, in October 2016, the Scottish Court of Session held that the 2012 Act was justified under Article 36 (*Scotch Whisky Association v Lord Advocate* [2016] CSIH 77; 2016 SLT 1141).

However, sometimes the defence fails. Defences tend be rejected for one of two reasons: (1) lack of evidence of a 'real' health risk or (2) failure to comply with the principle of proportionality (see below).

In general, the ECJ is vigilant to prevent Article 36 from being abused, hence the insistence of evidence of a 'real' risk. However, if the Member State whose legislation is being contested can point to international scientific research supporting them, then the ECJ is far more likely to accept that there was such a risk. In *Greenham and Abel* (2004), the ECJ stated:

JUDGMENT

'Since [Article 36] provides for an exception, to be interpreted strictly, to the rule of free movement of goods within the Union, it is for the national authorities which invoke it to show in each case, in the light of national nutritional habits and in the light of the results of international scientific research, that their rules are necessary to give effective protection to the interests referred to in that provision and, in particular, that the marketing of the products in question poses a real risk to public health.'

Member States may adopt different approaches to the same safety issue. What if there is disputed scientific opinion about whether or not there is a real health risk? In *Sandoz* (1983), the ECJ stated: 'Insofar as there are uncertainties at the present state of scientific research it is for the Member States … to decide what degree of protection of the health and life of humans they intend to assure.' This led the Court to conclude that Dutch rules prohibiting vitamin-enhanced muesli bars were 'justified on principle'.

In *Greenham and Abel* (2004), involving French legislation which prohibited the marketing of food and drink to which a substance called Q10 had been added, the ECJ laid down important guidelines on when the human health derogation would be available in such circumstances. The ECJ stated:

JUDGMENT

'A decision to prohibit the marketing of a fortified foodstuff, which is in fact the most restrictive obstacle to trade in products lawfully manufactured and marketed in other Member States, can be adopted only if the alleged real risk for public health appears to be sufficiently established on the basis of the latest scientific data available at the date of the adoption of such decision. In such a context, the object of the risk assessment to be carried out by the Member State is to appraise the degree of probability of harmful effects on human health from the addition of certain nutrients to foodstuffs and the seriousness of those potential effects. It is clear that such an assessment of the risk could reveal that scientific uncertainty persists as regards the existence or extent of real risks to human health. In such circumstances, it must be accepted that a Member State may, in accordance with the precautionary principle, take protective measures without having to wait until the existence and gravity of those risks are fully demonstrated. However, the risk assessment cannot be based on purely hypothetical considerations.'

The Court repeated this test in *Commission v Denmark* (Case C–192/01) [2003] ECR I–9693, deciding that Danish rules restricting the marketing of 'enriched' foodstuffs (described as any food to which had been added any substance designed to modify its nutritional value, shelf-life, colour, flavour or taste) were justifiable on human health grounds.

The protection of animal health was invoked by the House of Lords in *R (on the application of Countryside Alliance & Others) v HM Attorney General* [2007] UKHL 52; [2007] 3 WLR 922. The House was asked whether the ban on the hunting with dogs of wild mammals, in particular foxes, imposed under the Hunting Act 2004, infringed Article 34 and/or Article 56 (the freedom to provide services). The House accepted that the ban could hinder intra-Union trade. Lord Hope gave as an example horses bred in Ireland for sale to customers in England. However, the House agreed that the ban was justifiable under Article 36. Lord Bingham stated:

JUDGMENT

'I approach the issue of justification on the assumption that Articles 34 and 56 apply, but also on the basis that the measure to be justified is a measure of social reform.... In *Omega*, the German authorities considered, and the ECJ accepted, that "the exploitation of games involving the simulated killing of human beings infringed a fundamental value enshrined in the national constitution, namely human dignity". Parliament considered that the real killing of foxes, deer, hares and mink by way of recreation infringed a fundamental value expressed in numerous statutes and culminating in the 2004 Act. I am of the clear opinion ... that the 2004 Act is justifiable in Union law.'

(Note: Article 56 and the *Omega* case were examined in Chapter 13.)

Protection of national treasures

No case has yet succeeded on these grounds. In any event, it is more likely to apply to measures taken in respect of exports.

Protection of industrial and commercial property

In *Belgium v Spain (Rioja wine exports)* (Case C–388/95) [2000] ECR I–3123, the ECJ upheld provisions of Spanish law requiring Rioja wine intended for export to be bottled in the La Rioja region. Although *prima facie* in breach of Article 35, the legislation was justified. This was because Rioja wine enjoyed an international reputation for high quality, which might be tarnished if the wine could be transported out of the region in bulk and then bottled elsewhere. The ECJ stated:

JUDGMENT

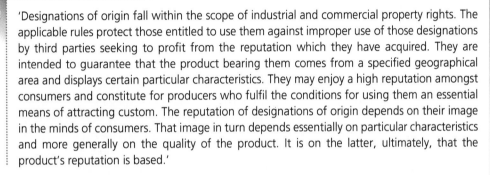

'Designations of origin fall within the scope of industrial and commercial property rights. The applicable rules protect those entitled to use them against improper use of those designations by third parties seeking to profit from the reputation which they have acquired. They are intended to guarantee that the product bearing them comes from a specified geographical area and displays certain particular characteristics. They may enjoy a high reputation amongst consumers and constitute for producers who fulfil the conditions for using them an essential means of attracting custom. The reputation of designations of origin depends on their image in the minds of consumers. That image in turn depends essentially on particular characteristics and more generally on the quality of the product. It is on the latter, ultimately, that the product's reputation is based.'

14.5.2 The second sentence of Article 36

As well as providing evidence to support the use of one of the six grounds of derogation under Article 36, the Member State in question must also satisfy the Court that no breach of the second sentence of Article 36 has occurred. There are two aspects to this. Any quantitative restriction or MEQR must not:

- discriminate against imports in an 'arbitrary' way; or
- be a restriction on imports for economic reasons but 'disguised' using one of the derogations (usually the 'health' derogation).

'Arbitrary discrimination'

National measures which only apply to imported goods (that is, quantitative restrictions in the strict sense, such as import bans; or distinctly applicable MEQRs) may be justified under Article 36. That is, Member States may discriminate against imported goods. An import ban is, by definition, discriminatory against imports. However, national legislation must not discriminate in an 'arbitrary' way. National legislation will be held to be 'arbitrary' if there is no objective basis for making the distinction (*Commission v France* (Case 152/78) [1980] ECR 2299). In *R v Henn and Darby* (1980) (in the context of the 'public morality' derogation) the ECJ said that 'the true function' of the second sentence of Article 36 was:

JUDGMENT

'To prevent restrictions on trade based on the grounds mentioned in the first sentence of [Article 36] from being diverted from their proper purpose and used in such a way as either to create discrimination in respect of goods originating in other Member States or indirectly to protect certain national products.'

In *Henn and Darby* (1980), the ECJ regarded s42 of the Customs Consolidation Act 1876 as discriminatory, since it prohibited the importation of material which was 'indecent or obscene', whereas domestic (UK-produced) pornography was only illegal under the

Obscene Publications Acts 1959 and 1964 if likely to 'deprave or corrupt'. Clearly, **some** foreign pornography, unlikely to deprave or corrupt, could still be described as 'indecent or obscene'. However, the ECJ held that, although discriminatory, the UK law was not **arbitrary**, and nor was there a disguised restriction on trade. The UK's anti-pornography laws, **taken as a whole**, did have as their purpose the prohibition (or at least the restraining) of the manufacture and marketing of articles of an indecent or obscene character.

The 1876 Act had, therefore, been genuinely applied for the protection of public morality, and not for the protection of national products, because there was no lawful trade in such goods in the UK. *Henn and Darby* was distinguished on that point in *Conegate* (Case 121/85) [1986] ECR 1007.

CASE EXAMPLE

Conegate (Case 121/85) [1986] ECR 1007

Conegate, a British company, was in the business of importing inflatable rubber dolls, and other articles, into the UK from Germany. A number of consignments of dolls and other articles were seized by Customs at the airport on the grounds that they were 'indecent or obscene' under s42 of the 1876 Act. However, there was no law preventing the manufacture of such dolls in the UK. Conegate brought an action for recovery of the dolls before the High Court, relying on Article 34. The Customs authorities relied on the 'public morality' defence under Article 36. The ECJ held that (1) there was a *prima facie* breach of Article 34 and (2) Article 36 did not apply because, although the sale of sex dolls was restricted in the UK, to licensed sex shops, it was not banned (unlike the explicit pornography in *Henn and Darby* (1980)). It would therefore constitute 'arbitrary' discrimination to ban the importation of love dolls from Germany when there was already a lawful (albeit restricted) trade in similar, UK-produced, dolls in the UK.

A 'disguised restriction on trade'

A national measure, ostensibly designed to protect human health (for example) may not be protected by Article 36 if, in reality, the measure is 'a disguised restriction on trade'. A good example is provided by *Commission v UK (French Turkeys)* (Case 40/82) [1982] ECR 2793. In 1981 the UK had banned poultry imports, ostensibly because of fears about a health risk. On closer examination, it transpired that the import ban had been imposed for economic reasons. The ECJ stated:

JUDGMENT

'Certain established facts suggest that the real aim of the 1981 measures was to block, *for commercial and economic reasons*, imports of poultry products from other Member States, in particular from France. The UK government had been subject to pressure from British poultry producers to block these imports. It hurriedly introduced its new policy with the result that French Christmas turkeys were excluded from the British market.... The deduction must be made that the 1981 measures did not form part of a seriously considered health policy ... these facts are sufficient to establish that the 1981 measures constitute a disguised restriction on imports of poultry products from other Member States.'

14.5.3 Article 36 and harmonising Directives

Where harmonising Directives in a particular subject (typically human or animal health) have been adopted, Member States may not unilaterally adopt, on their own authority, corrective or protective measures designed to obviate any breach by another state of EU law. Article 36 will not be available. In *Tedeschi v Denkavit* (Case 5/77) [1977] ECR 1555, the ECJ stated:

JUDGMENT

'Where … directives provide for the harmonisation of the measures necessary to ensure the protection of animal and human health and establish [Union] procedures to check that they are observed, recourse to [Article 36] is no longer justified and the appropriate checks must be carried out and the measures of protection adopted within the framework outlined by the harmonising directive.'

The ECJ confirmed this ruling in two cases involving measures taken allegedly in the interests of animal health: *Hedley Lomas (Ireland) Ltd* (Case C–5/94) [1996] ECR I–2553 (conditions in Spanish slaughterhouses) and *Compassion in World Farming Ltd* (Case C–1/96) [1998] ECR I–1251 (live animal exports in crates). In both cases the ECJ held that the measures could **not** be justified using Article 36 because harmonising Directives provided EU-wide protection.

KEY FACTS

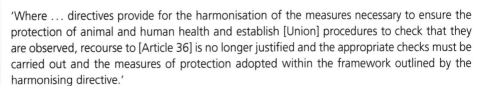

The Art 36 derogations	
Measures that restrict imports or exports can be justified on six grounds in the TFEU itself:	Art 36 TFEU
1. Public morality.	*Henn and Darby* (1979)
2. Public policy.	*R v Thompson* (1979); *Ahokainen and Leppik* (2006)
3. Public security.	*Campus Oil* (1984)
4. Protection of health and life of humans, animals or plants. Human health protection is the most important ground. Member States are allowed to adopt a precautionary principle, where there is scientific uncertainty. There must be a 'real risk' to human health based on the latest scientific data, and not 'purely hypothetical considerations'.	*Toolex Alpha* (2000) *Sandoz* (1983) *Greenham and Abel* (2004)
5. Protection of national treasures.	
6. Protection of industrial or commercial property. The list of grounds in Art 36 is closed and may not be added to. There must be no 'arbitrary discrimination' against imports. The grounds in Art 36 must not be used as a 'disguised restriction on trade'. Where harmonising directives exist, e.g. on animal health standards, Art 36 is not available.	*Belgium v Spain* (Rioja wine) (2000) *Commission v Ireland* (Souvenir Jewellery) (1981); *Leclerc* (1985) *Conegate* (1986) *Commission v UK* (French Turkeys) (1982) *Tedeschi v Denkavit* (1977); *Hedley Lomas* (1996); *Compassion in World Farming* (1998)

14.6 The effects of the *Cassis de Dijon* principle

14.6.1 Introduction

By 1979, Article 36 was already 22 years old and, never having been updated, was 'stuck' in 1957. By the late 1970s several Member States (in particular Germany and the UK) had enacted quite sophisticated consumer protection legislation. This legislation was quite capable of restricting the free movement of goods (especially given the wide scope awarded to Article 34 by *Dassonville* (1974)) but was incapable of being justified under Article 36 unless it could be brought under the 'protection of human health' heading. As only the Member States' governments had the power to amend the EC Treaty (and even then they must be unanimous) the wait for Article 36 to be updated was likely to be a very long wait indeed. In 1979, therefore, in *Cassis de Dijon* (Case 120/78) [1979] 649, the ECJ took decisive action. As the ECJ had no power to amend Article 36, it created a parallel set of derogations that Member States could plead as an alternative to Article 36. This is sometimes referred to as the 'rule of reason'.

CASE EXAMPLE

Cassis de Dijon (Case 120/78) [1979] ECR 649

German legislation laid down a minimum alcohol level of 25 per cent per litre for certain spirits, including cassis. Rewe-Zentral, a German company, applied to the Federal Monopoly Administration for Spirits for permission to import '*Cassis de Dijon*', a French blackcurrant liqueur about 15–20 per cent proof. Rewe was informed that the French cassis was of insufficient alcoholic strength. Rewe argued that this German law contravened Article 34. The German government argued that the legislation had been enacted in the interests of public health (by keeping alcohol levels high they were preventing an overall increase in alcohol consumption which would follow if the alcoholic content in drinks was lower) and to ensure fairness in commercial transactions (by denying the weaker, and so cheaper, French cassis an advantage over German cassis). The ECJ laid down the 'rule of reason', thereby establishing that national legislation could be justified on such grounds as consumer protection. However, the Court went on to hold that the German rules were not necessary to achieve these ends. Other means, less of a hindrance to trade, such as clear labelling, would have been sufficient.

The ECJ held:

JUDGMENT

'Obstacles to movement within the Union resulting from disparities between the national laws relating to the marketing of the products in question must be accepted in so far as these provisions may be recognised as being necessary in order to satisfy mandatory requirements relating in particular to the effectiveness of fiscal supervision, the protection of public health, the fairness of commercial transactions and the defence of the consumer.'

'Rule of reason': key points

▪ In *Cassis de Dijon* (1979), the ECJ described the derogations that Member States can plead as 'mandatory requirements'. It has used other, synonymous, expressions too, such as 'objectives of general interest' (*ADBHU* (Case 240/83) [1985] ECR 531). More recently, the ECJ has tended to describe the derogations as 'overriding interests' or 'overriding requirements' (*Familiapress* (Case C–368/95) [1997] ECR I–3689) or 'overriding reason in the general interest' (*Decker* (Case C–120/95) [1998] ECR I–1831).

- In *Cassis de Dijon* (1979), the ECJ gave four examples of 'mandatory requirements' but prefaced its list with the words 'in particular' – thus, there is no limit to the number of mandatory requirements that can be created. This contrasts with Article 36, which is a closed list.

- In subsequent case law the ECJ has added to the list, which now includes the improvement of working conditions (1981), the protection of culture (1985), the protection of the environment (1985), the diversity of the Press (1997), the maintenance of social security systems (1998), road safety (2000), the protection of 'fundamental freedoms' such as the freedom of expression (2003), the protection of children (2008) and the 'fight against crime' (2008).

14.6.2 The 'mandatory requirements'

The protection of public health (1979)

Although generally dealt with under Article 36, in one case at least, public health was dealt with under *Cassis de Dijon* (1979) principles (*Gilli and Andres* (1981)).

The fairness of commercial transactions (1979)

This was successfully argued in *Oosthoek's* (Case 286/81) [1982] ECR 4575. The Dutch government argued that legislation prohibiting the offering of free gifts as a means of sales promotion was justifiable on grounds of fair trading (and consumer protection). The ECJ agreed. The ECJ held that it was 'undeniable' that offering free gifts 'may mislead customers as to the real prices of certain products and distort the conditions on which genuine competition is based'. In *IDG* (Case 6/81) [1982] ECR 707, the ECJ agreed that Dutch legislation prohibiting the marketing of identical products (known as 'passing off' in English law) was justifiable on grounds of fair trading.

Fair trading was claimed, but rejected, in another 'passing off' case, that of *Prantl* (Case 16/83) [1984] ECR 1299.

CASE EXAMPLE

Prantl (Case 16/83) [1984] ECR 1299

Karl Prantl was prosecuted for importing Italian wine in bottles very similar in shape and design to traditional German bottles, *Bocksbeutele*, protected under German legislation as having a characteristic 'bulbous' shape that designated a particular quality wine. The ECJ acknowledged that the legislation did serve to protect consumers and protect German wine producers from passing off. However, the ECJ went on to conclude that because bulbous wine bottles had been traditionally manufactured in Italy for over a century, 'in accordance with a fair and traditional practice' meant there was no justification for excluding them from Germany.

The Court stated:

JUDGMENT

'National case-law prohibiting the precise imitation of someone else's product which is likely to cause confusion may indeed protect consumers and promote fair trading; these are general interests which ... may justify the existence of obstacles to movement within the Union resulting from disparities between national laws relating to the marketing of products.'

The defence of the consumer (1979)

The defence has been successfully raised in some cases, such as *Robertson and Others* (Case 220/81) [1983] ECR 2349, concerning Belgian legislation requiring the hallmarking of silver-plated goods. Another example of the defence being successfully raised is *A-Punkt Schmuckhandels v Schmidt* (Case C–441/04) [2006] ECR I–2093. The case involved an alleged breach by Claudia Schmidt, a jeweller, of the Austrian Trade and Commercial Regulations 1994, which prohibited the sale of silver jewellery to customers in their own homes. Although the Court held that the 1994 Regulations probably amounted to a 'selling arrangement', in which case Article 34 did not apply (see section 14.8), the ECJ also considered the possibility that the Regulations breached Article 34 and, if so, whether they could be justified using the consumer protection mandatory requirement. On that point, the Court stated:

JUDGMENT

'Consumer protection may constitute a justification for the prohibition at issue [taking into account] the specific features associated with the sale of silver jewellery in private homes, in particular the potentially higher risk of the consumer being cheated due to a lack of information, the impossibility of comparing prices or the provision of insufficient safeguards as regards the authenticity of that jewellery and the greater psychological pressure to buy where the sale is organised in a private setting.'

However, the defence has, in the majority of cases, proven to be unsuccessful. It is clear that the ECJ attributes a fair amount of intelligence and sophistication to consumers. Indeed, in *Estée Lauder v Lancaster* (2000) the ECJ held: 'It is necessary to take into account the presumed expectations of an average consumer who is reasonably well informed and reasonably observant and circumspect.'

In *Clinique Laboratories* (1994) and *Mars* (1995) the ECJ rejected the 'consumer protection' defence, which had been advanced by the German government in order to restrict the marketing of French goods (cosmetics and ice-cream bars, respectively). In *Mars*, the German authorities had objected to the sale of ice-cream bars bearing a '+10%' logo which covered substantially more than 10 per cent of the surface area of the wrapping. The ECJ stated:

JUDGMENT

'It is contended that the measure in question is justified because a not insignificant number of consumers will be induced into believing ... that the increase is larger than that represented. Such a justification cannot be accepted. Reasonably circumspect consumers are supposed to know that there is not necessarily a link between the size of publicity markings relating to an increase in a product's quantity and the size of that increase.'

A consumer protection defence was also rejected in *Clinique Laboratories* (1994):

CASE EXAMPLE

Clinique Laboratories (Case C–315/92) [1994] ECR I–317

German legislation – the Law on Foodstuffs and Consumer Items (1974) – prohibited the sale of cosmetics under misleading names, designations or presentations by which certain properties could be ascribed to products that they did not in fact have. German authorities regarded the name *'Clinique'*, a brand of cosmetics produced in France by Estée Lauder, as one such misleading name – it could mislead consumers into thinking that the product had medicinal qualities, as it evoked associations with the word 'clinic'. The consequence of this was that Estée Lauder had to repackage its product for the German market (it was renamed *'Linique'*) and advertise it differently from everywhere else, obviously increasing its costs greatly. The German authorities were challenged, alleging a breach of Article 34. The German authorities responded that the law was justifiable on public health and/or consumer protection grounds. The ECJ held that: (1) the German legislation *prima facie* infringed Article 34, because it required the manufacturers to incur expense in repackaging and re-advertising the product for different markets and (2) as far as consumer protection was concerned, the German rules were not necessary to achieve their objective. First, *Clinique* products were sold everywhere else under that name without causing confusion; second, *Clinique* products were sold in Germany (albeit as 'Linique') exclusively in perfumeries and the cosmetics departments of large stores – never in pharmacies. There was therefore no consumer risk to be protected against.

Often the defence will be rejected because the contested national legislation went beyond what was 'necessary' to protect consumers. Thus, in *Walter Rau v De Smedt* (1982), the ECJ held that the Belgian legislation requiring margarine to be packed in cubes was prohibited by Article 34, despite alleged consumer protection reasons, because Belgian consumers could have been adequately protected by less drastic means, e.g. clear labelling.

CASE EXAMPLE

Walter Rau v De Smedt (Case 261/81) [1982] ECR 3961

Belgian legislation required margarine to be sold only in cubes. This was ostensibly designed to help consumers distinguish between butter (not sold in cubes) and margarine. The case reached the ECJ after the German margarine producer, Walter Rau, was unable to deliver 30 tonnes of its margarine to the Belgian supermarket chain De Smedt. The supermarket refused delivery because the margarine was packaged in a 'truncated cone' shape, not a cube. When Walter Rau took De Smedt to court, seeking specific performance of the contract of sale, the ECJ held that this legislation was capable of hindering trade and went beyond what was necessary to achieve its alleged consumer protection objective – clear labelling would have achieved the same objective but would have imposed less of an obstacle to trade.

In *Alfa Vita Vassilopoulos* (Cases C–158 and 159/04) [2006] ECR I–8135, the ECJ emphasised that the mandatory requirement involved protection of the consumer, not the promotion of quality. The Court therefore held that the defence was unavailable to justify a provision in Greek law designed to help customers distinguish between fresh bread and 'bake-off' bread – meaning, bread which had previously been frozen – the former, apparently, being superior quality to the latter. The Court stated:

JUDGMENT

'A national measure which restricts the free movement of goods may not be justified solely on the ground that it aims to promote quality foodstuffs ... such an objective may be taken into account only in relation to other requirements which have been recognised as being imperative, such as consumer or health protection.'

The improvement of working conditions (1981)

The improvement of working conditions was added as a mandatory requirement in 1981 in *Oebel* (Case 155/80) [1981] ECR 1993, concerning German rules preventing bakeries from operating before 4 a.m. Although this was capable of restricting trade (in that it prevented German bakeries from producing bread early enough for export to pre-breakfast markets just over the border in the neighbouring states of Luxembourg and Belgium), the ECJ held that the restriction was justified. The Court stated: 'It cannot be disputed that the prohibition in the bread and confectionery industry on working before 4 am in itself constitutes a legitimate element of economic and social policy, consistent with the objectives of public interest pursued by the Treaty.'

The protection of the environment (1985)

The European Commission first mentioned this in a Practice Note in 1980. The Commission, ostensibly summarising the list of 'mandatory requirements' at that date, listed 'public health, protection of consumers or the environment, the fairness of commercial transactions, etc.'. However, environmental protection was only recognised as a mandatory requirement by the ECJ in 1985 in *ADBHU* (Case 240/83) [1985] ECR 531, involving French legislation restricting the movement of waste oil. The ECJ stated:

> Insofar as such measures ... have a restrictive effect on the freedom of trade ... they must nevertheless neither be discriminatory nor go beyond the inevitable restrictions which are justified by the pursuit of the objective of environmental protection, which is in the general interest.

The best-known case is *Commission v Denmark (the Danish Bottles case)* (Case 302/86) [1988] ECR 4607, where the ECJ stated:

JUDGMENT

'The protection of the environment is one of the Union's essential objectives, which may justify certain limitations of the principle of the free movement of goods ... it must therefore be stated that the protection of the environment is a mandatory requirement which may limit the application of [Article 34].'

CASE EXAMPLE

Danish Bottles (Case 302/86) [1988] ECR 4607

Danish legislation required that all beer and soft drinks sold in Denmark had to be packaged in re-usable containers, and that distributors of such products should establish deposit-and-return schemes and recycle the containers in order to protect the environment and conserve resources. The European Commission alleged a breach of Article 34. The ECJ agreed, holding: (1) the Danish rules were *prima facie* prohibited by Article 34, as they would restrict imports of non-recyclable bottles produced in other EU Member States; (2) environmental protection was recognised as a mandatory requirement. The deposit-and-return schemes, and the re-use requirements were, theoretically, legitimate under EU law. (3) However, the rules had not been shown to be strictly necessary to achieve their objective and therefore infringed the 'pro-portionality' doctrine (see below).

Environmental protection was also accepted as a defence in *Commission v Belgium (Walloon Waste)* (Case C–2/90) [1992] ECR I–4431, involving Belgian legislation restricting the importation of waste (for recycling purposes) and *Aher-waggon* (Case C–389/96) [1998] ECR I–4473, involving German legislation imposing strict noise levels on aircraft engines. The ECJ rejected an environmental protection defence in *Dusseldorp* (Case C–203/96) [1998] ECR I–4075, involving Dutch legislation restricting the exportation of waste oil filters, but only because the legislation was 'primarily' economic in nature.

Two more cases in which environmental protection was accepted as a defence, at least in principle, are *Commission v Germany (Waste Packaging)* (Case C–463/01) [2004] ECR I–11705 and *Radlberger & Spitz* (Case C–309/02) [2004] ECR I–11763. Both cases involved German legislation providing for a compulsory deposit-and-return scheme for waste packaging, which meant that manufacturers were obliged to charge a deposit for, and accept the return of, waste packaging. Although the Court accepted that the German rules were capable of hindering trade, they were justifiable. The Court stated:

JUDGMENT

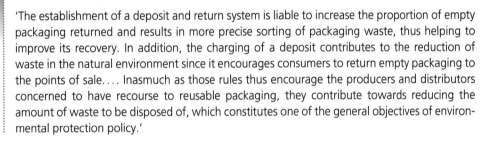

'The establishment of a deposit and return system is liable to increase the proportion of empty packaging returned and results in more precise sorting of packaging waste, thus helping to improve its recovery. In addition, the charging of a deposit contributes to the reduction of waste in the natural environment since it encourages consumers to return empty packaging to the points of sale. . . . Inasmuch as those rules thus encourage the producers and distributors concerned to have recourse to reusable packaging, they contribute towards reducing the amount of waste to be disposed of, which constitutes one of the general objectives of environmental protection policy.'

In *Mickelsson & Roos* (Case C–142/05) [2009] ECR I–4273, Swedish legislation prohibiting the use of 'personal watercraft' – jet-skis – except on water designated as a 'general navigable waterway' was held to breach Article 34. However, it was justifiable on environmental protection grounds. The Court held:

JUDGMENT

'A restriction or a prohibition on the use of personal watercraft are appropriate means for the purpose of ensuring that the environment is protected. . . . Member States cannot be denied the possibility of attaining an objective such as the protection of the environment by the introduction of general rules which are necessary on account of the particular geographical circumstances of the Member State concerned.'

In *Ålands Vindkraft* (Case C–573/12) [2015] 1 CMLR 10 and *Essent Belgium* (Case C–492/14) [2017] 1 CMLR 39, the Court examined whether national legislation encouraging the use of renewable energy was capable of justification under *Cassis de Dijon* in the event that the legislation was found to impose an obstacle to free trade. In both cases the answer was 'yes', at least in principle; although only the legislation in the former case passed the proportionality test and was held to be justified.

CASE EXAMPLE

Ålands Vindkraft (Case C–573/12) [2015] 1 CMLR 10

Swedish legislation encouraged the production of energy from wind farms by issuing 'electricity certificates', which could then be sold on to electricity suppliers and certain end users – but only if the wind farms were located in Swedish territory. This was challenged by a company that wished to import into Sweden electricity produced on a Finnish wind farm. The company argued that the Swedish legislation was an MEQR in that it hindered the importation into Sweden of electricity produced in other Member States. The ECJ agreed but went on to hold that the Swedish legislation was justifiable on environmental protection grounds, as it encouraged the production of renewable energy and contributed to the reduction in greenhouse gas emissions. The increase in the use of renewable energy sources constituted one of the important components of the package of measures needed to comply with the Kyoto Protocol to the UN Framework Convention on Climate Change, along with other EU and international greenhouse gas emission reduction commitments.

The protection of culture (1985)

This was added to the list in 1985 by *Cinéthèque* (Cases 60 and 61/84) [1985] ECR 2065, concerning French legislation temporarily restricting the availability of films on video, in order to encourage cinema attendance instead. The ECJ held that this policy was justifiable. (It is perhaps not insignificant that this case was heard at a time when cinema attendances were declining across Europe, largely because of the introduction of home video recorders in the early 1980s.)

CASE EXAMPLE

Cinéthèque (Cases 60 and 61/84) [1985] ECR 2065

French legislation prohibited the sale or rental of films on video until 12 months had elapsed since that film's debut at the cinema. This was challenged by the French video retail chain, Cinéthèque, and the case was referred to the ECJ. There it was acknowledged that this rule was capable of restricting trade (other Member States allowing films to be released on video much more quickly than that) but it was justified because it encouraged cinema attendance. The ECJ stated:

> It must be conceded that a national system which, in order to encourage the creation of cinematographic works irrespective of their origin, gives priority, for a limited initial period, to the distribution of such works through the cinema, is so justified.

In *Torfaen Borough Council v B&Q plc* (Case 145/88) [1989] ECR 3851, which concerned the legality of British Sunday trading legislation, the ECJ first coined the phrase 'sociocultural characteristics' to describe this mandatory requirement. The ECJ held that the prohibition on Sunday trading, although capable of hindering trade, was justifiable.

The protection of books as 'cultural objects' was recognised as an overriding interest in *Fachverband der Buch- und Medienwirtschaft* (Case C–531/07) [2009] ECR I–3717. Austrian legislation stipulated a minimum selling price for books. When challenged to justify this legislation, the Austrian government argued that, in the absence of a pricing system, there would be a drop in prices, which would cause a drop in profits, as a result of which it would become impossible to finance the production and marketing of more demanding but economically less attractive works. Moreover, small booksellers which normally offer a wider choice of specialist books would be driven out of the market by larger booksellers which sell primarily more commercial books. The ECJ accepted that books were 'cultural objects' deserving of protection, although the actual legislation was deemed to go beyond what was necessary to achieve that objective (in other words, it failed the proportionality test).

The diversity of the press (1997)

This was added to the list in 1997 by *Familiapress* (1997), concerning a prohibition in Austrian legislation on newspapers offering cash prizes to competition winners. The ECJ decided that the Austrian legislation was justifiable in the interest of helping smaller publishers to survive against fierce competition from larger publishers (who had the potential to offer bigger prizes), thereby promoting a diverse newspaper industry. The ECJ stated: 'Maintenance of press diversity may constitute an overriding requirement justifying a restriction on free movement of goods. Such diversity helps to safeguard freedom of expression.'

The maintenance of social security systems (1998)

This was added to the list in 1998, in *Decker* (Case C–120/95) [1998] ECR I–1831. D, a Luxembourg national, used a prescription obtained in Luxembourg to purchase a pair of spectacles from an optician in Belgium. When he tried to reclaim the cost from the Luxembourg social security authorities, this was refused as he had not sought prior authorisation. This rule only applied where spectacles were obtained abroad. D argued that this was contrary to Article 34. The ECJ held that the Luxembourg rules were *prima facie* in breach of Article 34, because they encouraged Luxembourg nationals to purchase or have their spectacles assembled in Luxembourg rather than another Member State, such as Belgium. However, the rules were justifiable under *Cassis de Dijon* (1979) principles. The Court stated that, 'the risk of seriously undermining the financial balance of the social security system may constitute an overriding reason in the general interest'.

Road safety (2000)

In *Snellers Autos* (Case C–314/98) [2000] ECR I–8633, the ECJ confirmed that road safety could be added to the list of mandatory requirements. This was confirmed in *Commission v Finland* (Case C–54/05) [2007] ECR I–2473, involving Finnish legislation under which a 'transfer licence' was required before cars registered in other Member States could be imported into Finland. The licence was not automatic but was regarded in practice as a formality. The European Commission alleged a breach of Article 34, and in response the Finnish government argued that the licensing requirement was justified on the grounds of promoting road safety (licences could be refused to cars not deemed to be road-worthy). The ECJ agreed (in principle, at least), stating:: 'It is not in dispute that road safety does constitute an overriding reason in the public interest capable of justifying a hindrance to the free movement of goods.'

In *Commission v Italy (Motorcycle Trailers)* (Case C–110/05) [2009] ECR I–519, involving Italian legislation prohibiting mopeds and motorcycles from towing trailers, the ECJ held that the legislation was capable of hindering trade in such trailers but was justified on grounds of road safety. The Court stated:

JUDGMENT

'In the field of road safety a Member State may determine the degree of protection which it wishes to apply in regard to such safety and the way in which that degree of protection is to be achieved ... Member States cannot be denied the possibility of attaining an objective such as road safety by the introduction of general and simple rules which will be easily understood and applied by drivers and easily managed and supervised by the competent authorities.'

In *Commission v Poland (Right-hand Drive Cars)* (Case C–639/11) [2014] 3 CMLR 26, the Court had to decide whether Polish legislation requiring drivers of imported right-hand drive cars to convert their cars to left-hand drive was compatible with EU Law on the free movement of goods.

CASE EXAMPLE

Commission v Poland (Right-hand Drive Cars) (Case C–639/11) [2014] 3 CMLR 26

Polish legislation required right-hand drive motor vehicles imported from other Member States (typically the UK and Ireland) to have their steering system transferred to the left-hand side. The Commission alleged a breach of Article 34 TFEU. The Polish government argued that the legislation was necessary because drivers would have a reduced 'field of vision' if driving a right-hand drive car on the right-hand side of the road. This in turn would make overtaking 'considerably more difficult, in particular on single-carriageway roads with two-way traffic' and would increase the risk of accidents. The Court held that the Polish legislation was a barrier to trade in such vehicles but was justifiable – in principle – on road safety grounds. However, the legislation failed the proportionality test (i.e. it was unnecessary), for several reasons. First, tourists visiting Poland and driving right-hand drive cars were permitted to do so (which suggested that Poland was prepared to tolerate that risk); second, the majority of Member States either explicitly allowed or at least tolerated the use of cars with steering systems on the same side as the direction of traffic; third, statistical data did not demonstrate a link between the use of right-hand drive cars and the number of road traffic accidents in Poland.

The protection of fundamental rights (2003)

In *Schmidberger v Austria* (Case C–112/00) [2003] ECR I–5659, the ECJ stated that the protection of fundamental rights 'is a legitimate interest which, in principle, justifies a restriction of … the free movement of goods'. The case involved a decision made by the Austrian authorities to allow a road to be closed for the purposes of a demonstration. The Court acknowledged that the authorities had been placed in a difficult position, having to balance the right of transport companies to enjoy the free movement of goods under Articles 34 and 35, on one hand, against the rights of the demonstrators to enjoy the freedoms of expression and assembly, under Articles 10 and 11 of the European Convention on Human Rights, on the other. The ECJ held that no breach of EU law had occurred.

CASE EXAMPLE

Schmidberger v Austria (Case C–112/00) [2003] ECR I–5659

The Austrian authorities had permitted an environmental group, Transitforum Austria Tirol, to stage a demonstration designed to raise awareness of traffic pollution. The effect of the demonstration was to block the Brenner motorway in Austria to all traffic for 30 hours and to heavy goods vehicles for even longer. Schmidberger, a German road haulage firm, alleged that this decision constituted a breach of Article 34. The ECJ agreed that this decision had the effect of imposing obstacles (however temporary) to the free movement of goods between Germany, Austria and Italy. However, the ECJ decided that the Austrian authorities were justified by considerations linked to respect of the 'fundamental rights' of the demonstrators to freedom of expression and freedom of assembly, both of which are protected by the European Convention on Human Rights.

The Court stated:

JUDGMENT

'The interests involved must be weighed having regard to all the circumstances of the case in order to determine whether a fair balance was struck between those interests … the competent authorities enjoy a wide margin of discretion in that regard. … Taking account of the Member States' wide margin of discretion, in circumstances such as those of the present case the competent national authorities were entitled to consider that an outright ban on the demonstration would have constituted unacceptable interference with the fundamental rights of the demonstrators to gather and express peacefully their opinion in public.'

Protection of Children (2008)

The case of *Dynamic Medien v Avides Media* (Case C–244/06) [2008] ECR I–505, involved a system under German law of compulsory classification and labelling of DVDs and videos in terms of their suitability for viewing by children. The Court accepted that, although capable of hindering trade, the German rules were justifiable. However, it is not entirely clear whether the Court dealt with the justification as an example of public policy under Article 36, or as a new mandatory requirement. At one point, the Court observed that the European Commission, along with the British, German and Irish governments, all agreed that 'the rules at issue … are justified in so far as they are designed to protect young people. That objective is linked in particular to public morality and public policy, which are grounds of justification recognised in [Article 36].' However, the Court then went on to state that 'the protection of the child is a legitimate interest which, in principle, justifies a restriction on a fundamental freedom guaranteed by the EC Treaty, such as the free movement of goods', which seems to suggest a new mandatory requirement.

Whichever is the true position, the Court accepted that the German rules ensured 'that young people are able to develop their sense of personal responsibility and their sociability. Furthermore, the protection of young people is an objective which is closely related to ensuring respect for human dignity'. The Court accepted that the German rules were 'designed to protect children against information and materials injurious to their well-being' and that, in such a case, in view of the divergence of 'moral or cultural views, Member States must be recognised as having a definite margin of discretion'.

CASE EXAMPLE

Dynamic Medien v Avides Media (2008)

German legislation prohibited the sale in Germany of videos and DVDs via mail order unless they had been examined for their suitability for viewing by young persons – such examination being undertaken by the authorities in Germany itself – and labelled accordingly. Avides Media, a German mail-order company, had imported into Germany from the UK a number of DVDs and videos featuring Japanese 'Anime' cartoons. These had been classified by the British Board of Film Control (BBFC) as suitable for viewing only by those aged 15 years or older. A rival German company, Dynamic Medien, sought to stop Avides from marketing the DVDs and videos in Germany as they had not yet been classified by the authorities in Germany. Avides alleged that the German legislation was in breach of Article 34. The ECJ agreed that the rules were 'liable to make the importation of image storage media … more difficult and more expensive', with the result that they may dissuade importers. However, the German government successfully argued that the purpose of the legislation – 'protecting young persons' – was sufficient justification.

The 'fight against crime' (2008)

The 'fight against crime' was added to the list in *Commission v Portugal (Tinted Film for Car Windows)* (Case C–265/06) [2008] ECR I–2245. The Portuguese government accepted that legislation banning the affixing of tinted film to the windows of cars and other vehicles was capable of hindering trade but argued that it was justified on grounds of public safety and/or road safety. The ban was:

> intended to enable the competent authorities to make a rapid external inspection of the interior of motor vehicles without the need to immobilise them, first, in order to ensure that the vehicle's occupants are wearing seat belts and, second, to identify potential criminals for the purpose of combating crime.

The ECJ accepted these arguments, at least in principle, stating: 'The fight against crime and ensuring road safety may constitute overriding reasons in the public interest capable of justifying a hindrance to the free movement of goods.'

14.6.3 Application to 'indistinctly applicable' measures only?

The traditional position of the ECJ has been that the 'mandatory requirements' are only available when national legislation is 'indistinctly applicable'. In *Gilli and Andres* (1981), for example, the ECJ stated:

JUDGMENT

'It is only where national rules, which apply without discrimination to both domestic and imported products, may be justified as being necessary in order to satisfy imperative requirements relating in particular to the protection of public health, the fairness of commercial transactions and the defence of the consumer that they may constitute an exception to the requirements arising under [Article 34].'

The ECJ confirmed this in *Commission v Ireland (Souvenir Jewellery)* (1981), rejecting a consumer protection defence on the basis that the contested Irish legislation only applied to imported jewellery.

CASE EXAMPLE

Souvenir Jewellery (Case 113/80) [1981] ECR 1625

Irish legislation, the Merchandise Marks (Restriction on Sale of Imported Jewellery) Order (1971), required imported jewellery which depicted motifs or possessed characteristics which suggested that they were souvenirs of Ireland – such as wolfhounds, shamrocks etc. – to bear an indication of their place of origin or the word 'foreign'. The ECJ held that the Irish legislation constituted an unjustifiable infringement of Article 34. Although intended to protect consumers, the legislation was distinctly applicable and therefore the *Cassis de Dijon* (1979) principle was unavailable.

This means that *Cassis de Dijon* (1979) should, logically, never be available in Article 35 cases, because the ECJ has held that national legislation only breaches Article 35 if it is 'distinctly applicable' (*Bouhelier* (Case 53/76) [1977] ECR 197 or if it has as its 'specific object or effect the restriction of patterns of exports' (*PB Groenveld* (Case 15/79) [1979]

ECR 3409, discussed below)). However, in two of the cases discussed above the ECJ accepted that *Cassis de Dijon* may apply in the context of Article 35 (*Oebel* (1981) and *Dusseldorp* (1998)).

This area of doubt has now been clarified by the ECJ. *Gysbrechts & Santurel Inter* (Case C–205/07) [2008] ECR I–9947 involved Belgian legislation under which it was illegal for Belgian retailers to require any payment from consumers within the seven-day 'cooling off' period allowed for distance-selling contracts. The ECJ accepted that the Belgian legislation had the effect of potentially restricting exports, as it deprived Belgian firms of an effective form of protection against defaulting consumers based in other Member States (given the difficulty of bringing legal proceedings in other jurisdictions). However, the Belgian legislation was held to be justifiable on consumer protection grounds, under *Cassis de Dijon* principles.

The Court stated:

JUDGMENT

'A national measure contrary to [Article 35] may be justified on one of the grounds stated in [Article 36], and by overriding requirements of public interest, provided that the measure is proportionate to the legitimate objective pursued.'

KEY FACTS

The *Cassis-de-Dijon* principles	
The ECJ introduced a parallel set of derogations in 1979. This is a far more flexible, open list of derogations – 'mandatory requirements'– to operate alongside Art 36.	*Cassis de Dijon* (1979)

The open list includes:
   i. the fairness of commercial transactions;
   ii. consumer protection;
 	
   iii. environmental protection;
 	
   iv. cultural protection;
 	
   v. road safety;
 	
   vi. the protection of 'fundamental rights';
   vii. the protection of children;
   viii. the fight against crime.
	Oosthoek's (1982); *Prantl* (1984)
	Walter Rau (1982); *Mars* (1994); *Clinique* (1994)
	Commission v Denmark (Danish Bottles) (1988); *Radlberger & Spitz* (2004); *Mickelsson and Roos* (2009)
	Cinéthèque (1985); *Fachverband* (2009)
	Snellers Autos (2000); *Commission v Finland* (2007); *Commission v Italy* (Motorcycle Trailers) (2009)
	Schmidberger v Austria (2003)
	Dynamic Medien (2008)
	Commission v Portugal (Tinted film) (2008)

It only applies to 'indistinctly applicable' measures, that is, national measures which apply without distinction to imports **and** domestic goods.	*Gilli & Andres* (1981); *Commission v Ireland* (Souvenir Jewellery) (1981)
Except, apparently, for distinctly applicable measures intended to protect the environment.	*Commission v Belgium* (Walloon Waste) (1992)
The mandatory requirements can be used in order to derogate from Art 35.	*Gysbrechts & Santurel Inter* (2008)

14.6 CASSIS DE DIJON

14.7 General rules concerning derogations: proportionality and mutual recognition

14.7.1 Proportionality

The ECJ has consistently held that the purpose of Article 36 is to allow certain national laws and rules to derogate from the free movement provisions only to the extent to which they are 'justified' in order to achieve the objectives in the Article. A measure may be justified provided it does what is **necessary** to achieve the objectives in the first sentence of Article 36, and further that it does **no more than necessary**. If there are other methods capable of achieving that objective which are less restrictive of intra-community trade, then they should be used instead. In *De Peijper* (Case 104/75) [1976] ECR 613, for example, the ECJ said:

JUDGMENT

'National rules or practices which do restrict imports ... or are capable of doing so are only compatible with the Treaty to the extent to which they are *necessary*.... National rules or practices do not fall within the exemptions specified in [Article 36] if [their objectives] can as effectively be protected by measures which do not restrict intra-Union trade so much.'

Many of the cases where Article 36 is invoked involve national measures introduced to protect against alleged risks to human health. Often, where a particular ingredient or additive has been restricted or prohibited altogether, the ECJ will pose the (rhetorical) question whether human health could still be protected by the simple expedient of requiring manufacturers of products to label the ingredients in their products clearly. Thus, in *Commission v France* (Case C–24/00) [2004] ECR I–1277, for example, the ECJ stated:

JUDGMENT

'It is naturally legitimate ... to seek to ensure that consumers are properly informed about the products which they consume. However, appropriate labelling, informing consumers about the nature, the ingredients and the characteristics of fortified foodstuffs, can enable consumers who risk excessive consumption of a nutrient added to those products to decide for themselves whether to use them.'

The same principles apply to attempts by Member States to justify legislation under *Cassis de Dijon* (1979) principles. The best example is perhaps *Walter Rau v De Smedt* (1982), discussed above, where the ECJ stated: 'if a Member State has a choice between various measures to attain the same objective it should choose the means which least restricts the free movement of goods'.

In *Commission v France* (2004), the ECJ summarised the proportionality principle as follows:

JUDGMENT

'The Member States must comply with the principle of proportionality. The means which they choose must therefore be confined to what is actually necessary to ensure the safeguarding of public health or to satisfy overriding requirements regarding, for example, consumer protection, and they must be proportional to the objective thus pursued, which could not have been attained by measures less restrictive of intra-Union trade.'

14.7.2 Mutual recognition

As well as creating the 'mandatory requirements' in *Cassis de Dijon* (1979), the ECJ went on to establish a presumption that, once goods have been 'lawfully produced and marketed in one of the Member States', they may be imported into any other state. This has become known as the 'mutual recognition' principle. The presumption may only be rebutted by evidence that the goods in question pose a threat to one of the heads or Article 36 or one of the 'mandatory requirements'. The net result is to place the burden of proof on the authorities of the Member States seeking to justify their domestic legislation. The best way to rebut the presumption is to identify specific national characteristics (usually involving dietary habits) which would justify different national legislative provisions. In *Muller* (1986), dealing with E475, a baking ingredient allowed in Germany but not in France, the ECJ stated:

JUDGMENT

'As far as ... E475 is concerned, there are serious doubts that it is harmless *in view of the specific eating habits of the French population*. It is clear from a recent survey carried out in France that there is a risk that the daily acceptable intake ... will be exceeded in France, particularly in children, *who are major consumers of pastry products....* In the present state of scientific research there is uncertainty as to the critical thresholds of harmfulness since such thresholds vary according to the quantities of additives absorbed with all the food eaten and *thus depend to a large extent on eating habits in the various Member States.*'

Similar principles are seen in these cases:

- *Bellon* (Case C–42/90) [1990] ECR I–4863: French legislation banned certain Italian pastries because they contained sorbic acid. The ECJ held that the legislation was justifiable on health grounds, but only after taking national dietary habits into account.

- *Aher-Waggon* (1998): German legislation set aircraft noise emission levels, which were more restrictive than in other states. The ECJ stated that these rules were justified because Germany 'is a very densely populated State' and therefore 'attaches special importance to ensuring that its population is protected from excessive noise emissions'.

- *Greenham and Abel* (2004): dealing with French legislation that banned, *inter alia*, an ingredient in fruit drinks called coenzyme Q10, the ECJ held that the ban would be permissible on health grounds only if the French authorities could show '*in the light of national nutritional habits* and in the light of the results of international scientific research, that their rules are necessary'.

In practice, rebutting the presumption will not be easy to do. In *Mars* (1995) and *Clinique Laboratories* (1994), German consumer protection arguments were rejected. The ECJ held in each case that the German legislation was in breach of Article 34. As the goods concerned (ice creams and cosmetics, respectively) were lawfully manufactured and marketed in France, the mutual recognition principle applied, and the German government had failed to show why it needed stricter laws than France. In *Commission v Germany* (the *Beer Purity* case) (1987), concerning German legislation on the additives permitted in beer, the German government tried to argue that it needed stricter rules on beer purity than other Member States because German nationals tended to drink more beer than nationals of other Member States. However, although not disputing that assertion, the ECJ did not accept that it justified stringent rules which made it practically impossible for French-made beer (containing banned additives) to be sold in Germany. The Court stated:

JUDGMENT

'Some of the additives authorized in other Member States for use in the manufacture of beer are also authorized under the German rules, in particular the regulation on additives, for use in the manufacture of all, or virtually all, beverages. Mere reference to the potential risks of the ingestion of additives in general and to the fact that *beer is a foodstuff consumed in large quantities* does not suffice to justify the imposition of stricter rules in the case of beer.'

CASE EXAMPLE

Beer Purity (Case 178/84) [1987] ECR 1227

German law, specifically Articles 9 and 10 of the *Biersteuergesetz* of 1952 (itself dating back to the *Reinheitsgebot* of 1516), provided that the name 'Bier' could only be used for products brewed using malted barley, hops, yeast and water. The use of other ingredients, such as rice or maize, did not preclude the marketing of a product, but it could not be sold as 'Bier'. The Commission alleged that the *Biersteuergesetz* was in breach of Article 34. The German government argued that the *Biersteuergesetz* was necessary in order to protect consumers (*Cassis de Dijon* (1979)). The ECJ disagreed. While it was legitimate to seek to

> enable consumers who attribute specific qualities to beers manufactured from particular raw materials to make their choice in the light of that consideration ... that possibility may be ensured by means which do not prevent the importation of products which have been lawfully manufactured and marketed in other Member States.

The Court suggested that 'the compulsory affixing of suitable labels giving the nature of the product sold' would suffice instead. The German government had argued that, as beer is not necessarily supplied to consumers in bottles or cans capable of bearing the appropriate details, such a system of consumer information was inappropriate. However, this argument was unsuccessful. The *Biersteuergesetz* went on to impose an outright ban on the marketing of all beers containing additives. The rule related to all beers, including those produced in Germany. Here, the German government argued for the protection of human health (Article 36). However, the additives in question were used in beers lawfully produced in the exporting states, and hence the mutual recognition principle applied. Undaunted, the German government pointed out that the high beer consumption of German people justified the ban. The ECJ said that, in such cases, the work of bodies such as the World Health Organisation and the Food and Agriculture Organisation of the United Nations, international scientific research and the dietary habits of the importing state should be referred to. However, the ECJ pointed out that the *Biersteuergesetz* led to a blanket ban on all additives, and not just those for which there was concrete justification. This was excessive, particularly given that the same additives were used lawfully in the manufacture of most soft drinks in Germany itself. Consequently, although the drinking habits of German people might have justified a ban on some additives in beer, the law as it stood was disproportionate.

Proportionality and mutual recognition	
Where Art 36 or the *Cassis de Dijon* principles are used, the measures must be the least restrictive option available.	*De Peijper* (1976); *Walter Rau v De Smedt* (1982)
The mutual recognition principle is a presumption that goods lawfully produced and marketed in one Member State should be available for sale in all other states.	*Cassis de Dijon* (1979)
The mutual recognition principle can be rebutted, by reference to specific national characteristics, e.g. dietary habits.	*Muller* (1986); *Commission v Germany (Beer Purity)* (1987)

14.8 The divisions in *Keck and Mithouard*: 'Selling arrangements'

14.8.1 Introduction

It has been noted already that Article 34 was widely defined in *Dassonville* (1974). However, in 1993, the ECJ acknowledged that the *Dassonville* 'formula' was so wide that it was leading importers and retailers to challenge a whole range of national laws whose likely impact on the free movement of goods was, at most, marginal. In the landmark ruling in *Keck and Mithouard* (1993), the ECJ announced that there was a distinction to be drawn between:

- **Product requirements:** these are laws regulating the goods themselves, which are still governed by Article 34 and the *Dassonville* formula and are prohibited. Such rules are *prima facie* contrary to EU law and require justification, under either Article 36 or *Cassis de Dijon* (1979) principles.

- **Selling arrangements:** these are laws concerning not the goods themselves, but rather how, when and where they are marketed. These rules fall outside of the scope of Article 34 altogether and hence do not require justification. In *Keck*, the ECJ said that these rules were *prima facie* lawful, although they were subject to two pre-conditions.

Strictly speaking, the decision in *Keck* was not entirely unprecedented. In a handful of earlier cases, the ECJ had held that national rules governing 'selling arrangements' are exempt from Article 34. In the earliest cases, *Blesgen* (Case 75/81) [1982] ECR 1211, involving Belgian legislation prohibiting the public consumption of strong alcohol, the ECJ stated: 'Such a legislative measure has no connection with the importation of the products and for that reason is not of such a nature as to impede trade between Member States.' Then, in *Quietlynn v Southend BC* (Case C–23/89) [1990] ECR I–3059, which involved UK law regulating licences for sex shops, the ECJ again ruled that Article 34 did not apply.

The logical conclusion of these developments occurred in *Keck*, which involved French legislation preventing the resale of goods at a loss, when the ECJ made a decisive statement on the legality of 'selling arrangements'. The ECJ began by conceding that the French legislation might have an effect on inter-state trade. It considered that such legislation 'may, admittedly, restrict the volume of sales of products from other Member States, insofar as it deprives traders of a method of sales promotion'. However, the ECJ then observed that 'national legislation imposing a general prohibition on resale at a loss is not designed to regulate trade in goods between Member States'. The ECJ concluded that, 'in view of the increasing tendency of traders to seek to avoid non-protectionist national laws' by relying on Article 34, it was necessary to review its position. It went on:

JUDGMENT

'Contrary to what has previously been decided, the application to products ... of national provisions restricting or prohibiting certain selling arrangements is not such as to hinder, directly or indirectly, actually or potentially, trade between Member States within the meaning of the *Dassonville* judgment, so long as those provisions apply to all relevant traders operating within the national territory and so long as they affect in the same manner, in law and in fact, the marketing of domestic products and of those from other Member States. Where these conditions are fulfilled, the application of such rules to the sale of products from another Member State meeting the requirements laid down by that State is not by nature such as to prevent their access to the market or to impede access any more than it impedes the access of domestic products. Such rules therefore fall outside the scope of [Article 34].'

You will note that the Court overruled any previous conflicting judgments but failed to identify what they are! Since 1993, therefore, there has been considerable discussion about which cases were overruled by *Keck* and which were not.

CASE EXAMPLE

Keck and Mithouard (Case C–267/91) [1993] ECR I–6097

French legislation banned the resale of goods at a lower than the purchase price, a form of predatory pricing. Such laws are designed to stop powerful companies from abusing their position and distorting the market by undercutting smaller rivals. Two supermarket managers, Bernard Keck and Daniel Mithouard, were prosecuted under this legislation for reselling products (coffee and beer, respectively) at lower than their purchase price. The two men argued that the French law hindered trade, and they relied on Article 34. The ECJ introduced the concept of 'selling arrangements'. In the present case, the French rules were held to be 'selling arrangements' and therefore fell outside Article 34. The Court noted:

National legislation imposing a general prohibition on resale at a loss is not designed to regulate trade in goods between Member States. Such legislation may, admittedly, restrict the volume of sales, and hence the volume of sales of products from other Member States, in so far as it deprives traders of a method of sales promotion. But the question remains whether such a possibility is sufficient to characterise the legislation in question as a measure having equivalent effect to a quantitative restriction on imports.

14.8.2 Examples of selling arrangements

Sunday trading legislation

Prior to *Keck*, the ECJ's policy was that national legislation regulating the freedom of retailers to trade on Sunday infringed Article 34 because it had the potential to reduce intra-Community trade. One such example was the UK's Shops Act 1950 (subsequently amended by the Sunday Trading Act 1994). In *Torfaen BC v B&Q plc* (1989) (discussed above in the context of the *Cassis de Dijon* principle) and *Stoke-on-Trent CC v B&Q plc* (Case C–169/91) [1992] ECR I–6635 the ECJ held that Article 34 was infringed. However, after *Keck*, the ECJ held that Article 34 did not apply to such legislation at all. This new approach was set down in a series of cases concerning Italian Sunday trading legislation (*Punto Casa and PPV* (Cases C–69 and 258/93) [1994] ECR I–2355, and *Semeraro Casa Uno and Others* (Cases C–418 to 421/93) [1996] ECR I–2975). In *Pelckmans Turnhout* (Case C–483/12) [2014] 3 CMLR 49, involving Belgian legislation which required retailers to close for one day per week, the ECJ confirmed that such legislation was a 'selling arrangement' (following *Punto Casa and PPV* and *Semeraro Casa Uno and Others*).

Opening hours

In *Tankstation t'Heukske and J B E Boermans* (Cases C–401 and 402/92) [1994] ECR I–2199, concerning Dutch rules on the opening hours of petrol stations, the ECJ stated the rules laid down in *Keck* were satisfied. National licensing legislation (such as that in England and Wales, whereby the normal closing hours for public houses is 11 p.m.) would also come within this heading.

Sale of goods only through specific outlets

With the benefit of hindsight, the case of *Quietlynn* (1990) (discussed above) falls into this category. UK legislation allowing only licensed retailers to sell alcohol would be classified as a selling arrangement. Another example is *Commission v Greece (Processed Milk)* (Case C–391/92) [1995] ECR I–1621, where Greek legislation prohibited the sale of processed milk for infants except from pharmacies. The ECJ stated that the Greek rules concerned selling arrangements, and not goods themselves, and were therefore exempt from Article 34.

Restrictions on certain forms of sale promotions

In a pre-*Keck* case, *Oosthoek's* (Case 286/81) [1982] ECR 4575, the ECJ ruled that Dutch legislation prohibiting the offering of free gifts as a sales promotion strategy was prohibited by Article 34. Similarly, in *Buet and EBS* (Case 382/87) [1989] ECR 1235, the ECJ ruled that very similar French legislation prohibiting door-to-door canvassing of educational materials could hinder trade. However, it can now be argued that the Dutch and French laws in question were 'selling arrangements'.

For example, in *Burmanjer & Others* (Case C–20/03) [2005] ECR I–4133, three Dutch nationals were accused of breaching Belgian legislation prohibiting the sale of subscriptions to periodicals (such as magazines) on the street without prior authorisation. In their defence they argued that the Belgian law was contrary to Article 34. The ECJ, however, held that the legislation was a selling arrangement and therefore exempt from Article 34. This was because the legislation did not ban the product, or even the sale of it, it simply banned one method of sale.

Restrictions on advertising

In *GB-INNO-BM* (Case 362/88) [1990] ECR I–667, the ECJ was asked to rule on the compatibility of Article 34 with Luxembourg legislation preventing advertising campaigns that made reference to the pre-sale price of a product. The ECJ held that the legislation was prohibited by Article 34 because it was capable of hindering trade. Similarly, in *Aragonesa and Publivia* (1991), the ECJ held that national legislation prohibiting the advertising of alcohol over a certain strength in mass media, on streets and highways, in cinemas and on public transport fell within the *Dassonville* formula.

After *Keck*, it has become clear that national rules imposing partial restrictions on advertising, at least, are not caught by Article 34. In *Hünermund* (Case C–292/92) [1993] ECR I–6787, concerning German legislation preventing pharmacists from advertising on the radio, on TV or at the cinema, the ECJ stated that the conditions in *Keck* were satisfied and the German legislation was therefore exempt from Article 34. The ECJ reached the same conclusion in *Leclerc-Siplec* (Case C–412/93) [1995] ECR I–179, concerning French legislation prohibiting TV advertising by the distribution sector (which included petrol companies) and in *PRO Sieben Media* (Case C–6/98) [1999] ECR I–7599, concerning German legislation on the division of time between programmes and advertising on German television. As will be seen below, however, national rules imposing total prohibitions on advertising are not 'selling arrangements' and continue to be caught by Article 34.

CASE EXAMPLE

Leclerc-Siplec (Case C–412/93) [1995] ECR I–179

French legislation prohibited the advertising on TV of, or by, the following: alcohol over 1.2 per cent proof; literary publications; the cinema; the Press; the distribution sector. The idea was to get those sectors to advertise in regional newspapers instead, thereby protecting that particular industry. L-S, petrol distributors, were denied access to French TV advertising by TF1 Publicité and M6 Publicité, two advertising companies. L-S argued that the French law was incompatible with Article 34. The ECJ held that Article 34 did not apply: it was a 'selling arrangement'.

Requirements as to how goods are presented in shops

It is well established that national rules imposing packaging requirements on products constitute measures equivalent to quantitative restrictions (*Walter Rau v De Smedt* (1982) being the classic example). However, in *Morellato* (Case C–416/00) [2003] ECR I–9343, the ECJ decided that a requirement under Italian law that bread had to be sold wrapped constituted a selling arrangement. The crucial difference between *Walter Rau* (Article 34 and *Dassonville* applies) and *Morellato* (2003) (*Keck* applies) seems to be that in the former case the onus is placed on the manufacturer, while in the latter situation the onus is placed on the retailer. In *Morellato*, the ECJ stated that the bread could be imported unwrapped and then sold wrapped, with the retailer carrying out the wrapping task. In this way, the wrapping could be regarded as 'a simple transformation process' and was therefore incapable of restricting the free movement of goods.

Price controls

Prior to *Keck*, it had been held that price controls (that is, national rules imposing either maximum or minimum prices on certain products, or rules preventing retailers from selling goods at a loss) could infringe Article 34. However, price controls have now been reclassified as selling arrangements. *Keck* itself is such a case, as is *Belgapom* (Case C–63/94) [1995] ECR I–2467, where *Keck* was applied. A recent example is *Colruyt* (Case C–221/15) (unreported), in which the Belgian supermarket chain Colruyt was prosecuted and fined for selling tobacco products at below cost price, a practice prohibited under Belgian legislation. The company challenged the fine, contending that the Belgian law was precluded by Article 34, but the ECJ held that the Belgian legislation was a 'selling arrangement' exempted from Article 34.

Restrictions on the display of goods

Although there is no ECJ case law on this point, in *Philip Morris v Norway* (Case E–16/10) [2012] 1 CMLR 24, the EFTA Court held that Norwegian law which banned the visible display of tobacco products and smoking devices in Norway was, in principle at least, a 'selling arrangement', provided that both *Keck* conditions were met (which was a decision for the national court). If one or both conditions were not met, then the Norwegian law would be an MEQR, albeit one justifiable on health grounds, subject to the proportionality test. (Note: the EFTA Court in Luxembourg hears disputes involving the interpretation of the European Economic Area Agreement in cases originating in Iceland, Liechtenstein and Norway.)

Philip Morris has valuable persuasive precedent value should a similar case arise in the EU. This is more than a theoretical possibility. There is equivalent legislation in the UK at least, in s7A(1) of the Tobacco Advertising and Promotion Act 2002, as amended, which states: 'A person who in the course of a business displays tobacco products, or causes tobacco products to be displayed, in a place in England and Wales or Northern Ireland is guilty of an offence.'

14.8.3 Failure to satisfy the conditions in *Keck and Mithouard*

If a provision of national legislation **appears** to be a 'selling arrangement' but **actually** fails one of the conditions in *Keck*, then the legislation falls to be dealt with under Article 34 as a measure having an effect equivalent to a quantitative restriction.

The first condition
The first condition is that the national rules alleged to constitute a selling arrangement 'apply to all relevant traders operating within the national territory'.

The second condition
The second condition is that those provisions must 'affect in the same manner, in law and in fact, the marketing of domestic products and of those from other Member States'. There have been several cases examining this condition. In *Ortscheit* (Case C–320/93) [1994] ECR I–5243, the ECJ ruled, distinguishing *Keck*, that a prohibition on advertising of all foreign medicinal products was caught by Article 34 (although justifiable on health grounds under Article 36). The second condition was not satisfied.

Similarly, in *De Agostini and TV-Shop* (Cases C–34 to 36/95) [1997] ECR I–3843, concerning Swedish legislation imposing an outright ban on advertising aimed at minors (children less than 12 years of age), the ECJ thought that the legislation might not satisfy the second *Keck* condition. It actually left the final decision on this issue to the Swedish court which had referred the case to the ECJ in the first place. In *Gourmet International Products* (Case C–405/98) [2001] ECR I–1795, involving an absolute prohibition in Swedish legislation on the advertising of alcohol, the ECJ decided that the second condition was definitely not satisfied.

Thus, the Swedish legislation constituted an indistinctly applicable MEQR, *prima facie* prohibited by Article 34 although theoretically justifiable under Article 36 on health grounds.

CASE EXAMPLE

Gourmet International Products (Case C–405/98) [2001] ECR I–1795

Swedish legislation provided:

> In view of the health risks involved in alcohol consumption.... Advertising may not be used to market alcoholic beverages on radio or television. Advertising may not be used to market spirits, wines or strong beers either in periodicals or in other publications.... That prohibition does not, however, apply to publications distributed solely at the point of sale of such beverages.

Gourmet International Products published a magazine entitled *Gourmet*. One issue, published in autumn 1997, contained three pages of advertisements for alcoholic beverages, one for red wine and two for whisky. The Swedish authorities applied for an injunction. GIP resisted and the case was referred to the ECJ. There, GIP contended that an outright prohibition did not satisfy the criteria established in *Keck*, on the basis that such a prohibition was liable to have a greater effect on imported goods than on those produced in the Member State concerned. The ECJ agreed. The blanket prohibition of all advertising was 'liable to impede access to the market by products from other Member States more than it impedes access by domestic products, with which consumers are instantly more familiar'. The Court observed that, although Swedish law allowed publications containing advertisements for alcoholic beverages to be distributed at points of sale, a company wholly owned by the Swedish State (*Systembolaget AB*), enjoyed a monopoly of retail sales in Sweden, so that the only magazines on sale were those promoting Swedish-made beverages. The Court concluded that the prohibition on advertising was caught by Article 34, although capable of justification on health grounds under Article 36.

The ECJ stated:

JUDGMENT

'In the case of products like alcoholic beverages, the consumption of which is linked to traditional social practices and to local habits and customs, a prohibition of all advertising … is liable to impede access to the market by products from other Member States more than it impedes access by domestic products, with which consumers are instantly more familiar. … A prohibition on advertising … must therefore be regarded as affecting the marketing of products from other Member States more heavily than the marketing of domestic products and as therefore constituting an obstacle to trade between Member States caught by [Article 34].'

It should be noted that the UK Parliament has adopted similar legislation in the field of tobacco advertising. Section 2(1) of the Tobacco Advertising and Promotion Act 2002, provides: 'a person who in the course of a business publishes a tobacco advertisement, or causes one to be published, in the UK is guilty of an offence'. Presumably this provision would be dealt with in the same way as that in *Gourmet* (2001) (that is, a *prima facie* breach of Article 34 but justifiable under Article 36 on health grounds).

Gourmet International Products was followed in *Douwe Egberts* (Case C–239/02) [2004] ECR I–7007. Belgian legislation prohibited any references on the labelling of food to the word 'slimming'. Douwe Egberts, a Dutch coffee producer, alleged that various statements, such as 'the absolute breakthrough in weight control' on the labels of 'DynaSvelte Café', a rival brand, infringed this legislation. One issue for the ECJ was whether the Belgian legislation was an MEQR, or whether it was a selling arrangement. The Court confirmed that a total advertising ban could not be categorised as a selling arrangement. The Court stated: 'An absolute prohibition of advertising the characteristics of a product is liable to impede access to the market by products from other Member States more than it impedes access by domestic products, with which consumers are more familiar.' Having categorised the Belgian legislation as an MEQR, the Court went on to consider whether it could be justified, on the grounds of the protection of human health, but rejected that on proportionality grounds.

Similarly, in *Deutscher Apothekerverband* (Case C–322/01) [2003] ECR I–14887, the ECJ again held that the second condition had not been satisfied.

CASE EXAMPLE

Deutscher Apothekerverband (Case C–322/01) [2003] ECR I–14887

German legislation prohibited the Internet sale of most medicines – the practical effect of which was that only pharmacists based in Germany could sell medicines to German customers. A Dutch Internet pharmacy, 0800 DocMorris, offered for sale via its website both prescription and non-prescription medicines to consumers in Germany. The German Pharmacists Organisation sought an injunction against DocMorris's activities, alleging a breach of the German legislation. The case was referred to the ECJ, which held that the German legislation could not be classified as a selling arrangement because the second Keck condition had not been satisfied. The German rule was 'more of an obstacle to pharmacies outside Germany than to those within it'. The Court stated that although pharmacies in Germany could not use Internet sales either, they were still free to sell the same products over the counter in their dispensaries. However, for pharmacies not estab-lished in Germany, that option was not available. For them, the Internet provided 'a more signi-ficant way to gain direct access to the German market'. The Court concluded: 'a prohibition which has a greater impact on pharmacies established outside German territory could impede access to the market for products from other Member States more than it impedes access for domestic products'. The German legislation was therefore an indistinctly applicable MEQR and *prima facie* in breach of Article 34, subject to justification under Article 36 on health grounds.

Deutscher Apothekerverband was followed in *Ker-Optika* (Case C–108/09) [2010] ECR I–12213, involving Hungarian legislation which stipulated that contact lenses could only be sold in specialist medical accessory shops or by home delivery. The effect of this was to prohibit the online sale, in Hungary, of contact lenses. The ECJ held that the Hungarian legislation was **not** a selling arrangement, because the second *Keck* condition was not satisfied. The ban on Internet sales had a greater impact, *in fact*, on traders based in other Member States than it did on traders based in Hungary itself. The Court stated (emphasis added):

> the prohibition on selling contact lenses by mail order deprives traders from other Member States of *a particularly effective means* of selling those products and thus significantly impedes access of those traders to the market of the Member State concerned.

The legislation was therefore an MEQR, prohibited by Article 34, subject to justification under Article 36 on health grounds. *Deutscher Apothekerverband* was again followed in *DPV* (Case C–148/15) [2017] 2 CMLR 1. This case involved a provision of German legis-lation which imposed a series of uniform prices for pharmaceutical products. This was held to be an MEQR, and not a 'selling arrangement', because the legislation did not affect the sale of all pharmaceutical products equally. The Court held that mail-order pharmacies based in other Member States were heavily reliant on 'price competition' as a means of gaining access to the German market, whereas pharmacies based in Germany had an alternative business model, i.e. selling medicines over the counter from a phys-ical pharmacy. The latter also had an advantage when it came to dispensing medicines in an emergency.

14.8.4 Academic reaction to *Keck and Mithouard*

Academic reaction to *Keck* has been mixed. Professor Stephen Weatherill has been a par-ticularly outspoken critic. He listed three principal objections ('After *Keck*: Some Thoughts on how to Clarify the Clarification' (1996) 33 *CMLR* 885):

- the categorisation of some national measures as 'selling arrangements' was 'inappropriately rigid';
- the distinction drawn between 'selling arrangements' and (his words) 'product composition' rules was 'artificial' and 'unworkable';
- the 'selling arrangements' test itself was 'out of line with the objectives of the Treaty'.

Professor Weatherill proposed a different test, based on the question of whether a national measure exerted 'a substantial restriction' on the access of imported goods to the market in that state. He contended that the national measures at issue in *Keck* (1993), *Hünermund* (1993) and *Tankstation t'Heukske* (1994) were not 'selling arrangements' but measures that exercised 'no direct impediment to access to markets of a Member State'.

The 'substantial restriction' test: is it workable?

Professor Weatherill's alternative test has itself been the subject of academic criticism. Peter Oliver ('Some Further Reflections on the Scope of Articles 28–30 (ex Articles 30–36) EC' (1999) 36 *CMLR* 783) has given three reasons for endorsing the ECJ's implicit rejection of a test based on whether or not a national rule 'substantially' restricts trade:

- 'any measure emanating from any branch of the State and whatever the level of government must be regarded as a matter of inherent importance, and must thus be deemed to have some incidence per se on inter-State trade';
- the free movement of goods is 'fundamental', and 'any restriction, even minor, of that freedom, is prohibited';
- 'the practical problems [with the "substantial restriction" test] are very considerable … it would introduce a new element of legal uncertainty and thus make it far harder for national courts to apply [Article 34]'.

Oliver concludes that the *Keck* approach is 'rule based' – by which Oliver means there is a legal formula against which national measures can be tested – and is thus 'far easier for national courts to apply', unlike the 'substantial restriction' approach, which requires 'evaluation of complex economic data'.

KEY FACTS

Keck and Mithouard: 'Selling arrangements'	
'Certain selling arrangements' are exempt from Art 34.	*Keck and Mithouard* (1993)
Selling arrangements are national rules that regulate the conditions under which goods are sold, not the goods themselves. Examples include: i. pricing restrictions; ii. Sunday trading rules; iii. opening hours; iv. restrictions on sale outlets/methods; v. partial advertising restrictions.	*Keck and Mithouard* (1993); *Belgapom* (1995) *Punto Casa and PPV* (1994) *Tankstation t'Heukske* (1994) *Commission v Greece (Processed Milk)* (1995); *Burmanjer and others* (2005) *Hünermund* (1993); *Leclerc-Siplec* (1995)

Selling arrangements must satisfy two conditions. First, they must apply to all relevant traders in the Member State. Second, they must not differentiate – in law or in fact – between the same of domestic goods and imports. A total advertising ban fails the second condition.	*Keck and Mithouard* (1993); *Gourmet International Products* (2001); *Douwe Egberts* (2004)
National rules breaching either or both conditions is an MEQR which will need to be justified using Art 36 or *Cassis de Dijon* principles.	*Gourmet International Products* (2001); *Deutscher Apothekerverband* (2003); *Ker-Optika* (2010); *DPV* (2017)

14.9 Article 35 and exports

There are some fundamental differences between the operation of Article 35 and that of Article 34. The case law relating to Article 35 draws an important distinction between distinctly and indistinctly applicable national rules.

14.9.1 'Distinctly applicable' rules

Measures which clearly discriminate against exports will usually be found to be in breach of Article 35. The most obvious examples are export bans, as in:

- *R v Thompson* (1979) – UK law prohibited the exportation of old coins. Held to be a *prima facie* breach of Article 35 (although justifiable under Article 36 on public policy grounds).
- *Hedley Lomas (Ireland) Ltd* (1996) – the Ministry of Agriculture, Fisheries and Food (MAFF) banned live animal exports to Spain. This was held to breach Article 35 (and the ECJ rejected a defence of protection of animal health under Article 36 for lack of evidence).
- *Dusseldorp* (1998) – prohibition in Dutch law on the exportation of waste oil filters. This was held to breach Article 35 (and was not justifiable under *Cassis de Dijon* principles on environmental protection grounds, because the ban was primarily motivated by economic considerations).

The same considerations apply to distinctly applicable MEQRs. Thus, in *Jongeneel Kaas* (Case 237/82) [1984] ECR 483, Dutch law requiring cheese exporters to be in possession of an export licence was held to be in breach of Article 35. Similarly, in *Bouhelier* (Case 53/76) [1977] ECR 197, concerning French rules requiring watchmakers to be licensed for export, ostensibly to ensure quality standards were maintained, the ECJ said that Article 35 had been infringed. The Court drew particular attention to the fact that the rules only applied 'to products intended for export' and were not imposed 'on products marketed within the Member State'. This leads to 'arbitrary discrimination between the two types of products which constitutes an obstacle to intra-Union trade'.

Similarly, in *Belgium v Spain (Rioja wine exports)* (Case C–388/95) [2000] ECR I–3123, Spanish rules on the transportation of Rioja wine drew a distinction between wine intended for export (this wine had to be transported in bottles) and wine intended for distribution to consumers in Spain (this could be transported in bulk). The ECJ held that this rule constituted a breach of Article 35, although justifiable on grounds of protection of commercial property under Article 36.

In *Jersey Potatoes* (Case C–293/02) [2005] ECR I–9543, the ECJ again held that national legislation which only applied to goods intended for export was capable of breaching Article 35. Under the Jersey Potato Export Marketing Scheme Act 2001, potato producers in Jersey were prohibited from exporting potatoes to mainland UK unless they were registered with the Jersey Potato Export Marketing Board. Failure to comply could lead to fines or imprisonment or both. The Jersey Produce Marketing Organisation contended that the provisions in the 2001 Act constituted a breach of Article 35. The Court agreed, stating: 'such legislation is, by its very nature, likely to interfere with the patterns of exports of potatoes grown in Jersey to UK markets'.

(Note: although the UK, the Channel Islands (including Jersey) and the Isle of Man are regarded as one Member State for the purposes of certain aspects of EU law, including the free movement of goods, the Court held that the provisions of the 2001 Act could act as a disincentive to exports of potatoes from Jersey to the mainland UK – and hence could potentially restrict *re-exports* from the UK to other Member States. Thus the provisions of the 2001 Act fell within the ambit of EU law.)

14.9.2 'Indistinctly applicable' rules

Where national rules are 'indistinctly applicable' MEQRs – that is, they do not distinguish between goods intended for the domestic market and goods intended for export – then there is simply no breach of Article 35. In *Groenveld* (1979), concerning Dutch rules banning sausage manufacturers in the Netherlands from using horsemeat (whether the sausages were intended for export or not), the ECJ stated that Article 35 did not apply.

CASE EXAMPLE

Groenveld (Case 15/79) [1979] ECR 3409

Dutch legislation, the Processing and Preparation of Meat Regulation (1973), prohibited, subject to express exceptions, any manufacturer of sausages in the Netherlands from having in stock or processing horsemeat. Groenveld, Dutch sausage manufacturers, brought a challenge to the Dutch authorities against their refusal to allow them to stock horsemeat, alleging a breach of Article 35. The ECJ held that no breach of Article 35 had been committed. The Dutch law made no distinction between domestic sales and exports of sausages.

The Court stated that Article 35 only:

JUDGMENT

'concerns national measures which have as their *specific object or effect* the restriction of patterns of exports and thereby the establishment of a difference in treatment between the domestic trade of a Member State and its export trade in such a way as to provide a particular advantage for national production or for the domestic market of the State in question at the expense of the production or of the trade of other Member States. This is not so in the case of a prohibition ... which is applied objectively to the production of goods of a certain kind without drawing a distinction depending on whether such goods are intended for the national market or for export'.

These principles were confirmed in *Jongeneel Kaas* (1984). Dutch law regulated the quality and content of cheese produced in the Netherlands. The ECJ held that, as the national rules drew no distinction between the ultimate destination of the goods concerned, there was no breach of Article 35.

However, this does not mean that an indistinctly applicable measure can never breach Article 35. An example is *Gysbrechts & Santurel Inter* (Case C–205/07) [2008] ECR I–9947, the facts of which were given above. Here, the Court decided that, although a provision of national legislation may be indistinctly applicable in the sense that it applies to all goods, if 'its actual effect is nonetheless greater on goods leaving the market of the exporting

Member State than on the marketing of goods in the domestic market of that Member State', then a *prima facie* breach of Article 35 has occurred. Such a measure was, however, capable of justification using *Cassis de Dijon* (1979) principles, such as consumer protection, as well as under Article 36, subject to satisfying the proportionality test.

KEY FACTS

Art 35 TFEU	
Quantitative restrictions and distinctly applicable MEQRs on exports are prohibited.	Art 35 TFEU
'Quantitative restrictions' involve measures such as export bans.	*R v Thompson* (1979); *Hedley Lomas* (1996); *Dusseldorp* (1998)
Distinctly applicable MEQRs are measures which only apply to goods intended for export, e.g. export inspections or licences.	*Bouhelier* (1977); *Jongeneel Kaas* (1984); *Jersey Potatoes* (2005)
Quantitative restrictions and distinctly applicable MEQRs on exports are potentially justifiable under Art 36, subject to satisfying proportionality.	*Bouhelier* (1977); *R v Thompson* (1979); *Hedley Lomas* (1996)
Indistinctly applicable MEQRs – measures which apply to all goods whether intended for export or not – do not, generally speaking, breach Art 35.	*Groenveld* (1979); *Jongeneel Kaas* (1984)
An indistinctly applicable MEQR whose 'actual effect' is greater on exported goods does breach Art 35.	*Gysbrechts & Santurel Inter* (2008)
An indistinctly applicable MEQR is potentially justifiable using Art 36 or *Cassis de Dijon*, subject to satisfying proportionality.	*Gysbrechts & Santurel Inter*

ACTIVITY

Applying the law

1. Prompted by developments in the United States, the British government is considering legislating to tackle the problems created by 'light pollution'. This is defined as the situation which occurs when excessive artificial light is allowed to block the light shining from the stars at night. According to research by pressure groups representing the country's amateur astronomers, light pollution in the UK has been steadily increasing for years and now affects virtually the entire population, even those living in rural areas. Numerous constellations are now effectively invisible to those living in major cities. In addition, some sleep experts have warned of the dangers of light pollution to the human body. Excessive exposure to artificial light can disrupt the body's melatonin levels, which can disrupt sleeping patterns and/or cause hyperactivity, especially in children.

   The government is considering banning the importation into and/or sale within the UK of all security lights which are unnecessarily powerful or which are not designed in such a way as to prevent light being projected upwards.

   Advise the government as to the compatibility of the above options with EU law on the free movement of goods.

2. Happihour, a Swedish drinks manufacturer, produces a non-alcoholic sports drink called 'Buzz' and an alcoholic version of the same drink called 'Fuzz'. The ingredients, packaging and taste of both drinks are very similar, the only differences being the names and the

presence of alcohol (specifically vodka) in 'Fuzz'. For several years, Happihour has sold both versions to retail outlets throughout Sweden and, six months ago, it also began selling the drinks to British retail outlets – off-licences, supermarkets and public houses. The UK government became concerned about this, as it envisaged that consumers, particularly in public houses, might easily confuse the two versions.

Subsequently, the UK Parliament passed legislation, the Alcoholic Drinks Act 2010, which allows the government to regulate the sale of alcoholic drinks in the UK. Using this new legislation, the government prohibited the sale of 'Fuzz' by all retail outlets in the UK, including public houses, with immediate effect. British retail outlets that had been importing 'Fuzz' are now refusing to take new deliveries and Happihour has seen a dramatic slump in trade with outlets in the UK. Last week, Happihour complained that the ban was in breach of EU law on the free movement of goods. A junior minister from the Department for Environment, Food and Rural Affairs (DEFRA) replied, refuting the complaint, and pointing out that a British company which made similar alcoholic and non-alcoholic versions of the same drink was subject to the same ban. The junior minister stated that the ban was still in force although it added that the government was now considering two alternative proposals:

i. lifting the ban on the sale of 'Fuzz' in the UK, but imposing an absolute ban on all forms of advertising of the product;
ii. allowing the sale of 'Fuzz' in the UK, but only from off-licences.

Advise the government whether its original ban on the sale of 'Fuzz', and whether its alternative proposals, are compatible with EU law on the free movement of goods.

SAMPLE ESSAY QUESTION

'According to the ECJ's decision in *Keck* (1993), "certain selling arrangements" fall outside the scope of Article 34 TFEU. The background to this decision was the "increasing tendency" of traders to invoke Article 34, which had forced the Court to expand the list of mandatory requirements under *Cassis de Dijon* (1979). Nearly two decades later, however, there is still uncertainty as to which national rules are subject to Article 34 and which are "selling arrangements". Arguably, the Court in 1993 should have narrowed the scope of Article 34 in another way: by redefining the *Dassonville* (1974) formula. Discuss.'

Explain scope of Article 34 TFEU:
- Article 34 TFEU prohibits quantitative restrictions and MEQRs on imports
- MEQRs defined as all trading rules enacted by Member States, capable of hindering, directly or indirectly, actually or potentially, intra-Union trade (*Dassonville*)
- Give examples, e.g. packaging rules (*Walter Rau*), origin-marking requirements (*Dassonville*), buy-national campaigns ('Buy Irish' *Campaign*), import licences (*Evans Medical*), import inspections (*UHT Milk*), contents and ingredients restrictions (*Cassis*), name restrictions (*Smanor, Guimont*), prohibitions on use (*Motorcycle Trailers*)
- Note that Article 34 applies to both 'distinctly' and 'indistinctly' applicable rules, i.e. even non-discriminatory rules are MEQRs caught by Article 34 if capable of hindering trade
- Observe that Article 34 has been defined very widely

Explain the introduction of the 'mandatory requirements' in Cassis de Dijon:

- In *Cassis* the ECJ authorised exemptions from Article 34 for rules which were necessary to satisfy 'mandatory requirements'
- The list of mandatory requirements is open ended. Give examples, e.g. consumer protection (*Walter Rau*), environmental protection (*Danish Bottles*), road safety (*Motorcycle Trailers*), cultural protection (*Cinéthèque*), the fight against crime (*Tinted Film*), protection of children (*Dynamic Medien*)
- Rules must be 'indistinctly' applicable to benefit under *Cassis* (*Gilli & Andres*, *Souvenir Jewellery*). Consider why this is the case
- Consider possible exception for environmental protection (*Walloon Waste*)

Explain the meaning and scope of the 'selling arrangements' concept:

- In *Keck*, the ECJ introduced 'selling arrangements', exempt from Article 34
- Explain that selling arrangements are rules which relate to the conditions under which goods are sold, not the goods themselves, although the distinction is blurred (e.g. *Morellato*)
- Give examples, e.g. rules on pricing (*Keck*), Sunday trading (*Punto Casa*), shops' opening hours (*Tankstation t'Heukske*), advertising (*Hünermund*), which shops can sell goods (*Processed Milk*), methods of sale (*Burmanjer*)
- Note the two *Keck* conditions. Give examples of cases where one or both were not satisfied, e.g. include total advertising bans (*Gourmet International*), bans on Internet sales (*Deutscher Apothekerverband*, *Ker-Optika*). Explain why these were not selling arrangements

Consider how Article 34 could have been redefined:

- Some academics have criticised *Keck* for being 'rigid' and 'artificial'
- Weatherill proposed a 'substantial restriction' test instead
- Oliver has pointed out that **any** national legislation has a 'substantial' effect
- Also, the meaning of 'substantial' is uncertain, and would lead to litigation involving decisions based on 'evaluation of complex economic data'

SUMMARY

- The ECJ defines goods very widely: 'products which can be valued in money, and which are capable, as such, of forming the subject of commercial transactions' (*Commission v Italy*).

- Article 34 TFEU prohibits quantitative restrictions (QRs) on imports and all measures having equivalent effect (MEQRs). Article 34 is directly effective (*Ianelli & Volpi v Meroni*).

- QRs are 'measures which amount to a total or partial restraint of … imports' (*Geddo v Ente Nazionale Risi*). QRs include import bans (*R v Henn & Darby*, *French Turkeys*, *Conegate*).

- The ECJ has defined MEQRs on imports very widely: 'All trading rules enacted by Member States which are capable of hindering, directly or indirectly, actually or potentially, intra-Community trade' (*Dassonville*). As far as establishing an MEQR is concerned, it is irrelevant whether national rules apply only to imports (distinctly applicable measures) or apply equally to domestic goods and imports (indistinctly applicable measures).

- Examples of MEQRs on imports: contents and ingredients restrictions (*Cassis de Dijon*, *Sandoz*, *Beer Purity*, *Muller*, *Red Bull*, *Greenham & Abel*); packaging requirements (*Walter Rau v De Smedt*, *Mars*); prohibitions on the use of goods (*Toolex Alpha*, *Tinted film*, *Motorcycle trailers*, *Mickelsson & Roos*); origin-marking requirements (*Dassonville*, *Souvenir Jewellery*); name restrictions (*Smanor*, *Guimont*); import inspections (*Commission v France (Italian Wine)*); authorisation requirements (*Dynamic Medien*).

- Article 35 TFEU prohibits quantitative restrictions (QRs) on exports and all measures having equivalent effect (MEQRs).

- 'Quantitative restrictions' on exports include export bans (*R v Thompson & Others*, *Dusseldorp*).

- Distinctly applicable MEQRs on exports are *prima facie* prohibited (*Bouhelier*, *Jersey Potatoes*). Indistinctly applicable MEQRs on exports only breach Article 35 if they have as their 'specific object or effect' the restriction of exports (*Groenveld*, *Gysbrechts*).

- Article 36 TFEU allows Member States to justify measures that restrict imports or exports on grounds of public morality, policy or security; protection of health and life of humans, animals or plants; protection of national treasures; protection of industrial and commercial property. It is a closed list. The burden of proof is on the national authorities to show (a) evidence that there is a risk and (b) that the restrictions imposed are 'proportionate' (*ATRAL*).

- Public morality is something for Member States to decide in accordance with their own values (*R v Henn & Darby*).

- Public policy was invoked in *R v Thompson & Others* and *Ahokainen & Leppik*.

- Public security was successfully invoked in *Campus Oil*. It covers both internal and external security (*Richardt & Les Accessoires Scientifiques*).

- Human health protection is the most important derogation under Article 36 (*Toolex Alpha*). Justification 'must be based on a detailed assessment of the risk to public health, based on the most reliable scientific data available and the most recent results of international research' (*Greenham & Abel*). Flexibility is permitted in situations of 'scientific uncertainty' (*Sandoz*).

- Even if a measure is covered by Article 36, it will still be unlawful if it is 'arbitrary', which will be the case if there is already a lawful trade in similar items in the importing state (*Conegate*).

- Member States must not use Article 36 as a 'disguise' for economic protectionism (*French Turkeys*).

- In *Cassis de Dijon*, the Court introduced two key principles. (1) The 'rule of reason': Member States may maintain or impose trade barriers where 'necessary' to satisfy 'mandatory requirements'; (2) the 'rule of mutual recognition': a presumption that goods lawfully sold in one Member State should be available in all others. This presumption is rebuttable, typically by referring to national characteristics, but the burden of doing so falls on the Member State which is resisting imports. The *Cassis* principles apply to both import and export restrictions (*Dusseldorp*, *Gysbrechts*).

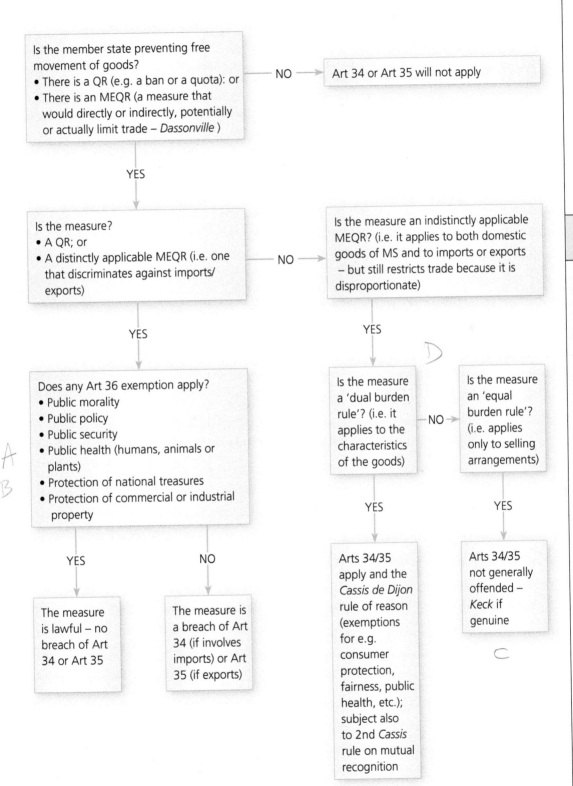

Is the member state preventing free movement of goods?
- There is a QR (e.g. a ban or a quota): or
- There is an MEQR (a measure that would directly or indirectly, potentially or actually limit trade – *Dassonville*)

NO → Art 34 or Art 35 will not apply

YES

Is the measure?
- A QR; or
- A distinctly applicable MEQR (i.e. one that discriminates against imports/exports)

NO → **Is the measure an indistinctly applicable MEQR?** (i.e. it applies to both domestic goods of MS and to imports or exports – but still restricts trade because it is disproportionate)

YES

Does any Art 36 exemption apply?
- Public morality
- Public policy
- Public security
- Public health (humans, animals or plants)
- Protection of national treasures
- Protection of commercial or industrial property

YES

Is the measure a 'dual burden rule'? (i.e. it applies to the characteristics of the goods)

NO → **Is the measure an 'equal burden rule'?** (i.e. applies only to selling arrangements)

YES

YES

The measure is lawful – no breach of Art 34 or Art 35

NO

The measure is a breach of Art 34 (if involves imports) or Art 35 (if exports)

Arts 34/35 apply and the *Cassis de Dijon* rule of reason (exemptions for e.g. consumer protection, fairness, public health, etc.); subject also to 2nd *Cassis* rule on mutual recognition

Arts 34/35 not generally offended – *Keck* if genuine

Figure 14.1 The means of establishing breach of Article 34

░ The list of mandatory ('imperative') requirements is open ended. Examples include: consumer protection (*Walter Rau v De Smedt*), the success of which depends on the 'presumed expectations' of the 'average ... reasonably well-informed ... reasonably observant and circumspect' consumer (*Mars, Clinique*); environmental protection (*Danish Bottles, Walloon Waste, Dusseldorp, Aher-Waggon, Radlberger & Spitz, Mickelsson & Roos*); cultural protection (*Cinéthèque*); protection of fundamental rights (*Schmidberger v Austria*); road safety (*Snellers Autos, Motorcycle trailers*); protection of children (*Dynamic Medien*); the fight against crime (*Tinted film*).

░ In principle, the 'rule of reason' is limited to 'indistinctly applicable' measures (*Gilli & Andres, Souvenir Jewellery*). However, there is an apparent exception for environmental protection (*Walloon Waste* (import ban) and *Dusseldorp* (export ban)).

░ All derogations are subject to a test of 'proportionality'. The test is failed if there is another method (e.g. clear labelling) capable of achieving the same objective which is less restrictive of trade (*Walter Rau*).

░ In *Keck & Mithouard*, the Court decided that 'Contrary to what has previously been decided ... certain selling arrangements' were exempt from Article 34.

░ Examples include rules on pricing (*Keck & Mithouard, Belgapom, Colruyt*), Sunday trading laws (*Punto Casa, Pelckmans Turnhout*), rules on shops' closing times (*Tankstation t'Heukske*), restrictions on which shops can sell goods (*Processed Milk*), rules on methods of sale (*Burmanjer & Others* – no itinerant sales; *A-Punkt Schmuckhandels* – no door-to-door sales), advertising restrictions (*Hünermund, Leclerc-Siplec*).

░ Selling arrangements are exempt from Article 34, provided they 'apply to all relevant traders' and 'affect in the same manner, in law and in fact, the marketing of domestic products and of those from other Member States'.

░ Total advertising bans are not selling arrangements because they have a greater impact (in fact) on the marketing of imported goods (*Gourmet International Products, Douwe Egberts*). The same is true of legislation banning Internet sales (*Deutsche Apothekerverband, Ker-Optika*). Such rules are MEQRs on imports, subject to Article 34.

Further reading

Articles

Connor, T, 'Accentuating the Positive: The "Selling Arrangement", the First Decade and Beyond' (2005) 54 *ICLQ* 127.

Davies, G, 'Can Selling Arrangements be Harmonised?' (2005) 30 *EL Rev* 370.

Hojnik, J, 'Free Movement of Goods in a Labyrinth: Can *Buy Irish* Survive the Crises?' (2012) 49 *CML Rev* 291.

Józon, M, 'The Enlarged EU and Mandatory Requirements' (2005) 11 *ELJ* 549.

Kaczorowska, A, 'Gourmet can have His *Keck* and Eat It!' (2004) 10 *ELJ* 479.

Krenn, C, 'A Missing Piece in the Horizontal Effect "Jigsaw": Horizontal Direct Effect and the Free Movement of Goods' (2012) 49 *CML Rev* 177.

Notaro, N, 'The New Generation Case Law on Trade and Environment' (2000) 25 *EL Rev* 467.

Snell, J, 'The Notion of Market Access: A Concept or a Slogan?' (2010) 47 *CML Rev* 437.

Szydlo, M, 'Export Restrictions within the Structure of Free Movement of Goods: Reconsideration of an Old Paradigm' (2010) 47 *CML Rev* 753.

15

Article 28 TFEU and Customs tariffs and Article 110 TFEU and discriminatory internal taxation

AIMS AND OBJECTIVES

After reading this chapter you should be able to:

- Understand the law relating to the prohibition of Customs duties and equivalent charges on imports and exports between Member States, in particular Articles 28 and 30

- Understand the law relating to the prohibition of discriminatory internal taxation on products of other Member States, in particular Article 110

- Apply the law to factual situations involving the prohibition of Customs duties and discriminatory taxation

15.1 The Common Customs Policy

In the previous chapter, the provisions of the TFEU dealing with 'quantitative restrictions' and 'measures having an equivalent effect' were examined. Articles 34 and 35 essentially deal with obstacles to trade caused by national legislation regulating the composition and/or packaging of goods. Articles 34 and 35 do not, however, apply to the situation when Customs officers in one Member State impose some form of financial charge on goods because they are crossing the border. Such charges are clearly capable of hindering trade, but they are tackled by different provisions of the TFEU. The key provision is Article 28, which creates the Customs Union. It has two parts:

- A prohibition on Customs duties and charges having equivalent effect. This deals with the imposition of charges on goods moving around the EU from one Member State to another. This prohibition on Customs duties and equivalent charges is reiterated in Article 30.

- A Common Customs Tariff. This deals with the movement of goods into the EU from elsewhere in the world, e.g. from China or the USA.

15.2 Article 30 and prohibition of Customs duties and charges having equivalent effect

15.2.1 Introduction

Article 30 prohibits Customs duties or charges having equivalent effect on all imports and exports between Member States. The ECJ has clarified that fiscal barriers to trade must be dealt with under Article 30 and not Article 34. In *Compagnie Commerciale de l'Ouest and Others* (Cases C–78 to 83/90) [1992] ECR I–1847, the Court stated:

JUDGMENT

'The scope of [Article 34] does not extend to the obstacles to trade covered by other specific provisions of the Treaty, and that obstacles of a fiscal nature or having an effect equivalent to customs duties which are covered by [Article 30] of the Treaty do not fall within the prohibition laid down in [Article 34].'

A 'Customs duty' is any charge of a fiscal nature that is imposed, directly or indirectly, on goods which cross a border. A simple prohibition of 'Customs duties' per se would have allowed Customs authorities to continue to charge importers through less obvious means. Hence, Article 30 also prohibits charges having an effect equivalent to Customs duties (CEE). In *Commission v Italy (Statistical Levy)* (Case 24/68) [1969] ECR 193, a CEE was described as:

JUDGMENT

'Any pecuniary charge, however small and whatever its designation and mode of application, which is imposed unilaterally on domestic or foreign goods by reason of the fact that they cross a frontier, and which is not a customs duty in the strict sense, constitutes a charge having equivalent effect ... even if it is not discriminatory or protective in effect and the product on which the charge is imposed is not in competition with any domestic product.'

In *Commission v Luxembourg and Belgium (Gingerbread)* (Cases 2 and 3/62) [1962] ECR 813, the ECJ emphasised that it is the **effect** of a charge, as opposed to its **name**, which is significant. Otherwise, Member States could disguise charges on imports easily, and use them to destroy any competitive advantage which cheaper imports would otherwise have over domestic products. Such charges need not necessarily be levied at a frontier. The key is whether the charge has been imposed **because the goods were imported** (*Steinike & Weinleg* (Case 78/76) [1977] ECR 595). In *Deutsches Milch-Kontor* (Case C–272/95) [1997] ECR I–1905, the ECJ expressly held that Article 30 applied even though the charges in question were in respect of Customs inspections carried out within Germany on lorries heading for Italy.

Many 'Customs duties' are imposed to make imports relatively more expensive and hence protect the domestic market. But there is no requirement that the charge be levied for protectionist reasons (*Commission v Italy (Statistical Levy)* (1969)). There may even be no domestic market in need of protection; but this will not stop the charge from infringing Article 30. This was seen in *Sociaal Fonds voor de Diamantarbeiders v SA Charles Brachfeld & Sons and Chougal Diamond Co* (Cases 2 and 3/69) [1969] ECR 211. Here, Belgian Customs officials imposed a charge on uncut diamonds imported into Belgium. There are obviously no Belgian diamond mines (the diamonds originated in southern Africa) but the ECJ nonetheless held that Article 30 applied.

15.2.2 Derogations from Article 30

Charge for services for the benefit of the importer/exporter

Even if the charge is for a service provided for the **benefit** of the importer or exporter, it may still breach Article 30. A charge for services which benefits the Union in general, e.g. health inspections or quality control, would not necessarily be compatible with Article 30 either (*Rewe-Zentralfinanz* (Case 39/73) [1973] ECR 1039). To escape Article 30, a charge must be capable of being regarded as a payment for services of tangible benefit to the importer: see *Commission v Italy (Statistical Levy)* (1969). The charge must not exceed the value or cost of the service (*Donner* (Case 39/82) [1983] ECR 19), nor a sum proportionate to the service provided (*Commission v Denmark* (Case 158/82) [1983] ECR 3573). A charge based on the value of the goods is not permissible (*Ford España v Spain* (Case 170/88) [1989] ECR 2305).

Charges for services imposed under EU law

Where the services charged for are imposed under EU law, then a charge could be regarded as a payment for services and therefore it would be permissible for the Member State concerned to require payment for it (*Commission v Italy (Statistical Levy)* (1969)). Similarly, where a service is mandatory under international agreement, a charge could be levied to cover the cost of the service (*Netherlands v P Bakker Hillegom* (Case C–111/89) [1990] ECR I–1735). Where the state is entitled to recover its service costs through a charge, it is only entitled to recover the actual cost of the service, and no more (*Denkavit Futtermittel v Germany* (Case 233/81) [1982] ECR 2933). Where a service is only **permitted** this is insufficient (*Commission v Belgium (Health Inspection Charges)* (Case 314/82) [1984] ECR 1543). It is essential that the service is **imposed** under EU law (*Germany v Deutsches Milch-Kontor* (Case C–426/92) [1994] ECR I–2757).

No other exceptions permitted

There is no correlation with Article 36 or the *Cassis de Dijon* (1979) principles (see Chapter 14). In *Commission v Italy (Export Tax on Art Treasures)* (Case 7/68) [1968] ECR 617, the Italian government argued, unsuccessfully, that a charge levied on those exporting works of art from Italy was required to protect artistic heritage. In *Diamanterbeiders* (1969), above, the Court rejected any suggestion that the social utility of the Belgian Customs charge provided a defence (it had been argued that any money generated by the import charge on the imported diamonds would be used to provide financial aid for diamond mine workers in Africa). This case was followed in *Kapniki Mikhailidis* (Cases C–441 and 442/98) [2000] ECR I–7415, involving the imposition of charges on exports of tobacco products from Greece, apparently designed to raise money for workers in the tobacco industry. The Court held that this was no justification for breaching Article 30.

15.2.3 Repayment of illegal duties and charges

In several cases examined above it was established that a Customs duty or equivalent charge had been imposed by the customs authorities of a Member State in breach of Article 30. When that happens, then the Member State in question is, in principle, obliged to repay the person subject to the charge, usually the importer or exporter (*San Giorgio* (Case 199/82) [1983] ECR 3595; *Dilexport* (Case C–343/96) [1999] ECR I–579). Moreover, national rules of evidence which have the effect of making it virtually impossible or excessively difficult to secure repayment of charges levied in breach of Article 30 are incompatible with EU law. However, EU law does **not** require the repayment of the duty or charge in circumstances where this would unjustly enrich the person concerned (*Just v Danish Ministry for Fiscal Affairs* (Case 68/79) [1980] ECR 501; *Kapniki Mikhailidis* (2000)). This would occur in a situation, for example, where the burden of the charge has been transferred in whole or in part to other persons. Thus, if an importer had paid the charge, but then passed on the cost to the distributor of the goods in the importing state, then to order the repayment of the charge to the importer would over-compensate that person (*Société Comatelo and others* (Case C–192/95) [1997] ECR I–165).

15.3 The Common Customs Tariff

Article 28 also provides for the creation of a Common Customs Tariff (CCT), which co-ordinates the duties imposed on to all goods imported into the EU. A single tariff 'wall' is erected against imports, which no state is free to breach. The CCT came into operation in July 1968. It lays down common rules on nomenclature, valuation and origin. CCT duties are fixed by the Council, following proposals made by the European Commission (Article 31).

KEY FACTS

Customs duties and equivalent charges (Art 30)	
• Creates the Customs Union.	Art 28
• There are two aspects to this: a prohibition on the imposition of Customs duties and equivalent charges on goods moving from one EU Member State to another, and the Common Customs Tariff, which co-ordinates the imposition of duties on goods entering the EU from elsewhere in the world.	
• Member States may not impose Customs duties or equivalent charges on goods when they are being imported or exported. There are very limited derogations from this principle – when charges are imposed to cover the cost (and no more) of a benefit of specific benefit to the importer/exporter, and when charges are imposed to cover the cost of services which are mandatory under EU law itself.	Art 30

15.4 Article 110 and the prohibition of discriminatory internal taxation

ARTICLE

'Art 110 No Member State shall impose, directly or indirectly, on the products of other Member States any internal taxation of any kind in excess of that imposed directly or indirectly on similar domestic products.

Furthermore, no Member State shall impose on the products of other Member States any internal taxation of such a nature as to afford indirect protection to other products.'

15.4.1 The scope of Article 110

Article 110 allows Member States the freedom to establish their own taxation system for any given product, provided that there is no discrimination against imports, or indirect protection of domestic products. The purpose of Article 110 is to remove discrimination against imports, not to accord them tax privileges (*Kupferberg* (Case 253/83) [1985] ECR 157). Therefore, internal taxation may legitimately be applied to a particular product even if there is no domestic production of that product, and the tax is effectively levied against imports only. However, this is permitted because the Member State is not **discriminating against** imports. It would only be discriminatory if it was imposing a different rate of tax on similar or competing domestic products, but if there are no similar domestic products, no breach of Article 110(1) can occur, and if there are no competing domestic products, no breach of Article 110(2) can occur either. This was seen in *De Danske Bilimportører* (Case C–383/01) [2003] ECR I–6065. A Danish company had bought and imported a new German-made Audi car. Under Danish law, all new cars must be registered and a 'registration duty' paid. The purchase price of the car was approximately €27,000; the duty came to just over €40,000, bringing the total price to some €67,000. The company could not believe that this was correct and brought a legal challenge. The ECJ decided that no breach of Article 110 had occurred, simply because there were no similar (or even competing) domestic products – Denmark does not manufacture cars. Finally, because Article 110 prohibits discrimination **against** imports, it does not preclude the imposition of higher rates of tax on domestic products than on imports: that is, discrimination **in favour** of imports (known as reverse discrimination) is permitted (*Grandes Distilleries Peureux* (Case 86/78) [1979] ECR 897).

It is very important to remember that internal taxation is only prohibited by Article 110 if it is either discriminatory or has a protective effect. To a very large extent, therefore, the 28 Member States of the European Union are allowed complete discretion whether or not to impose taxes – or 'excise duties' – on a range of goods and, if they do impose such taxes, at what rate. This can lead to significant differences in prices from one Member State to another. For example, in the UK, the most heavily taxed goods are cigarettes, alcohol and petrol. Indeed, the rates at which those products are taxed in the UK has produced some very interesting results:

- In the case of **cigarettes and alcohol**, significant differences in the rate at which those goods are taxed in the UK and France created the phenomenon of the 'booze cruise' – whereby UK nationals travelled across the English Channel by ferry to France in order to buy large quantities of much cheaper alcohol and cigarettes at huge supermarkets in Calais. Under UK law – the Customs and Excise Management Act 1979 – individuals are permitted to bring into the UK alcohol and cigarettes purchased in other EU Member States without having to pay UK excise duty, but only for their own use. HM Revenue & Customs officers are vigilant in seeking to catch people bringing back consignments of those goods which they think may be intended for commercial sale. Anyone caught may face criminal prosecution in a British court for evasion of excise duty, as well as having the goods confiscated.

- In the case of **petrol**, massive disruption was caused to much of the UK in 2000 when disgruntled lorry drivers (among others) blockaded British oil refineries, preventing fuel delivery trucks from getting in or out and thus causing many petrol stations throughout the country to run dry within a matter of days. The lorry drivers were protesting against the high cost of petrol in the UK, especially compared with petrol prices in much of the rest of the European Union. The lorry drivers eventually backed down when it appeared that public sympathy was beginning to turn against them.

'Products of other Member States'

Despite the clear implication of this phrase, the ECJ has held that the prohibition of discriminatory taxation must apply to goods manufactured or produced **outside** the EU, but which are in free circulation **inside** the EU (*Co-operativa Co-frutta* (Case 193/85) [1987] ECR 2085). Using even more expansive interpretation, the ECJ has held that Article 110 applies to exports, in order to guarantee the neutrality of national systems of taxation (*Larsen* (Case 142/77) [1978] ECR 1543). However, there are some limits. In *Air Liquide* (Cases C–393/04 and C–41/05) [2006] ECR I–5293, involving a

Belgian tax on the use of industrial, commercial, financial or agricultural motors, the Court held that Article 110 was inapplicable, because there was no tax on 'products' as such. The Court stated that the 'tax on motive force ... is not imposed specifically on exported or imported products. It applies to economic activities carried out by industrial, commercial, financial or agricultural undertakings and not to products as such'.

15.4.2 Distinguishing Customs duties and taxes

Charges imposed only on imports are clearly contrary to the provisions on Customs duties and are dealt with under Article 30. The position is different where a charge is applied to all goods: domestic products as well as imports. A charge levied indiscriminately on all products of a particular description, in all respects, regardless of the country of origin, is a **tax**, not a **Customs duty**, and should be dealt with under Article 110. The picture can be complicated because many Customs duties are disguised as taxes (e.g. *Commission v Luxembourg and Belgium (Gingerbread)* (1962); *Orgacom* (Case C–254/13) [2015] 1 CMLR 27).

It is important to distinguish genuine taxes from disguised Customs duties. A 'tax' was defined in *Commission v France (Reprographic Machines)* (Case 90/79) [1981] ECR 283 as one which related to a 'general system of internal duties applied systematically to categories of products in accordance with objective criteria irrespective of the origin of the products'. It follows that a charge which is **apparently** levied on all goods but which is imposed in a different **manner**, and/or which is subject to different **criteria**, for domestic and imported products, would fall to be dealt with under Article 30 (*Marimex* (Case 29/72) [1972] ECR 1309; *Orgacom* (2015)).

Moreover, 'taxes' which actually **benefit** domestic products are, in reality, Customs duties. In *Capolongo* (Case 77/72) [1973] ECR 611, a 'tax' was imposed under Italian law on all cellulose products, such as egg boxes. The proceeds were used to finance the production of paper and cardboard in Italy. The ECJ held that such a 'tax' may fall foul of Article 30 if the proceeds of the charge were used to benefit a domestic product. The Court went on to hold that this applied even where the product on which the charge was levied and the domestic product which benefited from it were **different**.

However, the very wide principle established in *Capolongo* (1973) has subsequently been restricted. In *Fratelli Cucchi* (Case 77/76) [1977] ECR 987, involving an Italian 'tax' on sugar, the ECJ held that a 'tax' would only constitute a CEE in breach of Article 30 if certain criteria were satisfied:

- the tax would need to have 'the sole purpose of financing activities for the specific advantage of the taxed domestic product';
- the taxed product and the domestic product benefiting from the charge must be the same;
- taxes imposed on the domestic product would need to be made good in full.

Thus, the charge that was the subject of the *Capolongo* (1973) litigation would not now be found to be in breach of Article 30, because the products involved were different. However, such a charge could very well be regarded as a discriminatory tax instead, in breach of Article 110 (*Co-operativa Co-frutta* (1987), concerning an Italian 'tax' on bananas). The *Fratelli Cucchi* (1977) criteria have been confirmed in a succession of cases subsequently. In *UCAL* (Case C–347/95) [1997] ECR I–4911 and *Fricarnes* (Case C–28/96) [1997] ECR I–4939, involving Portuguese 'taxes' on dairy products and meat, respectively, the position was summarised as follows:

JUDGMENT

'If the advantages stemming from the use of the proceeds of the contribution in question *fully* offset the burden borne by the domestic product when it is placed on the market, that contribution constitutes a charge having an effect equivalent to customs duties, contrary to [Article 30]. If those advantages only *partly* offset the burden borne by domestic products, the charge in question is subject to [Article 110]. In the latter case, the charge would be incompatible with [Article 110] and is therefore prohibited to the extent to which it discriminates against imported products, that is to say to the extent to which it partially offsets the burden borne by the taxed domestic product.'

15.4.3 Discrimination against imports: Article 110(1)

The ECJ has held that Article 110(1) must be construed broadly, to include all taxation actually and specifically imposed on a particular product. Article 110(1) prohibits the imposition of taxation on domestic products which discriminates against similar imported products. Discrimination may either be direct or indirect and still breach Article 110(1) – the difference is that indirect discrimination may be justified.

Direct discrimination

Discrimination may be 'direct', that is, the discrimination is visible on its face. *Alfons Lütticke* (Case 57/65) [1966] ECR 293 involved German tax legislation that discriminated against the same type of goods – dried milk – purely according to its country of origin. This clearly breaches Article 110(1). Moreover, in *Haahr Petroleum* (Case C–90/94) [1997] ECR I–4085, the ECJ rejected any suggestion that directly discriminatory taxation could be justified.

Indirect discrimination

Where a taxation system is *prima facie* non-discriminatory, but in practice discriminatory against imported products, this is known as indirect discrimination. It will nevertheless amount to a breach of Article 110(1). This is perfectly demonstrated in *Humblot* (Case 112/84) [1987] ECR 1367, a case involving French road tax.

CASE EXAMPLE

Humblot (Case 112/84) [1987] ECR 1367

French road tax operated on a sliding scale depending on engine capacity up to 16cv, with the top rate being about 1000 francs. For cars above 16cv, a flat-rate 'supertax' of about 5000 francs was payable. Michel Humblot, a French national, imported a 36cv Mercedes from Germany. He paid the 'supertax' but then sought repayment through the French courts. The ECJ held that the French system amounted to indirect discrimination based on nationality, contrary to Article 110(1). Although *prima facie* applicable without distinction in terms of nationality to all cars, in practice the tax policy discriminated against imported cars, because no cars exceeding 16cv capacity were manufactured in France. The Court also rejected the French authorities' argument that cars over 16cv were 'luxury' cars and therefore dissimilar to ordinary cars.

Note: the French franc was abolished when the single European currency, the euro, came into operation in 2002.

Indirect discrimination, unlike direct discrimination, may be justified, provided that the difference in treatment of domestic goods and imported goods is designed to achieve some acceptable outcome. The difference must be based upon objective criteria. In *Commission v France (Tax on Wines)* (Case 196/85) [1987] ECR 1597, sweet wines were taxed at a lower rate than ordinary wines. This was done in order to provide some economic assistance to rural areas in France that were dependent on sweet wine production. The ECJ held that the tax was *prima facie* in breach of Article 110(1) but, as the discrimination was indirect, it was capable of justification.

'Similar products'

It is not necessary that the imported products and the domestic products which are subjected to different rates of taxation are **identical**. They need only be '**similar**', and in *Commission v France (Taxation of Spirits)* (Case 168/78) [1980] ECR 347, the ECJ held this word should be construed broadly.

CASE EXAMPLE

Commission v France (Taxation of Spirits) (Case 168/78) [1980] ECR 347

Under French legislation, alcoholic beverages distilled from cereals (such as whisky and gin, which were largely imported) were subject to a much higher tax regime than spirits distilled from fruit or wine (such as cognac, armagnac and brandy), of which there was heavy domestic production. The Commission, arguing that all spirits were 'similar', alleged a breach of Article 110(1). The French government argued that a distinction should be drawn between aperitifs and digestives. The former were drunk, diluted with water, before meals and included all grain-based spirits. The latter were beverages consumed, neat, at the end of a meal, typically spirits obtained from fruit and wine. The French also argued out that cereal-distilled spirits were distinguishable from fruit- and wine-based spirits because of 'a number of organoleptic properties combining taste, aroma and smell'. The ECJ rejected the distinction between aperitifs and digestives. The 'products in question may be consumed before, during or after meals or even completely unrelated to such meals'; moreover, 'according to consumer preference the same beverage may be used indiscriminately as an aperitif or a digestive. Therefore it is impossible to recognise ... the objective value of the distinction upon which the French tax practice is based.' The Court also rejected any distinction based on flavour. There was 'no question of denying the reality of and shades of difference in the flavour of the various alcoholic products'. However, it was necessary to realise that this 'criterion is too variable in time and space to supply by itself a sufficiently sound basis for distinction'. The main problem was that the products in question could be consumed in very varied circumstances, either neat or diluted or with a variety of mixers. Hence, 'owing in particular to this flexibility of use' all spirits could be considered as 'similar' or in at least partial competition. The ECJ concluded that it did not need to decide whether the drinks were 'similar' because it was 'impossible reasonably to contest that without exception they are in at least partial competition', and hence Article 110(2) applied instead.

The Court held:

JUDGMENT

'The first paragraph of [Article 110], which is based on a comparison of the tax burden imposed on domestic products and on imported products which may be classified as "similar", is the basic rule.... This provision ... must be interpreted widely so as to cover all taxation procedures which conflict with the principle of the equality of treatment of domestic products and imported products; it is therefore necessary to interpret the concept of "similar products" with sufficient flexibility ... it is necessary to consider as "similar" products which have similar characteristics and meet the same needs from the point of view of consumers. It is therefore necessary to determine the scope of the first paragraph of [Article 110] on the basis not of the criterion of the strictly identical nature of the products but on that of their similar and comparable use.'

Most cases have arisen in the context of alcoholic drinks, primarily because they are taxed so heavily by most Member States' governments for social and/or revenue-raising reasons. There are also many fine distinctions that can be drawn between different drinks, depending on their raw ingredients, strength, method of manufacture, etc.

- *Commission v Denmark (Tax on Wines)* (Case 106/84) [1986] ECR 833 – wine and fruit wine were 'similar';

- *John Walker & Sons* (Case 243/84) [1986] ECR 833 – whisky and fruit liqueur wines were not 'similar', because whisky contained twice as much alcohol (40 per cent to 20 per cent).

FG Roders BV (Cases C–367 to 377/93) [1995] ECR I–2229 involved a very thorough examination of the similarity of a number of drinks, including French red wine and champagne, Italian vermouth, Portuguese madeira and Spanish sherry. BENELUX legislation (meaning legislation common to Belgium, Luxembourg and the Netherlands) taxed wines differently according to whether they were still or sparkling, and according to whether they had been made from grapes or from fruit. There were therefore four categories into which wine could fall for tax purposes:

- still grape wine;

- still fruit wine;

- sparkling grape wine; and

- sparkling fruit wine.

Still fruit wine was exempt from tax altogether (provided that it met certain requirements with regard to labelling and packaging) while sparkling fruit wine was taxed at a lower rate than sparkling grape wine. Various importers into the Netherlands of French red wine and champagne, Italian vermouth, Portuguese madeira and Spanish sherry (all of which are made from grapes) argued that their products were 'similar' to domestically produced fruit wine (whether still or sparkling, as the case may be) and should therefore be taxed at the lower rate. The Court made a number of findings, looking at each of the imported drinks in turn.

1. Red table wine is 'similar' to still fruit wine. It was in this specific context that the Court made its finding:

   > the two categories of wine possess similar organoleptic properties – in particular taste and alcohol strength – and meet the same needs of consumers, inasmuch as they can be consumed for the same purposes, namely both to quench thirst and to refresh, and to accompany meals.

2. Red quality wine may be 'similar' to still fruit wine, but this was a question for the national court, by examining the 'objective characteristics of both categories of beverage, such as their origin, their method of manufacture and their organoleptic properties, in particular taste and alcohol content', and, second, by considering 'whether or not both categories of beverage are capable of meeting the same needs from the point of view of consumers'.

3. Vermouth may also be 'similar' to still fruit wine, although again this was a question for the national court. However, the Court did point out two potentially significant differences: 'not only is ethyl alcohol added to grape wine but also a small quantity of mixed herbs which give vermouth its special flavour'.

4. Champagne may also be 'similar' to sparkling fruit wine, although that would be for the national court to decide. Again, the Court pointed out a number of differences between the two drinks:

> champagne is made sparkling by a natural method – by a second alcoholic fermentation in the bottle [but] sparkling fruit wines require the addition of carbon dioxide, a fermentation process which is not natural. Secondly, the organoleptic properties of champagne are not comparable to those of sparkling fruit wines. Thirdly, the two categories of beverage do not meet the same needs of consumers, particularly since the consumption of champagne is usually associated with special occasions.

5. Finally, sherry and madeira are not 'similar' to still fruit wines. There were two reasons for this; first, that the imported drinks were 'usually consumed as aperitifs or as dessert wines' and, second, because they had a higher alcohol content (17–18 per cent) than fruit wines (15 per cent).

15.4.4 Indirect protection of domestic products: Article 110(2)

It is unnecessary for the products in question to be 'similar' for the purposes of Article 110(2). Instead, it applies to 'all forms of indirect tax protection in the case of products which, without being similar within the meaning of [Article 110(1)], are nevertheless in competition, even partial, indirect or potential, with each other' (*Co-operativa Co-frutta* (1987)). It is thus much wider than Article 110(1). In several of the cases considered above under Article 110(1), the ECJ found that the products in question were not 'similar'. However, the Court then went on to discuss whether the dissimilar products may, instead, be 'in competition' with each other so that differential levels of taxation may have a protective effect for domestically produced goods. Hence:

- *Commission v France (Taxation of Spirits)* (1980) – brandy and cognac (domestically produced in France) and whisky and gin (imported) were not 'similar' to but were in competition.
- *Commission v UK (Tax on Beer and Wine)* (Case 170/78) [1983] ECR 2265 – beer (domestically produced in the UK) and wine (imported) were not 'similar' but beer was in competition with at least some wines.
- *Commission v Italy (Tax on Fruit)* (Case 184/85) [1987] ECR 2013 and *Co-operativa Co-frutta* (1987) – bananas (imported) were not 'similar' to other fruits (domestically grown in Italy) but were in competition with them.
- *Commission v Sweden (Tax on Beer and Wine)* (Case C–167/05) [2008] ECR I–2127 – strong beer (produced in Sweden) was in competition with at least some wines (imported).

It should be noted that, just because dissimilar products are in competition with each other, it does not mean that taxing one at a higher rate will have a protective effect on the other. It may be that the imported product is of such a significantly higher quality such that taxing it will have little or no impact on sales. Alternatively, as was the case in *Commission v Belgium (Tax on Wine and Beer)* (Case 356/85) [1987] ECR 3299, if the price differential between the imported product and the dissimilar domestically produced product is already quite substantial, differences in the rates of tax will not serve to protect the domestically produced product.

Finally, in *Commission v Sweden* (2008), the Court found that the difference in price between Swedish beer and imported wine was virtually the same after taxation as it was beforehand, and hence the fact that Sweden taxed wine more heavily than beer was not 'likely to influence consumer behaviour'. In other words, the tax system did not protect the domestic product (beer) against competition from the imported product (wine).

KEY FACTS

Internal taxation (Art 110)	
• The ECJ will first of all examine different domestically produced and imported products to see if they are 'similar'. This does not mean 'identical'.	Art 110(1); *Commission v France* (1980)
• If the answer is yes, then those products must be subject to the same rate of internal taxation or 'excise duty' otherwise there is a breach. This was seen where the Court held that French red table wine was 'similar' to Dutch fruit wine.	Art 110(1); *FG Roders BV* (1995)
• The only exception would be if any discrimination was 'indirect', and furthermore capable of objective justification.	
• If the same rate of internal taxation is applied to both domestically produced and imported products, but the revenue generated then finds its way back to the domestic producers, such that they are reimbursed in full, then the Article does not apply. Instead, this system would be regarded as imposing a charge equivalent to a Customs duty on imports, which breaches Art 30.	Art 110(1)
• If the answer is no the ECJ will examine whether or not the products are in competition with each other and, in addition, whether the differential rates of tax may have a protective effect.	Art 110(2)
• This was also seen in *FG Roders BV* (1995) where the ECJ held that Spanish sherry and Portuguese madeira were not 'similar' to Dutch fruit wines, but they were in competition with other.	*FG Roders BV* (1995)
• If there is a protective effect then the national legislation must be amended to remove the protective effect, otherwise there is a breach of Art 110(2).	
• Provided that any protective effect is removed, it is not necessary for the rates of tax to be equalised.	

SAMPLE ESSAY QUESTION

'The distinction between Customs duties and excise duties can be a difficult one to draw, but it is nevertheless a crucial distinction, as the legal implications are very different. Discuss.'

Explain the law relating to Customs duties:

- Article 30 TFEU prohibits Customs duties on imports and exports and all charges having equivalent effect
- Irrespective of its size, name or purpose, a charge imposed unilaterally on goods crossing one of the EU's internal borders breaches Article 30 (*Commission v Italy (Statistical Levy)*)
- Charges for services which benefit the importer/exporter (*Donner*), or which are imposed under EU law (*Statistical Levy*), may escape Article 30
- Otherwise, no derogations are available (*Sociaal Fonds, Kapniki Mikhailidis*)

Explain the law relating to excise duties:

- Article 110 TFEU prohibits discriminatory internal taxation (excise duties)
- Define taxes (*Commission v France (Reprographic Machines)*)
- Discriminatory excise duties are prohibited whether direct (*Alfons Lütticke*) or indirect (*Humblot*). Direct discrimination cannot be justified (*Haahr Petroleum*), but indirect discrimination is justifiable (*Commission v France (Tax on Wines)*)
- Article 110(1) prohibits the imposition of a higher rate of excise duty on imported goods vis-à-vis 'similar' domestic products. Products are 'similar' if they have 'similar characteristics and meet the same needs from the point of view of consumers' (*Commission v France (Tax on Spirits)*)
- Article 110(2) prohibits the imposition of excise duties on imported goods which afford 'indirect protection' to domestic goods. Products need not be 'similar' for Article 110(2) to apply but must be in 'competition, even partial, indirect or potential, with each other' (*Co-operativa Co-frutta*).

Compare/contrast Article 30 with Article 110:

- Article 30 and Article 110 are mutually exclusive
- It is crucial to distinguish between them. Under Article 30, Customs duties and equivalent charges are **prohibited** (subject to certain narrow derogations) but under Article 110, excise duties are **permitted** (unless they discriminate against similar imported products or afford indirect protection to competing domestic products)
- Examine the cases where a so-called 'tax' was found to be a charge having an effect equivalent to a Customs duty instead because it did not satisfy the Court's definition of a 'tax' (*Marimex, Capolongo, Fratelli Cucchi*)
- Observe that Article 30 applies when imports are subject to a charge even if there are no competing domestic products (*Sociaal Fonds*). However, for Article 110 to apply, there must be 'similar' or at least competing domestic goods (*De Danske Bilimportører*).

SUMMARY

- Article 30 TFEU prohibits 'Customs duties on imports and exports and Charges having equivalent effect.'
- Equivalent charges are defined very widely. All charges imposed on goods when they cross a national frontier, whether by the importing or exporting state, are prohibited. The size, and the name, of the charge are immaterial (*Commission v Italy (Statistical Levy)*).

- It is irrelevant why a Customs duty or equivalent charge has been imposed. It may have been for socially valid reasons (e.g. raising cash for disadvantaged workers) but this is immaterial (*Sociaal Fonds*, *Kapniki Mikhailidis*).

- Article 110 TFEU allows Members States to establish their own 'internal taxation' system, in the form of excise duties on goods, but prohibits discrimination against imported products. Discriminatory excise duties are prohibited whether direct (*Alfons Lütticke*) or indirect (*Humblot*). Direct discrimination cannot be justified (*Haahr Petroleum*), but indirect discrimination is justifiable (*Commission v France (Tax on Wines)*). 'Excise duties' are most frequently imposed on tobacco products, alcoholic drinks and fuel.

- 'Internal taxation' means a 'general system of internal duties applied systematically to categories of products in accordance with objective criteria irrespective of the origin of the products' (*Commission v France (Reprographic Machines)*).

- A so-called 'tax' which is apparently levied on all goods but which is imposed in a different manner, and/or which is subject to different criteria, for domestic and imported products, is therefore not a 'tax' and falls under Article 30 instead (*Marimex*). Similarly, a so-called 'tax' which actually benefits domestic products is not a 'tax' either and falls under Article 30 instead (*Capolongo*). However, the products in question must be the same (*Fratelli Cucchi*).

- Imported goods must not be taxed 'in excess' of the taxation imposed on 'similar' domestic products (Article 110(1)). 'Similar' products are 'products which have similar characteristics and meet the same needs from the point of view of consumers' (*Commission v France (Tax on Spirits)*). Hence products do not have to be identical for Article 110(1) to apply.

- Where different products are in 'competition' with each other, Member States may impose different excise duties but the level of taxation imposed on imported products must not afford 'indirect protection' to domestic products (Article 110(2)). Products need not be 'similar' for Article 110(2) to apply but must be in 'competition, even partial, indirect or potential, with each other' (*Co-operativa Co-frutta*). Beer and wine are not 'similar' products, but they are at least in 'competition' with each other (*Commission v UK (Tax on Beer and Wine)*).

- Article 30 applies when imports are subject to a charge even if there are no competing domestic products (*Sociaal Fonds*). However, for Article 110 to apply, there must be 'similar' or at least competing domestic goods (*De Danske Bilimportører*).

Further reading

Articles

Easson, A, 'The Spirits, Wine and Beer Judgments: A Legal Mickey Finn?' (1980) 5 *EL Rev* 318.

Easson, A, 'Fiscal Discrimination: New Perspectives on Article 95' (1981) 18 *CML Rev* 521.

Lonbay, J, 'A Review of Recent Tax Cases' (1989) 14 *EL Rev* 48.

Plender, R, 'Charges Having an Equivalent Effect to Customs Duties: A Review of the Cases' (1978) 3 *EL Rev* 101.

Snell, J, 'Non-discriminatory Tax Obstacles in Community Law' (2007) 56 *ICLQ* 339.

16

EU competition law

AIMS AND OBJECTIVES

After reading this chapter you should be able to:

- Understand why there are rules regulating anti-competitive practices
- Understand the prohibition under Article 101 TFEU
- Understand the necessary elements for showing a breach of Article 101 TFEU
- Understand the prohibition under Article 102 TFEU
- Understand the necessary elements for showing a breach of Article 102 TFEU
- Understand the enforcement procedures in EU competition law
- Understand the basis of merger control
- Evaluate the effectiveness of EU competition law
- Analyse the relationship between Article 101 TFEU and Article 102 TFEU
- Apply the rules under Article 101 TFEU and Article 102 TFEU to factual situations

16.1 The basis of EU competition law

16.1.1 The purpose of competition law

Article 2 EC Treaty originally identified the main task of EU law as being:

ARTICLE

'the promotion of harmonious development of economic activities by the creation of a common market and the progressive approximation of the economic policies of the member states'.

As well as this Article 3(g) also states that the EU must ensure:

ARTICLE

'competition in the internal market is not distorted'.

As a result, the framers of the EU Treaty included very specific rules regarding competition. To have rules on competitive, or rather anti-competitive, behaviour seems at first sight to be inconsistent with the whole idea of economic freedom that is demonstrated in the 'Four Freedoms' and the drive towards a Single Market unfettered by any national barriers to trade. Rules on competition would seem to be a restriction on business efficiency and a restriction on successful businesses and therefore on market forces. This is in fact not the case. The Treaty makers were not trying to restrict businesses from free competition but rather to prevent large powerful businesses from using unfair means to harm small- and medium-sized businesses.

The drafters of the Treaty realised that within a newly created Single Market companies would enjoy the benefit of a free and expanded market and might see this as a chance to get round former national policies on anti-competitive activities and operate on a much larger scale to maximise their potential. In other words, the framers of the Treaty recognised the point that unfettered market forces can lead directly on to monopolies. (A monopoly is where a single company or organisation enjoys almost unrestricted trade in a particular product or service.) Monopolies, almost by definition, defeat competition and ultimately, therefore, restrict consumer choice.

As a result, the framers of the Treaty inserted rules in the Treaty aimed at dealing with such practices. In doing so they took the same view as expressed in the Sherman Act of 1890 of the United States of America, that there should be prohibition of 'every contract, combination or conspiracy in restraint of trade' and also 'the monopolization of trade and commerce'. In other words, the rules should prevent the distortion of free competition resulting from either collusion between different businesses or the predominant power of a single business.

Therefore, the framers of the Treaty then drafted in a series of rules with three principal objectives:

- to avoid the possibility of restrictive practices and agreements;
- to prevent large businesses from abusing their economic dominance in the market;
- to ensure that, within certain limits, the public sector observes the same rules.

Set against the problems foreseen when framing the Treaty, these seem to be quite reasonable controls. Nevertheless, EU competition law has often been criticised in a number of different ways.

First, it has been said that the law is too general in its application. This is because all agreements and practices are treated alike, even if they would actually benefit the consumer.

Second, competition law has been criticised on the basis that it in fact only sacrifices equity and efficiency to political goals.

> [The existence of competition law] is 'a perversity' and 'the loud admission of defeat' and 'an admission that the market alone cannot effect competition'.
>
> Another danger, of course, is always that 'member states will continue to promote the national interest over that of the Community, cling rigorously to currency, sovereignty, and intensify economic divergences within the Community'.
>
> I Ward, *A Critical Introduction to European Law* (Butterworths, 2003), p. 126

Nevertheless, despite the apparent shortcomings, it is generally accepted that the EU institutions have succeeded in framing a cohesive and consistent set of objectives to be pursued in implementing competition policy. These are all identified in the Commission's Ninth Report on Competition Policy:

- to create an open and unified market which is not partitioned by restrictive and anti-competitive agreements between firms;

- to realise an appropriate amount of effective competition in markets, avoiding over-concentration or any abuses exercised by dominant companies;

- to achieve fairness in the marketplace, which involves giving support to small and medium-sized firms, measures for the protection of consumers and the penalising of unlawful state subsidies;

- to maintain the competitive position of the Community against its principal rivals in global economy, being mainly the USA and Japan.

16.1.2 The character of competition law

The rules on competition law cover all items capable of forming the subject-matter of commercial transactions. So it includes not only goods and services, but also intellectual property rights. The provisions are actually framed in quite broad terms and as a result have been the subject of much interpretation in the ECJ.

The competition rules can be used against firms regardless of the existence of a registered office in the EU, provided that its actions are capable of affecting trade within the Single Market. This was clearly identified in *The Woodpulp case, Ahlstrom Osakeyhtio and Others v Commission* (Cases 89, 104, 114, 116, 117 and 125–129/85) [1993] ECR I–1307. The rules are also pragmatic in order to preserve free trade. In this way they are subject to exceptions to preserve market efficiency.

EU law only requires that penalties should apply where the actions of 'undertakings' affect trade between Member States. Nevertheless, this means that they can apply even if the effect is actually quite small, and even if the undertakings involved are in the same Member State.

It is also possible, therefore, for EU competition law and national law to exist alongside each other.

CASE EXAMPLE

Wilhelm v Bundeskartellamt (Case 23/67) [1969] ECR 1

Here, firms were penalised under German law for engaging in an unlawful cartel. They complained, arguing that the German authorities were not in a position to bring such action against them because the matter was the subject of action under EU law also. The ECJ held that the two distinct laws in fact operated in different spheres and for different purposes and therefore that action under both was possible.

Articles 101 and 102 in fact complement each other, in that they pursue common objectives but by focusing on different types of activity in different situations.

It is evident, then, that EU competition law has three main objectives which may at times, nevertheless, appear to be incompatible:

- efficiency;
- protection of both consumers and small businesses;
- the creation of the Single Market.

It is also true to say that competition law is among the most highly developed of all EU law. In fact, as Josephine Steiner points out:

So pervasive is the influence of EU competition law and so severe are the sanctions for its breach, that business, whatever its size, whether or not their operations are currently confined to their domestic market, cannot afford to ignore Community law.

J Steiner, *Textbook on EC Law* (2nd edn, Blackstones, 1991), p. 106

16.2 Article 101 and provisions on restrictive practices

16.2.1 The scope of Article 101

Article 101 is concerned with restrictive trade practices. It sets out distinctly the nature of the prohibition:

ARTICLE

'The following shall be prohibited as being incompatible with the internal market: All agreements between undertakings, decisions of associations of undertakings and concerted practices which may affect trade between member states and which have as their object or effect the prevention, restriction or distortion of competition within the common market.'

Article 101(1) also goes on to identify specific examples of anti-competitive acts that would fall under the prohibition as anti-competitive practices. These are those which:

- Directly or indirectly fix purchase or selling prices or any other trading conditions. This covers any arrangement that directly or indirectly could hinder intra-Union trade. In this way it can include arrangements whereby undertakings agree on trading conditions applicable to their business dealings such as discounts or credit arrangements. It has, for instance, included a retail price maintenance agreement between Belgian and Dutch booksellers (*VBVB and VVVB v Commission* (Cases 43 and 63/82) [1984] ECR 19).

- Limit or control production, markets, technical development, or investment. This involves agreements where undertakings restrict their own growth in order to raise prices artificially and prevent those outside the agreement from entering the trade, as in the *Quinine Cartel case* [1970] ECR 661 (see below).

- Share markets or sources of supply. This refers to the situation where competitors agree to apportion markets on either a geographical or a product basis. This was in effect what was being done in *Consten and Grundig* [1966] ECR 429 (see below). It might be done in an oligopical market where competitors appoint each other as exclusive dealers of the other's product or in a particular region of the EU.

- Apply dissimilar conditions to equivalent transactions with other trading parties, thereby placing them at a competitive disadvantage. The object here clearly is to place the competing party at a disadvantage. It might obviously then involve providing advantageous conditions to one purchaser of a product over another.

CASE EXAMPLE

IAZ International Belgium and Others v Commission (Case 96/82) [1983] ECR 3369

A Belgian law meant that only those washing machines and dishwashers conforming to certain Belgian standards could be connected to the mains water supply. The standards had been set in an agreement between the national association of water suppliers and a trade association to which certain major suppliers of washing machines and dishwashers were affiliated. Clearly, this had the effect of disadvantaging those suppliers who were not affiliated to the trade association.

■ Make the conclusion of contracts subject to acceptance by the other parties of supplementary obligations which, by their nature or according to commercial usage, have no connection with the subject of such contracts. This refers to situations where in order for a party to enter a contract it is bound to fulfil other obligations which in fact have no real bearing on the contract. A classic example would be requiring a party buying one product or service to buy at the same time a completely unrelated product or service.

Article 101(2) makes all such agreements void. It is then possible for the Commission to grant exemptions in certain cases.

The prohibition under Article 101 has three key elements all of which need to be proved and therefore all of which need to be defined and understood:

■ the types of agreements that are prohibited;

■ the effect on inter-state trade;

■ the meaning of 'object or effect of preventing, distorting or restricting competition'.

Before looking at these it is important to understand the meaning of the word 'undertaking'.

16.2.2 The concept of 'undertaking'

Both Article 101 and Article 102 are concerned with the anti-competitive activities of 'undertaking'. The term 'undertaking', while used widely, is not defined anywhere in the Treaty and so again we have to look to the case law for interpretation of the term by the ECJ.

In fact, the ECJ has given a broad definition to the term: 'a single organisation of personal, tangible and intangible elements, attached to an autonomous legal entity and pursuing a long term economic aim' (*Mannesmann v High Authority* (Case 19/61) [1962] ECR 357). The term has also been defined in numerous other cases and in Commission Reports on Competition Law.

As a result, it can be seen that the term covers almost every type of entity regardless of its legal status, from an individual to a multi-national corporation, provided that it has legal capacity and is engaged in an economic activity. Therefore there is a wide spread of disparate economic activities to which the term has been applied over time:

■ an opera singer (*Re Unitel* (Commission Decision 78/516) [1978] 3 CMLR 306);

■ a sports federation (*Re World Cup 1990 Package Tours* (Commission Decision 92/51));

■ a state-owned corporation (*Italian State v Sacchi* (Case 155/73) [1974] ECR 409);

■ a public agency (*Höfner v Macrotron* (Case C–41/90) [1991] ECR I–1979);

■ a trade association (*FRUBO v Commission* (Case 71/74) [1975] ECR 563);

■ banking (*Zuchner v Bayerische Vereinsbank AG* (Case 172/80) [1981] ECR 2021).

It has been held that the definition does not depend on the activity involving a profit motive. Nevertheless, the General Court has recently refined the definition and stated that there must be some form of economic activity, however marginal, for the entity to be regarded as an 'undertaking' for the purposes of competition law.

CASE EXAMPLE

FENIN v Commission (Case T–319/99) [2003] ECR II–357

Spanish hospitals and other health bodies (known collectively as SNS), purchased supplies from FENIN, a Spanish association comprising the majority of firms marketing medical goods and equipment. When SNS delayed payment FENIN complained that this amounted to an abuse of a dominant position (now under Article 102 TFEU). The CFI rejected the claim on the ground that SNS was not an undertaking. This was because, even though a purchaser could be classed as an undertaking if the purchases were then used in what amounts to other than an economic activity, then there is no economic activity and no undertaking. SNS, financed by social security contributions, offered a free service to the public and so Article 102 TFEU could not apply.

Throughout its jurisprudence, the ECJ reaffirms that where a not-for-profit seeking activity operating for a social purpose on the principle of solidarity is not an undertaking (Joined Cases C–264/01, C–306/01, C–354/01 and C–355/01 *Aok Bundesverband and Others*).

The issue of whether a sporting body can be classed as an undertaking has also been considered. The *Bosman* ruling, of course, suggested that this would only be the case where an economic activity was involved. It could clearly impact upon the law governing free movement of workers for instance where rules of sporting associations limited the numbers of non-national players. However, rules that merely deal with sporting conduct are not within the scope of EU law, and this point has been considered in relation to the International Olympic Committee.

CASE EXAMPLE

Meca-Medina and Majcen v Commission (Case C–519/04P) [2006] ECR I–6991

Two distance swimmers were suspended by the International Olympic Committee after positive drugs tests. They complained that IOC anti-doping rules infringed both EC competition law and the law on provision of services. The Court of First Instance held that purely sporting rules were not covered by EC (now EU) law on either competition or provision of services. The swimmers appealed to the European Court of Justice to set aside the CFI's judgment. The ECJ affirmed the principle that rules of a purely sporting nature have nothing to do with economic activity and therefore are not covered by EC (now EU) law. However, the Court also identified that, where the rules concerned penalties as was the case with the IOC's anti-doping rules, then these might indeed have an adverse effect on competition law and so sporting bodies could be classed as undertakings on that basis. However, the swimmers had not complained on the basis of the excessive nature of the penalties so the ECJ rejected their claims.

It is clear in any case that the definition must be taken on a case-by-case basis.

16.2.3 The character of prohibited agreements

There are in fact three distinct types of agreement or restrictive practice which fall within the prohibition in Article 101:

- agreements between undertakings;
- decisions by associations of undertakings;
- concerted practices.

Agreements between undertakings

An agreement between undertakings must always carry with it some form of collusion. This is inevitably to distinguish it from unilateral acts.

CASE EXAMPLE

AEG Telefunken v Commission (Case 107/82) [1983] ECR 3151

Here, a refusal by a company to admit a trader to its distribution network was in fact seen as an agreement. This was because the refusal formed part of a system of contracts with existing distributors.

However, the agreement must also involve autonomous behaviour by the undertakings. For instance, Article 101 would not be infringed and it could not be classed as an agreement where national law imposed the agreement on the undertakings.

CASE EXAMPLE

Commission and France v Ladbroke Racing Ltd (Joined Cases C–359 and 379/95P) [1998] 4 CMLR 27

Here, French legislation required that companies engaged in off-course totalisator betting should be in the control of the Paris Mutuel Urbain (PMU). Ladbrokes complained that agreements between the companies and PMU were in breach of Article 101 TFEU. The ECJ identified that this could not be the case since the companies and PMU were operating according to the national law and not of their own initiative.

According to *Tepea v Commission* (Case 28/77) [1978] ECR 1391, it is clear that even informal, oral arrangements can be classed as an agreement for the purposes of Article 101. Indeed, while contractual arrangements would obviously be agreements there is no real requirement that the agreement should be binding for Article 101 to apply. In fact, the leading case has shown that the so-called 'gentlemen's agreements' could still fall foul of Article 101 and in any case the third type, concerted practices, would cover most collusive behaviour.

CASE EXAMPLE

ACF Chemiefarma v Commission (The Quinine Cartel case) (Case 41/69) [1970] ECR 661

Here, firms in France, the Netherlands and Germany agreed to sales quotas and even the prohibition of the manufacture of synthetic quinine. They did so in order to raise the price of the product artificially and this was thus a breach of Article 101 TFEU.

Decisions by associations of undertakings

Many industries collectively act within trading associations. Usually such associations co-ordinate behaviour and regulate standards in a trade and so incorporate a set of rules by which the members agree to be bound on membership. This is obviously usually beneficial. Nevertheless, when the rules of the association laid down are clearly aimed at harming free competition then they may amount to a breach of Article 101.

The obvious types of decision that could amount to a breach of Article 101 include ones fixing prices, or requiring specific discounts, or requiring collective boycotts of other undertakings, or the inclusion of any kind of restrictive contract clauses.

It has also been held, however, in *NV IAZ International Belgium v Commission* (1983) that even non-binding arrangements might count as a decision leading to a breach of Article 81 (now Article 101 TFEU). Neither does the body concerned have to be involved in commercial activity.

However, there will be no breach of Article 101 where trade associations are genuinely independent of their parent bodies.

CASE EXAMPLE

Germany v Delta Schiffahrts-und Speditionsgesellschaft GmbH (Case C–153/93) [1994] ECR I–2517

Here, both shippers and inland waterway ship operators were represented on freight commissions that were empowered to fix freight charges. These charges were then approved by the Minister of Transport and became compulsory. The shipper claimed that the charges were contrary to Article 101 TFEU but the ECJ rejected the claim since it felt that the state was entitled to provide tariffs for inland waterway freight traffic on recommendation from such a body, provided that the body was truly independent and the state still in effect retained control over the decision.

Concerted practices

The term 'concerted practices' has been defined both by academics and the ECJ. Academics have defined it as 'co-ordinated action between undertakings which, without amounting to an agreement, consciously substitutes co-operation for competition'. So the key characteristic of a concerted practice, by contrast with a straightforward agreement, is that it is more disguised or hidden and is generally informal.

In the leading case the ECJ has defined 'concerted practice' as:

JUDGMENT

'a form of coordination between enterprises that has not yet reached the point where it is a contract in the true sense of the word, but which, in practice, consciously substitutes co-operation for the risks of competition'.

CASE EXAMPLE

ICI Ltd v Commission (the Dyestuffs case) (Case 48/69) [1972] ECR 619

This case involved a decision by the major manufacturers of dyestuff, representing in excess of 80 per cent of sales of dyestuff, to raise prices at exactly the same time. The Commission concluded that there had been a concerted practice and imposed fines on the undertakings. The undertakings then challenged this decision, arguing that it was merely parallel behaviour in an oligopoly (similar to a monopoly but where the majority of a market is controlled by a few undertakings rather than a single body). The ECJ held that it was irrelevant that there was no formal agreement because the collusion could be identified in a series of telexes to subsidiary companies and phrased in the same terms. The Court identified:

JUDGMENT

'By its very nature a concerted practice does not have all the elements of a contract but may inter alia arise out of coordination which becomes apparent from the behaviour of the participants. Although parallel behaviour may not by itself be identified with a concerted practice, it may, however, amount to strong evidence of such a practice if it leads to conditions of competition which do not correspond to the normal conditions of the market.'

So the true test of a concerted practice is when the parallel behaviour can be shown to be co-operative such that the undertakings involved appear to be acting with a common design or purpose: *Co-operative Vereniging 'Suiker Unie' v Commission (the Sugar Cartel case)* (Cases 40–48, 50, 54–56, 111, 113 and 114/73) [1975] ECR 1663. Even a single meeting can amount to a concerted practice (*T-Mobile Netherlands BV* (Case C–8/08) [2009] ECR I–4529).

Horizontal agreements and vertical agreements

Agreements that may offend Article 101 may of course be of two different types: horizontal or vertical.

A **horizontal** agreement is one between undertakings at the same level, so would usually be one between competing manufacturers or distributors. This could, for example, be an agreement to divide up markets; or it could be a price-fixing arrangement as in the *Dyestuffs case (ICI v Commission)* (1972).

A **vertical** agreement, on the other hand, is one reached between undertakings at different levels in the process, for example between the manufacturer and the distributor, or between wholesalers and retailers. These would usually, of course, benefit the consumer because they are likely to streamline the process of trade. However, they may offend Article 101 if they involve exclusive distribution arrangements, or exclusive licensing agreements.

The principles were established in the leading case, commonly referred to as *Consten and Grundig*.

CASE EXAMPLE

Etablissements Consten and Grundig v Commission (Cases 56 and 58/64) [1966] ECR 429

This involved an exclusive dealership under which Consten was appointed sole distributor of Grundig's electrical goods in France in return for which there was a total ban on imports or exports of Grundig's products in any other EU country. Consten complained when another company, UNEF, sold Grundig's goods in France in breach of its exclusive rights. UNEF then complained to the Commission that the dealership was a breach of Article 81 and the Commission issued a decision on this basis. Consten and Grundig argued that the agreement was for the purpose of streamlining distribution of Grundig's products in France where Grundig had competition from other manufacturers and was not an interference with trade. The ECJ identified that vertical as well as horizontal agreements could fall under Article 101 TFEU and that this was in fact a breach since it might affect trade between Member States.

16.2.4 The effect on trade between Member States

In order to establish that there has been a breach of Article 101 the Article also requires that the agreement may affect trade between Member States. The important word here is 'may'. In other words, there is no absolute requirement that the agreement has in fact affected trade; merely that it has the potential to do so.

The capacity of the agreement to affect trade is ascertained by reference to the free movement of goods and attainment of a Single Market, the same basic test as that identified in the *Dassonville* formula (see section 14.4).

So an agreement is capable of affecting trade between Member States if it is capable of constituting a threat 'direct or indirect, actual or potential, on the pattern of trade'.

CASE EXAMPLE

Belasco v Commission (Case 246/86) [1989] ECR 2117

In this case a scheme fixing the price of cement in the Netherlands was held capable of affecting trade between Member States because it strengthened the existing divisions in the market.

In this way there is no need to prove any actual harm, as long as the agreement is likely to prevent, restrict or distort competition to a sufficient degree.

CASE EXAMPLE

Vereeniging van Cementhandelaren v Commission (Case 8/72) [1972] ECR 977

Here, a cartel in the Belgian roofing felt industry was held capable of affecting trade between Member States even though it was argued that there was no actual effect on trade. This was because it was capable of affecting inter-state trade, competitors from outside the cartel being at a potential disadvantage.

16.2.5 The object or effect of preventing, restricting or distorting competition

Article 101 requires also that the agreement must have as its 'object or effect the prevention, restriction or distortion of competition within the common market'.

'Object' and 'effect' in the context of the Article are clearly meant to be alternative tests. On this basis the test has as much to do with the practical outcomes of a business arrangement as it has to do with the intentions of the undertakings that are party to the arrangement.

The key issue then is whether competition has been stifled or affected, rather than whether there has been any actual movement in trade, whether up or down.

CASE EXAMPLE

Etablissements Consten and Grundig v Commission (Cases 56 and 58/64) [1966] ECR 429

As we have already seen, this leading case involved an exclusive distribution agreement between the German electrical goods manufacturer and a retailer/distributor in France. Consten was appointed sole distributor of Grundig's goods in France and also had exclusive rights to use Grundig's trademark. The case arose when another company, UNEF, sold Grundig's goods in France and Consten complained about the breach of its trademark rights. However, UNEF was successful in its counterclaim of breach of Article 101 TFEU since the arrangement had the potential to affect trade between Member States.

However, the ECJ nevertheless tries to apply the rules in a way that will not stifle business enterprise and initiative. The concern is not to prevent businesses from operating efficiently and effectively but to prevent a distortion of real competition.

CASE EXAMPLE

Bunce v Postworth trading as Skyblue [2005] EWCA Civ 490; [2005] IRLR 557

The claimant was a welder, who entered into an agreement with the agency which arranged regular welding work for him with Carillion Rail and other companies, amounting to 142 assignments during the year before the termination of his contract. Under his contract with the agency he was bound to accept the supervision of clients to whom he was assigned. At one point Carillion complained about his work and the agency terminated its contract with him. He claimed unfair dismissal. Both the tribunal and the EAT held that he was not an employee. The Court of Appeal agreed that he could not be an employee of the agency because it had no control over the manner in which he did his work and he was not an employee of Carillion as he had no contractual relationship with the company.

In the above case the ECJ identified the factors that will need to be taken into account to determine whether or not an agreement is capable of distorting competition:

- The nature and quantity of the product in question – so that the greater the market share of the product concerned, the more likely it is that an agreement may inhibit competition.

- The position and size of the undertakings involved – so that the greater the share of the market that they enjoy, the more there is a possibility of distorting competition.

- The relationship of the agreement to other agreements – so that the more isolated the agreement, the less likely it is to limit competition, but where it forms part of a network of agreements it is more likely to affect competition.

- The extent of the agreement – so that any agreement that extends beyond what is necessary to achieve the desired beneficial risk is likely to limit competition.

- The link with agreements on parallel imports or exports – so that where the agreement also includes bans on parallel imports or exports it will most usually be seen as stifling competition and lead to a breach of Article 101.

Market definition is clearly an important question and is one that the Commission has addressed in the Notice on Definition of the Relevant Market (1997 OJ C372/5). It has also been considered in the case law.

CASE EXAMPLE

European Night Services v Commission (Cases T–374/94 and 375/94) [1998] ECR II–3141

Railway services in France, Germany, the Netherlands and the United Kingdom decided to form European Night Services to provide overnight rail services through the Channel Tunnel between the UK and the other countries. The Commission was concerned that the agreement had the effect of restricting competition but granted it an exemption with strict conditions attached. The CFI (now the General Court) annulled this decision because the Court felt that the market share of the parties involved was in fact quite limited. The Court stated that, where an agreement does not include any obvious restrictions on competition, then it is necessary to examine the context in which the agreement actually operates, including the economic context.

Traditionally, in any case, the ECJ would apply the *de minimis* rule. The Court would not show interest in agreements which would have a disproportionately minor effect on competition and would only strike down agreements that might affect competition to a noticeable extent.

CASE EXAMPLE

Frans Volk v Establissements Vervaecke Sprl (Case 5/69) [1969] ECR 295

This case involved an agreement between a Dutch electrical goods distributor (Vervaecke) and a German washing machine manufacturer (Volk). The agreement gave the Dutch distributor exclusive distribution rights of the German company's washing machines in Belgium and Luxembourg. In return the agreement was reinforced by a ban on parallel imports of Volk's products by third parties, in other words a total protection. However, in examining the agreement the ECJ acknowledged that Volk only actually produced somewhere between 0.2 per cent and 0.5 per cent of washing machines in Germany and it sold considerably fewer in Belgium and Luxembourg. On this basis the agreement could not be said to have any real effect on competition, the *de minimis* principle applied and there was no breach of Article 101 TFEU.

In fact, the *de minimis* principle has been introduced by the Commission in the form of Notices on Agreements of Minor Importance. The first of these was in 1986. The most recent is the Commission Notice on Agreements of Minor Importance 2001 (OJ 2001 C368/13).

Under this Notice an agreement will not be in breach of Article 101:

- where the undertakings that are parties to the agreement are actual or potential competitors (in other words, in a horizontal agreement), the aggregate market share of the undertakings concerned does not exceed 10 per cent of the market; or

- where the undertakings that are parties to the agreement are not competitors (in other words, in a vertical agreement) the aggregate market share of the undertakings concerned does not exceed 15 per cent of the market.

However, there are qualifications to these basic rules:

- in horizontal agreements the agreement must not contain any restrictions on sale price, limitation of output, or allocation of markets or customers, otherwise the notice will not apply;

- in vertical agreements the agreement must not contain restrictions on the minimum resale price of goods or on the territory that the goods will be sold in or the consumers that the goods will be sold to, or the notice will not apply.

16.2.6 Exemptions

Not all agreements will be automatically found to be in breach of Article 101. There are in fact different ways of avoiding being caught by Article 101 and until recently these included the granting of exemptions by the Commission. Since 1 May 2004, under the operation of Regulation 1/2003 a different process is in operation involving the Member States.

Sensibly, the Treaty also provided the means by which it could be identified that certain agreements could be exempted from the operation of Article 101. This includes both individual exemptions (which follow individual applications) and block exemptions that can be applied to specific categories of agreement.

Article 101 paragraph 3 specifically creates the criteria for exempting agreements. There are four conditions that must be met in order for exemption to be granted. Two of these are phrased in positive terms and two are phrased in negative terms.

■ First, it must be possible to show that the agreement, decision or practice contributes in some way to **improving** the production or distribution of goods or alternatively to **promoting** technical or economic progress.

CASE EXAMPLE

Transocean Marine Paint Association v Commission (Decision 77/454) [1975] 2 CMLR D75

This involved collaboration between a number of marine paint manufacturers with a view to rationalising production. The agreement between them was granted exemption because a global distribution network was created under the agreement which was in fact beneficial to competition.

CASE EXAMPLE

Re Vacuum Interrupters (Decision 77/160) [1977] 1 CMLR D67

Here, a joint venture between manufacturers of switchgear was exempted. This was because the agreement meant that research and development of vacuum interrupters was made possible as a result of the agreement.

■ Second, a fair share of the resulting **benefit** must pass to the **consumer**. This need not merely be the end consumer.

CASE EXAMPLE

ACEC v Berliet (Decision 68/319) [1968] CMLR D35

This involved an agreement on production of a prototype bus by two French manufacturers. A benefit was gained by intermediaries in a distribution network in consequence of a commercial transaction. This was accepted as sufficient to justify exemption.

■ The agreement or practice must not impose any unnecessary **restrictions** that would go beyond the necessary positive aims. An example of a practice that would infringe this negative requirement and therefore mean exemption would be denied is an absolute territorial protection, such as the ban on parallel imports in *Consten and Grundig v Commission* (1966).

■ There must not be any possibility of the restrictions **eliminating** competition in respect of a substantial part of the product in question. Obviously, in respect of this requirement the market share of the parties concerned and the level of competition within the specific market will be crucial factors. In *Re Vacuum Interrupters* (1977) (above) the market stretched well beyond the EU because the undertakings faced significant competition from both the USA and Japan. However, where the competition is much more limited the market might be restricted to a single Member State.

Individual exemptions

Prior to 2004 individual exemptions were granted by the Commission under the procedure in Regulation 17/62. Application was by way of a 'notification' of the agreement or practice to the Commission. Individual exemption was then granted in the form of Decisions. These might be for only limited periods and they might also be conditional or depend on the fulfillment of certain criteria or certain obligations identified in the Decision.

Now, under Regulation 1/2003 it is no longer necessary to notify the Commission in order to obtain individual exemption. Article 1(1) of the Regulation instead places the burden on undertakings themselves to identify whether any of their agreements offend Article 101(1) but are in fact exempt under Article 101(3). The national authorities are then responsible for applying the criteria for determining whether a particular agreement is in fact exempt.

Unlike the former system where the Commission had to be notified for exemption to be granted there is no requirement to inform the national authorities in the same way for the exemption to take effect. National authorities will determine whether or not there has been an infringement of Article 101 by the agreement in question.

Block exemptions

Block exemptions were in any case a means of reducing the huge bureaucratic burden on the Commission of applications for individual exemptions. The process was introduced then for the purpose of streamlining competition law.

Inevitably, also, the process of making application for individual exemption left businesses in a state of uncertainty until a Decision was issued. On this basis the use of block exemptions allowed businesses to assess for themselves whether or not a particular type of agreement was exempt. If it was apparent that a particular type of agreement would fall under a block exemption then there would be no need for the businesses concerned to approach the Commission at all. It would only be if there was uncertainty that undertakings would approach the Commission for individual exemption. Nevertheless, the fact that a block exemption existed would not prevent the Commission from stating that particular aspects of individual agreements fell outside the scope of the exemption.

Block exemptions are introduced in the form of Regulations and are granted in respect of specific types of agreements. There are many examples and these have included:

- A block exemption on exclusive distribution agreements in Regulation 1983/83, replaced by Regulation 2790/99 on vertical restraints.
- Another on exclusive purchasing agreements in Regulation 1984/83, also later replaced by Regulation 2790/99 – in fact, Regulation 2790/99 (which came into force in June 2000) replaced exemptions on all vertical agreements with the exception of certain serious restraints.
- One also on patent licensing in Regulation 2349/84, later replaced by an exemption on technology transfer in Regulation 240/96.
- One on motor vehicle distribution in Regulation 123/85.
- Another on know-how licensing in Regulation 556/89.
- Another recent block exemption is that on research and development agreements in Regulation 2658/2000.

Inevitably, the issue of block exemptions is also affected by the introduction of Regulation 1/2003. The new block exemption Regulation 2790/99 creates an exemption for all vertical agreements as a category in their own right. There are limits to its application. There are special rules, for instance in the case of certain sectors such as petrol distribution. It does not apply also to certain types of clause such as non-compete clauses for over five years, those preventing buyers from manufacturing or selling certain goods after the agreement comes to an end, and 'hard core' restrictions, such as those covering resale price maintenance or restrictions on resale outside exclusive distribution networks. However, it is wider than the Regulations that it replaced, applying, for instance, to unfinished goods.

The new block exemption is applied according to a market share test. In this way it only applies if the buyer or seller has below 30 per cent of the market share. This does not mean that the agreement cannot gain exemption but an individual exemption will have to be applied for. It is on this basis that the new block exemption has been criticised for lacking the certainty of the previous system.

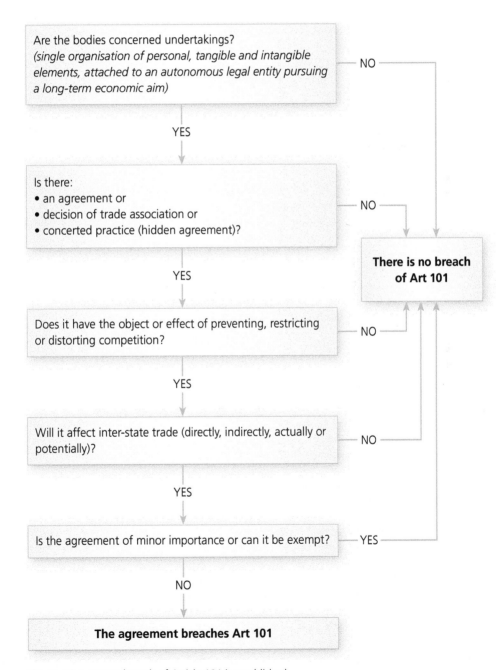

Figure 16.1 How a breach of Article 101 is established

ACTIVITY

Self-assessment questions

1. What is the definition of 'undertaking' in EU competition law?
2. What are the three main aspects of a claim under Article 101?
3. What three types of agreement will the Court of Justice accept amount to an agreement for the purposes of Article 101?
4. What types of agreement are prohibited under Article 101?
5. What was the basis of the decision in *Consten and Grundig v Commission*?
6. What is the difference in the *STM* case?
7. What test is applied in determining the effect on intra-Union trade?
8. What is the effect of the Commission Notice on agreements of minor importance?
9. What exemptions are available to undertakings under Article 101?

16.3 Article 102 and abuse of a dominant position

16.3.1 The concept of abuse of a dominant position

As we have seen, Article 101 concerns some form of collusive behaviour between undertakings that would have an effect on intra-Community trade and that in any case has as its object or effect the prevention, distortion or restriction of competition. Article 102, on the other hand, is usually concerned with the actions of a single undertaking rather than a combination of undertakings.

On this basis Article 102 was introduced to combat the perceived threat to competition posed by the negative effects of large concentrations of economic power in the hands of individual undertakings. It was also traditionally felt that Article 102 could not apply to oligopolies (large concentrations of economic power in the hands of a small number of undertakings). However, this reasoning has been challenged.

CASE EXAMPLE

Re Flat Glass (Decision 89/93) [1992] 5 CMLR 120

Here, the Commission decided that a group of undertakings that held a dominant position within the market for the production of 'flat glass' (between 79 and 95 per cent share) was in fact in a dominant position so that Article 102 TFEU could be applied when they engaged in concerted price fixing.

Article 102 is also applicable in the case of mergers and concentrations.

It must be remembered that Articles 101 and 102 are merely different mechanisms for dealing with what is essentially the same problem: the anti-competitive practices. The two Articles are, therefore, not mutually exclusive. Either may be alleged in a specific case and there is some overlap between the two. As a result, the Commission has a discretion how to apply competition law and which Article is in fact breached.

However, while there are overlaps with Article 101, it must also be remembered that there is no possibility of negative clearance in the case of Article 102. Neither are exemptions available (though they are for mergers). Once a breach has been proved then there is no further way of avoiding the consequences of the breach as there is in Article 101.

The basic prohibition is again spelled out in the Article itself. According to Article 102:

ARTICLE

'Art 102 Any abuse by one or more undertakings of a dominant position within the internal market or in a substantial part of it shall be prohibited as incompatible with the internal market insofar as it may affect trade between member states.'

Before moving on to analyse the separate elements of the Article it is important to emphasise that Article 102 does not in any way prohibit the existence of dominant positions. It is plain that the Article is not meant to punish efficient economic behaviour. Its purpose is rather to discourage practices that would cause damage to other undertakings by creating artificial conditions that distort competition. In this way it is the abuse of dominance that is significant more than the dominant position itself.

Looking at the wording of the Article, there are three distinct requirements all of which must be proved in order for there to be a breach of Article 102:

- The undertaking engaging in the practice complained of must have a dominant position in the appropriate market (which can be either the Single Market or a substantial part of it).
- The practice in question must amount to an abuse of that dominant position.
- Trade between Member States is affected as a result of the practice.

16.3.2 The concept of 'undertaking'

Articles 101 and 102 are both concerned with the anti-competitive activities of 'undertakings'. The definition given to the term 'undertaking' then is the same as under Article 101 (see section 16.2.2).

The term is thus defined broadly. Again, it is not defined anywhere in the Treaty, so again we have to look to the case law for interpretation of the term by the ECJ: 'a single organisation of personal, tangible and intangible elements, attached to an autonomous legal entity and pursuing a long term economic aim'.

Again, it covers almost every type of entity regardless of its legal status, from an individual to a multi-national corporation, provided that it has legal capacity and is engaged in an economic activity. However, as with Article 101, the definition is capable of evolving on a case-by-case basis.

16.3.3 The definition of 'dominance'

'Dominance' is not defined in the Treaty at any point. However, it was originally defined in the ECSC Treaty (European Coal and Steel Community Treaty). The definition given here was that dominance occurs where undertakings hold a position 'shielding them against effective competition in a substantial part of the common market'.

This is a fairly limited and imprecise definition and so as with other significant terms it has been left to the ECJ to define in the case law. The earliest possibility came in *Continental Can Co v Commission* (Case 6/72) [1973] ECR 215 where the ECJ identified that dominance amounted to:

JUDGMENT

'power to behave independently without taking into account their competitors, purchasers or suppliers because of their share of the market or ... availability of technical knowledge, raw materials or capital, they have power to control production or distribution for significant part of products'.

CASE EXAMPLE

Continental Can Co v Commission (Case 6/72) [1973] ECR 215

In this case Continental Can was a US multinational. Through its European subsidiary company, Europemballage, it possessed an 86 per cent share in another company, Schmalbach. This latter company enjoyed a dominant position in Germany in the market for tins for meat and fish products and also in metal lids for glass containers. When Europemballage proposed to engage in a takeover of another company, Thomassen, a Dutch packaging firm, this was challenged on the basis of being a breach of Article 102 TFEU. The Commission held that it did in fact amount to an elimination of potential competition and, therefore, a reduction in consumer choice, and that it was an abuse of a dominant position. The Commission's Decision was, however, overturned by the ECJ on the ground that the Commission had failed to identify the relevant product market and therefore had not proved dominance.

Two clear elements arise from the definition in the above case: the share of the market enjoyed by the undertaking and its ability to act independently. It was not long before the ECJ had the opportunity to review, re-affirm and supplement this definition.

CASE EXAMPLE

United Brands v Commission (Case 27/76) [1978] ECR 207

United Brands was one of the largest producers of bananas in the world, handling 40 per cent of EC trade at the time of the case. The company was alleged to have breached Article 102 TFEU and abused its dominant position by implementing a completely different pricing policy in different Member States. The ECJ held that there was such a breach and considered again the definition of dominance.

The ECJ, building on its definition in *Continental Can*, identified that dominance is:

JUDGMENT

'a position of economic strength ... which enables it to prevent competition being maintained on the relevant market by giving it the power to behave to an appreciable effect independently of its competitors, and ultimately its consumers'.

This again emphasises the significance of the ability of the undertaking to act independently without regard to competition. Another significant feature was added by this statement of the ECJ, the importance of the relevant market. In other words the ECJ was acknowledging that market share had to be analysed by reference to the specific market in which the undertaking was competing. In the case there was discussion whether the relevant market was fruit or whether there was a specific market for bananas.

Yet another extension to the definition was provided in the case of *Hoffmann La Roche v Commission* (Case 85/76) [1979] ECR 461:

'such a position does not preclude some competition but enables [it] . . . if not to determine, at least to have an appreciable effect on the conditions in which that competition will develop, and in any case to act largely in disregard of it'.

As a result of this gradual development of a definition it is possible to see that there are two critical concepts in determining dominance:

- the relevant market (this will be determined by analysing not only the relevant geographical market but the relevant product market also – other considerations include whether there is in fact a temporal market, and also cross-elasticity of supply may be important);
- calculation of the market share of the undertaking in question.

16.3.4 The relevant market

The relevant product market

Obviously, in terms of defending their position and avoiding a finding of dominance, undertakings will want to argue that the relevant product market should be defined as widely as possible. Inevitably the party complaining that it has been affected by the alleged breach of Article 102 will want the relevant product market to be defined narrowly so there is a greater possibility of dominance being found.

CASE EXTRACT

In the case extract below a significant section of the judgment has been reproduced in the left hand column. Individual points arising from the judgment are briefly explained in the right hand column. Read the extract including the commentary in the right hand column and complete the exercise that follows.

Extract adapted from the judgment in *United Brands v Commission* (Case 27/76) [1978] ECR 207

Facts

Here United Brands were charging different prices in different member states for the same goods. The company argued that the relevant product market was fresh fruit, in which case they would inevitably have a small market share and dominance could not then be considered. The Commission argued, and it was accepted, that there was in fact a separate product market for bananas themselves. The basis of this argument was that bananas had a very specific market usually being consumed by, according to evidence given, the sick, the aged and the young. They could not therefore be considered merely as a part of a much more general market.

Basic facts

Subject of the reference

Judgment

11 The opportunities for competition under Article [102 TFEU] . . . must be considered having regard to the particular features of the product in question and with reference to a clearly defined geographic area in which it is marketed and where the conditions of competition are sufficiently homogenous for the effect of the economic power of the undertaking concerned to be able to be evaluated.

Tests of dominance are relevant product market and relevant geographical market

Paragraph 1 The Product Market

12 As far as the product market is concerned it is first of all necessary to ascertain whether, as the applicant maintains, bananas are an integral part of the fresh fruit market, because they are reasonably interchangeable by consumers with other kinds of fresh fruit such as apples, oranges, grapes, peaches, strawberries, etc. or whether the relevant market consists solely of the banana market which includes both branded bananas and unlabelled bananas and is a market sufficiently homogenous and distinct from the market of other fresh fruit.

So question is – is the RPM bananas or fruit?

13 The applicant submits in support of its argument that bananas compete with other fresh fruit in the same shops, on the same shelves, at prices which can be compared, satisfying the same needs: consumption as a dessert or between meals.

United Brands argues it is fruit

14 The statistics produced show that consumer expenditure on the purchase of bananas is at its lowest between June and December when there is a plentiful supply of domestic fresh fruit on the market.

15 Studies carried out by the Food and Agriculture Organisation (FAO) (especially in 1975) confirm that banana prices are relatively weak during the summer months and that the price of apples for example has a statistically appreciable impact on the consumption of bananas in the Federal Republic of Germany.

And reason this is because of the low price of bananas in certain months

16 Again according to these studies some easing of prices is noticeable at the end of the year during the 'orange season'.

17 The seasonal peak periods when there is a plentiful supply of other fresh fruit exert an influence not only on the prices but also on the volume of sales of bananas and consequently on the volume of imports thereof.

18 The applicant concludes from these findings that bananas and other fresh fruit form only one market and that UBC's operations should have been examined in this context for the purpose of any application of Article [102 TFEU] . . .

19 The Commission maintains that there is a demand for bananas which is distinct from the demand for other fresh fruit especially as the banana is a very important part of the diet of certain sections of the community.

Commission argues bananas are a separate market

20 The specific qualities of the banana influence customer preference and induce him not to readily accept other fruits as a substitute.

This is because bananas have distinct qualities

21 The Commission draws the conclusion from the studies quoted by the applicant that the influence of the prices and availabilities of other types of fruit on the prices and availabilities of bananas on the relevant market is very ineffective and that these effects are too brief and too spasmodic for such other fruit to be regarded as forming part of the same market as bananas or a substitute therefor.

And other fruit does not affect the banana market significantly

22 For the banana to be regarded as forming a market which is sufficiently differentiated from other fruit markets it must be possible for it to be singled out by such special features distinguishing it from other fruits that it is only to a limited extent interchangeable with them and is only exposed to their competition in a way that is hardly perceptible.

To be an RPM the product must not be interchangeable with other fruit

23 The ripening of bananas takes place the whole year round without any season having to be taken into account.

Bananas are not seasonal

24 Throughout the year production exceeds demand and can satisfy it at any time.

And can satisfy demand at any time of year

25 Owing to this particular feature the banana is a privileged fruit and its production and marketing can be adapted to the seasonal fluctuations of other fresh fruit which are known and can be computed.

So are not affected by other fruit which is seasonal

26 There is no unavoidable seasonal substitution since the consumer can obtain this fruit all the year round.

And there is no substitute for a banana

27 Since the banana is a fruit which is always available in sufficient quantities the question whether it can be replaced by other fruits must be determined over the whole of the year for the purposes of ascertaining the degree of competition between it and other fresh fruit.

28 The studies of the banana market on the court's file show that on the latter market there is no significant long term cross-elasticity any more than – as has been mentioned – there is any seasonal substitutability in general between the banana and all the seasonal fruits, as this only exists between the banana and two fruits (peaches and table grapes) in one of the countries (West Germany) of the relevant geographical market.

29 As far as concerns the two fruits available throughout the year (oranges and apples) the first are not interchangeable and in the case of the second there is only a relative degree of substitutability.

30 This small degree of substitutability is accounted for by the specific features of the banana and all the factors which influence consumer choice.

31 The banana has certain characteristics, appearance, taste, softness, seedlessness, easy handling, a constant level of production which enable it to satisfy the constant needs of an important section of the population consisting of the very young, the old and the sick.

Bananas have important characteristics and a discrete market

32 As far as prices are concerned two FAO studies show that the banana is only affected by the prices – falling prices – of other fruits (and only of peaches and table grapes) during the summer months and mainly in July and then by an amount not exceeding 20%.

33 Although it cannot be denied that during these months and some weeks at the end of the year this product is exposed to competition from other fruits, the flexible way in which the volume of imports and their marketing on the relevant geographical market is adjusted means that the conditions of competition are extremely limited and that its price adapts without any serious difficulties to this situation where supplies of fruit are plentiful.

And the effect of other fruits on bananas is very limited

34 It follows from all these considerations that a very large number of consumers having a constant need for bananas are not noticeably or even appreciably enticed away from the consumption of this product by the arrival of other fresh fruit on the market and that even the personal peak periods only affect it for a limited period of time and to a very limited extent from the point of view of substitutability.

And consumers will not move to another fruit market

35 Consequently the banana market is a market which is sufficiently distinct from the other fresh fruit markets.

So the RPM is bananas not fresh fruit in general

Key Points from the case of United Brands v Commission (Case 27/76) [1978] ECR 207, above:

There are key points that result from the judgment of the Court of Justice:

- Dominance of a product is determined by testing the relevant product market (RPM) and the relevant geographical market (RGM).

- The relevant product market is one where there is no interchangeability of goods so a relevant product is the product in question plus anything that can be reasonably substituted for it.

- Bananas are not seasonal where other fresh fruit is so there is no seasonal substitute for bananas.

- Bananas also have unique characteristics and are consumed especially by the very young, the aged and the sick.

- For these reasons bananas are relatively unaffected by the competition of other fresh fruit.

- And consumers of bananas are not drawn away to other fresh fruit.

- So bananas are a relative product market in their own right.

ACTIVITY

In the following examples and using the reasoning from the judgment above try to determine what the relevant product market (RPM) is.

1. The major producer of a low alcohol strength sparkling fruit drink which is almost exclusively drunk by young women under the age of 25 is arguing that the relevant product market is alcoholic drinks generally of which they would have less than 0.1 per cent of sales. The Commission is arguing that the relevant product market is low alcohol strength sparkling fruit drinks.

2. The leading producer of a football boot called 'Playsafe' manufactured with a special carbon fibre lining which helps to reduce foot and ankle injuries is arguing that the relevant product market is footwear generally and if not that it is sportswear. Other manufacturers make 'Playsafe' football boots but only the leading producer makes the special lining and supplies it to the other manufacturers. The Commission is arguing that the relevant product market is 'Playsafe' football boots.

3. The leading producer of gunpowder for fireworks is arguing that the relevant product market is explosives of which it has a very small market share. The Commission is arguing that there is a discreet relevant product market for explosives which are only used in fireworks and nothing else.

As a result, in identifying what the relevant product market is it must be seen as including not only the specific product itself but also all products which may be perfectly substituted for it. Consequently a key factor for measuring on whether there is a specific market in the specific goods is the concept of 'interchangeability' of the goods in question.

As it was expressed in *Hoffmann La Roche v Commission* (1979) there must be:

JUDGMENT

'sufficient interchangeability between all products forming part of same market insofar as specific use of products is concerned'.

Relevant product market then is said to depend on 'cross-elasticity of demand' and 'cross-elasticity of supply'. Whether the relevant product market is viewed narrowly or broadly depends on whether there is no perfect substitute for the goods (narrow product market) or whether the goods can easily be substituted by an alternative (broad product market).

Seasonal factors may also be relevant in determining what the relevant product is. With seasonal goods there may be no possible substitute for the goods and therefore the market is likely to be viewed very narrowly. Seasonal fruits, *United Brands* (1978), are a classic example of a temporal market.

Examples of relevant product market have included:

- **Heavy goods vehicle tyres** (as opposed to tyres generally) in *Michelin NV Nederlandsche Baden-Industrie Michelin v Commission* (Case 322/81) [1983] ECR 3461. Here there was inevitably little to compare the very specific type of tyres concerned with tyres in general. Sheer size alone would have been sufficient to identify the tyres as a distinct product grouping. In any case the client group also differed widely.

- **Cash register parts** supplied by a Swedish firm to a UK firm through its UK subsidiaries, in *Hugin Kassaregister AB v Commission* (Case 22/78) [1979] ECR 1869. Again, these would be seen as very specific goods and not commonly transposed with spare parts generally.

- **Separate cartons for pasteurised and UHT milk** in *Tetra Pak v Commission (No 1)* (Case T–51/89) [1990] ECR II–309. The packaging here would not have been regarded as interchangeable by the consumers.

The relevant geographical market

Geographical market clearly refers to the range of territory within which the goods can expect to be sold. According to Article 102 the undertaking must be dominant 'within the single market or in a substantial part of it'.

In identifying just how far the relevant geographical market does in fact stretch in the context of the particular practice it has been identified that this is 'where the conditions of competition are sufficiently homogenous for the effect of economic power on the undertaking to be evaluated' (*United Brands v Commission* (1978)). In other words this is where the conditions for competition are the same for all traders in the product.

Clearly, then, while the relevant geographical market is generally assumed to be the whole of the EU, there are obviously other factors to be taken into account. Where there is a high level of cross-elasticity of demand or supply so that consumers have choice because other products can be substituted easily for the product in question then the relevant geographical market can in fact be large, indeed the whole EU.

However, this would depend on factors such as the cost and feasibility of transport arrangements. Producers in busy commercial areas may operate under entirely different conditions from those in remote rural areas, even if they enjoy the same market share. As a result, transport is a critical factor in determining the relevant geographical area.

CASE EXAMPLE

Eurofix and Hilti v Commission (Case T–30/89) [1990] 4 CMLR 602

Here, it was appreciated that transport was much easier and much cheaper in the case of the product in question, nail cartridges, than it would be for instance in the case of perishable foodstuffs. As a result, it was accepted that it would be appropriate to consider the whole of the EU as the relevant geographical market.

Another possibility identified as affecting the relevant geographical market is the pattern and volume of consumption. As a result, in *Suiker Unie* (1975) the relevant geographical market was limited to Belgium and Luxembourg. It has also been identified that if the product or service is only required in a single Member State then the relevant geographical market can even be as narrow as a Member State (*British Leyland plc v Commission* (Case 226/84) [1986] ECR 3263). However, it then has to be considered whether in fact there is an effect on trade between Member States.

16.3.5 Calculation of market share

Once the relevant market is established market share must also be considered in determining whether in fact the undertaking concerned is in a dominant position in that market. We have already seen from the definitions supplied in the *Continental Can* (1973), *United Brands* (1978) and *Hoffmann La Roche* (1979) cases that no particular market share is required in order to prove dominance. The statements of the ECJ in all three cases indicate that the most important element is the ability of the undertaking to act independently from the rest of the market. In *Continental Can Co v Commission* (1973) the subsidiary company owned by Continental Can had a share of nearly 80 per cent of the relevant product market in Germany. This was inevitably seen as a dominant position.

However, the market share does not need to be this large for there to be dominance.

CASE EXAMPLE

United Brands v Commission (Case 27/76) [1978] ECR 207

Here, the market share for bananas enjoyed by the company in Europe was between 40 and 45 per cent. This was still held to be a dominant position. However, as the ECJ noted where the market share is less than 50 per cent other factors must be considered, not least the share of the nearest competitors. In the case the two closest competitors held 16 per cent and 10 per cent of the market. United Brands owned its own fleet and was able to control the volume of other imports. The rest of the market was also highly fragmented. There was reasonably healthy competition in the relevant market but not enough to prevent United Brands being able to act independently of its competitors.

In any case the ECJ has suggested in *Hoffmann La Roche v Commission* (1979) that, while market share is clearly an important factor, it is not absolutely conclusive of dominance. Here, Hoffmann La Roche was offering loyalty rebates to purchasers of their vitamins, an obvious enough disadvantage to its competitors. The company enjoyed a market share in the relevant product amounting to more than 80 per cent. Again, this is a fairly obvious position of dominance. Nevertheless, the ECJ identified that there are a number of factors that might be considered apart from market share alone.

These have included:

▪ Possession of **superior technological knowledge and sales network**. An example would be *Michelin NV Nederlandsche Baden-Industrie Michelin v Commission* (1983) where the tyre company not only possessed the advanced technology but also had the history of supplying such specialist products by contrast to its competitors.

▪ The **length of time** for which the undertaking has enjoyed its position of dominance. As the ECJ pointed out in *United Brands* (1978), the longer a firm has enjoyed dominance, the more difficult it is for recent competitors to compete in the market.

- **Control of production and distribution**. This was indeed a key feature of the *Hoffmann La Roche* (1979) case.
- **Conduct or performance**. The loyalty rebates in *Hoffmann La Roche* are again a clear example of a 'predatory' policy aimed at stifling competition.

16.3.6 The character of abuse

As has already been identified (see section 16.3.1) it is not the existence of a dominant position which is seen as harmful and therefore prohibited. There is no breach of Article 102 unless an undertaking can be said to have abused its dominant position.

There is in fact no definition of abuse in the Article. So it is once again the ECJ that has supplied the definition, this time in *Hoffmann La Roche v Commission* (1979):

JUDGMENT

'The concept of abuse is an objective concept relating to the behaviour of an undertaking which is such as to influence the structure of the market where, as a result of the very presence of the undertaking in question, the degree of competition is weakened, and which, through recourse to methods different from those which conditions normal competition in products or services on the basis of the transactions of commercial operators, has the effect of hindering the maintenance of the degree of competition still existing in the market or the growth of that competition.'

In other words, it is behaviour by the undertaking in a dominant position which modifies the structure of the market in such a way that it reduces the level of competition or prevents the growth of competition in the particular market.

Although there is no definition in the Article, there are still several examples of abusive practices identified in it:

- Directly or indirectly imposing unfair purchase or selling prices or other unfair trading conditions, e.g.:
  - Price reduction to kill competition. In *AKZO v Commission* (Case 62/86R) [1986] ECR 1503 a company with a dominant position in the benzole peroxide market cut its prices over a long period of time in order to put a small British competitor out of business.
  - Differential pricing for different states, as in *United Brands* (1978).
  - Loyalty rebates, as in *Hoffmann La Roche* (1979).
- Limiting production, markets or technical development to the prejudice of consumers.

  In *Magill TV Guide and ITP v Commission* (Case C–241/91P) [1995] ECR I–743 a refusal by TV companies to supply information about television listings to a competing producer of a TV guide was an abuse. *Sot. Lelos kai Sia EE and Others v GlaxoSmithKline AEVE Farmakeftikon Proionton* (C–468/06 to C–478/06) also identifies that abuse includes refusing to supply medicinal products to Member States having higher selling prices in order to prevent parallel imports

- Applying dissimilar conditions to equivalent transactions with other trading parties, thereby placing them at a competitive disadvantage. In *British Leyland v Commission* (1986) different prices were charged for type-approval certificates for left hand drive cars. There was no objective justification for this discrimination so it was an abuse.

Making conclusion of contracts subject to supplementary obligations having no connection with the subject of such contracts – e.g. the 'tying arrangements' in *Tetra Pak International SA v Commission* (Case T–83/91) [1994] ECR II–755. Here, the firm had invented a process for filling cartons that would prolong the shelf life of the foodstuff to six months. It would only sell the machines for the process if customers also bought the cartons 'tetra paks' from its subsidiary company. This additional requirement in the contract was merely an abuse.

16.3.7 Affecting trade between Member States

As with Article 101, there must be an effect on trade within Member States. The effect must be one that is caused by the abuse.

In general the same conditions apply as those in Article 101. The abuse only has to have the potential to affect trade; it need not actually have affected trade. So the test is similar: the abuse of the dominant position is capable of affecting trade between Member States if it is capable of constituting a threat 'direct or indirect, actual or potential, on the pattern of trade'.

It is generally not hard to show that trade could be affected. In *British Leyland plc v Commission* (1986) the Court stated that specific effects do not have to be shown. It is sufficient to show evidence that trade might be affected.

16.3.8 Exemptions

As has already been stated, unlike Article 101, there are no possible exemptions for breaches of Article 102. What is possible is that it may be shown in the case of some of the abuses above that they are in fact objectively justified. Whether the Court accepts such an argument depends obviously on the facts of the individual case. Many of the factors that have already been seen in section 16.3.4 may be taken into account.

ACTIVITY

Self-assessment questions

1. What is the basic prohibition under Article 102?
2. How is dominance determined under Article 102?
3. What definitions of 'dominance' does the case law provide?
4. What is the significance of the 'relevant product market'?
5. What is the significance of the actual market share under Article 102?
6. What types of activity amount to an abuse of a dominant position?
7. What is the significance of the *United Brands* case?
8. What is the usual relevant geographical market?

16.4 Merger control

16.4.1 Merger control under Articles 101 and 102

EU competition law has also been used to control mergers, which in any case would concentrate economic power in fewer hands, and other concentrations of economic power. Both clearly require some form of control because the ultimate logical consequence of mergers and concentrations is to monopolies and by their very nature monopolies are anti-competitive.

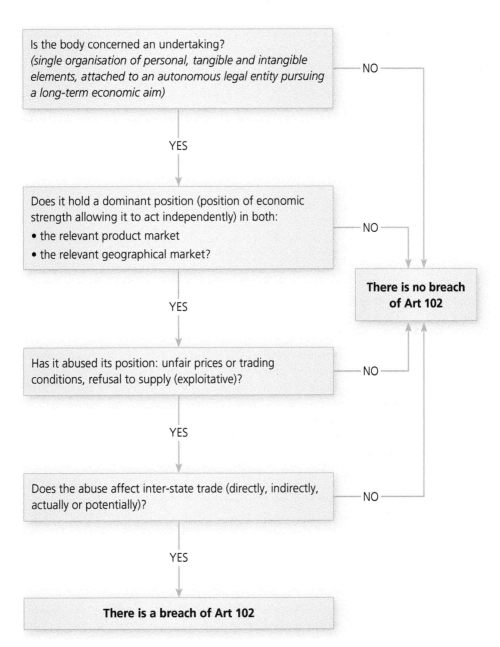

Figure 16.2 The means of establishing a breach of Article 102

Originally, prior to 1990, and the adoption of Regulation 4064/89, only standard competition law was available to deal with mergers and concentrations. The obvious means being an action under Article 102 for an abuse of a dominant position.

In this way it could be argued that Article 102 had been infringed if a dominant undertaking actually strengthened its dominance through a merger so that the only undertakings to remain in the relevant market were those whose behaviour actually depended on the dominant one. This surfaced in the *Continental Can* case (1973) and is identified by Josephine Steiner in *Textbook on EC Law* (8th edn, Oxford University Press, 2003), p. 453 as 'Perhaps the most surprising application of Article 82 [now Article 102 TFEU]'.

Europemballage Corporation and Continental Can Co Inc v Commission (Case 6/72) [1973] ECR 215

Here, as we have seen, Continental Can had an 86 per cent share in a German company, Schmalbach, which itself held a dominant position. Continental Can then proposed a takeover of a Dutch Company, Thomassen (the merger or concentration) and that both companies should then be placed under the control of Continental Can's European subsidiary, Europemballage. The Commission issued a Decision, identifying the transaction as a breach of Article 102 TFEU. Continental Can argued that Article 102 TFEU was inapplicable because it applied only to activities that were detrimental to consumers and that also there was no abuse because it had not used its dominance to secure the takeover. The ECJ held that it could amount to a breach of Article 102 TFEU because a merger could be a way of eliminating competition, and anything affecting the structure of competition could be said to affect consumers. Nevertheless, as we have seen already, the Commission decision was annulled because it had failed to show the relevant product market. However, the application of Articles 101 and 102 to mergers or any other form of concentration was established by the Court.

16.4.2 Merger control under Regulation 4064/89

Inevitably, pressure grew on the EU institutions for more effective legislation for the more effective control of mergers. By the late 1980s this pressure had increased and the EU acted in adopting Regulation 4064/89. The purpose of the Regulation was to identify mergers that were of such a size that they should be controlled by the EU rather than by individual national authorities.

In this way the Regulation identified a broader definition than mere mergers and instead would be applied to 'significant changes in ownership over companies which could distort competition', in other words 'concentrations'.

According to the Regulation, any 'concentrations' meeting certain criteria must be 'notified' to the Commission within one week of the agreement being concluded, provided also that they have a Union dimension. To require notification to the Commission:

- the undertakings concerned must have a combined world turnover of at least €5,000 million; and

- the total Union-wide turnover of at least two of the undertakings concerned must be in excess of €250 million. However, there will be no Union dimension and so no infringement where each of the parties does not derive two-thirds of its business in the EC within a single Member State.

An amendment to these basic requirements was added in Regulation 1310/97. This allowed that there could still be a Union dimension, and so the same controls could apply, where the requirements were not met but:

- the combined turnover of all of the undertakings worldwide is more than €2,500 million;

- the combined turnover of the undertakings in at least three Member States is more than €100 million; and

- the combined turnover of at least two of the undertakings in at least three Member States is more than €25 million; and

- the combined turnover of at least two of the undertakings in the Union as a whole is more than €100 million.

Where a concentration falls outside these two sets of requirements then it is subject to national rather than Union controls. Nevertheless, Member States may ask the Commission to intervene where the concentration would 'significantly impede' competition within its own territory.

16.4.3 Procedure

The test for the Commission is whether the concentration creates or enhances a dominant position that would lead to effective competition being substantially impeded.

Once the Commission has been notified of the concentration then it should take one of three decisions:

- it can decide that the concentration does indeed fall within the scope of the Regulation and that it gives rise to proceedings because it is potentially incompatible with the requirements of a Single Market; or

- it can decide that the concentration falls within the scope of the Regulation but that there is no need for proceedings because it does not 'create or strengthen a dominant position as a result of which effective competition would be impeded in the common market or a substantial part of it'; or

- it can decide that the concentration does not fall within the scope of the Regulation at all.

The Commission has a month in which to investigate and, if proceedings are initiated, then the Commission must reach a final decision within four months. The Commission can then declare the concentration compatible with the Regulation, or if it declares that it is not then it can be rescinded. The Commission can also fine undertakings which fail to notify a merger.

16.4.4 Reform of procedures on merger control

In 2003 the Commission published a proposal for a new regulation on mergers, reviewing the thresholds and the rules for notification. The underlying theme of the proposal was the same as for enforcement proceedings on Articles 101 and 102 generally, increased co-operation between the Member States.

The original proposal was not introduced immediately since a number of changes to it had to be accepted but the amended proposals have subsequently been introduced as Regulation 139/2004, the Merger Regulation. The Regulation in fact refers to 'concentrations' rather than 'mergers' despite the title given to it. As well as clearing up a lot of the bureaucracy it is also a recognition that national controls may be more effective than Union controls in allowing national industries to compete more effectively in the global market.

The Regulation defines concentrations as:

a. the merger of two or more previously independent undertakings or parts of undertakings; or

b. the acquisition, by one or more persons already controlling at least one undertaking, or by one or more undertakings, whether by purchase of securities or assets or by any other means, of direct or indirect control of the whole or parts of one or more undertakings.

The 2004 Regulation allowed for a simplification of the notification proceedings. Where a concentration could be reviewed under national law but this would involve notification in at least three Member States then the Commission can be informed instead.

Member States are informed of this and if there is no disagreement within 15 days then the concentration is deemed to have a Union dimension.

The Regulation has also introduced a case referral mechanism by which the case is referred to the most appropriate authority to deal with it. The characteristics of the case and the means of the authority to deal with it should both be considered. There is also a process for 'back referral' to the national authorities. A speedier appraisal system is also introduced, the overriding principle being based on 'compatibility with the common market'.

A simplified procedure has also been introduced for certain types of concentration that experience has shown are rarely in fact anti-competitive. A Commission Notice has identified types of concentration that should fall within this procedure:

- where undertakings gain joint control of a joint venture that has either no or only negligible activities within the European Economic Area (EEA);

- where none of the parties is engaged in business in the same product and geographic market (a horizontal relationship), or a product market that is related to that product (a vertical relationship);

- where, even though the parties are engaged in a horizontal or vertical relationship in a product market and geographic market their combined share of the market is not more than 15 per cent (horizontal) or 25 per cent (vertical);

- where a party gains total control over an undertaking of which it already has joint control.

16.5 Enforcement procedures and remedies in EU competition law

16.5.1 Introduction

The need for effective enforcement procedures was identified at a very early stage. Until very recently the powers and procedures for enforcement were found in Regulation 17/62. This was subsequently amended but in general the same mechanisms remained intact.

Inevitably, the enforcement procedures gave a great deal of power to the Commission. Inevitably too, it imposed a heavy burden on the Commission and enforcement of Articles 101 and 102 was a lengthy process and subject to lengthy delays. With enlargement looming, the EU felt the need to overhaul the procedures with a view to decentralising the system as far as possible and a Commission proposal was produced. This was then introduced in the main in Regulation 1/2003 which entered into force in May 2004.

Originally the Commission proposal suggested that exemption and notification should cease to be the responsibility of the Commission with national courts and competition authorities given the power to apply Article 101, including Article 101(3) and Article 102. Undertakings would need to take their own advice on whether their activities infringed competition law. The Commission would retain the right to intervene in competition cases being dealt with at a national level. The proposals did create some unrest, with the worry among businesses that national authorities would apply EU competition policy inconsistently.

The Regulation has decentralised enforcement proceedings, and the Commission has changed the focus of its attentions to the detection of serious cartels that are the major threat to competition policy. It has also adopted a 'leniency policy' by which immunity can be granted to undertakings that assist the Commission.

16.5.2 The Commission and enforcement of competition law

The powers of the Commission and Regulation 17/62

The Commission has always had wide powers to deal with actual as well as potential infringements of competition law. It could deal with breaches in a variety of ways:

- It could give negative clearance to agreements where Article 101 could be an issue (not in fact an exemption but merely a means of finding out from the Commission whether or not the agreement in fact was in breach of Article 101).

- It could grant individual exemptions under Article 101(3).

- It could create block exemptions from Article 101.

- The Commission might pursue investigations and conclude that there were no grounds to impose a penalty on undertakings following this investigation, although it would usually try to reach an informal conclusion first, for example by the issuing of 'comfort letters'.

In any case, all new agreements were required to be notified to the Commission. This might then prevent the imposition of fines, but of course it would not prevent an agreement which was an infringement from being invalidated by the Commission.

Changes under Regulation 1/2003

Now, under Regulation 1/2003 it is no longer necessary to notify the Commission in order to obtain negative clearance or individual exemption. Article 1(1) of the Regulation instead places the burden on undertakings themselves to identify whether any of their agreements offends Article 101(1) but are exempt under Article 101(3).

This means that the Commission no longer has to examine individual agreements to see if they justify exemption. However, the Commission is still responsible for issuing block exemptions, and can of course investigate anti-competitive agreements on its own initiative or those complained about by parties affected by them. However, its main focus should be on investigating the large price-fixing cartels.

National authorities instead will have the power to demand that a breach is brought to an end, and to order interim measures and accept commitments from undertakings, or indeed to fine or order any other penalty within national law. The Commission can of course issue decisions which are binding on the parties where it does investigate.

The investigative powers of the Commission

Under Regulation 17/62 the Commission could always instigate an investigation either on its own initiative or on the application of a Member State or of any interested parties. The Commission could only then take action after an 'appropriate preliminary investigation' had taken place. If it decided to act it was obliged then to notify the applicants.

In pursuing its investigation the Commission was given extensive powers under the Regulation to obtain information either from the governments of Member States, or their relevant authorities, or indeed from firms. As a result, it had the right to examine books and other business records, take copies or extracts from any of these, request on-the-spot oral explanations and to enter any premises or transport of an undertaking. Although in *Orkem v Commission* (Case 374/87) [1989] ECR 3283 the ECJ held that while the Commission was entitled to compel an undertaking to reveal all information of which it had knowledge it could nevertheless not compel it to incriminate itself by admitting to breaches of competition rules.

In brief, the Commission was entitled to undertake 'such investigations as are necessary' that would help to reveal a breach of either Article 101 or Article 102.

CASE EXAMPLE

Hoechst AG v Commission (Cases 46 and 227/87) [1989] ECR 2859

Here, the applicant challenged the legitimacy of a 'dawn raid' by the Commission, one that was unannounced and involved a search of his home and that he claimed deprived him of his right to a fair trial. The ECJ disagreed and held that it was for the Commission to decide on the necessity and character of the investigation.

Regulation 1/2003 has not significantly altered the investigative powers identified in Regulation 17/62. The Commission can ask undertakings to provide all relevant information either through a simple request or by a decision. There is also a power to impose fines for misleading information or failing to provide information within the declared time limit. It still has the power to enter undertakings, examine documents and take copies and conduct interviews, although written authorisation must be presented first. The Commission may also ask a national competition authority to conduct the investigation.

The available penalties

The Commission always had the power to impose financial penalties for breaches of Article 101 or Article 102. These were of two types:

- **Fines**: ranging from €1,000 to €1 million or a larger amount not over 10 per cent of annual global turnover, whichever is the greater. The amount would actually depend on certain criteria:
  - the seriousness and duration of the infringement;
  - the economic importance of the undertakings and their market share;
  - whether the breaches were deliberate or not;
  - whether the undertakings had previously breached competition rules;
  - whether the breach involved underhanded behaviour.

  These were later subject to the 1998 Notice on the method of setting fines.

- **Periodic payments or incentive-led penalties**. The penalty was a specific sum for every day or week that the breach continued and so was an incentive to stop quickly.

Regulation 1/2003 has made only minor changes:

- the Commission must first take advice from a newly constituted Advisory Committee on Restrictive Practices and Dominant Positions;
- the fine must not exceed 10 per cent of the undertaking's previous year's turnover;
- the Regulation includes an express power for the Commission to grant interim measures.

Review by the General Court

Regulation 17/62 provided that all Commission decisions were reviewable by the Court. The method of such review would take the form of either Article 263 or Article 265 actions. So, in effect it is a form of judicial review.

16.5.3 Enforcement of competition law by national authorities

Enforcement of competition law would never have been possible without the assistance of the national authorities in the Member States. As a result, they could be involved in various ways:

- national authorities could initiate an investigation into an anti-competitive practice by making an application to the Commission;
- under Article 13 of Regulation 17/62 national authorities could conduct their own investigations, and could also do so at the request of the Commission;
- besides this, in any case the national courts could also apply Articles 101 and 102 as well as their own competition rules. However, this was not possible where the Commission was already involved. National courts have this power because Articles 101 and 102 are both directly effective (*BRT v Sabam* (Case 127/73) [1974] ECR 51). Traditionally, only the Commission could issue exemptions, not the national courts, but they can award damages for parties affected by infringements, and also grant injunctive relief.

KEY FACTS

The basis of EU competition law	
States that the EU must ensure that 'competition in the internal market is not distorted'. Three principal objectives of competition rules: • to avoid possibility of restrictive practices and agreements; • to prevent large businesses from abusing their economic dominance in the market; • to ensure, within certain limits, that the public sector follows same rules. Aim is not to stop good business practice but unfair practice. Rules can be used against firms even if no registered office in EU if their actions could affect trade in the EU. So competition law has three main objectives which may appear at times to be incompatible: • efficiency; • protection of both consumers and small businesses; • the creation of the Single Market.	Art 3(g)
Art 101 and restrictive practices	
Basic Art 101 prohibition: • Rule prohibits 'agreements between undertakings, decisions of associations of undertakings and concerted practices which may affect trade between member states having as object prevention, restriction or distortion of competition within EU'. • Undertakings defined by ECJ as – single organisation of personal, tangible and intangible elements, attached to an autonomous legal entity and pursuing a long-term economic aim. Commission can grant exemption.	*Mannesmann v High Authority* (1962)
Elements for proving breach of Art 101:	
Agreements between undertakings, decisions by associations of undertakings, concerted practices: • must involve collusive behaviour; • decisions by undertakings are usually by trade associations on, e.g. fixing discounts, collective boycotts, restrictive contract clauses;	*AEG Telefunken v Commission* (1983)

• concerted practices are a form of co-ordination between enterprises that has not yet reached the point where it is a contract;
 • Art 101 identifies some prohibited arrangements, e.g.
    • price fixing
 	
    • limiting production
 	
    • sharing markets or suppliers
    • applying dissimilar conditions to equivalent transactions affecting trade between Member States;
 	
 • tested by reference to free movement and attainment of Single Market;
 • must be capable of constituting a threat, direct or indirect, actual or potential, on the pattern of trade;
 	
 • no need to prove harm; just that agreement may prevent, restrict or distort competition sufficiently.
	ICI v Commission (Dyestuffs case) (1972)
	
	 VBVB and VVVB v Commission (1984)
	 Quinine Cartel case (1970)
	
	 IAZ International Belgium v Commission (1983)
	 Belasco v Commission (1989)
	 Vereeniging van Cementhandelaren v Commission (1972)

Object or effect of preventing, restricting or distorting competition: • as much to do with practical outcomes as intentions; • key issue is whether or not competition is affected; • ECJ try to apply the rules so as not to stifle enterprise and initiative.	*Consten and Grundig v Commission (1963)* *Société Technique Minière v Maschinenbau Ulm (1966)*

Activities beyond scope of Art 101:	
De minimis rule: • and Commission Notice on Agreements of Minor Importance. Commercial agents and subsidiaries.	
Exemption if: • contributes to improving production or distribution of goods or promoting technical or economic progress; • consumer gets fair share of benefit; • no unnecessary restrictions; • no risk of eliminating competition; Exemptions can be individual or block.	*Transocean Marine Paint Association (1975)* *ACEC v Berliet (1968)* *Consten and Grundig v Commission (1963)*

Art 102 and abuse of a dominant position	
The basic prohibition:	
Article 102 involves the concentration of economic power in an undertaking.	
Any abuse of commercial dominance is prohibited if it would affect trade between Member States.	
Article 102 can also apply to oligopolies.	*The Flat Glass case (1989)*

Negative clearance and exemptions are not available.	
Three requirements: • dominant position in market; • abuse of dominant position; • affects trade between Member States.	
Existence of dominance:	

• 'Dominance' defined in ECSC Treaty – undertaking holds position shielding it against effective competition.
• ECJ has also defined dominance – power to control production or distribution for a significant part of the products in question.
• And a position of economic strength … which enables it to prevent competition being maintained.
• Need to consider:
  • relevant market;
  • market share.
• Relevant product market decided on whether there is sufficient inter-changeability between all products forming part of same market.
• So could be, e.g. separate cartons for pasteurised and UHT milk.
• Geographical market should be whole EU – but can take into account other factors, e.g. costs and feasibility of transport.
• Temporal market may involve, e.g. seasonal factors.
• No particular share needed for dominance – e.g. 40 per cent sufficient.
• Should consider, e.g.:
  • market share;
 	
  • competitor's share.
	Continental Can Co v Commission (1973)
	United Brands (1978)
	
	Hoffmann La Roche v Commission (1979)
	
	Tetra Pak (No 1) (1990)
	Hilti v Commission (1979) and (1989)
	United Brands (1978)
	United Brands (1978)
	
	Hoffmann La Roche (1979)
	United Brands (1978)

The abuse:	

• Defined in case law – behaviour which influences structure of market so that competition is weakened, and maintenance or growth of competition is hindered.
• So could include, e.g.:
  • differential pricing for different Member States;
  • 'tying arrangements';
  • dissimilar conditions;
  • limiting markets, technical development, production.
	United Brands (1978)
	Tetra Pak II (1991)
	
	Magill TV Guide and ITP v Commission (1995)

Affecting inter-state trade:	
• Must result from the abuse.	

'Discuss the ways in which EU competition law actually support the freedoms of the single market.'

Explain the basic prohibitions in Articles 101 and 102:

- Against collusive anti-competitive behaviour under Article 101
- Against abuses of dominant positions under Article 102

Explain that in both cases the bodies concerned must be 'undertakings'

Explain the essential elements of Article 101:

- An agreement between undertakings or a decision of an association of undertakings or a concerted practice
- With the object or effect of restricting, preventing or distorting trade
- Which affects trade between MSs 'directly, indirectly, actually or potentially'

Discuss the type of behaviour that is regulated:

- Price fixing, limiting production-sharing markets or supply applying dissimilar conditions; imposing supplementary obligations
- Note that the prohibition does not apply in the case of minor agreements, or where there is an exemption

Explain the essential elements of Article 102:

- The existence of a dominant position – measured against relevant product market, geographical market, temporal market if relevant and market share
- Abuse of that dominance by, e.g. predatory pricing, differential pricing, tying arrangements, applying dissimilar conditions, imposing supplementary obligations
- Affects intra-Union trade directly, indirectly, actually or potentially

Discuss the effects of Article 102:

- There is no problem with dominance
- It is the abuse of power that is prohibited
- Relevant product market can cause debate – so cross-elasticity of supply is important
- Market share is only one factor

SUMMARY

- EU competition law is not inconsistent with the freedoms of the Single Market.

- It is not about preventing competition but about preventing unfair competition.

- So it prohibits collusive behaviour and abusive behaviour by large powerful enterprises.

- The basic prohibition under Article 101 concerns agreements between undertakings, decisions of associations of undertakings and concerted practices which may affect trade between Member States and have as their object the prevention, restriction or distortion of competition within common market.

- The basic prohibition under Article 102 concerns any abuse by one or more undertakings of a dominant position within the Internal Market or in a substantial part of it insofar as it may affect trade between Member States.

- There are also controls on monopolies and mergers.

Further reading

Books

Furse, M, *Competition Law of the EC and UK* (4th edn, Oxford University Press, 2004).

Rodger, B J and MacCulloch, A, *Competition Law and Policy in the EC and UK* (3rd edn, Cavendish Publishing, 2004), p. 399.

Woods, L, Watson P and Costa M, *Steiner and Woods EU Law* (13th edn, Oxford University Press, 2017), Chapters 28 and 29.

17

Social policy

AIMS AND OBJECTIVES

After reading this chapter you should be able to:

- Understand EU social policy law, in particular the law relating to the protection of workers' health and safety, the protection of pregnant workers and the protection of young workers
- Understand the law relating to working time
- Analyse critically the law relating to social policy in the EU

17.1 Introduction

EU social policy law is designed to protect potentially vulnerable workers through a variety of measures:

- safety and health of workers at work: Directive 89/391;
- safety and health at work of pregnant workers: Directive 92/85;
- protection of young workers: Directive 94/33;
- parental leave: Directive 2010/18 (replacing Directive 96/34);
- protection for part-time workers: Directive 97/81;
- protection for fixed-term workers: Directive 1999/70;
- working time: Directive 2003/88 (replacing Directive 93/104).

These measures have dual social and economic aims. They have a **social** aim in that they clearly aim to protect vulnerable workers (those who are most at risk of exploitation: the young; part-time workers). But they also have an **economic** aim in that they are designed to co-ordinate employment policy across the EU. This means that companies in countries run by socialist, Left-leaning governments which would tend to have better worker-protection legislation are not placed at too much of a competitive disadvantage vis-à-vis companies in countries run by free-market, Right-leaning governments who would tend to try to maximise the operating freedom of companies. Without such co-ordination, employers might be drawn to setting up their businesses in countries run by Right-leaning governments because of reduced administrative burdens and operating costs (usually referred to pejoratively as 'red tape').

You will note that all of the EU legislation in this area is in the form of Directives, not Regulations. This is not coincidental. Directives allow Member States scope for manoeuvre, to lay down national rules within EU-wide parameters. Regulations, on the other hand, lay down specific EU-wide rules that have to be followed by all Member States. The use of Directives allows for some (but not too much) divergence between different Member States and indeed allows for divergence over time within the same Member State. To take one example: the maximum average working week, which is set out in Directive 2003/88, the Working Time Directive (WTD), at 48 hours. It must be stressed that this figure is a maximum: Member States are entirely free to set a different figure as long as it does not exceed 48 hours.

Bearing these dual social and economic aims in mind, the rest of this chapter provides an overview of the main social policy legislation introduced by the EU over the last 30 years.

17.2 Safety and health of workers at work: Directive 89/391

This is a 'framework' Directive which lays down general principles on health and safety of workers (Article 1). It applies to 'all sectors of activity, both public and private (industrial, agricultural, commercial, administrative, service, educational, cultural, leisure, etc.)' (Article 2(1)). Article 2 adds: 'the safety and health of workers must be ensured as far as possible in the light of the objectives of this Directive'. The bulk of the Directive is taken up with imposing obligations on employers to take steps to prevent risks to the safety and health of workers and to provide information and training.

17.3 Safety and health at work of pregnant workers: Directive 92/85

Directive 92/85, widely known as the Pregnant Workers' Directive (PWD), requires Member States to:

- introduce measures to encourage improvements in the safety and health at work of pregnant workers and workers who have recently given birth and are breastfeeding; and

- give special protection to women, by prohibiting dismissal during the period from the beginning of their pregnancy to the end of their maternity leave, save in exceptional circumstances unconnected with their condition.

This is legislation which clearly satisfies the dual social/economic aims identified above – the protection of vulnerable workers (pregnant women) combined with the establishment of a level legal playing field for all employers across the EU when faced with pregnant employees. In *Larsson v Føtex Supermarked* (Case C–400/95) [1997] ECR I–2757, the ECJ noted that the PWD had been introduced in view of the 'harmful effects' that the risk of dismissal may have on the 'physical and mental state of women who are pregnant, have recently given birth or are breastfeeding, including the particularly serious risk that pregnant women may be prompted voluntarily to terminate their pregnancy'.

17.3.1 Personal scope

Article 2 of the PWD applies to 'pregnant workers', 'workers who have recently given birth' and 'workers who are breastfeeding'. In each case the woman concerned is required to have informed her employer of 'her condition'.

The meaning of the phrase 'pregnant worker' was examined in *Mayr v Flöckner* (Case C–506/06) [2008] ECR I–1017. The case involved a woman who was undergoing *in vitro* fertilisation but whose fertilised eggs had yet to be implanted in her womb. The Court stated:

JUDGMENT

'It is clear ... that it is the earliest possible date in a pregnancy which must be chosen to ensure the safety and protection of pregnant workers. However, even allowing, in regard to in vitro fertilisation, that the date is that of the transfer of the fertilised ova into the woman's uterus, it cannot be accepted, for reasons connected with the principle of legal certainty, that the protection [against dismissal] established by Article 10 of Directive 92/85 may be extended to a worker when, on the date she was given notice of her dismissal, the in vitro *fertilised ova had not yet been transferred into her uterus.*'

By 'reasons connected with the principle of legal certainty', the ECJ meant the medical possibility that fertilised ova could be kept *in vitro* for several years, raising the possibility that a judgment in Ms Mayr's favour would protect women in that position from dismissal during that extended period of time.

As to the meaning of the word 'worker', in *Danosa* (Case C–232/09) [2010] ECR I–11405, the Court held that the case law on workers in the context of Article 45 TFEU (see Chapter 12) applied by analogy to cases under the PWD. Thus, a person who provided services in return for remuneration and who carried out their activities under the direction or control of another person satisfied 'prima facie the criteria for being treated as [a] worker'. It follows that a woman in self-employment is not a 'worker' for the purposes of the PWD (*Betriu Montull* (Case C–5/12) [2014] 1 CMLR 35).

17.3.2 Material scope

Exposure to risks

Under Article 4, an obligation is imposed on employers to 'assess any risks to the safety or health and any possible effect on the pregnancies or breastfeeding' of workers within Article 2 posed by having to undertake 'activities liable to involve a specific risk of exposure to the agents, processes or working conditions' listed (non-exhaustively) in the Directive itself, and then 'decide what measures should be taken'. The list includes the following:

1. 'Physical agents', in particular (a) shocks, vibration or movement; (b) handling of loads entailing risks; (c) noise; (d) ionising radiation; (e) non-ionising radiation; (f) extremes of cold or heat; (g) movements and postures, travelling, mental and physical fatigue and other physical burdens.
2. 'Biological agents'.
3. 'Chemical agents' including mercury and carbon monoxide.

Note: the Directive does **not** prohibit pregnant workers from carrying out such activities.

In *Otero Ramos* (Case C–531/15), not yet reported, the ECJ offered some guidance on the scope of Article 4(1). The Court stated that 'the risk assessment of the work of a breastfeeding worker must include a specific assessment taking into account the individual situation of the worker in question in order to ascertain whether her health or safety or that of her child is exposed to a risk'. The Court added that 'failure to assess the risk posed by the work of a breastfeeding worker in accordance with the requirements of Article 4(1) must be regarded as less favourable treatment of a woman related to pregnancy or maternity leave', and hence direct discrimination on grounds of sex, contrary to Directive 2006/54 (the Equal Treatment Directive (the ETD)), which is discussed in Chapter 18). Article 5(1) provides that if the assessment required by Article 4 reveals a risk to the safety or health or an effect on the pregnancy or breastfeeding of a pregnant worker, the employer must take the necessary measures to ensure that the exposure of that worker to such risks is avoided, by 'temporarily adjusting the working conditions and/or the working hours of the worker concerned'. Article 5(2) adds that if such an adjustment is not 'technically and/or objectively feasible', or cannot 'reasonably be required', the employer must move the worker concerned to another job. Article 5(3) then states that if moving the worker to another job is not technically and/or objectively feasible or cannot reasonably be required, the worker must be granted leave.

Article 5(2) was invoked in *Parviainen* (Case C–471/08) [2010] ECR I–6533. Sanna Parviainen, who worked as a chief flight attendant, was transferred to office work when she became pregnant until her maternity leave began. This was held to be in accordance with Article 5(2), because of the risks involved in working on planes. Article 5(3) was invoked in *Gassmayr* (Case C–194/08) [2010] ECR I–6281. Dr Susanne Gassmayr worked at the anaesthesia clinic of the University of Graz in Austria. She was given leave after she produced a medical certificate to the effect that continuing to work could endanger the life of herself or the unborn child.

Under Article 6, however, 'pregnant workers' and 'workers who are breastfeeding' are prohibited from certain activities and are also protected from exposure to various 'agents' listed in the Directive itself. In both cases, the workers may 'under no circumstances be obliged' to perform 'underground mining work', and are protected from exposure to 'chemical agents', specifically 'lead and lead derivatives in so far as these agents are capable of being absorbed by the human organism'. 'Pregnant workers' are further protected from any obligation to work 'in hyperbaric atmosphere, for example pressurized enclosures' and 'underwater diving'. They are also protected from exposure to two 'biological agents', namely toxoplasma and the rubella virus, 'unless the pregnant workers are proved to be adequately protected against such agents by the human organism'.

All of these specific protections are stated to be in addition to the general protections available to all workers under Directive 89/391.

'Night work'

Under Article 7, Member States are required to ensure that all workers listed in Article 2 'are not obliged to perform night work during their pregnancy and for a period following childbirth'. Where this happens, Member States must adopt measures which 'entail the possibility of (a) transfer to daytime work or (b) leave from work or extension of maternity leave where such a transfer is not technically and/or objectively feasible or cannot reasonably be required on duly substantiated grounds'.

'Maternity leave'

Under Article 8(1), pregnant workers are entitled to 'a continuous period of maternity leave of at least 14 weeks allocated before and/or after confinement'. Under Article 8(2), this must include 'compulsory maternity leave of at least two weeks allocated before and/or after confinement'.

The significance of Article 8 was emphasised in *Kiiski* (Case C–116/06) [2007] ECR I–7643, where the ECJ stated:

JUDGMENT

'Pregnancy follows its own inevitable course.... It is precisely that inevitable course which the Union legislature took into account when making available to pregnant workers a special right, that is to say a right to maternity leave, which is intended, first, to protect a woman's biological condition during and after pregnancy and, second, to protect the special relationship between a woman and her child over the period which follows pregnancy and childbirth, by preventing that relationship from being disturbed by the multiple burdens which would result from the simultaneous pursuit of employment.... The right to maternity leave granted to pregnant workers must be regarded as a particularly important mechanism of protection under employment law.'

In *Betriu Montull* (2014), the ECJ held that there was nothing in Article 8(1) of the PWD to prevent a woman transferring some of her maternity leave entitlement to the child's father. However, Article 8(2) precluded her from transferring the compulsory two week period specified in that paragraph. In *D* (Case C–167/12) [2014] 3 CMLR 15 and *Z* (Case C–363/12) [2014] 3 CMLR 20, the ECJ held that Article 8 did **not** apply to a woman who had entered into a surrogacy arrangement and who therefore had not, herself, been pregnant. In short, there was no entitlement to 'surrogacy leave' under the PWD. In *D*, the Court stated:

JUDGMENT

'The purpose of the maternity leave provided for in Article 8 is to protect the health of the mother of the child in the especially vulnerable situation arising from her pregnancy.... Whilst maternity leave is also intended to ensure that the special relationship between a woman and her child is protected, that objective concerns only the period after "pregnancy and childbirth".... The grant of maternity leave pursuant to Article 8 presupposes that the worker entitled to such leave has been pregnant and has given birth to a child.... A female worker who has had a baby through a surrogacy arrangement does not fall within the scope of Article 8, even in circumstances where she may breastfeed the baby following the birth or where she does breastfeed the baby. Consequently, Member States are **not** required to grant such a worker a right to maternity leave.'

The case of *D* is further examined in Chapter 18, as it was also contended that the refusal to allow D to take 'surrogacy leave' amounted to discrimination on grounds of sex.

Time off for ante-natal examinations
Article 9 guarantees that pregnant workers are entitled to 'time off, without loss of pay, in order to attend ante-natal examinations, if such examinations have to take place during working hours'.

Prohibition of dismissal
Article 10 prohibits the dismissal of pregnant workers and workers on maternity leave:

'Art 10 Member States shall take the measures necessary to prohibit the dismissal of workers, within the meaning of Article 2, during the period from the beginning of their pregnancy to the end of the maternity leave ... save in exceptional cases not connected with their condition which are permitted under national legislation and/or practice and, where applicable, provided that the competent authority has given its consent.'

Article 10 has been examined by the ECJ, first in *Jiménez Melgar* (Case C–438/99) [2001] ECR I–6915. The Court held that the prohibition on dismissal was directly effective, but the Court also held that the word 'dismissal' did **not** include an employer's failure to renew a short-term contract which had expired under the terms of the contract itself.

Article 10 was again examined in *Paquay* (Case C–460/06) [2007] ECR I–8511. Here the ECJ was asked whether the prohibition of the 'dismissal' of pregnant women covered the *notification of a decision* to dismiss. The Court held that it did, on the ground that a contrary interpretation would deprive Article 10 of its 'effectiveness' and 'could give rise to a risk that employers [could] circumvent the prohibition to the detriment of the rights of pregnant women'. Moreover, the Court held, even the *taking of a decision* to dismiss as well as *taking steps to prepare for* the dismissal, such as searching for and finding a permanent replacement, amounted to conduct caught by Article 10. The only exception would be where the defendant employer was able to prove – to the satisfaction of the national court – that the dismissal (including the decision to dismiss, etc.) was totally unconnected to the employee's pregnancy.

More recently, in *Danosa* (2010), the Court had little difficulty in holding that a provision of Latvian legislation permitting the dismissal of pregnant women on a company's Board of Directors was precluded by Article 10.

When you read Chapter 18 you will find a number of cases which deal with the legality of an employer's decision to dismiss a pregnant worker, either simply because she was pregnant (*Webb v EMO Air Cargo* (Case C–32/93) [1994] QB 718), or because she developed some form of pregnancy-related illness (*Brown v Rentokil Ltd* (Case C–394/96) [1998] ECR I–4185). These cases were dealt with under the Equal Treatment Directive 76/207 (ETD) because the facts occurred prior to the date of the PWD coming into force (1994). Such cases would now be dealt with under the PWD. The situation in *Hertz v Aldi Marked* (Case 179/88) [1990] ECR I–3979, which deals with the situation when an employer dismisses an employee because of a pregnancy-related illness manifesting itself after the end of her maternity leave, was held to fall outside the scope of the ETD and it would appear to fall outside the scope of the PWD as well.

Employment rights

Article 11 deals with the employment rights of pregnant workers and workers on maternity leave. Article 11(1) states that for some pregnant workers (specifically, those to whom Articles 5, 6 or 7 apply), their contractual employment rights 'must be ensured in accordance with national legislation and/or national practice'. In *Parviainen* (2010), the ECJ held that Article 11(1) did **not** entitle a pregnant woman, who had been temporarily transferred to another post during her pregnancy, to receive **all** of the remuneration to which she would have been entitled had she not been pregnant. Member States had 'a certain degree of latitude when defining the conditions for the exercise and implementation of the entitlement to an income for the pregnant workers'. Hence, in *Gassmayr* (2010), the Court held that Article 11(1) did **not** entitle a pregnant doctor to the 'on-call duty allowance' (a form of overtime payment paid to doctors in Austria, to compensate them for having to work anti-social hours, and to which Dr Gassmayr would have been entitled had she been at work) during the period of time when she was forced to take leave for pregnancy-related health reasons and/or whilst on maternity leave. However, in *Parviainen* the Court added that the pregnant worker's income must 'in any event' be made up of her 'basic monthly salary and the pay components or supplements relating to her occupational status such as allowances relating to the seniority of the worker concerned, her length of service and her professional qualifications'.

Article 11(2) requires that, in the case of workers on maternity leave, the following 'must be ensured': (a) 'the rights connected with the employment contract' of workers within the meaning of Article 2; (b) 'maintenance of a payment to and/or entitlement to an adequate allowance for' workers within the meaning of Article 2. In *Kiiski* (2007), where a provision of Finnish legislation allowed for modifications to be made to a worker's pre-arranged child-care leave, but only on 'unforeseeable and justified grounds', such as the serious illness or death of the child or of the other parent, and divorce, but not a new pregnancy, the Court held that this was in breach of Article 11(2)(a).

In *Lewen v Denda* (Case C–333/97) [1999] ECR I–7243, the Court held that the word 'payment' in Article 11(2)(b) was 'intended to ensure that, during maternity leave, female workers receive an income … irrespective of whether it is paid in the form of an allowance, pay or a combination of the two'. The case itself involved a disputed Christmas bonus, which the Court held could not be regarded as 'intended to ensure such a level of income' and hence could not be regarded as falling within the concept of 'payment'. In *Ornano* (Case C–335/15), not yet reported, the Court stated that 'when a worker is absent from work because she is on maternity leave, the minimum protection required by Directive 92/85 does **not** require that the person concerned should continue to receive full pay'. The Court pointed out that the PWD was designed to ensure that, during her maternity leave, a woman was entitled to 'an income of an amount at least equivalent to that of the allowance provided for by national social security legislation in the event of a break in her activities on health grounds', but not her full pay.

Article 11(4) states that 'Member States may make entitlement to pay or the allowance conditional upon the worker concerned fulfilling the conditions of eligibility for such benefits laid down under national legislation. These conditions may under no circumstances provide for periods of previous employment in excess of 12 months immediately prior to the presumed date of confinement'. In *Rosselle* (Case C–65/14) [2015] 3 CMLR 38, the ECJ emphasised the word 'periods' i.e. in the plural. The case involved Belgian legislation according to which a woman was only entitled to a maternity allowance if, during the six months preceding her maternity leave, she had worked for at least 120 working days. Charlotte Rosselle, a teacher in Belgium, changed her employment while she was pregnant. The result of this change was that she only had 120 working days prior to going on maternity leave if her two periods of employment were aggregated. The Court held that refusal to confer a maternity allowance on a worker who had changed employment during the six months prior to starting maternity leave would be a breach of Article 11(4), because that provision referred to 'periods' of employment. The Court stated:

JUDGMENT

'The "periods of previous employment" referred to in Article 11(4) cannot be limited solely to the employment ongoing prior to the presumed date of confinement. Those periods of employment must be understood as comprising the various successive posts occupied by the worker concerned prior to that date, including for different employers and under various employment statuses. … Member State may **not** impose a new six-month minimum contribution period prior to eligibility for a maternity allowance merely because the employment status or post of the worker concerned has changed.'

17.4 Protection of young workers: Directive 94/33

This Directive also satisfies the dual social/economic aims of protecting vulnerable workers (this time young workers) while simultaneously providing for a level playing field on which all employers operate.

17.4.1 Work by children

The Directive establishes a general – but not absolute – prohibition on work by 'children' (Article 1(1) and Article 4(1)), defined as persons of less than 15 years of age or who are 'subject to compulsory full-time schooling under national law'. However, Article 5 provides that children may be employed 'for the purposes of performance in cultural, artistic, sports or advertising activities', provided that prior authorisation is given by the 'competent authority' (Article 5(1)) and provided that the activities are not likely to be harmful to the 'safety, health or development of children' and are not such as to be 'harmful to their attendance at school' (Article 5(2)); or if authorised by legislation (Article 5(2)). If Article 5 had not been included in the Directive then it would, for example, have been illegal to recruit the young British cast to play the Hogwarts pupils in the *Harry Potter* film series, most of whom were aged 11 when the first film was released in 2001.

Furthermore, children of at least 14 years of age may perform 'light work', defined as all work not likely to be harmful to their 'safety, health or development' or such as to be 'harmful to their attendance at school'. Children aged at least 13 may also perform 'light work' for a 'limited number of hours per week' (Article 4(2)).

17.4.2 Work by adolescents

Article 1(2) provides that Member States must 'strictly regulate' all work by 'adolescents'. That term is defined as including any person of at least 15 but less than 18 years of age and who is no longer subject to compulsory full-time schooling under national law.

17.4.3 Work by young people

Article 1(3) provides that 'young people' should have working conditions which 'suit their age' and should be 'protected against economic exploitation and against any work likely to harm their safety, health or physical, mental, moral or social development or to jeopardize their education'. 'Young people' are defined as any persons under 18 years of age. These principles are elaborated upon in Article 7(1), which provides that Member States must ensure that young people are:

> protected from any specific risks to their safety, health and development which are a consequence of their lack of experience, of absence of awareness of existing or potential risks or of the fact that young people have not yet fully matured.

A list of prohibited activities is then provided in Article 7(2):

a. work which is objectively beyond their physical or psychological capacity;

b. work involving harmful exposure to agents which are toxic, carcinogenic, cause heritable genetic damage or harm to the unborn child or which in any other way chronically affect human health;

c. work involving harmful exposure to radiation;

d. work involving the risk of accidents which it may be assumed cannot be recognised or avoided by young persons because of their insufficient attention to safety or lack of experience or training;

e. work in which there is a risk to health from extreme cold or heat, or from noise or vibration.

17.4.4 Derogations

There are general derogations from the scope of the Directive for 'domestic service in a private household' and for 'work regarded as not being harmful, damaging or dangerous to young people in a family undertaking' (Article 2(2)).

17.4.5 Working time and night work

Article 8 sets out detailed limits on the working time of young people, with an absolute maximum of seven hours per day and 35 hours per week for children (those under 15) and eight hours per day and 40 hours per week for adolescents (those aged 15 or over but not yet 18). Article 10 sets out detailed rules on rest periods, which includes a daily rest period of 14 consecutive hours for children and 12 consecutive hours for adolescents, and a weekly rest period of two days (although this may be reduced 'where justified by technical or organization reasons' but may not be less than 36 consecutive hours). Article 11 also establishes an annual rest period, although it is not subject to any minimum duration. Article 12 also ensures a break of 'at least 30 minutes, which shall be consecutive if possible' where daily working time is more than four-and-a-half hours. Article 12 applies to all young people (children and adolescents).

Article 9 prohibits all work by children between 8 p.m. and 6 a.m. With adolescents, Member States have a choice: they may prohibit all work between 10 p.m. and 6 a.m. or between 11 p.m. and 7 a.m. Those restrictions on adolescents working may be relaxed by legislation, although there is an overriding and absolute prohibition on night work between midnight and 4 a.m.

17.5 Parental leave: Directive 2010/18 (replacing Directive 96/34)

Directive 2010/18, the Parental Leave Directive (PLD), implements the Framework Agreement on Parental Leave concluded between various 'cross-industry organisations' in June 2009. The key provision is Clause 2(1) of the Framework Agreement, which provides that a working parent – mother or father – has:

> an individual right to parental leave on the grounds of the birth or adoption of a child to take care of that child until a given age up to eight years to be defined by Member States and/or social partners.

Clause 2(2) adds that 'the leave shall be granted for at least a period of four months and, to promote equal opportunities and equal treatment between men and women, should, in principle, be provided on a non-transferable basis'. The 'modalities of application of the non-transferable period shall be set down at national level through legislation and/ or collective agreements'.

The scope of the PLD was examined by the ECJ in *Commission v Luxembourg* (Case C–519/03) [2005] ECR I–3067. The case involved a provision of Luxembourg legislation which stated: 'In the event of pregnancy or adoption of a child during parental leave giving entitlement respectively to maternity leave or adoption leave, the latter shall replace parental leave which comes to an end.' The Court agreed with the Commission that this was in breach of the PLD, holding that, as maternity leave and parental leave were designed to achieve different things, one could not simply substitute for the other. The Court stated:

JUDGMENT

'Parental leave is distinct from maternity leave. Parental leave is granted to parents to enable them to take care of their child. This leave may be taken until the child has reached a given age up to eight years. Maternity leave has a different purpose. It is intended to protect a woman's biological condition and the special relationship between a woman and her child over the period which follows pregnancy and childbirth.... It follows that each parent is entitled to parental leave of at least three months' duration and that this may not be reduced when it is interrupted by another period of leave which pursues a purpose different from that of parental leave, such as maternity leave.'

In *Chatzi* (Case C–149/10) [2010] ECR I–8489, the ECJ was asked how the PLD applied in the context of parents of twins. In May 2007, Zoi Chatzi, a Greek national, gave birth to twins. In accordance with Greek legislation implementing the PLD, she was granted nine months' paid parental leave. Subsequently, she applied for a second period of nine months' paid parental leave, in respect of the second twin, but this was refused. She challenged this refusal, arguing that the PLD conferred entitlement to a separate period of parental leave for each child. The Court held that Clause 2(1) did not *automatically* require that, in the event of the birth of twins, entitlement to a number of periods of parental leave equal to the number of children born be recognised. However, the Court acknowledged that 'parents of twins are in a special situation'. Clause 2(1) therefore obliged the national legislature to establish a parental leave regime which ensured that the parents of twins received treatment that took 'due account of their particular needs'. It was incumbent upon national courts to determine whether the national rules met that requirement.

In *Maïstrellis* (Case C–222/14) [2015] IRLR 944, the ECJ emphasised that the right to parental leave was conferred on both parents. The Court stated (emphasis added):

JUDGMENT

'Under clause 2.1, an "individual right" to parental leave is granted to men and women workers on the grounds of the birth or adoption of a child, to enable them to take care of that child, for at least [four] months. Moreover, under clause 2.2, in order to promote equal opportunities and equal treatment between men and women, that right to parental leave "should, in principle, be granted on a non-transferable basis". It follows from those provisions that **each** of the child's parents is entitled, ***individually***, to parental leave for at least three months.'

Clause 5(1) of the Framework Agreement provides that 'at the end of parental leave, workers shall have the right to return to the same job or, if that is not possible, to an equivalent or similar job consistent with their employment contract or employment relationship'. Clause 5(2) adds that 'rights acquired or in the process of being acquired by the worker on the date on which parental leave starts shall be maintained as they stand until the end of parental leave'. In *Meerts* (Case C–116/08) [2009] ECR I–10063, the ECJ said that Clause 5(2) 'must be interpreted as articulating a particularly important principle of [EU] social law which cannot therefore be interpreted restrictively'. Clause 5(4) provides that 'in order to ensure that workers can exercise their right to parental leave, Member States and/or social partners shall take the necessary measures to protect workers against less favourable treatment or dismissal on the grounds of an application for, or the taking of, parental leave'. In *Rogiers* (Case C–588/12) [2014] IRLR 656, the Court stated that Article 5(4), like Clause 5(2), articulated 'a particularly important European Union social right and it may not, therefore, be interpreted restrictively'.

17.6 Protection for part-time workers: Directive 97/81

Directive 97/81 follows the model of the PLD. The Directive implements the Framework Agreement on Part-time Work concluded between various 'cross-industry organisations' in June 1997. The Agreement is designed to 'provide for the removal of discrimination against part-time workers and to improve the quality of part-time work' and to 'facilitate the development of part-time work on a voluntary basis and to contribute to the flexible organisation of working time in a manner which takes into account the needs of employers and workers' (Clause 1). The key provision is Clause 4(1) of the Agreement, which provides that 'part-time workers shall not be treated in a less favourable manner than comparable full-time workers solely because they work part-time unless different treatment is justified on objective grounds'.

Under Clause 2(1) of the Agreement, it applies to 'part-time workers who have an employment contract or employment relationship' as defined by the national laws or collective agreements of practice in each Member State. In *O'Brien v Ministry of Justice* (Case C–393/10) [2012] 2 CMLR 25; [2012] IRLR 421, the ECJ was asked whether Recorders were protected by the PTWD. (Recorders are part-time, fee-paid judges who work in the Crown and county courts in England and Wales. A fee-paid judge is not paid an annual salary but is paid according to the number of days or sittings actually spent in court.)

CASE EXAMPLE

O'Brien v Ministry of Justice (Case C–393/10) [2012] 2 CMLR 25; [2012] IRLR 421

Dermod O'Brien was called to the Bar in 1962 and appointed QC in 1983. From 1978 until his retirement in 2005, he worked (part-time) as a Recorder. He then requested a retirement pension calculated *pro rata* to that which a (full-time) Circuit Judge would be entitled. The Department of Constitutional Affairs rejected his request. This was because the UK legislation implementing the PTWD, the Part-time Workers (Prevention of Less Favourable Treatment) Regulations 2000, excluded those holding judicial office on a fee-paid basis, which meant that Recorders were excluded. O'Brien challenged this, and the case eventually made its way to the UK Supreme Court. That Court observed that Recorders hold an office marked by a 'high degree of independence of judgment' and were not subject to the directions of any superior authority as to the way in which they perform the functions of judging. Nevertheless, the Supreme Court noted that judicial office partakes of 'most' of the characteristics of employment. It decided to refer a question to the ECJ as to whether judges were 'workers' for the purposes of the PTWD.

The ECJ held that although Clause 2(1) allowed Member States some flexibility to define concepts like 'worker' and 'employment relationship' in their implementing legislation, they could not do so in a manner which led to the 'arbitrary exclusion of a category of persons' and 'which were liable to jeopardise the achievement of the objects' pursued by the PTWD and hence 'deprive it of its effectiveness'. The Court further held that the sole fact that judges were treated as judicial office holders was insufficient in itself to exclude them from enjoying the rights provided for by the Framework Agreement. If judges were 'workers' then Clause 4(1) of the Framework Agreement precluded national law from establishing a distinction between full-time judges and part-time fee-paid judges for the purpose of access to the retirement pension scheme, unless such a difference in treatment was justified by objective reasons.

The UK Supreme Court applied the ECJ ruling in *O'Brien v Ministry of Justice* [2013] UKSC 6; [2013] 1 WLR 522. That court held that Recorders were in an 'employment relationship' within the meaning of Clause 2(1) and had to be treated as 'workers' for the purposes of the 2000 Regulations. Moreover, no objective justification had been shown for departing from the basic principle of equal treatment in Article 4(1). This meant that part-time judges, like Recorders, were entitled to be remunerated on terms *pro rata* to those applicable to full-time judges, like Circuit judges.

Under Clause 2(2), Member States are entitled to exclude 'part-time workers who work on a casual basis'. This point was addressed in *Wippel* (Case C–313/02) [2004] ECR I–9483, involving an employee of an Austrian company, whose contract of employment was based on a 'work on demand' principle. According to this principle, the employer offers work as and when it is required and the employee is free to accept or reject the offer, in the latter case without having to justify it. There were no fixed hours or fixed income. Eventually Ms Wippel was prompted to bring an action against her employer, and a question was raised as to her entitlement to rely, *inter alia*, on the Framework Agreement. The ECJ held that it was for national courts to determine as a matter of fact whether a particular worker was employed as a 'part-time worker' under Clause 2(1) or a 'part-time worker on a casual basis' under Clause 2(2).

17.7 Protection for fixed-term workers: Directive 1999/70

Directive 1999/70 also follows the model of the PLD by incorporating the Framework Agreement on Fixed-term Contracts concluded between various 'cross-industry organisations' in March 1999. A 'fixed-term worker' is defined as:

> a person having an employment contract or relationship entered into directly between an employer and a worker where the end of the employment contract or relationship is determined by objective conditions such as reaching a specific date, completing a specific task, or the occurrence of a specific event.

The Agreement on Fixed-term Workers is very similar to the Agreement on Part-time Workers, and again the key provision is Clause 4(1), which states: 'fixed term workers shall not be treated in a less favourable manner than comparable permanent workers solely because they have a fixed-term contract or relation unless different treatment is justified on objective grounds'. In *Impact* (Case C–268/06) [2008] ECR I–2483, the ECJ held that Clause 4(1) was sufficiently clear and precise to be capable of direct effect.

17.8 Working time: Directive 2003/88

Directive 2003/88, the Working Time Directive (WTD), is in fact the second such Directive. It replaces the original WTD, Directive 93/104. It is a lengthy piece of legislation and space here prevents anything other than an overview of its key provisions:

- **Daily rest (Article 3)** – all workers are entitled to a minimum daily rest period of 11 consecutive hours per 24-hour period.
- **Breaks (Article 4)** – all workers whose working day exceeds six hours are entitled to a rest break.
- **Weekly rest (Article 5)** – all workers are entitled to a minimum uninterrupted weekly rest period of 24 hours. This is in addition to the daily rest period in Article 3.
- **Maximum weekly working time (Article 6(2))** – for all workers, the average weekly working time (including overtime) must not exceed 48 hours. This allows for divergence between the Member States as to the actual maximum period. In the UK's implementing legislation (the Working Time Regulations 1998) the maximum is set at 48 hours, whereas in Austria it is 40 hours and in France it is only 35 hours. For the

purposes of calculating the average, a reference period not exceeding four months applies (Article 16). The WTD does not prevent workers from working in excess of the maximum average working week if they agree to do so (Article 22(1)). The same provision states that no worker must be 'subjected to any detriment by his employer because he is not willing to give his agreement to perform such work'.

- **Annual leave (Article 7)** – all workers are entitled to at least four weeks' paid annual leave.
- **Night work (Article 8)** – 'normal hours' for night workers must not exceed eight hours.

17.8.1 Rest periods: Article 3 and Article 5

A question was raised in *Jaeger* (Case C–151/02) [2003] ECR I–8389 regarding the situation of 'on-call' doctors who spent all their 'on-call' time at the hospital itself. The case concerned a doctor in a German hospital who spent part of his working week 'on call'. During this 'on call' time, he was present at the hospital, but was only required to actually carry out his duties when, or indeed if, the need to do so arose. When he was not needed, he was entitled to sleep in a bed in a room in the hospital. Dr Jaeger argued that his entire period 'on call' should be counted towards his average weekly working hours; the defendant authorities argued that periods of inactivity during 'on call' duty should be regarded as 'rest' periods. The case was referred to the ECJ, which agreed with Dr Jaeger, applying the earlier judgment in *SIMAP* (Case C–303/98) [2000] ECR I–7963, considered below. The Court stated:

JUDGMENT

'The objective of [the WTD] is to secure effective protection of the safety and health of employees by allowing them to enjoy minimum periods of rest. That interpretation is all the more cogent in the case of doctors performing on-call duty in health centres, given that the periods during which their services are not required in order to cope with emergencies may, depending on the case, be of short duration and/or subject to frequent interruptions and where, moreover, it cannot be ruled out that the persons concerned may be prompted to intervene, apart from in emergencies, to monitor the condition of patients placed under their care or to perform tasks of an administrative nature.'

The ECJ also dealt with the issue of 'rest periods' in *Commission v UK* (Case C–484/04) [2006] ECR I–7471. The case arose after the UK's Department of Trade and Industry issued guidance on the interpretation of various aspects of the Working Time Regulations 1998, the British legislation implementing the original WTD. The guidance stated, among other things, that 'employers must make sure that workers can take their rest, but are not required to make sure they do take their rest'. The Commission alleged that this did not adequately implement the WTD, and the ECJ agreed. The Court held that, although employers could not 'force' their workers to take rest periods, the guidance nevertheless contravened the WTD, because it threatened to 'render the rights enshrined in Articles 3 and 5 of that directive meaningless'. The Court stated:

JUDGMENT

'Each worker must, inter alia, enjoy adequate rest periods, which must not only be effective in enabling the persons concerned to recover from the fatigue engendered by their work, but also preventive in nature, so as to reduce as much as possible the risk of affecting the safety or health of employees which successive periods of work without the necessary rest are likely to produce.'

More recently, Article 3 was invoked in *Union Syndicale 'Solidaires Isère'* (Case C–428/09) [2010] ECR I–9961. The case involved casual and seasonal staff at holiday and leisure centres in France who were responsible for supervising children staying at the centres. Under French law, the staff had responsibility for the children's health and safety, as well as education, *day and night*, for the entire duration of their stay. The Court held that this denial of a daily rest period, even to casual workers, was in principle prohibited by Article 3. (However, see below for further discussion of this case.)

The ECJ considered the meaning and scope of Article 5 in *Maio Marques da Rosa* (Case C–306/16) (not yet reported). The case involved a worker in a Portuguese casino who was occasionally required to work seven consecutive days. He alleged a breach of Article 5, contending that no worker could be required to work more than six consecutive days. The casino disagreed, arguing that, as long as the worker had at least one 24-hour rest period *each week*, he could be required to work for seven (or more) consecutive days. Hence, for example, if the rest day in week one was on Monday and the rest day in week two was Friday, the worker could be required to work from Tuesday in week one to Thursday in week two (up to ten consecutive days) without breaching Article 5. The Court agreed with the latter interpretation. The Court noted that Article 5 'does not specify when that minimum rest period must take place and thus gives Member States a degree of flexibility with regard to the choice on timing'. It followed that 'the minimum uninterrupted rest period of 24 hours, plus the 11 hours' daily rest referred to in Article 3, may be provided at any time within each seven-day period'.

17.8.2 Maximum weekly working time: Article 6(2)

An issue concerning the interpretation of Article 6(2) of the WTD arose in *SIMAP* (2000). Litigation between the Spanish public doctors' union (SIMAP) and the Health Ministry in the Valencia region of Spain raised a question regarding whether time spent at home by doctors who were on call counted towards their working time. The Court held that it did not, distinguishing the situation of being on call at the hospital (which did count) and being on call at home (which did not). The Court stated:

JUDGMENT

'The characteristic features of working time are present in the case of time spent on call by doctors where their presence at the health centre is required.... Moreover, even if the activity actually performed varies according to the circumstances, the fact that such doctors are obliged to be present and available at the workplace with a view to providing their professional services means that they are carrying out their duties in that instance.... The situation is different where doctors are on call by being contactable at all times without having to be at the health centre. Even if they are at the disposal of their employer, in that it must be possible to contact them, in that situation doctors may manage their time with fewer constraints and pursue their own interests.'

Article 6(2) was also examined in *Pfeiffer & Others* (Cases C–397 to 403/01) [2004] ECR I–8835, which concerned seven employees of the German Red Cross. The workers all challenged provisions of German legislation implementing the WTD, under which periods of inactivity spent by emergency workers between call-outs was **not** counted towards their average weekly working hours. This was the case even though emergency workers were regarded as being 'on duty' throughout the entire time, whether actually engaged in responding to an emergency or not. The Court held that the German legislation had not correctly implemented the WTD. The Court stated:

'The 48-hour upper limit on average weekly working time, including overtime, constitutes a rule of Union social law of particular importance from which every worker must benefit, since it is a minimum requirement necessary to ensure protection of his safety and health and therefore national legislation which authorises weekly working time in excess of 48 hours is not compatible with the requirements of Article 6(2) of the Directive.'

The principles set out in *SIMAP* and *Pfeiffer* were applied in the cases of *Dellas & Others* (Case C–14/04) [2005] ECR I–10253 and *Vorel* (Case C–437/05) [2007] ECR I–331, both involving healthcare workers who spent part of their days 'on call'. The Court confirmed that, whenever an employee is required to be physically present at his or her place of employment, and available to do work, then that counted towards their weekly 'working time'. The fact that the employee might have 'some periods of inactivity' during this 'on call' time was 'completely irrelevant'. The ECJ stated, in *Dellas*, that the WTD 'does not provide for any intermediate category between working time and rest periods' and that 'the intensity of the work done by the employee and his output are not among the characteristic elements of the concept of "working time"'.

As a general rule, time spent commuting between home and work is **not** 'working time', because every worker is free (within reason) to choose where to have their home. It is the worker, and not the employer, who decides on the commuting distance between home and the workplace. It is also up to the worker, and not the employer, to decide on the mode of transport to and from work. The distance travelled, and the method of transport, dictate how much time it takes to commute. If commuting time was included in 'working time' then workers who chose to live a long distance from work and/or who chose a slow method of transport would spend longer commuting and would be entitled to spend less time at the place of work. However, in *Tyco* (Case C–266/14) [2015] ICR 1159; [2015] IRLR 935, the Court identified a derogation from this general rule, for workers who do not have a fixed or habitual place of work, but who are required to travel to visit customers at their homes or business premises. For these workers, time spent travelling to the first customer of the day, and returning home from the last customer of the day, can be considered to be 'working time'.

CASE EXAMPLE

Tyco (Case C–266/14) [2015] ICR 1159; [2015] IRLR 935

Tyco installed and maintained security systems at domestic, commercial and industrial properties throughout Spain. Tyco's employees were provided with company vehicles to travel directly from their homes to their customers' homes or place of business in the morning, and back home again in the evening. The employees were informed by phone on the eve of their working day the task list for the following day, including the various premises that they were required to visit and the times of their customer appointments. The distances travelled varied significantly but some employees travelled over 100 km. One employee apparently spent 3 hours travelling from home to his first client because of the volume of traffic. The employees were also required to travel at least once per week to the offices of a transport logistics company near their homes to pick up equipment, parts and materials needed for their work.

Tyco calculated their employees' daily 'working time' as starting when they arrived at the premises of the first customer of the day and ending when they left the premises of the last customer, with account being taken of the time spent at the customers' premises and on journeys getting from one customer to another, but not time spent travelling between home and the first and last customer each day. This was challenged. The ECJ held that, in circumstances in which workers do not have a fixed or habitual place of work, the time spent by those workers travelling each day between their homes and the premises of the first and last customers designated by their employer constituted 'working time'. For such workers, travelling was 'an integral part' of their work. The place of work of such workers could not be reduced to the physical areas of their work on the premises of their employer's customers. Moreover, not taking the journey times into account would distort the concept of 'working time' and jeopardise the objective of protecting the safety and health of workers.

KEY FACTS

- Time spent 'on call' counts towards 'working time' if the worker is required to be physically present at their place of employment and available to do work. Whether the employee is active throughout this 'on call' time is irrelevant (*SIMAP*, *Pfeiffer*, *Dellas*, *Vorel*).
- Time spent 'on call' but at home does not count towards 'working time' (*Jaeger*).
- There is no intermediate category between 'working time' and 'rest periods' (*Dellas*).
- Time spent commuting is, generally speaking, not 'working time'. However, it is for workers who do not have a fixed or habitual place of work, and who are required to travel to visit their employer's customers at their homes or business premises (*Tyco*).

17.8.3 Annual leave: Article 7

One of the first cases to reach the ECJ involving the WTD was *R (on the application of BECTU) v Secretary of State for Trade and Industry* (Case C–173/99) [2001] 1 WLR 2313. This case involved an allegation that the UK legislation implementing the Directive, the Working Time Regulations 1998, failed to give proper effect to Article 7. Regulation 13(7) of the 1998 Regulations made acquisition of the entitlement to annual leave conditional upon the employee having been continuously employed for 13 weeks by the same employer. The ECJ held that there was nothing in the WTD which allowed Member States to incorporate this provision.

CASE EXAMPLE

R (on the application of BECTU) v Secretary of State for Trade and Industry (Case C–173/99) [2001] 1 WLR 2313

The British trade union BECTU (the Broadcasting, Entertainment, Cinematographic and Theatre Union) represents about 30,000 people in jobs such as sound recordists, cameramen, special effects technicians, projectionists, editors, researchers, hairdressers and make-up artistes. The Union complained that, because the majority of their members were employed under short-term contracts, they tended to work under a series of separate, short-term contracts, either with the same employer or with different employers. Hence, most of the Union's members failed to qualify under Regulation 13 of the Working Time Regulations 1998 and thus did not become entitled to any paid annual leave. The case was referred to the ECJ, which held that the Article 7 had not been properly implemented.

The Court stated:

JUDGMENT

'Legislation of a Member State which imposes a precondition for entitlement to paid annual leave which has the effect of preventing certain workers from any such entitlement not only negates an individual right expressly granted by [the WTD] but is also contrary to its objective.

By applying such rules, [those] workers are deprived of any entitlement to paid annual leave. . . . Minimum rest periods are essential for the protection of their health and safety. . . . Furthermore, rules of the kind at issue in the main proceedings are liable to give rise to abuse because employers might be tempted to evade the obligation to grant the paid annual leave to which every worker is entitled by more frequent resort to short-term employment relationships.'

Article 7 was also considered in *Merino Gómez v Continental Industries* (Case C–342/01) [2004] ECR I–2605. The case raised a very interesting question regarding the relationship between annual leave (guaranteed by Article 7 of the WTD) and maternity leave (guaranteed by Article 8 of the PWD, considered above). The complainant worked for a company where all workers took their annual leave at the same time, during a 'factory shutdown' period. This shutdown period coincided with her maternity leave. The question, therefore, was whether she was entitled to take her annual leave at a different time of the year. The ECJ held that she was so entitled. The Court held that Article 7 'must be regarded as a particularly important principle of [Union] social law from which there can be no derogations'. It was designed to provide all workers with a 'rest', and therefore had an entirely different purpose to maternity leave guaranteed by Article 8 of the PWD, which was designed to 'protect women's biological condition during pregnancy and the special relationship that mothers have with their new-born children'. Hence, the requirements of Article 7 of the WTD were not met to the extent that they coincided with a period of maternity leave. Hence, a pregnant worker 'must be able to take her annual leave during a period other than the period of her maternity leave'. It was irrelevant that the maternity leave period coincided with an annual leave period fixed by collective agreement.

CASE EXAMPLE

Merino Gómez v Continental Industries (Case C–342/01) [2004] 2 CMLR 3

María Paz Merino Gómez worked at Continental Industrias del Caucho's tyre factory in Spain. Between May and August 2001, she was on maternity leave. She applied to have her four weeks' annual leave after the end of her maternity leave, in September 2001, but this was refused. Under a collective agreement between Continental and all employees, the latter agreed to take their annual leave in two four-week blocks, one in July and one in August. Every year, six workers were able to take their holiday in September, but priority was given to those who had not exercised this option the previous year. As María had taken her annual holiday in September 2000, she could not choose to do so in 2001. Nevertheless, she argued that the collective agreement was contrary to the WTD. The case was referred to the ECJ, which upheld María's claim.

In *Dominguez* (Case C–282/10) [2012] 2 CMLR 14, the Court held that Member States were precluded from unilaterally limiting the entitlement to paid annual leave by applying 'any preconditions whatsoever' to it, such as a minimum period of work. This meant that French legislation which stipulated that the right to paid annual leave only applied once the employee had been 'employed by the same employer for a period equivalent to a minimum of one month of actual work' was contrary to the WTD.

In *Russell & Others v Transocean International Resources Ltd* [2011] UKSC 57, the UK Supreme Court held (without referring the issue to the ECJ) that, while there could be no derogation from the Article 7 requirement of four weeks' annual leave, those weeks did not have to be either consecutive or uninterrupted. While the reference to 'four weeks' seemed to mean four uninterrupted seven-day periods, the conditions of the granting of such leave were left to national legislation or practice. The Supreme Court found that there was no breach of Article 7 in the defendant's working arrangements, according to which the appellants (all North Sea oil and gas workers) were effectively forced to take their annual leave in (at best) two fortnightly periods, because of their contractual obligations to work a two-weeks-offshore, two-weeks-onshore shift pattern throughout the year.

Calculating the amount of pay under Article 7

In *Williams & Others* (Case C–155/10) [2011] ECR I–8409, the Court was asked by the UK Supreme Court to provide guidance on the amount of annual leave pay to which workers were entitled. The case involved British Airways (BA) pilots, whose salary comprised three components: (i) a fixed annual sum; (ii) a supplementary payment which depended on the time spent flying, worth £10 per hour; (iii) another supplementary payment which depended on the time spent away from base, worth £2.73 per hour. The amount paid by BA in respect of annual leave was based exclusively on component (i), i.e. the fixed annual sum. The pilots challenged this, arguing that their annual leave pay should be based on their entire remuneration, including the supplementary payments.

The Court held that workers should receive their 'normal' remuneration for the duration of their annual leave. However, where remuneration was composed of several components, the determination of 'normal' remuneration and, consequently, of the amount to which a worker was entitled during his or her annual leave, required the application of the 'intrinsic link' test. According to this test, all workers had the right to enjoy, during their annual leave, 'economic conditions which are comparable to those relating to the exercise of his employment'. Accordingly, any 'inconvenient aspect' which was 'linked intrinsically to the performance of the tasks' which the worker was contractually required to carry out, and in respect of which a monetary amount was provided, 'must necessarily be taken into account' for the purposes of calculating the annual leave payment. On the other hand, any components of remuneration which were intended 'exclusively' to cover 'occasional or ancillary costs arising at the time of performance of the tasks' which the worker was contractually required to carry out did **not** need be taken into account when calculating the annual leave payment. Application of the 'intrinsic link' test was a matter for the national court.

Lock v British Gas (Case C–539/12) [2014] 3 CMLR 53 involved the question whether the amount of holiday pay paid to workers who received a basic wage, plus commission depending on their work, should either be based only on their basic wage or on the basis of the basic wage plus commission. The Court held that the worker's commission should be taken into account. Otherwise, a worker could be deterred from taking his annual leave because of the financial disadvantage that he would incur.

CASE EXAMPLE

Lock v British Gas (Case C–539/12) [2014] 3 CMLR 53

Lock worked for British Gas as an energy sales consultant. His salary comprised two elements: a basic fixed wage (representing around 40% of his total salary), and commission (representing the other 60%). The amount of commission was not fixed but varied every month according to the number and type of contracts that he persuaded businesses to enter into with British Gas. When he took his annual leave, British Gas calculated his holiday pay on the basis of his basic salary only. He challenged this, and the Court ruled that his commission should be taken into account when calculating his holiday pay.

'Rolled up' holiday pay

In *Robinson-Steele v RD Retail Services Ltd* (Case C–131/04); *Clarke & Others* (Case C–257/04) [2006] ECR I–2531, the ECJ was asked to examine the subject of 'rolled up' holiday pay and its compatibility with Article 7. 'Rolled up' holiday pay occurs when holiday pay is paid as part of an employee's normal wages, throughout the year, typically weekly or monthly, rather than paid when the worker is actually on holiday. All the cases involved men employed by companies in the UK. Under the terms of their employment contracts, they were not paid while on holiday; rather, part of their daily/weekly salary for work done throughout the year included a payment for holidays. The ECJ stated that these arrangements were in breach of Article 7 (emphasis added):

JUDGMENT

'The holiday pay required by Article 7(1) is intended to enable the worker *actually to take the leave to which he is entitled*. The term "paid annual leave" in that provision means that, for the duration of annual leave ... remuneration must be maintained. In other words, workers must receive their normal remuneration for that period of rest.... The directive treats entitlement to annual leave and to a payment on that account as being two aspects of a single right. The purpose of the requirement of payment for that leave is to put the worker, during such leave, in a position which is, as regards remuneration, comparable to periods of work. Accordingly ... the point at which the payment for annual leave is made must be fixed in such a way that, during that leave, the worker is, as regards remuneration, put in a position comparable to periods of work.'

Alan Bogg ('The Right to Paid Annual Leave in the Court of Justice: The Eclipse of Functionalism' (2006) 31 *EL Rev* 892) has argued that 'rolled up' holiday pay has advantages for both employers and employees. Employers may gain in terms of administrative convenience, while employees could gain by 'boosting' their holiday pay through working overtime (at, say, one-and-a-half times their normal hourly rate) and therefore 'securing a premium on the rolled up portion of pay'. However, Bogg acknowledges that there is a 'potentially darker side', in that some workers may not be careful or responsible enough to save their holiday pay throughout the year, so that when their annual leave period arrives they cannot afford to go on holiday. Given that the principles underpinning the WTD are those of workers' health and safety, and that the WTD aims to guarantee that workers get 'rest' (on a daily and weekly basis as well as an annual basis) it is not, therefore, surprising that the ECJ opted to outlaw 'rolled up' holiday pay.

Holiday leave may be carried over ... but cannot be 'sold' back

In *Federatie Nederlandse Vakbeweging* (Case C–124/05) [2006] ECR I–3423, the ECJ ruled that some or all of the four-week annual leave guaranteed by Article 7 may be carried over to the next year. But it is still subject to the WTD, and cannot be subsequently 'sold' back to the employer. The case began when the Dutch Ministry of Social Affairs and Employment published an information brochure indicating that employees could, if they wished, save up their holidays for perhaps two years in order to 'undertake a world tour'. It also stated that workers could then 'sell' some of these saved-up days back to their employer for cash, should the need arise (for example for emergency property repairs). The Netherlands Federation of Trade Unions brought a challenge to this, and the ECJ upheld the challenge. The Court explained the reasons behind its decision as follows:

- The minimum annual holiday leave entitlement is intended to have a 'positive effect' on the safety and health of workers.

- Carrying holiday leave over to the next year still contributes to a worker's health and safety, provided it is actually taken, and is therefore compatible with the WTD.

- The possibility of an employee selling their annual holiday leave back to the employer was 'incompatible with the objectives' of the WTD, as it created an 'incentive' not to take leave.

In *KHS* (Case C–214/10) [2012] 1 CMLR 46, the Court held that national legislation could provide that a worker's annual leave entitlement under Article 7 would eventually lapse (for example in the case of a worker on long-term sick leave). If a worker was on sick leave for several years and was allowed to accumulate annual leave entitlement, indefinitely, then eventually the entitlement 'would no longer reflect the actual purpose of the right to paid annual leave'. The dual purpose of annual leave was to provide workers with rest, and an opportunity for relaxation and leisure. If an annual leave entitlement was carried over for a long enough period of time, it would cease to serve the first of those purposes, i.e. it would no longer provide a rest but would be purely relaxation and leisure. Applying these principles, the Court held that German legislation restricting the carry over of holiday pay to the next year plus another three months, i.e. 15 months in total, was permissible.

Can a worker claim their annual leave and/or a payment in lieu while on sick leave?

In the joined cases *Schultz-Hoff* (Case C–350/06) and *Stringer & Others v HM Revenue & Customs* (Case C–520/06) [2009] ECR I–179, the ECJ was asked whether a worker on indefinite sick leave still accrued annual leave and/or a payment in lieu of annual leave (in the event that the employment relationship is terminated). The Court ruled as follows:

- Article 7 of the WTD did not preclude national legislation which prevented an employee taking annual leave whilst on sick leave.

- However, the right to take annual leave was accrued during sick leave and could be taken on the employee's return to work. Alternatively, if the employment relationship was terminated before then, the employee was entitled to a payment in lieu of annual leave.

This decision is consistent with that in *Merino Gómez*, discussed above. In that case, you will recall, the ECJ ruled that annual leave and maternity leave served different purposes; basically, a woman on maternity leave is not on 'holiday'. Hence, the fact that an employee had taken time off work on maternity leave did not prevent her from claiming her minimum annual holiday leave on her return to work. Similarly, *Schultz-Hoff and Stringer* decided that a worker off work on sick leave is not on 'holiday' either and is therefore perfectly entitled to take their annual leave once they regain their health and return to work. If they do not regain their health and their employment is terminated, then they are entitled to be compensated for the loss of that leave.

In *Bollacke* (Case C–118/13) [2015] 1 CMLR 4; [2014] IRLR 732, the Court held that a payment in lieu for annual leave that had not been taken (because the worker had been on sick leave) remained payable, notwithstanding the subsequent death of the employee.

CASE EXAMPLE

Bollacke (Case C–118/13) [2015] 1 CMLR 4; [2014] IRLR 732

Bollacke worked for the German supermarket chain Klaas & Kock for 12 years until his death in November 2010. During the last year of his life he had been seriously ill and had been off work for several months, as a result of which he had 140½ days of annual leave outstanding. In January 2011, his widow claimed a payment in lieu, but Klaas & Kock refused on the basis of German case law which held that an entitlement to a payment in lieu for annual leave that had not been taken ceased to be payable on the death of the employee. The Court held that the payment in lieu was still payable.

In *Maschek* (Case C–341/15) [2016] IRLR 801, the Court went further, holding that a worker who left employment with annual leave outstanding was entitled to a payment in lieu, regardless of the reason why the worker had left their employment. This was the case even where the worker 'terminates, at his own request, his employment relationship'.

17.8.4 Night work: Article 8

Another issue raised in *SIMAP* (2000) was whether doctors who were regularly on call at night could be regarded as 'night workers'. The ECJ decided that they did not qualify. The WTD itself defines 'night workers' as those who spend at least three hours of their working day during night-time 'as a normal course'. The Court held that on call doctors could not be regarded as working during the night 'as a normal course'.

17.8.5 Derogations

The WTD is subject to numerous derogations. According to Article 17(1), Member States may derogate from their obligations under Articles 3, 4, 5, 6 and 8 when 'the duration of the working time is not measured and/or predetermined or can be determined by the workers themselves', and particularly in the case of:

a. managing executives or other persons with autonomous decision-taking powers;

b. family workers;

c. workers officiating at religious ceremonies in churches and religious communities.

The scope and application of Article 17(1) was considered in *Hälvä & Others* (Case C–175/16) [2017] IRLR 942. The case involved four Finnish nationals who worked as 'relief parents' for foster parents. The Court held that the derogation for 'family workers' had to be strictly interpreted. It referred 'exclusively' to work carried out in a context in which the employment relationship between the employer and its employees was a 'family relationship'. The derogation was characterised by a 'personal relationship of trust and confidence between the parties'.

CASE EXAMPLE

Hälvä & Others (Case C–175/16) [2017] IRLR 942

Accommodation was provided in Finland for children who had been taken into care which was intended to be as close as possible to a normal family environment. It comprised seven villages, each with several houses; each house was home to between three and six children and one or two foster parents (or 'relief parents' when the foster parents were absent for whatever reason). When on duty, which might be for several days at a time, the 'relief parents' looked after the children, went shopping, took the children out on trips, etc. The number of days per year when 'relief parents' could be required to work was stipulated in their contract. Each village had a director who specified which days the 'relief parents' would be on duty and for whom the 'relief parents' had to produce a report on how they had implemented each child's care programme. Four former 'relief parents' brought an action seeking a declaration that their time spent looking after the children constituted 'work' and an order for a compensation payment in respect of overtime and work in the evenings, at nights and at weekends. The Supreme Court of Finland referred the case to the ECJ seeking guidance on the scope of Article 17.

The ECJ held that the fact that the 'relief parents' had a contractual limit on the days when they worked, were told which days when, and in which houses, they were working, and had to prepare a report on each child for the village director, all strongly suggested that Article 17 did not apply, although this was ultimately a matter for the national court. This finding was not undermined by the fact that the 'relief parents' had a 'certain degree of autonomy in the organisation of their time' and, more specifically, in the 'organisation of their daily duties, their movements and their periods of inactivity, without there appearing to be any supervision by their employer'. Furthermore, the 'relief parents' were not 'family workers'. The fact that the relationship between 'relief parents' and the children in their care was 'similar' to that between members of the same family was not enough to bring the derogation into play.

Article 17(3) provides that Member States may derogate from their obligations in Articles 3, 4, 5 and 8 in several areas, of which the following is a non-exhaustive sample:

- the emergency services;
- hospital staff, including doctors;
- security guards;
- dock and airport workers;
- Press, radio, TV, cinematographic production, postal and telecommunication services;
- utilities workers (gas, water, electricity production and transmission);
- refuse collection;
- agriculture;
- regular urban transport services.

Article 17(3) was successfully invoked in *Union Syndicale 'Solidaires Isère'* (2010). The ECJ accepted the French government's argument that workers at holiday and leisure centres in France had responsibility for the continual supervision of the children staying at the centres, which brought those workers within the 'security and surveillance activities' derogation (alongside security guards and caretakers).

Article 18 allows for derogation from Articles 3, 4, 5 and 8 'by means of collective agreements or agreements concluded between the two sides of industry at national or regional level'.

KEY FACTS

Social policy	
• EU social policy law is essentially designed to protect the health and safety at work of all workers in the EU.	
• Specific protection is provided for the health and safety at work of pregnant workers. It guarantees pregnant workers a minimum period of maternity leave, and protects pregnant women from the threat of dismissal during their pregnancy and beyond.	Directive 92/85
• In addition, young workers, part-time workers and fixed-term workers have specific protection under EU law.	

• The Working Time Directive, originally introduced in 1993, is designed to protect workers from the risks associated with long working hours. It guarantees, amongst other things:
  • a minimum daily rest period of 11 consecutive hours per 24-hour period;
  • a daily rest break for all workers whose working day exceeds six hours;
  • a weekly rest break of at least 24 hours;
  • an average maximum weekly working time of 48 hours (calculated over a 4-month period);
  • at least 4 weeks' paid annual leave.
	Directive 2003/88

• According to the ECJ this period of annual leave must be in addition to any maternity leave to which the worker is entitled under Directive 92/85. This is because they pursue different objectives. Annual leave provides all workers with a 'rest', while maternity leave protects 'women's biological condition during pregnancy'.	*Merino Gómez v Continental Industries* (2004); Directive 2003/88

SAMPLE ESSAY QUESTION

'Critically consider the extent to which EU law protects pregnant workers.'

Explain what is meant by a 'pregnant worker':

- Directive 92/85 protects 'pregnant workers' plus 'workers who have recently given birth' and 'workers who are breastfeeding'

- 'Pregnant workers' should be protected from the 'earliest possible date in a pregnancy' (*Mayr v Flöckner*)

- Note the position of women undergoing IVF treatment (*Mayr v Flöckner*)

Discuss the provisions of Directive 92/85:

- Employers' obligation to 'assess risks' (Article 4)

- Limitations on night work (Article 5)

- Minimum maternity leave guarantee (Article 8(1)). Explain the dual purpose of maternity leave (*Kiiski*)

- Paid time off for ante-natal examinations (Article 9)

- Protection from dismissal, from beginning of pregnancy to end of maternity leave (Article 10). Note the expansive interpretation of 'dismissal' in *Paquay* but contrast with the more restrictive interpretation in *Jiminez Melgar*

- Protection of contractual rights (Article 11)

- Entitlement to 'adequate' maternity benefits (Article 11)

Consider the application of other EU legislation (see Chapter 18):

- Although maternity benefits are 'pay' covered by Article 157(1) TFEU, pregnant workers are not entitled to full pay (*Gillespie, McKenna, Alabaster*)
- Explain why: women on maternity leave are not in a 'comparable situation' with male workers. Note how this can work in women's favour (*Abdoulaye*)
- The refusal to employ a pregnant woman because of her pregnancy is direct sex discrimination contrary to Directive 2006/54 (*Dekker, Mahlburg*). Pregnant women need not inform prospective employers of their pregnancy (*Busch*)
- The dismissal of a pregnant woman because of pregnancy (*Hebermann-Beltermann, Webb*), or because of a pregnancy-related illness during maternity leave (*Brown*), or because she is at an 'advanced stage' of IVF treatment (*Mayr v Flöckner*) is direct sex discrimination prohibited by Directive 2006/54
- Employment conditions are protected (Directive 2006/54, Article 15; *Thibault, Sass, Sarkatzis Herrero*)
- Explain and consider the significance of pregnancy-based discrimination being 'direct'. Discuss arguments that it could/should be classed as 'indirect'
- Consider the position of a woman dismissed because of a pregnancy-related illness manifesting itself after the end of maternity (*Hertz*)

SUMMARY

Directive 89/391 is a 'framework' Directive which lays down general principles on health and safety of workers.

Directive 92/85, widely known as the Pregnant Workers' Directive (PWD), is designed to improve the safety and health at work of pregnant workers. Pregnant workers are entitled to 'a continuous period of maternity leave of at least 14 weeks allocated before and/or after confinement' (Article 8). The dismissal of women from the beginning of pregnancy to the end of their maternity leave, save in exceptional circumstances unconnected with their condition, is prohibited (Article 10). Workers on maternity leave have their contractual rights protected and are also entitled to maternity benefits (Article 11).

Young workers are protected by Directive 94/33. Children under 15 or in full-time education are prohibited from working, subject to certain exceptions, while children aged 15–17 must have working conditions which 'suit their age' and must be 'protected against economic exploitation and against any work likely to harm their safety, health or physical, mental, moral or social development or to jeopardize their education'.

Directive 2010/18, the Parental Leave Directive (PLD), implements the Framework Agreement on Parental Leave. This provides that a working parent – mother or father – has 'an individual right to parental leave on the grounds of the birth or adoption of a child to enable them to take care of that child, for at least four months'.

- Directive 97/81 implements the Framework Agreement on Part-time Work, which is designed to 'provide for the removal of discrimination against part-time workers' compared to full-time workers.

- Directive 1999/70 incorporates the Framework Agreement on Fixed-term Contracts, which is designed to ensure that fixed-term workers are not discriminated against in comparison to permanent workers.

- Directive 2003/88, the Working Time Directive (WTD), provides that all workers are entitled to: a minimum daily rest period of 11 consecutive hours per 24-hour period (Article 3); a daily rest break if the working day exceeds six hours (Article 4); a minimum uninterrupted weekly rest period of 24 hours (Article 5); an average weekly working time (including overtime) not exceeding 48 hours (Article 6(2)); at least four weeks' paid annual leave (Article 7). Night workers' 'normal hours' must not exceed eight hours (Article 8). Time spent 'on call' at the workplace by workers such as doctors counts as working time whereas time spent 'on call' but at home or elsewhere does not (*SIMAP, Jaeger, Pfeiffer, Dellas & Others, Vorel*). Time spent commuting is not 'working time' except where the worker has no fixed place of work and is required to travel to their employer's customer's homes or business premises (*Tyco*). The annual leave entitlement contributes towards workers' health and safety. Although it can be carried over, it must actually be taken and cannot be 'sold' back to the employer (*Federatie Nederlandse Vakbeweging*).

- Annual leave (the WTD, Article 7) and maternity leave (the PWD, Article 8) serve entirely different purposes. A pregnant worker 'must be able to take her annual leave during a period other than the period of her maternity leave' (*Merino Gómez*). Similarly, annual leave and sick leave serve entirely different purposes, so that a worker on sick leave does not lose his entitlement to paid annual leave (*Schultz-Hoff, Stringer & Others; Bollacke*).

Further reading

Articles

Barnard, C, Deakin, S and Hobbs, R, 'Opting out of the 48-Hour Week: Employer Necessity or Individual Choice?' (2003) 32 *ILJ* 223.

Bogg, A, 'Of Holidays, Work and Humanisation: A Missed Opportunity' (2009) 34 *EL Rev* 738.

Caracciolo di Torella, E, 'Surrogacy, Pregnancy and Maternity Rights: A Missed Opportunity for a More Coherent Regime of Parental Rights in the EU' (2015) 40 *EL Rev* 52.

Geoghegan, F, 'Protective Measures for Pregnant Workers in the Workplace' (2011) 8 *IELJ* 36.

Jeffery, M, 'Not Really Going to Work? Of the Directive on Part-time Work, Atypical Work and Attempts to Regulate it' (1998) 27 *ILJ* 193.

McCann, D, 'Travel Time as Working Time: *Tyco*, the Unitary Model and the Route to Casualization' (2016) 45 *ILJ* 244.

Pavlou, V, 'Domestic Work in EU Law: The Relevance of EU Employment Law in Challenging Domestic Workers' Vulnerability' (2016) 41 *EL Rev* 379.

Prechal, S, 'Equality of Treatment, Non-Discrimination and Social Policy' (2004) 41 *CMLR* 533.

18

Discrimination law

AIMS AND OBJECTIVES

After reading this chapter you should be able to:

- Understand the law relating to the prohibition of discrimination on grounds of sex, in particular Article 157 TFEU and Directive 2006/54

- Understand the law relating to the prohibition of discrimination on grounds of race, in particular Directive 2000/43

- Understand the law relating to the prohibition of discrimination on grounds of age, disability, religion or belief and sexual orientation, in particular Directive 2000/78

- Analyse critically the law relating to discrimination on grounds of age, disability, race, religion or belief, sexual orientation and sex

- Apply the law to factual situations involving discrimination on grounds of age, disability, race, religion or belief, sexual orientation or sex

18.1 Introduction

Article 157 TFEU established the fundamental principle of equality of treatment for men and women. It applies most obviously in employment cases, that is, in disputes between employers and employees. However, it is not limited to that situation and can be used, for example, by individuals to challenge (allegedly) discriminatory national legislation. Following the signing of the Treaty of Amsterdam in 1997, the equal treatment principle has expanded into different areas, and now includes equal treatment regardless of age, disability, race, religion or belief and sexual orientation. The key legislative provisions are:

- equal treatment on grounds of sex in terms of pay: Article 157;

- equal treatment on grounds of sex in other conditions of employment: Directive 2006/54;

- equal treatment on grounds of sex in matters of social security: Directive 79/7;

- equal treatment on grounds of sex for self-employed persons: Directive 2010/41;

- equal treatment on grounds of race or ethnic origin in employment and certain other areas: Directive 2000/43;
- equal treatment on grounds of age, disability, religion or belief and sexual orientation in employment: Directive 2000/78;
- equal treatment on grounds of sex in access to and supply of goods and services: Directive 2004/113.

According to the ECJ, the principle of equal treatment for men and women is 'one of the fundamental human rights whose observance the Court had a duty to ensure' (*Defrenne v SABENA* (Case 43/75) [1976] ECR 455).

18.2 'Discrimination'

Discrimination, whether in terms of pay under Article 157, or more generally under one of the various Directives, can be 'direct' or 'indirect'.

18.2.1 'Direct discrimination'

Article 2(1)(a) of Directive 2006/54 (which deals with sex discrimination) defines 'direct discrimination' as occurring 'where one person is treated less favourably on grounds of sex than another is, has been or would be treated in a comparable situation'. Directives 2000/43 and 2000/78 provide similar definitions in the context of the other forms of discrimination. Direct discrimination can rarely be justified.

18.2.2 'Indirect discrimination'

Indirect discrimination may arise in many different ways. Article 2(1)(b) of Directive 2006/54 defines 'indirect discrimination' in the context of sex discrimination as occurring:

ARTICLE

'where an apparently neutral provision, criterion or practice would put persons of one sex at a particular disadvantage compared with persons of the other sex, unless that provision, criterion or practice is objectively justified by a legitimate aim, and the means of achieving that aim are appropriate and necessary'.

A typical situation of indirect sex discrimination is where an employer employs both full-time and part-time workers. The former group, comprised exclusively (or mostly) of men, is paid proportionately more than the latter, comprised exclusively (or mostly) of women. The fact that the adversely affected group contains both men and women does not prevent a particular measure from being discriminatory. Otherwise, the fact that there was one man doing the same work as a large group of women would prevent the comparison.

Unlike direct discrimination, indirect discrimination can be justified on 'objective' grounds. This point will be examined below (see section 18.5).

18.2.3 Discrimination based on 'sex'

It is obvious that EU sex discrimination law deals with discrimination on grounds of gender. But does it cover other situations? In *P v S* (Case C–13/94) [1996] ECR I–2143, the ECJ held that the dismissal of a post-operative male-to-female transsexual constituted discrimination based on 'sex'.

More recently, in *KB* (Case C–117/01) [2004] ECR I–541, the ECJ held that British legislation preventing post-operative transsexuals from marrying in their acquired gender could be regarded as an example of 'sex' discrimination. See also *Richards* (Case C–423/04) [2006] ECR I–3585, considered in section 18.8.3 below.

However, in *Grant* (Case C–249/96) [1998] ECR I–621, the ECJ held that EU 'sex' discrimination law did **not** cover sexual orientation discrimination. Such discrimination was later brought under the umbrella of EU discrimination law with the introduction of Directive 2000/78, which will be examined below.

18.2.4 Harassment

'Harassment' on any of the relevant grounds (age, disability, race, religion or belief, sex or sexual orientation) is also classed as discrimination. 'Harassment' as a form of discrimination prohibited by EU law was first introduced by Directives 2000/43 and 2000/78, and was only later applied to sex discrimination. Harassment on grounds of sex is now prohibited by Directive 2006/54. See Section 18.11.1 for a more detailed discussion of 'harassment'.

KEY FACTS

Discrimination	
Discrimination takes two forms: direct and indirect.	
Direct discrimination occurs where a person is treated less favourably than another person in a comparable situation on grounds of sex, race, age, disability, religion or belief, sexual orientation.	Directive 2006/54 (sex); Directive 2000/43 (race); Directive 2000/78 (age, disability, religion or belief, sexual orientation)
Indirect discrimination occurs when an 'apparently neutral provision' puts a person at 'a particular disadvantage' because of their sex, race, etc., unless that provision can be justified.	
'Sex' discrimination includes discrimination against transsexuals.	*P v S* (1996); *KB* (2004)
Harassment is treated as a form of discrimination. It is defined as 'any form of unwanted conduct' with the 'purpose of violating the dignity of a person'.	Directive 2006/54 (sex); Directive 2000/43 (race); Directive 2000/78 (age, disability, religion or belief, sexual orientation)

18.3 Article 157 TFEU and equal pay

ARTICLE

'Art 157(1) Each Member State shall ensure that the principle of equal pay for male and female workers for equal work or work of equal value is applied.

(2) For the purpose of this Article, "pay" means the ordinary basic or minimum wage or salary and any other consideration, whether in cash or in kind, which the worker receives, directly or indirectly, in respect of his employment from his employer. Equal pay without discrimination based on sex means:

(a) that pay for the same work at piece rates shall be calculated on the basis of the same unit of measurement;

(b) that pay for work at time rates shall be the same for the same job.

(3) The European Parliament and the Council ... shall adopt measures to ensure the application of the principle of equal opportunities and equal treatment of men and women in matters of employment and occupation, including the principle of equal pay for equal work or work of equal value.

(4) With a view to ensuring full equality in practice between men and women in working life, the principle of equal treatment shall not prevent any Member State from maintaining or adopting measures providing for specific advantages in order to make it easier for the under-represented sex to pursue a vocational activity or to prevent or compensate for disadvantages in professional careers.'

In *Defrenne v SABENA* (1976), the ECJ stated that Article 157(1) pursued a 'double aim', one economic and one social. The two aims are:

- **economic aim**: to ensure that employers in states which had already introduced their own principles of equal pay via national legislation did not suffer a 'competitive disadvantage in [intra-Union] competition', compared with employers in other states which had not yet eliminated discrimination against female workers;

- **social aim**: to ensure 'social progress and seek the constant improvement of the living and working conditions' of people in the EU.

Direct effect of Article 157(1)

In *Defrenne v SABENA* (1976), the ECJ held that Article 157(1) not only satisfied the conditions for direct effect (and hence it could be enforced in the national courts) but, moreover, that it could be enforced not just vertically but also horizontally. The Court stated that the prohibition on discrimination between men and women 'applies not only to the action of public authorities but also extends to all agreements which are intended to regulate paid labour collectively, as well as to contracts between individuals'.

CASE EXAMPLE

Defrenne v SABENA (Case 43/75) [1976] ECR 455

Gabrielle Defrenne was employed as an air stewardess with SABENA, the Belgian airline company. Eventually she brought an action against it, claiming that she was being paid less than her male colleagues. At the relevant time, there was no Belgian legislation prohibiting pay discrimination. Gabrielle therefore claimed that Article 157(1) applied. The ECJ agreed that Article 157(1) could be relied upon by individuals in national courts.

Scope of Article 157

One important limitation on the scope of Article 157 was identified by the ECJ in *Defrenne v SABENA* (1976) – individuals can only invoke Article 157 to challenge 'unequal pay for equal work which is carried out in the same establishment or service'. In other words, a woman working for company A cannot claim pay equality with a man employed at company B even if they are both doing exactly the same work. This point was confirmed in *Lawrence and Others* (Case C–320/00) [2002] ECR I–7325. The Court ruled:

JUDGMENT

'Where the differences identified in the pay conditions of workers performing equal work or work of equal value cannot be attributed to a single source, there is no body which is responsible for the inequality and which could restore equal treatment. Such a situation does not come within the scope of [Article 157]. The work and the pay of those workers cannot therefore be compared on the basis of that provision.'

This ruling was followed in *Allonby* (Case C–256/01) [2004] ECR I–873, where a group of part-time college lecturers (most of whom were female) employed by an agency were unable to claim equal pay with a group of full-time lecturers (most of whom were male) employed by the college itself. Even though the two groups worked in the same place, they had different employers and hence Article 157 did not apply.

18.3.1 The definition of 'pay'

The concept of 'pay' in Article 157(2) is generously worded. It is explicitly **not** restricted to 'wages' or 'salary'. Rather, it includes 'any other consideration' which the worker receives as a result of his employment relationship. Article 157 has also been generously construed by the ECJ.

Examples of pay

The following cases demonstrate the breadth of the word 'pay':

- **Sick pay:** see *Rinner-Kühn* (Case 171/88) [1989] ECR 2743.

- **Severance payments:** such payments are designed to help employees who became unemployed involuntarily, for example, following retirement or disability, to adjust to their new situation. See *Kowalska* [1990] ECR I–2591.

- **Compensation for unfair dismissal:** in *Seymour-Smith & Perez* (Case C–167/97) [1999] ECR I–623, the ECJ held that an award of compensation in the event of unfair dismissal was 'pay': it represented what the worker 'would have earned if the employer had not unlawfully terminated the employment relationship'.

- **Bonuses:** in *Krüger* (Case C–281/97) [1999] ECR I–5127, the ECJ held that an annual Christmas bonus amounted to 'pay'. This was confirmed in *Lewen v Denda* (Case C–333/97) [1999] ECR I–7243, where the Court held that a bonus was 'pay' whether or not it was regarded as an incentive to future work, or a retrospective reward for services performed.

- **Payment in lieu:** in *Bötel* (Case C–360/90) [1992] ECR I–3589, the Court held that compensation payable by an employer in lieu of wages when an employee was required to attend compulsory training was 'pay'.

- **Post-employment benefits:** in *Garland v BRE* (Case 12/81) [1982] ECR 359, the ECJ held that Article 157 could apply to benefits received by ex-workers, on the basis that it constituted consideration for work done during the employment relationship.

- **Redundancy payments:** see *Barber v Guardian Royal Exchange Assurance Group* (Case 262/88) [1990] ECR I–8889.

- **Maternity pay:** in *Gillespie* (Case C–342/93) [1996] ECR I–475, the ECJ held that money paid by an employer to a female employee on maternity leave was based on the employment relationship and therefore constituted 'pay'. In *Abdoulaye* (Case C–218/98) [1999] ECR I–5723, the ECJ confirmed that a lump-sum payment to women employees going on maternity leave was 'pay'.

- **Occupational pensions:** in *Bilka-Kaufhaus* (Case 170/84) [1986] ECR 1607, the ECJ held that **entitlement to join** such a scheme could be regarded as a form of 'pay', and in *Barber* (1990) the Court held that **benefits paid** under an occupational pension scheme also constituted 'pay'.

Barber was confirmed and extended in *Ten-Oever* (Case C–109/91) [1993] ECR I–4879. The Court held that Article 157 applied even if the pension benefits were paid to someone other than the employee who had earned them, namely the employee's survivor (typically a widow). Such benefits were still 'pay' because they derived from the contract of employment. In *Coloroll* (Case C–200/91) [1994] ECR I–4389, the Court held that Article 157 applied even if the scheme benefits, i.e. the 'pay', were paid by someone other than the employer, namely the pension scheme trustees. Thus, Article 157 applies:

- where 'pay' is provided by the employer **but not to the employee** (*Ten-Oever* (1993));

- where pay is provided to the employee **but not by the employer** (*Coloroll* (1994)).

18.3.2 Equal work or work of equal value
'Equal work'

At its most basic level, Article 157 TFEU requires employers to pay their male and female workers the same pay if they are doing 'equal work'. In the great majority of cases there is no dispute on this point as the workers in question are doing exactly the same jobs. However, in some cases, this apparently straightforward provision may require a sophisticated analysis of the facts. In *Wiener Gebietskrankenkasse* (Case C–309/97) [1999] ECR I–2865, the ECJ held that two groups of employees who were performing 'seemingly identical tasks', but whose **training and/or professional qualifications were different**, were not necessarily to be regarded as doing the 'same work'. This was because of the possibility that different tasks may be assigned to the different groups.

Wiener Gebietskrankenkasse was followed recently in *Kenny & Others* (Case C–427/11) [2013] 2 CMLR 50. The Court stated:

> where seemingly identical tasks are performed by different groups of persons who do not have the same training or professional qualifications for the practice of their profession, it is necessary to ascertain whether, taking into account the nature of the tasks that may be assigned to each group respectively, the training requirements for performance of those tasks and the working conditions under which they are performed, the different groups in fact do the same work.

In both cases, the ECJ stated that it was ultimately for the national court to decide whether work was 'equal'.

Similarly, in *Cadman* (Case C–17/05) [2006] ECR I–9683, the ECJ held that individual workers' different lengths of experience might justify differential pay rates for otherwise similar jobs. This was because 'Length of service goes hand in hand with experience, and experience *generally* enables the worker to perform his duties better' (emphasis added).

'Work of equal value'

This provision obliges employers to pay their male and female staff the same pay even if they are doing different jobs – if those jobs are of 'equal value'. In *Royal Copenhagen* (Case C–400/93) [1995] ECR I–1275, the ECJ made it clear that it was not for the Court to make decisions on whether different jobs were of 'equal value'. Instead, this was a question of fact for the national court. There have been problems in determining exactly **how** different jobs should be assessed to see if they are of 'equal value'. Article 4 of Directive 2006/54 (the Recast Directive) provides some guidance: 'where a job classification system is used for determining pay, it must be based on the same criteria for both men and women and so drawn up as to exclude any discrimination on grounds of sex'. Thus, although the directive refers to job classification schemes, it does **not** make them compulsory. However, it is essential that Member States ensure that some system is in place to decide whether work has the same value, whether as the result of a job classification scheme, **or otherwise**.

CASE EXAMPLE

Royal Copenhagen (Case C–400/93) [1995] ECR I–1275

Royal Copenhagen, a ceramics producer in Denmark, employed over 1,000 workers. Amongst these were two groups – the automatic machine operators and the blue-pattern painters. The former group, consisting of 26 men, received an average weekly wage of 104 Danish kroner. The latter group, consisting of 155 women and one man, received an average weekly wage of 91 kroner. A trade union brought an action to have the (predominantly female) blue-pattern painters brought up to the value of the (male) automatic machine operators. The ECJ held that it was for the national court to decide whether the work was of equal value. This would have to be done, bearing in mind that the automatic machine operators' job required muscular strength, while the blue-pattern painters' job relied heavily on dexterity; that the operators suffered 'inconveniences from noise and temperature', while the painters had problems caused by 'sedentary and monotonous' work. There were also differences in terms of paid breaks, and the freedom of the workers to organise their own work.

ACTIVITY

Applying the law

Apart from 'muscular effort', can you think of any criteria that an employer might decide to use to determine salary levels which would discriminate in favour of one gender and against the other?

In *North & Others v Dumfries & Galloway Council* [2013] UKSC 45, the UK Supreme Court held that it was possible that various employees of the defendant council could be regarded as performing work of equal value, even though their actual jobs were 'very different'. The complainants were 251 women who worked in schools and local authority nurseries; they wished to compare themselves with male groundsmen and refuse collectors who, unlike the complainants, were entitled to substantial bonuses and supplements. Lady Hale (with whom the rest of the Court agreed) stated:

JUDGMENT

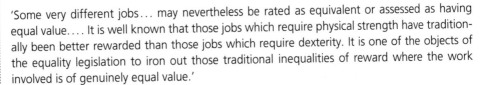

'Some very different jobs... may nevertheless be rated as equivalent or assessed as having equal value.... It is well known that those jobs which require physical strength have traditionally been better rewarded than those jobs which require dexterity. It is one of the objects of the equality legislation to iron out those traditional inequalities of reward where the work involved is of genuinely equal value.'

Equal pay for work of greater value
In *Murphy* (Case 157/86) [1988] ECR 673, a female factory worker discovered that she – along with 28 other women – was being paid less than a male store labourer in the same

factory. When she objected, she was told that because her work was of **greater** value than that of the male labourer, no comparison could be made. The ECJ held that although Article 157 referred to the principle of equal pay for equal work, or for work of equal value, but not to work of unequal value, it could nevertheless be applied in Ms Murphy's case. The Court said that to 'adopt a contrary interpretation would be tantamount to rendering the principle of equal pay ineffective and nugatory'.

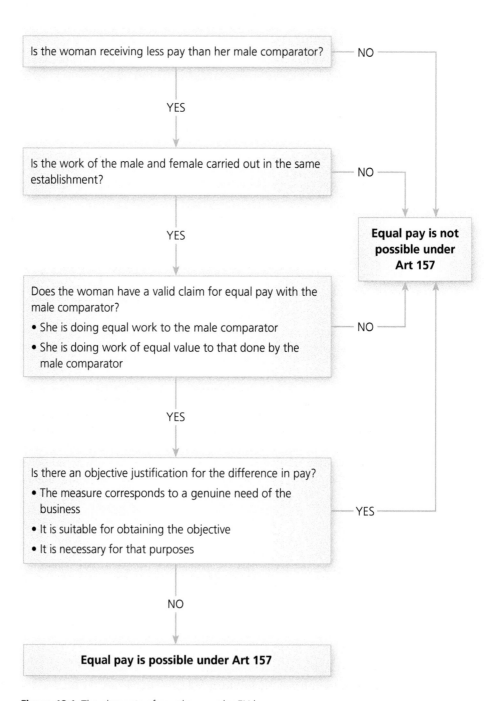

Figure 18.1 The elements of equal pay under EU law

Equal pay	
Men and women are entitled to equal pay for equal work.	Art 157 (1) TFEU
Art 157(1) TFEU is directly effective.	*Defrenne v SABENA* (1976)
In order to claim pay equality, the male and female employees must be working for the same employer.	*Lawrence & Others* (2002); *Allonby* (2004)
'Pay' is defined very widely. It includes, but is not restricted to, 'wages' or 'salary'. It includes 'any other consideration' which a worker receives as a result of his or her employment.	Art 157 (2) TFEU
'Pay' includes sick pay, bonuses and maternity pay.	*Rinner-Kühn* (1989); *Krüger* (1999); *Gillespie* (1996)
'Pay' includes post-employment payments such as severance payments, compensation for unfair dismissal, redundancy payments and occupational pensions.	*Kowalska* (1990); *Seymour-Smith & Perez* (1999); *Barber* (1990); *Bilka-Kaufhaus* (1986)
Employees performing 'seemingly identical tasks' but whose training, qualifications and/or experience is different may not necessarily be regarded as doing 'equal' work.	*Wiener Gebietskrankenkasse* (1999); *Cadman* (2006); *Kenny & Others* (2013)
Where a 'job classification system' is used to identify 'work of equal value' it must be based on the same criteria for men and women.	Directive 2006/54; *Royal Copenhagen* (1995)

18.4 Equal Treatment for men and women in employment – Directive 2006/54

Directive 76/207, widely referred to as the Equal Treatment Directive (ETD), first laid down a general principle for equal treatment in other conditions of employment, other than pay. The ETD was amended by Directive 2002/73 in October 2005, and then repealed in its entirety in August 2009. The principle of equal treatment is now found in Directive 2006/54, known as the 'Recast' Directive. However, some of the case law on the original ETD is still relevant today (see below). Article 1 of the Recast Directive states:

ARTICLE

'Art 1 The purpose of this Directive is to ensure the implementation of the principle of equal opportunities and equal treatment of men and women in matters of employment and occupation.'

To that end, the new Directive contains provisions to implement the principle of equal treatment in relation to:

a. access to employment, including promotion, and to vocational training;

b. working conditions, including pay;

c. occupational social security schemes.

It also contains provisions to ensure that such implementation is made more effective by the establishment of appropriate procedures.

The main substantive provisions of the Recast Directive are as follows:

- Article 3 – allows for 'positive action', defined as 'measures … with a view to ensuring full equality in practice between men and women in working life'.
- Article 4 – prohibits discrimination in terms of pay. This confirms Article 157 TFEU.
- Article 14 – provides for equal treatment as regards access to employment, vocational training, promotion and working conditions (including dismissals).
- Article 19 – sets out the burden of proof in sex discrimination cases.

Article 14(1) provides as follows:

ARTICLE

'Art 14(1) There shall be no direct or indirect discrimination on grounds of sex in the public or private sectors, including public bodies, in relation to:

(a) conditions for access to employment, to self-employment or to occupation, including selection criteria and recruitment conditions, whatever the branch of activity and at all levels of the professional hierarchy, including promotion;

(b) access to all types and to all levels of vocational guidance, vocational training, advanced vocational training and retraining, including practical work experience;

(c) employment and working conditions, including dismissals, as well as pay as provided for in [Article 157 TFEU];

(d) membership of, and involvement in, an organisation of workers or employers, or any organisation whose members carry on a particular profession, including the benefits provided for by such organisations.'

18.4.1 Access to employment and vocational training: Article 14(1)(a) and (b)

An example of a case which would now be dealt with under Article 14(1)(a) is *Meyers* (Case C–116/94) [1995] ECR I–2131. Here, the ECJ held that Family Credit, a British social security benefit intended to supplement the income of low-paid workers who were also responsible for a child, could be regarded as falling within the scope of the ETD. The benefit dealt with 'access to' employment because it encouraged people to take low-paid jobs. It followed that a refusal to pay the benefit to a single parent could amount to indirect discrimination (because the vast majority of single parents in the UK are women).

In *Kratzer* (2016), the Court held that the Recast directive did not apply when the person alleging discrimination in terms of the conditions for accessing employment had no actual intention of ever taking up employment in the first place.

CASE EXAMPLE

Kratzer (Case C–423/15) [2017] 1 CMLR 27; [2016] IRLR 888

Kratzer, an experienced lawyer in Germany, applied unsuccessfully for one of four graduate trainee jobs at an insurance company. He then alleged age discrimination (contrary to Directive 2000/78) on the basis that one of the selection criteria was experience as a 'student worker'. Later, when he found out that all of the four jobs had been awarded to female candidates, he made a further allegation of sex discrimination (contrary to Directive 2006/54). However, it then emerged that Kratzer was not sincerely interested in the job but had applied in order to provide the basis for a possible claim for compensation. Indeed it appeared that he had applied for 'countless' jobs with various firms and, when a negative response was forthcoming, he filed a lawsuit claiming he had suffered discrimination on grounds of age and/or gender, and seeking compensation. The ECJ held that neither directive applied to someone seeking to rely on them 'for abusive or fraudulent ends'.

18.4.2 Employment and working conditions, including dismissals: Article 14(1)(c)

'Working conditions'

This has been given a wide scope by the ECJ. In *Meyers*, the ECJ rejected an argument that 'working conditions' only referred to conditions in the contract of employment. Instead, the ECJ stated that 'working conditions' referred to the whole 'employment relationship'. A good example is provided by *Roca Álvarez v Sesa Start España* (Case C–104/09) [2010] ECR I–8661, in which the Court held that the right provided under Spanish law to working mothers, giving them time off work each working day for the purpose of feeding a child, was a 'working condition'. It was therefore contrary to Article 14(1)(c) not to give the same right to working fathers.

In *Coote* (Case C–185/97) [1998] ECR I–5199, the ECJ held that the ETD covered discriminatory measures occurring after the termination of the employment relationship (in this case, refusal to provide a reference). In contrast, in *D* (Case C–167/12) [2014] 3 CMLR 15, the ECJ said that there was no breach of Article 14(1)(c) when an employer refused to grant 'surrogacy leave' to an employee. D had entered into a surrogacy arrangement with another woman. However, when D applied for 'surrogacy leave' to spend time with her new baby, her application was refused. She contended that this was in breach of the Recast directive, but the ECJ held that here was no discrimination, either directly or indirectly, on grounds of sex. There was no *direct* discrimination because a father requesting surrogacy leave would have been treated in exactly the same way. Nor was there *indirect* discrimination, because there was nothing on the file to 'establish that the refusal of leave at issue puts female workers at a particular disadvantage compared with male workers'. Finally, although the Recast directive explicitly provided that 'any less favourable treatment of a woman that is related to pregnancy' constitutes discrimination on grounds of sex (Article 2(2)(c)), a woman like D, who had had a baby through a surrogacy arrangement, could not be subject to less favourable treatment 'related to pregnancy', given that she 'has not been pregnant with that baby'.

'Dismissals'

The word 'dismissals' is to be interpreted widely. In *Burton* (Case 19/81) [1982] ECR 555, the ECJ said that it extended to any termination of the employment relationship, even where this was part of a voluntary redundancy scheme.

Perhaps the most significant development in this context was the extension of what is now Article 14(1)(c) of the Recast Directive to cover discriminatory retirement ages in employment contracts. The leading cases are all British. This is because, prior to 1986, British legislation did not prohibit such discrimination. As a result, many British employers adopted a policy of allowing men to work until their 65th birthday whilst female employees had to retire at 60. This blatant discrimination against women could be explained on the basis that the British state pensionable age (that is, the age at which people could claim an old-age pension from the state) was itself discriminatory against men, who only became entitled to a pension at 65 whereas women could claim from 60. The best-known case is *Marshall* (1986), which has already been examined in Chapter 8. You will recall that Ms Marshall, who was forced to retire shortly after her 60th birthday, brought a successful challenge to her ex-employer's discriminatory retirement age in its contracts of employment. The ECJ held that forcing women to retire was tantamount to 'dismissal' and, therefore, in breach of EU law.

18.4.3 Derogations

Article 14(2) of the Recast Directive provides as follows:

ARTICLE

'(2) Member States may provide, as regards access to employment including the training leading thereto, that a difference of treatment which is based on a characteristic related to sex shall not constitute discrimination where, by reason of the nature of the particular occupational activities concerned or of the context in which they are carried out, such a characteristic constitutes a genuine and determining occupational requirement, provided that its objective is legitimate and the requirement is proportionate.'

Case law on the original ETD illustrates the type of situations in which Article 14(2) may apply. The ECJ has recognised that sex may be a 'genuine and determining occupational requirement' for posts such as those of:

- armed police officers (*Johnston* (Case 222/84) [1986] ECR 1651);
- prison warders in single-sex prisons (*Commission v France (Civil Service Employment)* (Case 318/86) [1988] ECR 3559);
- midwives (*Commission v UK (Private Households/Midwives)* (Case 165/82) [1983] ECR 3431);
- soldiers in specialist army combat units (*Sirdar* (Case C–273/97) [1999] ECR I–7403).

In *Sirdar*, the ECJ held that the exclusion of women from service in special combat units such as the British Royal Marines was justifiable under what is now Article 14(2). The Marines have a policy of excluding women from service on the ground that their presence is incompatible with the requirement of 'interoperability', that is to say, the need for every Marine, irrespective of his specialisation, to be capable of fighting in a commando unit. The Court ruled that the British Army was entitled:

> to come to the view that the specific conditions for deployment of the assault units of which the Royal Marines are composed, and in particular the rule of interoperability to which they are subject, justified their composition remaining exclusively male.

Ellis, in 'The Recent Jurisprudence of the Court of Justice in the Field of Sex Equality' (2000) 37 *CMLR* 1403, was critical of the *Sirdar* judgment. She commented that 'the degree of gender-stereotyping is little short of staggering'. This may be true, but the ECJ has since shown that it is unwilling to allow Member States to exploit similar arguments in order to prevent women serving in the armed forces in any capacity. In *Kreil v Germany* (Case C–285/98) [2000] ECR I–69, the ECJ distinguished *Sirdar* when it ruled that provisions of the German constitution barring women from all army jobs involving the use of arms was contrary to the ETD and could not be saved by what is now Article 14(2) of the Recast Directive. The case came to the ECJ when Tanja Kreil, an electronics expert, was turned down when she applied to join the German army to work with electronic weapons systems. She discovered that women were only allowed to serve in the German army either as medics or musicians. The ECJ held that this went too far. Indeed, the decision in *Kreil* actually supports *Sirdar* – the Court in *Kreil* pointed out that 'derogations remain possible where sex constitutes a determining factor for access to certain special combat units'.

18.4.4 Reversed burden of proof
Article 19(1) of the Recast Directive sets out the following principles relating to the burden of proof:

ARTICLE

'Member States shall take such measures as are necessary, in accordance with their national judicial systems, to ensure that, when persons who consider themselves wronged because the principle of equal treatment has not been applied to them establish, before a court or other competent authority, facts from which it may be presumed that there has been direct or indirect discrimination, it shall be for the respondent to prove that there has been no breach of the principle of equal treatment.'

KEY FACTS

Equal treatment for men and women	
Men and women are entitled to equal treatment in employment. This covers access to employment, working conditions and dismissals.	Directive 2006/54, Art 14(1)
Member States may derogate where a 'difference in treatment' can be justified by reference to 'the nature of the particular occupational activities concerned' provided it 'constitutes a genuine and determining occupational requirement'.	Directive 2006/54, Art 14(2); *Johnston* (1986); *Sirdar* (1999)

18.5 Justifications for indirect discrimination

Article 2(1)(b) of the Recast Directive states there is no breach of EU discrimination law if an indirectly discriminatory 'provision, criterion or practice is objectively justified by a legitimate aim, and the means of achieving that aim are appropriate and necessary'. This confirms principles established by the ECJ in cases such as *Bilka-Kaufhaus* (1986), where the ECJ stated that discrimination in terms of pay or other work conditions could be justified if the discriminatory measures 'correspond to a real need on the part of the undertaking, are appropriate with a view to achieving the objectives pursued and are necessary to that end'.

18.5.1 'A real need on the part of the undertaking'
Most of the cases involve employers with a mixed staff of men and women, some working full-time (mostly men) and some working part-time (mostly women). Often the full-time staff are paid more (on a *pro rata* basis) than part-time staff and/or receive additional benefits. This constitutes indirect sex discrimination – but can it be justified? The answer is 'yes', if it 'corresponds to a real need'. Over the years, employers have put forward a variety

of 'real needs'. A survey of the case law reveals that the ECJ regards the following as acceptable reasons (at least in principle) for indirectly discriminating against women:

- The need to encourage full-time workers – *Jenkins v Kingsgate* (Case 96/80) [1981] ECR 911.
- The need to discourage part-time workers – *Bilka-Kaufhaus* (1986).
- The need to alleviate constraints on small businesses – *Kirsammer-Hack v Sidal* (Case C–189/91) [1993] ECR I–6185.
- The need to reward specific qualities amongst the workforce, e.g. greater mobility, or extra training – *Danfoss* (Case 109/88) [1989] ECR 3199.
- The need to attract more staff to certain posts – *Enderby v Frenchay HA* (Case C–127/92) [1993] ECR I–5535.
- The need to recruit young workers by encouraging part-time work among older workers – *Kutz-Bauer* (Case C–187/00) [2003] ECR I–2741.
- The interests of 'good industrial relations' – *Kenny & Others* (2013).

For example, the employers in *Bilka-Kaufhaus* (1986), a large German department store, admitted that it deliberately operated a policy of discriminating in favour of full-time workers (the majority of which were men) by denying access to its occupational pension scheme to part-time employees (the majority of which were women). The policy was:

> intended solely to discourage part-time work, since in general part-time workers refuse to work in the late afternoon or on Saturdays. In order to ensure the presence of an adequate workforce during those periods it was therefore necessary to make full-time work more attractive than part-time work.

The ECJ left it to the national court to decide whether this policy was 'necessary' to meet a 'real need' on the part of the store.

18.5.2 Rejected examples of 'real needs'

In *Gerster* (Case C–1/95) [1997] ECR I–5253, it was argued that extra experience gained by full-time employees justified differential treatment compared with part-time workers. The Court rejected this view. It stated:

JUDGMENT

'It is impossible to identify objective criteria unrelated to any discrimination on the basis of an alleged special link between length of service and acquisition of a certain level of knowledge or experience, since such a claim amounts to no more than a generalisation concerning certain categories of worker. Although experience goes hand-in-hand with length of service, and experience enables the worker in principle to improve performance of the tasks allotted to him, the objectivity of such a criterion depends on all circumstances of each individual case, and in particular on the relationship between the nature of the work performed and the experience gained from the performance of that work.'

This must be right. Otherwise, employers could routinely pay full-time staff (mostly men) more than part-time staff (mostly female) and, when challenged, point out that the full-time staff were 'more experienced'. However, this is obviously not the case: a woman who has worked part-time (say on a 50 per cent contract) for 30 years is clearly far more experienced than a man who has worked full-time for five years.

Justifications for indirect discrimination	
There is no breach of EU discrimination law if an indirectly discriminatory 'provision, criterion or practice is objectively justified by a legitimate aim, and the means of achieving that aim are appropriate and necessary'.	Directive 2006/54
Examples of legitimate aims include the need to encourage full-time workers, the need to reward greater mobility or extra training, the need to attract staff to specific posts, the need to recruit young workers.	*Jenkins v Kingsgate* (1981); *Danfoss* (1989); *Enderby* (1993); *Kutz-Bauer* (2003)

18.6 Positive action and positive discrimination

Article 157(4) TFEU states:

ARTICLE

'The principle of equal treatment shall not prevent any Member State from maintaining or adopting measures providing for specific advantages in order to make it easier for the under-represented sex to pursue a vocational activity or to prevent or compensate for disadvantages in professional careers.'

Article 3 of the Recast Directive adds: 'Member States may maintain or adopt measures … with a view to ensuring full equality in practice between men and women in working life.' This policy is known as 'positive action'. However, the ECJ has been very careful to distinguish between 'positive action', which is tolerated (indeed encouraged) and 'positive discrimination', which is contrary to the principle of equal treatment.

18.6.1 Positive action

'Positive action' measures typically involve the removal of obstacles which prevent, or at least restrict, the 'under-represented sex' (which is typically women) from competing on a level playing field with the other sex. A good example of 'positive action' is *Lommers* (Case C–476/99) [2002] ECR I–2891. This case involved an employer's policy of giving women priority in terms of access to nursery places. The Court held that giving women priority in

> certain working conditions designed to facilitate their pursuit of, and progression in, their career, falls in principle into the category of measures designed to eliminate the causes of women's reduced opportunities for access to employment and careers and are intended to improve their ability to compete on the labour market and to pursue a career on an equal footing with men.

Typically, the 'under-represented sex' for whose benefit positive action measures may be taken will be women. However, Member States are permitted to adopt measures to prevent men from being disadvantaged too (see *Schnorbus v Lard Hessen* (Case C–79/99) [2000] ECR I–10997).

In *Roca Álvarez v Sesa Start España* (2010), the Court held that Spanish legislation (which gave working mothers, but not working fathers, time off work for the purposes of feeding a child) could **not** be justified as a form of 'positive action'. The Court stated that the refusal to allow fathers of young children time off work to feed their child was 'liable to perpetuate the traditional distinction of the roles of men and women by keeping men in a role subsidiary to that of women in relation to the exercise of their parental duties'.

18.6.2 Positive discrimination

'Positive discrimination' measures go further than 'positive action' by actually conferring an advantage on the 'under-represented sex'. This is not tolerated by the ECJ because it essentially substitutes one form of sex discrimination (against women) for another (against men). An example is provided by *Kalanke* (Case C–450/93) [1995] ECR I–3051. Here, provisions of German law provided that women who had the same qualifications as men applying for promotion to the same post were to be given priority if women were under-represented in that post. The ECJ held that national laws which guaranteed women absolute and unconditional priority for appointment or promotion went beyond the scope of 'positive action' measures and amounted to prohibited 'positive discrimination'.

Kalanke was followed in *Abrahamsson and Anderson v Fogelqvist* (Case C–407/98) [2000] ECR I–5539 and *Briheche* (Case C–319/03) [2004] ECR I–8807, where the ECJ again found that provisions of national legislation, in Sweden and France, respectively, conferred automatic priority on women and crossed the line into positive discrimination.

However, *Kalanke* (1995) was distinguished in *Marschall* (Case C–409/95) [1997] ECR I–6363. The ECJ took the view that, where men and women were equally qualified, men tended to be promoted particularly because of prejudices and stereotypes concerning the role and capacities of women in working life. These included, among other things:

- the fear that women would interrupt their careers more frequently;
- that view that, because of household and family duties, women would be less flexible in their working hours;
- that women would be absent from work more frequently because of pregnancy, child-birth and breastfeeding.

For those reasons, the 'mere fact' that a male and a female candidate were equally qualified did not mean that they had the same chances. Hence, national legislation which gave priority to women could be justified. However, it was crucial that such legislation contained what is typically referred to as a 'saving clause', that is, a provision allowing for men to be appointed nevertheless if the individual circumstances justified it.

CASE EXAMPLE

Marschall (Case C–409/95) [1997] ECR I–6363

German law provided that, where there were fewer women than men in a particular teaching post in a career bracket, women were to be given priority for promotion in the event of equal suitability, competence and professional performance 'unless reasons specific to an individual male candidate tilt the balance in his favour'. In 1994, Helmut Marschall applied for promotion at his comprehensive school. However, his application was rejected on the ground that there were fewer women than men in that career bracket. An equally qualified woman was promoted instead. He appealed against this but the ECJ distinguished *Kalanke* (1995) on the basis of the saving clause. The German law in this case was permissible.

Marschall was followed in *Badeck* (Case C–158/97) [2000] ECR I–1875, which involved various provisions of German legislation designed to remove obstacles affecting the employment of women in public administration. Crucially, the ECJ managed to identify a number of saving clauses which brought the legislation within *Marschall*.

As a result of these cases it is now possible to distinguish between two types of situation:

- National legislation conferring **automatic priority** on women in employment (known as a **hard** or **rigid quota** system) is prohibited: *Kalanke* (1995); *Abrahamsson* (2000); *Briheche* (2004).

- National legislation conferring priority on women in employment but subject to a **'saving clause'** whereby a male candidate could still be appointed or promoted if demonstrably the best candidate (known as a **soft** or **flexible quota** system) is tolerated: *Marschall* (1997); *Badeck* (2000).

KEY FACTS

Positive action and positive discrimination	
Positive action involves the removal of obstacles preventing the 'under-represented sex' from competing with the other sex on a level playing field.	Art (4) TFEU
Positive action is not only permitted but encouraged under EU law.	*Lommers* (2002); *Schnorbus* (2000)
Positive discrimination goes beyond positive action by conferring an advantage on the 'under-represented sex', such as prioritising employment or promotion. It is not permitted under EU law.	*Kalanke* (1995); *Abrahamsson & Anderson v Fogelqvist* (2000); *Briheche* (2004)
However, positive discrimination measures containing a 'saving clause' are permitted under EU law.	*Marschall* (1997); *Badeck* (2000)

18.7 Pregnancy

The application of EU discrimination law on equality between men and women has been somewhat strained when it comes to cases involving pregnancy. As a matter of biological fact, only women can become pregnant. Therefore, any rule which discriminates against someone because of their pregnancy constitutes discrimination against women. This much is not disputed. What has been disputed over the years is whether this form of discrimination constitutes direct discrimination (which is very difficult to justify) or indirect discrimination (which is much easier to justify). This section will deal with the following situations involving pregnant women:

- maternity pay;
- refusal to employ a woman on grounds of pregnancy;
- dismissal of a woman on grounds of pregnancy;
- dismissal of a woman on grounds of pregnancy-related illness;
- discrimination in conditions of employment.

18.7.1 Maternity pay and related issues

In *Gillespie* (1996), the ECJ held that benefit paid by an employer to a woman employee on maternity leave was based on the employment relationship, and therefore constituted 'pay' within Article 157 TFEU. However, the Court continued by stating that

Article 157 did **not** require 'that women should continue to receive full pay during maternity leave'. Nor did it 'lay down any specific criteria for determining the amount of benefit to be paid to them during that period'. However, the Court did say that 'the amount payable could not, however, be so low as to undermine the purpose of maternity leave, namely the protection of women before and after giving birth'.

In *Alabaster v Woolwich plc* (Case C–147/02) [2004] ECR I–3101, the ECJ decided that it was unlawful discrimination not to take account of a woman's pay rise awarded during the course of her pregnancy (but before the commencement of maternity leave) when the level of maternity pay was being calculated. In *Abdoulaye v Renault* (Case C–218/98) [1999] ECR I–5723 the ECJ ruled that a lump-sum payment given to pregnant employees at the commencement of their maternity leave did not breach Article 157. Although the payment was clearly a form of 'pay', the Court held that female workers going on maternity leave were not in a comparable situation with male workers and therefore no discrimination on grounds of sex had occurred.

(Note: rights to maternity leave and maternity pay are now set out in Directive 92/85, the Pregnant Workers' Directive (PWD), which was examined in Chapter 17.)

18.7.2 Refusal to employ a woman on grounds of pregnancy

In *Dekker v Centrum* (Case 177/88) [1990] ECR I–3941, the ECJ stated that refusing to employ a woman because she was pregnant was **direct** discrimination on grounds of sex, and was unjustifiable:

JUDGMENT

'It should be observed that only women can be refused employment on grounds of pregnancy and such a refusal constitutes direct discrimination. A refusal of employment on account of the financial consequences of absence due to pregnancy must be regarded as based, essentially, on the fact of pregnancy.... Such discrimination cannot be justified on grounds relating to the financial loss which an employer who appointed a pregnant woman would suffer for the duration of her maternity leave.'

Professor R Wintemute challenges the conclusion in *Dekker* that discrimination on grounds of pregnancy is automatically direct discrimination. He argues that it is not discrimination because **women have exercised a choice in becoming pregnant**. He writes:

It can be argued that the element of choice that intervenes between 'being female' and 'being pregnant' breaks the chain of causation with the result that these chosen conditions cease to be legally caused by the person's sex, even though they would not in fact exist 'but for' the person's sex. In other words, the discrimination is based on the choice to exercise a physical capacity unique to the chooser's sex, but not on the chooser's sex per se.

Professor R Wintemute, 'When is Pregnancy Discrimination Indirect Sex Discrimination?' (1998) 27 *ILJ* 23

Wintemute develops this hypothesis further. He poses the following (rhetorical) question:

Is dismissing a woman because she had an abortion also direct sex discrimination? Or does the element of choice have greater legal significance in the case of abortion, because pregnancy is necessary for the perpetuation of society in a way that abortion is not?

The Court, meanwhile, continues to follow *Dekker* (see *Mahlburg* (Case C–207/98) [2000] ECR I–549). In *Busch v Klinikum Neustadt* (Case C–320/01) [2003] ECR I–2041, the question for the Court was whether a pregnant woman (who also knew that she was pregnant) was under any obligation to tell a prospective employer of this fact when being interviewed for a job. The ECJ held that it would be direct discrimination to impose this obligation on to a pregnant woman.

The ECJ's firm stance with employers who refuse to employ pregnant women can be applauded for recognising and tackling the difficulties faced by pregnant women in trying to find employment. However, it can be criticised for imposing difficult burdens on employers, particularly small- and medium-sized companies, who may struggle to cope financially if forced by law to take on pregnant women. Despite this point, the ECJ has refused to allow employers to derogate from its view that discrimination against pregnant workers is direct sex discrimination.

18.7.3 Dismissal from employment on grounds of pregnancy

Dismissal of a pregnant woman also amounts to unlawful direct discrimination. In *Hebermann-Beltermann* (Case C–421/92) [1994] ECR I–1657, the complainant was sacked when it was discovered that she was pregnant. The ECJ held that she had been unjustifiably discriminated against on grounds of sex. In *Webb v EMO Air Cargo* (Case C–32/93) [1994] ECR I–3567, the Court confirmed that dismissal of a pregnant woman, regardless of the situation, amounts to unjustifiable, direct sex discrimination.

CASE EXAMPLE

Webb v EMO Air Cargo (Case C–32/93) [1994] ECR I–3567

Carole Webb was engaged by EMO Air Cargo, a small organisation with just 16 employees, to replace another employee, Mrs Stewart, who had become pregnant and was due to go on maternity leave. At the time it was envisaged that Mrs Webb's appointment was indefinite, and that she would remain even after Mrs Stewart returned to work. Two weeks after starting, however, she discovered that she was herself pregnant. She was promptly dismissed and brought a claim for unfair dismissal. The ECJ held that the dismissal of a pregnant woman – for the sole reason that she was pregnant – was unjustifiable discrimination on grounds of sex.

Workers on temporary contracts/seasonal workers

In both *Hebermann-Beltermann* and *Webb*, the ECJ explicitly referred to the 'termination of a contract for an indefinite period' because of pregnancy as constituting direct sex discrimination. Did this imply that the termination of a contract for a **definite** period would be treated differently? Contracts for a definite period could refer to workers on a temporary contract, or one held by a seasonal worker (for example someone employed to pick fruit during the summer, or someone employed in a shop during the weeks before Christmas). Would an employer be justified in sacking a woman employed purely for two months if she announced just after starting work that she was six months pregnant? The answer is 'no'. In *Jiménez Melgar* (Case C–438/99) [2001] ECR I–6915 the ECJ held that no distinction should be drawn between pregnant workers on definite, temporary contracts and those on indefinite contracts.

18.7.4 Dismissal from employment on grounds of pregnancy-related illness

Given the principles developed in the above cases – that dismissal of a pregnant woman from employment always amounts to unjustifiable, direct discrimination – you may think that the same principles would apply to the situation where a woman is dismissed because she has a pregnancy-related illness. However, in *Hertz v Aldi Marked* (Case 179/88) [1990] ECR I–3979, the ECJ held that EU law did not **necessarily** preclude dismissal of a woman because of pregnancy-related illness; it depended on when the illness manifested itself. The Court stated:

JUDGMENT

'In the case of an illness manifesting itself after maternity leave, there is no reason to distinguish an illness attributable to pregnancy or confinement from any other illness. Such a pathological condition is therefore covered by the general rules applicable in the event of illness. Male and female workers are equally exposed to illness. Although certain disorders are, it is true, specific to one or other sex, the only question is whether a woman is dismissed on account of absence due to illness in the same circumstances as a man; if that is the case, then there is no direct discrimination on grounds of sex.'

On the other hand, where the illness manifested itself **before or during** maternity leave, then the situation would be different. In *Brown v Rentokil Ltd* (Case C–394/96) [1998] ECR I–4185, the Court stated:

JUDGMENT

'Where a woman is absent owing to illness resulting from pregnancy or childbirth, and that illness arose during pregnancy and persisted during and after maternity leave, her absence not only during maternity leave but also during the period extending from the start of her pregnancy to the start of her maternity leave **cannot be taken into account** for computation of the period justifying her dismissal.'

The Court noted that pregnancy was a period during which specific disorders and complications may arise. These may lead to incapacity for work but, if an employer was to dismiss a woman because of them, it had to be regarded as 'essentially based on the fact of pregnancy'. As such dismissal could only affect women, it therefore constituted direct (and hence unjustifiable) discrimination on grounds of sex.

The case of *Mayr v Flöckner* (Case C–506/06) [2008] ECR I–1017, which was discussed in Chapter 17 in the context of the Pregnant Workers Directive (PWD), also raised a question regarding the application of the ETD (now the Recast Directive). Sabine Mayr, a waitress, had been dismissed from her job while off sick having undergone *in vitro* fertilisation (IVF) treatment. The Court held that it was possible that Ms Mayr's claim could be recognised under what is now Article 14(1)(c) of the Recast Directive. If Flöckner had dismissed her because she was off sick, which in turn was caused by her seeking IVF treatment, specifically the fact that she had just undergone a 'follicular puncture', then that would amount to direct discrimination based on sex.

18.7.5 Discrimination in conditions of employment

The ECJ has held that it is contrary to the ETD for an employer to deny to a woman on maternity leave any employment opportunities that she would have enjoyed had she not been on leave. For example in *Thibault* (Case C–136/95) [1998] ECR I–2011, Évelyne Thibault had been deprived of the right to an annual assessment of her performance and, therefore, of the opportunity of qualifying for promotion, because she had been away on maternity leave. This was held to be contrary to the ETD.

These case law developments have now been incorporated into legislation, in Article 15 of the Recast Directive, which states:

ARTICLE

'Art 15. A woman on maternity leave shall be entitled, after the end of her period of maternity leave, to return to her job or to an equivalent post on terms and conditions which are no less favourable to her and to benefit from any improvement in working conditions to which she would have been entitled during her absence.'

KEY FACTS

Pregnancy	
Although maternity pay is 'pay' under Art 157(1) TFEU, women on maternity leave are not guaranteed to receive full pay.	*Gillespie* (1996); *Alabaster* (2004); *McKenna* (2005)
This is because women on maternity leave are not in a comparable situation with men.	*Abdoulaye* (1999)
A refusal to employ a pregnant woman because of her pregnancy is direct sex discrimination, which is extremely difficult to justify.	*Dekker* (1990); *Mahlburg* (2000); *Busch* (2003)
The dismissal of a pregnant woman because of her pregnancy is also direct sex discrimination.	*Hebermann-Beltermann* (1994); *Webb* (1994)
The dismissal of a pregnant woman because of a pregnancy-related illness is also direct sex discrimination, but only if the illness manifested itself during the pregnancy or maternity leave.	*Hertz* (1990); *Brown* (1998); *Mayr* (2008)
It is prohibited for an employer to deny a woman on maternity leave any improvements in working conditions which she would have received had she still been at work.	*Thibault* (1998)

18.8 Equal treatment in matters of social security: Directive 79/7

Directive 79/7, the Social Security Directive (SSD) establishes a principle of equal treatment 'in the field of social security and other elements of social protection' between men and women (Article 1). Article 2 defines the Directive's personal scope and Article 3 its material scope. Article 4 amplifies on the equal treatment principle established in Article 1.

18.8.1 Personal scope

ARTICLE

'Art 2 This Directive shall apply to the working population – including self-employed persons, workers and self-employed persons whose activity is interrupted by illness, accident or involuntary unemployment and persons seeking employment – and to retired or invalided workers and self-employed persons.'

This definition gives the SSD a wide scope but it has been interpreted even more generously by the ECJ.

'The working population'

The ECJ has held that it is irrelevant whether or not the person is regarded under national law as being in 'minor' employment because of the small number of hours worked and/or the low wage earned (*Nolte* (Case C–317/93) [1995] ECR I–4625).

'Persons whose activity is interrupted'

In *Drake* (Case 150/85) [1986] ECR 1995, the Court held that the SSD applies even if a person in employment is forced to interrupt their activity in order to care for a relative. Thus, although the SSD refers to 'persons whose activity is interrupted by illness', the ECJ has interpreted that phrase to include someone else's illness, e.g. an elderly relative. The Court stated:

JUDGMENT

'There is a clear economic link between the benefit and the disabled person, since the disabled person derives an advantage from the fact that an allowance is paid to the person caring for him. The fact that a benefit is paid to a third party and not directly to the disabled person does not place it outside the scope of Directive 79/7.'

The same decision was reached in *Johnson* (Case C–31/90) [1991] ECR I–3723, where the claimant had given up work in order to look after her disabled daughter. However, in *Achterberg-te Riele* (Case 48/88) [1989] ECR 1963, the ECJ held that the SSD did not apply to a person who had given up work in order to care for children because that was not listed in Article 2. Similarly, in *Züchner* (Case C–77/95) [1996] ECR I–5689, the Court held that the SSD did not apply to someone who was caring for an invalid relative but who had not interrupted an 'activity' in order to do so. 'Activity' was defined 'as referring at the very least to an economic activity, that is to say an activity undertaken in return for remuneration in the broad sense'.

18.8.2 Material scope

This is set out in Article 3(1) of the SSD.

ARTICLE

'3(1) This Directive shall apply to (a) statutory schemes which provide protection against the following risks:

- sickness,
- old age,
- unemployment;
- invalidity,
- accidents at work and occupational diseases,

(b) social assistance, in so far as it is intended to supplement or replace the schemes referred to in (a).'

In *Smithson* (Case C–243/90) [1992] ECR I–467, the ECJ held that a benefit must be 'directly and effectively' linked to one of the specific 'risks' listed in Article 3(1) in order to come within the scope of the SSD. Cases in which Article 3(1) has been successfully invoked because such a 'direct' link was established include:

- exemption from prescription charges (*Richardson* (Case C–137/94) [1995] ECR I–3407) – linked to 'risk' of sickness;

- a winter fuel payment of £20 (*Taylor* (Case C–382/98) [1999] ECR I–8955) – linked to 'risk' of old age.

Conversely, in *Smithson* (1992), the ECJ concluded that Article 3(1) did not apply to housing benefit, because Article 3(1) did not explicitly refer to (lack of) housing as a 'risk' against which if protection was provided the 'equal treatment' principle would apply. Similarly, in *Hoever and Zachow* (Cases C–245 and 312/94) [1996] ECR I–4895, the Court held that a child-raising allowance was outside the scope of Article 3(1) because the SSD did not list responsibility for the cost of raising children as a relevant 'risk'.

In *Atkins v Wrekin DC* (Case C–228/94) [1996] ECR I–3633 the ECJ held that entitlement to concessionary travel on British public transport fell outside the scope of Article 3(1), because it did not afford 'direct and effective' protection against one of the 'risks' listed in Article 3(1). In *Jackson and Cresswell* (Case C–63 and 64/91) [1992] ECR I–4737, the Court held that the SSD did not apply because the benefits in question – 'supplementary allowance' and 'income support' – were designed to boost the earnings of low-paid workers (i.e. people already in employment) and were therefore not directly linked to the 'risk' of unemployment.

KEY FACTS

Benefits to which Art 3(1) has been held not to apply	
• Benefits paid to boost earnings of those in low-paid jobs – not directly linked to unemployment.	*Jackson and Cresswell* (1992)
• Concessionary travel benefits.	*Atkins* (1996)
• Child-raising allowance.	*Hoever and Zachow* (1996)
• Housing benefit.	*Smithson* (1992)

18.8.3 The principle of equal treatment

This is set out in Article 4(1) of the SSD.

ARTICLE

'Art 4(1) The principle of equal treatment means that there shall be no discrimination whatsoever on grounds of sex either directly, or indirectly by reference in particular to marital or family status.'

Direct discrimination

The case of *Drake* (1986), considered above, provided a very clear illustration of direct discrimination (invalid care allowance could be claimed by married men but not by married women). The ECJ held that this was contrary to both Articles 1 and 4 of the SSD.

A more recent – and unusual – example of direct discrimination occurred in *Richards* (Case C–423/04) [2006] ECR I–3585. Sarah Richards was born, as a man, in February

1942. She was subsequently diagnosed with gender dysphoria, and underwent gender reassignment surgery in May 2001. In February 2002, she applied for a retirement pension, having reached her 60th birthday, the pension age under the Pensions Act 1995 for women born before 6 April 1950. This was rejected, but the ECJ held that Ms Richards had suffered discrimination on grounds of sex, in breach of Article 4(1). The Court stated:

JUDGMENT

'The scope of Directive 79/7 cannot . . . be confined simply to discrimination based on the fact that a person is of one or other sex. In view of its purpose and the nature of the rights which it seeks to safeguard, the scope of that directive is also such as to apply to discrimination arising from the gender reassignment of the person concerned.'

In X (Case C–318/13) [2014] IRLR 975, the ECJ held that Article 4(1) precluded Finnish legislation under which the different life expectancies of men and women were applied as an actuarial factor for the calculation of a benefit payable due to an accident at work. The legislation was challenged by a Finnish man, X, who had been injured at work and was later awarded the benefit in the form of a lump sum. He alleged that the use of different male and female life expectancies meant that the lump-sum compensation paid to a man was less than that which would be paid to a woman of the same age and in a similar situation, and that this was in breach of Directive 79/7. The Court agreed, holding that the reference to life expectancy was a 'generalisation' based on 'general statistical data' which was 'likely to lead to discriminatory treatment of male insured persons as compared to female insured persons'. The Court stated that 'there is a lack of certainty that a female insured person always has a greater life expectancy than a male insured person of the same age placed in a comparable situation'.

Indirect discrimination and objective justification

Where discrimination is indirect (i.e. not based explicitly on gender) it may be justified by reference to overriding reasons in the public interest. In *Nolte* (1995), the ECJ held that German rules on entitlement to an old-age insurance scheme (where those in 'minor' employment were excluded) were indirectly discriminatory, because far more women than men were in 'minor' employment. However, the rules also exempted those in minor employment from paying contributions towards unemployment benefit. This led the ECJ to conclude that, overall, the rules were objectively justified.

18.8.4 Derogation regarding 'the determination of pensionable age'

Article 7 of the SSD provides a number of derogations, the most important of which is Article 7(1)(a). This allows Member States to exclude from the scope of the SSD 'the determination of pensionable age for the purpose of granting old-age and retirement pensions and the possible consequences thereof for other benefits'.

This derogation was designed to allow Member States to set differential ages at which men and women would become entitled to claim an old-age pension from the state. Many states had such a system in place, including the UK, where women were entitled to an old-age pension at 60 but men had to wait until 65. (In any event, the UK Parliament amended British law to equalise the pension age for men and women in the Pensions Act 1995, which raised the pension age for women to 65, the same as for men.)

Article 7(1)(a) was invoked in *Graham* (Case C–92/94) [1995] ECR I–2521. The ECJ held that British rules which provided for the payment of an invalidity benefit to those workers (male or female) forced to leave work because of ill-health up to the state pension age (60 for women, 65 for men), at which point the benefit would cease and be replaced with the state pension, were allowed under Article 7(1)(a).

However, in *Thomas* (Case C–328/91) [1993] ECR I–1247, the ECJ said: 'Art 7(1)(a) is limited to the forms of discrimination … which are necessarily and objectively linked to the difference in pensionable age'. This requirement had the effect of preventing the application of Article 7(1)(a) to the following benefits:

- *Thomas* (1993) – severe disability allowance and invalid care allowance;
- *Richardson* (1995) – exemption from prescription charges;
- *Taylor* (1999) – winter fuel payment.

As none of these benefits were 'necessarily and objectively linked' to the pensionable age, Article 7(1)(a) did not apply and it was therefore unlawful to set different ages in terms of eligibility for them (60 for women, 65 for men).

18.9 Equal treatment for self-employed persons: Directive 2010/41

All of the above discussion has concentrated on the rights of women (and men) to equality of treatment at work. It is self-evident that self-employed persons are much less likely to encounter discriminatory treatment than those in employment, as of course there is no chance of being made subject to discriminatory employment practices. However, self-employed persons are vulnerable to discriminatory national legislation, and hence EU measures are required. The legislation is Directive 2010/41 (which replaced the original legislation, Directive 86/613).

18.9.1 Personal scope

The Directive applies the equal treatment principle to self-employed persons (Article 1). It applies to 'self-employed workers', defined as 'all persons pursuing a gainful activity for their own account' (Article 2(a)). The Directive also applies to 'their spouses, or, when and in so far as recognised by national law, life partners, not being employees or business partners, where they habitually … participate in the activities of the self-employed worker and perform the same tasks or ancillary tasks' (Article 2(b)).

18.9.2 Material scope

The Directive eliminates sex discrimination in two areas:

- Member States are to ensure that equal treatment principles operate 'in respect of the establishment, equipment or extension of a business or the launching or extension of any other form of self-employed activity' (Article 4).
- Member States are to ensure that 'the conditions for the formation of a company between spouses, or between life partners when and in so far as recognised by national law, are not more restrictive than the conditions for the formation of a company between other persons' (Article 6).

18.10 Equal treatment on grounds of sex in access to and supply of goods and services: Directive 2004/113

The Goods and Services Directive 2004/113 (GSD) establishes a principle of equal treatment on grounds of sex in access to and supply of goods and services (Article 1), while Article 4(1) proscribes discrimination based on sex in terms of access to and supply of goods and services. Article 3 defines the scope of the GSD as follows:

ARTICLE

'Art 3(1) ...this Directive shall apply to all persons who provide goods and services, which are available to the public irrespective of the person concerned as regards both the public and private sectors, including public bodies, and which are offered outside the area of private and family life and the transactions carried out in this context.

(2) This Directive does not prejudice the individual's freedom to choose a contractual partner as long as an individual's choice of contractual partner is not based on that person's sex.

(3) This Directive shall not apply to the content of media and advertising nor to education.

(4) This Directive shall not apply to matters of employment and occupation. This Directive shall not apply to matters of self-employment, insofar as these matters are covered by other Community legislative acts.'

Article 4(2) allows for positive action. Article 4(5) provides that the GSD 'shall not preclude differences in treatment, if the provision of the goods and services exclusively or primarily to members of one sex is justified by a legitimate aim and the means of achieving that aim are appropriate and necessary'. The preamble to the GSD suggests five examples of 'legitimate aims' (with examples of single-sex services that might need to invoke the aim in parentheses):

- protection of victims of sex-related violence (shelters);
- reasons of privacy and decency (toilets, changing rooms, wards in private hospitals);
- promotion of gender equality or of the interests of men or women (voluntary bodies);
- freedom of association (private clubs);
- organisation of sporting activities (sports events).

Article 5(1) deals specifically with 'actuarial factors' (these are factors used by insurance companies, underwriters and pension schemes to calculate insurance premiums and benefits). Prior to the GSD, such factors could be used differentially between men and women (one factor, in particular, is that women's average life expectancy is longer than men's). Article 5(1) does not completely outlaw the use of such factors but it does state that 'the use of sex as a factor in the calculation of premiums and benefits for the purposes of insurance and related financial services shall not result in differences in individuals' premiums and benefits'.

Article 5(2) added that Member States were permitted to maintain 'proportionate differences' in insurance premiums and benefits 'where the use of sex is a determining factor in the assessment of risk based on relevant and accurate actuarial and statistical data'. However, in *Association Belge des Consommateurs Test-Achats & Others* (Case C–236/09) [2011] ECR I–773, the complainants (a Belgian consumer protection organisation, and two private individuals) sought a declaration that the Belgian legislation implementing Article 5(2) – and by extension Article 5(2) itself – was contrary to primary EU law, specifically Article 6(2) EU. The Court agreed, holding that Article 5(2) enabled the Member States which had chosen to take advantage of it to maintain, indefinitely, an exemption from the rule of unisex premiums and benefits contained in Article 5(1). As such, Article 5(2) was contrary to Articles 21 and 23 of the Charter of Fundamental Rights of the EU (which state, respectively, that any discrimination based on sex is prohibited and that equality between men and women must be ensured in all areas) and hence invalid.

18.11 Beyond sex: the EU's extended anti-discrimination agenda

In November 2000, the Council of the European Union adopted two Directives under powers conferred on the Council under what is now Article 19 TFEU.

- Directive 2000/43 (the Race Directive): this deals with discrimination on grounds of **race and ethnic origin**.
- Directive 2000/78 (the Framework Directive): this deals with discrimination on grounds of sexual orientation, religion or belief, disability and age.

18.11.1 Common elements
Although differing in certain important respects (which will be dealt with below), the Race and Framework Directives share a number of common elements.

Principle of equal treatment
Article 1 of each Directive establishes that its purpose is to put into effect in the Member States a principle of equal treatment.

Definition of 'discrimination'
Both Directives prohibit direct and indirect discrimination. Each provides a definition of both types of discrimination, in identical terms. Direct discrimination is defined in Article 2(2)(a) of each Directive as occurring: 'where one person is treated less favourably than another is, has been or would be treated in a comparable situation' on the grounds or race, religion, sexual orientation, etc. An example of direct discrimination on grounds of age was identified in *Palacios de la Villa* (Case C–411/05) [2007] ECR I–8531. The case involved a provision of Spanish legislation stipulating automatic termination of a worker's employment contract as soon as he or she reached retirement age. The ECJ stated that this 'must be regarded as directly imposing less favourable treatment for workers who have reached that age as compared with all other persons in the labour force'.

In *Hay* (Case C–267/12) [2014] 2 CMLR 32, the Court held that a provision of a collective agreement providing a salary bonus and leave entitlement to employees on their 'marriage' was directly discriminatory on grounds of sexual orientation.

CASE EXAMPLE

Hay (Case C–267/12) [2014] 2 CMLR 32

Under the terms of a collective agreement between Crédit Agricole (CA), the biggest bank in France, and its employees, the latter were entitled to a bonus (worth a month's salary) and special leave (10 days) payable to employees on 'marriage'. Frédéric Hay, a CA employee, had entered into a 'civil solidarity pact' with his male partner but the bank would not recognise this as a 'marriage'. The ECJ held that the payment of a bonus / conferral of leave entitlement on married couples, but not couples in a solidarity pact, constituted direct discrimination on grounds of sexual orientation. This was the case notwithstanding the fact that couples in both opposite sex and same-sex relationships could enter into a 'civil solidarity pact' under French law, because only couples in opposite sex relationships could enter into a marriage in that state.

In contrast, there was no discrimination (direct or otherwise) on grounds of sexual orientation in *Parris* (Case C–443/15) [2017] 2 CMLR 17; [2017] IRLR 173. Dr David Parris worked as a lecturer at Trinity College in Dublin until his retirement in 2010. Dr Parris was a member of the College's occupational pension scheme. In 2011, he asked the College to confirm that his civil partner would be entitled to a survivor's pension (in the event that Dr Parris died first). This was refused: under the pension scheme rules, a survivor's pension was only payable if the scheme member either married or entered into a civil partnership before reaching the age of 60, and Dr Parris had only entered into his civil partnership in 2009, when aged 63. Dr Parris challenged this refusal but the ECJ rejected the challenge: the pension scheme did not discriminate between same sex and opposite sex couples.

Similarly, there was no discrimination (direct or otherwise) on grounds of age in *O v Bio Philippe Auguste* (Case C–432/14) [2015] IRLR 1017. French legislation provided that, on the expiry of a fixed-term contract of employment, employers had to pay their staff 10 per cent of their salary in order 'to compensate for the insecurity of his situation'. However, this payment was not payable 'Where the contract is entered into with a young person for a period falling within the school holidays or university vacations'. Although this looked, superficially at least, like direct discrimination on grounds of age, the ECJ held that there was no breach of the Framework Directive. The Court held that, because direct discrimination occurs where one person is treated less favourably than another is, has been or would be treated in a 'comparable situation', it was necessary to compare school pupils and University students undertaking vacation work (on one hand) with other workers undertaking fixed-term employment (on the other). The Court decided that the former were not in a 'comparable situation' with the latter because the former were not in a situation of 'insecurity'; they intended to continue their studies at the end of their school holiday or University vacation. Therefore, the difference in treatment between those two categories of workers did not constitute discrimination on grounds of age.

'Indirect discrimination' is defined in Article 2(2)(b) of each directive as occurring where 'an apparently neutral provision, criterion or practice' would put persons of a racial or ethnic origin, or having a particular religion or belief, a particular disability, a particular age, or a particular sexual orientation at a 'disadvantage' compared to other persons. In *Achbita v G4S Secure Solutions* (Case C–157/15) [2017] 3 CMLR 21; [2017] IRLR 466 and *Bougnaoui v Micropole* (Case C–188/15) [2017] 3 CMLR 22; [2017] IRLR 447, the ECJ held that a rule banning the wearing of all visible signs of political, philosophical or religious beliefs was not direct discrimination. However, it could be indirect discrimination if it meant that persons adhering to a particular religion or belief were put at a particular disadvantage. These cases are examined in more detail below.

'Harassment'

Both Directives also prohibit discrimination in the form of 'harassment'. This is 'deemed' to be discrimination if certain criteria are satisfied. 'Harassment' is defined in Article 2(3) as follows (this is taken from the Race Directive):

ARTICLE

'Art 2(3) Harassment shall be deemed to be discrimination ... when an unwanted conduct related to racial or ethnic origin takes place with the purpose or effect of violating the dignity of a person and of creating an intimidating, hostile, degrading, humiliating or offensive environment. In this context, the concept of harassment may be defined in accordance with the national laws and practice of the Member States.'

In the Framework Directive the words 'any of the grounds referred to in Article 1' – that is, religion or belief, disability, age or sexual orientation – appear instead of 'racial or ethnic origin'.

The definitions of 'harassment' are wide. They obviously include the situation where, for example, a gay employee is attacked because of his sexuality, or where a black employee is taunted because of her skin colour. But it could also include the situation where a straight employee is attacked because he has gay friends, or where a white employee is taunted because she is married to a black man. In all of these hypothetical cases, there is 'unwanted conduct' which is 'related to' either racial origin or sexual orientation, and thus harassment has occurred.

The definition refers to unwanted conduct which has the 'purpose **or** effect' of violating the dignity of a person etc. Hence, purposeful harassment is one example of discrimination, but 'purpose' is not a precondition. Unintentional harassment is still discrimination – for example, where an employee makes homophobic remarks in front of fellow employees on the mistaken assumption that everyone present is heterosexual.

'Instructions to discriminate'

Both Directives also prohibit 'instructions to discriminate'. Article 2(4) in each Directive simply states that an instruction to discriminate on one of the relevant grounds is 'deemed' to be discrimination contrary to the Directives.

'Positive action'

Both Directives explicitly authorise 'positive action'. Article 5 of the Race Directive and Article 7(1) of the Framework Directive state that 'With a view to ensuring full equality in practice, the principle of equal treatment shall not prevent any Member State from maintaining or adopting specific measures to prevent or compensate for disadvantages' linked to the various grounds on which discrimination may occur within the scope of the two Directives.

'Victimisation'

Article 9 of the Race Directive and Article 11 of the Framework Directive deal with 'victimisation', that is, the possible negative repercussions of bringing a discrimination action. The Directives state that Member States must introduce measures to 'protect individuals from any adverse treatment or adverse consequences as a reaction to a complaint or to proceedings aimed at enforcing compliance with the principle of equal treatment'.

Derogation for 'genuine and determining occupational requirements'

Both Directives allow Member States to derogate from the principle of equal treatment established in Article 1 where there is a 'genuine and determining occupational requirement' (Article 4 of both directives). This is subject to the proviso that the requirement is 'proportionate' i.e. it does not go beyond what is strictly necessary. Most of the cases to date involve minimum or maximum age limits in employment. Article 4(1) was successfully invoked in *Wolf* (Case C–229/08) [2010] ECR I–1, a case of alleged age discrimination.

CASE EXAMPLE

Wolf (Case C–229/08) [2010] ECR I–1

Under German law, the maximum age for recruitment of 'intermediate' firemen (those who would actually be fighting fires, rescuing people and animals, etc.) was 30. Colin Wolf had applied for a job as a fireman in Frankfurt. However, his application was rejected because he would be 31 on the date of recruitment. He contended that the German legislation constituted direct discrimination on grounds of age. The Court, however, held that the maximum age limit for firemen was permitted by Article 4(1). The concern to 'ensure the operational capacity and proper functioning of the professional fire service' constituted a legitimate aim. Moreover, the 'possession of especially high physical capacities' may be regarded as a 'genuine and determining occupational requirement' for carrying on the occupation of fireman, at least for those whose tasks include fighting fires and rescuing people. The need to possess full physical capacity to carry on that activity was related to age, since (according to scientific data submitted by the German government), very few officials over 45 years of age have sufficient physical capacity to perform the fire-fighting part of their activities. Finally, the age limit was appropriate to the objective of ensuring the operational capacity and proper functioning of the professional fire service and was also proportionate to that objective.

Similarly, in *Vital Pérez* (Case C–416/13) [2015] IRLR 158 and *Salaberria Sorondo* (Case C–258/15) [2017] ICR 302; [2017] IRLR 162, the ECJ held that rules setting a maximum age limit for the recruitment of police officers in different regions of Spain was directly discriminatory but justifiable under Article 4(1). The ECJ accepted that the 'typical duties' of a police officer, involving the protection of people and property, 'requires a particular level of physical capability'. The 'possession of particular physical capacities' in order to be able to perform the 'essential duties' of the police may therefore be considered to be a 'genuine and determining occupational requirement'. However, whilst the age limit of 35 in *Salaberria Sorondo* was held to be justified, the lower age limit of 30 in *Vital Pérez* was held to be disproportionate, on the basis, *inter alia*, that stringent physical fitness tests were capable of achieving the same objective but in a less restrictive way.

In *Prigge & Others* (Case C–447/09) [2011] ECR I–8003, the Court held that the aim of 'guaranteeing air traffic safety' was a legitimate objective for the purposes of Article 4, in principle justifying a compulsory retirement age of 60 for airline pilots employed by the German airline Lufthansa. However, because German legislation authorised airline pilots to continue flying until 65, Lufthansa's age limit went beyond what was necessary to achieve its objective and hence failed the proportionality test.

Two recent cases involved the question whether religious discrimination could be justified under Article 4(1). In *Achbita* (2017), the Court held that an employer's 'desire to display, in relations with both public and private sector customers, a policy of political, philosophical or religious neutrality' was a legitimate aim capable of justifying a potentially discriminatory rule banning workers from displaying signs of political, philosophical and religious beliefs at the workplace. Such a conclusion was also consistent with the judgment of the European Court of Human Rights in *Eweida & Others v UK* [2013] IRLR 231. Ultimately, it would be for the national court to decide whether the rule was both appropriate and necessary. However, the rule would only be 'strictly necessary' if it only applied to 'workers who interact with customers'.

CASE EXAMPLE

Achbita v G4S Secure Solutions (Case C–157/15) [2017] 3 CMLR 21; [2017] IRLR 466

Samira Achbita, a Muslim of Belgian-Moroccan nationality, worked for G4S in Antwerp as a receptionist. One of their conditions of employment was that all employees were prohibited from wearing outward signs of political, philosophical and religious beliefs at the workplace. In 2006, Samira began wearing her Islamic headscarf to work. As this was contrary to G4S employment conditions, she was sacked. She challenged the dismissal, alleging that her rights to freedom from religious discrimination had been infringed. The ECJ held that the G4S rule was indirectly discriminatory on grounds of religion, but capable of justification because of the employer's legitimate aim of maintaining political, philosophical or religious neutrality in its relationships with customers.

The case of *Bougnaoui* (2017) was similar. Asma Bougnaoui worked for Micropole, a consultancy firm in Paris, as a design engineer. She routinely wore an Islamic veil at work. One day, a customer complained that Asma had upset a number of its employees after she visited their factory wearing the veil. Asma was summoned to appear before Micropole bosses and reminded that one of the conditions of employment was for her not to be veiled when working with customers. She refused to accept that condition and was sacked. She challenged the dismissal, alleging religious discrimination. The ECJ confirmed the principles set out in *Achbita*, above, but stressed that it was only in 'very limited circumstances' that a characteristic related to religion may constitute a 'genuine occupational requirement'. The Court held that the requirement had to be '***objectively*** dictated by the nature of the occupational activities concerned or of the context in which they are carried out'. It could not cover '***subjective*** considerations', such as 'the willingness of the employer to take account of the particular wishes of the customer'.

Meanwhile, it has been argued that cases where an employer asserts an 'occupational requirement' that employees have a particular 'sexual orientation' may pose considerable practical and theoretical difficulties.

> The concept of sexual orientation is in fact a very fluid one. Sexual orientation will often change over time, as people try out different sexual experiences. Although many individuals will clearly define themselves as heterosexual or homosexual, many others may not, and still more will have had experiences in the past that depart from their present sexual identity. On a more theoretical level, the idea of requiring individuals to 'label' their own sexuality in this way can be criticized ... Queer theory deconstructs categories of identity as applied to human sexuality. If a queer theory approach is applied, it appears to become impossible to state with any certainty whether a person is of a 'particular' sexual orientation.
>
> Hazel Oliver 'Sexual Orientation Discrimination' (2004) 33 *ILJ* 1

By way of contrast, a person's sex, race, religion (if any), disability (if any) and age should be relatively straightforward to establish. Although a person's sex or religion may change over time (and, obviously, their age will certainly do so), at any given moment these factors can be fixed. Oliver's point is that this is not necessarily the case with a person's sexual orientation, which might be in a state of flux. She goes on to argue that sexual orientation should have been recognised as posing unique issues.

Enforcement

Article 7 of the Race Directive and Article 9 of the Framework Directive provide for the enforcement of the rights established by the new Directives. The provisions state:

ARTICLE

'Art 7 Member States shall ensure that judicial and/or administrative procedures, including where they deem it appropriate conciliation procedures, for the enforcement of obligations under this Directive are available to all persons who consider themselves wronged by failure to apply the principle of equal treatment to them, even after the relationship in which the discrimination is alleged to have occurred has ended.'

It has been argued that enforcing claims of sexual orientation discrimination raises particular problems because of its 'extremely personal' nature (Hazel Oliver, 'Sexual Orientation Discrimination' (2004) 33 *ILJ* 1). The point is that, while persons claiming to have suffered sex or race discrimination have nothing to 'hide' when making a claim, persons making claims of sexual orientation discrimination might have to reveal extremely private personal details.

Reversed burden of proof

Article 8 of the Race Directive and Article 10 of the Framework Directive both establish a reversed burden of proof in certain circumstances. Specifically, the Directives state that when 'persons who consider themselves wronged because the principle of equal treatment has not been applied to them' are able to 'establish facts from which it may be presumed that there has been discrimination', then the burden of proof is reversed. This is consistent with the principles applicable to sex discrimination claims, set out by Article 19(1) of the Recast Directive.

In *Asociaţia ACCEPT* (Case C–81/12) [2013] IRLR 660, the ECJ accepted that Article 10 of the Framework Directive was applicable in a case where the alleged discrimination was not directly attributable to an employer. In February 2010, Gigi Becali, a shareholder in the Romanian football club Steaua Bucharest, issued a statement to the media which included the following words:

> Not even if I had to close Steaua down would I accept a homosexual on the team.... There's no room for gays in my family, and Steaua is my family. It would be better to play with a junior [player] rather than someone who was gay.

Steaua did not distance itself from the comments; to the contrary, the club's lawyer confirmed that that policy had been adopted at club level for hiring players because 'the team is a family' and the presence of a homosexual on the team 'would create tensions in the team and among spectators'. The Court held that Article 10 was applicable even though the club itself had not issued the statement.

18.11.2 Race and ethnic origin

Scope

The Race Directive prohibits direct and indirect discrimination based on 'racial or ethnic origin'. These words are not defined and litigation is inevitable to establish exactly what they mean. In *CHEZ Razpredelenie Bulgaria* (Case C–83/14) [2016] 1 CMLR 14, the ECJ held that the Race Directive could be invoked by people who 'suffered' the effects of discrimination against an ethnic group even though they were not themselves a member of that group.

In terms of scope, the Race Directive is much wider than both the Framework Directive and all EU law on sex discrimination. In particular, it is **not** limited to discrimination occurring in the context of employment. For example, *CHEZ Razpredelenie Bulgaria* (2016) involved alleged discrimination in terms of access to electricity and *Jyske Finans* (Case C–668/15) [2017] 1 WLR 3031; [2017] IRLR 665 involved alleged discrimination in terms of eligibility for a loan. Article 3(1) sets out the Directive's scope as follows:

ARTICLE

'Art 3(1) This Directive shall apply to all persons, as regards both the public and private sectors, including public bodies, in relation to:

(a) conditions for access to employment, to self-employment and to occupation, including selection criteria and recruitment conditions, whatever the branch of activity and at all levels of the professional hierarchy, including promotion;

(b) access to all types and to all levels of vocational guidance, vocational training, advanced vocational training and retraining, including practical work experience;

(c) employment and working conditions, including dismissals and pay;

(d) membership of and involvement in an organization of workers or employers, or any organization whose members carry on a particular profession, including the benefits provided for by such organisations;

(e) social protection, including social security and healthcare;

(f) social advantages;

(g) education;

(h) access to and supply of goods and services which are available to the public, including housing.'

None of these words or concepts is defined in the Directive, and so case law is inevitable. However, some of the words and concepts appear in pre-existing EU legislation, and thus it is possible to predict how the ECJ may interpret them. For example, the word 'pay' in Article 3(1)(c) appears in Article 157 TFEU and it is not unreasonable to expect the ECJ to apply its case law under that provision to the Race Directive. Similarly, the phrase 'social advantages' appears in Article 7(2) of Regulation 492/2011 (which was examined in Chapter 12 of this book).

The first case to reach the ECJ involving the Race Directive was Case C–54/07 *Feryn* [2008] ECR I–5187. The defendant firm, a manufacturer of up-and-over doors in Belgium, had advertised for new employees but, after getting no responses, one of the firm's directors was quoted in a newspaper saying 'Apart from these Moroccans, no one else has responded to our notice in two weeks … but we aren't looking for Moroccans.' It was alleged that the company had discriminated against potential employees on grounds of race. The ECJ held that the Race Directive had been breached even though there was no specific potential employee who had, or may have had, suffered discrimination. The Court stated:

JUDGMENT

'The objective of fostering conditions for a socially inclusive labour market would be hard to achieve if the scope of Directive 2000/43 were to be limited to only those cases in which an unsuccessful candidate for a post, considering himself to be the victim of direct discrimination, brought legal proceedings against the employer. The fact that an employer declares publicly that it will not recruit employees of a certain ethnic or racial origin, something which is clearly likely to strongly dissuade certain candidates from submitting their candidature and, accordingly, to hinder their access to the labour market, constitutes direct discrimination in respect of recruitment within the meaning of Directive 2000/43. The existence of such direct discrimination is not dependent on the identification of a complainant who claims to have been the victim.'

In *CHEZ Razpredelenie Bulgaria* (2016), the ECJ was asked whether a Bulgarian electricity distribution company's policy of placing electricity meters on 6–7 m high poles in districts where the majority (but not all) of the population were members of the Roma ethnic group amounted to direct or indirect discrimination prohibited by the Race Directive.

CASE EXAMPLE

CHEZ Razpredelenie Bulgaria (Case C–83/14) [2016] 1 CMLR 14

Anelia Nikolova owned a bakery in the Bulgarian city of Dupnitsa. More precisely, she lived in the district of Gizdova mahala, which was inhabited predominantly by people of Roma ethnicity. (Ms Nikolova was not herself Roma; she described herself as Bulgarian.) In that district, and others like it where the population was predominantly Roma, electricity meters were situated on poles at a height of between 6–7 m above the ground and were only visible by the consumer if they requested CHEZ (the electricity distribution company) to send out a special vehicle with a hydraulic platform. In non-Roma districts, however, electricity meters were placed at a height of up to 1.7 m, usually on the outside walls of the customer's property. Ms Nikolova alleged that the placing of electricity meters in the Roma districts constituted discrimination on grounds of ethnic origin. CHEZ responded that the meters had to be 7 m off the ground in 'Roma districts' because of tampering with electricity meters and illegal electricity extraction, which was apparently especially common in those districts.

The ECJ held that the Race Directive could be invoked by people who 'suffered' the effects of discrimination against an ethnic group even though they were not themselves a member of that group. The presence in the Gizdova mahala district of people like Ms Nikolova (who were not of Roma origin) did not in itself mean that CHEZ's policy was not discriminatory on grounds of ethnic origin against people of Roma origin. Whether CHEZ's policy constituted discrimination on grounds of ethnic origin was a matter for the Bulgarian court to decide, taking into account all of the circumstances surrounding that policy. If the policy had been adopted because most of the district's residents were Roma, which the ECJ said would be 'offensive and stigmatising', that would be **direct** discrimination. Alternatively, if the policy had been adopted in order to respond to abuse committed in the district concerned, it would be based on apparently neutral criteria while affecting persons of Roma origin in considerably greater proportions and hence **indirect** discrimination. Such discrimination was justifiable, because 'protection of the security of the electricity transmission network' and 'due recording of electricity consumption' constituted legitimate aims. Again, it was for the Bulgarian court to determine whether other appropriate and less restrictive measures existed for resolving the problems encountered.

By way of contrast, there was no discrimination (whether direct or indirect) on grounds of race or ethnic origin in *Jyske Finans* (2017). A Bosnian man (H) and his Danish girlfriend (X) wanted to buy a car. They applied to Jyske Finans, a Danish finance company, for a loan. Jyske asked H to provide proof of identity, but did not request any such proof from X, because the company had a policy requiring people from non-EEA states to provide proof of identity. H challenged this, alleging discrimination on grounds of ethnic origin, contrary to Directive 2000/43. The ECJ held that there was no breach of the directive. Jyske's policy was applicable without distinction to *all* persons born outside the territory of an EU or EFTA Member State, and was therefore neither directly nor indirectly connected with the ethnic origin of the person concerned.

18.11.3 The Framework Directive

Purpose

Article 1 states that the purpose of the Framework Directive is to lay down a 'general framework for combating discrimination on the grounds of religion or belief, disability, age or sexual orientation as regards employment and occupation'.

Scope

The scope of the Framework Directive (set out in Article 3(1)) is very similar to that of the Recast Directive, essentially covering working conditions and pay, access to employment and vocational training, and dismissal from employment. The Framework Directive's scope is therefore much narrower than that of the Race Directive.

'Pay'

The ECJ has been asked to explain the meaning of the word 'pay' in the context of the Framework Directive in a number of cases, coincidentally all originating in Germany. The first case, *Maruko* (Case C–267/06) [2008] ECR I–1757, involved a provision of German legislation which provided for (heterosexual) widows and widowers to receive pension benefits, but denied the same benefits to (homosexual) 'life partners'. The Court drew an analogy with the cases under Article 157 TFEU involving similar benefits, such as *Ten-Oever* (1993) and *Coloroll* (1994), and concluded that 'since survivor's benefit ... has been identified as "pay" within the meaning of [Article 157 TFEU it therefore] falls within the scope of Directive 2000/78'. Similar conclusions were reached in *Römer* (Case C–147/08) [2011] ECR I–3591 (also involving pension benefits) and *Dittrich & Others* (Cases C–124, 125 and 143/11) [2013] 2 CMLR 12 (involving sick pay).

'Access to employment and vocational training'

Article 3(1) was invoked in *De Lange* (Case C–548/15) [2017] IRLR 278. The case involved Dutch legislation which allowed, under certain conditions, persons under 30 to deduct from their taxable income the costs of vocational training in full. By contrast, for persons aged 30+, that right to deduction was limited to €15,000. The Court held that a system of tax deduction for the costs of vocational training, although not a precondition for 'access' to such training, nevertheless affected the 'accessibility' of it, and hence fell the scope of 'access to vocational training'. This meant that the Dutch legislation was *prima facie* contrary to the Framework Directive, being discriminatory on grounds of age, although potentially justifiable (see further below on this point).

'Dismissal'

The case of *Palacios de la Villa* (2007), an age discrimination case, examined the meaning of the word 'dismissal' in the context of compulsory retirement. The ECJ stated that 'the automatic termination of an employment relationship' under national legislation once a worker had reached a certain age was tantamount to a 'dismissal'.

'Employment' and 'Occupation'

There is no definition of 'employment' in the Framework Directive, but in *Jivraj v Hashwani* [2011] UKSC 40; [2011] 1 WLR 1872, the UK's Supreme Court held (without requesting a preliminary ruling from the ECJ) that it did not cover the situation where an arbitrator was appointed to resolve a contractual dispute. Rather, an arbitrator's role was that of an 'independent provider of services who is not in a relationship of subordination with the parties who receive his services' (*per* Lord Clarke).

Similarly, in *X v Mid-Sussex Citizens Advice Bureau* [2012] UKSC 59, [2013] 1 All ER 1038, the UK Supreme Court held (again, without requesting a preliminary ruling from the ECJ) that the activities of a volunteer adviser with the Citizens' Advice Bureau fell outside of the scope of the Framework Directive, not being an 'occupation'. *X* is particularly important as it establishes a precedent for the whole of the UK that those in the voluntary sector cannot rely on the Directive and/or the UK implementing legislation to challenge alleged discrimination on the grounds of religion or belief, disability, age or sexual orientation. As the UK's 'court-of-last-resort' the Supreme Court was, in principle, obliged to refer to the ECJ a question on the meaning of the word 'occupation' but invoked the *acte clair* doctrine instead (see Chapter 6). The Supreme Court did at least give serious consideration to the possibility that other national courts in the EU might reach a different conclusion, but Lord Mance's judgment was emphatic: 'there is no scope for reasonable doubt about the conclusion that the Framework Directive does not cover voluntary activity'.

'Disability'

As indicated above, there is no definition of 'disability' in the Framework Directive. In *Chacón Navas* (Case C–13/05) [2006] ECR I–6467, the ECJ was asked to provide one. The Court held that the word 'disability' had to be given an 'autonomous and uniform interpretation'. It went on to state:

JUDGMENT

'The concept of "disability" must be understood as referring to a limitation which results in particular from physical, mental or psychological impairments and which hinders the participation of the person concerned in professional life.'

More specifically, the Court was asked whether the Directive included the case of an employee who has been dismissed by her employer solely on grounds of sickness. Here the Court decided that 'disability' was not synonymous with 'sickness'. The Court stated:

JUDGMENT

'There is nothing in Directive 2000/78 to suggest that workers are protected by the prohibition of discrimination on grounds of disability as soon as they develop any type of sickness . . . a person who has been dismissed by his employer solely on account of sickness does not fall within the general framework laid down for combating discrimination on grounds of disability.'

In *Coleman v Attridge Law* (Case C–303/06) [2008] ECR I–5603, the Court was asked whether the Framework Directive's provisions on disability discrimination can be invoked, indirectly, by the carer of a disabled child. The ECJ answered 'yes'. The Court stated:

JUDGMENT

'Where it is established that an employee in a situation such as that in the present case suffers direct discrimination on grounds of disability, an interpretation of Directive 2000/78 limiting its application only to people who are themselves disabled is liable to deprive that directive of an important element of its effectiveness and to reduce the protection which it is intended to guarantee.'

In *Ring & Skouboe Werge* (Cases C–335, 337/11) [2013] IRLR 571, the ECJ again examined the meaning of the word 'disability' and laid down the following principles:

- The Framework Directive covers disabilities that are congenital, or result from accidents, or which are caused by illness. It would run counter to the very aim of the Directive to define its scope by reference to the origin of the disability.
- If an illness – whether medically diagnosed as curable or incurable – entailed a 'limitation' resulting from 'physical, mental or psychological impairments' which, in interaction with various barriers, may hinder the 'full and effective participation' of the person concerned in professional life on an equal basis with other workers, and the limitation was a 'long-term' one, such an illness could be covered by the concept of 'disability'. But an illness not entailing such a limitation was not covered, following *Chacón Navas* (2006).
- The fact that a person could work, albeit only to a 'limited extent', did not preclude reliance on the concept of 'disability'. A 'disability' did not necessarily imply 'complete exclusion' from work or professional life.
- The concept of 'disability' had to be understood as referring to a 'hindrance' to the exercise of a professional activity, not to the 'impossibility' of exercising such an activity. An alternative interpretation, based on impossibility, would be incompatible with the objective of the Framework Directive, which aimed in particular to enable a person with a disability to have access to or participate in employment.
- A finding that there was a 'disability' was not dependent on the provision of special equipment. The provision by an employer of such measures was intended to accommodate the needs of disabled persons. They are therefore the consequence, not the constituent element, of the concept of 'disability'.

The case of Z (Case C–363/12) [2014] 3 CMLR 20 involved an Irish schoolteacher who was unable to have children because of a rare genetic condition which meant that she had no uterus. Z and her husband entered into a surrogacy arrangement with a woman in California. Shortly before the surrogate was due to give birth, Z applied for either adoption leave or maternity leave, but this was refused. She challenged the refusal, alleging that it constituted discrimination on grounds of 'disability', but the ECJ disagreed. Z's inability to have children did not constitute a 'disability' as defined in cases like *Chacón Navas* (2006) and *Ring & Skouboe Werge* (2013). Z's inability to have a child by conventional means did not prevent her from having access to, participating in or advancing in employment. It did not make it impossible for her to carry out her work or constitute a hindrance to the exercise of her professional activity.

In *Kaltoft* (Case C–354/13) [2015] 2 CMLR 19, the ECJ was asked whether obesity could be classified as an example of 'disability'. The Court held that obesity did not 'in itself' constitute a 'disability' as defined in the case law. However, a worker's obesity could, potentially, be covered by the concept of 'disability' if it 'hindered full and effective participation in professional life on an equal basis with other workers on account of reduced mobility or the onset, in that person, of medical conditions preventing him from carrying out his work or causing discomfort when carrying out his professional activity'. The Court stated that the concept of 'disability' did **not** depend on the extent to which a worker may or may not have contributed to the onset of his disability.

In *Daouidi* (Case C–395/15) [2017] 2 CMLR 21; [2017] IRLR 151, the Court confirmed that a 'disability' could be caused by an accident, but only if it entailed a 'long-term' limitation resulting from a physical, mental or psychological impairment. If there was no 'clearly defined prognosis as regards short-term progress' and/or if the incapacity was 'likely to be significantly prolonged before that person has recovered' then this would be evidence to show that the limitation was 'long-term'.

CASE EXAMPLE

Daouidi (Case C–395/15) [2017] 2 CMLR 21; [2017] IRLR 151

Mohamed Daouidi worked as a kitchen assistant in a hotel restaurant in Barcelona. One day, he slipped on the kitchen floor and dislocated his left elbow, which meant he was temporarily incapacitated. Some six weeks' later, however, he was dismissed with immediate effect, allegedly because he 'did not meet the expectations of the undertaking or perform at the level the undertaking considers appropriate or suitable'. He challenged that dismissal, alleging that his dismissal was tantamount to discrimination on grounds of 'disability'. The ECJ held that his injury could qualify as a 'disability', which was a matter for the national court to decide by looking at the 'long-term' effects of the injury.

General derogations

Article 2(5) of the Framework Directive provides a set of derogations some of which are previously unseen in EU legislation. Curiously, there is no parallel provision to Article 2(5) in the Race Directive. Article 2(5) states:

ARTICLE

'Art 2(5) This Directive shall be without prejudice to measures laid down by national law which, in a democratic society, are necessary for public security, for the maintenance of public order and the prevention of criminal offences, for the protection of health and for the protection of the rights and freedoms of others.'

The 'protection of health' was invoked in *Petersen* (Case C–341/08) [2010] ECR I–47. Domnica Petersen, a dentist in Germany, reached her 68th birthday in April 2007, the maximum age permitted under German law. She was told that her entitlement to practise would lapse in June 2007. She complained that this was discrimination on grounds of age. The ECJ held that the maximum age limit for dentists was, in theory at least, permissible under Article 2(5) 'in order to protect the health of patients'.

Article 2(5) was also invoked in *Prigge & Others* (Case C–447/09) [2011] ECR I–8003, in an attempt to justify a mandatory retirement age of 60 (contained in a collective agreement) for airline pilots employed by the German airline Lufthansa. The Court held that a compulsory retirement age 'operates a difference of treatment based directly on grounds of age' but was justifiable (in theory). The aim of avoiding 'aeronautical accidents by monitoring pilots' aptitude and physical capabilities with the aim of ensuring that human failure does not cause accidents' satisfied public security and/or public health. However, the Court held that it was not actually necessary to force all Lufthansa pilots to retire at 60. It was significant that German legislation allowed pilots to continue flying until their 65th birthdays.

Article 3(4) creates a further derogation, albeit only in the context of discrimination based on disability and age, in stating that Member States may provide that the Framework Directive shall not apply to 'the armed forces'. That is yet another concept which is not defined in the Directive. It will be up to the ECJ to decide whether the phrase 'the armed forces' means a state's entire military service or whether distinctions can be drawn between, say, fighting units (where physical fitness might be essential) and other units such as transport and catering.

Special provisions regarding disability

'Reasonable accommodation'

Article 5 imposes an extra obligation on employers 'in order to guarantee compliance with the principle of equal treatment in relation to persons with disabilities'. Article 5 states:

ARTICLE
....

'Art 5 Reasonable accommodation shall be provided. This means that employers shall take appropriate measures, where needed in a particular case, to enable a person with a disability to have access to, participate in, or advance in employment, or to undergo training, unless such measure would impose a disproportionate burden on the employer. This burden shall not be disproportionate when it is sufficiently remedied by measures existing within the framework of the disability policy of the Member State concerned.'

Positive action

Article 7(2) of the Framework Directive contains further provisions with regard to disabled persons. It states that the principle of equal treatment does not prejudice the right of Member States to 'maintain or adopt provisions on the protection of health and safety at work or to measures aimed at creating or maintaining provisions or facilities for safeguarding their integration into the working environment'.

Special derogation regarding churches etc.

Article 4(2) provides an additional derogation 'in the case of occupational activities within churches and other public or private organizations the ethos of which is based on religion or belief'. Article 4(2) states:

ARTICLE
....

'Art 4(2) A difference of treatment based on a person's religion or belief shall not constitute discrimination where, by reason of the nature of these activities or of the context in which they are carried out, a person's religion or belief constitute a genuine, legitimate and justified occupational requirement, having regard to the organisation's ethos. . . . Provided that its provisions are otherwise complied with, this Directive shall thus not prejudice the right of churches and other public or private organizations the ethos of which is based on religion or belief, acting in conformity with national constitutions and laws, to require individuals working for them to act in good faith and with loyalty to the organisation's ethos.'

Special derogation regarding age

Article 6(1) establishes an additional derogation for Member States in the context of age discrimination. According to Article 6(1), Member States may provide that 'differences of treatment on grounds of age shall not constitute discrimination' if they are 'objectively and reasonably justified by a legitimate aim' and if 'the means of achieving that aim are appropriate and necessary'. Three examples of such 'differences of treatment' are given:

a. the 'setting of special conditions' in the employment context for 'young people, older workers and persons with caring responsibilities in order to promote their vocational integration or ensure their protection';

b. the 'fixing of minimum conditions of age, professional experience or seniority in service for access to employment or to certain advantages linked to employment';

c. the 'fixing of a maximum age for recruitment which is based on the training requirements of the post in question or the need for a reasonable period of employment before retirement'.

The ECJ was asked to interpret Article 6(1)(a) in *Mangold v Helm* (Case C–144/04) [2005] ECR I–9981. The case involved a provision of German legislation which allowed employers to conclude fixed-term contracts if the employee in question was over a certain age (52). Although *prima facie* discriminatory on age grounds, the Court stated that the provision was, at least in principle, 'objectively and reasonably justified by a legitimate aim'. The Court ruled that the purpose of the German legislation was 'plainly to promote the vocational integration of unemployed older workers, in so far as they encounter considerable difficulties in finding work' and that the 'legitimacy of such a public-interest objective cannot reasonably be thrown in doubt'. The Court added that an 'objective of that kind must as a rule, therefore, be regarded as justifying, objectively and reasonably, a difference of treatment on grounds of age' in accordance with Article 6(1)(a).

However, the Court then went on to consider, as required by Article 6(1)(a), whether the 'means of achieving that aim are appropriate and necessary'. The Court held not:

JUDGMENT

'In so far as such legislation takes the age of the worker concerned as the only criterion for the application of a fixed-term contract of employment, when it has not been shown that fixing an age threshold, as such, regardless of any other consideration linked to the structure of the labour market in question or the personal situation of the person concerned, is objectively necessary to the attainment of the objective which is the vocational integration of unemployed older workers, it must be considered to go beyond what is "appropriate and necessary" in order to attain the objective pursued.'

Mangold v Helm was distinguished in *Palacios de la Villa* (2007). This case involved a provision of Spanish legislation which stated that clauses contained in collective agreements providing for compulsory retirement in the event of workers reaching the Spanish retirement age were lawful. The ECJ held that, although compulsory retirement was tantamount to dismissal and, hence, a *prima facie* breach of the Framework Directive, the Spanish legislation was justifiable under Article 6(1)(a), in that it pursued a 'legitimate aim', namely, 'the promotion of full employment by facilitating access to the labour market' (i.e. it created job opportunities for younger people). Moreover, the Spanish legislation also satisfied the test of being both 'appropriate and necessary'. On this point the Court emphasised the flexibility built into the Spanish system.

Palacios de la Villa was followed in *Rosenblat* (Case C–45/09) [2011] 1 CMLR 32 and *Fuchs & Köhler* (Cases C–159 and 160/10) [2011] 3 CMLR 47 (both involving German legislation which provided for the automatic termination of employment contracts when the employee reached the age of 65), *Georgiev* (Case C–250/09) [2010] ECR I–11869 (involving Bulgarian legislation which provided for the compulsory retirement of university professors on reaching the age of 68) and *Commission v Hungary (Compulsory Retirement)* (Case C–286/12) [2013] 1 CMLR 44 (involving Hungarian law which imposed a compulsory retirement age of 62 for judges, prosecutors and notaries). In all four cases the legislation constituted direct discrimination on grounds of age, *prima facie* prohibited by Article 2, but was potentially justifiable, under Article 6(1)(a), on the basis that it freed up positions for the younger generations.

In *Age Concern England* (Case C–388/07) [2009] ECR I–1569, it was argued that the UK government had failed to properly implement the Framework Directive by providing that it was not unlawful for an employer to impose compulsory retirement on any employee aged 65 or over. The ECJ rejected the argument, holding that the legitimate aims and the differences in treatment referred to in Article 6(1) were not exhaustive but were purely illustrative.

An Article 6(1) derogation was rejected in *Hütter* (Case C–88/08) [2009] ECR I–5325. Austrian legislation precluded employment service completed prior to the age of 18 when calculating salary increments. David Hütter, who had spent two-and-a-half years working as an apprentice between the ages of 16 and 19, challenged this, alleging age discrimination. The Austrian court which referred the case to the ECJ suggested that the legislation was necessary in order to avoid three undesirable situations:

1. placing persons who had obtained a secondary education at a disadvantage;
2. discouraging pupils from pursuing secondary education; and
3. making apprenticeship costly for the public sector (and thereby promoting the integration of young apprentices into the labour market).

The ECJ held that the Austrian legislation did discriminate on grounds of age but that the aims of the Austrian legislation were (when looked at individually) legitimate. However, those same aims (when looked at collectively), were mutually contradictory. Aims (1) and (2) were designed to encourage young people to pursue secondary education (rather than vocational education); whereas aim (3) was designed to do the exact opposite. The Court stated that it was therefore 'difficult ... to accept that national legislation ... can, simultaneously, be of advantage to each of those two groups at the expense of the other' and concluded that the means of achieving the (otherwise legitimate) aims were not 'appropriate and necessary'.

Article 6(1) was also rejected in *Kücükdeveci v Swedex* (Case C–555/07) [2010] ECR I–365. German legislation provided that the notice periods which employers were required to observe on termination of employment were to be increased incrementally with the length of service, but periods of employment before the age of 25 were to be disregarded. For younger employees, employers were only required to observe a basic period of notice. The ECJ held that the German legislation constituted direct discrimination on grounds of age and rejected the purported justification of affording employers greater flexibility by making it easier to dismiss younger workers. The Court held that the German legislation was 'not appropriate' for achieving its purported aim, since it applied to all employees who joined the undertaking before the age of 25, whatever their age at the time of dismissal.

Article 6(1) derogations were also rejected in *Specht & Others* (Cases C–501–506, 540, 541/12) [2015] 1 CMLR 7 and *Unland* (Case C–20/13) [2016] 1 CMLR 24. Both cases involved German legislation which provided that a newly-appointed civil servant's starting salary was determined according to his/her age at the time of appointment. The Court rejected the German government's justification that the legislation was designed to reward previous professional experience. Although the Court agreed that, in principle, rewarding experience was 'a legitimate aim of wages policy', the German legislation was not 'appropriate and necessary'. Instead of rewarding service, 'the sole criterion' used to determine a new employee's position on the pay grade at the time of appointment was age, irrespective of his/her 'professional experience'.

In two recent cases, Article 6(1) justifications were accepted. In *De Lange* (2017), the ECJ held that Dutch tax legislation, which allowed workers under 30 (but not those aged 30 or over) to deduct the full cost of vocational training from their taxable earnings, was justifiable under Article 6(1) because it encouraged young people to obtain vocational training in order to improve their job prospects.

CASE EXAMPLE

De Lange (Case C–548/15) [2017] IRLR 278

In 2008, when he was 32 years old, Mr de Lange started training as a commercial airline pilot. In 2009, when he filed his income tax form, he deducted from his taxable income the costs of that training (€44,057). However, the Dutch authorities informed him that he was only allowed to deduct €15,000, being the maximum amount permitted under Dutch legislation for workers aged over 30. Mr de Lange alleged unlawful age discrimination. The Dutch government responded that the Dutch legislation offered tax concessions to people under 30 in order 'to promote the access of young people to training and to improve their position on the labour market'. Conversely, the exclusion of those aged 30+ from the same entitlement was justified on the basis that such 'persons have generally had the opportunity to undertake prior training and to pursue a professional activity, with the result that, being in a better financial position than young people who have recently left the school system, they are able to bear at least in part the financial burden of new training'. The ECJ accepted that the legislation was justifiable under Article 6(1).

In *Abercrombie & Fitch Italia* (Case C–143/16) [2017] IRLR 1018, the Court was asked whether Italian legislation, which provided that workers under the age of 25 and employed under 'on call' contracts (i.e. zero hours contracts) would have their contracts automatically terminated on their 25th birthday, was capable of being justified. The Italian government argued that the legislation was 'intended to facilitate the entry of young people to the labour market'. The government contended that 'the lack of professional experience is a factor which hampers young people' and so 'the possibility of entering the world of work and of acquiring experience, even if it is flexible and limited in time, could constitute a springboard towards new employment opportunities'. It was further argued that the availability of 'on call' contracts helped to 'increase the adaptability of employees to the labour market and give access to that market to persons in danger of social exclusion, while eliminating forms of illegal work'. The employer in this case, the fashion house Abercrombie & Fitch, agreed with the government. They submitted that, in a 'context of a persistent economic crisis and weak growth' it was better to be able to offer a 'flexible and temporary employment contract' to a young worker who might otherwise end up unemployed. The ECJ held that the Italian legislation was justified under Article 6(1).

KEY FACTS

Directive 2000/43	
Race discrimination (whether direct or indirect, and including harassment) is prohibited.	
The Directive applies in the public and private sectors and includes discrimination in employment, vocational training, social security, healthcare, education and housing.	Art 3
A 'difference of treatment' on race grounds may be justified where, by reason of the nature of the 'particular occupational activities', there is a genuine and determining occupational requirement.	Art 4

KEY FACTS

Directive 2000/78	
Discrimination (whether direct or indirect, and including harassment) on grounds of age, disability, religion or belief and sexual orientation is prohibited.	
The Directive applies in employment and vocational training.	Art 3
A 'difference of treatment' on grounds of age, disability, religion or belief and sexual orientation may be justified where, by reason of the nature of the 'particular occupational activities', there is a genuine and determining occupational requirement.	Art 4; *Wolf* (2010); *Prigge* (2011); *Vital Pérez* (2015); *Achbita* (2017); *Bougnaoui* (2017); *Salaberria Sorondo* (2017)
'Disability' means a 'limitation' resulting from 'physical, mental or psychological impairments' which hinder 'the participation of the person in professional life'. It can include accidents leading to 'long-term' limitations, and obesity, but does not include sickness.	*Chacón Navas* (2006); *Ring & Skouboe Werge* (2013); *Z* (2014); *Kaltoft* (2015); *Daouidi* (2017)
Age discrimination may be justified if 'objectively and reasonably justified by a legitimate aim', provided that the means adopted are 'appropriate and necessary'. In principle, this provision allows, e.g. employers to offer shorter contracts to older workers and for compulsory retirement ages.	Art 6; *Mangold v Helm* (2005); *Palacios de la Villa* (2007); *Age Concern England* (2009); *Georgiev* (2010); *Rosenblat* (2011); *De Lange* (2017); *Abercrombie & Fitch Italia* (2017)

SUMMARY

- Discrimination comes in various forms: direct (which is very difficult to justify), indirect (which can be justified by reference to a legitimate objective) and harassment.

- Article 157(1) TFEU sets out the principle of equal pay for men and women for equal work. 'Pay' is defined very widely, both in the TFEU itself and in subsequent case law. Article 157(1) TFEU is directly effective (*Defrenne v SABENA*).

- Positive action is permitted (indeed encouraged) by EU law but positive discrimination is prohibited.

- Directive 2006/54 sets out the principle of equal treatment on grounds of sex in employment (including access to employment and dismissal). There is a derogation for 'genuine and determining occupational requirements'.

- Discrimination against a pregnant woman (including refusal to employ and dismissal of a pregnant woman) constitutes direct sex discrimination.
- Directive 2000/43 sets out the principle of equal treatment on grounds of race and ethnic origin in employment (including access to employment and dismissal) and other areas including education, social services and housing. There is a derogation for 'genuine and determining occupational requirements'.
- Directive 2000/78 sets out the principle of equal treatment on grounds of age, disability, religion or belief and sexual orientation in employment (including access to employment and dismissal). There are general derogations for 'genuine and determining occupational requirements' and special derogations. In particular, age discrimination may be justified by a 'legitimate aim' which is 'appropriate and necessary'.

KEY FACTS

The development of EU discrimination law	
• In 1957, the EC Treaty was signed. It contained the original version of Art 157, which forced Member States to protect the principle that 'men and women should receive equal pay for equal work'. The Article was introduced for economic, as opposed to social, reasons.	Art 157 TFEU
• By 1976, however, the ECJ acknowledged that Art 157 pursued a 'double aim', that is, one economic and one social. The Court also elevated sex equality to the status of a 'fundamental right'.	*Defrenne v SABENA*
• In the mid-1970s, detailed secondary legislation on sex equality appeared for the first time. The first of these, the Equal Pay Directive, merely expanded the scope of Art 157 to cover work of equal value. The second, the Equal Treatment Directive (ETD), introduced new substantive legal rights of equality in the employment context covering conditions of employment, access to and dismissal from employment. It also introduced provisions allowing for 'positive action', but not 'positive discrimination'.	Directive 75/117; Directive 76/207
• At this time, EU sex discrimination legislation still focused exclusively on employment rights. This changed with the introduction in 1979 of a new Directive conferring rights of equality in social security matters.	Directive 79/7
• In 1986, the Court held that discriminatory retirement ages in employment contracts were contrary to the ETD. This has had a significant impact on employment rights in the UK in particular.	*Marshall* (1986)
• In 1990, the ECJ held that discrimination against a pregnant woman constituted direct discrimination and was therefore incapable of justification. This ruling has influenced several subsequent ECJ cases on the topic of pregnancy.	*Dekker* (1990)
• In 1995, the ECJ held that national 'positive discrimination' legislation breached the ETD.	*Kalanke* (1995)
• The signing in 1997 of the Treaty of Amsterdam marked a new level for EU discrimination law. Until this point, EU law dealt only with discrimination on grounds of sex. Although the ECJ had been prepared to extend the coverage of the ETD to cover discrimination against transsexuals, the Court refused to extend the scope of Art 157 to tackle sexual orientation discrimination. The Treaty of Amsterdam inserted Art 13 into the EC Treaty (now Art 19 TFEU), authorising the Council of Ministers to combat virtually any form of discrimination.	Treaty of Amsterdam; *P v S* (1996); *Grant* (1998)

- Two pieces of legislation issued under (what is now) Art 19 TFEU appeared in 2000.

The first of these, the Race Directive, tackles race and ethnic origin discrimination. It applies to discrimination in the employment context and beyond, covering matters such as education, housing and social services. The Directive came into force in December 2003.

- The second Directive issued under (what is now) Art 19 TFEU, the Framework Directive, tackles discrimination on grounds of age, disability, religion or belief and sexual orientation. It only applies in the context of employment. The provisions on religion and sexual orientation discrimination came into force in December 2003. Member States were given the option of deferring implementation of the provisions on disability and age discrimination by three years 'if necessary'. These provisions came into force in December 2006.
- A second Equal Treatment Directive came into force in October 2005. It updated the original ETD and extended its coverage in certain respects, e.g. to encompass 'sexual harassment'.
- Directives 75/117, 76/207 (the ETD), 86/378 and 97/80 are all repealed, replaced by the 'Recast' Directive, in August 2009.

(margin references: Art 19 TFEU; Directive 2000/43 — Directive 2000/78 — Directive 2002/73 — Directive 2006/54)

SAMPLE ESSAY QUESTION

'Critically compare and contrast the protection provided by EU law to victims of "discrimination" based on "sex", "race" and "age".'

Explain the meaning and scope of 'discrimination' in EU law:
- Define 'direct' discrimination
- Define 'indirect' discrimination
- Explain that 'discrimination' includes 'harassment' and an instruction to discriminate
- Define 'harassment'

Explain the provisions of EU law on 'sex' discrimination:
- Article 157 TFEU prohibits differential pay for men and women doing equal work or work of equal value. 'Pay' is defined widely in the Treaty and in case law. Give examples, e.g. *Garland*, *Barber*
- Directive 2006/54 provides for equal treatment of men and women in the workplace
- Directive 2004/113 prohibits sex discrimination in terms of access to/supply of goods and services
- Sex discrimination includes discrimination against pregnant women (*Dekker*, *Webb*, *Brown*) and against transsexuals (*P v S*), but not discrimination on grounds of sexual orientation (*Grant v SW Trains*)

Explain the provisions of EU law on 'race' discrimination:

- Directive 2000/43 prohibits discrimination on grounds of 'race' in the workplace
- It also prohibits race discrimination in the context of social security, healthcare, education, 'social advantages' and access to/supply of goods and services available to the public, e.g. housing
- This is the widest scope of any form of EU discrimination legislation

Explain the provisions of EU law on 'age' discrimination:

- Directive 2000/78 prohibits discrimination on grounds of 'age' in the workplace
- Derogation is available on grounds of health protection, e.g. maximum age limits for dentists (*Petersen*)
- Compulsory retirement ages are justifiable (*Palacios de la Villa, Age Concern England, Rosenblat*)

Compare/contrast:

- Race discrimination has the broadest scope, covering areas not covered by the others. Age discrimination has the narrowest scope, and is the only one where health grounds may justify discrimination
- In all areas, derogation is permitted on the basis of a 'genuine and determining occupational requirement', e.g. male only fighting units in the army (*Sirdar*); maximum age limits for fire-fighters (*Wolf*)
- All areas provide for 'positive' action, i.e. the adoption of measures to ensure full equality in practice (*Marschall*), but not 'positive' discrimination (*Kalanke*)

SUMMARY

- EU Law tackles discrimination on grounds of sex, race or ethnic origin, age, disability, religion or belief, and sexual orientation. However, the scope and level of protection varies from one area of discrimination to another. There is also EU law tackling discrimination based on nationality (see Chapters 11, 12 and 13 for discussion).

- Discrimination comes in various forms: direct, indirect and harassment.

- 'Direct' discrimination occurs when one person is treated less favourably than another person is, has been or would be treated in a comparable situation.

- 'Indirect' discrimination occurs where an 'apparently neutral provision, criterion or practice' gives one person a 'particular disadvantage' compared with another person because of a difference in age, race, sex, etc., unless that provision, criterion or practice is 'objectively justified by a legitimate aim', and the means of achieving that aim are 'appropriate and necessary'.

- 'Discrimination' includes 'harrassment', where 'unwanted conduct' on grounds of age, race, sex, etc., occurs with the 'purpose or effect of violating the dignity of a person, and of creating an intimidating, hostile, degrading, humiliating or offensive environment'.

- Discrimination includes an instruction to discriminate.

- Indirect discrimination is capable of justification by reference to 'a legitimate aim'. Examples (in the context of sex discrimination) include the need to encourage full-time workers (*Jenkins v Kingsgate*); the need to attract more staff to certain posts (*Enderby*); the need to recruit young workers (*Kutz-Bauer*).

- Discrimination on grounds of 'sex' essentially means discrimination on grounds of gender. It also includes discrimination against transsexuals (*P v S, KB*). Discrimination against pregnant women amounts to direct sex discrimination (*Dekker*).

- Sex discrimination is tackled by several provisions of EU law, the most important of which are Article 157 TFEU and Directive 2006/54 (the 'recast' directive).

- Article 157(1) TFEU provides for equal pay for men and women doing equal work or work of equal value. This provision is directly effective, vertically and horizontally (*Defrenne v SABENA*). It pursues a 'double aim' – economic and social (*Defrenne*).

- 'Pay' is defined widely in the Treaty, as 'the ordinary basic or minimum wage or salary and any other consideration, whether in cash or in kind, which the worker receives, directly or indirectly, in respect of his employment from his employer' (Article 157(2) TFEU). It has been broadly interpreted by the Court of Justice, to include post-employment benefits (*Garland*), sick pay (*Rinner-Kühn*), severance payments (*Kowalska*), compensation for unfair dismissal (*Seymour-Smith & Perez*), bonuses (*Krüger*), payments in lieu (*Bötel*), redundancy payments (*Barber*), maternity pay (*Gillespie, Alabaster*), membership of occupational pension schemes (*Bilka-Kaufhaus, Barber*).

- Article 157(1) only applies to pay discrimination that is the responsibility of a single employer. It cannot apply if the alleged pay discrimination involves different employers (*Lawrence, Allonby*).

- 'Equal work' does not mean identical work. However, employees performing similar tasks but whose level of experience, training and/or qualifications are different should not necessarily be regarded as doing 'equal work' (*Wiener Gebietskrankenkasse, Kenny & Others*). In particular, rewarding experience which enables a worker to perform his or her duties better constitutes a 'legitimate objective of pay policy' (*Cadman*).

- Whether work is of 'equal value' is ultimately a question of fact (*Royal Copenhagen*). Where a 'job classification system' is used, it must be based on 'the same criteria for both men and women and so drawn up as to exclude any discrimination on grounds of sex' (Directive 2006/54, Article 4).

- Directive 2006/54 provides for equal treatment of men and women in the workplace. It prohibits sex discrimination in the context of access to employment, working conditions, promotion, dismissal and vocational training (Article 14). The imposition of different contractual retirement ages for men and women constitutes 'dismissal' and is prohibited (*Marshall*).

- The refusal to employ, or the dismissal of, a pregnant woman because of her pregnancy is direct sex discrimination (*Dekker, Webb*). The same applies to the dismissal of a woman who is at an advanced stage of IVF treatment (*Mayr v Flöckner*), or because of a pregnancy-related illness (*Brown*), but not if the illness manifests itself after the end of the maternity leave period (*Hertz*).

- Women returning to work after maternity leave have their terms and conditions of employment protected (*Thibault*). They are also entitled to benefit from any improvement in working conditions to which they would have been entitled during their absence (Article 15).

- Directive 79/7 prohibits direct or indirect sex discrimination 'in the field of social security and other elements of social protection'. In terms of personal scope, it applies to the 'working population', which is very widely defined, including the self-employed, the retired and the involuntarily unemployed. In terms of material scope, it applies to statutory schemes which provide protection against sickness, invalidity, old age, accidents at work and occupational diseases, and unemployment. There is an important derogation for the 'determination of pensionable age for the purpose of granting old-age and retirement pensions and the possible consequences thereof for other benefits' (Article 7).

- Directive 2010/41 prohibits sex discrimination in the context of self-employed persons.

- Directive 2004/113 prohibits sex discrimination in terms of access to/supply of goods and services.

- Directive 2000/43 prohibits discrimination on grounds of 'race and ethnic origin' in the workplace. Race discrimination may be established without the need to prove that there was any specific potential employee who had, or may have, suffered discrimination (*Feryn*). A person may 'suffer' discrimination even if they were not a member of the racial or ethnic group subject to the discriminatory rule (*CHEZ Razpredelenie Bulgaria*).

- It also prohibits race discrimination in the context of social security, healthcare, education, 'social advantages' and access to/supply of goods and services available to the public, e.g. electricity (*CHEZ Razpredelenie Bulgaria*) or loans (*Jyske Finans*). This gives Directive 2000/43 the widest scope of any form of EU discrimination legislation.

- Directive 2000/78 prohibits discrimination on grounds of 'age', 'disability', 'religion or belief' and 'sexual orientation' in the workplace.

- 'Disability' refers to 'a limitation which results in particular from physical, mental or psychological impairments and which hinders the participation of the person concerned in professional life' (*Chacón Navas*). 'Disability' is not synonymous with 'sickness' (*Chacón Navas*). Disability can arise from an accident where there is a 'long-term' limitation (*Daouidi*) or obesity when it hinders the participation of the person concerned in professional life (*Kaltoft*).

- Disability discrimination may occur indirectly (*Coleman v Attridge Law*).

- Derogation is available on grounds of public security, public order, crime prevention, health protection, e.g. maximum age limits for dentists or airline pilots (*Petersen, Prigge*), and 'for the protection of the rights and freedoms of others'.

- Age discrimination may be justified if 'objectively and reasonably justified by a legitimate aim', provided that the means adopted are 'appropriate and necessary'. In principle, this provision allows, e.g. employers, to offer shorter contracts to older workers and for compulsory retirement ages (*Mangold v Helm, Palacios de la Villa, Age Concern England, Rosenblat, Georgiev*).

- In all areas of EU discrimination law, derogation is permitted on the basis of a 'genuine and determining occupational requirement', e.g. male only fighting units in the army (*Sirdar*); maximum age limits for fire-fighters, airline pilots and police officers (*Wolf, Prigge, Vital Pérez, Salaberria Sorondo*); an employer's wish to present political, philosophical or religious neutrality (*Achbita, Bougnaoui*).

- All areas of EU discrimination law provide for 'positive' action, i.e. the 'adoption of measure to ensure full equality in practice' (*Lommers, Marschall*).

- 'Positive' discrimination – involving conferring advantages on an under-represented group – is prohibited (*Kalanke, Briheche*).

- EU legislation provides for a reversed burden of proof in discrimination cases. Thus, when a person, who considers themselves to have been the victim of a form of discrimination covered by EU law, is able to establish facts from which it may be presumed that there has been direct or indirect discrimination, it shall be for the respondent to prove that there has been no breach of the principle of equal treatment (see e.g. Directive 2006/54, Article 10).

Further reading

Articles

Beck, G, 'The State of EC Anti-Sex Discrimination Law and the Judgment in *Cadman*, Or How the Legal can Become the Political' (2007) 32 *EL Rev* 549.

Burrows, N and Robinson, M, 'An Assessment of the Recast of Community Equality Laws' (2006) 13 *ELJ* 186.

Dewhurst, E, 'The Development of EU Case-Law on Age Discrimination in Employment: 'Will You Still Need Me? Will You Still Feed Me? When I'm Sixty-Four' (2013) 19 *ELJ* 517.

Driessen-Reilly, M and Driessen, B, 'Don't Shoot the Messenger: A Look at Community Law relating to Harassment in the Workplace' (2003) 28 *ELR* 493.

Howard, E, 'Reasonable Accommodation of Religion and Other Discrimination Grounds in EU Law' (2013) 38 *EL Rev* 360.

Masselot, A, 'The State of Gender Equality Law in the European Union' (2007) 13 *ELJ* 152.

Oliveira, A and King, S, 'A Good Chess Opening: Luxembourg's First Roma Case Consolidates its Role as a Fundamental Rights Court' (2016) 41 *EL Rev* 865.

Schiek, D, 'Age Discrimination before the ECJ: Conceptual and Theoretical Issues' (2011) 48 *CML Rev* 777.

Schiek, D, 'Intersectionality and the Notion of Disability in EU Discrimination Law' (2016) 53 *CML Rev* 35.

Vickers, L, 'Achbita and Bougnaoui: One Step Forward and Two Steps Back for Religious Diversity in the Workplace' (2017) 8 *ELLJ* 232.

19

The wider social influence of the EU

After reading this chapter you should:

▨ Have a basic understanding of the wider influence of the EU on Member States

The original EC Treaty was economic in character and while it had a broad range of economic objectives, characterised by the 'Four Freedoms' and the addition of restrictions on anti-competitive practices, as well as a limited form of social policy in the form of Article 119 (now Article 157 TFEU), it was still relatively limited in its focus.

However, a number of different policy areas have become important since the Treaty was first signed in 1957. Social policy has become a significant area in its own right and has been subject to major development (see Chapter 17). Even as early as 1972 discussion between the Member States identified the need for a distinct policy on the environment and environmental protection. As an extension to the 'Four Freedoms' and with a view to making the Single Market more effective a number of developments have also concerned consumer protection.

The SEA and the TEU both included measures to include a wider range of policies now identified as both tasks and as activities (under Article 3). Specifically, the TFEU now includes provisions to include within the legal order of the Community policies on:

▨ consumer protection – Article 169 TFEU;

▨ the environment – Articles 191–193 TFEU;

▨ transport – Articles 90–100 TFEU;

▨ trans-European networks – Articles 170–172 TFEU;

▨ research and technological development – Articles 179–190 TFEU;

▨ social policy, education, vocational training and youth – Articles 151–161 TFEU;

▨ public health – Article 168 TFEU.

In moves towards closer integration economically, socially and politically it is inevitable that the scope of EU law must grow. It is worth looking briefly at how some of these policies have developed and the extent of EU influence. These are areas that are not normally included in mainstream syllabuses on EU. As a result, this chapter provides only a brief overview of the areas covered for a general understanding of how the EU has developed beyond its early economic programme.

19.1 Protection of consumers

The EC Treaty did not contain any specific provisions for consumer protection because it was felt that the free competition created by the 'Four Freedoms' would inevitably benefit the consumer as well. Indeed, any measures that were introduced had as much to do with protecting free competition as anything else.

In fact, prior to the SEA there were only two specific references in the Treaty to consumer protection. Article 33 (formerly Article 39) identified that under the Common Agricultural Policy (CAP) produce should reach the consumer at what was described as 'fair prices'. Also under Article 101, prohibiting restrictive trade practices, one of the criteria for granting exemptions under Article 101(3) was that the agreement contributed to the improvement of the production or distribution of the goods and that this passed a fair share of the benefit on to the consumer (see section 16.2.3).

The ECJ also of course recognised the importance of protecting the consumer within the so-called 'rule of reason' in the case of *Rewe-Zentral AG v Bundesmonopolverwaltung für Branntwein* (Case 120/78) (*Cassis de Dijon*) [1979] ECR 649 in relation to providing exemption for Member States breaching Article 34 TFEU (see Chapter 14).

A Consumer Programme was eventually accepted in 1975 and this set out a plan for implementing five fundamental consumer rights. These were:

- the protection of health and safety;
- the protection of the consumer's economic interests;
- the right of the consumer to both information and education;
- the right of a consumer to redress;
- the right of a consumer to representation and participation.

Before the SEA measures concerning consumer protection were introduced under the old Article 100 (now Article 116). In fact, 18 measures were adopted in 1976 under Article 100 covering a range of specific products including for instance motor vehicles. The purpose of the measures was the harmonisation of national laws with the focus very much on avoiding distortion in competition as much as on consumer protection itself. The process was also very slow because it required the unanimous vote of Council.

Probably one of the most significant of the measures introduced by this process was the Product Liability Directive 85/374. This imposed strict liability on producers for all damage caused by defective products. The term 'producer' was defined broadly so that it could include anyone in the chain of supply and distribution, including manufacturers, importers and suppliers. Under the Directive the claimant need only show the defect in the goods, the damage caused and the causal relationship between the two. Although there are a number of defences also available. In the UK the Directive was introduced as Part 1 of the Consumer Protection Act 1987.

A number of other measures were introduced by the same procedure under the old Article 100:

- The Misleading Advertising Directive 84/450: this gives consumers rights of redress when they have entered into contracts on the basis of misleading advertisements. It therefore imposes high standards of business practice on sellers.

- The Doorstep Selling Directive 85/577: this protected consumers by introducing the right to a cooling-off period of seven days for contracts made in their homes or away from the business premises of the seller. A consumer has the opportunity to reflect and cancel the contract.
- The Consumer Credit Directive 87/102.

This provides a range of protections to consumers purchasing goods or services on credit. In fact, UK consumers already enjoyed similar protections under the Consumer Credit Act 1974.

While the SEA did not specifically include provisions for consumer protection it did recognise the need to speed up this process of harmonisation in order to provide greater consumer protection. As a result, it developed the processes already available under the old Article 100a (now Article 114) and made use of qualified majority voting by Council in order to adopt measures.

A number of measures were subsequently introduced by using Article 100a and Article 95 (now Article 114 TFEU). These included:

- The Toy Safety Directive 88/378: this was inevitably aimed at preventing the sale of dangerous toys within the Community by harmonising laws in the Member States. In fact, it introduced a European standards body, the CEN which both introduced a standard for different toys with accompanying certification as well as the requirement for national safety standards to conform to the EC (now EU) model. A further requirement was that all toys supplied in the EC (now EU) should carry a CEN approved mark. In the UK this was implemented as the Toy Safety Regulations 1995.
- The Price Indication Directive 88/314: this required that certain goods, particularly foodstuffs, should be displayed together with their selling price or in some cases with a unit price.
- The Package Travel Directive 90/314: this includes minimum standards of protection in the case of package travel, package holidays and package tours. It has been implemented in the UK as the Package Travel, Package Holidays and Package Tours Regulations 1992. The Regulations following the Directive impose minimum requirements in respect of the information given to consumers prior to contracting and liability for sub-standard or no performance.
- The Unfair Terms in Consumer Contracts Directive 93/13: the basic aim of the Directive is to remove inequalities in consumer contracts that would act as a detriment to the consumer. Any inequality in the contractual terms that would create an imbalance in the respective rights of seller and consumer or any requirement contrary to the requirement of good faith will be seen as unfair and be considered invalid. The Directive applies only to standard terms and not those that are individually negotiated. The Directive is incorporated into English law now as the Unfair Terms in Consumer Contracts Regulations 1999.

The TEU inserted consumer protection as a distinct policy of the EU. In fact Article 153 (now Article 169 TFEU) (Article 129a under the TEU) called for a 'high level of consumer protection'. In fact Article 153 (now Article 169 TFEU) states:

ARTICLE

'Art 169 In order to protect the interests of the consumer and to ensure a high level of consumer protection, the Community shall contribute to protecting the health, safety and economic interests of consumers, as well as promoting their right to information, education and to organise themselves in order to protect their interests.'

This would be achieved according to the Article by internal market measures under Article 114 TFEU, and also by specific actions using the co-decision procedure. This commitment was carried into the Treaty of Amsterdam. Significantly, the Article provides for minimum standards so that a higher level of consumer protection within individual Member States is accepted that is still compatible with the provisions of the Treaty.

CASE EXAMPLE

Buet v Ministère Public (Case 382/87) [1989] ECR 1235

Here, French law actually outlawed doorstep selling of educational materials. Directive 85/577, on the other hand, only provided that consumers might withdraw from contracts made at home within a defined period. The ECJ held that the French law did not breach EC (now EU) law under Article 30 but merely offered a greater level of consumer protection which was not inconsistent.

An important measure introduced following the TEU and the inclusion of Article 153 (now Article 169 TFEU) is the Distance Selling Directive 97/7. This is clearly an important development because of the difficulties associated with modern methods of contracting and their potentially international scope. This is a problem already highlighted in the law of many Member States and one of the key purposes of the Directive was the harmonisation of the rules within the Member States. The Directive applies to contracts for the sale of goods and for the provisions of services made by a variety of modern methods, e.g.:

- telephone
- fax
- Internet shopping
- mail order
- e-mail
- television shopping.

The Directive requires a seller to provide purchasers with certain minimum information, before any contract can be considered to be validly formed. Minimum terms should also be implied into contracts formed in this way for the protection of the consumer including the right to cancel. The Directive is implemented in English law as the Consumer Protection (Distance Selling) Regulations 2000.

Other measures introduced through Article 95 as a result of the new Article 153 (now Article 169 TFEU) include:

- the Timeshare Directive 94/47; and
- the Cross-Border Transfer Directive 97/5.

Recently, the Electronic Commerce Directive 2000/31 (e-commerce) has also been introduced to regulate the formation of contracts by electronic means. Article 11 of the Directive identifies:

> where [a purchaser] in accepting [a seller's] offer is required to give his consent through technological means, such as clicking on an icon, the contract is concluded when the recipient of the service has received from the service provider, electronically, an acknowledgement of receipt of the recipient's acceptance.

This would appear to clear up some of the problems formerly encountered in determining when such agreements are actually complete and a contract is formed.

Directive 2005/29, the Unfair Commercial Practices Directive, introduces an overall ban on misleading trading practices. The Directive identifies a number of practices which are misleading and therefore unlawful. Examples include describing a product as free when there is in fact a hidden charge, and so called 'buy one get one free' (BOGOF) offers.

19.2 Environmental protection

Again, there was no specific provision within the EC Treaty for the protection of the environment. Nevertheless, even before the SEA the Community did adopt three individual Environment Action Programmes. The first two of these were aimed basically at action to remedy existing environmental problems. The third was more proactive, calling for environmental action that would assist economic growth through non-polluting industries. Even before the SEA, then, the EC (now EU) issued numerous Regulations, Decisions and more than 100 Directives with environmental protection as their purpose.

These were usually introduced under the power given in Article 308 (now Article 352 TFEU) (formerly Article 235). This was a general power allowing the Council following a proposal of the Commission and after consultation to take the appropriate measures to ensure the attainment of a Treaty objective.

The SEA recognised the need for specific measures aimed at environmental protection since pollution, although it may be caused by individual states is even a global problem and certainly the effects of pollution can be felt in more than one state.

As a result, specific environmental policies were introduced in the SEA under Articles 174–176 (now Articles 191–193 TFEU) (formerly Articles 130r–130t). The objectives contained in the former Article 130r were:

- to preserve and improve the quality of the environment;
- to contribute towards the protection of human health;
- to ensure that there should be both a prudent and a rational use of natural resources.

Under the SEA the EC (now EU) would introduce measures under the old Article 130r on a preventive basis with the provision of removing the source of the problem and making the polluter pay for the damage caused. It was also possible to introduce environmental measures under the old Article 100a (now Article 95) if they could be shown to be associated with the function of the Internal Market.

One limitation of Article 130r was that it was linked to subsidiarity so that EC (now EU) action could only be taken where the problem could not be resolved better by the Member States themselves. Inevitably, the worst polluters were likely to argue against EC (now EU) involvement.

CASE EXAMPLE

Commission v Council (Case C–300/89) (the Titanium Dioxide Directive case) [1991] ECR I–2867

Here, argument focused on the application of Directive 89/48 on titanium dioxide waste. The ECJ accepted that since the Directive was essentially a harmonising Directive it should not have been introduced under the old Article 130r (now Article 191 TFEU) but should have been introduced under Article 95 (ex-Art 100a). As a result, the measure was annulled.

The TEU, on the other hand, specifically included environmental policy as a policy of the EU by inclusion within the amended Treaty. Following the Treaty of Amsterdam the environment is now included within the activities identified in Article 3. The introduction of a specific title covering the environment, Title XIX covering Articles 174–176 (now Articles 191–193 TFEU), means that there is no longer a need to introduce measures by the older more artificial means either of Article 130r or Article 95 (now Article 114 TFEU) (ex-Article 100a).

Article 191 TFEU recognises that introduction of environmental measures must take account of:

- regional variations within the Union;
- the availability of scientific and technical data;
- the relative costs and benefits of action to be taken or if it is not taken;
- the general economic and social development of the Union.

As has been said above, EU environmental policy has been introduced as the result of a series of Environmental Action Programmes. A fourth programme was introduced in 1987 following the SEA. The legislation that has resulted from these programmes tends to have focused on distinct areas:

- Water and air pollution – as a result of which, for instance, Directive 75/324 on the use of CFCs was introduced.
- Noise pollution – an example of this is Directive 80/51 on noise from aircraft.
- Chemical pollution – an example of this is Directive 77/728 which requires labelling of paints to identify pollutants.
- Protection of the natural environment – this is possibly one of the most important but also one of the most controversial areas – one of the earliest measures introduced was Directive 76/160 on bathing water.

Protecting the natural environment is, not surprisingly, controversial. Many of the activities carried out by industry have the potential to affect the environment adversely and many vested interests are therefore at stake in legislating for its protection.

One of the most important of the developments in this field is Directive 85/337 on the use of land. The Directive introduces guidelines under which local planning authorities are supposed to assess in advance the effect of both private and public proposals for the use of land according to the effect that they will have on the environment before they consider any planning applications. The likely impact on the environment should be considered in the light of the size of the project and the nature of the location. Obviously, projects such as the building of power stations or of new transport systems fall within the scope of the Directive but smaller projects must be considered also. In the case of the latter, however, the Member States do have some discretion in terms of introducing the controls. In the UK the Directive was implemented by the Town and Country Planning Regulations 1988.

Other measures introduced with the general objective of protection of the natural environment include:

- Regulation 3258/86 and Regulation 2158/92 concerning the protection of forests both from rain and from fire.
- Directive 96/61 which integrates pollution prevention and control policies and which is mainly concerned with regulating the licensing of industrial appliances.

Enforcement of environmental law is generally against Member States through Article 258 proceedings. One possible problem is that associated with Directives generally, that they may not be directly effective against the bodies causing the pollution. However, the *Francovich v Italy* (Case C–6/90) [1991] ECR I–5357 principle of state liability may be used where the Directive has not been properly implemented or not implemented at all and thus allowing the alleged breaches of EU law.

A fifth Environmental Action Programme was also introduced in 1993 and expired in 2000. This programme focused on five main areas:

- industry
- energy
- transport
- agriculture
- tourism.

One interesting feature of the programme was a change from traditional regulatory practices to measures based on economic benefits such as tax reductions for achieving environmental targets.

19.3 Transport

Transport was actually included in the original EC Treaty. Article 70 (now Article 90 TFEU) (formerly Article 74) simply stated that the objectives of the Treaty should be carried out within the framework of a common transport policy.

Furthermore Article 71 (now Article 91 TFEU) (formerly Article 75) identified how this Common Transport Policy should be provided. This would be by the introduction of:

- the creation of common rules on transport;
- the introduction of conditions for carriers who were not resident in the Member State;
- the introduction of measures to improve safety within transport; and also
- the implementation of any other appropriate measure needed to satisfy these aims.

However, in the early days Council did very little to develop transport policy. A significant development came in the case law of the ECJ. In *Commission v Council* (Case 22/70) [1971] ECR 263 there was disagreement between the Commission and Council over the second European Road Transport Agreement. The first agreement was entered into by five of the original six members of the EC together with some other European states. A second agreement was then proposed because of problems ratifying the first. However, Council in the meantime had issued a Regulation covering the same areas as the agreement. The Commission was seeking to annul the second agreement but the ECJ held that, because Council was charged with the obligation to create a common transport policy the agreement was valid.

The TEU introduced a number of measures concerning transport including trans-European networks under Title XV and contained in Articles 154–156 (now Articles 170–172 TFEU). Nevertheless, a Common Transport Policy is developing much more slowly than other areas. Following the Treaty of Amsterdam, transport is an area that falls within the co-decision procedure so Parliament may well be more influential in this area. Certainly there is a need to develop a standard safety policy.

19.4 Research and technological development

Again, there was no specific provision for this within the original EC Treaty. There was limited early progress. For instance, guidelines were introduced in 1974 to co-ordinate national policies for the participation in a European Science Foundation and to develop an EC programme for scientific and technological research.

Research was included as a policy within the SEA and this was also retained in the TEU. Following the Treaty of Amsterdam this is now under Title XIX and Articles 179–190 TFEU.

The policy again is aimed at harmonisation and cohesion. Article 181 TFEU states:

ARTICLE

'Art 181 TFEU The Community and the Member States shall co-ordinate their research and technological development activities so as to ensure that national policies and Community policies are mutually consistent.'

19.5 Education

There was no specific provision for education in the EC Treaty. However, there were still references to education in the Treaty. Article 35 (now Article 41 TFEU) (formerly Article 41) did refer to the co-ordination of vocational training in agriculture. Article 151 (now Article 167 TFEU) (formerly Article 128) also required general principles for the implementation of a Common Vocational Training Policy.

In fact, an Education Action Programme was put in place as early as 1974 and this led on to a number of different studies and reports. This gradually led to the development of an education policy and in 1989 the Commission introduced guidelines for education and training.

In any case, education and training had already been the subject of legislation because of the nature of certain Treaty Articles. Rights of establishment under Article 43 (now Article 49 TFEU) required first harmonisation of professional qualifications through the introduction of a variety of sectoral Directives. Because the process was so slow-moving, Directive 89/48, in the case of three-year degree equivalent qualifications leading to a professional qualification, and Directive 92/51, in the case of vocational qualifications of at least one year, were introduced to simplify matters through the process of mutual recognition. These were later placed under the umbrella of the 'Slim Directive' 2001/19 which increased the factors to be taken into account in assessing qualifications and widened the actual procedural safeguards (see Chapter 13). Now there is Directive 2005/36, the recognition of professional qualifications directive.

Besides this, education was identified as a social advantage in relation to the rights of workers' families under Regulation 1612/68 (now Regulation 492/2011) in relation to the free movement of workers guaranteed by Article 39 (now Article 45 TFEU) (see Chapter 12).

Another aspect of the Community education policy has been the ERASMUS programme which provided for co-operation between universities of different Member States to aid exchange programmes. Later there was the SOCRATES programme which through the LINGUA programme promoted the development of foreign language skills.

The TEU added education as a Community policy, now in Title X under the heading of 'Education, Vocational Training and Youth' in Articles 165–167 TFEU.

19.6 Public health

Public health did have a context in the original EC Treaty as a derogation under Article 39(3) (now Article 45 TFEU), later amplified in Directive 64/221 (replaced by Directive 2004/38), from the free movement of workers under Article 39 (now Article 45 TFEU) (see Chapter 12). The same derogation applies in the case of Article 43 rights of establishment (see Chapter 13). Similarly, there is a public health derogation in Article 36 TFEU from the free movement of goods in Articles 34 and 35 TFEU. Here, however, the derogation is inevitably broader and refers to the health of humans, animals and plants. Such a public health exemption is also accepted within the *Cassis de Dijon* rule of reason (see Chapter 14).

Health is also referred to in Article 153 TFEU under which Member States are required to co-operate in areas such as occupational hygiene and the prevention of occupational diseases and occupational injuries. The so-called 'six pack' of Regulations on health and safety in employment are a result of compliance with EU health and safety law.

Otherwise, the major responsibility still lies with the Member States and this is indicated in Article 168 TFEU. However, the Article does indicate that there should be co-operation between Member States in harmonising standards and that health protection should form a consistent part of the other policies of the EU. Usually EU influence on public health is through recommendations which, of course, while influential, are non-binding.

ACTIVITY

Self-assessment questions

1. What level of consumer protection existed in the EC (now EU) prior to the SEA?
2. How were measures aimed at consumer protection introduced at that time?
3. What changes did the SEA make?
4. In what ways did the TEU alter the area of consumer protection?
5. How did the EC (now EU) impact upon environmental protection prior to the SEA?
6. What effect did the SEA have on environmental protection?
7. In what ways has the TEU altered environmental protection within EU law?
8. What difficulties are associated with the protection of the 'natural environment'?
9. What part did transport play in the original EC treaty?
10. What methods have been used to create a 'Common Transport Policy'?
11. How successful has the transport policy been?
12. How has the TEU affected transport policy?
13. When was research and technological development introduced as a policy of the EC?
14. What methods are used in this area to develop policy among Member States?
15. In what ways does the EU support education in the Member States?
16. In what areas of EU law is public health important?
17. To what extent is there an EU public health policy?

Consumer protection	Only two aspects in original Treaty: • Art 33 (now Art 39 TFEU) – requirement for 'fair prices' under CAP; • possible exemption for breach of Art 81 (now Art 101 TFEU) under Art 81(3). But measures introduced under Art 94 (now Art 115 TFEU) (ex-Art 100) through harmonising Directives: • Product Liability Directive 85/374; • Misleading Advertising Directive 84/450; • Doorstep Selling Directive 85/577; • Consumer Credit Directive 87/102. SEA used Art 95 (now Art 114 TFEU) (ex-Art 100a) through qualified majority voting: • Toy Safety Directive 88/378; • Price Indication Directive 88/314; • Package Travel Directive 90/314; • Unfair Terms in Consumer Contracts Directive 93/13. TEU inserted 'high level of consumer protection' as a policy in Art 153 (now Art 12 TFEU) – to be introduced by co-decision procedure: • Distance Selling Directive 97/7; • Timeshare Directive 94/47; • Cross-Border Transfer Directive 97/5; • Electronic Commerce Directive 2000/31.
Environmental protection	Nothing in Treaty but three Environment Action Programmes before SEA: • and Directives introduced under Art 308 (now Art 352 TFEU) (ex-Art 235). SEA introduced environment as policy: • used Arts 174–176 (now Arts 191–193 TFEU) (formerly Arts 130r–130t) to introduce largely preventive measures; • but based on subsidiarity. TEU inserted environment as a distinct policy under Title XIX in Arts 174–176 (now Arts 191–193 TFEU): • Directive 75/324 on the use of CFCs; • Directive 80/51 on noise from aircraft; • Directive 76/160 on bathing water; • Directive 85/337 on the use of land; • Regulation 3258/86 and Regulation 2158/92 on protection of forests from rain and fire. Enforcement usually through Art 258 TFEU proceedings.
Transport	Art 70 (now Art 90 TFEU) (formerly Art 74) called for 'Common Transport Policy'. TEU included as Title V in Arts 70–80 (now Arts 90–100 TFEU) and also inserts transEuropean networks under Title XV in Arts 154–156 (now Arts 170–172 TFEU).
Research and technological development	Nothing in original Treaty but guidelines introduced in 1974 to co-ordinate national policies for participation in a European Science Foundation. Included in SEA as policy. Now in TEU under Title XVIII in Arts 163–173 (now Arts 179–190 TFEU). • Art 181 TFEU based on harmonisation so that Member States' policies are 'mutually consistent'.

Education	Only references in original Treaty were: • Art 35 (now Art 41 TFEU) (formerly Art 41) co-ordination of vocational training in agriculture; • Art 151 (now Art 167 TFEU) (formerly Art 128) general principles for implementation of Common Vocational Training Policy; • also important in harmonising, then mutual recognition, for Art 49 TFEU; • also social advantage under Regulation 1612/68 for Art 45 TFEU rights. Education Action Programme from 1974. See also ERASMUS, SOCRATES and LINGUA.
Public health	In original Treaty, appears as: • derogation from Art 39 (now Art 45 TFEU) rights under Art 39(3) and Directive 64/221 (replaced by Directive 2004/38); • derogation from Arts 34 and 35 rights under Art 36. Art 153 TFEU requires co-operation on occupational hygiene and health and safety. Art 168 TFEU obligation for public health is on Member States.

SUMMARY

▨ The programme of the EU is usually associated with the Four Freedoms and the creation of the single market.

▨ However, there are other significant areas of legislation deriving from the Treaties as amended.

▨ These include consumer protection, environmental protection, transport, research and technological development, education and public health.

Index

Page numbers in **bold** denote figures.

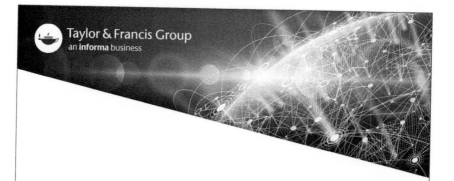